SPECIAL EDUCATION

FOR THE EXCEPTIONAL

VOL. I   INTRODUCTION AND PROBLEMS

VOL. II   THE PHYSICALLY HANDICAPPED AND
SPECIAL HEALTH PROBLEMS

VOL. III EMOTIONAL AND MENTAL DEVIATES AND SPECIAL
PROBLEMS

EDITED BY

MERLE E. FRAMPTON, PH.D., LL.D., LITT.D.

PRINCIPAL, NEW YORK INSTITUTE FOR THE EDUCATION OF THE BLIND

AND

VISITING LECTURER, DEPARTMENT OF EDUCATION
HUNTER COLLEGE OF THE CITY OF NEW YORK

AND

ELENA D. GALL, M.A., ED.D.

ASSISTANT PROFESSOR, DEPARTMENT OF EDUCATION,
AND COORDINATOR OF SPECIAL EDUCATION
HUNTER COLLEGE OF THE CITY OF NEW YORK

PORTER SARGENT PUBLISHER

11 BEACON STREET   BOSTON 8 MASSACHUSETTS

SPECIAL EDUCATION

FOR THE

EXCEPTIONAL

VOLUME I

INTRODUCTION AND PROBLEMS

`SPECIAL EDUCATION FOR THE EXCEPTIONAL`

VOLUME I

INTRODUCTION AND PROBLEMS

Elbert

EDITED BY MERLE E. FRAMPTON

AND *"*

ELENA D. GALL

CONTRIBUTING AUTHORS

NORMAN ACTON

SALVATORE G. DiMICHAEL

KARL C. GARRISON

HERMAN R. GOLDBERG

I. IGNACY GOLDBERG

CHRISTINE P. INGRAM

MAMIE J. JONES

FRANCES G. KOENIG

GEORGE LAVOS

DARRELL J. MASE

HAZEL G. McINTIRE

VELMA Y. MORTON

FRANCES A. MULLEN

FRANK J. O'BRIEN

H. E. ROBINSON

MABEL ROSS

DOROTHY SEBALD

GEORGE SINGER

CURTIS G. SOUTHARD

RUTH STRANG

MARY E. SWITZER

EUGENE J. TAYLOR

WARREN T. VAUGHAN

DONALD V. WILSON

PORTER SARGENT PUBLISHER

11 BEACON STREET • BOSTON 8 MASSACHUSETTS

DEDICATION

To the Managers of the New York Institute for the Education of the Blind, whose generosity has made this volume possible, — a group of laymen whose services to the exceptional child are unheralded, although unsurpassed by any professional contribution.

TABLE OF CONTENTS

VOLUME I
INTRODUCTION AND PROBLEMS

TABLE OF CONTENTS—VOLUME I

Aging, Building and Equipment, Camping, Cardiac, Cerebral
Palsy, Charities, Child Education and Welfare, Chronically
Ill, Deaf, Dental Education, Diabetics. Employment, Epilep-
tics, General, General Education, Guidance, Health, Heredity,
Juvenile Delinquents, Medicine, Mental Health, Mentally Re-

TABLE OF CONTENTS

VOLUME II

THE PHYSICALLY HANDICAPPED AND SPECIAL HEALTH PROBLEMS

TABLE OF CONTENTS

VOLUME III
EMOTIONAL AND MENTAL DEVIATES AND SPECIAL PROBLEMS

CONTRIBUTING AUTHORS

SPECIAL EDUCATION FOR THE EXCEPTIONAL

VOLUME I

Edited by

MERLE E. FRAMPTON and ELENA D. GALL

In collaboration with the following contributing authors

Norman Acton, A.B.
Executive Director, United States Committee for UNICEF, and Consultant, International Society for the Welfare of Cripples, New York City.

Salvatore G. DiMichael, Ph.D.
Executive Director, National Association for Retarded Children, Inc., New York City

Karl C. Garrison, B.S., M.S., Ph.D.
Professor of Education, University of Georgia, College of Education, Athens, Georgia

Herman R. Goldberg, B.S., M.A.
Director of Special Education, Board of Education, Rochester, New York, and Instructor in Education, University of Rochester, Rochester, New York

I. Ignacy Goldberg, Ed.D.
Director, Department of Rehabilitation, Muscatatuck State School, Butlerville, Indiana

Christine P. Ingram, M.A., Ed.D.
Professor of Education and Psychology, Illinois State Normal University, Normal, Illinois

Mamie J. Jones, B.L.I., A.B., M.A., Ph.D.
Coordinator, Education of Exceptional Children, State Department of Education, Atlanta, Georgia

Frances G. Koenig, B.S., M.A.
Lecturer, Psychology and Special Education, Hunter College of the City of New York; Teacher, Health Conservation, and Consulting Psychologist

George Lavos, M.A.
Administrative Aid, Michigan School for the Deaf, Flint, Michigan

Darrell J. Mase, M.A., Ph.D.
Coordinator, Florida Center of Clinical Services, Gainesville, Florida

Hazel G. McIntire, Ed.D.
Director, Division of Special Education, Ohio State Department of Education, Columbus, Ohio

Velma Y. Morton, B.S.
Teacher, Abraham Lincoln School, Park Ridge, Illinois

Frances A. Mullen, Ph.D.
Assistant Superintendent in Charge of Special Education, Chicago Public Schools, Chicago, Illinois

Frank J. O'Brien, M.D., Ph.D.
Associate Superintendent of Schools, Division of Child Welfare, New York City

H.E. Robinson, B.S., M.S., Ed.D.
State Director of Special Education, Texas Education Agency, Austin, Texas

Mabel Ross, M.D.
Mental Health Consultant, Health, Education, and Welfare, Regional Office, New York City

Dorothy Sebald, Ed.D.
Assistant Professor of Education, Hunter College of the City of New York

George Singer, M.D.
Attending Physician, New York Institute for the Education of the Blind, and Instructor of Surgery, New York Medical College, New York City

Curtis G. Southard, M.D.
Chief, Community Services Branch, National Institute of Mental Health, Department of Health, Education, and Welfare, Washington, D.C.

Ruth Strang, Ph.D.
Professor of Education, Teachers College, Columbia University, New York City

Mary E. Switzer, A.B.
Director, Office of Vocational Rehabilitation, Department of Health, Education, and Welfare, Washington, D.C.

Eugene J. Taylor, M.A.
Associate Professor, Department of Physical Medicine and Rehabilitation, New York University College of Medicine, and Editorial Staff, *New York Times*, New York City

Warren T. Vaughan, M.D.
Director, Division of Mental Hygiene, Department of Mental Health, Boston, Massachusetts

Donald V. Wilson, A.B., LL.D., M.A.
Secretary General of the International Society for the Welfare of Cripples, New York City

CONTRIBUTING AUTHORS

SPECIAL EDUCATION FOR THE
EXCEPTIONAL

VOLUMES II AND III

Edited by

MERLE E. FRAMPTON and ELENA D. GALL

In collaboration with the following authors

Georgie Lee Abel, B.S., M.A.
Consultant in Education, American Foundation for the Blind, New York City

Leslie R. Angus, M.D.
Director, The Woods School Child Research Clinic and Treatment Center, Langhorne, Pennsylvania

M. Robert Barnett, B.A.
Executive Director, American Foundation for the Blind, Inc., New York City

Lauretta Bender, B.S., M.A., M.D.
Professor Clinical Psychology, New York University College of Medicine, and Senior Psychiatrist in Charge of Children's Service of the Psychiatric Division, Bellevue Hospital, New York City

E.T. Boulter
Field Director, American Foundation for Overseas Blind, New York City

Mildred Brazier
Principal, Institution School, Walter E. Fernald State School, Waverly, Massachusetts

Florence Brumbaugh, Ph.D.
Associate Professor, Hunter College of the City of New York, and Principal, Hunter College Elementary School, New York City

Claire Burrell, B.A., M.A.
Director, Bureau for Education of the Visually Handicapped, Board of Education, New York City

Catherine E. Chipman
Psychologist, Walter E. Fernald State School, Waverly, Massachusetts

Kathleen Coogan, M.A.
Teacher, Children with Retarded Mental Development Classes, P.S. 24, Brooklyn, New York

Chris J. De Prospo, B.S., M.A.
Assistant Professor of Education, The City College, New York City

Powrie V. Doctor, Ph.D.
Editor, *American Annals of the Deaf*, and Chairman, Department of History and Political Science, Gallaudet College, Washington, D.C.

Leonard M. Elstad, LL.D.
President, Gallaudet College, Washington, D.C.

Robert L. Erdman, B.S., M.S.
Associate Professor of Special Education, Wisconsin State College, Milwaukee, Wisconsin

Malcolm J. Farrell, M.D.
Superintendent, Walter E. Fernald State School, Waverly, Massachusetts

Margaret Fitzgerald, B.S., M.A.
Instructor, Hunter College of the City of New York, and Principal Teacher, Grasslands Hospital, Valhalla, New York

Ernest J. Fleischer, B.S., A.M.
Chairman, Department of English, Fashion Institute of Technology sponsored by the New York City Board of Education

Irving S. Fusfeld, B.S., M.A., Litt.D.
Vice President in Charge of Research, Gallaudet College, Washington, D.C.

Clyde Getz, M.A.
Executive Director, Children's Home Society of California, Los Angeles, California

Valerie Hawkins, B.S., M.Ed.
Visiting Professor, Hunter College of the City of New York

Harold M. Henderson, B.A., M.A.
General Secretary, American Leprosy Missions, New York City

Lois T. Henderson, A.B.
Author of "The Opening Doors."

Arthur S. Hill
Educational Director, United Cerebral Palsy Association, New York City

Seth Hoard, A.B., A.M.
Instructor, Hunter College of the City of New York, and Instructor, The New York Institute for the Education of the Blind, New York City

Ruth B. Irwin, B.S., M.A., Ph.D.
Associate Professor of Speech, and Supervisor of Student Training in Speech Therapy, Speech and Hearing Clinic, The Ohio State University, Columbus 10, Ohio

Ellen Kerney, A.B., M.A.
Instructor, Hunter College of the City of New York, and Instructor, The New York Institute for the Education of the Blind, New York City

Milton Lewis
Reporter, *The New York Herald Tribune*

Marty Mann
Founder and Executive Director, National Committee on Alcoholism, Inc., New York City

Boyd McCandless, A.B., M.A., Ph.D.
Professor and Director, Iowa Child Welfare, Research Station, State University of Iowa, Iowa City, Iowa

Harriet S. McLaughlin, B.A., M.A.
Acting Assistant Supervisor, New York Board of Education, and Principal, Junior High School 47, New York City

Paul C. Mitchell, A.B., M.A.
Assistant Principal, The New York Institute for the Education of the Blind, New York City

Gladys M. Park, R.N., B.S.
Director, Health Advisory Service, Tuberculosis and Health Association, Inc., New York City

Eleanor C. Ronnei, B.A., M.A.
Head, Educational Services, New York League for the Hard of Hearing, and Instructor in Special Education, Teachers College, Columbia University, New York City

Lillian Rosenson, B.A., M.A.
Consultant to the Bureau for Physically Handicapped Children, Board of Education, New York City

Harry Sands, Ph.D.
Executive Director, Epilepsy Association of New York, New York City

Beatrice Schenk de Regniers, Ph.B., M.Ed.
Educational Materials Specialist, American Heart Association, New York City

Harry J. Spar, B.S., M.A.
Director of Services, The Industrial Home for the Blind, Brooklyn, New York

Harvey A. Stevens, B.S.
Superintendent, Southern Wisconsin Colony and Training School, Union Grove, Wisconsin

Ernst H. Suerken, A.B., A.M., M.A.
Supervising Principal, The Echo Hills School, UFSD Greensburgh #11, Dobbs Ferry, New York

Morton D. Schweitzer, Ph.D.
Scientific Director, Muscular Dystrophy Associations of America, Inc., New York City

Martha Taber, B.S., M.A.
Director, Nursery School, New York Institute for the Education of the Blind, New York City

Helen M. Wallace, A.B., M.D., M.P.H.
Director, Bureau for Handicapped Children, New York City Department of Health, and Associate Professor of Pediatrics, New York Medical College

NEED FOR SERVICES TO EXCEPTIONAL CHILDREN

SAMUEL MILLER BROWNELL

COMMISSIONER OF EDUCATION

DEPARTMENT OF HEALTH, EDUCATION AND WELFARE

We all appreciate the necessity of having more and having better educational provisions for the children we call exceptional. We call them exceptional either because they have talents or handicaps sufficient in degree to make it important to provide opportunities, treatment, instruction, facilities, and/or programs different at least in part from those afforded to most children.

To meet all of these specialized needs — for the blind, the partially seeing, the crippled, those with special health problems, the deaf, and hard-of-hearing, the speech handicapped, the socially maladjusted, the mentally retarded, and the gifted — there are today in the service of the Nation's schools, not more than twenty-five thousand who are designated as "special teachers." Roughly, this means an average of 180 exceptional children for every "special teacher" in this field in the United States. It means in fact that many, many children who need the services of a teacher with preparation to help them with their special problems get no such help.

Many children with physical handicaps are in hospitals where no program of instruction is provided. Many others are confined to their homes without the opportunity for instruction from which they could profit and which they will need. Some with vision, hearing, and speech problems are in classes which cannot give them the services they require. Many children with mental limitations, or special health problems could become able to care for themselves and even to contribute to home or community well-being if the school program was such as to prepare them to be as useful adults as they were capable.

Failure to serve both the handicapped and gifted results in an unnecessary loss of manpower and womanpower — a loss which this country can ill afford to have.

*Excerpts from a speech delivered before the Working Conference on the study, "Qualification and Preparation of Teachers of Exceptional Children," at the Department of Health, Education, and Welfare, Room 5022 South, October 25, 1954, used by special permission of Dr. Samuel Miller Brownell, Commissioner of Education, U.S. Department of Health, Education, and Welfare.

PREFACE

Services of an educational, psychological, social, vocational and spiritual nature have been planned and carried out for child and adult deviates since the beginning of civilized man's social conscience.

The beginnings of these services were often clouded with superstitions, idealogies, and philosophies conditioned by tribal customs, religious beliefs, economic circumstances, and political experience. Good or bad, these services were attempts to meet a problem ever current in organized society: What to do with the child or adult who, because of physical or mental deviation, cannot benefit from the available and accepted pattern of educational services.

Although methods of census were not satisfactory centuries ago, and are still inadequate for our present servicing needs, we know that the incidence of this problem at any stage in human society has never been small. The magnitude of the problem has varied with the flow of history. Famine, disease, epidemics, intermittent and extended wars and great social movements such as the industrial revolution have in one way or another added to the number of exceptional children and adults whom we now classify as individuals in need of special education.

Churches, public and private agencies, legislative bodies, schools, and industry have in a measure responded to the challenge to provide services of varying nature for the exceptional child and adult.

For the most part, the great advances in the development of a professional program for the area have been made by individuals and groups fired with a 'categorical imperative' to serve their fellow man. From their ranks have come the professional and lay leaders of special education in our century.

Special Education for the Exceptional, Volumes I, II and III, have been prepared to inform a new generation of leadership, lay and professional, of services now available to individuals needing special assistance, treatment, or education.

Each volume is a unit in itself. The first constitutes a general treatment of the entire field of special education and includes a detailed survey and summary of those problems and methods which are common to all phases of special education. There are chapters by authorities, comprehensive bibliographies, extensive lists of agencies, periodicals, and other reference materials.

In the second and third volumes, each area of special education is treated separately by professionals who are experts on the particular subject under consideration. Volume II is devoted to the physically handicapped and to special health problems; Volume III, to the neurologically impaired, the emotionally disturbed, the mentally retarded, the intellectually gifted, and to special areas, including the aged, the alcoholic, and the narcotic.

While these three volumes do not pretend to cover all the technical subject matter of all areas currently included in special education for the exceptional, they do form a comprehensive introduction to the field. If the young college student desires to know what his culture has produced in services for the exceptional, he will find here a summary of these, as well as adequate source references for further study of each area. If the prospective teacher, social worker, educational administrator, interested parent or layman wishes a rapid survey of special education, he will here find a resumé of objectives and procedures for teaching the exceptional child, and a listing of the major current problems of the various areas for our time.

The recent rapid growth of the profession of special education has produced many pamphlets, brochures, manuals, doctoral theses, and technical articles which are of importance to the parent, student, teacher, and professional. The editors have attempted to select for reference from this large collection those most suitable as supplementary reading. A goodly proportion of this material can still be procured from the sources indicated, and it is recommended that the serious student avail himself of the opportunity to enlarge his personal library.

The editors have not considered it possible to separate the medical and educational approaches to special education problems. While the emphasis in these volumes is on the educational, there is no attempt to minimize the importance of medical service. Equally important to a 'whole' program are the services of social workers, rehabilitation personnel, therapists, and counsellors, — in short, the 'team.'

The editors have also not always clearly delimited the areas of services for children or adults. This has been intentional. Most, if not all, of the areas of special education are concerned with both children and adults, and therefore with the general field of adult rehabilitation. Many of the teaching methods, service programs, technical aids and prostheses can only be considered in the light of servicing both areas. While these volumes do not pretend to cover the general field of rehabilitation, civilian or veteran, its close relationship is obvious. The editors are conscious that the chapters on the aged, the chronically ill, the narcotic, and the alcoholic in Volume III, deal almost wholly with adults. It is, however, their studied decision that special education must soon plan an effective program for these areas, and for this reason they have been included.

The nature of such a work makes us beholden to hundreds of authors, associations, and institutions for the results of their research projects and successful programs, and for illustrative materials. Every effort has been made to give credit for such contributions. Any failure on our part to give such recognition will be due solely to our shortcomings and we will appreciate having such omissions brought to our attention for correction in subsequent editions.

Special mention should be made of the services of Dr. Hugh G. Rowell, experienced teacher, scientist, friend of children and leader of men. Dr. Rowell has through his long years of experience rendered the editors invaluable aid in the preparation of these volumes.

The editors are indebted to the following authors, publishers, and organizations for use of reprints and quotations in Volume I: Samuel Miller Brownell, Dr. Leonard Mayo, Dr. Romaine P. Mackie, Dr. Arthur J. Lesser, Dr. Eleanor P. Hunt, Dr. L. M. Dunn, Dr. William M. Cruickshank, Mr. Henry M. Light, Mr. Isaac Jolles, Dr. Julius B. Richmond, Dr. J. Wayne Wrightstone, Dr. Helen M. Wallace, Verna S. Carlisle, The Association for the Aid of Crippled Children, The American Journal of Public Health, The U.S. Office of Education, The American School and University, The U.S. Department of Public Health, and The Department of Public Instruction of the State of Illinois. To the staff of the New York Institute for the Education of the Blind and to Mr. E. Nelson Hayes, and the staff of Porter Sargent, Publisher, the editors owe a debt of gratitude for their aid in the preparation of the manuscript.

Opinions expressed by contributing authors are not necessarily the opinions of the editors. Nor do contributing authors necessarily subscribe to the opinions of other authors with whom their contributions appear.

MERLE E. FRAMPTON
ELENA D. GALL

New York, N. Y., May, 1955

CREED FOR EXCEPTIONAL CHILDREN

LEONARD MAYO

WE BELIEVE in the American promise of equality of opportunity, regardless of nationality, cultural background, race, or religion.

WE BELIEVE that this promise extends to every child within the borders of our country no matter what his gifts, his capacity, or his handicaps.

WE BELIEVE that the nation as a whole, every state and county, every city, town, and hamlet, and every citizen has an obligation to help in bringing to fruition in this generation the ideal of a full and useful life for every exceptional child in accordance with his capacity: the child who is handicapped by defects of speech, of sight, or of hearing, the child whose life may be adversely influenced by a crippling disease or condition, the child whose adjustment to society is made difficult by emotional or mental disorders, and the child who is endowed with special gifts of mind and spirit.

WE BELIEVE that to this end the home of the exceptional child, the schools, the churches, and the health and social agencies in his community must work together effectively in his behalf.

WE BELIEVE that for the most exceptional children their parents and teachers are the master architects essential to the planning and building of their future.

WE BELIEVE, therefore, that every appropriate resource of the community must be mobilized, if need be, to aid in maintaining his family life at an adequate social and economic level, and in furnishing guidance and encouragement to his parents.

WE BELIEVE that the teachers of exceptional children must possess the personality, develop the understanding, and acquire the knowledge and skill through special preparation that will enable them to inspire and motivate, as well as teach the art of making a living and a life.

WE BELIEVE that the cooperative efforts of parents and teachers must be encouraged, sustained, and supplemented: by teacher education institutions with curricula and programs based on the knowledges and skills needed in

---

*This creed, presented to the Conference on the Qualification and Preparation of Teachers of Exceptional Children, October, 1954, by Dr. Leonard Mayo, Director of the Association for the Aid of Crippled Children, New York City, is used by special permission of Dr. Leonard Mayo and the Association for the Aid of Crippled Children, New York City.

the education of exceptional children; by State departments that will develop challenging standards of program operation, and work with teachers in establishing sound certification procedures; by local school systems that will recruit and employ teachers who are qualified by personality and special preparation; by health and welfare agencies that will provide diagnosis and evaluation, medical and psychiatric care, and social service.

WE BELIEVE that research designed to increase present knowledge of personality and the learning process, and studies aimed at the improvement of programs of special education are essential to further progress.

WE BELIEVE in the sensitive interpretation of the exceptional child and his needs by teachers and others in order that an attitude favorable to his acceptance and development may be engendered and sustained in the community.

ABOVE ALL, WE BELIEVE in the exceptional child himself; in his capacity for development so frequently retarded by the limits of present knowledge; in his right to a full life too often denied him through lack of imagination and ingenuity on the part of his elders; in his passion for freedom and independence that can be his only when those who guide and teach him have learned the lessons of humility, and in whom there resides an effective confluence of the trained mind and the warm heart.

SECTION I

CHAPTER I

HISTORICAL BACKGROUND

HISTORICAL BACKGROUND

Special Education, both as a phrase and as a service program, has taken on new and expansive meaning during the past twenty-five years. Our present decade has seen phenomenal development of medical, vocational, educational, psychological, recreational and socio-economic services, all claiming in one way or another to be part of the field of special education or related areas. The rapid growth of this new educational emphasis has been accomplished despite confusion, overlapping services, some pseudo-scientific programs and projects, lack of proper coordination, inaccurate classification of cases, and much literary license with definitions.

The term 'Special Education' today has no concise definition limiting its objectives and field of function. Perhaps it does not need such definitive treatment. It is always difficult with a new discipline to limit clearly its field of functions or define concisely its objectives. Special education is by its very nature a composite of many interrelated medical and non-medical services. These are offered to both children and adults who are to some extent handicapped by physical, mental, educational, economic or social factors which set them apart as individuals who need one or more of the wide variety of services of special education now available from federal, state, municipal and private agencies and individuals. Depending upon the nature of the handicap and the environment in which it is found, the need of such services may exist for a limited or extended period of time.

Even at present it is often felt that exceptional children or adults are more the problem of the physician than the educator. Certainly medical treatment seems to be provided for them, even under modern social and medical plans, long before their education is considered. If the history of service to the exceptional is closely allied with medical history, it must be remembered that medical history was never recorded in the manner of national political conflicts or the complex social activities of an age. Mysticism and secrecy prevailed among the ancient Aesculapians. It may well be that, in addition to the lost medical arts of certain nations like the Egyptians, there have disappeared the record of their actual care and training of the handicapped and exceptional. On the other hand, it is generally felt that the type of social and educational motivation that underlies real care for the exceptional is of recent origin.[1]

The history of the care and training of the exceptional must of necessity follow social and educational trends rather than create them. The injured do not form the advance guard for an army. It must be added that, as often as not, it has been impossible for the educator of the exceptional to follow an educational trend, at least for a long period. The reason is simple enough. With the exceptional there are physical, social and psychological problems which do not exist with the nonhandicapped. It is the solution of these problems that actually constitutes the special education. To solve or attempt to solve these, we must know their nature. This implies that medical science must first analyze the problem, which may be impaired or lost vision, or a similar difficulty with the hearing or speech, or some other physical, emotional or mental disability. Scientific medicine is recent. The day of the 'humors' as an explanation of pathology is only just past. Tests and measurements are relatively new. The application of a truly scientific method to the field of special education is still in the future. We are making progress, but our profession is an infant discipline just learning to walk along the pathways of the older disciplines.

Having learned the physical or psychological problems to be solved, and something of their nature, we must next find the means of solving them. For example, in the education of the blind, carved letters and other devices were invented and tried unsuccessfully until the advent of braille produced a medium by which the problem of lost vision could be overcome. Even then, disagreements as to technical matters prevented the adoption of a universal braille until a very few years ago.

In the case of the deaf and the hard-of-hearing, the stupidity and cupidity of man stand out. Here was lip reading, a device known to the monks. Here, too, was sign language. Yet for years these valuable methods of communicating and of socially short-circuiting impaired hearing seem to have been unused. And then the methods came into conflict!

As for the situation with speech defects, there was confusion worse confounded, and still is. Theory after theory, and classification after classification, and treatment after treatment have been proposed and defended. Although the real answers are distant, many are those who propose solutions.

The fact is, all these problems have been studied and their true nature often discovered. Remedial measures have been worked out on a trial-and-error basis. The historical record of such experimentations is important if only because those working for the advancement of the various areas should not and need not repeat the errors of the past. Just why any particular remedy was found at a given time seems to have been a combination of interest and accident, thereby following the trend of other scientific discoveries. As often as not the discovery has come from someone, himself handicapped, who has sought some means of self-improvement, found it, and made it generally available. Likewise, when the work with the exceptional has attracted persons at all, it seems to have won devoted professional and volunteer workers. One reason may have been that, in any age, some of its most distinguished persons were in one way or another handicapped.[2] Nor may the social role of the fool be forgotten, for it was a large and influential one in many instances. More often than not, these individuals were severely handicapped.

From a misty past, from the attempts to overcome or go around handicaps, from the slow arrangement of the parts of the picture puzzle, from the efforts and devotion of interested persons, sometimes themselves handicapped, through all historic periods, and in spite of the strangest sort of opposition at times, have come the modern care and education of the exceptional — a fascinating evolution.

THREE DISTINCT HISTORIC PERIODS

The history of the care and treatment of the exceptional is greater than the aggregate of its separate areas and periods. It deals with the humanities of every age, for the exceptional have been problems of all periods of cultural development. Different societies have dealt with them differently. Social treatment as such apparently preceded educational procedures.

Historically, references to services for the handicapped, or the exceptional, or special education for deviates extend back into the most ancient of cultures.[3]

There are three general periods of the work with the exceptional whether as a whole or by distinct areas, though in the latter case there may be individual variation in bracketing dates. These periods are approximately as follows:

1. *Primitive and Ancient Times, dating from about* 1550 B.C. *to about* 476 A.D. This period may be analyzed principally for its philosophy of social treatment of the exceptional as revealed through authentic records and accounts.

2. *The Middle Ages, approximately* 500-600 A.D. *to around* 1500 A.D. The interest of outstanding personalities, if roused at all, assumed a more philanthropic aspect, notably in the case of the blind and deaf.

For both these earlier periods, the record we have is confused and easily misinterpreted. There has always been, and it is still increasing, a trend toward recognizing the handicapped as a horizontal (taking all groups together) as well as a vertical (by areas) problem. The exceptional were more likely to be viewed as a group, i.e., horizontally, rather than with emphasis upon any divisional areas, although the areas were known, recognized, and sometimes specially considered. For these reasons the story of the exceptional before 1400 A.D. is best presented as a unit.

3. *The Modern Period, after* 1400-1500 A.D. In this period most of the real progress has been made in the care and education of the exceptional, beginning with basic scientific investigations which pointed the way toward the solution of some of the more baffling problems. Modern special educational procedures had their beginnings during this era.

PRIMITIVE, ANCIENT, AND MEDIEVAL TIMES

Probably from man's earliest thinking moments the exceptional have been recognized as a group of individuals needing treatment. In prehistoric days, and among animals, nature herself eliminated the handicapped and exceptional by the process of the survival of the fittest. As they were incapable of combating nature and equally unable to detect and adequately combat enemies, death came upon them rapidly.

As tribes developed from small hunting groups, a formal process of elimination was favored. The handicapped, owing to their inability to assume responsibility even for their own persons, slowed the movements of the roving tribe. They neither joined the hunt nor contributed to the meager production of food supplies. Thus they constituted an actual economic hazard to the entire group. Their lives were constantly in danger from wild beasts and human foes. In attack they were helpless and depended upon the protection of their tribesmen. If they were deserted by the fleeing tribe, they were easily captured by the enemy and often became the victims of ceremonies, rites, and practices more cruel than death at the hands of their own associates. In some primitive tribes, similar treatment is even today accorded the aged, for similar reasons.

Such a protective and possibly merciful practice continued with the ancient Greeks and Romans, though possibly it has not been accurately chronicled. Since the family was the social unit in these civilizations, the head of the family determined the fate of any exceptional child. The decision was based, in all probability, upon the degree and type of impairment, with emphasis upon the social and economic prognosis. It is quite possible that society, even at that time, was not equipped for any form of treatment. The practice, at any rate, was selective and gradually came into disuse when these nations turned from strictly warlike pursuits to become the centers of the culture of their times. There is no conclusive historical evidence that abandonment or destruction of the unfit was a universal practise in the ancient world. It is claimed that handicapped individuals were thrown into rivers, or left in the mountains to perish or to be destroyed by wild beasts. It is usually reported that imperfect children were exposed in Sparta under Lycurgus, and that the Athenians put deaf children to death and the Spartans consigned them to the great pit in Taygetus. In Athens, exposure supposedly occurred under Solon and Plato. Aristotle is claimed by some to have approved. The laws of Lycurgus permitted abandonment of idiots. In Sparta, a socially handicapped individual was not allowed to exist because he imperiled the lives of the group.

Nevertheless, many of these reputed practices do not tally with the proper ages of children for expected discovery of certain physical defects. It is hardly possible scientifically, even today, to determine whether a child at birth or in early infancy possesses or does not possess hearing. Mental handicaps, likewise, are often discovered late. On the other hand, blindness and crippling are obvious very early in life. Conceivably, early destruction may have been practiced in some cases by some societies. But it is not known that the Spartans or other Greeks destroyed children two or three years of age.

In summary, discovery of a defect or variation had to precede the elimination of the individual. Abandonment and similar practices had to be confined to infants whose defects could be found or the age for such destruction extended into young childhood. Again, in certain instances, it is known that various limitations were placed upon different types of the exceptional — the mentally handicapped, for example, being given no social rights. If destroyed, what need could there be for controlling practices?

Early Desire for Remedial Measures. That the practice of elimination was not satisfying, even though selective, is evident at a very early stage in the growing social conscience. There developed attempts at treatment by ceremony, by social practice, and by other means. Treatment implied the employment of experts, and curious experts and methods they were.

Logically, as various remedial groups appeared in society, attempts were made to treat the various types of the exceptional. This was true, whether the healers were medicine men, priests, or Asclepiads (those famous physician-priests of Epidaurus, third century B.C.). Quite probably some of the sadistic practices of the Middle Ages were actually offshoots of some un-chronicled theories of treatment. Instead of medical diagnosis, there came classifications as demon-possessed, accursed of the gods, or even protected by the gods. Superstitions arose around these explanations of the phenomena of deviation. Some have persisted over long periods. The witch hunts of Salem may have found their origin in this remote past. Touching a cripple's hump to insure good luck may be but a survival of medieval superstition. The explanation of such practices may no longer be known, but the sources are old indeed.

Judging from ancient and primitive idols, the bizarre were worshiped most of all, possibly on the basis of fear and propitiation. The exceptional, if of high degree, were sufficiently bizarre to meet this standard. If of less degree, they were perhaps accepted as reasonably normal members of society.

Both medicine and education of today are heritages from the religious, — from the primitive medicine man; the priest in Egypt, whose many skillful arts and sciences for the most part have been lost; the Babylonian groups; and the monk of the Middle Ages, caring for body and mind as one more means of saving the soul. The barber-surgeon and the physician-philosopher are a comparatively late development. The handicapped, from very early times, were obviously the wards of the religious. Yet neither the disciples of Aesculapius nor the followers of Christ, even in combination, came anywhere near solving their problems.

Treatment of the exceptional as a group or by areas might or might not follow or influence the culture of any world period. For example, the Chinese principle of family loyalty was extended to the more unfortunate members of the family. Parents must protect their children, and children obey their parents, even at the expense of larger social loyalties. "Everyone calls his son his son," said Confucius, "whether he has talents or has not talents." In other words, shortcomings should be viewed charitably and judgment with-held until the youth grew up. The same philosophy applied to all the exceptional.

The Hebraic Law. The Hebraic laws concerning the unfortunate and dependent represent the high-water mark of prophetic thought and teaching. It is true that Hebrew law is unmethodical and unclassified, and reflects in-consistencies of thought and practice. Nevertheless, it is in marked contrast with some of the harsh and pitiless practices of antiquity. The law recognizes the unfortunate, the handicapped, the needy, and the dependent. It admon-ishes the people to aid these helpless classes. Widows and orphans, the blind, the deaf, and the needy are to have special consideration. (Exodus XII, 21-24; Duteronomy XXIV, 17, 18 and XXVII, 18; Leviticus XIX, 9, 10, 14 and XXIII, 22.)

The Talmud and Midrash mention four categories, — deafness, dumbness, blindness, and lameness, — blindness being regarded as the most severe. Certain definite social limitations placed upon the exceptional related to the laws of ceremonial uncleanness which excluded defective persons from sacred places. Jesus was condemned for healing a lame man in the synagogue on the Sabbath. Such infirmities were considered as possibly outcomes of sin, though the Talmud and Midrash enjoined compassion and benevolence.

The Code of Hammurabi. Occasionally, inspired social remedies are revealed; e.g., the modern practices of vocational guidance and workman's compensation laws are of ancient origin. That vocational guidance existed early is shown from the Egyptians' use of the blind as professional mourners.

The principle of compensation for injuries dates back to the Code of Hammurabi. The Babylonian attitude toward the exceptional can, with some difficulty, be inferred through indirect references to the unfortunate in the Code of Hammurabi. The responsibility rested upon an involved family loyalty system in a civil code which was harsh and severe. The 'lex talionis' which prevailed throughout, recognized class distinctions but demanded that injuries be requited in kind. Thus —

> If a man destroy the eye of another man (a patrician),
> they shall destroy his eye.
> If he shall destroy the eye of a workingman or break a
> bone of a workingman, he shall pay one miva of silver.
> If a slave deny his master, he shall cut off his ear.

The basis of this code came from the quasi-scientific practice of medicine in Babylonia, where physicians were severely punished for bungling an operation. "If a physician operate on the eye socket of a man with his bronze lancet and destroy the man's eye, they shall cut off the physician's hand." The same principles were applied to other forms of medical treatment.

The Christian Era. With the coming of Christ came also compassion and care for the poor, the lame, the blind, the demon-possessed, and the mentally afflicted, — in fact, for all our known deviates. No attempt, however, was made to educate them, nor is it clear how far the teachings of Christ were actually practiced toward the exceptional in His day. Certainly He **was** criticized for aiding them on the Sabbath.

The Middle Ages. In the early Middle Ages, there arose a curious contrast between the treatment of the exceptional by the religious orders, and by the nobility. To the religious orders they undoubtedly represented souls to be saved through a certain amount of extra effort. The nobles, on the other hand, used the exceptional, as had certain nations previously, for the purpose of amusement. Imbeciles, though not having the shrewdness to create jokes, continued to be the butts of them. But there also arose Merry Andrews and Grimaldes, — sometimes rachitic dwarfs, sometimes true dwarfs and cripples, — of great cleverness and influence. These might have, in addition to their wit, a certain bizarre appearance amusing to their owners. Some have been immortalized through literature, especially drama and song. Even today certain types of dwarfs are considered good raw material for circus clowns.

The keynote of the Middle Ages was cruelty and confusion. There is no reason to believe that the cause of the exceptional was much advanced during this period.

THE MODERN PERIOD

With the advent of the modern era, innumerable important figures appeared in the pageant of the exceptional. The keynote of the succeeding work has been the development of both the horizontal and the more international point of view. Modern science and the invention of means of faster communication have made this possible. The compassion of Christ has been united with the latest discoveries of science for service to the exceptional.

The gradual stepping into the lead by the United States has characterized the last century. The greatest developments have been in perfection of organization rather than in improvements of methods or the development of a truly scientific approach to the solution of the problems of the exceptional.

Religious literature (Talmud, Midrash, Vishnu), legal codes (Justinian), public service programs, all give clear evidence of mankind's interest in the welfare of those who because of marked physical or sensory deviation from a standard in any period of a given civilization, need special services.[4-16]

FOOTNOTES

1. See the historical resume for each area (i.e., Blind, Deaf, etc.) in *Special Education for the Exceptional*, Vols. II & III, edited by Frampton, M. E., and Gall, Elena D., published by Porter Sargent, 11 Beacon St., Boston, Mass.
2. Bett, W. R., *Infirmities of Genius* (Philosophical Library: N.Y.C., 1952).
3. See Frampton, M. E., and Rowell, H. G., *Education of the Handicapped*, Vol. I. History (World Book Company: Yonkers, N. Y., 1938).
4. French, S. F., *From Homer to Helen Keller* (American Foundation for the Blind, Inc.: N. Y., 1932).
5. Best, H., *Blindness and the Blind in the United States* (Macmillan: N.Y.C., 1934).
6. Best, H., *Deafness and the Deaf in the United States* (Macmillan Co., N.Y.C., 1943).
7. Vives, Juan Luis, *On the Subvention of the Poor* (1526).
8. See the story of Tobit in the *Apocrypha*
9. St. John Chrysostum, *Sermon on the Poor*.
10. St. Ambrose, *Address to Anexentius*.
11. Condillac, *Traite des Sensations* (1755).
12. Fay, E. A., "What Did St. Augusine Say?" *Annals of the Deaf*, Jan., 1912.
13. Locke, John, *Essay Concerning Human Understanding* (1690). See also the so-called "Problem of Molyneux. "
14. Diderot, D., *Essai sur les Aveugles* (1798).
15. Pliny, *Natural History* (23-79 A. D.).
16. Berkeley *Essay toward a New Theory of Vision* (1709).

SECTION I

CHAPTER II

WHAT IS SPECIAL EDUCATION?

WHAT IS SPECIAL EDUCATION

THE CLINICAL APPROACH IN SPECIAL
EDUCATION BY DARREL J. MASE

WHAT IS SPECIAL EDUCATION?

The obviously handicapped — the blind, the deaf, the mentally deficient — were the first to be recognized as needing services, and the term 'Physically Handicapped' or 'Handicapped' soon became associated with such deviates and used loosely to describe them. The terms 'Exceptional Children and Adults' and 'Special Education' are of relatively recent origin in their present usage, while the consciousness of a special profession is an even later development in the terminology of educational circles. Some recent research indicates that the use of the term 'Special Education' in the United States probably dates not earlier than 1884.

Joseph C. Gordon remarked in his Presidential Address to the National Educational Association in 1898 that:

The time is too short to go into the history of the organization of this department. I will say, merely to put the matter on record, that the initiative came from the National Educational Association, at a meeting in Madison, Wis., in 1884. The matter was taken up there joining hands with the educators of the deaf; and immediately after the meeting adjourned an invitation came from the officers of the National Educational Association for the teachers of the deaf *to form a department;* but nothing came of it at that time. In planning this organization, it seems to have been laid out upon broad lines. It is, you may say, all-embracing for it embraces the beginnings of all things. While it was primarily intended for the educators of the deaf, it soon came to include the educators of the blind, and afterward it took in those who are interested in the education of backward and feeble-minded children. It invites to attend the meetings of the department all who take an interest in the growth and progress of education for these classes. We feel that we are entitled to march along the same road, and that we must do so if we would keep up with the procession.
I will only say that we who are engaged in these *special lines* have also been urgently invited to join our forces with the body of associated charities.[1]

At the same meeting of the N.E.A., Dr. Alexander G. Bell pointed out special treatment for the deviate in his Closing Address:

Now, all that I have said in relation to the deaf would be equally advantageous to the blind and to the feeble-minded. We have in the public-school system a large body of ordinary children in the same community. We have there children who cannot hear sufficiently well to profit by instruction in the public schools, and we have children who cannot see sufficiently well to profit by instruction in the public schools, and we have children who are undoubtedly backward in their mental development. Why should not these children form an annex to the public-school system, receiving special instruction from special teachers, who shall be able to give instruction to little children who are either deaf, blind, or mentally deficient wihout sending them away from their homes or from the ordinary companions with whom they are associated?[2]

In 1902 Dr. Bell further developed the subject and referred to the action of the Board of Directors of the N.E.A. in his President's Address at their meeting held July 8-12, 1901, at Detroit, Michigan, when a 'Department of Special Education' was established:

At a meeting of the Board of Directors of the Association yesterday, the request for the change of the name of the department was presented, and it gives me pleasure to announce that the request was granted by unanimous vote. So we are now and will hereafter be known as the *Department of Special Education*.[3]

In 1902, at its forty-first annual meeting, the N.E.A. adopted a definite program for the 'Department of Special Education':

A number of names were proposed for the department, but none seemed to satisfy. Finally, at the Detroit meeting last summer a committee was appointed consisting of the executive officers of the department, to reorganize the department and to make effort to have its name changed. This Committee acted and it adopted the following platform:
1. The name of the department shall be: *'Department of Special Education—Relating to Children Demanding Special Means of Instruction.'*[4]

It would seem from these references that special education in its broader meaning had its auspicious beginnings in 1901-02, giving the educational field in the United States[5] a virile new professional offspring fifty-three years of age in 1954. The rapid growth of this new discipline toward the status of a full-fledged, acceptable member among the older established disciplines of learning has been dynamic and substantial. Our sister sciences may look askance at some of our early productions, and cast a critical eye on some of our current efforts to come of age; but special education can look with just pride on its accomplishments and hope our distinguished colleagues will remember that theirs were once fledgling disciplines. The next half century will find the profession of special education as accepted and definitive as our older disciplines.

What do we mean when we use the term 'Special Education'? Who are these individuals the profession of special education attempts to serve? Approximately how many individuals in the United States need special education services according to latest available census figures or formulae? An answer, if one is possible and desirable, is to define the field of service in which special education is engaged.

There are some professionals who believe it is useless to engage in what they call "fruitless search in semantics." These leaders feel strongly that to attempt to define and delimit too closely merely means "an effort to find the most pleasing connotation"; that our main effort should be expended on "changing parental and community attitudes toward the exceptional"; that when these broad problems have been solved "our problem of phraseology" will also have been solved.

There are others who feel our field needs a definitive statement of each of the areas of special education, clearly indicating the scope, objectives, methodology, and specific programs designed to serve the exceptional child. This group of professionals realize the difficulty inherent in applying more scientific measuring rods to a new and complex field such as special education, but they are also aware of the confusion, lack of scientific methods, overlapping, and gross misunderstanding which this 'tyranny of words' has caused when released upon the public and in the profession with such profusion and such intensity.

The rapid growth of our means of propaganda through press, radio and television has made hereto professional language more commonplace among the American public. This is a welcome development in the education of the public. It also places an obligation upon the educator to be certain his pupil, public or patient, not only gets the right pill, but that he knows what the pill contains as well as how to administer the medicine and what the remedy is expected to prevent or cure. It is, therefore, imperative that we crystallize our thinking concerning the field of special education. It would be well for the reader to review some of the attempts to define the field of special education, or the education of the exceptional.

We give here six basic definitions, as well as references to others which are of particular interest and import.

SIX DEFINITIONS

National Society for the Study of Education (1950):

> In every school system there are pupils who, because they deviate markedly from the so-called "normal" child, require special skills and services on the part of teachers and other school personnel. These children cannot adjust to the school program without such special services. Some of them are physically handicapped — blind, deaf, epileptic, or crippled. Some differ mentally to a significant degree, being either seriously retarded in intellectual development or exceptionally gifted. Some are emotionally disturbed or are unable to make a proper social adjustment in school and community; among these are children with serious behavior problems which may result in a disturbed personality or in delinqency.
>
> All these are called "exceptional children," the term being used to refer to those who deviate from what is supposed to be average in physical, mental, emotional, or social characteristics to such an extent that they require special educational services in order to develop to their maximum capacity. Those special services may include a radical modification of the curriculum, special methods of instruction, special equipment, or an adjusted school schedule. Under present conditions of school organization, they can sometimes be offered best through the medium of a special class or school; but, in many cases, they may be provided for individual pupils in a regular class. Whatever the type of exceptional condi-

tion and wherever the child may be, the important matter is that the child's needs be identified and satisfactorily met.

Exceptional children do not profit sufficiently from the group education techniques used in most of our schools for teaching children of average ability. Society has not constructed enough classrooms, has not kept classes small enough, and has not provided enough highly qualified teachers. For this reason, it is necessary to furnish special services for exceptional children, either in the regular classroom or in special schools and classes, if we expect them to grow according to their potentialities.

A child with seriously defective vision requires different techniques of instruction than the child who has normal vision. So, also, a child with a marked hearing loss requires additional services and special instruction. The crippled child requires special facilities for his physical care and must have appropriate adjustments of his daily schedule if he is to make satisfactory progress. Even when all of these are provided, exceptional children in the same class with normal children and with the same teacher, all trying to learn under the same methods of instruction, do not have equality of opportunity with others. Educational equality demands the consideration of individual differences and needs and the provision of special services to meet those needs.[6]

U.S. Department of Health, Education and Welfare (1952-53):

One of the most vital and significant developments in American education is the extension of instructional services to exceptional children. The term "exceptional children" is applied to those pupils who need special adjustive services because of their physical, intellectual, or personal-social differences from other children. Included in this broad category are the unusually bright or gifted children; the mentally retarded; the crippled (including the cerebral-palsied); those with special health problems, such as cardiac involvements, epilepsy, and other debilitating conditions; the blind and partially seeing; the deaf and the hard-of-hearing; those with speech defects; and the socially and emotionally maladjusted.

The special adjustive school services for exceptional children are usually referred to as "special education." Special education includes several types of services, depending upon the needs of the children and the policies of the administrative staffs of the schools. In general, however, the most commonly found organizational patterns are as follows:

1. Special schools and classes for long-time placement. — This type of program is designed for the child whose differences represent a permanent disability or exceptionality and who needs an especially adapted curriculum. Ordinarily the child spends all, or most, of his time in the special class, although at the upper age levels many schools assign special class children to some experiences in the regular school program. These assignments are

usually in areas of learning in which the exceptional pupil may benefit from such instruction and in which his differences will not cause him to be a misfit.

The special-class approach for children in need of a long-time program has been employed to the greatest extent in providing for children with intellectual differences. The mentally retarded child's differences become greater as he grows older, and it is usually considered necessary to plan an adjusted curriculum that will extend to or beyond the school-leaving age. However, some schools have also provided for intellectually gifted children, as well as for socially and emotionally maladjusted pupils, through part- or full-year special classes extending over a long period of years.

For the child who is physically handicapped by severe crippling or debilitating conditions, long-time placement in special facilities may also be employed. This is ordinarily due to the ease of providing physical adjustment in a special school rather than because of the pupil's intellectual disability. Many of the traditional facilities for crippled children — as well as for the deaf, the blind, and those handicapped by other severe physical disabilities — involve special elementary schools and, sometimes, special schools which include the high-school grades. Nevertheless, more recently established programs for many of these children involve short-time assignments to special classes, and eventual absorption of the handicapped into regular elementary and secondary school classes.

2. Special classes for short-time placement. — It is probable that recent years have brought considerable emphasis to the provision of temporary adjustive facilities for many handicapped children whose intellectual differences are not a major consideration. If the educational services are provided at the nursery school and kindergarten levels, most severely crippled and otherwise physically disabled children may develop improved coordinations and better speech habits, and learn to live with their handicaps to the extent that they may be absorbed in the regular schools and classes at a relatively early age. For the deaf or blind child the period of special class placement may need to be longer, since children who are deaf or blind must learn special techniques of communication. Nevertheless, it has been demonstrated that both normally intelligent deaf and blind children may achieve well in the regular school classes after they have mastered communicative skills, especially if they are provided periodic guidance and assistance by a specialist in their area of disability.

3. Special supplementary instruction services. — Many exceptional children make adequate adjustments to the program of the regular schools and classes if they are given supplementary assistance and instruction. These include children with speech defects, who are usually provided speech training at regular intervals by specialists in speech correction; hard-of-hearing pupils, who may profit from periodic lip-reading instruction or assistance in the use

of hearing aids; and the partially sighted, who may meet with a specialist for supplementary instruction or guidance. For partially sighted children considerable differences exist in the types of services provided by various schools. Some schools continue to provide full- or part-time special classes; others provide supplementary assistance by a specialist who may work with children at intervals according to their needs; and in other schools the specialist is considered primarily as a counselor to classroom teachers.

4. Home or hospital instruction. — A large number of schools have extended their instructional programs beyond the confines of school buildings and into the homes and hospitals where many severely disabled children are found. These programs may involve daily group instruction in hospitals and convalescent homes, itinerant bedside instruction, and the use of electronic devices in homes. The children served are those who are temporarily or permanently incapacitated to the extent that they cannot be served in regular schools or special classes, even when transportation is provided, or for whom no special adjustive services are available in nearby schools.

5. Residential school programs. — Many handicapped children can only be served by residential school programs. Because of the absence of local facilities, of individual problems of social adaptability, or of severity of handicaps, institutional and residential schools are maintained for thousands of mentally deficient, blind, deaf, and socially maladjusted children. While many of these institutions and schools come under the administration of welfare and mental hygiene commissions rather than departments of education, they constitute an important field of special education. Their functions are primarily educational and rehabilitative.[7]

Harry J. Baker (1953):

There is no single term which appropriately describes all the types of children to be discussed in this book. The term "exceptional" is probably the most suitable of several which might be selected. But even this term immediately gives the impression of something very unusual, outstanding, extraordinary, or rare, according to dictionary definitions. On the contrary it is the purpose to relate the education of exceptional children to normal, average children in logical and meaningful ways. One of the greatest obstacles to a better and more complete program of education for exceptional children arises from the widespread misconception that they are a class, separate and distinct from normal children. As a matter of fact some exceptional children are characterized by handicaps so minor that they continue to be taught mainly in regular grades. The types of exceptional children embrace a much wider group of children than has usually been included by most authors and for two reasons: (1) to bridge a gap between the normal, average child and the extremely handicapped or exceptional, and (2) to interpret the needs of the mildly handicapped who are often more neglected and misunderstood than are those with severe deviations.

'Exceptional' is a more inclusive term than 'handicapped,' since it embraces children at both extremes of various scales. This use is particularly true in the case of mental variations in which the mentally gifted are included. There should be a greater emphasis and development of the exceptional in the direction of talents of all kinds in addition to those disclosed by mental tests. The committee of the National Society for the Study of Education dealing with the education of exceptional children proposed the following definition: 'Those who deviate from what is supposed to be average in physical, mental, emotional, or social characteristics to such an extent that they require special educational services in order to develop to their maximum capacity.'[8]

National Foundation for Infantile Paralysis and National Society for Crippled Children and Adults (1952):

Public education is for all children who are capable of profiting by instruction. The American public schools recognize that no two children are alike and that programs must be adjusted to meet individual differences and needs. Special education is the direct outgrowth of the emphasis on the individual differences of children. The present trend in education shifts away from the teaching of subjects, and toward teaching of children with consideration for all of their special abilities, or disabilities, in an environment created to meet their needs. Between four and five million children of elementary and secondary school age are in need of specialized programs because of physical, mental and emotional and social handicaps. These children who deviate from the hypothetical so-called 'normal' child are called exceptional children. These children must have special educational services if they are to develop to their fullest capacities. These special services may consist of a complete program in a special school, a special class within a regular school, a specially trained individual for needed educational services, special consideration for the child within the regular class or various other provisions adapted to the child's needs and capacities. Special education is planned to make use of highly specialized methods in order to provide all exceptional children with the specific type of educational service they need.

Children needing these services are the deaf, the hard of hearing, the blind, the partially seeing and the speech defective. They are crippled children with cerebral palsy, poliomyelitis, congenital deformities and other orthopedic handicaps. They are children with cardiac difficulties who are often referred to as those with 'crippled' hearts. Still other exceptional children are those with physical disorders such as epilepsy, tuberculosis, diabetes, and endocrine disorders. They are those children who cannot follow the regular school program because of intellectual retardation but who can profit by a restricted and adjusted program. They are those children with extremely high intellectual capacity who need a specialized program or an adjusted curriculum if their potentials are to be utilized. They are children with emotional and/or social maladjustments, including those with serious behavior disorders or emotional instability.

These exceptional children comprise the 10 to 12 per cent of our school population who require special services and procedures if they are to take their rightful place in society. Their educational goals are the same as those for the 'normal' child. Their educational programs must be adjusted to fit the restrictions imposed by their handicaps. According to the U.S Office of Education in 1947-48, only 441,000 handicapped children of all types were reported as enrolled for special educational services in day or residential schools, at home, or in hospitals and convalescent homes. This is not more than 10 to 11 per cent of the number that should be given such special educational services.[9]

Romaine P. Mackie (1952):

In far corners of the world today unprecedented interest is being focused on the education of the handicapped. This is particularly true in the United States where the movement now known as education of exceptional children has been developing for more than 100 years. Progress in the beginning, of course, was slow and limited mainly to the deaf, blind, and mentally deficient. The motive back of the present movement is to bring suitable educational opportunity to all exceptional children so that they can have optimum benefits from their educational experiences. Specifically, the purpose is to make sure that the school program is sufficiently flexible and individualized so that it will meet the needs of children with marked variations of a physical, emotional, and mental nature. This is a high goal. If this goal is to be reached, the services of public-school systems must be greatly improved and increased.

Many children who are born with handicaps or who become disabled in early years have conditions that could be improved, compensated for, or fully corrected if adequate services were made available to them early in childhood. The number of adult handicapped individuals could thus be decreased and the load to society lessened.

The school — because it is responsible for the education of all children — has an unusual opportunity to help find the handicapped and provide the services they need. Through the years it has been the ideal of the American people to give educational opportunity to all children. However, many children with severe handicaps, such as cerebral palsy, partial vision, epilepsy, mental deficiency, or combinations of such conditions have been unable to take either partial or full advantage of the opportunity the school offers to them. For more than a half century a movement known as 'special education' has been developing. In the United States this movement is generally referred to as the 'Education of Exceptional Children.' The term 'exceptional' includes the various types of physically handicapped such as the crippled, the blind and partially seeing, the deaf and hard of hearing, the speech defective, and those with special health problems; the socially handicapped and emotionally disturbed; the mentally retarded; and the gifted. The purpose of the movement is to find new ways to meet the problems of children with severe limitations and thus to make good the belief that every child has the right to that kind of educational opportunity from which he will benefit.[10]

Darrel J. Mase (1952-53):

Special education as applied through the services provided by residential schools is well over a century old in the United States. The day school movement which is now well developed in a majority of the states is primarily a product of the present century. Thousands of children are receiving special instruction through these two services. Special education as represented by both of these programs is a part of a large public school movement to provide education for all American youth.

In order that the education of the handicapped might have recognition and status there has been a tendency to over-emphasize the ways in which it differs from regular education. Fundamentally, special education techniques are the result of the application of the principles of adaptation of instruction and services to the individual needs of pupils. This principle is basic in all education but when applied to the handicapped and the gifted results in some marked differences in (1) teaching techniques, (2) curriculum adjustments, and (3) special therapeutic services. These adaptations spring primarily from the special problems associated with serving children who vary markedly in mental capacities, in sensory capacities and in motor abilities. Most of these problems of adaptation are found to a certain degree with so-called normal children. They are, however, intensified in and more universally associated with exceptional children.

It is widely recognized that the general education objectives are applicable to exceptional children. For example, the general objective of economic security is appropriate for retarded children, gifted children, and crippled children. The degree of attainment of this general objective will vary considerably from that of normal children. The retarded adult may be able to obtain only marginal security for himself while the gifted adult may obtain maximum security for himself, his family, and make notable contributions to the economic needs of the general welfare.

The deaf child and the retarded child may obtain a minimum efficiency in communication as a part of the general goal of social efficiency. The retarded child's attainment is reduced by his capacity to learn while the deaf child is limited by his lack of opportunity to learn from oral imitation.

Successful teachers of exceptional children are obligated to employ a clinical approach to the study of children. Such children present learning difficulties, sensory and motor impairments which require careful study in order to adapt instruction successfully. Furthermore, teachers of exceptional children are called upon to integrate professional information from psychology, education, and medicine into working hypothesis for instruction and therapeutic services. Consequently, special education as applied to each type of exceptional child has developed some rather distinctive techniques and materials which distinguish it from regular education.[11]

FOOTNOTES

1. *National Educational Association Proceedings,* 37th Annual Meeting, Washington, D.C., July, 1898, pp. 1031-1033.
2. *Ibid.,* pp. 1057-1059.
3. *National Educational Association Proceedings,* 40th Annual Meeting, Detroit, July, 1901, pp. 828, 829.
4. *National Educational Association Proceedings,* 41st Annual Meeting, Minneapolis, July, 1902, pp. 828, 829.
5. There is some evidence that 'special classes' were attempted in Scotland as early as 1834. Definite attempts were made in 1868 in Glasgow, and in 1879 in London. See Campbell, Lady, "Schools and Other Agencies Aiding the Blind in Great Britain and Ireland", *Outlook for the Blind,* Spring, 1921, pp. 50-58; and Bryden, S.F., "Societies and Missions for the Blind in Scotland, 1857-1908", *Outlook for the Blind,* Autumn, 1909, pp. 95-100.
6. *The Education of Exceptional Children,* 49th Yearbook, Part II, National Society for the Study of Education (University of Chicago Press: Chicago, 1950), pp. 3, 5.
7. *Statistics of Special Education for Exceptional Children,* 1952-53 (U.S. Department of Health, Education and Welfare: Washington, D. C.: 1954).
8. Baker, Harry J., *Introduction to Exceptional Children,* Revised Edition (Macmillan: New York City, 1953), pp. 11, 12. Used by permission of the Macmillan Co. The passage quoted by Baker is from: *The Education of Exceptional Children, op. cit.,* p. 3.
9. *Careers in Service to the Handicapped,* (National Foundation for Infantile Paralysis and National Society for Crippled Children and Adults: Chicago, 1952), pp. 24, 25.
10. Mackie, Romaine P., *Some Problems in the Education of Handicapped Children,* Pamphlet No. 112 (Federal Security Agency, Office of Education: Washington, D.C., 1952), Foreword and p. 1.
11. Mase, Darrel J., *What is Special About Special Education?* (Reprint from *Exceptional Children,* Dec., 1952, Jan., May, 1953), pp. 3, 4.

For other definitions of the field of special education, and the education of the exceptional consult:

12. Mackie, R.P., and Dunn, L.M., *College and University Programs for the Preparation of Teachers of Exceptional Children,* Office of Education Bulletin No. 13 (Department of Health, Education and Welfare: Washington, D.C., 1954), p. 2.
13. Frampton, M.E., and Rowell, Hugh Grant, *Education of the Handicapped,* Vol. II Problems (World Book Co.: N.Y.C., 1940), pp. 2-6.

14. Heck, A., *The Education of Exceptional Children* (McGraw Hill: N.Y.C., 1953), pp. 4-5.
15. See "Announcement of Teachers College of Columbia University", *University Catalogue 1936-37*, pp. 90-103, for definition.
16. *Special Education in the Chicago Public Schools: A Manual of Procedures and Policies* (Board of Education: Chicago, 1953), Foreword.
17. "The Handicapped Child in the Mainstream", *Proceedings of the Tenth Governor's Conference on Exceptional Children*, Illinois Commission for Handicapped Children: 160 N. LaSalle St., Chicago, 1953).
18. *Is Your Child Exceptional?* (Indiana State Department of Public Instruction: Indianapolis, 1951), pp. 1, 2.
19. Jenks, William F., editor, *Special Education for the Exceptional Child* (Catholic University of America Press: Washington, D. C., 1953), Foreword.
20. Carrington, Evelyn M., *The Exceptional Child — His Nature and Needs* (Texas State College for Women: Denton, 1951).
21. *The Physically Limited Child* (Board of Education: N.Y.C., 1953).
22. Horn, J.L., *The Education of Exceptional Children* (Century: N.Y.C., 1924).
23. Brownell, Samuel M., "Need for Services to Exceptional Children", *Exceptional Children*, Jan., 1955, p. 138.
24. Mayo, Leonard, "Creed for Exceptional Children", *Exceptional Children*, Jan., 1955, p. 139. Reprinted earlier in this volume.

THE CLINICAL APPROACH IN SPECIAL EDUCATION

DARREL J. MASE

Special Education is a program which prepares youth with problems and handicaps to become as productive to themselves and to society as they are capable of becoming. The goals are the same as for all education. The procedures for achieving these goals must vary according to the problems and handicaps of those who are to profit by a program of special education. There is nothing very special about special education except in respect to the limitations imposed by the specific needs of those with vision deficiencies, hearing impairments, speech defects, crippling conditions, emotional disturbances, mental retardations, and superior abilities. The clinical approach includes nothing in principle that is not desirable for all youth. Those with problems and handicaps *must* have this consideration if they are to take their rightful places in society.

The clinical approach implies that we see the individual as an individual. It requires thorough and complete examination, treatment, and education of the subject as an individual. The boy who is blind should not be treated as twelve year old boys who are not blind should be treated, but rather in respect to the abilities, capacities, interests, and needs of this specific twelve year old boy who is blind. The minister, the social worker, the counselor, the parent, should use the clinical approach when attempting to aid an individual. The better all who are to aid the individual understand clinical procedures, the better can individual needs be met. This does not imply that people other than professionally trained personnel should become clinicians and diagnosticians. However, they can be taught some of the techniques, skills, philosophies, and limiting factors which enter into diagnostic and treatment procedures of the professionally trained individual.

Special education implies the development of a healthy, well-adjusted personality who can adapt to a society in which he can know successes. This individual does not *have* a personality; he *is* a personality. This physically, intellectually, emotionally, socially functioning individual must be taught in the light of how he feels, thinks, and acts—not as another with a similar handicap behaves. Such teaching and training implies that we must know all that is to be known about this individual if our program in special education is to operate at maximum efficiency.

The fact finding report of the Midcentury White House Conference on Children and Youth for 1950, in the book *Personality in the Making,* states

Knowledge about personality comes from no one source of information. The anthropologist's knowledge of personality differences from culture to culture, the sociologist's knowledge of the social process, the physiologist's knowledge of the growth of the nervous system, the geneticist's knowledge of heredity, the psychiatrist's knowledge of the process of emotional illness and health, the psychologist's knowledge of changes in mental functioning with development and with all manner of physical and social circumstances —these and other kinds of knowledge are needed if we are to understand human behavior.[1]

The individual is a product of both nature and nurture. Too often our nurture of the child who needs special education services has not permitted him to function at the level nature intended he should. This growing, changing personality must be seen in relation to his own needs and goals, not in relation to the needs and goals of his loved ones. He must be challenged up to his capacities but not beyond his potentials. He must be seen in the socioeconomic structure in which he can be a contributing, well-adjusted adult rather than the one his parents might desire for him. The clinical approach will assist in providing realistic goals.

Information is gathered through the various methods of measurement, analysis, and observation used in physical, psychological, aid social histories and examinations. Those who live and work with the subject contribute their knowledges to the understanding of the individual. It is then necessary to integrate the findings and make recommendations and suggestions for the adjustment, training, and education of the individual. Professional personnel are never final in their diagnoses. They conclude that with all the information at their disposal it would appear that perhaps the reason for the behavior is because of this and that. Diagnosis implies that we must treat but continue to seek, and that with further study and observation we may find other causes for the behavior pattern.

However, the parent, the teacher, the neighbor may be very definite in assigning a cause to the behavior. Common remarks may include: "Of course the child is undernourished. The mother is never home to cook a meal." "The parents are separated and naturally Jane is emotionally disturbed." Once a cause is assigned they fail to look, and thus may fail to see. The professionally trained person recognizes that the obvious cause for the behavior pattern is generally not the real cause. He also recognizes that there are generally multiple causes, some of which may not now be present. He gathers all available facts from all known sources and qualifies his diagnosis with "maybe", "perhaps", "possibly". This is an approach that could and should be applied by all.

The clinical approach implies that all that can be known about the subject shall be determined but that we should continue to seek further. This knowledge shall then be communicated to others capable of applying and using it. The clinical approach demands that those who are to work with the subject shall agree upon procedures and goals. It is, therefore, important that not only the psychologist who evaluates the level of functioning, but the parent who cares for the child, and the teacher who imparts knowledge to the child, shall follow similar patterning insofar as this is feasible. The society to which the children in special education are to adjust will then be determined by agreed upon limitations, acceptances, understandings, and opportunities.

It was stated previously that we must first see the individual and then see the problem or handicap. Too often with the child we have seen an I.Q. or a mental age and have failed to see the potentials for social adequacy, economic security, and emotional stability. When we speak of a blind child, we may see blindness and fail to see the child. Never speak of a blind child, deaf child, cerebral palsied child. If we think and speak of disability first, we may fail to see ability. The clinical approach demands that first we see abilities, capacities, strengths, and then turn to disabilities and weaknesses. When we apply this principle, we change our own thinking as well as the thinking of those to whom we speak. Let us talk about a child, a person, and individual first, last, and all the time: a child with cerebral palsy — a child who is deaf — a child with freckles — a child who is mentally deficient. Let us speak of the child first and this will permit our listeners to see abilities before looking to disabilities.

Whether our role be that of teacher, parent, physician, psychologist, social worker or physical therapist, we all have the same job of developing healthy, well-adjusted personalities. The individual with a healthy personality is one who masters his environment, demonstrates a unity of personality, and perceives himself and the world in which he lives in a proper frame of reference. Henry Viscardi who is the head of J.O.B. (Just One Break), an organization to convince businessmen that the disabled will and can handle many jobs as well as or better than many not disabled, insists that no one is handicapped when he has become rehabilitated. He contends that when the right job has been found for the person with a handicap, he is neither handicapped nor disabled. This is a clinical approach which could and should be applied by everyone. If society would accept this premise in the same way those with handicaps must accept it, we would find many more individuals with handicaps able to take their rightful places in society.

Dr. Karl Menninger states that "the rehabilitation worker should continually remind himself that he is treating not a body, a disabled organ, an impaired function, but a fellow human being whose disability is an integral part of his total personality." We are in this rehabilitation process when we are in special education. Dr. Menninger continues, "the disability is not so much what the examiner perceives it to be, as it is what the patient perceives it to be."[2] We can not perceive as the subject perceives until we learn to know him. Clinical procedures can help us in knowing those in special education programs.

Rehabilitation demands that we not only do all we can for the handicapping condition, but that we take care of what the individual has done to himself because of the condition, and what society has done to him because of the condition. Getting to the focus of the infection which caused a hearing loss in not enough. Fitting the individual with a hearing aid is not sufficient. Teaching him lip reading and improving his speech pattern is not all he needs. We must help him in respect to what he did to himself while he heard only the vowels and missed the consonants, or heard only the consonants and missed the vowels, or heard only distortions of both. We must help him with what society has done to him while he did not hear. We should leave to the physician the treatment of the infection; to the audiologist the fitting of the hearing aid; and to the speech and hearing therapist the teaching of lip reading and improvement of speech. However, it must be the business of all who come in contact with him to help with what he has done to himself and what society did to him while he could not hear.

Lest we minimize the problem of those who are exceptional, let us be mindful that there is no tragedy in the world like the tragedy of being different. Let us be mindful that children who are deaf or blind, who have speech defects, all children who are exceptional, fall into a minority group with all the pressures and problems encumbent on any minority group. This minority group is going to be stared at, ridiculed, misunderstood, even as are other minority groups. It takes those who are crippled, handicapped, or otherwise exceptional, working side by side with so-called normals, to make democracy work, with equal opportunities for all. We need to recognize the extent of the tragedy of being different, and we may need to remember our own personal experiences of being 'different', inconsequential as they may seem to be, to multiply them 100 or 1000 times over, in order to understand some of the feelings and reactions of the individual who is different.

Let us through our abilities in communication help to educated the citizenry to accept those who are exceptional. Curiosity is a natural thing. Somehow all of us should have an opportunity to put on hearing aids, try crutches, wear the artificial eye as a monocle, try to manipulate one of the artificial hands to pick up objects as the bucket grab bags do at Coney Island. This would satisfy our curiosity and would stop a lot of staring.

The clinical approach demands teamwork. This term 'team-work' is used with some trepidation because of its misuse and abuse. It has become a hackneyed and overworked phrase which at times has covered a multitude of sins. Yet the team approach is essential, so let us define and describe its operation. Teamwork means simply a close, cooperative, democratic plan of action by various individuals working together for a common purpose—the best program for the individual. Teamwork is not a collection of ideas from various professional consultants, but a group of individuals representing the needed disciplines, with comparable skills and training for the discipline each represents. The clinical approach implies considerable experience working with subjects in respective areas of specialization. Sometimes we have had a member of the Yankees' pitching staff throwing to a sand lot catcher. Too often our teams have had some members who had not received the necessary conditioning, had not taken the necessary courses, internships, training. Too often we have teams consisting of a plastic surgeon, a pediatrician, a prosthodontist, a student in training in speech pathology, a psychometrician, and a teacher who has yet to see her first child with cleft palate when she comes into class on the opening day of school. Those representing medicine and dentistry do not know what the Doctor of Philosophy in clinical psychology and speech pathology and the instructor trained to teach the orthopedically handicapped can contribute to the team evaluation, if they have known only psychometrists, speech therapists, and teachers without special training.

Teamwork is not an easy thing. Lay people, to say nothing of professional people, are not inherently cooperative. We do not always have as much respect for the other person's profession as we have smugness and security for our own. The third grade teacher is sure the second grade teacher accomplished little; the high school teacher is convinced the elementary schools accomplished nothing; and the college professor cannot fathom how his students could have spent the previous twelve years. And we seldom hear professional people running down their own profession as easily or as frequently as they run down other professions. We need to remember that very often professional people have had to work individually without the opportunity for teamwork. Too often their training has not permitted the bringing of various disciplines together to see what one profession could contribute to another. One specialist may have to give some of his previously assumed activities because there is now a member on the team who can perform more competently than he can. Diagnostic, therapeutic, and educational teams must meet the requirements of comparable skills and training for this disciplines each represents in order that one member of the team may have respect for and confidence in another member of the team. We should remember that any time we point our index finger at anyone else, three of our fingers are pointing at ourselves.

Leonard W. Mayo has been a pioneer in espousing the team concept. In his annual report of 1954, as Director of the Association for the Aid of Crippled Children, he says —

The gains made in rehabilitation in the last decade have been due in large measure to those who have been able to see handicapped people as people, and to deal with them on the basis of their total needs, mobilizing the appropriate specialities and calling upon all available resources in the community on their behalf. The fact that this philosophy and method are effective, means that a new ingredient or dimension has been added to the old concept of the treatment and prevention of human ills. It would seem to establish beyond reasonable doubt that in the confluence of several specialities, and in the impact of a number of professions working in unison, there exist new and as yet unexplored possibilities for the common good. The whole may indeed be greater than the sum of its parts.[3]

One of the major deterrents to the team concept in providing total diagnosis and treatment has been the relative segregation from each other of those disciplines promoting total health. This segregation has existed in professional training programs and so it was quite natural that such segregation would continue or at least be difficult to overcome in practice. Recently, the various disciplines involved in reaching the goal of total health have come to realize that they have a greater chance for success when they work together, each stressing the competence of its own field.

The idea of coordinating rather than separating the clinical sciences is being developed in training centers and in many other ways. The necessity for this coordination has been obvious for some time to many working in physical, biological, and behavioral sciences. The success of this venture demands that the individual shall be the core of the treatment.

In the previously quoted report Leonard Mayo also says —

The realization by any one profession that the fundamental problems it faces defy solution until they are attacked by several professions working in unison is a strong incentive to cooperative effort. One of the clearest lessons science has taught us in the last half century is that the key to basic problems in any phase of human life is not to be found in one discipline or profession, but in a synthesis of many.

Professions are like nations in that no one can 'go it alone.' In the solution of every problem and in the daily experience of every profession there are times and places for the solo, the duet, and the chorus. To insist on a solo when the time for a duet has arrived, or to continue the duet when all voices and instruments should be merged in a chorus of united effort is to jeopardize further advance. To know when and how long to continue the solo and duet, and how to participate effectively in the chorus requires that combination of wisdom and skill that is the unfailing mark of mature professional leadership.

The present emphasis on the team method in rehabilitation is an indication that the need for 'choral' work has been recognized. We shall be more effective in the use of the professional team, however, when it is generally recognized as a means rather than an end, and when the social aspects are more fully integrated with the physical in diagnosis, evaluation, and treatment.[4]

This team concept must also be applied to the public and private agencies and organizations now assisting those with problems and handicaps. While agencies must keep their identities, they must also coordinate their activities. In too many instances the overhead of maintaining a state or local office is greater than the direct service from that agency. How can we expect nations to cooperate and peoples to live happily together when public agencies serving those with handicaps do not get along with other public agencies serving the handicapped; when private agencies cannot sit down to a table to consider problems with other private agencies; and when public and private agencies are not able to work together for the welfare of children who are exceptional. When personalities so affect the thinking of individuals representing public and private agencies that there cannot be planning and teamwork, there are many who suffer; and when those personalities are considering extending and advancing programs for the welfare of the handicapped, then it is the person with the handicap who suffers. If we had the money and time now being expended because individuals will not see the child and his needs because they want something for themselves or for their organization, we could indeed extend our services considerably.

The team concept, which is indeed a clinical approach to special education, becomes a problem of communication. We must think as our correspondent thinks if we would understand him. This is true if we are to communicate with the three year old. It is equally true if the psychologist is to communicate with the physician; the speech pathologist with the physical therapist; the social worker with the parent. Let us see the problems inherent in communication in just one area: the use of psychological test data by the speech therapist or teacher in special education. The primary aim of such test data is presumably to assist in the satisfactory adjustment or readjustment of an individual to an environment. If we accept this hypothesis, it follows that this information, in a form which is meaningful, should reach those who are to help the adjustment or readjustment. Such does not always follow. Communication lines may not be open, with the result that the reports are not meaningful and therefore are not very useful to the teacher, parents, and therapists. The psychologist must be able to communicate with those representing various disciplines and stations in life as well as to use the tools in his kit to make the appraisal and evaluation.

Too often therapists, teachers, and parents do not know what the psychologist can contribute. They ask for "an I.Q.". That is not what they need. They need to know about the individual and his variations; his abilities and his disabilities; his deviation from accepted behavior patterns; his general emotional state. Communication is essential if the therapist, teacher, and parent are to receive from the psychologist all he can contribute to them concerning learning, behavior, and personality patterns. The clinical approach demands that we learn all we can about the individual and then that we communicate as much of this information as can be presented in a meaningful manner to those who are to work and live with the subject.

One of our problems in special education is in not having sufficient and adequate diagnostic and evaluation centers to provide the necessary evaluations as indicated by the team concept. We have established many units and classes in special education, but too often have not provided needed funds for adequate evaluations of the children in the special classes. More diagnostic and evaluation centers are needed to provide the necessary studies as indicated by the team concept. Classes continue to be established in special education without there being a means to learn all that is to be known about the children to be assigned to these programs. Classroom teachers are then forced into the untenable role of having to become diagnosticians without knowledge or experience for such a responsibility. The teacher of the special class cannot meet the needs of the children in her classes without all the physical, social, and psychological information which science can provide.

About two years ago *Exceptional Children,* the Journal of the International Council for Exceptional Children, had four articles on clinical services for exceptional children. In the first of the series, Jack W. Birch, Director of Special Education in Pittsburgh, says the two purposes of the article are: "(1) to describe certain important kinds of clinics which provide diagnosis, treatment, and various interpretative services for exceptional children, in urban and rural areas, and which are closely identified with educational programs for children; (2) to provide, by inference, some criteria that might be found useful in selecting or planning such clinics. Broad general knowledge about clinics should provide a sounder basis for the special class teacher to advise parents regarding the selection and use of clinical facilities, and what realistically to expect from clinics." The author proceeds to describe and discuss the operation and role of the child guidance clinic, psychological clinic, educational clinic, reading clinic, eye clinic, cerebral palsy clinic, and psychiatric clinic. He emphasizes the need which special education personnel have for "broad and well-rounded services."

However, he speaks of these clinic services as being 'ancillary' to special education. In reality, they must be an essential integral part of special education. One of the reasons adequate clinical facilities have not been provided for special education is that they have not been considered as essential as the instructor who is to teach the special class or the equipment to be used in the classroom. State funds have been available for the teacher but often have not been available for adequate clinical evaluations. Too often the schools have turned to already over-loaded clinic programs to provide them with needed diagnostic work-ups, to provide more intensive treatment and therapy than can be provided in the school, and to do needed follow-up. Staff time has not been budgeted in the established clinic programs, with the result that service is inadequate and communication is very poor.

In many instances those in special education have turned to universities and colleges in their areas for these needed clinical services. Such institutions of higher learning often have limited services to offer which generally must relate to training programs, and cannot begin to meet the demands of the surrounding communities. The primary task of colleges and universities is to train students. They cannot be expected to provide extensive and comprehensive clinical services. They cannot go very far beyond their training and research needs.

We must plan to establish the needed clinic facilities as an integral part of special education rather than as programs apart from special education. If it is necessary to use established programs, then budgetary provisions should make staff time available for the needs of the special education program. A state program of clinical services in the State of Washington is described by Ruth I. Levy. While the author stresses that they have far to go in providing comprehensive clinical services, especially to the rural areas, they have some fine programs which merit careful consideration. She emphasizes that these clinical needs had to be met in Washington by legislation.[6]

D. A. Worcester, of the University of Nebraska, made a tour of thirty states in studying current programs and needs for the exceptional child. He draws a very realistic picture of the needs for special education of children in rural areas. He explains the team approach and the traveling clinic and he contends that the diagnosis of exceptional children for the rural areas is easier to accomplish than is the establishment of special classes. Since special classes generally cannot usually be established, it is necessary in most instances to communicate findings to local physicians, teachers, parents, welfare workers, and others who are concerned with the welfare of the child.[7]

Rutherford B. Porter, Chairman of the Division of Special Education at Indiana State Teachers College, Terre Haute, has had considerable experience in respect to rural needs. In respect to clinical needs he summarizes as follows:

(1) A qualified leader who can set up adequate clinical services should be employed first, so that initial surveys can be made and particulars for starting a program can be discovered.

(2) After the original survey is completed, a special education program, perhaps for one type of exceptionality at a time, can be put into operation.

(3) Continued clinical services must be available for further diagnosis, check on progress of individuals, and re-evaluation.

(4) Outpatient services offered by college clinics and other specialized non-local organizations should be used on a consulting basis for difficult cases, and for technical assistance. Complete dependence on such facilities should be avoided.[8]

Diagnostic and evaluation centers should be geographically located that they would be accessible to all citizens of the state. They should be staffed with personnel representing the medical, behavioral, and social sciences in order for a complete evaluation to be made. The author expressed this need in respect to those who are mentally retarded in the following manner:

We need such evaluation centers geographically located where parents would feel secure in the findings and recommendations. With such a feeling of security professional personnel would be in a better relationship to tell parents the results of their findings and to offer realistic programs of training for the child. In such evaluation centers we would have the team approach to diagnosis, treatment and research which is so basic to understanding. Early and accurate diagnoses are essentials to successful programs for those who are mentally retarded. Adequately staffed evaluation centers are the answer to this need.[9]

The staff of such centers should spend the major portion of their time with diagnostic procedures and treatment. However, staff time should be available for prevention, education, and research. Current programs of special education should be continually assessed and evaluated. Staff from clinic centers with training in research techniques could provide such studies.

Evaluation centers should have housing facilities whereby the subject could remain for a week, a month, or longer, if indicated. Such careful and prolonged study is necessary with difficult problems if a realistic prognosis is to be made. Such prolonged study and team evaluations will permit professional personnel to be more secure in their findings and to communicate much better with those who are to relate to the child in his growth and development.

Such evaluation centers, staffed with comprehensive diagnostic, treatment and research teams, can provide a new way of life for children in special education programs.

The team approach applied to private and public agencies now serving those with problems and handicaps can assist in the development of these centers and extend services in other ways. Transference of findings by those on the team to those who are to participate in the growth and development process of the child must be accomplished by improving communication techniques. The assessment of abilities as well as the treatment of disabilities is essential if desired ends are to be achieved. Teaching the individual to accept his limitations and to learn to live with what is left is an essential part of this growth process. These and other considerations as discussed in this chapter are essential if those with problems and handicaps are to have equal rights in our democratic society.

FOOTNOTES

1. Witmer, H. L., and Kotinsky, Ruth, *Personality in the Making* (Harper: N.Y.C., 1952), p. 4.
2. Menninger, Karl A., *Psychological Aspects of Physical Disability*, Rehabilitation Service Series, No. 210 (Office of Vocational Rehabilitation, Federal Security Agency: Washington, D.C.), pp. 15-16.
3. *Synthesis*, Annual Report (Association for the Aid of Crippled Children: N.Y.C., 1954), pp. 13-14.
4. *Ibid.*, p. 18.
5. Birch, Jack W., "Patterns of Clinical Services for Exceptional Children", *Exceptional Children*, vol. 19, no. 6, 1953, pp. 214-222.
6. Levy, Ruth I., "Clinical Services in the State of Washington", *Exceptional Children*, vol. 20, no. 2, 1953, pp. 69-77.
7. Worcester, D. A., "Clinical Services: Making the Best of Resources in the Rural Community", *Exceptional Children*, vol. 21, no. 4, 1954, pp. 176-179.
8. Porter, Rutherford B., "Clinical Service Extensions for Rural Area Exceptional Children", *Exceptional Children*, vol. 20, no. 3, 1953, pp. 105-110.
9. Mase, Darrel J., "The Scientific Basis of Selection", *The Adolescent Exceptional Child - A Realistic Approach to Treatment and Training*, Proceedings of the 1954 Spring Conference of the Child Research Clinic of the Woods Schools, Langhorne, Pa., p. 41.

SECTION I

CHAPTER III

CLASSIFICATION AND CENSUS

WHO ARE THE EXCEPTIONAL? HOW MANY?

THE NUMBER OF EXCEPTIONAL CHILDREN
BY ROMAINE P. MACKIE AND L. M. DUNN

THE NATION'S HANDICAPPED CHILDREN
BY ARTHUR J. LESSER AND ELEANOR P. HUNT

WHO ARE THE EXCEPTIONAL? HOW MANY?

The educational definition of any one group of the exceptional is based on medical definitions (in which are included any parallel psychological definitions), legal definitions based on existing statutes, and a further attempt at some type of classification which will result in a reasonably homogenous group which may be organized, served and taught together in a class or group of classes.

Among the many areas of activity which the field of special education serves are these: The Blind, The Partially Sighted, The Deaf, The Hard of Hearing, The Speech Defective, The Mentally Retarded, The Feeble-minded, The Cerebral Palsied, those with Muscular Dystrophy, Multiple Sclerosis, individuals with Special Health Problems, The Tuberculous, The Cardiopathic, The Intellectually Gifted, The Emotionally Disturbed and others with acute psychopathic conditions, The Neurologically Impaired, The Socially Maladjusted, The Orthopedically Handicapped, those with Lowered Vitality, The Delicate, The Epileptic, The Multiple-Handicapped, The Aged, The Chronically Ill, those with Endocrine Disturbances, The Narcotic, The Alcoholic, The Hemophiliac, The Juvenile Delinquent, those with Dental Defects, Leprosy, Brain Injuries, Spina Bifida and allergies, Paraplegia, Diabetes, Poliomyelitis, Asthmatic conditions, Chorea, Tics, Lateral dominance, Osteomyelitis, Legg-Perthis disease, Encephalitis, and many other medical, psychopathic and emotional defects.

Various authorities in the field of special education have established several different groupings of these areas for servicing purposes. No definitive classification has been accepted for the field as a whole. The current literature shows some overlapping of categories and treatment; in each instance, the reasons given seem logical for the specific purposes of those making the classifications. It is sufficient for our purposes to list the areas for which service programs are available and in which current medical and educational problems are the motivating forces for active service programs.

Time, strangely enough, does not always seem to clarify definitions, although it may crystalize and standardize the content of a discipline. Much too often some outstanding leader, whether individual or community, insists upon creating and defending the 'only' suitable terminology or classification. Scholarship and the application of a more effective scientific method to the field of special education will in time create something more than inventiveness in augmenting the dictionary, for terminology does vitally affect the patient, his family, and his community.

How Many Individuals Needing Special Education Are There in the U.S.?

The discovery of cases is one of the most difficult problems in all work with the exceptional. Probably the basic reason is the parental philosophy of long standing, that the presence in the family of a physically or mentally handicapped child is a distinct punitive visitation from Providence. There is also the prevalence of ill-planned attempts to screen the unfortunate child from a curious and not too sympathetic world. That the existence of a congenitally or adventitiously handicapped child is a terrific blow to the morale of the parents and the home cannot be denied. The shock of the onset of a disabling condition in childhood is devastating; the fear of inadequate adjustments to marked physical and sensory changes resulting from chronic diseases brings about confusion and despair. Rationalization and amateurish planning too often take the place of consultation with experts.

The answer to this problem is, of course, wider education of all parents, as to the true status of the exceptional and what can be done for them through educational programs. There is also the need of being certain that physicians and allied groups are informed concerning facilities available and that a close team approach is developed. Since any mother or father may at any time become the parent of an exceptional child, either through a new birth or by some disease or accident to an existing child, it follows that parent education must include all parents, with further services to those in whose family such a child already exists.

In any program for discovery of exceptional children it seems reasonable to believe that the most economical and basic mechanism would be a census covering all types of the exceptional, combined with routing the various types to suitable services for further investigation and classification.

Without attempting to specify the exact setup, it is highly desirable that an annual census of the exceptional of all types should be taken.[2] Such a census would enable both the educator and the medical man to take up their respective problems of rehabilitation at an early period in the life of the child and at the incipient stages of the state of disability. In actual practice this service is often widely divided, thus adding both cost and confusion and sometimes bringing competition into the picture.

The best census or discovery results from wide understanding and positive cooperation of all concerned. To secure this, definite plans of organization are required and must be generally known to those who may profit by this service. Since the human mind is prone to forget, such services must be regularly and repeatedly publicized.

In actual practice, knowledge of an exceptional case of any type may come from any one of many sources. The visiting nurse may observe the child in his home; a case may be reported by the family doctor, a social worker, neighbors, or others. It is of greatest importance, however, to secure knowledge of the case as early as possible in order to begin a service program at once.

It is reasonable to believe that the clearing station on these cases should be some official agency rather than a private one, the latter being successful chiefly when on a semi-official basis. It is unfortunate that at present some of the educational programs for the exceptional have been sacrificed, in terms of government grants for statistical studies, to the equally important need for direct medical and other non-educational services. This criticism is equally applicable to some private organizations devoted almost entirely to securing medical care for certain types of the exceptional. A more general, better-balanced program would recognize that education is the mental hygiene required by the case and that the exceptional child is more than an animal needing only certain physical restoration.

There should also be some definite clearing station for information which would afford assurance that the case would receive the interest of physicians and local educators at the earliest possible moment, and that planning for the child's future would be begun as soon as possible. Since the school will direct the child's activities more than any other agency during many years of his life, the clearing station should be part of the regular school program. Where the problem is rural, and therefore extends outside the child's own community for solution, the state department of education seems the logical group for responsibility. It is assumed that the educator in all cases will definitely cooperate with and inform any and all other servicing agencies.

There has never been a complete census of individuals in the various categories of special education. We do know, however, from various sources, even though they do not agree, that the incidence in our total population of the various areas of special education is a very substantial one. Some authorities have arrived at census estimates on the bases of census reports from their cooperating agencies; others have developed formulae for gross estimates and still others have made "rough guesses"; finally, some have said "We do not know how many, nor how to estimate with any accuracy." The following sources and references have been consulted, to prepare as complete a statement on incidence as can probably be made at this time. Reference is usually made to the 1930 White House Conference on Child Health and Protection.[3]

CHILDREN (1930)

Blindness (under 20)	14,400
Partial Sight	50,000
Impaired Hearing	3,000,000
Defective Speech	1,000,000
Crippled	100,000
Tubercular	382,000
Suspected Tubercular	850,000
Weak or Damaged Heart	1,000,000
Undernourished	6,000,000
Behavior Problems	675,000
Mentally Retarded	450,000
	13,521,400

The Federal Security Agency-Public Health Service during the winter of 1935-36 made a survey of the health of our nation and attempted a correlation with social and economic factors by means of a house to house canvass of over 700,000 households in urban areas and 37,000 in rural communities. Their sample was based on the 1930 Federal Census. A large number of studies have since been made of the findings, scope and methods of this survey.[4-20]

Sanders, Barkev, and Federman[21] conclude "That results from four sample surveys indicate a rate of disability only half as great as that found by the National Health Survey. Differences in definition of disability and in time and scope of surveys are given as reasons for differences." They conclude results of check sample as "roughly comparable."

Heck[22] makes a tabular estimate based on figures from various sources[23-4] showing a figure of 13,407,000.

The biennial survey of Education in the U.S. 1952-54, Department of Health, Education, and Welfare, in their report[25] give figures for Special Education services (rural and urban) in all 48 states and the District of Columbia. The response to the questionnaires was 99.44% of those circularized. The report does not include data on "residential schools for exceptional children, data on home or hospital instruction" nor "information on the class of children designated as 'truant, delinquent or maladjusted.'" Public school data is the only data included. Two tables are significant for our consideration of the incidence reported for each area.

Enrollment in Special Schools and Classes, Elementary and Secondary, by type of Exceptional Children in the U.S. 1952-53:[26]

EXCEPTIONAL CHILDREN IN PUBLIC SCHOOLS (1952-53)

Mentally Retarded	113,565
Speech Defective	306,747
Crippled	17,813
Hard of Hearing	11,932
Partially Seeing	8,014
Special Health Problems — (Delicate and Epileptic)	11,455
Deaf	3,935
Blind	839
Mentally Gifted	22,916
	497,216

As compared with figures for 1947-48, these studies point clearly to a substantial increase in service programs for special education throughout the United States. Gains in special education enrollments were 2.7 greater than the rate of increase in public school enrollment. This indicates, at least a greater public awareness of the size and extent of the field of special education, and perhaps better census, case discovery, classification, and expanding service programs.

Table showing percentage increase in total Public School enrollment:[26]

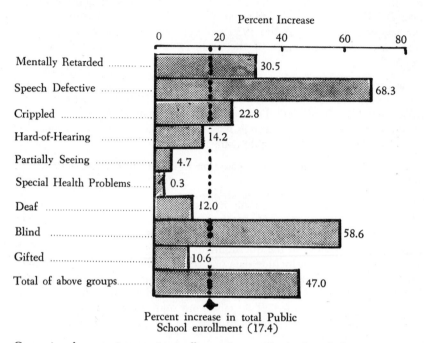

Percent Increase

	Percent Increase
Mentally Retarded	30.5
Speech Defective	68.3
Crippled	22.8
Hard-of-Hearing	14.2
Partially Seeing	4.7
Special Health Problems	0.3
Deaf	12.0
Blind	58.6
Gifted	10.6
Total of above groups	47.0

Percent increase in total Public
School enrollment (17.4)

Comparison between increase in enrollments in special schools and classes and increase
in total enrollment in public elementary and secondary day schools

It is obvious from the above studies that only gross estimates can be used
to indicate the incidence of cases needing special education. The editors, in
an attempt to arrive at some gross figures for estimate of current incidence of
exceptionality, communicated with all major National Agencies serving the
respective areas and list the results of their correspondence:

ALL AGES (1954)[27]

Blind—Both Eyes	270,000
Blind—One Eye	1,000,000
Sight Saving and	
Partially Sighted	600,000
Deaf (total)	185,000
Hard-of-Hearing	2,188,000
Poliomyelitis (1953) acute	35,592
Mentally Defective	950,000
Emotionally Disturbed	700,000 to 800,000
Gifted (5-17)	700,000 to 800,000
Epileptic	1,500,000

Muscular Dystrophy	100,000
Speech Defective	20% children under 3
	15% children 3 to 18
	7% adults[28]
Cardiac Conditions	5,000,000
Arteriosclerosis and High Blood Pressure	4,600,000
Nephritis	950,000
Cardiovascular (renal)	9,200,000
Tuberculosis	1,200,000
Cancer (under treatment)	700,000
Diabetes	2,000,000
Cerebral Palsy	500,000

The National Society for Crippled Children and Adults issued a pamphlet[29] for estimating the extent of Physical Disability based on estimates from the various voluntary agencies. This report gives some sound counsel on the use of current estimates and totals. The report lists:

ALL AGES (1954)

Arthritis	1,500,000	
Multiple Sclerosis	200,000	
Muscular Dystrophy	100,000	(over half aged 3-13)
Paraplegia	82,500	(2,500 veterans)
Major Amputee	400,000	
Hemiplegia	1,000,000	
Heart Disease	9,200,000	(adults & children)
Rheumatic Fever	500,000	to 1,000,000
Tuberculosis[30]	500,000	(active)
Speech Disorders	2.5%	of all adults
	7%	of all children
Cerebral Palsy[31]	7	per each new 100,000 population
Poliomyelitis[32,34,35]	14.4	per 10,000 population under 21 years
Epilepsy	800,000	(300,000 children; 500,000 adults)
Mentally Retarded[33]	4,520,000	
Blindness	308,000[36]	(6,000 children under 7 yrs.[37])

	(adults)	1953	
		(52) Residential Schools[38-39]	5,574
		(45) Day Classes	1,447

Deaf—Children in Residential Schools & Classes
Day Schools   22,362[40]
Hard-of-Hearing 1,500,000[41-42] Children 5-18
Sight-Saving   1 to every 500 of school enrollment
  (Partially Seeing)   (app. 3-17)[43-45]
Cancer[46]   237,000
Emotionally Disturbed[47]   500,000
Aged   13,500,000[48]
Narcotics   50,000 - 60,000[49]

It is evident that these estimates, covering all age groups, and differing in numerous instances, are not amenable to accurate statistical analysis. However, taken together they do present to the layman and the professional the stark fact that the field of special education is large and its problems formidable. It is probably not possible at the present to secure a reasonably accurate census of each of these areas, but we can hope by carefully planned research and the adoption of standard definitions and definite classification greatly to improve the quality and usefulness of future studies on the incidences of exceptional children and adults in our population and thereby make our planning of service programs more effective and economical.[50] A program planned to provide the variety of services, methods, and techniques inherent in an optimum program of special education for from 9 to 14% of the children of school age in this country[51-52] is a ringing challenge to the professionals and the serious immediate responsibility of the public.

FOOTNOTES

1. The reader is referred to *Special Education for the Exceptional*, Vols. II & III, edited by M.E. Frampton and E.D. Gall (Porter Sargent Publisher: 11 Beacon St., Boston, Mass., 1955) for a more complete treatment of these areas of special education.
2. The American Federation for the Physically Handicapped, Washington, D.C., has introduced several bills in Congress to provide a census for the handicapped as of 1954. None as yet have become law. The Editors.
3. *Special Education: The Handicapped and Gifted, White House Conference on Child Health and Protection* (Appleton-Century-Crofts: N.Y.C., 1931) pp. 5-6.
4. Holland, Dorothy F., "The Disabling Diseases of Childhood, Their Characteristics and Medical Care as Observed in 500,000 Children in Eighty-three Cities Canvassed in the National Health Survey of 1935-1936", *American Journal of Diseases of Children*, Dec., 1939. 58:1157-1185.
5. Collins, Selwyn D., "The Incidence of Poliomyelitis and its Crippling Effects, as Recorded in Family Surveys", *Public Health Reports*, March 8, 1946. 61:327-355. Reprint No. 2696.
6. Collins, Selwyn D., "The Incidence of Rheumatic Fever as Recorded in General Morbidity Surveys of Families", *Public Health Reports*, Supplement 198 (Federal Security Agency, U.S. Public Health Service: Washington, D.C., 1947).
7. Lawrence, P.S., "An Estimate of the Incidence of Chronic Disease", *Public Health Reports*, Jan. 16, 1948. 63:69-82.
8. Beasley, Willis C., "Characteristics and Distribution of Impaired Hearing in the Population of the United States", *Journal of Acoustical Society of America*, July, 1940. 12:114-121.
9. Beasley,Willis C., "The General Problems of Deafness in the Population", *Laryngoscope*, Sept., 1940. 50:856-905.
10. Beasley, Willis C., "Partial Deafness and Hearing-Aid Design, I. Characteristics of Hearing Loss in Various Types of Deafness", *Journal of Society of Motion Picture Engineers*, July, 1940. 35:59-85.
11. U.S. Public Health Service, "Generalized Age and Sex Trends in Hearing Loss, Preliminary Reports National Health Survey, 1935-1936", *Hearing Study Series*, Bulletin 7 (National Institute of Health: Washington, D.C., 1938).
12. U.S. Public Health Service, "Sex Differences and Age Variations in Hearing Loss in Relation to State of Deafness. Preliminary Reports, National Health Survey, 1935-1936." *Hearing Study Series*, Bulletin 6 (National Institute of Health: Washington, D.C., 1938).
13. Sanders, Barkev S., "The Blind - Their Number and Characteristics", *Social Security Bulletin*, Oct., 1943. 6:17-26.

14. Spiegelman, Mortimer, and Marks, Herbert H., "Age and Sex Variation in the Prevalence and Onset of Diabetes Melitus", *American Journal of Public Health*, Jan. 1946. 36:26-33.

15. Collins, Selwyn D., "Statistical Studies of Heart Disease. V. Illness From Heart and Other Cardiovascular-Renal Diseases Recorded in General Morbidity Surveys of Families", *Public Health Reports*, Nov. 18, 1949. 64:1439-1492. Reprint No. 2978.

16. Woolsey, Theodore D., "Statistical Studies of Heart Disease. VI. Age at Onset of Heart and Other Cardiovascular-Renal Diseases", *Public Health Reports*, April 28, 1950. 65:555-571. Reprint No. 3017.

17. Karpinos, Bernard D., "The Physically Handicapped", *Public Health Reports*, Oct. 22, 1943. 58:1573-1592. Reprint No. 2521.

18. Perrott, George St. John, "Medical Needs Revealed by the National Health Survey", *National Conference of Social Work Proceedings*, 1938. (University of Chicago Press: Chicago, 1939).

19. Cumming, Hugh S., M.D., "Chronic Disease as a Public Health Problem", *Milbank Memorial Fund Quarterly*, March, 1936. 15:125-131.

20. U.S. Public Health Service, "An Estimate of the Amount of Disabling Illness in the Country as a whole. Preliminary Reports, National Health Survey, 1935-1936." *Sickness and Medical Care Series*, Bulletin 1 (National Institute of Health, Washington, D.C., 1938).

21. Sanders, Barkev S. and Federman, David, "The Prevalence of Disability Recorded Through Four Monthly Sample Surveys", *Social Security Bulletin*, August, 1943. 6:5-11.

22. Heck A., *Education of Exceptional Children*, 2nd edition. (McGraw-Hill: N.Y.C., 1953), pp. 5-6.

23. American Association of Social Workers, *Social Work Year Book* (N.Y.C., 1951), p. 63.

24. *The Education of Exceptional Children*, National Society for the Study of Education, 49th Year Book, Part II, (University of Chicago Press: Chicago, 1950), pp. 6-7.

25. U.S. Office of Education, "Statistics of Special Education for Exceptional Children, 1952-1953", Biennial Survey of Education in the U.S., (U.S. Department of Health, Education, and Welfare: Washington, D.C., 1954), chapter 5, page 18.

26. *Ibid.*, pp. 11, 19.

27. From an unofficial estimate provided the editors by the Morbidity and Health Statistics Branch, Division of Health Methods, Washington, D.C., 1954.

28. From unofficial estimate of the Editor of the *Journal of Speech Disorders*, 1954.

29. Institute on Rehabilitation Centers, *Estimating Extent of Physical Disability* (National Society for Crippled Children and Adults: Chicago 1954).

30. Communication from the Field Consultant, Social Research Division, National Tuberculosis Association, 1954.

31. Communication from United Cerebral Palsy Association, 369 Lexington Ave., N.Y.C. 1954. Under 3—43,000; 3-18—160,000; Adults—347,000.

32. Sevfling, Robert E., and Sherman, Ida L., "Poliomyelitis Distribution in the United States", *Public Health Reports*, Vol. 68 #5, May 1953 (U.S. Dept. of Health, Education and Welfare: Washington, D. C.), Reprint pp. 153-66.

33. Based on Merrill and Terman I.Q. under 75 - 3% of 1950 Census for Total Population. "The socially inadequate and borderline—if considered (78-79) the percentage would rise to 7% of the population. From unofficial correspondence with the Executive Director of the N.Y. State Association for the Help of Retarded Children, Inc., 323 Fourth Avenue, N.Y.C., 1954.

34. Early descriptive accounts of poliomyelitis outbreaks in the United States have been reviewed and an analysis made of State Morbidity Reports since 1907. "Poliomyelitis, a comparatively rare disease in the early years of this century, has since been recognized as a communicable disease problem in every state of the nation. During the last 20 years the trend of the annual case rate has been upward, particularly during the last decade, during which a marked increase has occurred. The death rate has shown a slight but definite increase. In 1952, for the nation, both the case rate and the estimated death rate were the highest since the 1916 epidemic. The ratio of reported deaths to reported cases has decreased over the last 20 years. "Earlier observers noticed that rates had been higher in the northern than in the

southern regions of the country. In recent years this difference had diminished and an East-West differential is more prominent. In recent years both average and maximum rates have been higher in the western and north central divisions of the United States than in the northeastern and southeastern divisions. Over extended periods of time geographic concentration has not been consistent.

"In southern regions of the country, seasonal rise in incidence occurs earlier and the epidemic span is longer than in the northern regions."

35. The recent announcement of the success of the Salk vaccine will without question have an important influence on reducing the incidence of poliomyelitis in the years ahead. The Editors.
36. Hurlin, Ralph G., *Estimated Prevalence of Blindness in the U.S.* (American Foundation for the Blind: N.Y.C., 1953). Reprint.
37. Kerby, C. Edith, *Blindness in Preschool Children* (National Society for the Prevention of Blindness: N.Y.C., 1954).
38. American Printing House for the Blind, *Report on Schools and Classes* (Louisville, Ky., 1954).
39. Frampton, M. E. and Kerney, E., *The Residential School* (Edwin Gould Printery: N.Y.C., 1953), p. 35.
40. *American Annals of the Deaf*, Jan., 1955. v. 100, no. 1, pp. 160ff.
41. *Education of Exceptional Children*, p. 156.
42. Hardy, William G., *Children with Impaired Hearing*, Children's Bureau Publication #326. (Federal Security Agency: Washington, D. C., 1952), pp. 3-4.
43. *Communication with Associate for Statistics and Analysis* (National Society for Prevention of Blindness, N.Y.C., 1954).
44. Young, M., "Certification of Teachers for Sight Saving Classes", *Exceptional Children*, April, 1952. Miss Young says 50,000 partially seeing children in school population.
45. Kerby, C. Edith, in *Exceptional Children*, Feb., 1952, pp. 137-142.
46. Communication with the American Cancer Society, 1954. Under 3 - 1,075; 3-19 - 3,675; adults - 232,250.
47. Communication from the League for Emotionally Disturbed Children, Inc., 10 West 65 Street, N.Y.C., 1954.
48. New York State Joint Legislative Committee on Problems of the Aging. "Growing with the Years." Albany, N.Y., 1954. "Since 1940, the people 65 and over have increased by nearly 50% in the U.S.A., and now total about 13,500,000." Page 4.
49. Congressional Record. Proceedings of the 83rd Congress, First Session, Remarks of Congressman Samuel W. Yorty, March 23, 1953. Mayor's Committee on Drug Addiction, N.Y.C., estimated in 1951 one addict for every 88 to 177 individuals in the population.
50. Lesser, Arthur J. and Hunt, Eleanor P., "The Nation's Handicapped Children", *American Journal of Public Health*, Feb., 1954.
51. There are approximately 42,000,000 children three to seventeen years of age (1954 Census estimate). The gross estimate of exceptional children, exclusive of adults, needing special education in the United States would range from 9% or 3,780,000 to 14% or 5,880,000. Estimates and percentages are ours. Editors.
See also U.S. Office of Education, F.S.A. release D. 42, Jan., 1952. States 5,000,000 exceptional children in U.S., of whom not more than 15% receiving aid.
52. Mackie, R.P. & Dunn, L. M., *College and University Programs for the Preparation of Teachers of Exceptional Children*, Off. of Educ. Bul. #13 (U.S. Department of Health, Education and Welfare: Washington, D.C., 1954), p. 2.

THE NUMBER OF EXCEPTIONAL CHILDREN*

ROMAINE P. MACKIE AND L. M. DUNN

When administrators of colleges and universities are considering the establishment of programs to prepare special education personnel, they recognize that this is a field which merits attention because of the great human need. Nevertheless, they face the practical problem of whether or not the number of exceptional children is large enough to warrant the financial investment necessary to maintain a worthwhile program for the preparation of special teachers.

No complete census has ever been made of the number of exceptional children in the United States. The best that can be done is to use the percentage of incidence based on spot studies made by national organizations and local communities. The figures are presented with some reluctance, since there is need for research to determine better estimates. If such investigations were to be undertaken, it would be important to take into consideration multiple deviations which occur in the same child. In the estimates which follow, it is assumed that the exceptional child is included once—under the major handicapping condition, although it is known that many of these children have secondary disabilities. For example, hard-of-hearing and cerebral-palsied children may also have speech handicaps. Taking into consideration such factors, it has been estimated[1] that at least 5 percent of the school population (as compared with 2 percent in the following data) are in need of help from speech correctionists.

A conservative estimate of the percentage of incidence, and the estimated number of children of school age, follows:

---

*Excerpt from Mackie, R. P. and Dunn, L. M., College and University Programs for the Preparation of Teachers of Exceptional Children, Office of Education Bul. #13 (U.S. Dept. of Health, Education and Welfare: Washington, D.C., 1954). Used by special permission.

Areas of exceptionality	Percent of incidence	Estimated number of school-age children (in round numbers)
Visually handicapped	.20	10,000
Blind		10,000
Partially seeing		58,000
Crippled	1.50	510,000
Special health problems	1.50	510,000
Deaf and hard-of-hearing[1]	1.50	510,000
Speech-handicapped	2.00	680,000
Socially maladjusted	2.00	680,000
Mentally retarded	2.00	680,000
Gifted	2.00	680,000
Total	12.7	4,318,000

[1]Many studies have been made attempting to differentiate the deaf and hard-of-hearing. Because of variations in definitions, no attempt has been made to provide separate incidence figures.

It seems safe to say that the number of exceptional children of school age in the United States is between 4 and 5 million. Accepting a minimal estimate of 12 or 13 percent (one-eighth) of the school-age population as exceptional, then this figure can be defended. The Bureau of the Census reported approximately 34,000,000 children between the ages of 5 and 17 in the United States for the year 1952. Using the percentage of incidence as 12.70, the number of exceptional children would be 4,318,000.

This, however, is not the complete story. To include only children in the age group 5 through 17 would not give an adequate picture of those in need of assistance from the schools. Many under age 6 should have help; others require it after 17. As is often pointed out, nursery schools and kindergartens are very important for such young children as the deaf and cerebral-palsied. At the other end of the age range, there is also need for more service from the schools. For example, many adolescents with handicaps drop out of school at a time when their social and vocational needs are greatest, simply because the school program is not adequate for them. Many of these youths would have profited from education extending beyond the 17-year-old level.

It is easy to see that the problem is large enough to command the interest, not only of State and local school systems, but also of colleges and universities and the citizenry as a whole.

THE NATION'S HANDICAPPED CHILDREN*

ARTHUR J. LESSER AND ELEANOR P. HUNT

Historically the term "crippled children" has meant children with orthopedic handicaps. Today, we recognize that the lives of children may be crippled by a variety of other kinds of handicaps. The problem is becoming one of equal provision of comparable care for handicapped children, regardless of whether the impediments to their progress are orthopedic or of another nature.

One of the things we would like to know about the problem of handicapped children is its size. How many handicapped children are there in the United States? The most cautious and perhaps most realistic answer to this question is that nobody knows exactly, even within a measurable amount of error. The available fragments of information, while numerous, were not designed to fit together. Differences in basic definitions of handicaps, in observational methods, and in statistical procedures stand in the way of combining many of the reported facts. All of these and similar limitations are important to recognize, not so much to caution against faith in current estimates as to show clearly where we are in attacking the question at issue. Statistically speaking, we are in the initial planning stage, where the question is raised, and we are casting about for such pieces of information as may be at hand to assist us in planning a reasonably good way of getting a proper answer.

From this point of view, we have reviewed a number of surveys concerned with prevalence or incidence of those handicapping conditions of children which are of increasing concern. The particular conditions covered are: rheumatic fever and rheumatic heart disease, cerebral palsy, epilepsy, cleft palate and cleft lip, eye conditions, hearing impairments, speech defects, and orthopedic conditions. In each case, nothwithstanding the weight of uncertainty, some estimate is advanced on prevalence in the United States in 1952 and

---

*Reproduced, with permission from the American Journal of Public Health February, 1954. Bibliography appended has been omitted.

what appears to be a reasonable figure for a prevalence rate. Child population estimates used are those reported by the Bureau of the Census.

Rheumatic Fever. This condition is responsible for about 90 per cent of the defective hearts in childhood. In the mid-1940's, the Children's Bureau estimated that there were some 500,000 children under 18 suffering from rheumatic fever or its effects. This estimate rested upon reports from the states where rheumatic fever demonstration programs were under way, upon probable needs in other states as seen by the bureaus, and the size of the child population at that time. Today, the figure may be greater since the child population has greatly increased in size, and prevention of this disease has probably not kept step with this growth. In the light of size of the child population in 1952, children who have rheumatic fever or its aftereffects may now number 675,000 under 21 years of age.

These speculations are fairly consistent with results obtained in recent surveys of school-age children in which initial examination was made by a cardiologist or other physician especially interested in heart disease. The results of these surveys have recently been summarized and lead to an estimate for school-age children at 604,550.

Cerebral Palsy. The number of children with cerebral palsy in the United States who received physician's services under crippled children's programs reached 22,397 in 1952, or 10 per cent of all crippled children who were served that entire year. While practically all states provide services for children with cerebral palsy, these programs are far from state-wide in many areas. Probably not more than one child in 10 with cerebral palsy is receiving care under these programs.

Recent studies on cerebral palsy have, on the whole, tended to confirm estimates proposed by Dr. Winthrop M. Phelps. The survey in New York State reached a birth incidence rate at 5.9 per 1,000 births, which can be interpreted as not significantly different from incidence implied in Dr. Phelps' estimates, four per 1,000 births.

Age-specific prevalence rates found in the New York study in Schenectady County, if assumed to be generally applicable, would suggest that about 512 children per 100,000 under 21, or somewhere in the neighborhood of 285,000 children under 21 in the United States in 1952 have cerebral palsy either from birth or as a result of subsequent brain damage. Some allowance is made here for the poor reporting of cases under five years of age. With an anticipated annual birth population at 3.8 million during the remaining years of the 1950's, nearly as many children will be born each year with congenital cerebral palsy as are now receiving physician's services in any one year under the crippled children's programs in the United States.

Epilepsy. About 1,000 children in the United States received physician's services under crippled children's programs in 1952 for this condition. Prevalence of epilepsy among children under 21 in the United States was estimated in 1954 at about 200,000 on the basis of the literature then current. Recent experience of the Maryland State Health Department in their epilepsy program suggests a minimum incidence of two per 1,000 under 21, while more intensive study of one county led to an estimate of five accurately diagnosed cases of epilepsy per 1,000 children under 21. The latter prevalence rate, if generally applicable, would mean that there are now about 275,000 children under 21 in the United States who have epilepsy.

Cleft Palate and Cleft Lip. Four per cent of all the children who received physician's services under the state's crippled children's programs in 1952 were treated for cleft palate or cleft lip, or both. This group numbered about 9,500 children in 52 different states and increased 20 per cent in size in the biennium 1950-1952.

Data reported on official birth certificates place the incidence of these conditions among newborn at about 1.3 per 1,000 live births, or roughly one for any 770 births. Since supplemental items on the birth record are not always reported completely, this rate is probably conservative. With the annual number of births in the United States at approximately 3.8 million, this incidence at birth, if generally applicable, would mean that in the United States nearly 5,000 infants are born each year with this malformation. In Wisconsin about 52 per cent of the children with this type of handicap had cleft lip as well as cleft palate, 26 per cent had cleft palate alone, 22 per cent cleft lip alone.

If we assume an incidence rate at birth of 1.3 per 1,000 live births has prevailed for some time and has general significance beyond the several states where surveys have been made, the number of children with cleft palate or cleft lip, or both, under 18 years of age in the United States would be in the neighborhood of 64,000 in 1952. More than one-third of these children, or 23,000, would be under five years of age, and perhaps 33,000 in the age group 5 to 14 years. These estimates of prevalence assume that mortality of infants and children with cleft palate or harelip is the same as among other children in these age groups.

Eye Conditions. The National Society for the Prevention of Blindness estimates 7.5 million school children in the United States are in need of eye care. This estimate is consistent with the findings in the St. Louis study on vision testing methods, cosponsored by the National Society, the Division of Public Health of the State of Missouri, the Children's Bureau, and other organizations. In this study the prevalence rate of children with eye conditions requiring observation or treatment by an eye specialist was 27 per cent among first and sixth graders.

Children with visual handicaps so serious as to require special educational help are estimated at 60,000. Facilities for this help were available to 8,000 of these partially seeing children during 1952-1953 in the public school system. In 1952, about 5,800 children under seven years of age, or one in 4,000, were blind; in the school-age group, in the neighborhood of 6,600 were so handicapped, or one in 5,000. Many of these children are in residential schools for the blind; a small number are in special classes in the public school system.

Hearing Loss. Available crude statistics on hearing loss have usually been reported on the basis of children whose hearing appears sufficiently impaired to warrant further study. Typical of such statistics are those of the Committee on Hard of Hearing Children of the American Hearing Society (1945), which indicated a prevalence rate among school children of about 5 per cent. In 1952, at this prevalence rate, an estimated 1.3 million children, five to 14 years of age, in the United States were in need of further observation to determine accurately the extent of impairment and indications, if any, for treatment. Estimates of prevalence of handicapping hearing loss among children have been given in the neighborhood of 0.5-1.0 per cent of the total child population, or from about one-quarter to one-half a million children under 21 in the United States if applicable in 1952. This is probably a conservative estimate. Under a standardized screening program, with well qualified personnel, prevalence of major hearing defects has been found to be as high as 3.3 per cent of elementary school children in one of the southeastern states. Major hearing defects included impairment below 15 db in any frequency between 250-8,000 cps, and a history or evidence of chronic pathological condition.

Speech Handicaps. About two million children or 5 percent of those five to 20 years of age have speech disorders of such severity as to interfere with their educational progress and social and emotional development. Among this handicapped group 16 per cent, approximately, have speech disorders associated with other handicapping conditions. Ten per cent are children with impaired hearing, 4 per cent are children who have cerebral palsy, and 2 per cent of these children have cleft palate. Stuttering handicaps about seven per 1,000 children in this age range and in 1952 the number of such children is estimated as 270,000. Over half of the children with speech disorders have functional articulatory defects.

Orthopedic. Estimates on prevalence of orthopedic handicaps among children vary widely, due in large part to type of inclusions, methods of examination, and type of observer. If we assume a prevalence of 3.2 per cent for orthopedic defects, except foot defects, about one million children in the school age population (five to 17 years) would indicate the number with orthopedic defects or conditions of sufficient severity to justify referral to a physician for treatment. This estimate stems from the results of school health examinations of 83,019 children in 19 school systems in New York State, 1945-1946, and is intermediate among others derived on somewhat similar types of surveys.

All of these estimates taken together suggest that the burden of physical handicaps in childhood is formidable. To improve our knowledge of its dimensions, distribution, and composition we need continuing study. We also need greater uniformity of approach and procedures in different studies on the same conditions, as well as between studies on different conditions. Comparable and deliberate designs in studies to yield among other things age-specific estimates of prevalence and incidence will also facilitate the estimating process.

SECTION I

CHAPTER IV

PUBLIC EDUCATION

EDUCATION OF THE PUBLIC

THE ROLE OF MASS MEDIA IN SPECIAL EDUCATION BY NORMAN ACTON AND EUGENE J. TAYLOR

EDUCATION OF THE PUBLIC

Through the history of mankind we have learned that only when our common populace fully understand the needs of their society, then and only then do they take action. The growth of our moral consciousness of the dignity of human personality and the educational needs and rights of all our children, including the exceptional, has been proclaimed in articles and textbooks of the professionals for some years.[1] It has been recent that the educator of the exceptional has become conscious of the tremendous power of the press, radio, television, and other means of presenting to the public the urgent needs of our field. Many individuals and communities still treat the exceptional as social outcasts or ignore them as socially and economically useless. The educator of the exceptional is still too inept at utilizing all means of education of the public as a whole, and too slow in using the interested segments of the population, such as the parent of the exceptional child, the general school administrator, the various allied community agencies and the exceptional themselves.

Many of the problems pressing for solution in the area of special education could move ahead toward solution if the interested professional and parent or agency concerned would utilize high quality programs of public relations leading to more effective public education.

Our society is a constantly changing one in which new social and economic conditions necessitate a flexible educational program which will fit the current need.

Most, if not all, critical administrative problems which face the parent, the teacher, and the administrator dealing with the exceptional individual can be solved with a more aggressive and effective public education program. The acceptance by general educators of their responsibility for special education services of high quality; the answer to the administrator for adequate financing; the different opinions as to where and how the exceptional shall be educated; the proper union of the disciplinary or authoritarian, and self-expression of 'freedom of action' approach; adequate trained teaching and administrative leadership; proper housing and equipment; adequate research, — all these pressing problems would benefit immediately and substantially by the application of the right kind of 'sales promotion' program properly timed for public consumption.

It is high time the leadership in the field of special education utilize these invaluable aids to the development of a rich service program for the exceptional so they, too, may become more nearly self-supporting and self-respected citizens of our nation.

FOOTNOTE

1. Grace, J. F., and Doctor, P. V., "A Better Understanding of the Deaf Through a Public Relation Program", *Exceptional Children,* Jan., 1955, 21:4:130-131.

THE ROLE OF MASS MEDIA IN SPECIAL EDUCATION

NORMAN ACTON AND EUGENE J. TAYLOR

One of the important developments of the twentieth century has been the tremendous growth of the means and techniques of reaching the attention of and seeking favorable response from the public. We who are engaged in programs for the welfare of the handicapped are not strangers to this process. From the early beginnings of our work, it has been necessary to depend on the understanding and support of the communities in which we function, and we have long recognized the need to inform the people of the community what we are doing and why it is important.

Today, however, we are confronted with a new challenge; never before have the people of the world, and particularly of the United States, been subjected to so extensive, effective, and highly-financed barrage of demands for their interest and support. If we are to succeed in promoting understanding and support of special education, we must accept these facts and prepare ourselves to compete in the most effective possible manner with other groups seeking public interest, understanding and support.

Every human institution or group, including your own, has a public relations program, whether or not it be called by that name. The question to be asked is, "Is your public relations program good, bad, or indifferent?" Every contact you and your colleagues in special education have with a child, parent, another teacher or other professional person, or the 'man on the street' results in the creation of some type of impression of special education and your own organization. Taken collectively, all contacts you have with the public constitute your public relations program. Your responsibility is to ensure that all of these contacts contribute to the development of a public impression which is in accord with your objectives.

Two Levels of Public Relations

For convenience, it is possible to identify two levels of public relations actions in programs for the exceptional child. The first is what may be called the sociological level.

Special educators have long recognized that their responsibilities to the exceptional child are not limited to the provision of special educational programs directly affecting such children, but include a responsibility for 'educating' the parents of exceptional children and the public as a whole. They recognize that if the child with a severe physical, mental, or emotional disability is to realize his life's ambitions, the attitudes, concepts and values of the social milieu in which he will grow up and live are important factors in his eventual adjustment to that milieu. The responsibility for changing attitudes, concepts, and values through eradication of prejudice, misunderstanding, and discrimination rests with those who know the capabilities and potentialities of the exceptional child and who are free of these negative social reactions. Nothing will accomplish this more effectively than in telling the story of the successfully rehabilitated or adjusted child; than in making certain that the public has the facts about the processes by which disability or maladjustment is eliminated or minimized; than in being realistic and objective.

The second level of public relations is the hard fact of financial support for special education.

Special education frequently faces the very important problem of 'selling' the social and economic values of special education programs to school administrators, school boards and other groups. Public education, public relations or whatever term may be used, therefore, has greater significance for the special educator than for teachers, supervisors and administrators who may be working in some other aspects of education.

PUBLICITY AND PUBLIC EDUCATION

Although the two words are frequently used interchangeably, there is a great difference between 'publicity' and 'public education'. Publicity is drawing public attention to a particular person, group, place, event, or product. Its purpose is name identification, or public recognition of the name of your special school, program, or organization.

Public education, on the other hand, involves much more than publicity. Its purpose is not only to create name identification in the minds of the public but also to create an interest in and understanding of special education, its program, purposes, and value.

In formulating a public education program, one must first determine objectives. Publicity in itself is valid if one recognizes clearly the purposes for which such publicity is sought. Our national voluntary organizations, for example, are dependent upon publicity so that the symbols they use immediately connote the objectives of their organizations. Through good publicity, the identification of the Christmas Seal with the National Tuberculosis Association, and of the March of Dimes with the National Foundation for Infantile Paralysis, has become as clear in the minds of the public as similar brand names of the business world. When the United Nations International Children's Emergency Fund recognized that the 'emergency' aspects of its program were over and it became a permanent long-range organization under the name United Nations Children's Fund, it still kept the familiar short identification "U.N.I.C.E.F." because it had become so firmly fixed in the minds of the peoples of the world.

Special education in a strictly professional sense does not have the same need for general name identification, but there are numerous ways in which such specific identification is desirable in order to standardize certain terminology in the minds of the general public to the point where these words as symbols of expression provoke similar connotations. Among such terms are 'exceptional child' rather than 'crippled children', and 'cerebral palsied' rather than 'spastic'.

In seeking valid publicity of the term identification type, however, publicity per se is much more important in meeting the general objectives of special education if it is used as but one of a number of methods of professional, parent, and public education. Continuing to strive for publicity for publicity's sake rather than making publicity a part of a planned public education program is to scatter the shot and waste ammunition. It may get scores of newspaper stories and radio spots, but it is only meeting a part of the objective.

NEWSPAPER AND MAGAZINES

Two of the most readily available and effective mass media to promote special education are newspapers and magazines. The special educator's role, whether he is acting as a representative of the school system itself or of a professional organization such as the International Council on Exceptional Children, is getting the newspaper or magazine interested in special education and providing them with material. Before contacting your local newspapers, first consult one of the many available books on public relations techniques in your local library. The journalism teacher in your local high school or college will also probably be very glad to discuss public relations techniques with you. And be sure you have thought the 'whys' of your objective.

Usually special education programs receive the most attention when one of the national or a local voluntary organization concerned with services to the handicapped are conducting their fund-raising drives. Such groups usually have had some experience and possibly some volunteer or paid professional public relations personnel working with them and are well able to handle the mechanics of public relations. Instead of waiting for these groups to approach you, think through some of the activities in special education in your school which are worthy of publicizing and in which attention on the positive side would aid in spreading public understanding. Analyze your own programs in their relationship to special drives for heart disease, tuberculosis, poliomyelitis, hearing, cerebral palsy, crippled children, muscular dystrophy and other crippling conditions. Then, if you have something you consider newsworthy and worthwhile, contact the representatives of these groups to see if you can discuss it with them. Frequently, professional people working in special education are disappointed when they cooperate in such projects and then find the side of the story of what is being done by the schools is minimized in the sincere and earnest desire of the voluntary organizations to play up the needs. In such instances, there is frequently disappointment that credit is not given where credit is due. When this happens, your sense of true public or human relations really comes into focus, for your job then is attempting to show those responsible that emphasis on the positive side is desirable not only from your point of view but from theirs as well. Even though you may at first resent the efforts of the professional and voluntary workers in these organizations to 'take advantage' of your school program for what you may interpret to be their own ends, working closely with them will result in the type of desirable public relations that promotes both your objectives and theirs, for those objectives in the last analysis are the same.

Do not, however, limit your public relations program to working with the voluntary organizations during their campaigns or to such special weeks as Education Week or National Employ the Physically Handicapped Week. Study your newspapers carefully. Consider the special departments such as the women's page, home page, book reviews, school page, sports news and other, and the possible angles that might be of interest to the readers of those sections. For example, the sports page editor may be interested in your recreational program for exceptional children. The editor of the women's page may want to write up the homemaking activities you conduct, or the school page editor may want to do a column on career opportunities in special education.

When you have developed an idea which you think may be of interest, make an appointment with the editor of that particular page of the news-paper, and invite him to visit your school. Remember the editor is the judge of what is news. Don't try to force stories on him. Even if you happen to know the publisher's wife, go directly to the person at the paper who is responsible. By pressure methods you may gain your immediate objective on a particular story, but advancing public understanding of the handicapped and of special education is a long range program. Don't jeopardize your chances for future interpretation.

Don't try to use the high pressure methods you may sometimes see depicted in motion pictures or books about newspapers or public relations. Newspaper people are familiar with such tactics. There is no substitute for sincerity and facts in telling your story to anyone, particularly an experienced editor or reporter. The newspaper editor or reporter may be depicted in fiction as a hard-boiled, cynical person; but in reality, he realizes the great responsibility he bears in the selection, presentation, and analysis of news. He usually is a person with a high degree of civic consciousness and social responsibility who will be deeply interested in aiding in any way possible the advancement of public understanding of the problems of and programs for exceptional children.

As a professional teacher, you will probably never have occasion to prepare or send out press releases concerned specifically with announcements about your own school. Each local chapter of the International Council on Excep-tional Children and other professional organizations, however, should have a public relations committee and a single person who has the specific respon-sibility of seeing that professional news of his organization's activities is made available to the press. If you bear that responsibility, consult one of the books from the library on the technical aspects of preparing press releases. But remember in preparing such releases that you are concerned with public education. Attempt to include some general information material in your release. For example, instead of just a simple meeting announcement, give your president or chairman a quote of this type:

The Blank Blank Chapter of the International Council for Exceptional Children will hear Dr. John Doe, Professor of Pediatrics, Upstate Medical College, speak on 'New Developments in Cerebral Palsy' at a public meeting at the library of the Blank Blank School, Independence and Fourth Avenues, Tuesday evening, February 1st, at 8:00 P.M. In announcing the meeting, Miss Mary Moe, chapter president, said, "Although medical science cannot prevent or cure the condition known as cerebral palsy, experience has shown that through therapy and special education much can be done to aid the cerebral palsied, particularly if treatment, training and education are started early enough".

Thus, if the newspaper carries the quote, in addition to the necessary facts about the meeting, the readers will have learned several basic concepts concerning cerebral palsy.

When a particularly effective news story or feature has appeared, write a note to the publisher or editor or reporter who prepared the story telling him of the number of comments you have received on the story and how helpful it was. Newspapers like to know their stories have received attention and have made a social contribution.

Don't be disappointed if some of the releases you send the newspaper are not used. The editor has many factors to evaluate in selecting which stories are to be published or to receive special attention. An announcement of a meeting may not get in today, but it may the next time you have a meeting. Your job is to furnish clearly typed, factual releases of your organization's activities to him. His job is to decide whether they should be printed.

When you are releasing a story which has particular interest, send a photograph if one is available. Be sure the photograph is one which has spot news value or pictorial interest and will amplify your news release.

Don't send snapshots or artistic, mat finish photographs. For reproduction, the newspaper needs an eight by ten inch glossy finish photograph. Be sure to include a short caption which identifies the persons and the place of the photograph, and the activity shown. Type the caption on paper and paste it on the back of the photograph. Do not write on the back of the photograph.

When a particularly outstanding guest is visiting your chapter or your school, telephone the newspaper and suggest they may be interested in taking a photograph. Cooperate with the photographer if they send one, but don't try to tell him what type of picture to take. That is his business. Yours is special education.

These same principles in arranging for stories in newspapers should also be followed in contacting and working with magazines.

RADIO AND TELEVISION

Although the techniques vary considerably, the same general approach is used in promoting public education by radio and television. Radio and television are specialized fields, and those who plan, write and produce radio and television programs recognize that in all probability, you are inexperienced in such matters. Don't read a book on radio or television and then sit down and try to plan a program or write a script. You can't do that, anymore than the radio ad television specialists can teach blind, deaf, or orthopedically handicapped children after reading the other chapters in these two volumes.

For spot news programs, send the news editor of your local radio and television stations the same releases you send to the newspapers. For other programs, make an appointment with the station's program director or those responsible for the production of certain programs, and then approach them in the same manner you approached the editor of the newspaper. Tell them your story simply and sincerely, bringing in as much factual and human interest material as possible. They will be able to suggest the treatment of your story if it commands their interest. Again, remember, it is your responsibility to make the contacts and present the material. It is their responsibility to evaluate the material and suggest the best method of treatment.

Listen to a certain radio program or watch a certain television program critically over a period of several broadcasts before you approach the station. Be thoroughly familiar with the format of the program before you make your appointment. If it is a women's show, a breakfast human-interest show, or a program featuring interviews or roundtable, be sure you have the names of some locally prominent persons who have already agreed in advance to participate. Remember also that radio and television programs are planned for some time in advance.

If arrangements are made for a broadcast, send out postal cards to your membership and other interested groups telling them about it. As you did with the newspaper editor, write the persons responsible for the program a letter of appreciation after the broadcast. Suggest to your colleagues and friends that they, too, write expressing their interest.

Both in newspaper and in radio-television approaches, you may be able to tie in stories on special education with local fund raising programs. During the March of Dimes, Easter Seal, Christmas Seal, or other campaigns, contact the persons in charge of publicity for these drives and discuss with them the possibilities of feature stories, picture spreads, and radio and television programs on the part that special education plays in the rehabilitation of the patients with whom the particular campaign is concerned.

SPEAKERS

Although newspapers, magazines, radio, and television provide the most effective means of contacting large groups of persons, probably the most effective methods of a concentrated approach to a small group is through lectures, demonstrations, discussions, and similar meetings. In your community there are scores of professional groups such as public health, nursing, medical, personnel, education, social work and safety organization; civic groups; church organizations; parent teachers groups; employer and employee groups; women's clubs farm organizations and others to whom you could profitably tell the story of special education.

Make certain that before contacting such groups you not only have a story to tell, but that you have someone who can tell it effectively. You may want to use a member of your own group who is a good speaker, an older student or adult who previously participated in a special education program, the parent of a child who has benefited from a special education program, or some other interested and informed person. But remember the old adage of 'the proof of the pudding'; be sure your speaker not only knows the subject but can hold the interest of your audience and get over the information you want covered. An outstanding orthopedic surgeon, a clever prosthetic technician or even an able classroom teacher or supervisor of special education is not necessarily an effective speaker for such groups.

There are a number of excellent films, film strips, and slides which can be used in connection with such meetings. Familiarize yourself with them so you know which visual materials would be of interest to different groups. Demonstrations by the children themselves, when they are well done and in good taste, are growth experiences for both the children themselves and the audience. As with radio and television, let your members know about such meetings if they are open to the public.

With the current shortage of teachers, it is the responsibility of all in education to help interest qualified young men and women to consider teaching as a career. This is especially true in special education and the professions of physical therapy, occupational therapy, and speech and hearing therapy. Effective aids to this goal are films, talks, demonstrations and discussions to Hi-Y Clubs, Girl Reserves, 4-H Club groups, Y.M.C.A. and Y.W.C.A. meetings, church and school groups and other organizations of youth and young adults.

Meetings, exhibits and public demonstrations may also be held in connection with voluntary agency fund campaigns, National Employment of the Physically Handicapped Week, hobby shows, fairs, and other public gatherings.

A Last Word

In all of your public relations activities, don't be reticent about asking for help. After hearing your story, most people will recognize the importance of special education and will want to help you tell its story. But remember that factual knowledge and sincerity go a great deal further in your contacts with the press, radio and television and community groups than some 'so-called' public relations techniques.

SECTION I

CHAPTER V

COORDINATION OF THE SERVICES OF OFFICIAL AND VOLUNTARY SERVICES

COORDINATION OF THE SERVICES OF OFFICIAL AND VOLUNTARY AGENCIES

Today, and probably in the future, the keynote of the program for serving the exceptional is cooperation along a broad front.[1] There must be clear understanding of the contributions of both official and voluntary agencies.

Among the official agencies are city, state, and Federal, county, town, and village groups, or some parallel setup. These agencies may be considerable in numbers, especially under present methods of organization, where many Federal, state, and local bureaus and departments serve the exceptional in one way or another.[2] This shared responsibility leads frequently to conflicts of authority and opinion, with the result that the exceptional suffer. Likewise, the cost of care and education of the exceptional is sometimes unnessarily increased without corresponding improvement in service and results.[3]

Voluntary agencies are many. Various organized groups exist in every area of the exceptional, and each of these has taken upon itself in a national and local way to present its case to the public and to officials. An unfortunate danger from this, and one to be avoided, is overlapping of programs among voluntary agencies and between voluntary and official groups, which causes confusion and conflict. Each type of agency has a contribution which it can make in some unique and economical way. Better coordination needs to be developed through the agencies themselves, and closer cooperation with local service agencies is necessary.[4]

The Official Agencies[5-6] dealing with the work with the handicapped are many and varied. Their influence or scope may be national, intrastate, or local.

OFFICIAL AGENCIES:
FEDERAL GOVERNMENT

Legislative. The underlying function of the Federal government in relation to work with the exceptional is both investigative and supportive when viewed from the legislative angle. There has been a trend toward presenting the educational problems and needs of the exceptional to the Federal authorities as applied to limited areas rather than to all the exceptional areas as a unit. Much legislation has been introduced into the Congress in recent years to develop special programs for certain areas. Each session brings in new bills, or amendments to existing acts.[7] Legislative provision on a Federal level for the exceptional is necessary. But much caution must be used or we will have confusion and overlapping of services far greater and more costly than we can afford to carry.[8-9]

Executive. While it is impossible to predict what trends the Federal government may take in an age of changing social conditions, it is the present and probably the future feeling that in this country the further function of the Federal educational action will be coordinating, advisory, and supportive in the sense of augmenting state and local financial provisions for increased service. Support by grants places the Federal authorities in a strategic position to develop a coordinated and reasonably standardized minimum program through the states, with uniform methods of organization and administration, yet with full recognition of local needs and preferences.[10]

A threefold program of this kind already exists in the United State Office of Education.[11] It functions somewhat as follows: (1) assistance by the Office of Education to representatives of various official and voluntary groups that deal with exceptional children; (2) assistance to the Office of Education by such groups; (3) assistance extended to one another under the guidance of the Office of Education, or with its cooperation, by various groups dealing with exceptional children in given geographical areas.

The objectives to which this triple program leads include bringing about a better understanding of the educational needs of the different groups of the exceptional and fostering a greater coordination of effort on the part of national private organizations and state agencies. There is need in all probability for the creation of some type of coordinating council for the field of the exceptional and rehabilitation such as exists in the National Health Council. It is recognized, for instance, that many problems in work with the exceptional are common to all areas and closely related.

It has been suggested that the Office of Education might be of much use in handling the following: (1) conducting surveys and making legislative and other studies that would be of great value to those concerned with the education of exceptional children; (2) formulating suggestive standards for teacher training and selection,[12-17] for curriculum, teaching methods, teaching organization, admission to special schools and classes, state plans of supervision, and for the solution of other pertinent problems; (3) developing more extensive 'on call' service for informational, advisory, and technical assistance; (4) promoting progressive movements that involve the following: legislation for and enumeration of exceptional children; better provision for the care of exceptional children in rural communities; better coordination between day schools and residential schools administrative setups that will bring the education of all types of exceptional children under the same general direction; inauguration of pre-service training in the essentials of special education of all teachers and continued in-service training which will help them to recognize and to take steps toward the correction of serious maladjustments in all the children.

Representatives of various groups under state, municipal, or private control should cooperate with the Office of Education by: (1) keeping before their respective organizations the needs of all types of exceptional children; (2) interpreting the problems of the respective groups to the Office of Education; (3) suggesting research problems for study; (4) giving and encouraging prompt and complete replies to all requests for information; (5) encouraging local organization for the education of exceptional children as a unit, with all groups under the same administrative direction; (6) using the resources of all existing local organizations in the interest of a coordinated program.

This accomplished, state and local organizations, whether official or voluntary, may then be considered as coordinators of action for the exceptional.

OFFICIAL AGENCIES:
STATE DEPARTMENT OF EDUCATION

The functions of a state department of education[18-21] in handling the education of the exceptional include: (1) cooperation with Federal and voluntary national agencies in promoting national programs; (2) a plan for finances, advice, and help regarding them, and to some extent administration of interstate programs, always including full recognition of the work of other state and voluntary agencies charged with responsibilities in the same field; (3) consideration of both the general and common problems peculiar to one or several areas, with the objective of sound, economical, up-to-date solutions utilizing all available facilities.

From another point of view,[22] the functions of a state bureau or department include: (1) Stimulation of the public in local communities, together with stimulation of educational leaders to the realization of existing needs;[23] (2) standardization of special-class organization, instructional procedures, requirements of special equipment, teacher preparation, and teacher certification; (3) clinical work for psychological study, medical inquiry, and educational diagnosis, all directed toward making the needed adjustment in the life of the child; this should include a complete medical examination of the individual and a diagnosis of his needs, looking toward his best placement; (4) organization, including organization of the clinical program just mentioned; organization of curricula; organization of teacher-training facilities with definite cooperation with both state and private setups; organization of special schools and classes in districts where interest and needs have found expression; (5) supervision of work already organized, including instruction and classroom procedure; this work includes methods, instructional devices and units of work, teaching materials, and equipment; (6) administration, including special surveys, careful supervision of expenditures allocated to the education of exceptional children, and general supervision of the whole statewide program, with due recognition of peculiar local needs and problems; special education, and the funds with which to administer it; also improve-(7) coordination with other portions of the state department of education, with other state departments, with state and community agencies, — public and private, — concerned with the problems of the exceptional; (8) promotion, such as that of state legislation calculated to increase the facilities for ments in community practices and promotion of opportunities for teacher preparation.

In the final analysis, the objective of any official state organization for the exceptional is a completely coordinated program. In 1933 Martens published an analysis of outstanding state programs and also certain conclusions. She stressed the dangers of a laissez-faire policy where by state functions were allowed to develop in a haphazard fashion in one or another division of the state government. As can be seen, such policy may result in lack of coordination, competition, limited cooperation, and increased costs. No state organization can be effective without: "(1) a thorough understanding of the problems involved on the part of those responsible for meeting them; (2) wholehearted cooperation among all agencies contributing to the final result; (3) adequate facilities for carrying on the work."[24]

Following this study, Martens developed a tentative ideal ten-point program, which may be summarized as follows:

There should be delegation of responsibility for the administration and general supervision of educational facilities for all groups of handicapped to a centralized educational authority, represented by the Director of a Division of Education of the Handicapped in the State Department of Education.

The Director should present qualifications along the lines of: (a) general educational and psychological background, including considerable personal culture; (b) thorough familiarity with educational objectives, curricular needs, and methods for all children; (c) intensive professional training in psychology and in the education of all or most types of handicapped children; (d) understanding of clinical practice (medical and psychological) diagnosis; (e) successful teaching and supervisory experience; (f) administrative ability. Specialized or technical assistance must be given the Director, as required, in carrying on a statewide program. There are, in addition to professional qualifications, certain personality requirements which must not be overlooked if the Director is to reveal true leadership.

There should be coordination with other state departments and voluntary agencies which render valuable aid. Such agencies include the Department of Health, Department of Public Welfare, Bureau of Vocational Rehabilitation, and various groups concerned with the social welfare and health of children. Duplication of effort must be avoided. Each cooperating agency must make a contribution in keeping with its special field.

The establishment of a state coordinating council composed of representatives of the various agencies involved is probably the best step toward participation of each one in matters of common concern. Such a council supplies a channel through which active cooperation must be secured. It leads, if properly handled, to a willingness to understand one another's problems, it provides a forum for the discussion of common problems and the delegation of responsibility to the organization to which it belongs, and it goes far to insure the interest of each agency in the progress of the total program.

The program developed must include consideration of and provision for every type of handicapped child, including the physically, mentally, and socially handicapped.

The subject of care is the whole child, his physical, mental, and spiritual needs, his social, vocational, and educational problems.

The program involves clinical, instructional, and social service for the handicapped child, since each cooperating agency has much to give in one or more of these fields.[25]

There is no particular gain to be achieved in presenting various state programs in detail. Once the principles of operation and the basic necessity of cooperation are understood, the actual program may be built, giving due consideration to many special factors that are peculiar to the state involved.[26-27]

No state can provide a better program than that made possible by available funds. Furthermore, in some states one group of the exceptional may be in more pressing need of services than others, and its problems require more immediate attention.

The actual building and successful operation of a state program involves the work of years. Likewise, in times like the present, when taxation has been an overwhelming and protested burden, it is not an uncommon experience to have an educational program wrecked through unconsidered, short-sighted, and truly expensive economies.

OFFICIAL AGENCIES:
MUNICIPAL DEPARTMENTS OF SPECIAL EDUCATION

Scores of cities throughout the country have developed and are developing departments of special education.

In Section II, Chapter III of this volume will be found detailed descriptions of special education programs in Chicago and in New York City. In addition, in the various chapters in Volumes II and III devoted to the different areas of handicaps, there are a number of readings outlining the services for these areas in several metropolitan centers.

It is impossible here to list all the cities that are now offering programs in special education. But a representative list, by no means inclusive, would give the following: Boston, Mass.; Springfield, Mass.; Providence, R.I.; Hartford, New Haven, Conn.; Albany, Buffalo, New York, Rochester, Syracuse, N.Y.; Newark, N.J.; Erie, Harrisburg, Philadelphia, Pittsburgh, Pa.; Wilmington, Del.; Baltimore, Md.; Washington, D.C.; Charlotte, Winston-Salem, N.C.; Jacksonville, Miami, Fla.; Chattanooga, Nashville, Tenn.; Jackson, Miss.; Dallas, El Paso, Forth Worth, Houston, Tex.; Akron, Cincinnati, Columbus, Dayton, Toledo, Ohio; Indianapolis, Ind.; Battle Creek, Dearborn, Detroit, Flint, Grand Rapids, Lansing, Mich.; Champaign, Chicago, Elgin, Evanston, Normal, Peoria, Rockford, Springfield, Ill.; Beloit, Milwaukee, Racine, Wis.; Duluth, Minneapolis, St. Paul, Minn.; Cedar Rapids, Davenport, Des Moines, Iowa; Kansas City, St. Louis, Mo.; Little Rock, Ark.; Lincoln, Neb.; Denver, Colo.; Spokane, Wash.; Salem, Ore.; Bakersfield, Los Angeles, Oakland, Pasadena, San Francisco, Calif.

VOLUNTARY AGENCIES

Voluntary agencies[28-29] make a very definite contribution not only to the education of any type of the exceptional but also to the welfare of the field as a whole. They are of great assistance, too, in providing service which for various reasons cannot be rendered by the official agencies. Voluntary agencies are more able than official agencies to develop their program as they choose. They are better able to select top administrations and change inefficient ones. Adequate leadership is paramount to the voluntary agency. Since their function is to a considerable extent the dissemination of propaganda, these agencies sometimes divert to dramatic but unimportant activities the interest and funds that might be employed in some more significant direction. The outstanding agencies have survived because of far-seeing programs based on cooperation and definitive service programs.

The primary function of voluntary agencies is exploratory, cooperative, advisory, and informative. When the chosen field has been studied and its needs are determined, a second function arises, the scientific selection of the point or points of approach and a determination as to services required.

The field having thus been determined, and having been justified as meeting some need, a program must be presented and promoted, perferably on a temporary research, exploratory, or demonstration basis.[30] The really far-sighted agency is constantly abandoning those products which other official agencies can take up and seeking new horizons that may lead to the programs of tomorrow. This is a difficult procedure for official agencies, since they lack facilities for even the problems of the moment and are limited in the necessary time, personnel, or resources for exploratory endeavors.

Most voluntary organizations are supported by memberships and contributions, and they find themselves quite often in direct competition for financial aid from sources of funds that are common to them all. They are sometimes over enthusiastic to the extent of magnifying problems which are minor or creating ones which do not exist. In addition, they are at times dependent on patrons who are peculiarly interested in only one area or problem. Frequently it is necessary to offer 'interesting' projects for support rather than projects that meet basic needs of the work. This is probably due to failure to educate the public to the objectives of the work in general. Where publicity has been promoted, it has too often been conceived on a sentimental and bizarre basis which in the end tends to injure the work rather than aid it.[31]

FOOTNOTES

1. Mayo, Leonard, "The Art of Synthesis", *Assn. for the Aid of Crippled Children, Annual Report*, Oct., 1954, N.Y.C.
2. See Section III of this volume for list of Official and Voluntary Agencies.
3. *The Handicapped Child in His Home and His Community*: Proceedings of the Ninth Governor's Conference on Exceptional Children, 1952, (Illinois Commission for Handicapped Children: Chicago, 1952).
4. *Report of the Task Force on the Handicapped* (Office of Defense Mobilization: Washington, D.C., 1952), Part VI, pp. 43 ff.
5. *Ibid.*, pp. 17, 18.
6. See Section III of this volume for list of Official Agencies serving this area on a national basis.
7. See Public Law 565, 83rd Congress, Chapter 655, 2nd Session, "Vocational Rehabilitation Amendments of 1954".
8. Frampton, M.E., "Assistance and Rehabilitation of the Physically Handicapped, Hearing Before a Special Sub-Committee on Education & Labor, House of Representatives, 83rd Congress, First Session, July and August, 1953." pp. 79 ff.
9. *The U.S. Program for Crippled Children, What It Does and What Congress and the States Need to Do about It* (American Parents Committee, Inc.: N.Y.C., 1954).
10. *Report of the Task Force on the Handicapped*, pp. 45 ff.
11. Martens, Elise H., *Coordination of Effort for the Education of Exceptional Children*, Bulletin No. 7 (United States Office of Education: Washington, D.C., 1935).
12. Mackie, R.P. and Dunn, L.M., *College and University Programs for the Preparation of Teachers of Exceptional Children* Bul. #13 (U.S. Office of Education, Washington, D.C., 1954).
13. *College Symposium on the Education of the Exceptional*, Feb. 25-28, 1952; *Teachers and Other Professional Personnel, Their Selection and Education* (Hunter College: N.Y.C., 1953).

14. *Opportunities for the Preparation of Teachers of Exceptional Children* (National Society for Crippled Children & Adults: Chicago, 1949).
15. *Teachers of Children Who Have Special Health Problems—Their Qualifications and Professional Preparation* (U.S. Office of Education: Washington, D.C., 1954), 70 pp. mimeo.
16. MacKenzie, G.N., and Corey, S. M., *Instructional Leadership* (Bureau of Publications, Teachers College, Columbia University: N.Y.C., 1954).
17. McGeoch, D.M., *Direct Experiences in Teacher Education* (Bureau of Publications, Teachers College, Columbia University: N.Y.C., 1953).
18. *State Plan for Education of Physically Handicapped Children*, Bulletin #1025 (Michigan Department of Public Instruction: Lansing, Michigan, 1954).
    A comprehensive plan setting an administrative standard — Editors.
19. *Is Your Child Exceptional?* Circular Series H, No. 12 (Illinois Supt. of Public Instruction: Springfield, Ill., 1950).
20. *Include All the Children*, Biennial Report, 1951-53 (Illinois Commission for Handicapped Children: Springfield, Ill., 1953).
21. *Special Services for Handicapped Children* (The Commonwealth of Virginia: Richmond, 1953).
22. Martens, Elise H., *Organization for Exceptional Children Within State Departments of Education*, Pamphlet No. 42 (U.S. Office of Education: Washington, D.C., 1933).
23. *Is Your Child Exceptional?*
24. Martens, Elise H., *Organization for Exceptional Children Within State Departments of Education.*
25. *Ibid.*
26. *The Handicapped Child in the Mainstream*, Proceedings of Tenth Governor's Conference on Exceptional Children (Illinois Commission for Handicapped Children: Chicago, Ill., 1954).
27. Reynolds, M.G., "Minnesota Has Done Well in Education for the Handicapped, But We Must Do More", *Minnesota Journal of Education*, Feb., 1954. 34:7:24-25, 36.
28. See Section III of this volume for list of Voluntary Agencies.
29. *Report of the Task Force on the Handicapped.*
30. *Hunter College Summer Vacation and Demonstration School for the Exceptional* (Office of Special Education, Hunter College: N. Y. C., 1953).
31. See results of an extensive study of N. Y. State Charities in *Report of The Joint Legislative Committee on Charitable and Philanthropic Agencies and Organizations*, State of N.Y., Legislative Document #26, 1954 (William Piers: Albany, N.Y.). See also: *Amendments to N.Y. State Social Welfare Laws*, Article 10A, Chapter 418, 419, and 420 of the Laws of 1954 (N.Y. State Dept. of Social Welfare: 112 State Street, Albany, N.Y.).

SECTION I

CHAPTER VI

SPECIAL EDUCATION AND INTERNATIONAL

COOPERATION BY DONALD V. WILSON

SPECIAL EDUCATION AND INTERNATIONAL COOPERATION

DONALD V. WILSON

A major handicap confronting the exceptional children of the world is the attitude of teachers and educators, as well as other professions, toward the child who is physically or mentally different. In many parts of the world this inability to give more attention to special education is partly explained by the urgent need to provide fundamental education. In many countries, illiteracy is a pressing problem and it is not surprising, therefore, that a high priority is given to providing basic education for the masses of children who have been long neglected. However, educators in many parts of the world recognize the necessity of taking action for the exceptional child, and some small beginnings are being made in even the most backward countries. In many places these undertakings are the result of the interest of parents and non-professional persons who are the first to recognize that the exceptional child must also be included in the newly developed social, educational and health programs.

The health and educational needs of the so-called normal child are so great, and economic resources are so limited in many parts of the world, that it is impossible for priorities to be established with assurance that the most important needs are being met first. Some beginnings have been made, however, in most countries of the world to meet the educational needs of those persons who cannot participate in regular educational programs.

In recent years, distinct progress has been made on a world level in the development of services for the handicapped. Experience indicates that in an international program it is not possible to separate the educational needs in a particular community, from related needs in social and economic areas. This means that the problems of special education cannot be separated from the total pattern of social and economic development in a particular community and nation. Facilities for the handicapped must be closely related to other services in the fields of health, social welfare and employment which each community develops. In every community a first requirement is the development of public opinion and public attitudes toward the exceptional child so that deviations from the normal will be recognized and accepted as 'normal.' It is also essential that as special educational programs are developed, consideration also be given to the need for related medical, vocational and social services.

International programs to aid the disabled are being carried out by the United Nations and several related specialized agencies such as UNESCO. In addition to these governmental programs, a large number of voluntary organizations are interested in special education as a part of their total effort to develop international understanding among the various countries of the world.

The different standards of living prevailing in different parts of the world must be taken into account when planning a program of international action for the handicapped. It is not possible to establish services for the disabled until public opinion is such that it will support such measures and there are satisfactory hospitals, other health services, schools and social welfare programs, as well as facilities for vocational training and employment which are all needed in order to provide the comprehensive services required by the handicapped.

United Nations Program

The prevention of disability and the rehabilitation of handicapped persons are problems to which the United Nations has given attention. The aim of the United Nations is primarily to assist the member governments to establish and expand services for the handicapped. This is carried out in close cooperation with other governmental as well as non-governmental international organizations. In order to coordinate the activities of the many international organizations engaged in work for the handicapped, the Economic and Social Council in 1950 requested the Secretary General of the United Nations "to plan jointly with the specialized agencies and in consultation with the interested non-governmental organizations, a well coordinated programme for the rehabilitation of the physically handicapped persons". This coordinated programme of the United Nations is carried out in cooperation with a number of specialized agencies including the World Health Organization (WHO), the International Labour Organization (ILO), the United Nations Educational, Scientific and Cultural Organization (UNESCO), and the United Nations Children's Fund (UNICEF).

The Secretariat of the United Nations drafted plans for a comprehensive international programme after drawing upon the counsel of representatives of the Specialized Agencies at a meeting in February, 1950. The Secretariat's report was submitted to the Social Commission in April, 1950, and the resulting programme was agreed to by the Commission and approved by a resolution adopted by the Economic and Social Council in July of that year.

This resolution, which is the basis for the present United Nations programme, seeks to establish a broad, coordinated programme for the social rehabilitation of the physically handicapped. The salient points of the resolution are:

1. Joint planning with the Specialized Agencies and in consultation with the interested non-governmental organizations to develop a well coordinated

international programme for the rehabilitation of physically handicapped persons;

2. Providing fellowships, scholarships and experts under the regularly established United Nations programmes;

3. Expanding facilities for the dissemination of information on rehabilitation and the preparation of training materials.

The resolution also recommends to the member governments of the United Nations that they: (1) continue their efforts in the field of rehabilitation; (2) consider establishing or encouraging governmental or other organs to take the lead in studying and solving the problems confronting physically handicapped persons; and (3) consider appropriate measures, including legislation, for helping physically handicapped persons to solve the special problems with which they are faced.

Several steps have been taken to ensure the cooperation and coordination which is essential to the United Nations programme. A special unit was established in the Bureau of Social Affairs of the Secretariat of the United Nations; the unit, of which Mr. Kurt Jansson of Finland is Chief, serves a coordinating function for international programmes for the handicapped. There is also a Technical Working Group composed of representatives chosen by the United Nations and interested Specialized Agencies, which is charged with planning the implementation of the coordinated program. The Social Commission reviews the program when it meets every two years and makes definite recommendations for future action.

Specialized Agencies

The coordination of activities provided by the Secretariat of the United Nations is extremely important because, as indicated above, the programs of several other international, inter-governmental organizations include services for the handicapped. Some of the interest and activities of these specialized agencies affiliated with the United Nations are indicated here.

The education of the handicapped is a matter of particular concern to the United Nations Educational, Scientific and Cultural Organization (UNESCO). Although a primary concern of UNESCO is the development of educational systems and opportunities for all adults and children, the agency has been able to give some attention to the needs of exceptional children. Through the UNESCO Gift Coupon program, materials and equipment to be used in the education of handicapped children have been provided to needy institutions in several nations. The UNESCO Book and Film Coupon plans facilitate the international exchange of teaching materials and the Organization's Education Clearing House compiles and distributes data concerning regional and international conferences devoted to exceptional children.

The United Nations International Children's Fund (UNICEF) has provided supplies and equipment to various nations to aid in the development of pilot services for handicapped children. The health of millions of children throughout the world has been improved through UNICEF's mass campaigns against tuberculosis, yaws, trachoma, and malaria and by the Fund's work in the development of maternal and child health centers in remote areas.

Fellowships and scholarships provided by UNICEF have enabled a number of persons to secure training in services for handicapped children. Technical guidance in the planning and execution of UNICEF activities is provided by the World Health Organization.

The World Health Organization has been especially effective in the prevention of disability through campaigns against various infectious diseases. By means of training fellowships, the assignment of expert consultants and the sponsoring of technical meetings, the WHO has done much to advance the level of medical rehabilitation in many areas of the world.

In 1951, the World Health Organization established a Joint Expert Committee on the Physically Handicapped Child. Organized with the participation of the United Nations, the International Labour Organization and UNESCO, the Committee met in Geneva, Switzerland in December 1951. The participating agencies selected twelve experts from several countries and various professions including education, medicine, and social work. The Committee's report emphasizes that the central problem is to bring the necessary professional services and facilities to the handicapped child, without disturbing the equilibrium of normal growth and development. The integration of services, — medical, educational, social and vocational, — is considered as a basic prerequisite of adequate care, and the need to relate programs for handicapped children to services provided for the community as a whole is stressed. In its report the Committee discusses special education as a right as well as a necessity for the handicapped child and urges that adequate standards be maintained in the selection and training of teachers to work with impairments.

The World Health Organization also convened an Expert Committee on the Mentally Subnormal Child which met in Geneva in 1953. The report of this Committee emphasizes preventive and remedial measures which can be carried out during childhood and the need to provide adequate educational opportunities and special facilities for subnormal children of school age. The principles set forth in this report provide a sound basis for further action for this particular category of the handicapped.

The International Labour Organization (ILO) has long been interested in the problems of disability and particularly the prevention of industrial and vocational accidents; it has also done valuable work in the development of vocational guidance services and training and placement of disabled persons. In recent years the ILO has given attention to the preparation of a proposed international recommendation concerning vocational rehabilitation of the disabled. This recommendation recognizes the need for special provisions for disabled children and young persons and specifically recommends that vocational rehabilitation services for disabled children and young persons of school age be organized and developed by the education authorities in cooperation with those responsible for vocational rehabilitation.

It is also urged that education programmes take into account the special problems of disabled children and young persons and their need of opportunities equal to those of non-disabled children and young persons to receive vocational preparation best suited to their age, abilities, aptitudes and interests.

Voluntary Organizations

Many international non-governmental organizations (NGOs) are interested in extending services to the handicapped although this interest is usually incidental to the main purpose of the organization. For example, in 1953 the World Association of Girl Guides and Girl Scouts held in Finland a training course concerning work with the handicapped. More recently, the Boy Scouts International Bureau has established an International Advisory Committee on Scouting with the Handicapped. Both of these organizations are developing programs to enable handicapped children to participate more fully in informal education activities.

Cooperation between the various non-governmental international organizations and the governmental programs is facilitated by the Conference of World Organizations Interested in the Handicapped. This Conference held its first meeting in Geneva, Switzerland in October 1951 and has subsequently met at the United Nations Headquarters in New York in February 1953 and also in Geneva in September 1954. The purposes of the Conference are: to assist the United Nations and the specialized agencies in their programs: to provide liaison between the non-governmental organizations and the United Nations and Specialized Agencies; and to develop cooperation among the non-governmental organizations.

The existing wide interest in the handicapped is indicated by the action taken at the most recent meeting in 1954 when the Conference urged that steps be taken to encourage and assist training schools for teachers to include information concerning disabling conditions, in their curricula. The need for further research into all problems of the subnormal child was also stressed by the Conference, and each country was urged to undertake research and devise tests and other criteria appropriate to its special conditions.

Although not a member of the Conference, the World Confederation of Organizations of the Teaching Profession was represented at one of the meetings. The diversity of interest in international action to assist the handicapped, is indicated by the number of organizations which are members, including: World Veterans Federation, International Confederation of Free Trade Unions, The World Council for the Welfare of the Blind and the International Catholic Child Bureau, the World Federation of Mental Health, International Organization of Employers, International Hospital Federation and the World Federation of Trade Unions. A total of twenty-three international organizations are members of the Conference.

These voluntary organizations assist in the exchange of information through their publications, through conferences, and through providing expert guidance and material assistance. They provide channels of communication to their national affiliated organizations and in cooperation with governmental bodies, frequently provide the stimulus for the organization and development of services in local communities.

International Society for the Welfare of Cripples

The International Society for the Welfare of Cripples is a federation of national voluntary organizations in thirty countries which provide services for disabled persons. The Society, founded in 1922 as the International Society for Crippled Children, has been for more than thirty years the principal international voluntary organization concerned with the medical, educational, social, and vocational problems of handicapped persons in all parts of the world. An extensive program is maintained to promote the exchange of information concerning services for the handicapped, to stimulate the development of programs to provide such services and to provide assistance to persons and organizations throughout the world interested in the welfare of the disabled.

The functions of the Society on the world level include publication and film distribution programs, assistance in the international exchange of experts and students interested in services for the disabled, guidance in the development of voluntary programs, and the holding of international meetings. The Society works in close cooperation with other international organizations and particularly with the United Nations with which it has consultative status granted by the Economic and Social Council.

The World Congresses held by the ISWC every three years serve to bring together persons from all parts of the world who are interested in special education, as well as other professional persons engaged in work for the handicapped. The Fifth World Congress of the ISWC held in Stockholm in September, 1951, was attended by a number of educators, and the program included consideration of "Education of the Crippled Child"; various papers concerning this subject were presented at the Congress. Again at the Sixth World Congress held at The Hague in September 1954, papers were presented concerning the development of "Special Schools for the Handicapped."

The Society's Committee on Education for Crippled Persons serves as a specific means for the exchange of information concerning educational programs. The members of this Committee live in various parts of the world and are particularly interested in the problems of education.

METHODS OF ACTION

In order to carry out international programs to aid in the development of more adequate services for the handicapped, various methods of action are used. All these programs aim to stimulate and assist the development of services and in order to do this, organizations are needed. In fact, the establishment of organizations, local, national, and international, is an important part of the work being done to stimulate services and more attention needs to be given to type of organizations needed, the purposes of existing organizations and their relationship to each other. An organization, however, is merely a means to an end, and perhaps more important is the methods used by the organizations to achieve their purposes.

The methods of international action for the handicapped are not particularly new, for they are the same methods used within nations to secure the improvement of educational and other services for the handicapped. What is new is the increased use of these methods on a world-wide basis.

Special educational services for the handicapped usually are, and certainly should be, a local responsibility. The principal aim of international programs is to encourage the local acceptance of responsibility and to help make it possible for organizations within nations to provide the best possible services.

In international programs the media used to achieve this aim includes international conferences, publications, films, and study and observation in a foreign country. International agencies try to assist in the development of more effective national and local organizations and in the preparation of well-qualified personnel to provide better educational services.

INTERNATIONAL CONFERENCES

Since there is no international organization devoted primarily to the educational problems of exceptional children, the need for exchange of information and experiences in the field of special education must be met by other groups. The large number of international meetings held in recent years which have given consideration to these problems of education attests to the real interest which exists and the desire for current information. The following are some examples of the meetings which have been held:

The International Union for Child Welfare, because of its general interest in all problems of children, has given particular attention to the matter of education of handicapped children. A conference of experts on the educational problems of Orthopedically Handicapped Children was held in Geneva, Switzerland in February, 1950, under the auspices of the IUCW in cooperation with UNESCO. Representatives from seventeen countries attended this meeting. The conference emphasized that handicapped children need integrated medical, educational and other services to enable them to develop their abilities and be effective, contributing members not only of their communities and nations, but also of the world.

An International Study Conference on Child Welfare was held in Bombay, India in December, 1952, under the sponsorship of the International Union for Child Welfare and the All India Save the Children Committee. A special session of the conference, held in cooperation with the International Society for the Welfare of Cripples, considered "The Care and Education of the Handicapped Child". This meeting considered the problems affecting mentally retarded, orthopedically handicapped, blind, deaf, and other handicapped children. Particular attention was given to the problems of South East Asia and to the importance of prevention and early detection and treatment of the mentally and physically handicapped child. This Conference in 1952 extended the work undertaken by the United Nations Conference of Experts on Physically Handicapped Children for Countries in South East Asia held in Jamshedpur, India in December, 1950.

At the World Child Welfare Congress held in Zagreb, Yugoslavia in September, 1954, under the auspices of the International Union for Child Welfare, considerable attention was given to the needs of disabled children, the mentally deficient and the socially maladjusted child. The Findings and Resolutions of this Congress contain specific and definite action that each nation and community of the world is urged to take concerning these groups of exceptional children. This conference was attended by more than four hundred persons and from thirty-two countries.

Group training courses are an effective method to keep professional personnel informed of developments. One of the first such courses sponsored by the United Nations was held in London in 1951 and considered the subject "Treatment and Aftercare of Physically Handicapped Children". This course was attended by 49 persons from seven countries (Austria, Finland, France, Germany, Greece, Italy and Yugoslavia). Teams of persons attended from each of these countries including educators, doctors, therapists and social workers. This course was jointly sponsored by the United Nations, World Health Organization, and UNICEF.

An International Conference of Educators of Blind Youth was held in Bussum, Holland in the Summer of 1952. The Conference gave consideration to the education and social needs of the pre-school blind child, the needs of the average blind child, and other related problems. Resolutions adopted by the Conference set forth specific recommendations concerning various aspects of special education for the blind. It was decided that the conference be continued as a permanent organization under the name of the International Conference of Educators of Blind Youth, and an Executive Committee consisting of representatives of eleven countries was established.

THE CHALLENGE TO SPECIAL EDUCATION

Each professional group devoted to serving the handicapped has an obligation not only to improve its own knowledge and techniques, but also to contribute to wider efforts being made to increase and improve services for the handicapped in all parts of the world. Education is an integral part of the total international effort which is being made, and special educators have a responsibility not only to aid the development of educational programs in their local communities but also on the national and international levels.

In many communities of the world which are now designated as 'underdeveloped', services for the handicapped begin with special activities in the schools for pupils with mental and physical limitations. In many countries where services for the handicapped have not existed in the past, the first symptoms of an awakening interest in social and education problems is the appearance of special education programs. The best results will be secured from these new efforts only when maximum use is made of the experience of other parts of the world where such activities are more fully developed. In order to do this, professional people must develop and support international organizations which facilitate the exchange of information and experiences.

All truly professional people are now recognizing more clearly than ever before that their responsibilities are not met by programs and organizations that are limited in scope to a single community or nation. Indeed, it has been suggested that international understanding will come about more rapidly through the development of world-wide groups of particular professional persons than through governmental programs. Such international organizations make it possible to serve others in a wide area and also to benefit from the experience of others.

Although special educators have made valuable contributions to international efforts in the past, no real or concerted effort has been made by the workers in the field of special education to develop a truly international organization. The sum total of international effort in this field has been quite limited in comparison to the magnitude of the problem. It is to be hoped that more effective ways can be developed so that those in the field of special education in all parts of the world can share their knowledge and benefit from the experience of others.

In developing special education programs, some thought can well be given to the question as to whether it is primarily a problem confronting one school, one community, one province or a single nation. When one is faced with many immediate and difficult problems in the home community, it is difficult to consider at the same time the problems of a distant community. It frequently happens, however, that the solution to local problems can be most readily found by looking to the experience of other places. For several centuries the United States benefited by the experience of other places, particularly European countries, and the feeling of superiority which many persons in the United States now possess does not prevent the honest seeker of improvement to "go abroad" for new and different ideas in the same manner as followed by their forefathers.

Each profession devoted to serving the disabled is called upon to make its contribution, not only to the improvement of its own knowledge and techniques, but also to the general organization of effort to increase the services which are available to the handicapped in every part of the world. Special education, as a profession performing a fundamental role in the rehabilitation of the disabled, has an important responsibility in the development of international programs. The very nature of special education requires that differences between people be recognized. For this reason, special education has an important contribution to make internationally, for one of our most difficult international problems is to recognize and apply this philosophy of differences among people.

BIBLIOGRAPHY

Cruickshank, William M., "The President's Message. Exceptional Children - A World-Wide Responsibility", *Exceptional Children,* Vol. 19, No. 4 (Jan., 1953), pp. 129-130.
The Education of Orthopaedically Handicapped Children. Report of the International Conference of Experts organized by the International Union for Child Welfare, with the help and under the auspices of UNESCO; 21-25 February 1950, Geneva.
International Society for the Welfare of Cripples, *The Disabled in the Modern World.* Available from the ISWC, 701 First Avenue, New York 17, N.Y.
International Socitey for the Welfare of Cripples, *Changing Attitudes Towards The Disabled.* Available from the ISWC, 701 First Avenue, New York 17, N.Y.
International Union for Child Welfare, "*Reports of Sections Findings and Resolutions*". World Child Welfare Congress, Zagreb (Yugoslavia) 30 August to 4 September, 1954.
United Nations Conference of Experts on Physically Handicapped Children for Countries of South East Asia. Available from Int'l. Documents Service, Columbia Univ. Press, 2960 Broadway, New York 27, N.Y.
United Nations, *Modern Methods of Rehabilitation of the Adult Disabled.* Available from Int'l. Documents Service, Columbia Univ. Press, 2960 Broadway, New York 27, N.Y.
United Nations, *Rehabilitation of the Handicapped.* Social Welfare Information Series, Special Issue. United Nations, September 1953.
United Nations, *Services for the Physically Handicapped.* Dept. of Social Affairs, United Nations, 1954.
World Health Organization, *Joint Expert Committee on the Physically Handicapped Child.* First Report. WHO Technical Report Series No. 58. Available from Int'l. Documents Service, Columbia Univ. Press, 2960 Broadway, New York 27, N. Y.
World Health Organization, *The Mentally Subnormal Child.* Report of a Joint Expert Committee convened by WHO with the participation of United Nations, ILO, and UNESCO. WHO Technical Report Series No. 75. Geneva, April 1954.

SECTION II

INTRODUCTION

SOME PROBLEMS COMMON TO ALL AREAS OF SPECIAL EDUCATION

SOME PROBLEMS COMMON TO ALL AREAS
OF SPECIAL EDUCATION

Special education presents a wide variety of medical, social, vocational, educational, and administrative problems for treatment. Specific answers to the technical problems of the various areas must be left to the authors of chapters and articles dealing with the special area under discussion.[1] There are, however, some common problems which are to be found in all areas of special education.[2-5] In dealing with these, we find ourselves in less carefully charted areas in which much is challenging and controversial; in fact, for some areas the general problems are being faced by the educator of the exceptional for the first time. There is always a certain amount of satisfaction in exploration. In the field of special education it is gratifying indeed to feel that a sincere effort to explore the many problems that face the educator is an effort to provide a more effective program for the exceptional child.

It is hardly possible to treat the many general and specific problems of the area of special education without relating them to methods and techniques of teaching and servicing each area. An adequate treatment, however, of teaching methods and techniques would require a volume for each area, and in spite of the urgent need of more definitive works of this nature, it did not seem feasible to the editors to include, to any considerable extent, materials dealing with teaching methods and techniques. The excellent presentation by Baker[6] and others[7-9] of the nature of exceptional children, the objectives of education for exceptional children, and the importance of special education in the total educational picture of our democracy will give the student sufficient material to evaluate the current thinking of our profession on the subject of special education. We must turn our attention to the practical problems facing the administrator, teacher, parent, and other personnel interested in this subject.

Earlier we discussed the general problems of adequate census and case discovery. These are two common problems to be found in every area of special education.

Granting that reasonably accurate or practical methods of census and classification are in operation, then the question of servicing becomes not only immediate but imperative.

Such servicing will have complete success only under conditions that assure full coordination or the child's program as affected by his home, community, church, school, physicians, and all other individuals concerned with his case.

While accepting always the doctrine of control by the best agencies available, it should also be an accepted concept that whenever possible the school ought to be that agency.[10] Far too frequently it is not. There are, of course, duties which no parent nor home should delegate to others. It must be recognized, however, that most parents have had little professional experience to draw upon for techniques in dealing with the specific problems of the exceptional, and that in the past there have been available few private advisors with the essential training and experience the community is likely to provide through its schools.

A vital function of the parents is, therefore, one of cooperation in an endeavor to make the teaching processes fully effective. Compared with the school, the rest of the community, including the medical profession, has little contact with the child. The school, accordingly, should be readily recognized as the best coordinating agency, and the entire program for the exceptional should be planned around it.

Many of the problems that arise among the exceptional, in both sparsely and in thickly populated areas, are no different, except in degree, from those to be met among normal children. Yet such problems are often overemphasized by those who deal with these deviates. In any rural locality or in the outlying districts of a city, medical service, particularly of a highly specialized type, may not be easily available. Likewise, the school, even though convenient in situation, may have but meager remedial facilities. In the case of a consolidated rural type of school, transportation problems may be involved. Here the chief difference in dealing with non-handicapped and exceptional children, at least in the physical types, is that the latter may be somewhat frail, and therefore travel back and forth to school, clinic, and elsewhere more difficult.

Problems concerned with meager local provision of any sort are logically of interest to city, state, and Federal bureaus or agencies. They are of interest also to those voluntary agencies that may employ propaganda to ensure greater flow of public funds, or to provide the needed service through private funds on a demonstration or permanent basis. Either of these tasks is going to be increasingly difficult unless taxation of the donors and diversion of public funds for other and possibly less meritorious purposes can be definitely reassigned.

We now turn our attention to the most important problems facing the field of Special Education in our era.

FOOTNOTES

1. See *Special Education for the Exceptional*, Vol. II, edited by Merle E. Frampton and Elena D. Gall, published by Porter Sargent, 11 Beacon St., Boston, 1955.
2. Baker, M.F., *Introduction to Exceptional Children*, revised edition (Macmillan: N.Y.C., 1953), pp. 455-468.

3. Henny, N., Ed., *The Education of Exceptional Children*, 49th Year Book, National Society for the Study of Education (University of Chicago Press: Chicago, 1950), Section I, Chapters I-VIII.
4. Heck, Arch O., *Introduction to Exceptional Children* (McGraw-Hill: N.Y.C., 1953).
5. *The Education of the Handicapped and Griften Pupils in the Secondary Schools*, National Association of Secondary School Principals Bulletin, Jan., 1955, vol. 39, no. 207.
6. Baker, *op. cit.*, pp. 455-458.
7. Henry, *op. cit.*, Section I, Chapters I-VIII.
8. Educational Policies Commission, *Policies for Education in American Democracy* (National Education Association: Washington, D.C., 1946).
9. Olsen, Willard C., and Hughes, Byron O., *The Education of Exceptional Children*, National Society for the Study of Education (University of Chicago Press: Chicago, 1950).
10. New York State Education Department, *Removing Blocks to Mental Health in School* (Mental Health Committee: Albany, 1954), Introduction.

SECTION II

CHAPTER I

MEDICAL SERVICES

MEDICAL SERVICES

SCHOOL HEALTH SERVICES BY GEORGE SINGER

MEDICAL SERVICES

A problem common to all areas of special education is the provision of adequate medical services. In accordance with the statutes of most states, most school systems have some provision for health surveys, varying from an annual examination of vision and hearing to more complete health clinical services.[1] Such a program is usually provided through the school health services.[2-4] In rural situations, several special variations of this service exist. Interest in such programs for this text is due to the fact that they offer a basic health service to all the children. Likewise, every classroom teacher in the public schools is expected to give certain instruction in personal and community hygiene. This, plus various services involving school housekeeping and sanitary inspections, constitute such a health program as may usually be expected from the regular school services.[5,6]

Advantage cannot be taken of the regular instructor in physical education, since the exceptional have very definite special needs and problems that require the supervision and services of a specially trained personnel; for example, there is need for physiotherapists, recreational leaders, and special programs for the severely disabled.

Since school health service at best is largely preventive and protective rather than diagnostic and remedial, contacts with various treatment centers are necessary for professional care where no family physician is available. Basically, the same mechanism which secures such service for the non-handicapped child should be used or paralleled for the exceptional child.[7]

Special medical service for the exceptional is secured in several ways: (1) The responsibility is placed upon the parent. This is usually unsuccessful, frequently because of the high cost of medical service for the severely handicapped. (2) Use is made of existing clinics of various types in the community. These are often overcrowded, wasting a great amount of the time and energy of the pupil and of those who accompany him. (3) Use is made of special consultants and clinics within the school buildings. This plan, it is generally agreed, is most successful in conserving a maximum of time for the child's education and necessitating a minimum of time in getting to and waiting for medical service. (4) Medical diagnosis and treatment are sought in rehabilitation centers, sheltered workshops, hospitals, sanitaria, and institutions for the mentally ill.

There is no reason for the opposition to such services which exists on the part of certain medical groups, provided there is no interference with relationships existing between the private practitioner and his patients.[8] In most instances, a clear understanding with the local medical society will secure not only valuable advice in setting up such medical services but also splendid cooperation in operating them.[9,10]

In most communities, public clinics are not geared to take expeditious care of school-age exceptional children. And even if such service were expeditious, the school usually does not have the personnel to supervise the children properly at the clinic.

In many instances, as in the case of the severely handicapped, there may be definite inability to pay for the highly specialized and expensive medical and allied services over the long period of time usually required for the needs of these severely handicapped. Few private physicians can afford the type of special equipment needed in many of these cases, and few patients can afford to pay the fees necessary for the special services. Nevertheless, unless these services are provided, and are continually available, certain types of exceptional children are distinct and definite sufferers, and eventually the public itself is handicapped by their physical limitation.[11,12]

Two types of specialized services are needed for the severely disabled requiring continuing treatment: (1) periodic checkups both of special defects and of general health; (2) emergency service.

Few physicians realize to what extent the education of the exceptional, including the mentally and socially handicapped, is medically controlled. In work with the exceptional, not only is the bond between the physician and the educator closer, but also the understanding and cooperation are much better than they once were,[13] although still meriting closer cooperation and understanding. Proof lies in the fact that the exceptional child who has undergone a combined medical and educational program emerges into the world of economic and social activity surprisingly able to compete with so-called normals, both in health and training.

Actually, the medical service in schools is often much better for the exceptional, in terms of planning, personnel, and accomplishments, than it is for the non-handicapped. Frequently the highest-grade specialists serve as consultants at minimum fees or even as dollar-a-year clinicians. Here the 'team' approach is most important and should work.

In general, the teacher appreciates the value of this service to her pupils and cheerfully shares the child's time with the physician, even though she often wishes she knew more about the physician's recommendations and point of view and that clinic appointments interfered less with her classroom program. These opposing claims on the pupil's time form one of the commonest conflicts between the classroom and the health office. Ordinarily, the relationship between the physician and the educator is a happy and cooperative one; and it is now recognized by the medical profession that the educational program is actually therapeutic in nature, especially in those phases dealing with mental hygiene, and that it therefore adds greatly to the success of purely medical measures.

There are certain common problems of a medical nature that exist all through the work with the exceptional. Some are being well handled with considerable understanding, and others poorly treated.

The first of these problems is the extent to which specialized medical service should be furnished to the child at his school. No one denies that specialized medical service is necessary, often for the entire period of the child's life. Not only the high original cost of this service but the long period over which it must continue places it beyond the current budgets of schools and the purses of families with even liberal incomes. For this reason, such care is recognized as a community responsibility, without relationship to or establishment of any precedent in regard to so-called state or socialized medicine.

Without doubt the most convenient place to serve the child is at the school. He is there most of the week. He can be reached there easily at nearly any working hour of the day. Transportation difficulties and attendant service are simplified. These services are provided, often in most ambitious fashion, at schools in most communities which have programs for the exceptional.

Where nothing but educational service is provided, the program is wholly inadequate, and many inconveniences and complications result. However, it is recognized, first, that the wishes of the local medical profession and con-sultive medical services probably will be paramount; and second, that under no circumstance should the professional relationship between the private practitioner and his patient be disturbed.

A second problem is the cost to the city, state, and community of such medical service. Aid is obtained through the provisions in the various Federal, state, and municipal legislative provisions, and from private organizations. Intelligent conservation of the time of highly trained and expensive personnel reduces costs without sacrificing service.

A third problem, allied to the first two, is the struggle for the child's time between the classroom and special medical or other necessary services. The obvious answer is that the medical services must come first, the classroom teacher second, and other services, even if time is wasted, thereafter.[14,15]

A fourth problem is the failure of many persons to recognize that education is actually a form of medical therapy. Often this serves as mental hygiene. Sometimes simple natural activities, such as the use of table cutlery or of musical instruments serves as an ingenious form of physical and mental therapy. The neuromuscular tension characteristic of the exceptional is largely overcome by properly and hygienically planned educational programs, though these may be augmented by the more formal and pressure types. Since the prevocational and rehabilitation programs lead to the hope of economic security, they are in themselves forms of mental hygiene, vocational guidance, and socialization.

A fifth problem is the ever present danger that both physicians and teachers will consider the children as specimens in the medical museum rather than as children under protective care, with personality and other special problems that require solution. Protecting the child's personality is an extremely important factor in any program, even though the exceptional child must have some understanding of his own problems in order to cooperate and to face life realistically.[16]

A sixth problem involves a subtlety of judgment between protecting an exceptional child against injury or delayed medical improvement on the one hand, and overprotecting him on the other, with a resulting development of laziness, lack of self-reliance, and even neuroses. The exceptional child will eventually have to face the competition of the non-handicappd and must learn to live in the society of his time.

A seventh medical problem is that of control of fatigue. It is educational folly to believe that an exceptional child can, in a school day of fewer hours than that of a non-handicapped and with interruptions in certain types of cases for medical and allied service, cover the same ground as the so-called normal of similar mental capacity. Yet this is often attempted, without considering the fact that each child has an individual factor of safety and that the first objective in the education of the exceptional is that he have as good health as possible, both at the present time and, if possible, in the future.

An eighth problem involves the cooperation of the family and the home in medical as well as in educational programs. The answer lies, of course, in parental education[17-20] properly directed, plus definite professional follow-up into the home.

A ninth problem comes from one-track thinking on the question of whether special programs and classes are needed and determining which children should or should not receive them. Such matters cannot be settled on medical bases alone, since they also involve practical problems of educational administration. Accordingly, a pronouncement in regard to certain types of children may be sound enough medically, but not produce the expected and desired result in terms of protective care or health when applied practically. It is by no means certain that the existing programs for children with special health problems should be abandoned, even though it might seem medically sound to do so. There is no dispute as to the services needed. Only the mechanism of providing them is under discussion. Time and experience will bring a solution that is satisfactory, since it is well recognized by those who actually deal with the exceptional that the best practices result from the conference table at which all interests and points of view are represented.

A further problem is the provision of adequate occupational and physical therapy services.[21-24] The American Medical Association notes that the following types of technicians are most commonly required by hospitals and the medical profession: clinical laboratory technicians, X-ray technicians, physical-therapy technicians, and occupational therapists. The last two are of special interest to the educator of the exceptional.[25,26]

Physical-therapy technicians are employed not only in hospitals, but in institutions and schools which deal with the exceptional, where they render a most important service. It is generally felt that the preliminary training of these technicians should follow the standards set by the American Physical Therapy Association and the American Occupational Therapy Association.[27-31] Physical-education teachers are trained in some of the measures used in physical therapy, as also are nurses. Since the services of the physical-therapy technician are of a highly specialized nature and are carried out under the direct supervision of a physician, teacher-training institutions for the exceptional have not seen fit to affiliate any of the various training schools for these specialists. It is a question whether the general educational requirement for degrees in teacher-training institutions would benefit this group particularly or improve their chances of securing positions or subsequently of rendering more valuable service.

On the other hand, occupational therapy is distinctly more educational in nature and involves definite educational techniques. This may eventually be accepted as part of the training program of departments of education of the exceptional in teacher-training institutions.

FOOTNOTES

1. See Kilander, H.F., *Health Services in City Schools,* Bul. 1952, no. 20 (Federal Security Agency, Office of Education: Washingon, D.C., 1952). Presents a brief but excellent history of school health programs and other pertinent data on administration and financing. Ninety-one per cent of all school systems with populations of 2500 and above report health services.
2. *Child Health Is Everybody's Business* (New York State Department of Health, Office of Public Health Education: Albany, 1952). A joint publication of the N. Y. State Study Committee of American Academy of Pediatrics, Medical Society of the State of N.Y., and Bureau of Maternal and Child Health.
3. Great Britain, Ministry of Education, *The Health of the School Child,* Report of the Chief Medical Office, Ministry of Education, for years 1950-51 (London 1952).
4. *Distribution of Health Services in the Structure of State Government* 1950, Public Health Service Publications no. 154, part 3 (U.S. Public Health Service: Washington, D.C., 1953).
5. Smiley, Dean F., and Hein, Fred V., *Health Appraisal of School Children,* A report of the Joint Committee on Health Problems in Education of the N.E.A. and the A.M.A.
6. See excellent school health material from Board of Education, New York City, Bureau of Health Education, of which Dr. I. H. Goldberger is director, especially *The Activities of the School Health Education Program in the Public Schools of the City of New York,* Joint Policy on Procedures for Health Services in the Secondary Schools, Revised Edition, 1954.
7. Ridenour, Nina, *Health Supervision of Young Children,* Committee on Child Health (American Public Health Association: 1790 Broadway, N.Y.C.).
8. Culbert, R.W., Jacobziner, H., and Ollstein, P., "Training Programs in School Health Services", *American Journal of Public Health,* Feb., 1954. 44:2:228-234.
9. *Today's Health* (American Medical Association: Chicago, Ill., Nov., 1954).
10. *Educating for Healthful Living* (Association for Childhood Education International: Washington, D.C., 1950).
11. N.Y.C. Welfare and Health Council, *Score Card for Welfare and Health Service,* May, 1954.
12. *Helping the Physically Limited Child,* Curriculum Bulletin Series No. 7 (N.Y.C. Board of Education: N.Y.C., 1953), Chapters 1 and 2.
13. Rusk, H., and Taylor, E., "Team Approach in Rehabilitation and the Psychologist's Role", in Garrett, J.F., ed., *Psychological Aspects of Physical Disability* (U.S. Office of Vocational Rehabilitation, Department of Health, Education, and Welfare: Washington, D. C., 1954) Chapter 1.
14. Some educators feel that all or most of the important services should be in operation about the same time or closely correlated and carefully timed. This concept represents the ideal team approach with a scientifically designed time schedule. The concept is an ideal yet to attain. - Editors.
15. Cruickshank, William M., "Team Action with Exceptional Children", *Exceptional Children,* May, 1952. 18:8242-244.

16. *Helping the Physically Limited Child*, Chapter 2.
17. *Parent's Study Guides A Manual for Parents of Cerebral Palsied Children* (National Society for Crippled Children and Adults: Chicago, 1951).
18. *Helping Parents Understand the Exceptional Child* (Woods School: Langhorne, Pa., 1952).
19. *The School Psychologist Aids the Parents of the Crippled Child* (National Society for Crippled Children and Adults: Chicago, 1954). A joint publication of American Psych. Assn., American Speech and Hearing Assn., and National Society for Crippled Children and Adults.
20. Burgess, Caroline B., "Counseling Parents of Handicapped Children", *New Outlook for the Blind*, Jan., 1955. 49:1:1:15.
21. Stauco, Clarice, *The Atypical Child* (Catholic University of America Press: Washington, D.C., 1954), pp. 231 ff.
22. Willard, Helen S., and Spackman, Clare S., eds., *Principles of Occupational Therapy*, 2nd Edition (J.B. Lippincott: Philadelphia, 1954).
23. "Administrative Practices and Personnel Policies", *American Journal of Occupational Therapy*, May-June, 1954. 8:3:128-129. Reprint.
24. Wade, B., "Organizing an Occupational Therapy Department", *Hospitals*, Nov., 1954. 28:11:92-96, 98.
25. Abbott, Marguerite, "Professional C.P. Training for Occupational Therapists", *Cerebral Palsy Review*, Jan.-Feb., 1953. 14:142:6-8.
26. American Occupational Therapy Association, *Manual on the Organization and Administration of Occupational Therapy Departments* (McBrown: Iowa, 1951). Planographed.
27. See Occupational Therapists requirements for registration, American Occupational Therapy Association, N.Y.C. As of March 1, 1954, there were 4,073 registered Occupational Therapists. See list of schools offering courses in Occupational Therapists, Section III of this volume.
28. *The Outlook for Women as Occupational Therapists*, Medical Service Series, no. 203-2, Rev. (U.S. Woman's Bureau, Federal Security Agency: Washington, D.C.).
29. *The Job of the Physical Therapist* (American Physical Therapy Association: Broadway, N.Y.C., 1954).
30. *Physical Therapy—A Service and a Career* (American Physical Therapy Association: N.Y.C., 1953).
31. For registration requirements for Physical Therapists, see *State Registration for Physical Therapists* (American Physical Therapy Association: N.Y.C.). See list of schools offering courses in Physical Therapy approved by the Council on Medical Education and Hospitals of the A.M.A. Section III of this volume. The American Physical Therapy Association estimated 6,000 graduates of approved schools in 1955.

SCHOOL HEALTH SERVICES

GEORGE SINGER

Handicapped students, except for their defects, are normal human beings who are subject to all types of illnesses and respond to therapy in the same manner as other individuals. The majority are interested in being taught how to help themselves and to be of value to the community in which they live, regardless of their inability to see, hear, talk or walk properly. The health of these students must be constantly observed and protected in order to permit an uninterrupted course of study. Keeping them in a satisfactory physical condition presents an important problem to all medical and nursing staffs affiliated with these special schools of learning. The cooperation of the teachers, house supervisors and social service workers is essential.

People of all ages with disabilities present problems that are definitely characteristic of individuals who know that their sensory or motor organs are damaged and react in proportion to the degree of impairment. Although these students wish to be treated as normal people and resent any reference to their handicap, they are, nevertheless, subconsciously cognizant of their impaired status and reveal great concern about any additional attack upon their physical condition. This emotional behavior is the same regardless of whether the handicap occurred congenitally or was acquired later in life. Therefore, in addition to medication and kind words when sick, all ailments should be minimized regardless of their gravity and reassurance given of a speedy recovery. Illness will produce interruptions in their studies which in turn create problems for the teachers. Any absence from their classrooms frequently requires personal assistance to bring them up to date, whereas non-handicapped students can help themselves.

Competent nursing care is of the utmost importance and should be available day and night whenever students are in the school, dormitories or on the campus. A nurse should be kind, tolerant, qualified in first aid to handle all kinds of emergencies, and must gain the confidence of the students so that they will never hesitate to consult her about their health. She assists the medical staff with the examinations and treatments of the students and executes their orders for any follow-up care. A nurse's clinic should be arranged at a certain hour daily to permit students to go to the infirmary for any prescribed medication, various minor complaints, change of small dressings, et cetera. The nurse is required to keep a folder with a complete health record of each student in the infirmary as well as a daily register listing the names of the students seen, their disability, treatment, time of visit and disposition of each case. A nurse's report must be sent to the principal's office every day, and a summary at the end of each month.

A medical staff consists of a school doctor, dentist, and consultants representing each specialty. The school doctor should have at least one clinic session each week at the infirmary, and he or his assistant must be available at all times when called. A dental clinic should be arranged twice a month or more often, depending on the number of students for an annual examination and required treatment. Certain specialists, such as an ophthalmologist in a school for the blind or an otologist in a school for the deaf, may also have weekly sessions throughout the school year. All other consultants whose services are not frequently required at the school could be available to the students at their offices if and when needed.

Arrangments with a nearby hospital are necessary to care for those students who cannot be treated in the infirmary or transferred to their homes. Friendly and co-operative relations with the hospital authorities will prove very helpful to the medical staff at the school when the need for hospitalization arises.

Everyone at the school should be acquainted with the location of the infirmary because it is the center for all the health services and its very presence produces peace of mind. The students come here for their annual physical examination, specialized care, illness, emergencies, trauma and minor disorders. Considerable thought and care must be used in planning an infirmary that will offer the proper facilities for the type of handicapped students to be treated.

For the most satisfactory results, an infirmary should be divided into male and female sections with separate lavatories and washrooms. It should have a waiting room, treatment room and an office which could also double as an examining room. A three or four bed room and one or more single bed isolation rooms in each section are necessary. The infirmary must be light, well ventilated, painted in a pleasant color, kept absolutely clean, easily accessible and located in the ground floor level. All the rooms should be equipped with proper artificial lighting and various means of diversion, such as radio, books, toys and games.

The treatment room should have a basin with hot and cold water, a refrigerator for vaccines and other medications requiring low temperatures, a small sterilizer, scale, cabinets for supplies, sterile gauze, bandages, instruments, drugs and all other necessities required by a school doctor. The addition of an examining table in the office permits the school doctor to perform all routine examinations in this room. However, the dentist, ophthalmologist, and various other consultants require special equipment to properly examine and treat the students. Such facilities must be made available in the infirmary unless the students can be taken to the offices of these specialists without any difficulty.

A family doctor will frequently forward a letter recommending that a particular medication be continued daily in certain chronic conditions. Such advice should be followed as directed and complete assurance given to the physician of the fullest cooperation on the part of the school's medical staff. The school doctor is responsible for the health of the students and should prescribe all treatment when necessary until the sick individual can consult his private physician. If it is impossible to return to his own doctor because of a great distance between school and home, gravity of the ailment, emergency surgery or any other reason, then the school medical staff treats the patient until he recovers. Parents must be notified at once when an injury or ailment occurs regardless of the severity of the condition. Their written consent for any medical procedure should always be obtained unless it is an emergency. Such cooperation among the school, parents and family physician is in the best interest of the student and will often help to prevent any discord or lawsuits.

A complete history is necessary for each student and must include all details about his health up to the time of admission. All diseases, their dates of occurrence and recurrence, should be listed. Childhood diseases such as measles, german measles, chicken-pox, mumps, whooping cough and scarlet fever can be recorded but any complications must be fully described. Rheumatic fever, acute anterior poliomyelitis and other ailments that are inclined to produce permanent damage in various organs of the body should be completely detailed. Any injury, operation or period of hospitalization must also be included and it may occasionally be necessary to request a transcript of a hospital or a doctor's record in order to thoroughly evaluate the student's physical status. It is important to know when the student was vaccinated against small pox and injected against tetanus, diphtheria, pertussis, poliomyelitis and other contagious diseases. He should be immunized without delay if any injections have not been given.

Every student, on admission, is kept in an isolation room for twenty-four hours during which time a nose and throat culture should be examined for the presence of diphtheria bacilli. He is checked by the nurse for evidence of pediculosis, skin rash, rhinitis or other manifestations of a possible contagious condition and permitted to associate with the other students if found to be negative.

A complete medical examination of every student on admission and once a year thereafter is absolutely essential. The height and weight are checked for normal growth and obesity. The heart may have rheumatic involvement and the lungs show signs of a tubercular lesion. Blood pressure readings are taken to rule out a hypertensive condition. The mucous membranes may indicate an anemia. The spine and posture may require correction for abnormal curvatures. The feet may reveal fallen arches, corns, callouses or a fungus infection. The skin and scalp should be checked for a dermatitis. Abnormal lymph glands can be palpated in the cervical, axillary and inguinal regions. The nose may have a deviated septum or large turbinates which can predispose to sinusitis. The ears should be examined with an otoscope for a discharge or perforated drum, and the throat inspected for enlarged or diseased tonsils. The presence of an umbilical or inguinal hernia and the need for a circumcision should be detected and recorded. Any abnormal nervous manifestations must become part of the record. The functioning of the upper and lower limbs should be tested. A thorough eye examination should be done by an ophthalmologist, and the teeth carefully checked by a dentist.

The examination on admission should include a urine analysis, blood typing and Wassermann, Rh factor determination and tuberculin or skin patch test for the presence of tuberculosis. An annual X-Ray of the lungs of each student must be done, and it is also advisable to have chest plates taken of the entire school personnel. The local health department will usually assist the school in obtaining the necessary laboratory and X-Ray examinations.

Abnormal findings and the doctor's recommendations are recorded on the student's health form, and the parents should be notified of his advice. If they are financially unable to obtain the necessary treatment, the school doctor may procure these services from the consulting staff or a hospital if so requested. The physician's examination must guide the teaching staff and coaches of the various athletic teams as to the physical ability of those students with cardiac involvement, abnormal blood pressure, anemias, et cetera. His judgment must be final in deciding what a student may be permitted to do in competitive sports and the gymnasium.

Being on the alert to prevent or control any outbreak of disease is very important, and the medical staff cannot be too cautious. A student who is ill should be sent to the infirmary immediately by the house supervisor or teacher. He should be kept isolated if the disease is of a communicable nature until he recovers or can be sent home, and must not return to the school unless examined by the doctor and found free of contagion. All contacts of the sick student are closely observed and referred to the nurse when any signs or symptoms appear. Injecting everyone at the school against influenza must be considered at the time of a local epidemic, and immune globulin should be given to all contacts of a measles case. A laboratory report of a smear from any genital discharge must be obtained without delay, and all students using the same lavatory and washroom should also be examined.

The school health services should not only be available at all times but the students should be encouraged to avail themselves of it. Constant vigilance is necessary to maintain the good health of the student body and requires complete cooperation among the school personnel, nurses and doctors. Special education for the exceptional can only be realized when their health is satisfactory and they are able to devote themselves to their studies.

SECTION II

CHAPTER II

MENTAL HEALTH AND GUIDANCE

MENTAL HEALTH AND THE HANDICAPPED

WARREN T. VAUGHAN, JR.

The mental health movement began in 1909 following the publication of Clifford Beers' classic book, *A Mind That Found Itself*. It has moved from the initial focus on treatment and care of mentally ill patients, through efforts at preventing major breakdowns, to the present day positive approach of promoting the mental health of all persons. This evolution in the mental health field parallels an evolution in public health in general. The public health aim has been restated in recent years with a positive definition of health. "Health is more than simply the absence of disease . . ." according to the World Health Organization definition.

The field of mental health cannot point to the eradication of any disorders, although there has been a striking decrease in the incidence of general paresis (syphilis of the brain) and of the psychosis associated with the deficiency disease, pellagra. Why, then, has mental health turned to a positive concept and why are we now concentrating on the promotion of mental health in the general population? The reason is simple, namely, that psychiatric disorders seem indeed most closely related generically to that large group of chronic states of ill health with which public health in general is concerned today when it speaks of "more than simply the absence of disease." These states of ill health seem largely associated with the stresses of modern life, especially stresses in human relations. Given our present limited knowledge concerning psychiatric disorders, we must conclude that the most effective means available for prevention of psychiatric disorders within a population is to promote the positive mental health of the entire population.

How can we promote the mental health of a population? Do we have any principles or guides to lead us? What scientific evidence do we have to support our theories concerning mental health? First, we must state that there are excellent theories to guide us, theories which have behind them a substantial body of scientifically sound facts. Mental health theories are primarily concerned with (1) the fields of emotional growth and development and (2) interpersonal relations. We have knowledge of growth and development which gives us important information concerning the emotional and physical needs of children at different ages. We learn from the field of interpersonal relations how these emotional needs may or may not be met during various critical stages of growth and development.

It is obviously impossible in this chapter to discuss in detail the specific mental health problems posed by various types of handicaps. We can immediately see, however, that the nature of the emotional impact of any handicap upon an individual will depend upon the following factors: (1) the nature of the handicaps and its influence on physical growth and development; (2) the meaning which the handicap itself and its resultant limitation of function may have to the individual; (3) the stage of emotional growth and development at which the handicap occurs, or, in older persons, the personality structure of the victim; (4) the nature of the human relations surrounding the victim, and the influence of the handicap itself on the human environment.

The emotionally relevant human environment of the handicapped person, — his family, relatives, social acquaintances, job or schoolmates, — reacts to the handicap in various ways. Some of these may be helpful, some harmful. The environment of the handicapped individual may materially change as a result of the handicap. Special environmental settings often accompany attempts to relieve the handicap, to rehabilitate and re-educate. Reactions of the human environment may lead to interpersonal relations between the handicapped individual and the key people in his life which may or may not meet the immediate and long-term emotional needs which the handicapped person may have in order to promote his mental health.

The National Association for Mental Health, in its pamphlet *Mental Health is* 1, 2, 3, characterizes mentally healthy people as follows:

1. *They feel comfortable about themselves.*
   They are not bowled over by their own emotions—by their fears, anger, love, jealousy, guilt or worries.
   They can take life's disappointments in their stride.
   They have a tolerant, easy-going attitude towards themselves as well as others; they can laugh at themselves.
   They neither under-estimate nor over-estimate their ability.
   They can accept heir own shortcomings.
   They have self-respect.
   They feel able to deal with most situations that come their way.
   They get satisfaction from the simple, every-day pleasures.
2. *They feel right about other people.*
   They are able to give love and to consider the interests of others.
   They have personal relationships that are satisfying and lasting.
   They expect to like and trust others, and take it for granted that others will like and trust them.
   They respect the many differences they find in people.
   They do not push people around, nor do they allow themselves to be pushed around.
   They can feel they are part of a group.
   They feel a sense of responsibility to their neighbors and fellow men.
3. *They are able to meet the demands of life.*
   They do something about their problems as they arise.
   They accept their responsibilities.
   They shape their environment whenever possible; they adjust to it whenever necessary.
   They plan ahead but do not fear the future.

They welcome new experiences and new ideas.
They make use of their natural capacities.
They set realistic goals for themselves.
They are able to think for themselves and make their own decisions.
They put their best effort into what they do, and get satisfaction out of doing it.[1]

Each one of these statements represents important ideals as goals for parents and professional persons to bear in mind when working with handicapped individuals in various settings.

In order to relate emotional needs to interpersonal relations during various stages of growth and development, we shall arbitrarily divide growing-up into five stages, infancy, early childhood, preschool years, grade school years, adolescence. Obviously, the characteristics of any child during a certain stage depends upon his life experiences during the preceding stages. In almost every child one can find conflicts from earlier stages manifesting themselves in various complex fashions. There are both healthy (successful) and unhealthy (unsuccessful) modes of resolution of childhood emotional conflicts. Growing up is usually not a smooth process; it takes place with 'fits and starts.' In all children there are spurts ahead and regressions. There are frustrations for parents and children alike, handled for the most part successfully by virtue of the love, support and understanding which members of families usually have for each other. Family solidarity, exemplified by the attitude, 'we stick together,' enables most frustrations to become positive learning experiences. The models which children have to guide them are, of course, the parents themselves.

Mature parents who have 'emotional reserve' and who are capable of giving with love and understanding to their children represent the best assurance the child may have that he will enjoy good mental health. Children who lack a home life conducive to good mental health are in dire need of help from outside the home. Children with handicaps carry an added burden, as well as place an added stress on the family. All professional people working with handicapped children must strive to understand the place of the child with his handicap in the family setting, and his relationship to the parents themselves need a tremendous amount of help and understanding to enable them to cope successfully with the terrible problem before them.

INFANCY (Birth to c. 1½ years)

The infant is an oral creature, first knows the world through contact with its mouth and in relation to the feeding process. Frustration and discomfort are relieved through feeding and the very important interpersonal processes surrounding feeding, such as being held close, being rocked, being snug and warm. Basic needs, the needs to be cared for, sheltered, fed and loved are met in these crucial early years. Indeed, basic attitudes are set in children during their infancy, attitudes towards the world being a friendly, loving accepting place or being a frustrating, hostile and potentially harmful place. The foundation for good mental health in later years, the ability to master crises and handicaps, the capacity to feel right about oneself, about others and to meet the demands of life are laid in the earliest years.

Interpersonal Relations. The important human relationship of infancy is, of course, the mother-child relationship. The infant is in a completely dependent relationship to mother. He cannot be left. He cries to attract his mother. He responds to warmth and bodily contact with her. In some cultures infants stay close to mother all day, as with the Indian papoose. In the first month the infant gradually becomes able to distinguish between himself and the outside world. He is first able to recognize mother, begins to laugh and smile in relation to mother's mood and facial expression. This is related to the stage of development of the infant's central nervous system as well as to characteristics of the mother-child relationship. As a child begins to recognize mother to be the special person in his life, he goes through another phase towards the end of the first year of not understanding that mother will be returning when she is out of his sight. He begins to cry when left. The intuitive, sensitive mother will talk to the baby when she is out of his sight, or sing songs. The baby only gradually develops a time sense and a concept of the future. It takes some time for the infant to know that mother will return and that he will be fed and cared for soon. The first game to be played with infants is peek-a-boo, which helps the infant solve this basic problem of loss. There is tension release with a hearty laugh when the missing face returns.

Infants who are deprived of loving mothers or mother substitutes or who have a serious disturbance in the mother-child relationships are found to be profoundly damaged, often both psychologically and physiologically. Maternal care is most important for good mental health.[2]

Implications for the Handicapped. Some children are born with handicaps which are recognizable at birth. Other handicaps become evident only during the first years of life. Many Mongoloid children and blind children are recognized at birth, some only later. Children with brain damage due to birth trauma or other causes, children with cerebral palsy, may be recognized at birth or soon thereafter. There are a number of children born with congenital defects, gross defects such as failure to develop limbs and cleft palate, which are recognized at birth. Certain orthopedic defects, such as club foot and congenital dislocation of the hips, may be recognized only later. Many children with mental retardation are only recognized later when they fail to progress along a normal growth curve.

Many of these infants must have special treatment settings which necessitate other caretakers than the mother. Some have to be hospitalized. The institutionalization of infants is a hazardous proposition for the optimum growth and development of the infant because there is usually not a satisfactory means to meet the basic emotional needs of the infant. The classic study of Anna Freud and Dorothy Burlingham describes this process in a nursery setting and suggests ways of solving it.[3]

Most important for handicapped children is to protect and reinforce the positive healthy components in the mother-child relationship. This is accomplished through guidance and case work with the mother and father. The attitude of mother towards the handicapped child and the meaning of the defect itself to the mother are of extreme importance to the child's mental health. Of course, the attitude of other members of the family, — father, older brothers and sisters, in-laws, — is of extreme importance, for as they rally around the mother and support her emotionally, the mother may successfully sort out her feelings about the handicapped infant and develop a personal philosophy which will sustain her during the trying years which lie before her.

Early Childhood (c. 1½ years to c. 4 years)

These are fast moving years for the growing child during which he is acquiring new skills daily and learning very rapidly about the world around him. He is exploring and testing with respect to what he can do with this world. He is testing his ability to shape his environment and to control it. His first move out of the world of infancy and into that of childhood occurs when he begins to walk. And whom does he have to help him, encourage him and support him in this new world but his parents! He begins to want to feed himself and he is taught methods of feeding. He is also exposed to toilet training, and during these years he masters his basic body functions. The psychological process of identification, the drive of the child to copy adults and older children, provides a mechanism for the process of socialization.

The child learns from his parents what he should do and what he should not do. The child begins to realize that certain activities are praiseworthy and others are blameworthy. After certain actions the child receives love, affection and warmth from the parents; other actions result in scoldings, withholding of warmth and love, and punishment. The child wants his parent's love and begins to seek it out. The earliest formation of a conscience begins at this age. Most children know when they have been naughty. This stage of growth and development is no less important to personality and character formation than the period of infancy. The secure child gets great pleasure out of learning to be a successful member of his family group.

During early childhood there are many issues which are loaded with tension for parent and child. The child is testing out his wings, his power. He gives up pure pleasure-seeking with some reluctance. The child enjoys 'messing around', is naturally destructive. Play becomes the important medium through which the child expresses its feelings and discharges its tension. Blocks are piled up and knocked down. Water is splashed about. Mud, dirt and, more lately, finger paints are smeared indiscriminately on self and elsewhere. The child is learning to use language. Language is used to communicate not only ideas but also feelings. Disturbances in interpersonal relations in the home or difficulty within the child in handling aggressive impulses during these years may block language development.

Learning to get along with siblings becomes important. The little child disturbs older children. New babies may disturb the little child. Childhood illnesses at this period have their important emotional aspect, especially in relation to the severity of the illness and the manner in which it is handled by parents and others.

These are the years when the child learns what the world expects of him. These are years of overcoming frustrations, of being able to wait for the rewards which come a little later. The child comes through these years with healthy and strong supports for his future mental health, again, only with the love, help and understanding, tolerance and patience of his parents.

Interpersonal Relations. The father-child relationship now joins the mother-child relationship as a matter of some interest to the child. He begins to distinguish between the roles of mother and father. Father traditionally plays the more active role in discipline and limit setting. Fathers of today are being encouraged to participate more actively in baby care and no longer have full responsibility for setting standards and discipline. Authorities on family life feel that the flexible partnership arrangement of modern parents is more conducive to good mental health in the growing family, but agree that it demands more of the parents in the way of patience, understanding and mutual confidence.

The child can now control, to some extent, the frequency of interactions in his family setting. He moves about from room to room. He can go to mother himself; he can come into parents' bedroom in the mornings; he can leave his nap and get out of bed after being placed there at night. Accordingly, mother can no longer control the frequency and amount of interaction she has with the child. This becomes of special importance when another baby is born into the family. Mother's energy may be sorely sapped, and her patience exhausted by an active, inquisitive, demanding young child.

The behavior of the child and how to mold it is a topic of some importance between parents, between parents and grandparents (in-laws), and in the neighborhood. Considerable anxiety and guilt may build up in parents concerning their own actions, growing out of frustrating experiences with their children. Parents react to their own childhood experiences as they raise their children. Those parents who are 'enlightened' and who do not necessarily accept 'old-fashioned' ways or those stereotyped rules for child rearing, which are deeply engrained in some ethnic culture patterns, are more liable to uncertainty, anxiety and guilt with respect to how their children are being raised.

Implications for the Handicapped. Many handicapped children between the age of 1½ and 4 have only a dim awareness, if any at all, of their handicaps. This may be especially true if the handicap has been present from birth. These children are very resourceful as they begin to explore the world about them in the family and neighborhood setting and are striving to carve out a niche for themselves in the scheme of things. In no less degree than the average child, the handicapped child will test limits, test the endurance of the parents, will 'mess around', will be angry, frustrated, pleasure-bent. It seems that the parents' task is to resolve for themselves their own feelings about the handicap, to face it realistically, to aid the child in his maximum growth and development, and to encourage the development of skills and interest which may serve as compensations for the handicap. The parents of the handicapped child must, nevertheless, set limits and help the child to develop sound relationships with siblings. They must also help siblings to find satisfying relationships with the handicapped child. Some handicapped children, in particular blind children and severely mentally handicapped, brain-damaged, and Mongoloid children, may need special community settings, such as day nurseries or institutionalization. Such a move may be necessary in many instances, not only for the health of the handicapped child, but also for the benefit of the family, especially the other siblings. Parents can get the best help with these difficult decisions through the offices of the family physician or the special medical clinic. In recent years, nurseries have been developed in institutions for the mentally handicapped. Most authorities, however, do not recommend that all children be placed immediately in institutions, but feel that infancy and some part of early childhood in the family setting with the mother is to the best interest of the mental health of the handicapped child who will later be institutionalized, as well as providing a positive experience for the parents and family. Of course, all such generalizations must fall by the wayside when one is dealing with the individual problem situation which demands its own solution based upon the unique factors involved.

THE PRESCHOOL CHILD (c. 4 years to 5½ years)

This is an age of great events in the emotional growth and development of children. Early needs have been more or less met, and the child has a more or less secure, positive feeling towards the world around him. We have seen him begin to walk and mold his own environment. We have seen how society, as represented by his parents, begins to demand things of him in exchange for love and care. We have seen how it is with some difficulty that the child is able to learn to stem his pleasure seeking and learn conformity to basic standards of behavior. We have noted how the child begins to communicate his thoughts and feelings to others through the development of speech.

During the preschool years the child begins to be concerned with the basic 'mysteries of life.' He begins to ask "Why?" He begins to be more aware of the differences between his father and mother, begins to realize that there are two types of people in the world, men and women, boys and girls. These are the years when the child's unconscious mental life is consumed with the emotional problems which psychiatrists embrace under the famous term 'Oedipus complex.' This was first described by Freud half a century ago when he startled the world with his theories concerning the origins of neuroses and the unconscious psychosexual life of children. Freud's theories have been substantiated not only by further work with adults but also in direct work with young children in psychiatric clinics. Nevertheless, controversy still rages today in some circles concerning these fundamental theories.

In essence, Freud postulates that in the deep emotional life of children at this age they fall in love with the parent of the opposite sex and have, in consequence, desires to replace the parent of the same sex and to be rid of that parent. Of course we do not see the Oedipus complex displayed by the child in any pure form, for as stated above, these 'wishes' are emotional strivings deeply buried in the unconscious. This is as it should be. However, we see the results of this matter in many ways. The most striking form which demonstrates itself is seen in childhood anxieties, nightmares, the development of phobias in children. These reactions come from the fear of retaliation that the child has for his strong aggressive wishes. We find that some children are very concerned with the meaning of death, afraid themselves of dying, afraid of punishment in the hereafter, afraid of the dark and of going to bed.

The positive strivings in the Oedipus complex are manifest in another characteristic set of behaviors. Children want to be big, want to do grown-up things, want to dress in grown-up clothes. They will want to win, will begin competitive games with other children, will want to be Superman, will listen to stories of heroes doing great things and making good win over evil. Many children in their fantasy life and in their play act out scenes, over and over, day after day, which represent the power strivings of the Oedipus complex. Little girls at this age, likewise are aware of sex differences, not infrequently will wonder why they do not have the genital organ of older brother or baby brother. They may not have so much fear of being harmed as boys, but may feel that they have already been harmed, been deprived. Compensations are readily found by girls for the fact of being a girl. Some go in the direction of enhanced feminity, interest in dresses, clothes, hairdo, dancing. Others go in the direction of tomboyishness, which may in a sense represent a denial of the whole problem of being a girl. Preschool girls often begin to play 'mother', using the doll house and dolls to act out their anticipated special role, a role awaiting them when they grow up.

Good mental health suggests that when children of this age begin to ask about sex differences, about how babies are made and where they come from, simple, straightforward, truthful answers within the comprehension of the child provide the best foundation for later mature attitudes towards sex. Little girls know almost intuitively that the function of the mother is to make the baby, and that they will grow up to be mothers. Girls tend to be much more creative than boys at this age. This tendency carries over into early school years.

How is this great emotional storm resolved? It is resolved through the powerful mental mechanisms of identification and repression, with the aid of an increasingly developed sense of reality. The small boy, in essence, gradually 'wakes up to reality.' He says to himself, "I'm just a little boy; I cannot replace father; but what I can do is grow up to be like father." The child takes into himself, then, the sets of values and standards of the parents; he begins to have a conscience and to experience more grown-up feelings of personal responsibility and guilt. Of course, the parents are extremely important as models for healthy identification. Children lacking such parents are later often shown to be disturbed in community settings, — such as school systems, — and the community has to provide substitute models for identification. When a child has completed the resolution of the Oedipus complex, he is ready for school, for he is psychologically motivated to grow up, to learn, to strive to be a success. Children come into first grade only more or less finished with the Oedipus phase, many bringing with them into the school "unfinished emotional business of early childhood." Crises in early childhood, — illnesses, family disruptions, handicaps of various sorts, — may cause the child to have special problems when he begins school.

Interpersonal Relations. There is considerable intensification of emotions in the relationship between the preschool child and the parents. The striving of the child to take over the father's or the mother's job represents more than the tension of several years before when the child was just 'naughty.' Now the parents may feel the need to 'put the child in his place.' When the parent is cross with the child at this time, he may feel somewhat personally threatened himself by the child. The task before the parents is not only to set limits, but also to strengthen the sense of reality in the child, to teach him about many things. Patience with children of this age is essential.

Many communities now have kindergartens where these tyros can try their wings in the company of their peers. Some four and five year olds are completely involved in their own fantasy world, do not participate with other children in the kindergarten. Other children will be primarily involved in creative work, using clay, crayons and other media. This is especially true of girls. There are some who are well adjusted and aggressive children who will play together in active games, not infreqeuntly with a destructive aim, such as building forts and then knocking them over. Occasionally in a kindergarten, one will see a small group of boys and girls actually playing house, acting out through identifications with their parents and other models, playing at being grown-up.

Implications for the Handicapped. It is during these years that the handicaps of children begin to have special meaning to them. Children with orthopedic handicaps or congenital defects begin to feel the fact of the defects tremendously. Just as parents have an opportunity to begin enlightment concerning sex, so the parents of the handicapped child are faced with interpreting the handicap to the child, trying to help him arrive at an emotionally satisfying adjustment to it, be that ever so difficult. Hospital experiences, surgery, and other medical procedures on children during these years when they are especially susceptible to anxieties and fantasy-distortions of reality must be handled with great care. In some instances, it may be better to avoid the medical procedures altogether. This seems especially true of dental work with some children.

At this age, children with emotional disturbances can usually be detected by trained workers in the public or private kindergarten setting. Mental health programs which have case-finding elements may concentrate much effort with this age group. During these years, children who are having great adjustment difficulties can often be helped, through work with the parents as well as through individual work. Mental health and psychiatric clinic work with children of this age is very rewarding inasmuch as help can be given in a very much shorter period of time usually than would be necessary several years later.

THE GRADE SCHOOL YEARS (c. 5½ years to c. 12 years)

The grade school child is very busy continuing the growing up processes set in motion by the resolution of the Oedipus complex. He is busy learning more about the world; he is busy mastering new skills. He is concerned with himself, his own and other's view of himself. He becomes judgmental and critical of himself. His place in the social group, especially with respect to his peers, is important to him. He also has much practice in school conforming to standards of behavior set by the authority figures. He rubs elbows with many people outside the family circle.

Child development specialists speak of these years as the latent years. The psychosexual drives, for the most part, lie dormant through these years until adolescence, the energy derived therefrom pouring into the broad development of new skills and acquisition of new knowledge. In early latency the emphasis is on personal development and self awareness, while in later latency, the emphasis is on group participation and control of basic instinctual drives, especially aggression. Organized social groups, such as the Cub Scouts and Brownies, and organized sports, with the concept of 'team play', enter the lives of children around age eight. If left to their own devices, children at this age will organize their own neighborhood clubs. Girls usually move ahead faster than boys in the maturation process. It seems easier for them to learn in the school situation, especially during the primary years, and they move into adolescence several years before most boys.

Interpersonal Relations. During the grade school years, children spend a good part of their time in the school where they are 'on their own' and where both the school and their parents hold certain expectations with regard to what their behavior and academic achievement will be. New human relationships with peers and adults are entered into. The socialization process is extended to participation as a member of the broader community group. The child's place in the group, his status, depends upon many factors. Most important are his performance in specific tasks and his basic 'human relations skills,' which he has developed during earlier years. We begin to use the concepts of leadership and 'followership' as we try to understand the social life of grade school children.

The models for social relationships with peers comes from life with siblings at home and life with other children in the neighborhood. Children who have been to nursery school and kindergarten usually know how to play together better than children first leaving the home. First grade teachers can spot these children very readily among a group of, say, 25 new school children. Needless to say, some children need special help and understanding throughout the grade school years as they develop their social skills with their peers.

Relationships with adults are reflections of the emotional life children have in relation to their parents. The teacher is a parent substitute. Relationships run the gamut from overdependency and a passive compliant attitude, through complete indifference to teacher with most energy poured into peer group relations, to hostile — demanding attitudes toward teacher with daily testing of classroom rules and the teacher's patience and endurance.

Implications for the Handicapped. The handicapped child finds his adjustment to the handicap during these years. The nature of the adjustment is of greatest importance to the mental health of the child. How to attain the optimum adjustments for each child is the concern of many persons, — the parents, educators, physicians, nurses, occupational therapist, physiotherapist, and many others. Supportive relationships with adults represent the key to the problem for most handicapped children. Confidence in the child helps him to acquire compensatory skills and interests, helps him develop a healthy and satisfying self-image, a realistic orientation to the handicap. Adults help the handicapped child to develop human relations skills in both his adult and peer relationships.

Agencies which are available to handicapped children and their parents are numerous. In recent years, psychiatric personnel has been added to the teams of many agencies. Among these are cerebral palsy clinics, poliomyelitis treatment centers, and orthopedic rehabilitation centers. There is a trend toward development of special classes for all mentally retarded children in school. Some educators fear stigmatization of children by special classes, while others believe that the special curriculum designed for these children will spare them from the development of overwhelming inferiority feelings and other emotional disturbances.

ADOLESCENCE (c. 12 years to c. 21 years)

Adolescence is ushered in by profound physical changes which prepare for the mature sexual function. Each child meets the 'crisis of maturing,' with its concomitant emotional reactions, in his own unique way, dependent upon his emotional growth and development through the years preceding. Emotionally healthy children are striving for physical and emotional maturity. They anticipate the 'coming of age' and feel proud of their maturation. Physical appearance begins to be of some importance as boys and girls alike begin to want to be 'attractive' to the opposite sex. Naturally, however, this desire is often accompanied by worry, feelings of inferiority, anxiety and guilt. Physical achievement, especially on the athletic field, becomes extremely important to teen-age boys and girls alike. Throughout the teen-age years, and even into adult life, growing boys and girls, men and women, are concerned about their body, their appearance, and their accomplishments.

The increased instinctual energy which accompanies the physical and glandular development in teen-agers poses real problems for them. The raw expression of 'sex urge' is accompanied by tension, anxiety and guilt. The energy of teen-agers is unbounded. The problem is to channelize it into satisfying and constructive activities. Emotional storms and chronic emotional difficulties among teen-agers may represent the inability of the teen-ager to successfully channelize his energies. Excitement and thrill-seeking through new and daring experiences is natural. Trouble lies ahead when the child does not have the sound home relationships to help him make sound judgments.

Conflicts with parental authority and questioning of parents' way of life, their mores, their standards are normal in adolescence. Teen-agers want to make their own decisions and take responsibility for themselves. However, they are more often not really ready for this. They are adult one day, child the next. The struggle over authority is especially present during the early teen-age years. The parents are helped by extra-familial community institutions, such as school, church, scouting, where boys and girls are closely involved with other adults who convey authority and at the same time are personally interested in teen-agers. The early teen-ager is very concerned with himself as a person, but may care little for parental standards in relation to dress and cleanliness. This comes later, as the teen-ager begins to be interested in what other people think of how he looks. Then he may begin to wash up and dress up without parental prodding.

In the early teens the peer life is characterized by attachment to own sex. In junior high schools the boys have their own gangs and groups, as do the girls. Dating begins at various ages but becomes a normal social institution in the high school. Children begin dating with varying degrees of anxiety, heightening of the concern over self. The emphasis is on personal achievement and how one is regarded by others. Mature concern with the partner comes only later in true courtship and marriage, but may even be lacking then. Children who are delayed in developing relationships with the opposite sex may have special emotional problems that need attention.

During adolescence, boys and girls are seriously preparing for their place in the adult world, are concerned about their own capabilities and their future. School failure is a serious problem among teen-agers. Many youngsters need the most skilled vocational guidance to help them to face and plan for their future. Children run through these various phases of adolescence at much their own pace. Some are mature early, some much later. The latter often need much reassurance. Secondary school educators speak of 'late bloomers,' children who appear extremely immature as they go through their first two years of high school, but suddenly around age 16 will blossom out. The striving towards adult ways is strong in most every teen-age boy and girl. Dean Kerr of Phillips Exeter Academy once told the writer that his formula, developed out of the experience of many years working with teen-age boys, was always to treat a boy as if he were at least one year older than you know he really is. The teen-ager responds to the dignity, respect and understanding which characterize mature adult relationships.

Interpersonal Relations. The preceding section contains many references to interpersonal relations during adolescence, for the psychology of the adolescent cannot be discussed apart from the human environment about him. He uses his interpersonal relations to develop his perception of himself. Some teen-agers are more peer group-oriented than adult-oriented. There are a certain few who are social isolates, but who have meaningful relationships with adults and who have special skills and interests, such as in studies, science, art and music. They may be well adjusted from the mental health point of view. However, in the main, the peer group life of the teen-age years, from the gang formation of early adolescence to dating of the later years, is intimately related to healthy emotional growth and development. The development of social skills and a satisfying self-percept is achieved not only through peer group activities, but also through the availability of helpful adults in the form of parents and others.

The relationshps of teen-agers with the grown-up world revolves around authority and authority-conflicts. Teen-agers express this problem by using the word 'fair.' Teen-agers are delighted to have limits clearly set by authority, for they have anxiety and uncertainty with respect to whether they can themselves successfully set limits to their behavior. The fact that authority-conflicts exist does not mean that parents and other adults should not exercise authority, set standards for group and individual behavior.

Implications for the Handicapped. During adolescence, handicapped children face the same emotional adjustment problems with which their fellows are struggling. These are the years when the security and self-confidence gained in childhood from parental and other supportive relationships are so important. The development of the self-percept, with its attendant anxieties and inferiority feeling, causes physical defects and handicaps to be exaggerated in their importance. Group life and group participation, both so important, may be difficult for handicapped children to achieve. Yet teen-age groups often include or exclude individuals not on the basis of specific attributes but on general personality factors related to social skills. If the group 'likes' an individual, it will overlook any handicaps. Children with handicaps need special help in education and vocational guidance. They need help in gaining a realistic view of themselves, their assets and liabilities. They need to formulate a satisfying life plan which is within their capabilities. Their increased energies need channelizing into constructive and satisfying pursuits. This is difficult, inasmuch as the handicap becomes a central limiting factor.

Many community agencies are interested in these problems and can be called upon by the family and school to help. The ideals expressed in the beginning of this chapter in the pamphlet *Mental Health is One, Two, Three,* focus in the minds of the grown-ups and the handicapped child himself as he prepares for entering the adult world.

Conclusion

A preparatory commission of the World Federation for Mental Health has prepared a statement on the prophylactic aspects of the mental health of the physically disabled. They stress the fact that social attitudes towards physical disabilities impede progress as much as anything.

Throughout recorded history, in civilized and in primitive areas of the contemporary world, social attitudes are such that the physically handicapped are assumed to have a variety of other liabilities just because they are physically handicapped. There are many prevailing social attitudes which reflect disapproval, fear, superstition, and prejudices, sometimes manifested in overt, sometimes in disguised forms of discrimination and hostility.[4]

The commission speaks of the direct approach to the handicapped individual, striving to help him to a realistic appraisal of his problems, his limitations and the attitudes of people towards him and his handicap. However, it states the first approach is directed towards society. We must work towards the acceptance of handicapped persons in the community, with communities treating the handicapped as *equals* rather than as special members of society. Handicapped individuals, despising pity and fearing rejection, respond to warm, friendly relationships when they are treated with respect and dignity. Nothing should surprise us here, for this is no less true of all of us.

FOOTNOTES

1. *Mental Health is 1, 2, 3.*
2. Bowlby, John. *Maternal Care and Mental Health.* Monog. of The World Health Organization, Series 2 (Geneva. 1952).
3. Freud, Anna, and Burlingham, Dorothy T. *Infants Without Families.* (National University Press: N.Y.C., 1943).
4. "Prophylactic Aspects of the Mental Health of the Physically Disabled", *A.M.A. Arch. of Ind. Hygiene Occup., Med.,* V: 389-394, 1952.

MENTAL HEALTH OF EXCEPTIONAL CHILDREN

CURTIS G. SOUTHARD AND MABEL ROSS

Mental Health is a part of our total health, which is described by the World Health Organization as "A state of complete physical, mental and social well-being, and not merely the absence of disease or infirmity."[1] There appears to be no single standard for a healthy personality. Successful adaptation may be made by a wide variation in kinds of personality, and the so-called abnormal personality is usually considered as a deviation from the average. The person with a normal personality: (1) has the capacity to work or play satisfactorily; (2) is able to love others; (3) has a feeling of well-being most of the time; (4) has the ability to meet ordinary stressful situations successfully; (5) is relatively free of symptoms of pathology; and (6) is without disabling mental conflicts.[2]

The average person is able to make decisions without too much worry or delay, enjoy work to a certain extent, get pleasure out of social activity, and understand the needs and points of view of others without developing too much anxiety. It is true we are born with certain inherent characteristics, but our personality make-up depends a great deal on experiences we have while growing up.

BRIEF HISTORY

Understanding the personality from a scientific point of view is relatively new. The philosophers and ancient writers, including Plato, Aristotle, and authors of the Bible, had a rich understanding of human nature from which they suggested sound principles by which to live. These have guided the human race in achieving a more civilized and perhaps a happier existence. However, it was only in the early part of the nineteenth century that so-called psychological activity could be predicted and measured.

Pavlov and others demonstrated that animal behavior is associated with physiological changes. This stimulated other research in physiology and psychology. Messmer, Morton Prince, and Charcot created considerable attention with their experiments with hypnotism, dreams, and dissociated states. In the latter part of the nineteenth century many groups became interested in personality structure and development. Freud and his co-workers began a series of observations on neurotic patients in the hope of constructing a scientific theory about personality structure. and development. They developed a theory of the conscious and unconscious; called attention to mental mechanisms utilized daily by everyone — including repression, displacement, rationalization, projection, introjection; and advanced the libido theory accounting for the source of psychic energy existing from birth. These findings, and all the experimental work since, point to the formation of feeling and behavior patterns early in childhood. These patterns seem to form as a result of interplay between the child and his environment, in which his mother is most significant.[3]

These new insights into man's make-up brought about a change in the attitudes and management of the mentally ill throughout the world. They are no longer considered 'the creatures of the devil'.

Furthermore, it is now felt by most people that all types of behavior are explainable by earlier experiences between man with his hereditary make-up and his environment. If this be true we should expect rapid advancement in methods of treatment and the promotion of mental health. Universities, hospitals, and government at all levels throughout the world are devoting more time and funds for research, training, and services for the promotion of mental health and the cure of mental illness. In the United States, the National Mental Health Act, enacted in 1946, has stimulated this work through grants to States and institutions. The World Health Organization is actively interested in many aspects of mental health.

Basic Principles of Mental Health

If the principles of mental health are to be fully understood, one must have some understanding of personality development. Studies in psychology and the biological and social sciences have given us some appreciation of the highly impressionable nature of the child at birth and perhaps before. His need for comfort, love, attention, and a general feeling of security as well as physical care, is obvious from the beginning. These needs continue to exist throughout life, although they may be modified as he grows older. The interaction at first is between child and mother or her substitute. The child 'feels' with his mother. Eventually he relates with other members of the family and becomes less dependent upon his mother if his initial efforts to relate with others are successful. In time the child's feelings become differentiated into the same general emotional pattern as that of his mother and other members of the family. After this pattern becomes fixed, the individual tends to react to a situation characteristic of his family. His feelings or emotions tend to spill over into the family and are shared by it. An injury to a member is shared in some degree by all.

The interplay of these psychological and social forces as the personality develops may result in the average or normal personality, in the withdrawn, or in the aggressively maladjusted, for example. Dr. Hargreaves of London aptly states that a human personality must be thought of as the sum total of present relationships and effects of past relationships which the individual has incorporated into himself.[4] Some of the basic principles of mental health may be stated in terms of human needs: (1) food, shelter, and clothing[5]; (2) to be loved and wanted by individuals and groups; (3) to be important; (4) to be useful; (5) to be recognized as an individual.[6] There are, of course, many other basic principles of mental health, but for the present discussion these will suffice.

APPLICATION OF THE PRINCIPLES OF MENTAL HEALTH
TO THE EXCEPTIONAL CHILD

The exceptional child's mental health needs are essentially the same as the average child's.

A fairly new concept in mental and personality development which should be kept in mind while thinking about the exceptional child is that all people have their own rate of development, even though all tend to follow a similar pattern. The gifted child at seven may resemble to a remarkable degree the average child of eleven or the retarded child of fourteen. Furthermore, the IQ may not be a fixed phenomenon. Studies have shown that there are more gifted children in kindergarten than prove to be the case when they reach high school.[8] This concept may change our attitude toward the potentialities of the retarded as well as all exceptional children. Skeels' work with babies isolated from parental love and stimulation showed that many children who appear to be retarded begin to show average intelligence after they are provided with a mother substitute.[9] Lack of stimulation is apt to occur with other exceptional children, and as a result their potentialities for development are never realized.

It is of no consequence whether we are speaking of average children or of exceptional children. All are young human beings, with the same basic needs and the same human reactions. It is necessary to remember that the exceptional child is not of a different species; he is only a variation from the usual human. Perhaps it would be well if the phrase "He is different" could be abolished in all discussions. This phrase implies a complete difference which is far from the truth; he is merely different in speech, walking, motor control, or in ability to see or hear, but not in his basic humanness. Even more, his being different in that one area is only a matter of degree — the child who wears glasses for astigmatism, the one who wears thick lenses for myopia, the child in a sight-saving class, and the child who is blind, suffer disability in the same sensory field to a different degree and have many of the same problems of being considered by their peers as 'odd' or 'different', of feeling inferior or queer or mistreated by fate, and of being overprotected or shelved by parents and teachers. The parents of the exceptional child often feel it necessary to insist upon their child being just like all the others, as a reaction to his being considered 'different'. Because of their own fears and because they sense the implication in other's use of the term, they may try to prove their child is not of a different order of beings and in doing often seem to, or do, deny the existence of his particular handicap. This may lead to the parents being labeled as 'unrealistic', 'unable to face reality', or 'negative'. Understandably, this only increases the child's problem in trying to find an area of functioning adjustment between his disability and the world.

Every child has many problems of growth and development to solve. The child with a handicap has all of these plus the particular ones incident to his disability. Even the most seriously handicapped child is striving toward a state of balance where he can live, grow, and function at his level with the minimum of tension and the maximum of satisfaction. All living things have a basic drive toward healthy functioning, according to their own needs and abilities. Much is made of the force of growth in plants — of how a sunflower can break through pavement or how seedlings can lift a sheet of glass. How rarely is the same growth force recognized in humans, particularly in exceptional children. Often society is irritated by the child and sees only the equivalent of the cracked pavement instead of admiring the growth force and helping channel it in a personally and socially more effective direction. It is not easy to accomplish this re-direction, but it is less difficult if the basic requirements for physical and mental health are kept in mind.

Some Basic Needs for Mental Health

1. *Food, shelter, clothing and reasonable freedom from epidemic diseases.*
    In the report of the International Preparatory Commission[10] to the International Congress on Mental Health in London in 1948, it is stated that these "are indispensible prerequisites and must be maintained before any consideration of education, social standards, or personality redirection can be effective." The hungry or cold child cannot see beyond his immediate need, and the natural drive to live requires satisfaction of these at any cost. In an adult, social values can sometimes outweigh for a time the hunger or cold, but not so with a child. Furthermore, the child recognizes that adults should supply these fundamental needs, and their failure to do so may be interpreted by the child as rejection, with rejection in turn by him of all overtures by adults. True, it is rare today in our country to hear of a child being literally cast out by his family because of a handicap, but it is not so rare to find his care neglected or resented. The ungrudging satisfaction of his basic needs is his right and is necessary to his mental health.

2. *To belong to and be wanted by a group.*
    Man is a gregarious animal who, since the beginning of time as far as can be determined, has lived and hunted in groups. In addition to this, the human infant is helpless, and the child dependent for a relatively long period of his life span. In the early stages of his dependency the child acquires his pattern of relationship with others. Some modification of this can and does occur throughout life, but the basic attitude of warmth, trust, suspicion, fear, or whatever, remains the core of the eventual adjustment. Every teacher has met the over-affectionate child who seems forever hungry for attention but never confident of finding it. This is a frequent personality pattern in children repeatedly placed in foster-homes or relatives' homes and who have no sense of belonging anywhere. The handicapped child who has spent much of his life in a hospital or institution may show this behavior or may show passivity or hostility as a result of long experience of being merely a 'case'. Basic to good mental health is not only being in an 'own-group', ideally the family, but also being wanted and owned by that group. Even the stern, scolding, or nagging parent or parent-substitute can give the child a

sense of belonging. At the other pole, the attitude of enduring a burden is sensed by any child, and particularly by the exceptional child, as meaning he is unwanted, and he responds according to his personality and experience.

3. *To be important.*

No human being can endure the thought that his disappearance would never be noted. Every child needs to feel that he is important to someone for something, that he has a unique place in his world. A boy of eleven with a severe reading disability described his years of experiencing frustration and disgrace in school, along with his belief that he was "plain dumb", but added that he was "the best fighter in school", a reputation which his teachers sadly corroborated. To have nothing he could do well was more than he could endure. Many exceptional children struggle with this same problem, and in too many instances family, school, and community conspire to convince them that their handicap is their only possible source of importance in the group, thus robbing them of any incentive to work around the particular disability.

4. *To be useful.*

Everyone has the need to feel of use in his world. The sense of being 'on the shelf' is one of the most serious problems in rehabilitation at any age. Usually we think of this in relation to people who have had a place which they can no longer hold, but with children it is also important since they see usefulness as part of the adult world which they wish to enter. "Let *me* do something" is the frequent expression of this need at all ages. To be told that he is incapable of doing anything is difficult for the child who can believe that next year he will be "big enough", but for the exceptional child who hears it as a sentence for life it can be soul-destroying. The sense of having contributed to group activity, and therefore of having ensured his place in the group, is essential to his mental health. The school and family often find it difficult to allow the necessary time for the handicapped child to carry out his task, or are so disturbed by the obvious effort it takes that they interfere through mistaken kindness; either situation may add to his sense of utter incompetence, or being a piece of junk. His subsequent disinclination to try is understandable.

If the need to be useful and the need to be important seem very similar, it is not surprising. They can be compared to having an unusual hat which is yet in the height of style. All people of all ages need to feel uniquely set apart in some one thing, but also intimately part of the activity of their world otherwise.

5. *To be a person.*

Everyone at least in our Western culture, has the need to be recognized as an individual human being, rather than to be lost as a particle in an amorphous mass of humanity. Society has recognized this in the culminating disgrace of taking away a man's name and giving him only a number when he is imprisoned. In the development of the individual the sense of 'I', of the self, is central. A widely held theory of personality development states that to the infant the whole world is part of himself, that gradually he sees his mother as not part of him, then becomes aware of still other beings who are separate, and finally begins to be aware of himself as an individual in a world of individuals. Throughout childhood, he is trying to find the limits of his power, rights, and responsibilities with relation to his peers and to the adults of his environment. With his intense awareness of himself, he reacts strongly to lack of respect for him as a person. A seven-year-old boy trying to describe his feeling about a teacher finally burst forth, "She *pushed* me, — she just *pushed* me!" All the sense of outrage at being treated as a piece of furniture, a thing, was in his voice. The child who experiences limitations because of a handicap may be very sensitive about his personal dignity and interpret many kindly-meant actions as invading or belittling his individuality.

All of these basic needs are as essential for the exceptional child as for the average child. The symptoms of deficiency vary in both groups but are always determined by the personality of the child, the situation in which he finds himself, and the understanding of the adults. The bitter, complaining chronically ill child, the suspicious, antagonistic deaf child, the fearful, withdrawn blind child, are all expressing a deficiency in these basic needs. Similarly, the happy, laughing child with cerebral palsy, delighted at accomplishing a few steps, and the active, friendly boy with arms and legs but no hands nor feet have somehow, somewhere, had these needs met. A person may experience repeated denial of his personality, with constant battering of his individuality, until he seems lost in the mass, but even then he responds to individual attention and may achieve unexpected levels. A child of six in a large institution for the feebleminded was utterly helpless and unable to walk. Through an unusual series of circumstances, he was placed in a group home for the adult feebleminded, where one resident took a maternal interest in him. After a year of constant and patient care the boy was walking after a fashion, kept himself reasonably clean, and fed himself to a slight extent. Each step was proudly pointed out by his 'mother', who in turn received the special attention and commendation which she merited for her achievement. Every human can attain more when he feels in his own mind that he is truly a person and knows that he is a person of importance to someone else.

The Exceptional Child and His Relationship to His Parents

Of first importance to the mental health of the exceptional child is his place in his family; of prime importance to the family is their place in the community. The individual and the family need the sense of belonging to and being wanted by the group. The meaning of the disability to the family and to the community is vital to the mental health of the child and important in any school program for the exceptional child. The acceptance within the school setting cannot entirely counteract rejection in family and community. Important as peer acceptance is to every child, this is only part of the story. The reverse is equally true. If the school rejects him, while the family and community accept him, he will still find the going rough. All three, — family, community and school, — must work together, must share the responsibility for broad public education regarding the needs of exceptional children.

In the development of the exceptional child, many factors affect the attitude of the adults responsible for his care, and these in turn directly affect the personality of the child. Some of these factors can be controlled by taking thought, and others are ingrained in our culture.

From time immemorial, the myth of the sins of the fathers being visited upon the children by crippling handicaps and illness has persisted. Rarely do we meet today the attitude that no treatment should be attempted for the child because his handicap was decreed by God and must be accepted. However, other residuals of this attitude are seen in the sense of guilt and failure expressed by parents. In extreme instances this leads to the sacrifices of all members of the family to the care and support of the exceptional child and the inability to accept any plan implying self-responsibility by the child. When the parent sees the child as his punishment or as his failure, the child absorbs enough of this attitude to affect his concept of his own value as a person and of his role in his world. This will be translated in terms of his personality and family culture, and will directly affect his attitude toward peers, teachers, tasks, authority, social experience. The attitude of the child in turn affects the family, and the cycle may become a vicious one.

It is natural to focus our sympathy on the child, but the greatest stress is apt to be on the closest well relative (the significant person) whose responsibility it is to be a helper and partner of the handicapped.

The professional worker who contacts families in distress because a member is handicapped with a crippling illness or condition expects to observe manifestations of anxiety and other symptoms of distress. It is only natural for those faced with such unfortunate circumstances in a loved one to suffer enormously, but with even the slightest encouragment most parents live through these experiences and become more mature people. We must admit that many do not, and we see everyday accounts where a family literally falls apart. Perhaps they have not been sufficiently fortified or perhaps they have not had the opportunity to reach emotional maturity and when misfortune comes they react in an immature fashion leading to panic.

How does the exceptional child wish to be treated by the family? He has the same desires, yearning, and in general his emotional needs are the same as the non-handicapped. He needs recognition, companionship, but not too much sympathy. He wants a chance to develop skills which may still be possible. Over-protection, too much attention and sympathy, encourages increased dependency which the handicapped already recognizes as his own worst enemy. He is likely to appear too touchy on this point. Therefore, in dealing with the handicapped, one must be sensitive to the things he cannot do for himself and give help without too much ado, but leave all things of which he is capable for him to demonstrate. In this manner he is allowed to win his recognition as a human being. It is only in this way that he will realize his limited ambitions. One of the great social advances of our time is the realization that the handicapped persons have tremendous possibilities as useful, happy citizens. This is not accidental, nor the result of sentimentality, but more likely is due to the application of knowledge about human feelings, motivations, and behavior. Industry has proved that most handicapped people are valuable employees.

The parent needs to guard himself from the conscious feelings of guilt which are likely to haunt him. He may feel he is responsible in some way for the handicapping condition, or he may feel that some of his thoughts and dreams about the handicapped person are sinful. In his guilt he may over-compensate and be over-sympathetic, thereby robbing the handicapped of his independence or the will to do for himself. This guilt and worry may lead to mental and physical fatigue and depressions of varying severity. The effect on the handicapped is damaging, for as pointed out in the beginning, the emotional tone of each family member tends to reach a common level. The solution to this stressful situation is not easy.

In working with the handicapped child during this stage, in an effort to bring about rehabilitation, we should be conscious of these emotional states in other family members, especially the ones closest to the member. The parent or relative responsible for the support of the handicapped child must be given time to work out this new relationship. The suffering is a two-way affair. If the disability is of a permanent nature, he must have time to accept reality — every means for a hopeful solution must be explored before the responsible person can accept things as they are. It is a mistake for those of us who can observe objectively that, for example, the mongoloid will always be handicapped, to try to convince a mother that her child is below average. She must work through it herself.

This may give the impression that relatives are considered a stumbling block to the rehabilitation process. In reality, they are additional people who must work through this emotional process pervading the whole family, and the relative who at first is a helpless 'helper' to the handicapped one, becomes the key to the new lives all must build.

His Relationship to the Educator

The professional mental health worker in most instances is not consulted by the family. Instead, understanding friends, relatives, and the teacher are contacted, and they will have to offer support in their own way. It is extremely helpful if they know the resources in the community and where this professional help can be obtained.

The handicapped child needs to have others outside the family with whom he can relate, not in a dependent fashion, but to demonstrate worth, independence, and love, and to realize his limited goals. Those of us who work with the handicapped must detect who the significant persons are. When we find this relationship, our goal is to strengthen it. The teacher should not try to replace the mother in this relationship. After a feeling of security is established, rehabilitation and education can begin. The blind may be taught to read, the deaf to communicate, the cripple to perform in a satisfactory manner.

It is a mistake to classify the basic problems of the handicapped person in terms of the illness or condition affecting them. True, the educational needs are different for each, and special types of training are needed for them, but everyone has the same basic needs for relating to others, to prove his worth, to give and receive love.

The increasing knowledge of personality development and of the important roles of significant adults in the early life of a child carries with it the responsibility to consider carefully the role of the teacher in the life of the exceptional child as well as the average child. It is necessary to recognize some of the factors which have affected the child before he reaches the school and those which affect him outside of school and therefore to consider the extent of the teacher's influence on the child's continued development, with a realistic and objective examination of the limits of her responsibility. The eventual life adjustment of the individual is of importance to the teacher as an ultimate goal, but it is equally, or perhaps even more, important to consider the day-by-day mental health of the child in school. To attend only to the long-range goal may be to miss important steps on the way. It is especially important for the teacher dealing with exceptional children to take notice of the day-by-day accomplishments. 'Resting points of satisfaction' are essential in a program requiring such a high degree of patience, faith, and concentrated effort.

The adjustment of the exceptional child in school is often dependent upon the attitude of the teacher. To the teacher who has responsibility for a class, partly or entirely made up of exceptional children, the meaning of the various disabilities to her is important in her success. Without intent, pity, revulsion, irritation, anxiety created in the teacher by a particular disability will be felt by the children and affect their relation with the teacher and with each other. If such a group exacts too much from the teacher, it is better for her not to force herself to continue unless she can receive expert help in understanding her reaction.

School efforts toward social integration may be defeated if the child believes that he is a malformed monster, or if he believes he has no disability. The body image held by the individual is important to his life adjustment. He may set totally unrealistic standards for himself or be unable to allow for the necessary adjustments in his environment. A girl with a severe congenital dislocation of the hip denied its existence and believed it was not noticeable when she was walking or dancing. Far from making life easier for her, she believed others to be deliberately trying to embarrass her if they made allowances for her disability, and deliberately making matters more difficult for her if they did not. Although the body image is largely a reflection of family and community attitude, it is also a very personal matter. It is difficult but especially important for the teacher to assist the exceptional child in developing a realistic, tolerant, and optimistic attitude toward himself as a basis for satisfactory personality development and functioning.

His Relationship to the Community

It has been pointed out how important it is to know the resources for help with exceptional children in the community. What is most encouraging is the fact that one of the good sources of help come from organizations which have been formed by parents who have lived through stressful periods with handicapped loved ones. They have banded together and have founded organizations which provide professional guidance as well as being a source of relief and comradeship to those parents who have felt alone with their worries.

The adjustment of the exceptional child is directly related to the meaning of his disability to the community, family, and individual. In a few cultures it has been believed that convulsive disorders were indicative of divine visitation, but in more they have been considered to be leagued with the devil. Some leftover of this is seen in the fear and abhorrence seen in many communities today. Where this attitude is present, the child with convulsive disorder reacts with shame, confusion, sense of inferiority, and defiance, according to the person and the situation. Although a few cultures have considered that the mentally retarded person was special because half of his mind was obviously in Paradise, more often he has been considered to be a derelict, an outcast, with no feelings, no future, and no value. In addition to the usual complexities of growing up, most of these children face the indifference of the community to their special problems of adjustment. Too often they struggle, with inadequate equipment, to fit into the complex world about them with minimum understanding and help from the social institutions of the community.

Conclusion

Mental health can no more be subdivided into particular programs to meet the need for individual types of disability than can general health. The child with diabetes or one who is unable to swallow has the same nutritional requirements as does every other child, but the methods of supplying these is different. It is sometimes easy to confuse the method with the need. Mental health cannot be subdivided into mental health for the crippled, mental health for the deaf, mental health for the blind, mental health for the mentally retarded, mental health for the chronically ill., The same basic requirements for food, shelter, clothing, reasonable freedom from epidemic disease, belongingness, usefulness, importance, and individuality obtain; it is only the methods of satisfying these needs that differs. Herein lies the challenge to adults responsible for programs directed toward the goal of the greatest possible personal satisfaction and social functioning as a constructive citizen for each exceptional child.

Rules or a set of formulae will not guarantee mental health. It has been pointed out that the individual does not stand alone in sickness or health, that mental health tends to strike a common level among the members of a family. Getting well or rehabilitating the handicapped requires a working through by more than one person. How well this is done depends a great deal on the motivation of each individual. Where there is strong motivation to live constructively, there is already a certain amount of emotional maturity which can be depended upon to carry one through many trying circumstances. It is the duty of those of us who are not involved in the handicapping situation to give understanding help.

Relationship of general physical health to emotional well-being has not been discussed. Suffice it to say that research has shown, as we have long believed, that there is a strong interrelation between them. In fact one is dependent upon the other, and we cannot separate the mind from the body. We will be most successful in our approach to exceptional child when we treat him as a whole feeling person rather than a child without legs, or vision, or hearing. These things cannot be true of a person without involving his emotions. The main avenue to rehabilitation lies in the recognition of his emotions. Only as we consider how he feels, how we feel, and how the family and community feel, can we hope to meet the exceptional needs of the exceptional child.

FOOTNOTES

1. *Constitution*, the World Health Organization.
2. Weiss, Edward, and English, Spurgeon, *Psychosomatic Medicine* (W. B. Saunders: Philadelphia, 1949).
3. Lewis, Nolan D. C., *A Short History of Psychiatric Achievement* (W. W. Norton: N.Y.C., 1941), pp. 167-168.
4. Hargreaves, G. R., *Mental Health Aspects of Pregnancy and Childbirth* (World Health Organization).
5. Report of International Preparatory Commission.
6. Plant, James, *Personality and the Cultural Pattern* (Oxford University Press: N.Y.C., 1937).
7. Henry, Nelson B., *The Education of Exceptional Children*, 49th Yearbook, Part II, National Society for the Study of Education (University of Chicago Press: Chicago, 1950), p. 10.
8. Bayley, Nancy, "Consistency and Variability in the Growth of Intelligence from Birth to 18 Years", *Journal of Genetic Psychology*, 1949. 75:2:192-194.
9. Skeels, Harold, and Dye, Harold B., "A Study of the Effects of Differential Stimulation on Mentally Retarded Children", *Proceedings of the American Association of Mental Deficiency*, 1939. 44:1:114-136.
10. Report of International Preparatory Commission.

MENTAL HEALTH FOR THE EXCEPTIONAL

I. IGNACY GOLDBERG

Throughout the ages the dictum "A healthy mind in a healthy body" inferred "An unhealthy mind in an unhealthy body". The stress that was put on the physical health and fitness of an individual set aside all those who differed physically, mentally, emotionally or socially from those who were considered normal.

Today a more liberal attitude has evoked. As a result, we are more and more aware of the "unhealthy mind in a healthy body", as well as of the "healthy mind in an unhealthy body". We have become aware as much of maladjustments, emotional blocks, overprotection, rejections, sibling rivalries, etc., as we are of flat feet, round shoulders, visual defects, speech defects, etc.

Since the beginning of this century, the door of our educational facilities has opened to all children and youth regardless of their physical, mental, emotional and social efficiencies. We have developed special education services for those who require them because of their disabilities and handicaps. Through these efforts we have reclaimed a vast army of human resources back into our society. However, many exceptional individuals who could have been helped to become contributing members in their communities have been lost in spite of all our tremendous efforts. Just a rough survey of the hundreds of state institutions would reveal thousands of children who are physically handicapped, mentally retarded or emotionally disturbed who are not receiving any education and training, who have been separated from their families, very often only because the schools in their respective communities could not cope with their problems.

It has been repeated over and over again that exceptional children do not differ in their basic needs, motivations, goals, etc. from the so-called normal, although they do require special educational facilities to take care of their specific disabilities. Yet we still consider many of them to be problems of a special nature with which we cannot cope in a normal community environment.

In order to better understand the basis of this barrier to our progress in more effective help to the exceptional individuals, the consideration of the mental health point of view in relation to the exceptional was chosen in this chapter. It is believed that this is a neglected area in the preparation of the special classroom teacher, as well as in the professional literature.

Mental health in its broadest sense has come to mean the adjustment of a human being to the world, to others, and to himself, with a maximum of effectiveness. In other words, the mental health of an individual takes into account his personality, his environment, the interaction between his personality and other personalities, as well as the interaction between his personality and his constantly changing environment. Mental health thus conceived applies to any individual, normal as well as exceptional.

There are, however, certain hazards besetting the wholesome development of personalities of the exceptional that very often prevent attainment of good mental health. Erik Erikson in his *Childhood and Society* describes eight stages of personality development.[1] In each stage, he says, there is a central problem that has to be solved, temporarily at least, if the person is to proceed with confidence to the next stage. Witmer and Kotinsky interpret these central problems as: the sense of trust, the sense of autonomy, the sense of initiative, the sense of duty and accomplishment, the sense of identity, the sense of intimacy, the parental sense, and the sense of integrity.[2]

Let us review these stages, relating each one to the developmental hazards of exceptional individuals:

Eight Stages of Personality Development

The Sense of Trust. The component of the healthy personality that is the first to develop is the sense of trust. "The first demonstration of social trust in the baby is the ease of his feeding, the depth of his sleep, the relaxation of his bowels".[3]

Witmer and Kotinsky add that

Experiences connected with feeding are a prime source for the development of trust. At around four months of age a hungry baby will grow quiet and show signs of pleasure at the sound of an approaching footstep, anticipating (trusting) that he will be held and fed. This repeated experience of being hungry, seeing food, receiving food, and feeling relieved and comforted assures the baby that the world is a dependable place.[4]

One cannot help but think about the cerebral palsied babies with feeding difficulties, or the congenitally deaf who do not hear the sound of an approaching footstep, or the blind who do not see the food. Furthermore, the exceptional child senses the anxieties in his family unit that develop on account of his condition. There may also be frequent visits to doctors, shorter or longer separation from the family due to hospitalization, etc. All these experiences may handicap the child in having his sense of trust deeply rooted in his total personality development.

The Sense of Autonomy. When the child is twelve to fifteen months old, he begins the struggle for the next component of the healthy personality. He starts to expend his energy to ascertain that he is a human being with a mind and will of his own. Erikson describes this as a child's striving toward becoming an independent human being and yet one who is able to use the help and guidance of others in important matters.[5] It is obvious that before the sense of autonomy can develop, the sense of trust must be reasonably well established. At this stage of development the child experiments with 'trying out' his right to choose. He tries to learn the boundaries of autonomy: 'holding on and letting go'. If his physical or mental disabilities prevent him from his basic right to choose, for example, "whether to sit or whether to stand . . . whether to accept offered food or whether to reject it, whether to use the toilet or to wet his pants"[6], then there is the great danger that he will not discover the frontiers that mark off what is approved, what is tolerated, and what is forbidden in our society.

The Sense of Initiative. Another hazard to the development of healthy personality of the exceptional child occurs at the time when his normal peers start to find out what they can do. Witmer and Kotinsky call this "the period of enterprise and imagination".[7] The child tries to imitate the behavior of everybody he observes. He asks questions. He is making discoveries constantly. The sense of initiative that is so much prized in our society starts to develop.

The child who is crippled, deaf, or blind, depends very much on others. Very often the development of his sense of initiative is discouraged or prevented by his condition.

The Sense of Duty and Accomplishment. A child who has not achieved the three stages so far described enters his school years very much handicapped. He is apt to experience a sense of inadequacy and inferiority. It should be remembered that children need and want real achievement. To help them develop a sense of accomplishment does not mean merely praising them, giving them all good marks and passing them on to the next grade. School, of course, becomes at this stage the core of the child's life.

The exceptional individual needs, more than others, the reconfirming of his sense of trust, autonomy, and initiative as well as help in developing his sense of duty and accomplishment.

The Sense of Identity. The adolescence of an exceptional individual is the most trying period of his development. Unfortunately, in our present educational setup this is when he ends his formal special education. At this period, he seeks to clarify who he is and what his role in society is to be. The exceptional adolescent becomes more aware of his shortcomings, whether physical, intellectual, emotional, or social. He is in need of very careful guidance to help him to accept himself.

The Sense of Intimacy. The sense of intimacy infers, according to Erikson, intimacy with persons of the same sex or of the opposite sex or with oneself.[8] The exceptional youth not fairly sure of his identity may shy away from interpersonal relationships and is apt to become enmeshed in himself. During this period self-pity may become deeply seated and well-nigh ineradicable, and the presence of a defect may also interfere with sex love. Intimacy with persons of the opposite sex cannot be developed in the lives of many handicapped.

The Parental Sense. This stage of development is characterized by an individual entering his adulthood and his craving for others more than for himself. It is characterized by accepting the fact that giving is higher than receiving, and loving than being loved. Many exceptional individuals do not ever achieve this stage in their development. If they do, the danger represented here is that they have accumulated experiences of constant getting, receiving and being loved. It is very difficult to change this pattern.

The Sense of Integrity. The final component of the healthy personality, the sense of integrity, depends very much on all the others mentioned previously. If the individual experienced failure throughout his life, he will not be able to accept his life cycle. One of the goals of special education should be the preparation of the exceptional individual for accomplishing his sense of integrity.

This, then, is a summary description of some of the hazards besetting the healthy personality development of exceptional individuals ,and which should be taken into account in working with them.

In discussing personality development, one has to remember that it denotes the totality of an individual's behavior as shown in his conduct, reputation, temperament, and character as judged by others, and the inner organization of his drives, purposes and attitudes. Some of the components of personality are observable, e.g., physical characteristics, physique, etc. Some of the components are measurable, e.g., aptitudes, skills, intellectual abilities, etc. But the most important ones are neither observable nor measurable. Jersild calls them the subjective or 'inner' components: the individual's motives, aspirations and feelings; his ideas and attitudes regarding himself; and the manner in which his 'inner life' is organized.[9]

THE TEACHER'S ROLE

Because of the subjective, nonobservable components of our personalities, it is very difficult for teachers to help their pupils to understand and accept themselves as they are. It is even more difficult to achieve this with exceptional children. In spite of these difficulties, the teacher should stress helping them toward self understanding, thus also helping them more effectively to overcome some of the hazards in their personality development.

When an effort is made to promote self understanding, which is the basic principle of mental health in any group of exceptional children, one of the most impressive effects is the emotional impact of such work upon the teacher. Very often exceptional pupils, when encouraged, will reveal a wide range of emotional problems. According to Jersild,[10] children who have been considered 'problems' in the school, in the home, and in the community for several years, often will display various aspects of their hostility, anxiety, and despair. These can be very threatening even to the most experienced teacher. In other words, the child who is mentally retarded, physically handicapped, or socially maladjusted, provides many mental health hazards for the teacher himself. One of the most commonly found is that the teacher may be overwhelmed by the terrific needs that are laid bare. The needs of the exceptional children are so great, and the teacher may realize that his ability to help is so limited that it seems hopeless even to try.

There was once a belief that the best teachers of exceptional children were those who themselves were handicapped, because they had a better insight into the problems besetting those children. As far as problems related to the disability per se are concerned, this might be true, but it is more important to gain insight into the child's inner life. In order to be able to do this, one has to gain insight into one's own inner life. To be able to sympathize with the child who is hostile, the teacher must face his own hostile tendencies and try to accept the implication of his anger as its occurs, say, in his annoyance with his pupils, his impatience with himself, his likes and dislikes of other teachers, his complaints against parents or school authorities, or others on whom he fixes his ire. To realize the fears and anxieties of children, the teacher must try to examine his own fears and anxieties. To do so may be more painful and threatening at the moment than to pretend that they do not exist. Unless he can understand his own fear of making mistakes and the fear of what others may think of him, his ability to perceive that others are frightened will be limited.

One of the most common phenomena found in the attitudes of handicapped people toward themselves, and one which most often develops into a serious mental disorder, if not caught at an early stage, is what Horney calls "feeling abused." Very often a child who is disabled in one way or another may dwell on the harm done to him by heredity, physicians, his parents, schools, or by society in general. I remember talking to a young man afflicted with cerebral palsy who blamed his condition on the physician who had delivered him into the world by means of instruments and who had, according to this boy, "damaged his brain". Now at the age of twenty he was trying to find this doctor to make him pay back for all his sufferings.

This "feeling abused" may convince a person that everybody is better off than he. "Others find a better job, get a raise in salary; their clocks always keep correct time, their cars never need repairs, their sorrows are negligible".[12] It may also convince him that everybody is against him. Everybody expects something impossible of him and if he does not measure up to their expectations, it makes him feel guilty.

Sometimes these feelings are justified, sometimes they are imaginary. One thing, however, is certain. If a child lives in an environment in which he is opposed, thwarted, or rejected, as happens often with the exceptional, he will begin at an early age to develop the kind of behavior which we find in a person who perceives himself as one who is being abused. He will feel hostile and probably will project his hostility onto others.

When we face a person who expresses the feelings of being abused, this may become threatening to our own feelings of mistreatment. We might tend to keep it from our awareness, being afraid of its disruptive effect on human relations.

The teacher should help his students in the process of self understanding. However, to help others to understand themselves, one must understand oneself. "Love thy neighbor as thyself" becomes meaningful and applicable only as one comes to "love thyself". One must first know himself, and accept himself for what he is. It is not a matter of loving some illusion of oneself. When one accepts his limitations, then, and *only* then, can he accept the limitations of others. It is important to note that the ability

which enables a person to be wise to himself does not necessarily show a very high correlation with the kind of ability we measure by means of our intelligence tests. . . A person can have a very high IQ and still thoroughly fool himself and people with modest IQ's sometimes achieve a very canny and healthy picture of themselves.[13]

An exceptional child most often is influenced by the anxieties of his parents. There is a tendency on the teacher's part to use cliches, — this parent is rejecting, that one is overanxious, another one is overprotective, — and leave it at that. When dealing with parents of exceptional children, the teacher must again have enough of self understanding to be able to grasp the fundamental facts of parental problems. The birth of any new child involves a shift in family relationships for which parents have to be prepared. However, parents in most cases are not prepared for what will be involved with a handicapped child. Some hold themselves or each other responsible for the cause of the child's handicap, and their feelings of guilt or blame affect their approach to the child and to each other. The handicapped child introduces a severe strain which often intensifies the weak spots in the relationship between the parents.

The problem becomes more complex when other siblings are involved. How can parents find time to meet the ordinary day-to-day needs of their nonhandicapped children, without neglecting the handicapped one? How can they manage to care adequately for the handicapped child without depriving the rest of the family of their time and interest? The parent of a child with a handicap has been deeply hurt. No matter how brave, stoical or even cheerful he appears, he feels he has been deprived, through no fault of his own, of many of the normal satisfactions of parenthood, especially the expectation that his child will grow up and take his place in society to work, to marry, to participate in the life of the community.

The education of the exceptional cannot be carried on in complete isolation from other children and youth. Even though special classes and special schools, and special services are often required, an attempt has to be made to mix exceptional children with their normal peers. This process, it is said, prepares the exceptional child to live in a world consisting of normal individuals. One question, however, has been neglected.

Who teaches the normal youngsters to adapt their activities, their wishes, their preferences to the interests, needs, limitations, and preferences of the exceptional youngsters? Who teaches them that they must learn to live in a world that includes blind, deaf, crippled, and mentally retarded people, and that these people have the same right to a voice in how the world is run as do those who can see and hear, and who have strong bodies and nimble minds?[14]

In order to minimize the difficulties endangering the mental health of exceptional individuals, special education practices and processes should include as a planned feature psychological instruction that would help students gain in understanding themselves and in understanding of others in relation to them. According to Jersild,

nearly everything in the curriculum is charged with psychological meaning when viewed from the standpoint of what it might do to help learners find themselves, realize their potentialities, use their resources in productive ways, and enter into relationships which have a bearing on their ideas, and attitudes toward themselves.[15]

Every teacher, therefore, becomes in his own way a psychologist. "Everything he does, says, or teaches has or could have a psychological impact.

I. IGNACY GOLDBERG

What he offers helps children to discover their resources and their limitations. He is the central figure in countless situations which can help the learner to realize and accept himself or which may bring humiliation, shame, rejection, and self-disparagement".[16]

FOOTNOTES

1. Erikson, Erik, H., *Childhood and Society* (W.W. Norton: N.Y.C., 1950), pp. 219-233.
2. Witmer, Helen L., and Kotinsky, R., *Personality in the Making* (Harper: N.Y.C., 1952), pp. 8-26.
3. Erikson, *op. cit.*, p. 219.
4. Witmer and Kotinsky, *op cit.*, p. 9.
5. Erikson, *op. cit.*, p. 222.
6. Witmer and Kotinsky, *op. cit.*, p. 12.
7. *Ibid.*, p. 15.
8. Erikson, *op cit.*, p. 229.
9. Jersild, Arthur T., *Child Psychology*, Fourth Edition (Prentice-Hall: N.Y.C., 1954), p. 576.
10. Jersild, Arthur T., *In Search of Self* (Bureau of Publications, Teachers College, Columbia University: N.Y.C., 1952), pp. 104, 105.
11. Horney, Karen, "On Feeling Abused", *The American Journal of Psychoanalysis*, 11:5-12, 1951.
12. *Ibid.*, p.
13. Jersild, Arthur T., "Self-Understanding in Childhood and Adolescence", *The American Psychologist*, 6:122-126, 1951.
14. Featherstone, William B., "The Education of Exceptional Children", *Teachers College Record*, 51:512-520, 1950.
15. Jersild, *In Search of Self*, p. 103.
16. *Ibid.*, p. 125.

THE ROLE OF PSYCHOLOGY IN SPECIAL EDUCATION

KARL C. GARRISON

A satisfactory program for the education of exceptional children must be based upon the needs, abilities, and dynamics of the individuals concerned. Increasingly, the psychological aspects of the problems of the exceptional child are being recognized as extremely important. Thus, one finds as part of the staff of a complete clinic for exceptional children one or more individuals trained in clinical psychology, as well as others with some understanding of the function of psychology in special education.

The role of the psychologist will vary in accordance with the nature of the individual problems involved in special education programs. In some cases his role is a major one, while in others it will be of less importance.

IDENTIFYING CHILDREN NEEDING SPECIAL HELP

Although the teacher is in the best position to study the individual child, the help of psychologists and other specialists will be needed in identifying those children in need of special help. The teacher will, therefore, refer children suspected of being mentally retarded or otherwise handicapped to specialists for further study. A competent psychologist is the proper one to administer individual mental tests and otherwise appraise the educability of the pupil. He is best equipped to classify the pupil as mentally deficient, mentally retarded, or slow learning. He is the key figure in identifying those children who are too retarded in their mental development to profit from the educational program designed for children with normal mental development. Shultsky, Justman, and Wrightstone report that a short form of the Stanford-Binet intelligence test has been devised for screening children for admittance to special classes in New York's public schools.[1]

One of the major responsibilities of the psychologist is to administer psychological examinations to children in hospitals, special classes, and elsewhere. An examination of 67 cerebral palsy cases in special class units in regular public schools of New York revealed 16 to 24 per cent to have an IQ of 110 or above.[2] The data presented in Table 1 shows that 51 per cent of the group were of average intelligence. As a result of the examinations, arrangements were made to transfer the 6 mentally defective children to more appropriate community services, thus providing better for their needs.

TABLE 1
Intelligence Status of Sixty-seven Cerebral Palsy Children Enrolled in School

IQ Classification	Number	Per cent
Superior (110 IQ and above)	16	24
Average (90 to 109 IQ)	34	51
Borderline through Dull — Normal (70 to 89 IQ)	11	16
Mental Defective (below 70 IQ)	6	9

DIAGNOSIS AND CLASSIFICATION

Accurate diagnosis and classification is essential for a sound educational and guidance program. Such a diagnosis should furnish information about the degree, classification, and probable cause of the condition. The use of mental tests alone is inadequate for such a diagnosis. A comprehensive clinical appraisal would combine the evidence obtained from mental tests with results obtained from other tests and a case study of the individual. Thus, specialists from different areas are essential for a complete clinical study of the individual child. A complete evaluation includes a thorough case history, and physical, neurological, psychiatric and psychological examinations. The physically handicapped, socially and emotionally maladjusted, and gifted should be located, and an educational program developed in harmony with their needs and abilities. The child who is severely handicapped would combine the evidence obtained from mental tests with results obtained from other tests including previous tests, and a case study of the individual. Thus, specialists from different areas are essential for a complete clinical study of the individual child. A complete evaluation includes a thorough case history, and physical, neurological, psychiatric and psychological examinations. It is the function of psychology to recommend how the educational program should be structured and implemented so as to produce the optimum development of the individual child.

The psychologist plays a major role in the diagnosis of the mental ability of children. The diagnosis and classification of those at the lowest level of mental deficiency is not so difficult. The child who is classified as severely retarded mentally should then be placed in the classes where he will be able to function to the best of his ability. It is at the moron level where pseudo-feeblemindedness and marginal normality appear that inaccurate diagnosis are often made. It is with these individuals in particular that the use of the criterion of social adequacy, or results from sources other than intelligence is very important.

One of the weakest links in the mental diagnosis of physically handicapped children is the inadequacy of instruments for evaluating the general intellectual level. This is brought out in a report by Blum, Burgemeister, and Lorge of their studies at the Institute of Psychological Research, Teachers College, Columbia University.[3] The practice of psychologists has been to use existing tests for diagnosing and classification, pending the development and validation of instruments which would take into account certain inadequacies inherent in the handicapping condition. A review of the literature shows that much progress has been made in the development of tests with items better suited to the limitations imposed by certain physical or sensory handicaps.

A number of psychological studies of epileptics have been made during the past several decades. Two techniques of evaluation have been used with some success. These involve (1) the Rorschach test, and (2) the scatter or pattern analysis on an intelligence test. For several decades psychologists have made use of the latter in an effort to diagnose certain mental states, such as schizophrenia. A number of extensive studies have dealt with the characteristic patterns of responses given to items on intelligence tests by individuals suffering from some organic condition, such as that found in the case of epileptics. The results of these studies, although revealing in terms of recognized signs, are not sufficiently valid for a clear-cut diagnosis. The psychological diagnosis has been found to be valuable in supplementing findings from observations and a careful medical diagnosis.

Adjustment Problems of the Handicapped

Many factors operate jointly in affecting the adjustments of physically handicapped children. Cruickshank and Dolphin have suggested that crippled children, as a group, "show personal socio-emotional adjustments which deviate from those which are considered healthy."[4] For most children the disabling condition exerts a psychological as well as physical influence. A comparison of the social and emotional adjustments of crippled and non-crippled children by Gates showed that the crippled children obtained scores which compared to those obtained by non-crippled children at inferior adjustment levels.[5]

The psychological problems of the exceptional child arises from two sources: (1) the limitations placed upon the child by the handicapping conditions; (2) the attitudes and personality characteristics developed as a result of environmental forces related to the handicapping condition. The exceptional child, like other children, craves the affection of others, and has a keen desire to win the approval of his classmates and teachers and to attain a fair degree of self esteem. He has the same basic needs as other children. Too often he is looked upon as an individual to be guided and manipulated into low-level pursuits rather than as a human being capable of reacting to affection and hostility, acceptance and rejection, approval and disapproval, failure and success. Mental hygienists and psychologists emphasize the importance of the relation of these needs to the personal and social adjustments of the individual child. The behavior of the child is symptomatic of failures in the satisfaction of certain basic needs. The early emotional climate as well as the immediate situation must be taken into consideration in the evaluation and guidance of the emotionally disturbed child.

An important role of psychology is to assist parents and teachers of exceptional children to recognize their needs and to understand more completely the nature of psychological adjustments faced by these children. In the group of 87 children studied by Cruickshank and Dolphin it was observed that the need to share in decision-making and the need for love and affection were being over-met by parents, teachers, and other adults.[6]

Handicapping conditions affect behavior in both a direct or primary way and an indirect or secondary way. These secondary or psychological effects superimposed upon a primary organic defect are more serious than the primary effect. Fears, resentments, lack of motivation, inattention, and various personality distortions may appear as secondary results of a handicapping condition. The problem of differentiating primary and secondary effects is a difficult one, and there are no simple rules to guide the teacher or specialist. However, it is extremely important that it should be made in order to guide the individual child in his personal and social development. Such a differentiation requires the services of a psychologist or clinician who can bring together the life history, testing data, and his own observations of each individual case and from this constellation arrive at more accurate differentials of primary and secondary effects.

A good illustration of the secondary effects is that reported by Lashley of a patient who, after a brain operation, failed to learn the alphabet with 900 repetitions.[7] A bet of 100 cigarettes was made with the patient that he could not learn the alphabet during the period of a week. This furnished the necessary incentive for the patient, and he promptly learned the alphabet in 10 trials. Thus, an increased motivational condition produced a significant change in the learning behavior of the subject.

A crippling condition tends to limit the activities and achievement of the crippled child. Likewise, the hard-of-hearing or visually handicapped child is restricted by his sensory handicaps. The mentally retarded child in regular classes is not only handicapped in his educational achievement, but the needs for belongingness and social approval are often not satisfactorily met. Thus, there is a preponderance of problem behavior found among pupils with an IQ of 80 or less in regular classes. Concerning this Maberly has pointed out:

Where no special steps are taken to assist the handicapped to accept or to overcome their difficulties, there follows a distortion of normal development whereby the child fails to make personal relationships and is very liable to display anti-social behavior. He sets out to satisfy his own needs at the expense of those towards whom he feels neither affection nor loyalty.[8]

The role of the psychologist in a study of maladjustments among these children extends beyond the school into the home. Nearly one-fourth of a random sample of 165 cerebral palsied children studied by Miller were reported emotionally maladjusted.[9] Adjustment problems of the parents were recognized as frequently as those of the cerebral palsied children.

CLINICAL SERVICES TO THE TEACHER

The teacher is the key figure in the special education program, especially after the child has been carefully examined and recommendations made relative to his educational needs. Although the teacher of the exceptional child should be acquainted with the contributions of anthropology, sociology, psychology, social case work, and other related fields, he will find many opportunities for seeking help from medicine, psychology, psychiatry, and social case work. For example, when the emotionally disturbed child is referred to the psychologist or psychiatrist, the teacher need not feel that his ability to deal with the child is being questioned or even minimized. Teach-ing the exceptional child is a team affair, with the teacher as the central figure of the team. Certain behavior activities may well be regarded as sympto-matic. The trained and experienced teacher will recognize these as symptoms and seek further help from the specialist who can be of most service in diagnosing the difficulty and in suggesting remedial measures. The teacher of exceptional children, like others with a scholarly attitude, will find it neces-sary to face the fact that because of lack of specific knowledge, training, and experience, his effectiveness will be limited unless he secures help from other sources. Such an attitude is an indication of emotional and professional maturity.

The case study is the most comprehensive of all methods available for studying the individual child. It is especially useful in dealing with mal-adjusted children, children exhibiting signs of undeveloped ability, and chil-dren who are often referred to as 'delinquents'. Although complete case studies require the services of a specialist, teachers are finding an increased need to gather accurate information about their pupils and to study carefully the past history and present status of those confronted with difficult problems. The developmental concept of the child emphasizes the need for complete and accurate records in an effective educational program.

The help of the psychologist will be needed in making a thorough study of an individual child presenting special problems. A complete case history will include the family background, health history, physical growth record, social development, mental and educational development, interests and hobbies, special abilities and disabilities, and problems. This information will be supplemented by interviews with and observations of the individual.

The psychologist assists the teacher in dealing with problems arising from learning difficulties, faulty personality structuring, personal and social adjust-ments, and unfavorable home conditions. He is particularly concerned with curriculum materials and teaching procedures appropriate for the individual child.

The psychologist plays an important role as a therapist, although the teacher is the key figure in the instructional program. Many children will need special help; the psychologist either works with the teacher in provid-ing for this special need or works directly with the child. His role in this connection will depend largely upon his training, the training of the teacher, and the facilities available.

Need for Continuous Appraisal and Re-evaluation

The physically handicapped child admitted to an inpatient hospital or convalescent institution or to a special class for exceptional children, or assigned to a teacher for instruction at home, may remain there longer than this service is necessary. Such a practice is not only a costly one, but is a potential source of psychological injury to the individual child. There is a basic need for a careful and continuous evaluation of the progress of each child. This evaluation should emphasize particularly the advancement made in meeting the physical needs of the child and secondary effects that may appear as a result of the handicapping condition or of the special program designed for his benefit. The psychologist plays an important role in preventing or alleviating secondary effects resulting from the handicapped condition. For example, it is noted that the polio child of school age is subject to many very real fears. He needs to be shielded from the worry growing out of or closely related to the crippling condition. The services of a qualified psychologist with clinical training and experience should be available as part of the team that evaluates the physical development and personality structure of the child.

The investigations of the psychologist should take into account any sensory deficiencies present, including the finer sensory abilities such as perception of form and spatial relations or the perception of pitch, tonal qualities, and the like. A differentiation should be made between the child's present functional level and his potential. When the actual functioning level is below the suspected potential, an analysis of possible causes must then be made.

Vocational Guidance and Adjustment

The amount of intelligence required of different jobs has been studied by many investigators. This is most important in connection with the vocational guidance and placement of the mentally handicapped. In a study by Ball, a high correlation was found between intelligence and gross occupational areas.[10] Cookley found that the mentally retarded person can do the repetitious, monotonous type of work with greater efficiency than the bright person.[11] In order to ensure better vocational adjustment on the part of the mentally handicapped, the vocational counselor should make a practical use of intelligence test scores. Through the application of psychological findings relative to job requirements and job satisfaction the mentally and physically handicapped can be placed on jobs for which they are best suited. These studies have shown that there are many jobs available for the physically handicapped and mentally retarded. An educational and guidance program should have as one of its goals vocational adjustment on the part of the individuals concerned.

Research in Special Education

The psychologist is well equipped through training in experimental methods and statistics to conduct needed research with children requiring special education. He makes use of devices available for the assessment of the developmental characteristics and abilities of children. These include such instruments as Gesell Developmental Scales, the Vineland Social Maturity Scale, anecdotal records, varied projective techniques, as well as standardized verbal, non-verbal, and performance tests. He develops new tests and modifies existing tests for use with handicapped children. He studies the developmental characteristics of the exceptional child and makes recommendations relative to a suitable educational program.

There is a need for additional research on the development of nonhandicapped children in order to make a more accurate diagnosis of the deficiency or dysfunction of the exceptional child. For example, the lack of sufficient data on the auditory-perceptual development of children makes the task of accurately differentiating deafness and disturbances of auditory perception of the elementary-school child a difficult one.[12] The Interim Hayes-Binet Intelligence Tests for the Blind is an illustration of the development of test items and the adaptation of many items for use in testing the blind. The development of two forms of the Stanford-Achievement Test, Intermediate Battery in large type, made it possible to evaluate more accurately the educational achievement of those children with visual difficulties. The five verbal tests and the vocabulary test of the Wechsler-Bellevue Scale can be used with the partially seeing and the blind with only slight variation. Handicaps among the crippled are so varied that the choice of tests must be made on an individual basis. The cerebral-palsied child presents the most difficult problem, for wide variations in their ability to respond manually or verbally will be found. Obvious difficulties appear from any attempt to determine their mental development on the basis of scores made on existing instruments for measuring intelligence.

Within recent years considerable research has been conducted dealing with the personal and social adjustment of the exceptional. Psychologists are continuously evaluating therapeutic methods of alleviating personality disorders. However, there is a need for additional research bearing on problems involving the mental hygiene of exceptional children.

The psychologist, teacher, and counselor should work together as a team in studying teaching procedures, curriculum provisions, and therapeutic measures for the exceptional. Research is in progress dealing with the vocational possibilities of various exceptional children. There is also needed research in occupational satisfaction, and other problems connected with the exceptional after they have completed a program of education. Such research will furnish a sound basis for an educational and guidance program which will contribute to the optimum development of exceptional children.

FOOTNOTES

1. Shultsky, J.E., Justman, J.E., and Wrightstone, J.W., "Screening Children for Placement in Special Classes for the Mentally Retarded: A Preliminary Report", *American Journal of Mental Deficiency*, 1953, Vol. 57, pp. 687-690.
2. Wallace, Helen M., Slater, Beatrice S., and Steinberg, David, "Checking Pupil Progress in Classes for Cerebral Palsy", *Journal of Exceptional Children*, 1954, Vol. 21, pp. 51-54, 70.
3. Blum, Lucille Hollander, and others, "Trends in Estimating the Mental Maturity of the Cerebral Palsied Child", *Journal of Exceptional Children*, 1951, Vol. 17, pp. 174-177.
4. Cruickshank, W.M., and Dolphin, Jane E., "A Study of the Emotional Needs of Crippled Children", *Journal of Educational Psychology*, 1948, Vol. 39, pp. 295-305.
5. Gates, M.F., "A Comparative Study of Some Problems of Social and Emotional Adjustment of Crippled and Non-crippled Boys and Girls", *Journal of Genetic Psychology*, 1946, Vol. 68, p. 219.
6. Cruickshank and Dolphin, *op. cit.*, p. 304.
7. Lashley, K.S. "Factors Limiting Recovery After Central Nervous Lesions", *Journal of Nervous and Mental Diseases*, 1938, Vol. 88, pp. 733-755.

8. Maberly, Alan, "Delinquency in Handicapped Children", *The British Journal of Delinquency*, 1950, Vol. 1, p. 128.

9. Miller, Melba M., *An Investigation of Secondary Defects Potentially Affecting the Educability of Children Crippled by Cerebral Palsy*, (Ed. D. Dissertation, University of Southern California, 1952), p. 147.

10. Ball, R.S., "The Predictability of Occupational Level from Intelligence", *Journal of Consulting Psychology*, 1938, Vol. 2, pp. 184-186.

11. Cookley, F., "Study of Feebleminded Wards Employed in War Industry", *American Journal of Mental Deficiency*, 1947, Vol. 51, pp. 441-451.

12. Myklebust, Helmer R., "Differential Diagnosis of Deafness in Young Children", *Journal of Exceptional Children*, 1951, Vol. 17, pp. 97-101, 117.

BASIC PROBLEMS IN GUIDANCE IN THE FIELD OF THE EXCEPTIONAL

VELMA YOWELL MORTON

Many of the guidance problems for the exceptional child are not problems because he is an exceptional child, but rather because he is a child. The exceptional child will have to meet all of the problems that the so-called average child will meet; in addition, he will be required to meet some other problems. We are all exceptional in that we have our own peculiarities and our own particular restrictions and limitations.

The term 'guidance', as used in this chapter, refers to those services rendered to the individual for the purpose of assisting, as much as possible, the individual to adjust to his present situations and to plan for the future so that he may be able to support himself and, perhaps, a family.

To plan for the future, ALL children must consider their needs, abilities and limitations, their interests, their opportunities, and their social responsibilities. In considering some of these, the exceptional child will be required to adjust to definite limitations which are beyond his control.

GUIDANCE SERVICES FOR THE EXCEPTIONAL CHILD

If we are to provide a complete guidance service for all individuals, we must include provisions for: (1) helping each individual to analyze himself and understand that analysis; (2) promoting in each individual the development of interests and desires that are attainable for him; (3) helping him to learn those things about his environment that are important in his planning for the future; (4) allowing him to experience actual planning and choosing in his activities; and (5) aiding him in gaining access to opportunities for putting into his daily living those ideas which will help him in his long time planning for the future.

All of these services must be provided to all of the children. The exceptional child will need other guidance services because of the existence of his handicaps. The school will be able to furnish the services that are needed by all; but for the exceptional child, the school may not be able to assume the responsibility for all needs. Some of these services can come best through the participation of an outside agency which can work closely with the school and which has at its disposal special resources for the handicapped beyond those that the school can supply.

GUIDANCE FOR THE PHYSICALLY HANDICAPPED

The behavior of children both at home and in school has attracted more interest in exceptional children than in any other type. This is because malbehavior disturbs classes and upsets the routine of school and the home.

Malbehavior arises from conditions within the child or from external influences that are not even understood by most people. If a child is totally blind or totally deaf, those conditions are obviously the reason for his major behavior. We are inclined to make allowance for a blind child or deaf child, but not for the actual behavior.

There is a distinction between behavior problems and personality problems. This was pointed out by Ackerson, who mentioned that personality problems which affect others to some degree may be considered behavior problems. Recessive or withdrawing behavior, which mainly affects the individual, is an example of a personality problem.[1]

Every individual has his own needs, motives and drives; these are the basis for his behavior. A physical handicap does not mean an intellectual handicap. A severe handicap of physique often imposes very definite restrictions upon the range of choices open to an individual. This means a very definite problem as far as his personal adjustment is concerned. A very young child may struggle and even exhibit rage when his bodily movements are restricted. As he grows older he is more able to control and show mastery over many of his movements.

Physical handicaps all tend to reduce the range of activities in which an individual may participate or lower the level of performance. This may cause frustration.

The presence of an obvious handicap may lead the parents to devote an extraordinary amount of attention to a child. This over-protection may produce an over-inhibited and dependent personality. Hypersensitiveness, shyness and withdrawing behavior may be expected in children who have been over-protected.

Other parents may reject the handicapped child. This extreme rejection has a very definite effect upon the child. The feeling of "not being wanted" causes the child to retire into a far corner and give up.

Then we have families who refuse to recognize a handicap as such — this refusal may be on the part of a parent or it may be the child. We often see children attempting activities which he will experience failure just because there is a physical blockage. This experiencing failure often has a marked influence on a child's behavior.

If the child who is physically handicapped is to achieve the one big goal in life, that of taking his place in society and to make the most of his possibilities, he will need much guidance to overcome some of his special problems.

GUIDANCE FOR THE MENTALLY DIFFERENT

A mentally retarded child may have a much greater effect on the parent than on himself. The more retarded the child, the less he realizes his condition. The effect on the parents may cause them to react in many ways that definitely affect the behavior and wellbeing of the child.

The attitude parents take toward the mentally handicapped child varies. Some have great pity for him and over-protect him. They may shower him with affection. Others may be ashamed of him and reject him completely. Either reaction will cause the child to develop traits that may be very difficult to overcome.

The mentally handicapped child is essentially narcissistic in nature. He seldom has very deep feeling toward others. This has been pointed out by Harms.[2] He lacks foresight and judgment, naturally he cannot comprehend abstract situations. Changes are difficult for him. He is different from the physically handicapped child in that he is often unaware of his limitations. With the physical handicap the child was forced to see his limitations by his failure at being able to do some things. This failure to realize his limitations may cause him to experience failure a great number of times. Repeatedly experiencing failure and finding no means of progress toward acceptable goals leads to the disintegration of personality.

The gifted child has been defined and selected in accord with high I.Q. L. Terman referred to those children whose intelligence quotients 130 or higher, as 'gifted'. We may not be able to identify all gifted children with intelligence tests. Expression might have been blocked in some children by insecurity which may be traced to the home. The gifted child has been shown to be a physically superior, attractive, well -rounded individual. Typically he is modest and socially well-adjusted. Anderson[3] has reported in a study that there are five types of discipline problems somewhat common among gifted children: (1) disorderly discussion in classrooms; (2) expressions of disappointment at not being heard; (3) egotism; (4) indolence; (5) truancy. Disciplinary cases are common and criminal records occur.

Brilliant minds sometimes use their wits for success in unprofitable pleasures and pursuits. The gifted child is often neglected and this may affect considerably his mental, social and normal life.

The gifted were superior when compared in personality traits with the average child. In behavior adjustments and moral traits the gifted as a group compare favorably with the average.

Guidance for the Socially Handicapped

The term 'socially handicapped' includes children who are usually spoken of as truants or delinquents and who often are educated in parental or farm schools or in state industrial schools. It also includes those who are potential truants or delinquents. We may find this group of children among the physically handicapped, the mentally handicapped, or the so-called normal. They have many of the same problems. There may be many causes for this child being labeled as a socially handicapped child. There are those who claim that such traits are inherited; others believe that there are inherited traits which give an ideal background for growth. Perhaps it is low intelligence, lack of adjustment, emotional instability, physical inferiority, superabundance of physical energy, or abnormal psychic tendencies. These traits are found in varying degrees and combinations that it has been thought that it is the abnormal combination of these traits that causes truancy and delinquency.

SPECIAL GUIDANCE FOR THE EXCEPTIONAL CHILD

The preceding paragraphs have offered us some of the basic problems of the various types of exceptional children. If we are going to render the services to these individuals that are necessary for the purpose of assisting the individuals to adjust to his present situations and to plan for the future so that he may be able to support himself and, perhaps, a family, then we are going to have a definite program in guidance.

Guidance must take into account the unique qualities of the individual. There must be a very careful diagnostic study which will reveal these qualities. It is very necessary that we assemble the information necessary for a detailed picture of each child's interest, abilities, and problems in such a way that it may help a child succeed. It will be necessary to classify the needs and potentialities of children. These will, in turn, have to be interpreted to the parents and community. If this is done it will be possible to bring to bear all resources in meeting the needs of children. Then it will be necessary to give experiences which will produce confidence. This must be done in such a way that children may help themselves.

The exceptional child needs guidance, whether it be the formal type as offered by many schools or the kind that can be given in schools that lack these services. Some of the steps that can be taken to guide these children toward the attainment of their goals are:

1. Give the child a chance to feel success by giving him tasks that he can perform as effectively as his classmates.
2. Recognize the handicapped child's successes whenever possible.
3. Present new activities to the exceptional child so that he may experience new interests.
4. Teach for increased tolerance. It is very important that this type of child be appreciated.
5. Give as much remedial instruction in basic school skills as possible.
6. Give as much corrective treatment for the specific handicaps as possible. Provide equipment necessary to correct the handicap as much as possible.
7. Give placement in special groups if that placement is going to give these individuals a chance for improvement.
8. There must be vocational guidance for all types of exceptional children. A great deal of this can be done in schools, but there is a very valuable contribution to vocational adjustment by non-school agencies, — The Division of Vocational Rehabilitation Agency and many private and public rehabilitation agencies.

FOOTNOTES

1. Ackerson, L., *Children's Behavior Problems* (University of Chicago Press: Chicago, 1931).
2. Anderson, R. G., "The Problem of the Dull-Normal Child", *Mental Hygiene*, 1927.
3. Harms, M., "Casework with Adult Mental Defectives in a Placement Program", *American Journal of Mental Deficiency*, 1947, pp. 510-518.

GUIDANCE FOR EXCEPTIONAL CHILDREN AND YOUTH

GEORGE LAVOS

Guidance for exceptional children and youth is a many-sided process involving both the rational and the emotional. From one view, guidance involves a description of the personal mechanisms used in psychological adjustment. From another, guidance includes the description of reactions of others to the exceptional individual. Guidance is also a process by which the exceptional individual may realize suitable goals for himself and by which those in whose world the exceptional individual lives may adjust to his conditions and aid him in his growth. Entwined in guidance are the historical attitudes toward disabling conditions that stem back hundreds of years, highly personal feelings about physical and mental integrity within the concept that the individual develops about himself, and cultural standards of personal attractiveness and strength. Appeals for aid, publicity highlighting a unique aspect, and professional accentuation on special needs enter into the guidance of exceptional individuals. Guidance has been confounded by the rapid plunge from observations to systems of amelioration, by the gap between what is rationally known and what is emotionally felt, and by the multiplicity of helpful suggestions which may sometimes be contradictory.

Guidance pervades the child's life within the home, extends into his acceptance of himself as well as his status with others, and broadens into the expanding physical and social worlds he enters after leaving the home. It deals with self understanding, with achieving socially acceptable goals consistent with his capacities and interests, in addition to gaining experiences that foster the two.[1]

THE OUTCOMES OF EXCEPTIONAL CONDITIONS

Although some exceptional conditions are temporary while others are progressive or static, any condition which affects the child for a time may have an aftermath in his adjustment which must be encompassed in a guidance program. These adjustments become part of the child, remaining with him as an adolescent, a youth, and an adult. The extent to which these adjust-ments arising from the exceptional condition expedite or hinder his growth is a guidance problem confronting parents and educators.

The effects of an exceptional condition may be described from three view-points: the physical or the immediate, the reactions of others or the societal, and the reactions of the individual himself or the personal. These outcomes may operate within a short time or be extended through many years of the child's life. They may be only partially operative. Some of the conditions may be immediately apparent as in an orthopedic child, or disclosed only under certain conditions as in a hard-of-hearing child. Some are revealed only in special examinations such as cardiac impairments.

Immediate Outcomes. The immediate outcomes are primarily physical in nature and are commonplace in the inability to walk, see, or hear as others do. There are secondary outcomes that follow restricted use of arms and heart, eyes and ears. Although a child with a disabled leg may be able to walk and stand, he may be unable to plane a piece of wood because he cannot lean over sufficiently to put his weight behind the movement. The triology of the deaf child who cannot hear ordinary speech and consequently does not learn without special instruction to talk or to use the ordinary symbols of language is well known. Blindness, too, has secondary outcomes in limited perceptions, control of the environment, and in other ways.[2]

The primary outcomes may be described in terms of physiology and anatomy. Some have even yielded to measurement in an easily understood scale. The secondary outcomes lie within the area of control of objects, in mobility in the environment, in the extent of experiences, in the perception of objects, and in establishing duplicating cycles of communication.

Societal Outcomes. Even before the primary and secondary outcomes of an exceptional condition are felt in the child's life, outcomes of its presence arise from the reactions of parents and other family members as well as from those of peers and neighbors. One group of reactions are rationally based; these often take the form of restrictions on the child's behavior for his own safety. At some point, however, personal judgment may become erroneous and establishing restrictions in areas in which the child can actually function. On the basis of judgment alone an impairment may be considered more extensive than it is. No thought may be given to alternate ways of meeting the situation. For the child's own good, actual or supposed, limits may be set on the range of his exploring activities, and from such limits it is but a step into rationalizations for underlying emotional reactions of a distance-main-taining nature, disbelief in abilities, and others.

On the other hand, there are reactions of a more subtle nature, often shown in attitudes of those in intimate contact with the child. Barker has outlined several of these.[3] Because of guilt feelings, for example, "the parents of a crippled child are . . . prone to over-protect or reject him or to do both". Meyer has pointed out that in a home in which the level of communication is verbal, and physical demonstration of affection is restricted, deaf children become aloof and withdrawn, turning their interests to objects rather than people.[4] The penetration into the child's life of certain types of emotional and attitudinal response on the part of the family may result in the develop-ment of behavior within the child which may not be healthful or desirable.

In a broader perspective, there are reactions of groups in less intimate contact with the child which have a bearing on his growth. When asked to rate the disabled in various ways, sophisticated people, — college and high school students and professional men, — indicated a favorable attitude. On the other hand, in 80% of the jokes surveyed in a study, the disabled were clearly depreciated. Barker, on the bases of these facts and of nicknames, religious practices, and characters in novels, concluded that although expressed attitudes of sophisticated people are often favorable, an undercurrent of hostility or depreciation was present.[5] Tenny also outlined the devaluated status of the exceptional child in present-day society.[6] And Johnson and Kirk brought the attitude of the non-exceptional to the classroom itself in their study of the maintenance of social distance between the typical child and his mentally handicapped fellow classmate on the grounds of undesirable behavior in the handicapped child.[7] Whether the same or similar reactions develop when other exceptional children are placed in non-segregated classes has yet to be demonstrated.

In yet another way society sets the stage for the role that an exceptional condition may play in a child's life. Through pity society places some exceptional children in a somewhat privileged and yet devaluated status. Laycock said that such a sentiment is "found in the members of many organizations which help handicapped children. From their own 'normality' they look down upon such children as inferior beings who need help".[8]

Popular conceptions have a force in society's attitude toward the exceptional child. Society has attributed a considerable number of qualities to the exceptional, ranging from the extra-normal to the negative and undesirable. To the blind, capacities have been attributed beyond the physiological limits of their tactual sense although some studies reveal a lower-than-normal capacity. Another instance was the affirmation of an obstacle sense before study showed the true nature of how obstacles were perceived by the blind. To the deaf have been given a visual and vibration sensory capacity greater than normal.

In the social sphere the attribution of qualities continues. Studies of personality traits attributed to crippled youths showed that their fellow students regarded them as closer to realizing ideals of behavior in such areas as kindness, conscientiousness, unselfishness, average in others, and farthest in social adaptability, sensitiveness, self-confidence, and others.[9] In citing opinions of authorities Brunschwig showed that attitudes toward the deaf run a gantlet from 'as good as the next fellow' to the undesirable or derogatory such as suspicious, persecution-minded, and so forth.[2]

Not all exceptional are equally favored. Strong showed that while crippled and blind were liked by 29% and 25% of a group of professional men, only 16% liked deaf mutes. The converse was true about the dislikes of the group: 19% and 16% liked the first two, while 25% disliked the last.[10]

Popular conceptions play a role within the home as well. Unusual, annoying, immature, or emotionally disturbed behavior in exceptional children may be accepted by parents as invariable concomitants of the condition in somewhat the same fashion that certain theories link physical defects and personality traits so that the terms "crippled personality," "tuberculous personality," would be acceptable.[11] More than one parent has taken a deaf child for his first day of school thinking that a temper tantrum was a normal way of behaving on his part.[12] Such permissive attitudes on the part of the family may encourage behavior which will be unfavorable at a later time.

The societal outcomes of an exceptional condition in a child often operate earlier than the physical. Stereotyped thinking and emotions predominate in these outcomes, reactions to the condition obliterating reaction to the individual and his particular situation. Society's behavior toward the exceptional is both devaluative and restrictive although there are verbalized traces of a more favorable nature. At times a compensation is thought to exist beyond normal limits.

Personal Outcomes. The exceptional child's growth is not only bounded by the physical and social outcomes but circumscribed by his own reactions. Before he can verbalize to any extent, he reacts emotionally to rejection and over-solicitude within his family and in broader social worlds. He may accept a role based on the expectations of those he associates with. He develops his concepts of what he can and cannot do from those of the people with whom he lives. From his perceptions of himself in relation to other people and objects in the environment, concepts of personal capacity, status, and membership develop.

Because the child mingles with other groups as he leaves the family circle and because groups differ in their reactions to him, these concepts may develop ambiguously or even in a contradictory way. If, on the other hand, his world is limited to his immediate family in which he may be highly cared for, he finds satisfaction in this and may not wish to leave it.[13,14] Or if he leaves it, he may believe he does not have to meet the same standards others do, as Bauman showed is true of some blind youth.[15]

The social setting in which exceptional children and youth find themselves may result in establishing superficial relationships with others. The exceptional individual restrains himself from intimacy because he fears a lack of understanding on the part of others.[16,17]

Another facet of the interaction of the exceptional child and his social world lies in the sources of his motives. Both Barker in writing of the loyalty of disabled employees[18] and Cruickshank in introducing the problem of fear in crippled children[19] raised the question of fear, guilt, inadequacy, and insecurity as sources of behavior in exceptional individuals. Although such tension-producing feelings are powerful, they may not be healthful because they may have physical effects. On the other hand, society may abet an exceptional individual in his desire not to assume responsibilities by maintaining that his condition is so severe that he need not seek employment or other goals common to his social group, thus constricting motivation.

These are illustrations of some of the dynamic aspects of the personal outcomes of the interaction of the exceptional individual and the social worlds in which he lives. His role is ambiguous; sometimes his is depreciated, at other times favored. His path may be narrowed and expectations reduced to the minimum; he may be required to meet every-day standards.

The effects of this ambiguous role lie within his personal feelings and his behavior. Commonly mentioned effects are feelings of inadequacy, incompetence, lack of status, and lack of membership. On a deeper level, as Smock has shown, frustrations are reacted to as threats to the whole personality rather than localized to the specific instance. The child's status is so precariously balanced, that it can be easily tumbled.[20] Feelings of fear, guilt, and hostility have been shown to exist.[21,22] Barker and his associates, after an extended survey of studies, concluded that among the exceptional, while 35% to 45% are as well adjusted as the typical, there is a greater incidence of behavior termed maladjusted or undesirable. Except in extreme instances of long term disabilities or those requiring special care, the kinds of maladjusted behavior parallel those of other persons and cannot be attributed to a specific condition in the exceptional individual. Among the more specific types of behavior commonly observed were those of withdrawal, timidity, and personal sensitiveness and, to a lesser extent, their opposites.[23]

Adjustment for Exceptional Children

Efforts leading toward the personal integration of an exceptional child into the community of his family, neighborhood, and larger social circles have numerous ramifications. Outlining the adjustment for an exceptional child so that he can be at peace within himself, responsive to and accepted by his associates, and able to realize his interests and fulfill his capacities, the previous trichotomy can be profitably repeated. On the immediate level the efforts are numerous: medical and surgical care including plastic surgery, physical and speech therapy, instruction in Braille, establishment of communication methods for the deaf, hearing aids, prosthetic devices, adaptations in work surface heights for chair-bound persons, instruction in heart conservation for housewives running their own homes. These and more are all part of the adjustment efforts designed to duplicate or circumvent physical losses in control of the environment and control of one's self in it. While such efforts are not uniformly effective nor as great in one area as in another, they do exist and have resulted in the reduction of the immediate outcomes of an exceptional condition.

Adjustment efforts have extended into the societal aspects as well. Among the first were the endeavors to convince the public that deaf and blind were intellectually capable of education; even today the campaign must be continued. Because societal attitudes have hit employment of exceptional youth and adults so hard, active campaigns to educate employers as to the work capacity of disabled are now in progress. Gaining acceptance of deaf, blind, and cerebral palsied as well as other groups of exceptional youth as college students in competition with typical students would be another instance. These efforts are characterized by the attempt to overcome the supposed rational restrictions on the range of activities of exceptional children and youth.

More immediate for the problems of childhood are the parent-education programs of many agencies for exceptional children. Such programs, most of which were started within the past 15 years, range from 'round robins' of letters, correspondence courses, or one- or two-week institutes to year-round associations of parents. These groups seeks through either their own initiative or the programming of the sponsoring agency a greater rational understanding first of the child's condition so that his capacities are more clearly seen, and second of resources through which the capacities may be realized. They may also be of some therapeutic value in showing that no family is alone in its problems although question has been raised about the psychological value of a common interest in stressing a pathological condition while possibly neglecting the numerous normal conditions in an exceptional child. From another view there is a danger that the exceptional child may usurp all of the parent's energy, preventing full family living for the parents and siblings. Question may also be raised as to the efficacy of a group approach in reaching such inner feelings as hostility or guilt feelings.[24,25]

Parents have repeatedly raised the question of how they can extend their rational understanding and emotional acceptance of their exceptional child to the neighbor across the back hedge, the corner storekeeper, and others in the immediate environment of the child. Laycock offered several suggestions usable at this point. These suggestions, aimed at the educator of typical children, members of a church, lodge or service club, and others, are carried out through films, panel discussions, skits, calling upon such groups to act as participants in programs for exceptional children and visits to centers for such children.[26] Through these devices a rational understanding and possibly even an emotional acceptance may be gained.

On a broader plane than parent efforts are more formal educative attempts. To a greater extent than earlier, teachers' colleges are offering general survey courses in special education. Nurses and doctors have available literature on the socio-emotional aspects of exceptional conditions.[27] Psychologists are beginning to recognize work with the exceptional as a distinct aspect of their field.[28] For many years before campaigns were taken up by others than special educators and vocational rehabilitation workers, these two professional groups had been educating the public. As Kerr pointed out for a single school for the deaf, education of the public can be established in numerous ways ranging from offering services to the community, acting as host, and concluding with sponsoring of community activities.[29]

There are already in existence programs, and suggestions for many more, to reduce societal misconceptions and emotional reluctance to accept exceptional children to the extent that a rational understanding can influence emotional acceptance. Since attitudes toward exceptional children and adults in times past differed from those of today and since the changes were made by those interested in the exceptional child in spite of possible deep hostility, hope is offered for extension and intensification of this change. In this change the rational understanding will probably outstrip emotional acceptance, and care must be taken that more than lip service is rendered.

In securing emotional acceptance on the part of society, probably the behavior of the exceptional child or youth will have more influence than any other single factor. While a rational understanding of exceptional conditions and the capacities of such children can be shown by demonstration, accounts of accomplishments, and other means, it is in the day-by-day contact which initially may be won by such a rational understanding that emotional acceptance takes place. Consequently, as a final facet of the guidance problems of exceptional children, the personal adjustments of such children to themselves and those they meet day by day must be included.

In entering into a discussion of the personal aspects of adjustment certain basic tenets may be mentioned: (1) The exceptional child is not excluded or exempted from development in achieving an appropriate pattern of dependent-independent behavior; receiving and giving affection; relating himself to changing social groups such as his peers, his fellow workers, his neighbors; conscientious behavior; accepting his sex role; adapting to a growing body; understanding and controlling the physical world; using symbols and conceptual abilities; and relating one's self to beliefs and values. These are the mental hygiene goals for all children, including the exceptional, for their integration into society.[30] (2) His exceptional condition, after all physical restorative efforts have been made, is a permanent characteristic and must be coupled with other characteristics he has in his guidance. (3) He will grow up to become an adolescent, a youth, and an adult leaving behind the worlds of his parents, his special school, and his doctors and other therapists. (4) Psychological studies have not shown that exceptional children develop any compensatory capacities to counterbalance their losses.[31] (5) The World in which they will compete for jobs, membership in social circles, and material success is seldom hospitable toward them, often indifferent or callous economically, probably pitiful otherwise, and possibly even hostile. (6) Personal adjustments are the outcome of the interplay of the individual and adjustment efforts for his benefit on the immediate and societal levels.

Basic to personal adjustment is the acceptance of the exceptional condition as permanent. The individual cannot cope with any problem of vocational adjustment, of marriage, or of any other major decision if he does not recognize emotionally that the condition is permanent. Some may echo parents, relatives, and others who do not wish to be harsh that some medical or other aid may alleviate the condition. Others may base their decisions on a rejection of the presence of the condition.

If the condition is accepted as permanent, no matter how hard the hope to the contrary dies, the next step becomes feasible. This lies in the rejection of the concept of an absolute standard of normalcy. If an absolute standard is the only standard, then the possession of an exceptional condition is a stigma to be hidden by doing all things in the same words and actions that typical people use. Inward anxieties about keeping face, about being discovered, about suffering further privation and greater expenditure of energy may be the outcome.[32]

If, on the other hand, a relative definition of normalcy is accepted, this would be in keeping with trends in medicine, education, and psychology which consider normalcy as a range, not a pinpoint, and as having a changing nature, not a fixed one. Alternates in expressions, in actions, and in thoughts becomes acceptable and necessary. Achievement is made within a range or normalcy, not either success or failure.

In moving toward a relative definition of normalcy, probably the first step would be a clarification of the concept of the right to be different, to be an individual within one's self, not imitating the value systems of those who are typical. While examples of this imitation may be rare, more subtle imitations exist, leading Meirs, in writing of exceptional children, to declare: "Difference is the norm in human experience and our egos play us false in forcing upon us, especially in our youth, a pitiful rejection of our right to be different."[33] Over a decade earlier Pintner had made a similar declaration in writing of educational aims for the deaf.[34]

In accepting range of normalcy and its correlate of the right to be a different individual, there must be a shift in the values attributed by the person to his body or his mind. In vocational adjustment of the exceptional, the slogans are "abilities count," "cross the 'dis' out of disabilities." In a more personal way Barker, in citing research by Dembo in the acceptance of an exceptional condition, said "The larger the scope of values within which a particular loss is evaluated, the less will be the self-devaluation on the basis of a single misfortune".[35] If the meaning of the loss can be defined in words relating it to other characteristics and qualifications such as appearance, cooperativeness, integrity, level of education, technical training, and others valued socially and economically, then the loss is a diminution of an asset, not a liability that causes a bankruptcy of a life. Breadth of interests plays a significant role at this point, for they provide an abundance of activities within which re-evaluation may be made.

Accepting an exceptional condition is not a passive affair of changing definitions of values for that would appear to be almost a rationalization or 'sour grapes' attitude. Acceptance is an active and positive process, not a resignation.[36] As an active process its first step may be using an appliance, learning new skills such as Braille or speechreading, or undergoing lengthy therapy. To use an appliance or to learn a special skill is to accept the fact that some condition can be aided by such use or learning. An aid, to select an extreme example, is often visible and as such is a flag of an exceptional condition. By the same token, when used it is an objective sign of an acceptance. Another aspect of acceptance can be seen in the youth's vocational plans. In such plans he leaves behind him the ordered life of a school in which his condition may have put him on a track with no choice at the switches since he becomes his own switchman in vocational planning. The realism of his planning in terms of his condition and other qualities he may have is an indication of his acceptance of his condition. Other aspirations that he may have, if expressed in terms of his condition and qualifications, are other views of the process.

In addition to planning and learning new skills, the process is identifiable in other avenues of behavior. For the want of another term, one of these avenues may be described as the art of being handicapped gracefully. The form this art will take depends upon the nature of the condition. For the blind it may involve arranging the storage of clothing so that outfits can be harmoniously selected; handling of a checking account techniques for identification of denominations of bills in one's purse and for accepting bills in change and so forth.[37] For the orthopedic it may include maintenance of an appliance so that it does not cause annoyance because of a lack of lubrication; storage of crutches so that they are not in the aisle in bus or subway car; care of clothing so that pressure spots do not become shabby; use of balms for skin pressure spots; etc. For the hard of hearing it may include planning to rest to reduce fatigue; accepting social invitations in terms of the size of the group; keeping the hearing aid in peak operating condition; etc.[38] These are inward adjustments which reduce the annoyance of the conditions to the individual himself and to others with whom he may come in contact. In a certain sense they are compensatory.

Another view of the process lies in the exceptional child and youth's 'public relations program', to adopt a current term. Regardless of what they may do, some exceptional children and youth are conspicuous by reason of their condition and, while others are not noticeable upon sight, they are upon limited acquaintance. Those who notice the individual may respond in certain ways. Staring at those with startling conditions, covertly glancing, or strained avoidance of looking or mentioning, offers of solicitous help or of advice about faddist cures, excessive praise for every-day accomplishments are the ingredients of some of these responses for which the exceptional individual must be prepared. He must develop a pattern of responses to these reactions which will maintain his status, not put him and others who appear as he does in an unfavorable light, and enable him to handle his feelings without emotional harm to himself. By the same token, he must learn that any of these reactions to himself may not be related to his condition at all. They may be the mere notice, cordial courtesy, casual interest, or mannerly behavior accorded any person, exceptional or typical. For this reason, the response of the exceptional child or youth should be premised on the latter rather than the former as the source of behavior.

In a particular way the exceptional child and youth must develop a pattern of response, both inwardly and outwardly, to the offer of help. Because certain physical restrictions on manipulation or mobility inevitably follow as an immediate outcome of the condition, there may be times when help is necessary. The problem for the exceptional arises in the way 'necessary' is perceived by the typical and the exceptional individual. The former may wish to speed the attainment of a goal, the latter may wish to have the satisfaction of accomplishment even if the task is not completed in the same way or as speedily. If the former learns to offer help in terms of the particular situation and the limitations of the exceptional individual rather than the presence of a disability per se, acceptance of help may be eased and the exceptional condition less readily denied.[39]

A part of public relations is the ease with which the exceptional individual makes contact with others. Passing the time of day, extending greetings and courtesies are aspects of recognizing other people as people. The extent to which exceptional youth show such interest in others by entering casual relationships is another indication of the process of acceptance. Going outward, while it calls attention to one's self, is disarming and compels a socially acceptable response.

The use of inspirational literature telling the stories of the accomplishments of handicapped is of special import in motivation. Such biographies and autobiographies have come from the presses in great number within the recent years. While no systematic evaluation of their use has been made, Baker pointed out that the use of such literature with patients recovering from some major handicapping condition may leave something to be desired.[40] Although such writings may have therapeutic value to the writer, further study of such literature as an aid in the establishing of goals, compensation, or overcoming defects is definitely needed. At present it appears that such literature may have value in the extent to which the exceptional individual can identify himself with the leading character and to which the situations for the two are related.

In a deeper and more pervasive way, the exceptional individual may find in religion an adjustment he can secure in no other way as extensively or as permanently. Both Laycock and Garrett reiterate the thought that in the spiritual world the exceptional may gain some measure of security and acceptance.[41-43] Although the actual situation as seen through the eyes of a group of orthopedic individuals with apparent disabilities may leave something to be desired,[44] yet the weight of experience clearly indicates that acceptance of an exceptional condition may be aided by identification with a religious group.

CONCLUSIONS

The guidance of exceptional children cannot be achieved through the development of programs at any one level, whether it be that of the school or clinic. Guidance is a web in which are entwined numerous strands of our culture, some abetting and some hampering adjustment. It extends from technology and social groups of many kinds to the innermost feelings of human beings. In guidance the multiplicity of the facets requires the cooperative efforts of many people, of whom many may have only casual contact with the exceptional individual, as well as the support of the exceptional individual himself.

While the trends that have been traced have not been statistically verified in most instances, many observations, including autobiographical, have been made. Not all trends apply to all exceptional conditions. As time passes some will undoubtedly have to be discarded as untrue. Others may be more adequately defined. Trends in relation to specific conditions, degrees of conditions, and particular situations will be worked out which, when translated with guidance, will aid in adjustment.

FOOTNOTES

1. Henry, N., ed., *The Education of Exceptional* Children, 49th Yearbook National Society for the Study of Education (University of Chicago Press: Chicago, 1950), pp. 83-102.
2. Lowenfeld, B., "Effects of Blindness on the Cognitive Functions of Children", *The Nervous Child*, 1948. 7:45-54.
3. Barker, R., *et al.*, *Adjustment to Physical Handicap and Illness*, Science Research Council, Bulletin No. 55, Revised, 1953, pp. 85-93.
4. Meyer, E., "Psychological and Emotional Problems of the Deaf Child", *American Annals of the Deaf*, 1953. 98:472-77.
5. Barker, *op. cit.*, p. 84.
6. Tenny, J., "The Minority Status of the Handicapped", *Exceptional Children*, 1953. 19:260-4.
7. Johnson, O., and Kirk, S., "Are Mentally Handicapped Children Segregated in Regular Grades?", *Exceptional Children*, 1950. 17:65-69.
8. Laycock, S., "Community Understanding of the Exceptional Child", *Exceptional Children*, 1954. 21:47-49.
9. Barker, *op.cit.*, pp. 71-73.
10. Garrett, J., ed., *Psychological Aspects of Physical Disability* (Office of Vocational Rehabilitation, Department of Health, Education, and Welfare: Washington, D.C., 1952), p. 136.
11. Block, W., "Personality of the Brain Injured Children", *Exceptional Children*, 1954. 21:92.

12. Garrett, *op. cit.*, p. 143.
13. Hayward, E., *Psychological Problems of the Physically Disabled* (Office of Vocational Rehabilitation, Department of Health, Education, and Welfare: Washingon, D.C., 1947).
14. Grossman, M., "Emotional Aspects of Rehabilitation", *American Journal of Psychiatry,* 1953. 109:849-52.
15. Bauman, M., *A Comparative Study of Personality Factors in Blind, Other Handicapped, and Non-handicapped Individuals,* Rehabilitation Service Series, #134 (Office of Vocational Rehabilitation, Department of Health, Education, and Welfare: Washington, D.C., 1950).
16. Cholden, L., "Group Therapy with the Blind", *Group Psychotherapy,* 1953. 6:21-29.
17. Garrett, *op.cit.*, p. 21.
18. Barker, *op. cit.*, p. 370.
19. Cruickshank, W., "Relation of Physical Disability to Fear and Guilt Feelings", *Child Development,* 1951. 22:291-98.
20. Smock, C., and Cruickshank, W., "Responses of Handicapped and Normal Children to the Rosenzweig P-F Study", *Quarterly Journal of Child Behavior,* 1952. 4:156-64.
21. Bauman, *op. cit.*
22. Cruickshank, *op. cit.*,
23. Garrett, *op. cit.*, p. 5.
24. Greenberg, H., "Problems of Parents of Handicapped Children", *Exceptional Children,* 1950. 17:1-7.
25. Levy, J., "A Study of Parent Groups for Handicapped Children", *Exceptional Children,* 1952. 19:19-26.
26. Laycock, "Community Understanding of the Exceptional Child".
27. Seidenfeld, M., *Psychological Aspects of Medical Care* (C. C. Thomas: Springfield, Ill.,: 1949).
28. Brower, D., and Abt, L., *Progress in Clinical Psychology* (Grune and Stratton: N.Y.C., 1952), Vol. I, Section 2.
29. Kerr., M., "A Program of Community Relationship Activities at the New Jersey School for the Deaf", *American Annals of the Deaf,* 1945. 90:193-205.
30. Association for Supervision and Curriculum Development of the N.E.A., *Fostering Mental Health in Our Schools,* Yearbook, 1950.
31. Pintner, R., et al., *The Psychology of the Physically Handicapped* (Crofts: N.Y.C., 1941).
32. Garrett, *op. cit.*, pp. 21, 22.
33. Miers, E., "The Right to be Different", *Exceptional Children,* 1952. 18:225-8.
34. Pintner, *op. cit.*, p. 180.
35. Barker, *op. cit.*, p. 82.
36. *Counseling for Psychological Acceptance of Disability* (U S. Office of Vocational Rehabilitation, Department of Health, Education, and Welfare: Washington, D.C., 1954.
37. Bindt, J., *Handbook for the Blind* (Macmillan: N.Y.C., 1952).
38. McGrath, F., "The Psychology of the Hard of Hearing", in *Handbook of Information for the Hard of Hearing,* California State Department of Education, 1947.
39. Barker, *op. cit.*, p. 79.
40. Baker, L., "Personal Experience Books", *Hospital Book Guide,* 1952. 13:32-6.
41. Laycock, S., "Problems in the Adolescence of Exceptional Children", *Exceptional Children,* 1943. 9:263-7.
42. *The Church and the Handicapped* (National Council of Churches of Christ: 1954).
43. *Counseling for Psychological Acceptance of Disability.*
44. Wendland, L. "Some Religious Feelings of the Post-Poliomyelitic",*Journal of Social Psychology,* 1953. 38:99-108.

CONTRIBUTION OF GUIDANCE TO THE FIELD OF SPECIAL EDUCATION

RUTH STRANG

The definition of guidance given in the author's *The Role of the Teacher in Personnel Work* (Columbia, 1953) as "a process of interaction in which every individual is helped, through his own efforts, to discover and develop his best potentialities for his personal happiness and social usefulness"[1] applies to exceptional children as well as to their more normal schoolmates. But are there differences in emphasis in the case of exceptional children?

By 'exceptional' we mean the mentally retarded as well as the gifted, those with visual and orthopedic impairments, those with auditory and speech handicaps, the socially and emotionally maladjusted. In fact, it is impossible to draw any hard and fast dividing line between exceptional children and other children. As one teacher said when asked to list the gifted children in her class, "All my children are gifted." Every child has some talent; most children have some degree of physical, intellectual, emotional, or social impairment. And even the most seriously handicapped child has within him some potentialities for growth.

The guidance worker should have a background knowledge of the dynamics of behavior, which is so helpful in understanding the individual child. In general, he should recognize that the secondary emotional effects of a handicap are often more difficult to cope with than the primary difficulty. For example, cerebral palsy or a marked mental deficiency may seriously affect the child's relationship with his parents and teachers and other adults, as well as with his peers. Their attitude toward him and their expectations of him, in turn, affect his idea of himself.

As the child with a serious defect grows older, he often feels more and more misunderstood and rejected. He becomes increasingly lonely. In certain institutions one notices a marked difference between the attitude of very young children with hearing and speech defects, for example, and the attitude of adolescents with the same impairments. At an early age they are hardly distinguishable in general appearance and behavior from normal children; fourteen years later they are quite different from normal adolescents. They tend to be more withdrawn, less secure, more discouraged and frustrated.

Another basic consideration is the effect it has on the child when we label him as 'retarded,' 'a remedial case,' 'a stutterer,' or some other designation that implies inferiority or defect. Wendell Johnson has reported evidence that stuttering becomes worse after the child has been diagnosed and designated as a stutterer. Unskillful or unnecessary referral to clinics may also increase a child's anxiety about himself.

In view of the preceding chapters, it is unnecessary to include here any detailed discussion of the characteristics and common problems of different types of exceptional children. Such information, if used wisely, would make the guidance worker more alert to the special needs of individual children.

In our definition guidance is described as a *process*, not an end result. This does not mean that we are not interested in solving a particular problem or helping the child to make a particular adjustment. It does mean that we are concerned with helping children to learn problem-solving methods. The counselor will see that his charges become acquainted with the process of stating the problem, analyzing the situation, suggesting and evaluating various solutions, choosing the most feasible, and trying it out. Able learners will 'catch on' quickly and learn to solve their own problems with less and less help. Slow learners will need more concrete experience before they are able to apply the method to new situations.

The phrase 'through his own efforts' is especially important for exceptional children. Gifted and talented children are eager to take initiative and responsibility. For their best growth they need freedom with responsibility. But handicapped children also need to solve their own problems. A counselor who *gives* them insights which they could discover for themselves, and suggests plans which they could have thought out, is depriving them of the exciting experience of self-realization. To do something for a handicapped child that he could do for himself is to make him feel less adequate as a person. Underlying all guidance procedures is a philosophy of respect for each person, an appreciation of his assets, an understanding of his desire to make himself as 'good' and complete as possible, and a faith in his ability to use his latent resources.

A constructive relationship between guidance worker and child is basic to the development of self-direction and self-confidence. The counselor establishes such a relationship by presenting himself as a helping, accepting person. This is especially important with children who have experienced multiple rejection by family, teachers, classmates, and playmates. These children fear to venture again into any relationship. Because of this fear they may rebuff the counselor's friendly approach. He should never take such a rebuff personally. Instead, he should patiently persist in his warm feeling toward the child and, in time, convince him that the world is not so hostile and rejecting as his earlier experiences may have indicated. The child grows in the warmth of such a relationship. To maintain the relationship, he will try to behave acceptably.

Children, especially handicapped children, are sensitive about people's feelings toward them. Some rural children made the following spontaneous comments about their teachers:

"Last year I had a teacher who was very unqualified. She called us 'dumb bunnies' and other ugly names."

"My first-grade teacher was nice, and tried to help me in every way she could. She did not have anyone who was her pet. When I was in the first grade I was bashful and she taught me not to be bashful. She liked us and showed us that she liked us, which made us like her."

"In the second grade my teacher was gentle about things that usually make people angry. She always found a way to use pupils, even dumb ones. She could make them feel at home and that they were welcome."

The elementary teacher, who also serves as counselor for his class, guides as he teaches. If he likes and understands his pupils, he helps them to realize their potentialities through living fully day by day at each stage of their development.

Guidance in learning is especially important for mentally retarded children; one must prevent any occurrence which would reinforce their idea that they are failures. One teacher of emotionally disturbed pupils wrote personal directions for each member of the group. For example, one boy received a card which read, "The boy with red hair will sing a song." He could read these directions because all the words were among those which the group had learned, and singing was the thing the red-haired youngster enjoyed most. He read the sentence and carried out the directions, to the delight of all.

Teachers of all exceptional children should know more about the psychology of learning as it applies to these particular pupils. Gifted children, for example, need instruction in critical thinking, enjoy the subtler aspects of the appreciation of literature, and are interested in other high-level reading skills.

Helping children "to discover their potentialities" involves many guidance techniques. The most basic is systematic, accurate observation over a period of time. This is possible in a school situation. In England and Scotland at one time, and this is probably still true, no child was placed in the special schools for the mentally and physically defective until he had been observed for about a year in a regular classroom. This day-by-day observation shows how a child is actually functioning in a school situation; the alert observer will find clues to possible conditions that may be interfering with his optimum learning. Observation can reveal trends in social and emotional as well as in academic development.

Tests, precisely administered and astutely interpreted, yield valuable information about mental ability and achievement, under specified conditions. Sociometric tests reveal patterns of social relationship at a particular time. Of course, interpersonal relations change with circumstances: one youngster might be chosen by many on the day he was giving a party and rejected by many on a day when he had been annoying the other children. Modified sociometric tests and questionnaires may be particularly valuable in indicating other children's relationships with the handicapped child, — how they feel about him, and why they behave as they do toward him. Projective techniques may reveal much of the child's inner world of feeling and meaning, and throw light on his basic personality structure.

The interview offers the individual an opportunity to reveal his feelings. Both parent and child may welcome this opportunity. However, too little consideration is usually given to the client's feelings. Interviews are too often counselor-centered; the counselor is concerned with his own success. In the following case, the counselor accepted and responded to a mother's feeling. The mother knew that her child was mentally defective. She had accepted this fact intellectually but not emotionally. At each interview she would express a hope that some miracle would happen. By recognizing the mother's emotional need to have a normal child, and by constantly emphasizing the things the child could do, the counselor gradually helped the mother to accept both herself and the child.

Since the parents' attitude is such an important factor in the child's adjustment, child guidance often becomes largely parent guidance. Parent conferences should recognize the feelings of fear, anxiety, guilt, and hostility that often beset the parents of exceptional children. In guiding the parents of gifted children, the object is usually to overcome or prevent one or two common detrimental practices — exploitation of the child's talent, or failure to provide sufficient stimulation and suitable experience.

As an indication of vocational aptitude, work samples and try-out experiences are valuable. They are the most direct way of assessing proficiency and interest in a given kind of work. Follow-up studies of exceptional children who have taken certain jobs give a realistic view of their proficiency. For example, many years ago Dr. Emily Burr obtained information on the kinds of work that could be done by adolescent girls with mental ages as low as three years. At the lowest mental age, if they were emotionally stable, they could pack Christmas tree ornaments of the same color in a box. They could not handle the job of packing different-colored balls in a certain pattern.

Tools for synthesizing and interpreting information from various sources include the cumulative record, case study, and case conference. The cumulative record, properly kept, shows trends in academic achievement, school relations, interests, purposes, and health over a period of years. The case study gives still more detailed understanding. The case conference is a valuable method of in-service education as well as an effective means of sharing information and developing insights about an individual.

No item of information should be used singly. A single anecdotal record may only raise the question, "Why?" No important decision should be made on the basis of a single test score. Although the average fluctuation on individual intelligence tests is only about six points, in certain cases test scores of the same individual have fluctuated as much as forty points. Any personal data should be interpreted in the light of all the other information available. There is no other way to protect the child from the discrepancies or inconsistencies of his own records.

Having helped the individual to discover his potentialities, the guidance worker should then help him to develop them — whether the individual possesses one talent or ten talents. Much can be done indirectly by creating conditions favorable to growth. A favorable classroom atmosphere is one in which we find children learning and growing, succeeding in suitable tasks, enjoying more freedom, and engaging in more purposeful activity than is possible in the ordinary classroom. In such an atmosphere there are limits, too, — limits that are necessary to reinforce a child's still inadequate self-control.

Even in a 'lush environment', one that provides the experiences every child needs, some guidance in the use of these experiences is necessary. For example, the teacher can encourage a slow-learning child to choose at first projects that are very easy, that require no special skill or understanding of a process, that can be finished in a short time, and can be displayed for others to admire. Such projects should be somewhat creative, and their end-products should be attractive and useable, though inexpensive. At the other end of the scale, the reading of gifted children may be guided into more varied and deeper channels.

Service activities are especially important for handicapped children. So much has always been done for them; they need the experience of helping others. For example, one cooking class made large quantities of various foods and served them as lunches for younger children whose mothers went out to work during the day.

Many handicapped children have difficulty in making the transition from the special classes in elementary school to high schools where no special provision has been made for them. Hayward High School, California, has made marked progress in overcoming this difficulty.

The suggestion has been made that the duration of the high school program be adjusted to the ability of the pupils — three years for the able learners, four years for the slow learners, and a five-year course for average students who would like to have a year of advanced study while still in high school.

Since reading is such an important tool for life adjustment, the guidance worker should see that all groups of exceptional children who are retarded in reading have the opportunity to reach their optimum efficiency. Surprising progress has been made even with pupils who tested as low as 50 IQ. It is important that the reading teacher use materials and techniques that appeal to the particular pupil and motivate his best effort. Slow learners are usually interested in reading road signs, safety and health signs, labels on cans, ads in newspapers, addresses on envelopes, menus, road maps, and mail order catalogues. Those who are more proficient will read simple stories about teen-agers like themselves, driver education material, simple agricultural bulletins, and pamphlets about vocations. Much more of this simplified material is needed to develop fluency and to convince these pupils that reading can be enjoyable and useful to them.

The last phrase in the definition — "for their personal happiness and social usefulness" — emphasizes the special social responsibility of the gifted, and the possible social contribution of all exceptional children.

The foregoing description of guidance suggests the following trends:
Toward developmental rather than remedial guidance
Toward increasing guidance of parents
Toward recognition of the social purpose of guidance
Toward respect for each individual — his reticence and his resources
Toward client-centered counseling
Toward guidance through the environment, with recognition of the influence of family, community, and world conditions on the individual

Toward placing increased responsibility for guidance on the teacher, as part
    of an all-school team

Toward freedom of choice with responsibility

Toward coordination and continuity of guidance.

All these aspects of guidance can be applied in the field of special education. Exceptional children's need for guidance is very much the same as that of the rest of the school population.

TESTS AND MEASUREMENTS*

MARIE A. CORRIGAN

By definition the exceptional child is one who deviates in some way from what is looked upon as "average". This deviation is sufficiently pronounced to warrant treatment or attention which differs from that offered to the "average" group of children of the same age or educational status.

One readily recognizes the necessity for different attention or treatment in the case of physical handicaps. The visually handicapped are not pitted against those with normal vision in tasks requiring the use of the eyes nor is the crippled child expected to use his body in the same way in which the physically normal child uses his.

The distinction between normal performance and that to be expected from the exceptional child should also be made in the use of test and measurements. Perhaps a little background discussion will serve to underline this factor. Measurement of human qualities involves two things: The designation of a task which will test the quality under consideration, and the evaluation of the performance turned in by a given individual. If, for example, one is interested in knowing how well informed an individual is in anthropology, one must design some task which will test that information; it may be a series of questions, a written discussion on a topic in the field, or the indentification of a series of objects. That, however, is only half the task of testing. When the individual performs the task, one must evaluate the results: Do ten correct answers out of a total of twenty-five represent a poor, fair, or excellent grasp of anthropological information? Although the author of the test may decide arbitrarily that ten is poor or is excellent, the usual procedure is to set an individual's performance against that of a group who have performed the same task. If the group average were twenty correct answers, ten might be rated as poor.

---

*Used by special permission of the Catholic University Press of America. This article first appeared in *Special Education for the Exceptional Child,* edited by the Rev. William F. Jenks (Catholic University Press: Washington, D.C., 1953).

Obviously the group selected must have certain features in common with the individual who is matched against it. The group may, for instance, be fifty persons selected at random from the general population. In that case, all one can say is that the individual seems to be less well informed in the field of anthropology than is the general public. This might be merely an interesting comment about an ordinary citizen. If, however, the individual has just completed a few courses in the field, the fact that his performance was poor when compared with that of the general population would be a serious reflection on the test, the courses, or the individual.

The point to be established here is this: A test or other measurement of a human quality consists not only of the task which checks that quality but it also consists of norms for evaluating the individual's performance. These norms are usally established by the performance turned in by a selected number of other individuals. The suitability of these norms as applied to a particular person is determined, to a considerable extent, by his conformity in other respects to the norm group. This point is particularly important in the choice and the evaluation of tests used with the exceptional child.

To insure proper selection and use of these measures certain questions ought to be answered: (1) What do we wish to measure; (2) What tasks have already been set up for measuring this quality; (3) What group of persons were chosen to establish the norms for the test; (4) Does this child's deviation place him outside that group to such an extent that he cannot fairly be compared with them? (5) Is there any reason why he *should* be compared with the group?

What do we wish to measure when we are working with the exceptional child? First, we wish to identify those deviations which are not readily discernible by ordinary observation; second, we wish to measure specific physical, mental, and social qualities and skills, to diagnose a difficulty, assess a quality, or gauge improvement.

MENTAL TESTS

Since we are dealing with exceptional children in an educational setting, the first information that is important is the mental ability of the child. The common practice is to administer group tests to children in the elementary school. Usually a group intelligence test does not adequately measure the mentally handicapped or the mentally gifted, but close observation of the conduct of the child during the examination; his speed, interest in the task, reaction to directions—these and other test behavior may point out children who can be tested by individual tests—such as the Stanford-Binet.

It is important to discover as early as possible those who deviate. The gifted child should be identified early before he develops poor work habits. His easy success in early grades may lead him to expect the same easy success throughout his life, or it may lead to intellectual pride and snobbery. And, of course, from an intellectual point of view, he ought to be developing his superior ability. Likewise, the dull child who is overlooked may develop feelings of general inferiority, hopelessness, and unwarranted guilt when he is forced to compete with those of much greater ability. The sooner either deviation is discovered, the sooner the school can begin to assist the child to use his own peculiar abilities. There are many group mental tests in use. Among them are these: Terman-McNemar Test of Mental Ability, Otis tests, the National Intelligence Tests, the Pintner General Intelligence Test, and others. The individual test of greatest value at this level is probably the Stanford-Binet. The exceptional child ought to be retested from time to time even on the individual tests since his general adjustment and cooperation may affect his early scores. Many of the tests include some performance, and the dull or crippled child who has been over-protected up to this point may have had little or no experience with simple tasks such as stringing beads or following directions, tasks commonly performed by the average child of the same age. The child's deviation may place him outside the norm group to such an extent that he cannot be compared with them. In this case his experiences are not yet comparable to those of the average child so he may not perform as effectively merely because of lack of experience rather than lack of basic ability.

Likewise certain physical handicaps may render the child unable to perform as average children do on mental tests. The slightly deaf child may not hear directions; the child with poor eyesight may not be able to see pictures or other test media. It is also possible that the examiner will not readily recognize these defects.

If the defect is recognized, the examiner may secure intelligence tests which are designed for persons with defective vision or hearing, or with other handicaps. Dr. Samuel Hayes has adapted the Stanford-Binet for use with the blind. His test, the interim Hayes-Binet Intelligence Test for the Blind, may be secured through the Perkins Institute for the Blind, Watertown, Massachusetts. For the older pupils and adults, parts of the Wechsler-Bellevue Scale may be used without much adaptation. Both the Stanford-Binet and Wechsler-Bellevue tests, of course, require special training to administer and interpret; but they are mentioned here so that those dealing with the exceptional child may know of their usefulness.

There are also Braille adaptations of some of the group intelligence tests used for normal persons. The Kuhlman-Anderson, Otis Classification, and Pressey Mental Survey Test have been so adapted by workers in the field. These group tests are not practical, however, if the individual tests can be administered.

There are several individual performance tests for use with deaf children: The Pintner-Paterson Performance Scale, the Grace Arthur Point Scale, and the Nebraska Test of Learning Aptitude. The latter test has been standardized on deaf children and is available from Dr. Marshall Hickey, the author, who is at Southern Illinois University, Carbondale, Illinois.

Obviously, the testing of crippled children must take into consideration the peculiar disability involved. Limited hand or arm movement, for instance, might affect a performance test. One must be particularly careful in administering and interpreting intelligence tests for children with cerebral palsy. There are some psychologists who doubt the reliability of any mental test score reported for a child with this handicap.

It should be noted that there is a difference between mental or other tests which have been adapted *in form* for use by the handicapped and which have been standardized on such a group. Which is preferable? That depends on the purpose of the test. From a guidance point of view, there are four reasons for trying to gauge the mental ability of a pupil or student. First, to determine whether or not he can profit by the education offered by a particular school or program within that school. Second, to judge the level of achievement to be expected of the pupil within the program to which he has been admitted; third, to discover what the child can do by way of a succeeding educational or occupational step; and fourth to judge the ability of the pupil to advance within that second step.

No doubt, it is clear at this point that the norm groups used should be those which correspond most closely to the group with whom the child will be competing. If the handicapped child is to attend classes with normal children and is to have little or no special assistance, the tests should be those by which one can gauge his ability or aptitude when placed with normal children. If, however, his education is to be carried on within special groupings, the norms should be based upon groups handled in a special manner.

This observation should be made for the first two purposes of mental and achievement testing. The situation may change if one is interested in knowing whether or not the child can leave the special classes and go—let us say—into normal high school or college classes, or into occupations in which normal persons are engaged. If that is planned, the norms used should be those of the normal student or worker.

Achievement Tests

Not only does the teacher or counselor wish to know the mental ability of the exceptional child but he also wishes to know the extent to which the child has profited by any formal or informal learning experiences. This may be gauged by achievement tests which are available in batteries covering several subjects or in individual tests for specific subjects. Much of what has been said about mental tests also applies here. That is, the child should be measured against those with whom he will compete, and the handicap of the child must be taken into account in selecting the test. At present sufficient work has not been done in this area to provide us with an adequate selection of achievement tests for the handicapped. It is well, however to be realistic about the academic demands upon the handicapped child. What will he be doing in five, ten, fifteen years; in the light of that, what is necessary in the way of educational background? What will he be doing with his leisure? What occupations might he enter? What manner of life will he follow? Skill in reading, for instance, will play a greater part in the future life and happiness of some types of handicapped than with others. Likewise with mathematics or other basic learnings. For that reason difference in achievement may well be analyzed in terms of future needs.

The purpose of an achievement test is to gauge the informational background and proficiency in basic skills needed for academic work, to plan remedial work, and to judge the progress of the pupil in learning.

Sensory Tests

Those working with the handicapped are especially interested in tests for sight, hearing and speech defects. Most of these defects require the type of diagnosis which only a medical specialist can give. However, teachers often give screening tests in all these areas, and by this means select those persons who need closer examination by the highly trained diagnostician. The Minnesota Mobile Speech Clinic offers one example of these two kinds of examiners. In 1946 the Mobile Clinic was set up at the suggestion of the Minnesota Society for Crippled Children and Adults. A public health nurse preceded the unit and instructed lay persons in the use of the audiometer with groups. The traveling unit, consisting of four clinicians, speech and hearing therapists, followed and retested the referrals. You may, incidentally, be interested to know that in the first two and half years of their work, they found that 9 per cent of the children contacted had some impairment of hearing and that about 4 percent needed special education because of this impairment. About the same proportion of the child population had serious speech defects requiring special attention.

There are several tests available for general screening of visual defects. The most commonly used, perhaps, is the Snellen E-Chart. While this is simple to use, it reveals only a limited range of visual defects. The Massachusetts Vision Test, used by the Massachusetts Department of Public Health, probably reveals a wider range of visual defects. Another instrument commonly used for this purpose is the Betts Telebinocular.

Audiometers are available for both group and individual testing. Speech defects can be detected by listening to the pupil and the written material given to the child under observation can be selected to sample letter and sound combinations in which speech defects are most pronounced.

Lowered vitality is another health defect which may set a child apart from his companions. This, of course, is the result of some other health problem: malnutrition, tuberculosis. an infection, lack of proper rest, emotional disturbances, etc. The tests for lowered vitality may be those which check the physical condition, such as X-Ray, dental examination, blood tests, or tests of basal metabolism. Or they may consist of checks on the child's eating and sleeping habits, or his emotional adjustment. The former tests must, of course, be given only by medical specialists. The latter will be discussed in the next section of this paper. Physical defects can be detected in many cases by careful observation of the child: his response when addressed, his approach to printed material, his complaints of pain, etc. The classroom teacher can train herself to be observant of all children and in this way she can often detect the exceptional child so that he can be given more intensive study.

Personality and Adjustment Tests

Perhaps no other area of diagnosis has aroused more interest and more criticism than that centered on the human personality. Those who work with others in an educational, psychological, or medical capacity are aware of the fact that personalities differ and that the differences are not only marked but also may seriously affect the health, social relations, and intellectual and spiritual life of the persons. The personality differences are particularly difficult to describe and sometimes hard to detect since many of them do not manifest themselves in striking, overt ways. Or at least not in ways recognized by the average person. For this and other reasons, one is apt to look hopefully at any objective description of personality or measure of adjustment.

Our initial interest is to detect personality deviates who might not reveal their difficulties until much later in their school or adult lives. When test or behavior reveals strong deviations, we are interested in diagnosing the nature of the difficulty and later in evaluating the progress toward adjustment.

Personality and adjustment testing is fraught with many difficulties: The wide variation in the definitions of personality and of adjustment makes it inevitable that those who design measures of personality will differ in that which they try to measure. The highly subjective and personal nature of the questions or items of a test may lead the subject to "fake" his answers in order to give a socially acceptable picture of himself. The moods and variations which mark the human personality make it dangerous to establish any stable quantitative or qualitative description of a given personality and to act upon this description for any length of time. When personality tests are used for screening purposes, it may easily happen that a given number of pupils will fake the test and that others will not be currently involved in any particular stress situation which tries the human personality. Both of these groups may, therefore, appear to be better adjusted than they actually are; normal scores may lull the teacher into indifference even in the face of some later manifestations of maladjustment.

The weakness of many personality scales need not, however, lead one to conclude that the study of personality is hopeless or that all tests in this area must be avoided. Rather, it should lead one to exercise caution in their selection, administration, and interpretation; and it should encourage one to assume some responsibility, if possible, for furthering the research that is being done in this field.

There are several approaches to personality study. First, one may secure the opinions of others regarding the specific traits under observation. This is commonly done by means of rating scales, case histories, verbal reports, and anecdotal records. In the first group there is, for example, the Haggerty-Olson-Wickman Behavior Rating Scale, which may be checked by the respective teachers of the pupil. Other rating scales are available or may easily be designed. Anecdotal records consist of a brief description, usually under seventy-five words, of a child's behavior in a particular situation. This may or may not be accompanied by the writer's interpretation of the behavior. Obviously, isolated reports have much less value than consistent reporting of many aspects of behavior as observed by several persons.

The second approach is that of the child's own fairly free report of his attitudes, feelings, experiences, interpretation of events or situations. Diaries, letters, and autobiographies are useful here. The autobiography is especially useful if the topics or chapter headings are well chosen: My Greatest Disappointment, My Favorite Friend, The Most Unhappy Day of My Life, If I Had a Thousand Dollars, If I Could Run Our Home (or School) for One Week, Teachers I Have Had. These and similar topics often reveal the thoughts and feelings of the child. Care, however, must be exercised in their interpretation: The child with a vivid imagination may be inspired by certain topics. The child who finds it difficult to express himself in writing may produce little or nothing, and this in commonplace terms.

The third approach is through the questionnaire or test. Items are selected to tap specific areas of adjustment. The Bell Adjustment Inventory, for example, makes an attempt to study the adjustment in home, health, social, and emotional areas. A second test has been designed by Bell to check only school adjustment.

The Vineland Social Maturity Scale, and Rath's Self-Portrait N test have been used by various persons who have done research in the adjustment of exceptional children.

The fourth means of appraising personality and adjustment is through the unstructured and association tests. This may be called the projective approach in that the child interprets a picture or responds to a word in terms of his own experience and feelings. Among these tests are Rogers' Word Association Test for Children, Schwartz' Social Situation Pictures for Children, as well as the better known Rorschack ink blot test and the Murray Thematic Apperception Test, which has pictures for older children.

Tests of Special Aptitudes

Test of special aptitudes for normal children are limited in number and scope, and of these only a few have been adapted for the handicapped child. The Seashore Measures of Musical Talents, the MacQuarrie Mechanical Ability Tests, the Pennsylvania Bi-Manual, and the Minnesota Rate of Manipulation Tests have been given to exceptional pupils. Mrs. Mary K. Bauman, for example, has done considerable work in adapting existing aptitude tests for the blind. More should be done for those with other kinds of handicaps.

The Use of Test Information

While the scope of this paper does not extend to the guidance of exceptional children, it is important to dwell at least briefly on the use of the information obtained through tests.

The information may be used to adjust the curriculum and teaching procedures so that the exceptional child may use his peculiar abilities to the greatest advantage and overcome his handicap wherever possible. The information may also be used in assisting him to make his vocational choices.

It is especially important in the guidance of the exceptional child that the counselors and teachers themselves have a comprehensive grasp of the meaning of vocation. The word must not be narrowed so that it become synonymous with *occupation* or even with the *religious state in life*. Rather, it must include man's total vocational life: his call to personal sanctity, his invitation to achieve this in one of three states of life, and his personal fitness to serve his fellow men in a particular occupation. It is of the utmost importance to keep the comprehensive picture in mind when advising or guiding the handicapped. When vocation means occupation, the handicapped finds his vocational life constricted. Many doors are closed to him and others open only reluctantly. Even when vocation means the choice of a state in life, the handicapped finds his vocational life difficult and sometimes frustrating: Religious life is frequently denied him; marriage is often an unattainable goal;

and single life must be lived within limits prescribed by the handicap. When, however, the vocational concept is based on personal sanctity, the vocational world of the handicapped holds tremendous possibilities. In no other concept does deprivation and suffering have any value, except insofar as it arouses scientific or social efforts to relieve it. But in the Christian pursuit of sanctity, suffering is a coin which has untold value for personal and social good. The state of life and the occupational limitations become acceptable if one can see that any state, properly lived, and any legitimate occupation suited to the ability of the worker and the needs of society are the raw material with which one works out the same destiny as that sought by the physically favored, the mentally brilliant, or the socially well-placed person who enters a more popular state of life or follows an occupation having greater worldly prestige.

Not only ought the counselor of the handicapped help the individual to appreciate the value of suffering even when it means inactivity, but also to know the value of poverty. The handicapped may never know the joy of giving freely of his abundance, for his occupational opportunities will be limited. Their cost of living may be far greater than that of normal workers. The blind or the crippled cannot save money on home conveniences, shopping, transportation, mending and other personal short-cuts. They may have to pay higher insurance; their education may cost more because of personal services needed. Their working years may be shorter than those of others, and their illnesses or accidents more frequent and expensive, so the ordinary handicapped person will have to face the possibility of poverty; and he should know that poverty is another coin of great value in the Christian economy. Perhaps more than this he needs to learn to accept the help of others in a charitable manner. Independence is an ideal in our day, and the handicapped are taught to strive toward it. And rightly so. But the pendulum can swing too far. The total concept of vocation will lead one to recognize that others in *their* attainment of sanctity must serve Christ in the poor, the suffering, and the handicapped. And although the poor and the suffering and the handicapped individual will not covet this service, when it comes to him he will receive it with a graciousness suitable to one in whom Christ is being served. In no other way may one receive the frequent ministrations of others without lapsing into dependence or cultivating resentment at one's condition.

The basic vocational attitudes so important for all, but especially for the handicapped, can be developed from early childhood. Later one may begin to train for, choose, and enter upon some specific occupation in which one may use his abilities and allow for his handicaps. The occupational counselor of the handicapped ought to be very well informed on the abilities of his client and the work available to one with those abilities. He must rid himself and assist others to rid themselves of unfounded prejudices and fears regarding the occupational placement of the handicapped. Slowly, there is being built a collection of occupational literature for this purpose. The United States Employment Service has a publication on *The Selective Placement of the Handicapped*. The Overbrook School for the Blind has put into Braille a book covering over two hundred occupations open to the blind. Bridges has an extensive volume on *Job Placement of the Physically Handicapped*. Articles have been written on the success of the handicapped and mentally retarded in various lines of work. Those who are interested in the handicapped ought to make every effort to add to this body of material so that a substantial amount of information will be available for the guidance of the handicapped. Marriage counselors ought to be alert to ways in which they can assist the handicapped to enter upon and succeed in the married state. Those interested in religious vocations should not overlook whatever possibilities there are in the religious life.

Those who are charged with the care or direction of the exceptional child can not think in terms of five easily discernible talents but now of the single talent and then of the ten. Either extreme brings with it problems of discovery, for the possessors of such talents often appear to have less than they really have, and easily deceive themselves and those about them. And there are problems in the wise use of talents, for the extremes are easily tempted to bury all or some of their talents. They need help and encouragement to avoid this tragedy. Who shall predict the reward reserved for those who assist the child to make a praiseworthy accounting of every talent entrusted to his care?

SECTION II

CHAPTER III

EDUCATIONAL PROBLEMS

EDUCATIONAL AND ADMINISTRATIVE
PROBLEMS

A STATE PROGRAM OF SPECIAL EDUCATION
BY HAZEL G. MC INTIRE

A METROPOLITAN AREA PLANS FOR SPECIAL
EDUCATION BY FRANCES A. MULLEN

SPECIAL EDUCATION IN NEW YORK CITY
BY FRANK J. O'BRIEN

SPECIAL CLASSES FOR HANDICAPPED
CHILDREN BY HELEN M. WALLACE, J. WAYNE
WRIGHTSON, AND ELENA GALL

THE DEVELOPMENT OF INSTRUCTIONAL
MATERIALS FOR SPECIAL EDUCATION IN A
CITY SYSTEM BY HERMAN R. GOLDBERG

COMMUNITY PLANNING FOR SPECIAL
EDUCATION BY MAMIE J. JONES

RESEARCH IN SPECIAL EDUCATION

EDUCATIONAL AND ADMINISTRATIVE PROBLEMS

The educational program, in one sense, covers the entire servicing of the child. For convenience of organization in this chapter, educational servicing is interpreted as instructional service to the exceptional child.[1]

CURRICULUM

If the theory is accepted that the basic philosophy in the education of the exceptional is preparation for living in a world of non-handicapped people, then the same basic principles of curriculum construction[2] apply to both the exceptional and the non-exceptional, except for such changes as are indicated by special needs and the conditions arising therefrom. There must be a core of content of learning and experience; there must be definitely revealed goals at various points; there must be possibilities for enrichment.[3] It is further recognized that the curriculum must be flexible enough to be adaptable to the needs of the group and to the needs of each individual in it.[4-9]

The normal curriculum as applied to the education of the exceptional need not be varied at all in some cases. This is true for certain individuals who, while exceptional in some way, may be able to accept the regular program in classes with non-handicapped children.[10]

When variation is necessary, the principle of individual and group differences applies, and the principles of educational guidance enter. For, in a sense, the curriculum for the exceptional is a form of educational guidance, built largely with a definite aim toward cultural achievement and socio-economic independence. At present this guidance is still too often directed mainly along the line of manual skills.

For certain groups of the exceptional it is necessary to augment the curriculum with special instruction. Examples of this are braille work with the blind; eyesight conservation techniques with the partially-seeing; lip reading, speech and voice work with the deaf and hard-of-hearing; special hygiene instruction with the tuberculous; and special adjustments and enrichment of the curriculum with the cerebral palsied, the gifted, the mentally retarded, the emotionally disturbed, and other severely handicapped individuals.[11-21]

With some groups, such as the mentally retarded, there must be modifications in the direction of a minimum academic work, with the introduction of prevocational programs and other means of determining special non-academic abilities, and with subsequent change or adjustment to a program better fitted to the individual's abilities and needs.

For all groups, mental hygiene[22-24] must be emphasized and a definite place found for it in the core of content. Physical education programs must be modified on the basis of the physical limitations characteristic of each group. Physical and occupational therapy and rest periods must be available for such groups as the motor handicapped, and rest periods for most of the physically handicapped. This becomes necessary because of the added fatigue imposed by learning under difficulties due to personal physical restrictions.[25-31]

The classroom instruction for some groups of the exceptional seems to tend toward emphasis on drill rather than toward the modern progressive teaching for the non-handicapped. Since society holds all types of the exceptional to stricter standards of accomplishment than the non-handicapped, this emphasis on drill, where employed in competition with the non-handicapped, may be viewed in the light of better work habits. Drill, practically speaking, is not incompatible with a progressive program. There is no one method or curriculum.

Very definitely there must be curricula modifications based upon whatever individual limitations are set by the student's handicap. Many factors enter into the progress of the child in sight-saving classes, though successful normal progress is made by many of these pupils.

It is admitted that in the case of the deaf a special curriculum emphasizing speech, voice training, and lip reading, plus training of residual hearing, makes it difficult for the child to keep up to normal grading. However, in some cases the deaf and hard-of-hearing are able to reduce the educational lag through better teaching methods, an earlier start in language training, and parent institutes cooperating with the school program in providing language opportunities outside school hours. The hope here is that at the end of elementary school, in the less acute cases, the admitted retardation of three years will have been offset.

A similar situation holds with the spastic and athetoid groups. The progress of these children cannot at present be determined by the child's personal health and attendance record.

In the special health groups fatigability is the defeating factor, since it is believed that most of these individuals are potentially the mental equals of the non-handicapped. However, the added rest periods, plus the special instruction in hygiene and the diminished school day, all defeat a complete mastery of a standard core of content. In many instances the use of audio-visual aids, together with ingenuity on the part of the teacher, may make it possible to give the individual the necessary standard curriculum.

In an attempt to offset retardation and to eliminate 'isms' as rapidly as possible, nursery schools for the exceptional have been widely advocated.[32-34] This experience for the blind, the deaf, the cerebral palsied, and the hard-of-hearing has been successful when early discovery of the case makes the service possible. There is a trend in such instances toward placing the exceptional child with non-handicapped for the social effects thus obtained. In such cases special instruction along approved lines, — lip reading, speech, etc., — is given individually to the exceptional child, while both he and the non-handicapped carry out a regular nursery-school program.[35-39]

Extracurricular activities of the exceptional should be directed more than with non-handicapped toward the goal of economic independence. There is also extra emphasis in cultural directions, since the time is short until the educational facilities provided by society must release the child because of age limits.

On the other hand, natural and suitable interests are encouraged. The life of the exceptional child, as a whole, is probably much more carefully guided during the educational period than is the case with the non-handicapped. It should not be otherwise.

The exceptional individual who desires, — and is sufficiently gifted, — to pursue higher education usually does so in the company of, and in competition with, the non-handicapped. This he often carries through with considerable success, though subsequent employment remains far more difficult to obtain than is the case with non-handicaps. The exceptional individual in higher education almost invariably requires special services, such as readers for the blind, corresponding aides for the deaf, or physical help for the crippled. In many instances such service is provided by members of their own classes.

SPECIAL CURRICULA

Among special curricula[40] are those for home instruction, those involving recreational and occupational therapy, and those for use in hospitals and sanatoria. All of these are based more upon the special needs and preferences of the individual than upon any standard curriculum as such.[41-44]

The child in the hospital welcomes something to do, but medical services must come first, and limited physical resources must not be overtapped. The child at home is limited principally by the comparatively few hours a week a teacher can visit him, plus existing physical difficulties that result from the illness. While it is customary in New York City to offer graduation and a diploma for this work, and while many such children eventually return to school, curricular concessions have to be made. Occupational and recreational therapy for the exceptional[45-49] are still in the developmental stage.

The training of the child and adult who are unable to go to a regular school is not yet fully accepted as the community's educational and social responsibility.[50,51] This type of exceptional individual is found in everv area of special education. A surprising range of educational and semi-educational projects exists in various private homes, convalescent homes, and hospitals and institutions for nonambulatory or otherwise confined persons.[52] Even in hospitals where individuals are confined whose span of life is possibly short or whose educability is limited, some attempt is made to provide recreational, occupational, and physical therapy closely allied to academic or manual education.[53-57] This is first of all for the personal satisfaction and pleasure of the individual who is expected to return to society or to regular classes in public schools or other educational institutions. The programs are planned generally on some elementary level, it being accepted that the higher education or specialized education that follows elementary school should usually be pursued either with normals or in advanced and specialized situations requiring previous preparation.[58]

For the mentally retarded, various recreational programs are provided in most schools and institutions.[59,60] Occupational therapy also is usually furnished. In many instances, however, the theory of occupational or physical therapy is not thoroughly understood by the medical or educational fraternity; therefore the practice of it is less thoroughly used.[61] One reason for this may be that some physicians feel that technicians do not have sufficient background or do not understand the problems confronting the medical staff. The result of this is that occupational and physical therapy in such institutions as these physicians serve is frequently confined to simple forms of arts and crafts work and superficial physical therapy. Social, educational, and recreational programs are available for inmates who can benefit by them, but here again there is considerable untilled soil.[62–67]

Child and adult programs in hospitals have not been highly developed.[66] In general they are concerned first of all with teaching the individual how to protect himself and society upon his return to his home and employment. There does not seem to be sufficient stress upon the idea that the patient should maintain an interest in the outside world and its events, not alone for present information but in preparation for future participation.[67] There is at times too much of a tendency to capitalize upon the patient's momentary and pathological interests in his own illness and that of similar cases, in the expectation that some encouragement may result from knowing that medical science has been able to bring about successful rehabilitation in other like patients.

Convalescent home and hospital programs are at their best in the case of the severely handicapped child. Nursery schools and kindergartens are conducted in some hospitals.[68–71] Many convalescent programs have definite school organizations which, as in New York City, are regular parts of the public school system.

Hospital programs are of two general types: the abbreviated type for children whose stay is short, and a longer and more standard curriculum for those who are likely to remain hospitalized for the greater part of the school year. In the short program, recreation rather than education is stressed, the attempt being to have the child pass his stay pleasantly and without the self-conceived activities or boredom otherwise possible.[72–78] But in severe cardiac, orthopedic, and chronically ill cases, when hospitalization is to be for any length of time, instruction is provided according to the physical capacity of the child as determined by the visiting medical staff. In convalescent homes practically everything found in a school for non-handicapped may be available. The size of hospital classes varies greatly. In some instances, such as at Grassland Hospital, in Valhalla, Westchester County, N. Y., a school is maintained. Such schools are found in many institutions where the children will remain for a long period of time.

The policy in regard to hospitals and convalescent homes that house New York City exceptional children, as elsewhere in the United States, is to permit the children to proceed with their instruction without interruption. Promotion is on the same basis as for normal children, — namely, mastery of the courses of study. Children are expected to progress at the normal rate, provided, of course, their physical condition allows such a program.

A program for exceptional children at home is also provided. Special visiting teachers give home instruction in elementary subjects and in industrial arts. The type of children served in this way is apparent in the New York City list:[79] cripples, spastics, encephalitis cases, cardiacs, epileptics, chronic medical cases, cerebral palsied, etc., for whom junior and senior high school work and diplomas are available.

In some cities the multiple-grade curriculum is pointed toward a thorough elementary education that provides the exceptional child with a rich course of study. These courses lead to graduation and the privilege of attending general commercial or vocational high schools or classes for industrial training, according to the mental and physical ability of each pupil.

In addition to the common branch subjects, hand training is provided for the purpose of improving motor ability and coordination, and also as a means of studying the exceptional child with regard to his subsequent potentialities for occupational training and placement. Thus the curriculum includes as objectives the skillful use of tools and the study of form, color, and construction on the elementary level. In the homebound child this finds expression in an equivalent of shopwork, hand lettering and poster work, domestic science, sewing, dressmaking, lamp-shade making, flower making, rug making, embroidering, weaving, and crocheting. Some success has been experienced in home telephone, radio and television service programs.[80-82]

Beyond these points noted, the same situation prevails as with other programs for exceptional children. The main objective is to provide a continuous and interrupted program of education through classes in hospitals and convalescent homes and by home instruction and special classes.[83-86]

Whether the child is in a hospital class or at home, it is agreed first of all that this education process keeps up the child's morale and encourages the parents' cooperation. Hospitalized and home bound education is an inducement to the parent to be willing to have the child remain under the doctor's care sufficiently long for the medical program to be effective since worry about the child's loss of school instruction is removed.[87,88] And with education assured, parents are willing to have the child hospitalized until he can be physically adjusted to the home.

In pursuing these courses, the child proceeds according to his ability. Since the majority of children with physical defects reach an optimum of medical treatment at some time or are so greatly improved as to render return to regular classes possible, this program makes such a return feasible without such retardation as would otherwise follow a loss of school attendance for a period all the way from one term to many years. Naturally all this is reflected in the child's return to health and happiness and in the actual medical recovery or improvement. In some instances, children are placed under these programs after long absences from school through illness, with consequent backwardness in grading and adjustment.

Experience with these programs has shown that the young, properly trained teacher, endowed with ingenuity, is often the most successful. Home or hospital teaching does not offer the most attractive career for an older teacher; nor may she feel the full challenge and opportunities of a hospital or home teaching situation. Unfortunately, also, these positions at present are sometimes less well paid than regular classroom teaching. There is a need to recruit teachers for children with contagious diseases and with careful selection and professional support for those who enter the field willing to run the risk of contagion. Some protection for the teacher, such as special health precautions and insurance coverage, should be a part of the offerings for those serving active tuberculous patients and other cases with infectious diseases. In hospital or home teaching programs the necessary interruptions because of medical services for the children, plus the abbreviated school day, make either bedside or classroom teaching discouraging unless the teacher realizes that even slight progress is distinct gain.

In some cities a regular teacher is often drafted for the work. She may be an enthusiastic newcomer who gives the work both freshness and originality, or she may be a teacher who brings with her wide experience with normals. In either case special training and supervision are essential, though too rarely are these available or given.

The responsibilities of this specialized teaching are greater than those of regular work. The teachers not only must know how to give instruction, but also should be trained to administer diagnostic tests and set up remedial programs for each child, looking forward to adjustment. Educational and vocational guidance work goes along with their instruction.

PROBLEMS ARISING FROM SPEECH DEFICIENCIES

Few persons realize that impairments of speech may exist simultaneously with, or arise secondarily in practically all types among the exceptional.[1-8] One reason for this is the presence of fatigue and neuromuscular tension in individuals who are trying to meet normal competition with certain senses that function at anywhere from zero to perhaps near normal expectancy. Introduce nervous tensions and it is only a question of their amount before speech disorders having a nervous basis will arise. There are also, in certain types of the exceptional, speech defects arising from intrinsic causes.

Speech, it will be recalled, is learned by imitation. If there are either distorted patterns or inability to form words correctly for physical reasons, a speech defect results. In some deaf individuals there are few or no speech patterns until they have been taught. The hard-of-hearing have memory of speech heard before the advent of the impairment. But they may subsequently develop speech defects through distortions in hearing. Both the deaf and the hard-of-hearing must be given speech patterns either through sufficiently clear amplification or through the other distinctive methods used in teaching the deaf and hard-of-hearing by use of the eye and the sense of touch and feeling.

Both the blind and the partially-seeing must be watched closely in the matter of speech. The basis for their poor speech is not too clear and needs further study.[97-100] It is possible that in some instances a mildly poor quality of speech organs may accompany the poor quality of seeing organs. Nervous tensions are factors, as are also certain psychological elements peculiar to both groups.

In the athetoid types of cerebral palsied,[101] speech is a major problem, as it is in the case of the deaf, but for different reasons. The palsied understand the word perfectly unless there is also a mental deficiency involved. But the motor speech areas do not have normal function. They tend to follow the rest of the body in what are often unpurposed, spastic movements resulting in word distortion and often accompanied by movements of the rest of the body.[102]

In the case of the mentally retarded,[103–105] the speech defect is probably due to slow learning ability. A retardation in learning speech, and definite inaccuracies and slovenliness, are as logical in these cases as similar slowness in subject-matter learning.

It follows that since actual or potential speech impairments are definitely a part of the problem of the exceptional child, a program must be planned which is both preventive and corrective, with the classroom teacher at the front line, fortified with specialists trained for definitive speech service with the exceptional.[106,107] In some instances, as in the case of the deaf and the hard-of-hearing, this work becomes a definite part of the training of the special teacher. In the case of the deaf, speech is the first educational objective, and in the case of the hard-of-hearing, speech correction and lip-reading instruction are commonly handled by the same person.[108]

The use of music as an aid in speech correction is very important, and considerable progress in this area has been made. It is certainly worthy of careful study and adaptation to the needs of practically all exceptional children.[109,110]

PROBLEMS OF PHYSICAL EDUCATION AND RECREATION

The fields of physical education and recreation for the exceptional are very promising, but for the most part they are still in their infancy.[1–3] It is the custom in many cases to employ for this work persons who have had training in physical education and recreation work for the non-handicapped. Many of these are trained in service as employees in work with the exceptional. These persons, of course, are not to be confused with the physical therapists and the occupational therapists. The result of their guidance is usually a subjective attempt to transfer the non-handicapped program to a specialized field without having had the necessary training in the technical background of the latter. Indeed, even persons with experience in physical education and recreation in some area of the exceptional fail on the one hand to realize opportunities for special service, and on the other to meet or recognize genuine danger.

Physical education in relation to the exceptional is a professional specialty. It requires first of all a sound background and experience with the non-handicapped, and in addition, specialized training, possibly for each area.[114–117]

The opportunities for the use of what may be called a natural program with the exceptional are marked. There is every reason to believe that efforts should be made, far more than with non-handicapped, to introduce life situations into the program and to take advantage wherever possible of opportunities to bring to the exceptional individual experience that has previously been denied him by the presence of the defect. During recent years many camp programs for the exceptional have been developed, and these offer excellent opportunity to develop more natural situations.[118,119]

Work with the blind, deaf, cerebral palsied, and severely disabled requires a considerable basic knowledge of the particular field. When this is available, programs of great merit may be the outcome. Opportunities in work with the mentally retarded, — whether in special day or residential schools, or in institutions for commitment, — have grown rapidly during the past decade.[120–122]

There is great opportunity in this work with the exceptional for utilization of those values which physical educators have maintained make their work definitely educational, values that are highly useful in character training as well as in the development of a healthy body.

In each exceptional area there are certain dangers to be avoided. Some of them are real; some are more apparent than real. The physical education program for sight-saving classes has been greatly limited by the belief that actual damage to the vision of the child might result from bending and from certain other activities. Other areas have similar problems. Obviously, to the child who has chronic osteomyelitis there is very real danger to fracture, and even occasionally the possibility of amputation, as a result of an unwisely planned physical education program. The cerebral palsied child, or the child with multiple sclerosis or polio presents very real and practical problems.[123] It is probably true that it is better for the exceptional, even in nonsegregated situations, to have separate physical education programs. It is also probably true that contact activities should be permitted only when they can be definitely defended. The deaf and mentally retarded seem to be able to enjoy such sports and excel in them somewhat more than other severely disabled children.

Problems of coordination and rhythm are common. These are met through programs of music, rhythm, and physical education.[124,125] The same problems are present where the handicap involves neuromuscular tension. Indeed, this is a problem common to all types of the exceptional, and it is one which must definitely be met by a suitable program.

The problems of recess time are considered best met not only by separate hours for the exceptional but also by considerable subdividing of the exceptional themselves, either by area or within an area, on the basis of functional grouping through physical limitations. The answer to the problem is rarely the elimination of the physical education program. The true answer lies first of all in encouraging desirable persons to undertake the work and training necessary to carry through successfully a well planned and carefully tailored physical education program for the exceptional. One solution lies in research, undertaken by those who are entering the field and by those who have already accepted such work as a career, pursuing it often under most difficult circumstances.[126]

SEGREGATION AND NONSEGREGATION

Any discussion of the so-called segregated and nonsegregated plans of education of the exceptional involves programs both within day schools and in different types of residential schools. There has been a tendency toward developing dogma and cultism in the discussion of this problem, where what is needed is a careful and objective analysis of the situation based on the individual needs of the exceptional.[127,128]

The first need of the exceptional is an education of as good quality and as suitable for him as is available for the non-handicapped child. This implies a high quality of physical environment and equipment, often of a special nature, and an adequately trained teaching staff.

The question which must be answered for the exceptional child is his degree of adjustment to his defect. Likewise, it must be known how well he is adjusted socially. The probable answer lies in the type of individual profile; for individual situations will usually determine the kind of school program by which the child can best be serviced. Thus the elements of transportation and transportability and the quality of educational and other services available must all be considered in determining where and how the educational program for the exceptional should be conducted.

In the day school situation at last two philosophies exist in regard to the operation of classes; namely, the segregation and the nonsegregation of exceptional children. On analysis, the basic philosophies and aims of each are the same. The only question is the means of attainment.

The difference in the two schools of thought lies in the fact that the segregationists feel that an exceptional child is better serviced in a group of similarly afflicted pupils and in the hands of one teacher; while the nonsegregationists prefer to have the child in a room with non-handicapped or in a special room used as a 'home room', with the exceptional child taking all possible subjects in a class with non-handicapped children. In sight-saving work the nonsegregation policy has been the more approved in theory, but it has not always been carried out in practice. With the mild and moderately hard-of-hearing, the child is actually placed in a room with normally-hearing pupils, but he receives special instruction in lip reading and speech correction, plus special guidance. The orthopedically handicapped are segregated for motor reasons, as are individuals with special health problems and the severely handicapped, if their cases are of sufficient degree to require special services. The mentally retarded have been largely handled on a segregated basis; but experiments with a partial nonsegregation program have proved successful when children selected are fairly well adjusted socially and when suitable activities are chosen.[129,130]

In some instances special schools exist for one type of the exceptional. In other instances several types are found in one school.[131,132]

In some communities classes for the exceptional are placed in certain schools with the non-handicapped.

The exceptional child, whether in a day school class, special school, or residential school, and whether in a segregated or nonsegregated plan, should be placed in about the same general educational situation, with various classes, recreational activities, assemblies, medical services, and other activities as with the nonhandicapped. For the segregated class there are always many social functions in which the whole school, including the exceptional, participate. Therefore, segregation is rarely total.

The dispute regarding segregation can for the most part be confined to the elementary school age. The trends with the semi-blind and the hard-of-hearing are toward nonsegregation. In the cases of the motor-handicapped and the deaf the trend has been toward segregation. The bases of these trends are as follows: There is, first, as stated, greater safety for the individual in a segregated program. Second, in the sensory handicapped of high degree there is need of immediate and intensive training if the pupil is to be ready for high school work and for life among the non-handicapped. Third, in the case of the motor handicapped, when of sufficient degree to require special class services, the necessary rest periods and time for special medical service cut down the available school-day hours. Fourth, the availability of adequate service equipment and personnel. Fifth, there are possibilities for experimental research in methods and techniques.

The fact that the exceptional child is to any degree physically inferior and unable to stand as much work as the non-handicapped creates a problem. So does the fact that these motor-handicapped children, even under the best of circumstances, cannot attend school as regularly as the non-handicapped affect the situation. The program, therefore, for these pupils must be a specially modified one, covering only the high points of the standard curriculum. For them segregation for individualized instruction can be held, for the present, to be the best answer.

At the moment, experimentation is under way to determine what shall be done with the best adjusted exceptional children. The trend is toward trying them in classes with non-handicapped to whatever extent is practicable in terms of the educational profile of the child.

Where the nonsegregated home room plan is used, the first necessity, in addition to adequate equipment, is a highly trained special teacher who understands the needs of the exceptional child. The second requirement is the cooperation and interest of the regular classroom teacher and the supervisory personnel of the school. The special teacher must not only know what her pupil is doing in the regular room in terms of lesson assignments, but she must actually see him in that room and determine for herself his shortcomings and how she can aid him in meeting them.

As has been said before, a consideration in favor of segregated programs is the element of safety. It is true that in the end the exceptional child learns how to take care of himself, but it is mere sentimentalism and poor pedagogy not to realize the danger to these children, particularly those with poor vision or with severe orthopedic disabilities, in participating with the non-handicapped in free play, or in moving through crowded hallways or on elevators. The educator must have a realistic approach to these problems when determining the relative merits of segregation and nonsegregation.

When viewed from a common-sense standpoint, there is very little of real controversial issue in the question of whether or not an exceptional individual shall attend a residential school, a special class, or a special school.[133] The determining factors are the classification of the case, the current needs of the child, and the facilities available.

The special school, whether of day or residential type, is intended primarily for exceptional individuals with the more severe disabilities, where highly specialized equipment and personnel are needed. In situations where population is scattered, the residential school offers something which really parallels the modern consolidated rural school. The opportunities in terms of highly specialized personnel and equipment, with splendid physical surroundings, are all made available to both residential and day pupils.

In the past it has been customary to place the following in the residential or special day schools for the exceptional:

1. The deaf child or adult whose degree of defect or other personal guidance requirements make it evident that the abbreviated schedule of the regular day school will be inadequate to compensate for the retardation. In the day school are placed the hard-of-hearing, either with programs involving lip reading and other special services or in intensive training classes. Though this is not the rule, there are also classes for the deaf in many progressive school systems, such as those of New York, Minneapolis, Chicago, Los Angeles, Cincinnati, and other cities. The majority of deaf children and the high degree deafened are still educated in residential or special day situations. With the latter type this applies particularly where the advent of deafness has been so early as to prevent the establishment of the speech patterns.

2. In the cases of the blind and the partially-blind, both residential schools and public day school classes are used with combinations of both. The partially-seeing are placed in segregated or nonsegregated types of sight-saving or partially-blind classes. In some instances the blind and partially-blind are educated in day schools, notably in the large metropolitan areas.[134] In such instances success must depend upon the equipment, environment, leadership, and personnel, and also upon the ability and willingness of the public school system to set up a program as satisfactory in every way as that available in the residential or special day school.

3. In the case of the motor handicapped, children with special health problems, the severely disabled, and those with special mental and emotional problems, the trend is definitely toward the special day school, excepting the case which must be taught in hospital or home, and with the further exception of the extreme case which requires very special attention or in which the span of life is expected to be comparatively short.

4. With the mentally retarded, usually institutionalization involves commitment, and is based on the medical and psychological diagnosis and prognosis plus the safety and comforts of society. On this basis, commitment usually occurs when there is an IQ of below 50, in cases of dangerous mental states and patterns with inability to care for personal hygiene, and in other anti-social situations.[135]

The day school tends to establish elementary and junior and senior high school programs, with some interest in nursery and kindergarten levels.

The arguments presented against the use of residential schools are the same as those presented against the special day schools and the segregated or partially segregated type of certain day school classes. The difficulty here lies in separating sentimentalism and education dogmatism from sound educational philosophy. The real question is whether or not the goal of special education, — namely, sound educational and socialization at the end of elementary school or secondary school, — shall be achieved by a route of intensive training of a specialized sort in a selected group with all necessary equipment and trained personnel. The alternative is that the route may be traveled, probably a little more slowly in the technical sense, in surroundings where contacts with non-handicapped pupils can be emphasized. The only reasonable solution is to place the exceptional child in the educational situation which best meets his needs to achieve maximum growth at a normal rate. There is a delicate and subtle difference between educating and socializing an exceptional child and trying to maintain the thesis that he is not in contact with reasonably non-handicapped-thinking individuals when in a residential or semisegregated situation. In some instances it has been shown that the residential school or special day school products among the exceptional have proved to be better adjusted socially when in contact with the non-handicapped in high school, and of greater help to the non-handicapped than the non-handicapped are to him.

In the final analysis, the quality of product resulting from any of these educational programs is the only basis for judgment. It is obvious that the education of the exceptional requires special environment, special equipment, and specially trained personnel. The objective is to produce a reasonably happy individual who is socially acceptable and economically effective. The best program is the one that best meets these requirements.

RURAL PROBLEMS

The care and education of the exceptional child in rural areas offer many complex and difficult problems.[136] First of all, rural communities are not usually in a position to finance their own educational program for the exceptional. The first justification for state aid for education is based on this inability of sparsely settled populations to provide training facilities for children in districts where the school year has to be based on periods when farm service problems are least pressing. As demands have arisen for a more comprehensive curriculum, the Little Red Schoolhouse has given way to the more adequate consolidated school.

For these reasons the program for the exceptional in rural areas must in general follow that for rural non-handicapped. However, as in urban situations, facilities for non-handicapped must be modified, augmented, and otherwise changed on the basis of the needs of each individual child, plus possible group requirements. A consolidated school for children may be within reasonable transportation distance for all children; but such travel might be too much of a daily hardship for certain of the more severely handicapped. Likewise, even in a consolidated district there may not be a large enough number of exceptional children to make possible the establishment of special classes—such as, for example, classes for the partially-sighted or for the crippled, or the cerebral palsied. When the school population is sparse, it must be recognized that there will be very few needing special education. Yet the needs of these few are individually as great as those of each exceptional child in a larger group.

The basis of all rural problems is sparse population. The attempted answer in a day of rapid transportation has been centralization of services. Administratively most rural problems are solved on this basis, the local control giving way to county or state setups. It is recognized that because there are differences in weather and climate, because the term "sparsity of population" is comparative, because distances between homes and service setups vary from rods to miles, no one type of program will meet all needs. In some of the compact suburban sections of Westchester County, New York, problems are relatively simple in solution. In regions like North Dakota and Texas, where farms are miles apart, the problems created by distance, plus weather and climate, are very great. Likewise, the type of population is a considerable factor, the better the quality, the more successful is any solution.

The problem of discovering the exceptional child in rural areas is a marked one. Perhaps the most successful attempts at solution have been through providing special clinics,[137] where the cooperation of voluntary and official organizations with the medical profession in official and private capacities has brought to light many cases which might otherwise be without aid. The rural newspapers are most cooperative and interested in programs for the exceptional and aid greatly in making them both possible and effective. This is definitely in line with modern trends in public education or constructive publicity.

Probably the traveling medical clinic, visiting teachers, or an equivalent, in cooperation with private physicians or public health authorities, are the opening wedge for the educational program. Certainly medical examination and classification of cases is the first step. Consecutive to it is psychological testing in a broad sense. Quite possibly a psychologist with special training in work with all types of the exceptional should be attached to a traveling medical clinic. His services might also be made available for consultation with private physicians and public health officials.

Medical diagnosis and educability having been determined, the next question is where the training shall take place. It may be at home, in a residential school; or in a special program in a regular or special class in a public school. It could be in some local setup, or in a consolidated school. Or it might be in an approved boarding home for the school days of the week.

Since the number of the exceptional is small both numerically and proportionately, there arises the question of whether, on this basis, it is best: (1) to provide a traveling teacher, where distances permit; (2) to transport the child to a school in which he may be placed in a regular classroom with a modified curriculum set by an expert, as is the custom in rural Ontario under Inspector Amoss;[138] (3) to transport the child to a consolidated school for admission to a regular or a special class; or (4) to provide some other appropriate plan.

Special classes must be multigrade under such circumstances, because of the small number of the exceptional. They may have to be multitype as well, thus creating, as has been proved in practice, a difficult training situation.

In connection with educable exceptional children who are very backward, psychopathic, or mentally defective, auxiliary training units may be established.

TRANSPORTATION

It is the custom of school systems to transport to the school children who for any reason would have difficulty in reaching it otherwise.[139-142] In terms of a normal or ambulatory child, about half a mile is considered an allowable distance without transportation being provided. The location of schools today and the availability of public transportation systems usually make transportation of non-handicapped pupils unnecessary. But the child with crippling deformities of the legs cannot travel even the normal distance.

Handicapped children make up the largest single special group transported to school in cities both from the standpoint of number of children transported and the number of schools transporting. Of the 906 reporting schools, 334 are transporting 28,499 mentally and physically handicapped children to and from school.

As might be expected, the percent of cities transporting handicapped children is closely related to size of city. Almost 80 per cent of the reporting cities of more than 10,000 population are transporting them, while the percent of the cities of 30,000 to 100,000 population is about 55 and drops to 25 percent for cities of 10,000 to 30,000 population. There is also a marked difference between geographical areas. In the Northeastern quarter of the country and in the Pacific region 40 to 50 percent of the reporting cities transport handicapped children while in the Southeastern quarter it ranges from 3 percent to 15 percent. The other Central and Mountain regions range from 14 percent to 30 percent.[142]

There is a serious question as to the justification, even for a normal child, of having to be ready for school more than a half or three quarters of an hour before the opening hour, or of arriving home an hour later than his brothers. Transportation should not add heavily to the length of the school day.

In some instances bus and other transportation services are operated by the school department; in others, by contract. Much discussion of costs has been carried on.[143] Since the costs of operation vary widely in different communities, we can only refer to studies which present current geographic conditions.[144,145]

It is commonly recognized that parents cannot be expected to transport children to school or to call for them. Lack of means of transportation, the need of earning a living, and duties toward the other members of the family make this additional responsibility in most cases out of the question. The principle, therefore, is to provide transportation where public facilities and the facilities of the family of the exceptional child are inadequate.

There has been considerable discussion during the last few years of the use of specially designed busses for the transportation of handicapped children. Though there has been considerable interest the use of such busses is not yet very common. Fewer than 30 cities report the use of specially designed vehicles and apparently only a few cities have more than one. Most of these busses are owned by the schools, although about 40 percent are privately owned. No attempt was made to determine the degree to which these busses deviate from the standard bus, but it is known that in some cases the chief changes are the removal of some seats and possibly the provision of a ramp so that wheel chair pupils may be accommodated.[146]

There are available busses with rear and side doors and ramps that give access to the loading platforms of the same height as the floor of the bus. These are excellent for any group of children, especially since the loading platform removes difficulties resulting both from inclement weather and the hazard of steps.[147] It is regrettable that the expenses of these improvements, especially the one involving construction at the school of the loading platform and special entries, probably prevents their more universal use.

Pupil transportation, then, is today a necessary adjunct to the school system. It is particularly necessary in connection with the care of the exceptional child, and to a very large degree it has come to be in part a state responsibility.[148] With this fact recognized, many states have developed standards for such bus construction and operation as seem best fitted to the needs of the local situation.[149]

FOOTNOTES

1. See *Special Education for the Exceptional*, Vols. II & III, edited by Frampton, M.E., and Gall, E.D., published by Porter Sargent, for fuller treatment of each subject discussed here.

2. *The Education of Handicapped and Gifted Pupils in the Secondary School*, Bulletin #207, v. 39 (National Association of Secondary School Principals: Washington, D.C., Jan., 1955), Ch. 1.

3. *The Education of Exceptional Children*, 49th Yearbook, Part II (National Society for the Study of Education (University of Chicago Press: Chicago, Ill., 1950), pp. 3 ff.

4. Lindberg, L., *The Democratic Classroom* (Bureau of Publications, Teachers College, Columbia University: N.Y.C., 1954).

5. New York State Citizen's Committee of One Hundred for Children and Youth, *The Four Million* (Albany, N. Y., 1951), pp. 35-185.

6. Baker, H. J., *Introduction to Exceptional Children*, Rev. Ed. (Macmillan: N.Y.C., 1953), Introduction, Part I.

7. Gaus, R. Stendler, C., and Almy, M., *Teaching Young Children* (World Book: Yonkers-on-Hudson, N. Y., 1952).

8. McNerney, C. T., *The Curriculum* (McGraw-Hill: N.Y.C., 1953), Chapters 1, 2, 13, 14.

9. Wiley, R. D., *Guidance in Elementary Education* (Harper: N.Y.C., 1952).

10. Frampton, M. E., and Rowell, H. G., *Education of the Handicapped* (World Book: Yonkers-on-Hudson, N. Y., 1940), p. 25.

11. *Removing Blocks to Mental Health in School* (N. Y. State Education Department, Mental Health Committee: Albany, N. Y., 1954).

12. *Curriculum Adjustments for the Mentally Retarded*, Bulletin #2 (U. S. Department of Health, Education, and Welfare: Washington, D. C., 1953). Reprint.

13. *The Forward Look, The Severely Retarded Child Goes to School*, Bulletin #11 (U. S. Department of Health, Education and Welfare: Washington, D. C., 1953). Reprint.

14. Featherstone, W. B., *Teaching the Slow Learner*, Rev. Ed. (Bureau of Publications, Teachers College, Columbia University: N.Y.C., 1951).

15. Frampton, M. E., ed., *Education of the Blind* (World Book: Yonkers-on-Hudson, N. Y., 1940).

16. Mackie, R. P., *Education of Visually Handicapped Children* (U. S. Office of Education: Washington, D.C., 1951).

17. Hopkins, Thomas W.; Bice, Harry V.; and Calton, Kathryn C., *Evaluation and Education of the Cerebral Palsied Child: New Jersey Study* (International Council for Exceptional Children: Washington, D.C., 1954).

18. *Special Education for Children with Cerebral Palsy* (Division of Supervision and Curriculum, Nebraska Department of Public Instruction: Lincoln, 1951).

19. Lassman, Grace H., *Language for the Pre-School* (Grune and Stratton: N.Y.C., 1950).

20. Myklebust, Helmer R., *Your Deaf Child* (Charles C. Thomas: Springfield, Ill., 1950).

21. *Realistic Planning for Children with Cerebral Palsy* (United Cerebral Palsy Association: N.Y.C., 1952-53), Pamphlets #1, 2, 3.

22. Hobby, O. C., "Address Before Arizona's Third Annual Mental Health Institute" (U. S. Department of Health, Education, and Welfare: Washington, D. C., Nov., 1954), Mimeo.

23. *Emotional Problems Associated With Handicapping Conditions in Children*, Bulletin #336 (U. S. Department of Health, Education, and Welfare: Washington, D.C., 1952).

24. *The School Psychologist Aids the Parent of the Crippled Child* (National Society for Crippled Children and Adults: Chicago, Ill., 1954). A joint publication of the National Society for Crippled Children and Adults, Division of Psychologists and Division of Educational Psychology of the American Psychological Assn., and American Speech and Hearing Assn.

25. *Mental Health Pamphlets and Reprints,* Public Health Service Series #2 (Federal Security Agency: Washington, D.C., 1951).
26. Schwartz, F. F., "Physical Therapy for Children with Cerebral Palsy", *Journal of International College of Surgeons,* Jan., 1954. 21:1:84-87. Reprint.
27. Willard, H. S. and Spackman, S. C., eds., *Principles of Occupational Therapy,* 2nd edition (Lippincott: Philadelphia, 1954).
28. Kille, E. C., Therapy and Training Programs for Middle Grade Epileptic, Physically Handicapped, and Emotionally Disturbed Children", *American Journal of Mental Deficiency,* July, 1953. 58:1:88-92.
29. Krusen, F. H., "Relationships Between Occupational Therapy and Physical Medicine and Rehabilitation", *Canadian Journal of Occupational Therapy,* March, 1954. 21:1:3-9.
30. Daniels, A. S. *Adapted Physical Education:Principles and Practice of Physical Education for Exceptional Students* (Harper: N.Y.C., 1954).
31. Stafford, G., *Sports for the Handicapped,* 2nd ed. (Prentice-Hall: N.Y.C., 1947).
32. Almy, M., "Principles and Practices of Nursery Education", *Exceptional Children,* Oct., 1954. 21:1:18-21.
33. Denhoff, E., "The Physically Handicapped Child and the Nursery School", *Exceptional Children,* Feb., 1954. 20:5:202-208.
34. Boynton, M. S., and Drennan, *The Pre-School Exceptional Child in Illinois* (Department of Public Instruction: Springfield, 1949).
35. *Report of the National Work Session on the Pre-School Blind* (American Foundation for the Blind: N.Y.C., 1951), Reprint.
36. *The Exceptional Child in Infancy and Early Childhood* (The Woods School: Langhorne, Pa., May, 1950).
37. Heilman, G. C., *Needs and Resources for Group Learning of Cerebral Palsied Children of Pre-Elementary School Age in New York City* (Coordinating Council for Cerebral Palsy in N.Y.C.: N.Y.C., 1954). Mimeo.
38. Shane, P. J., "Slow Learning Pre-School Child", *American Childhood,* May, 1953. 38:14-15.
39. "Nursery and Pre-School Panel—June, 1952", *Volta Review,* Nov., 1952. 54:9:421-434;464.
40. See *Special Education for the Exceptional,* Vol.II., edited by Frampton, M. E., and Gall, Elena D., for further materials in these areas.
41. Brooks. G. L., "The Care of Children in Hospitals", *Pediatrics,* Oct., 1954. 14:4:401-419.
42. Barckley, V., "They Go to School in the Hospital", *American Journal of Nursing,* March, 1954. 54:3:328-330.
43. Mackie, R. P., and Fitzgerald, M., "Enriching the Curriculum of the Hospitalized Child", *Exceptional Children,* Nov., 1950. 17:2:33-34; 61-62.
44. *A study of Home Bound Physically Handicapped Individuals* (U.S. Department of Health Education, and Welfare: Washington, D.C., 1954).
45. Falkner, F., *The Convalescent Child* (University of Liverpool: Liverpool, England, 1952).
46. *Diseases and Disabilities of the Home Bound Child and Education of the Home Bound* (Hunter College: N.Y.C., 1952, 1953).
47. *Advancing the Education of the Hospitalized Child,* Publication #72 (National Foundation for Infantile Paralysis: N.Y.C., 1948).
48. *Rehabilitation Programs for the Homebound Child* (U. S. Office of Vocational Rehabilitation, Federal Security Agency: Washington, D.C., 1952).
49. McMullin, M. D., *How to Help the Shut-In Child* (E. P. Dutton: N.Y.C., 1954).
50. See *Special Education for the Exceptional,* Vol. II, edited by Frampton, M. E., and Gall, E. D., for additional material on Homebound.
51. See recent report to the Congress of the Department of Health, Education, and Welfare on *Study of the Home Bound, Programs for Physically Handicapped Homebound Individuals,* Eugene J. Taylor, Consultant, Feb. 2, 1955, Washington. D.C.
52. U. S. Office of Education, U. S. Office of Vocational Rehabilitation, Public Law 565, 83rd Congress, Chapter 655, 2d Session, Vocational Rehabilitation Amendments of 1954, 665 Section 7—Provides for greatly expanded services to the homebound. A Study, currently being made by the Office of Vocational Rehabilita-

tion and the U. S. Department of Health, Education, and Welfare. It should provide the basis for greatly expanded services for this group—Editors.

53. Crawley, W. H., "Friends of the Homebound Disabled", *Occupational Therapy,* Oct., 1953. 16:4:221-214.

54. Jenks, William, "Homebound Catholic Children Take on New Hope", *The Catholic Educator,* Oct., 1953. Reprint.

55. Shieff, F. L., "Occupational Therapy for the Chronically Ill Children", *Cerebral Palsy Review,* Nov., 1953. 14:11:8-9, 10.

56. Quibell, E. P., "The Child in the Long Stay Hospital, A Medical Social Problem", *Almoner,* July, 1954. 7:4:142-149.

57. *Supervised Correspondence Instruction in the Secondary School,* Bulletin #190, v. 36 (National Association of Secondary School Principals: Washington, D.C., Dec., 1952).

58. Widdowsen, D. C., "30 Cardinal Requisites for and Adequate Educational Program for Hospitalized Children", *Exceptional Children,* March, 1954. 20:6:251-252, 258.

59. Cianci, V., "A Program for the Home Training of Mentally Retarded Children", *Training School Bulletin,* June, 1948. 45:4:63-68.

60. Cianci, V., "Objectives of Home Training", *Training School Bulletin,* April, 1953. 50:2:23-29.

61. Willoughby, M. G., "Education of the Physically Home Bound Child", *Occupational Therapy and Rehabilitation,* June, 1948. 27:3:186-190.

62. *Entertaining the Convalescent Child* (American Medical Association: Chicago, Ill., 1944).

63. *Diversion for the Sick* (John Hancock Life Insurance Company: Boston, 1950).

64. Parker, C. S., *Your Child Can Be Happy in Bed* (Thomas Crowell: N.Y.C., 1952).

65. Culbertson, Polly, *Kindergarten in the Kitchen* (Bancroft School: Haddonfield, N. J., 1954).

66. Gall, Elena D., *The Adult Education Program at Goldwater Memorial Hospital,* Doctoral Thesis, Teachers College, Columbia University, N.Y.C., 1949.

67. Prugh, D. G., "A Study of the Emotional Reaction of Children and Families to Hospitalization and Illness", *American Journal of Orthopsychiatry,* Jan. 1953. 23:1:70-106.

68. Gordon, E. E., *A Home Program for Independently Ambulatory Patients* (National Multiple Sclerosis Society: N.Y.C., 1952). Published in cooperation with the Institute of Physical Medicine and Rehabilitation and the University-Bellevue Medical Center.

69. *Education of the Homebound.*

70. *Advancing the Education of the Hospitalized Child.*

71. See excellent description of programs in action in *The Education of Handicapped and Gifted Pupils in the Secondary School,* pp. 45-55.

72. *A Study of Education of Hospitalized Children in Urban Areas* (American School Health Assocation: Buffalo, N. Y., 1950). Mimeo.

73. *Iowa Hospital School for Severely Disabled Children* (State University of Iowa: Iowa City, 1950).

74. *The Kansas Plan for Home and Hospital Instruction for Homebound and Hospitalized Children,* Bulletin #4 (Kansas Division of Special Education: Topeka, 1951).

75. Mathesson, L., *Hospital Schools in the United States,* Bulletin #17 (U. S. Office of Education: Washington, D.C., 1939).

76. Mackie, R. B., and Fitzgerald, M., *School in the Hospital,* Bulletin #3 (U. S. Office of Education: Washington, D.C., 1949).

77. *Education of the Homebound Child* (Superintendent of Public Instruction: Lansing, Michigan, 1952).

78. Walton, M. H., *Report on a Survey of 559 Hospitals in the U. S.* (Committee on the Hospitalized Child, International Council for Exceptional Children: Washington, D.C., 1954). Mimeo.

79. "Helping the Physically Limited Child", *Curriculum Bulletin #7,* (New York City Board of Education: N.Y.C., 1952-53), Chapter 4.

80. Dry, L. O., "A School to Hospital", *Telephone Service Hospitals*, June, 1952. 26:6 pt. 1:52-54.
81. Richards, J. A., "Teaching Homebound Children by Telephone", *Exceptional Children*, Dec., 1953, v. 20, #3.
82. "Helping the Physically Limited Child".
83. Mullen, Frances A., *Special Education in the Chicago Public Schools, A Manual of Proceedings and Policies* (Chicago Board of Education: Chicago, Ill., 1953), pp. 9 ff.
84. *The Child with Cardiac Limitations*, Publication #32 (Bureau of Educational Research, New York City Board of Education: N.Y.C., June, 1953), p. 154.
85. *The Child with Orthopedic Limitations*, Publication #33 (Bureau of Educational Research, New York City Board of Education: N.Y.C., June, 1954), p. 132.
86. Mackie, Romaine P., and Fitzgerald, Margaret, *School in Hospital*, Bulletin #3 (Federal Security Agency, Office of Education: Washington, D.C., 1949).
87. *Home Instruction for Crippled Children—A Handbook for Parents* (Oregon Superintendent of Public Instruction: Salem, Ore., 1951), Mimeo.
88. *Study of the Home Bound.*
89. Johnson, W., ed., *Speech Problems of Children* (Grune & Stratton: N.Y.C., 1950), Chapters 4, 5, 6, 7, 8, 11.
90. VanRiper, Charles, *Speech Therapy, A Book of Readings* (Prentice-Hall: N.Y.C., 1953).
91. *Speech Problems of School Children* (National Society for Crippled Children and Adults: Chicago, Ill., 1953).
92. Whitehurst, M. W., and Morisees, E. K., *Auditory Training for the Deaf* (The Volta Bureau: Washington, D.C., 1952).
93. Gottlober, A. B., *Understanding Stuttering* (Grune & Stratton: N.Y.C., 1953.
94. Hessler, H. E., "The Relationship of Dentistry to Speech", *Journal of the American Dental Association*, Jan., 1954.
95. Westlake H., "What Is Special About Special Education" and "The Speech Defective Child", *Exceptional Children*, Nov., 1953. 20:2:56-69; 86.
96. See Chapter on Speech Defects in *Special Education for the Exceptional*, Volume II, edited by Frampton, M. E., and Gall, E. D., published by Porter Sargent, 11 Beacon St., Boston, Mass.
97. Brieland, D. M., "A Comparative Study of Speech of Blind and Sighted Children", *Speech Monographs* 17, #1, 1950. pp. 99-103.
98. Stinchfield, Hawk, *Psychology of Speech* (Boston Expression Company: Boston, 1928).
99. Cutsforth, T. D., *The Blind in School and Society* (American Foundation for the Blind: N.Y.C., 1951), pp. 103-120.
100. Fladeland, Waterhouse, "Speech Therapy for Blind Pupils", *Outlook for the Blind*, Vol. 45, 1951, pp. 22, 23.
101. Cass, Marion T., *Speech Habilitation in Cerebral Palsy* (Columbia University Press: N.Y.C., 1951).
102. Westlake, H., *A System of Developing Speech With Cerebral Palsied Children* (National Society for Crippled Children and Adults: Chicago, Ill., 1952).
103. Schlanger, Bernard B., "Speech Examination of a Group of Institutionalized Mentally Handicapped Children", *Journal of Speech and Hearing Disorders*, Dec., 1953. 18:4:339-49.
104. Gwens, George W., "The Speech Pathologist Looks at the Mentally Deficient Child", *Training School Bulletin*, April, 1951.
105. Karlin, Isaac W., and Strazzulla, M., "Speech and Language Problems of Mentally Deficient Children", *Journal of Speech and Hearing Disorders*, Sept., 1952. 17:3:286-294.
106. Irwin, R. B., *Special Education for Children With Speech and Hearing Disorders* (Division of Special Education: Columbus, Ohio, 1948).
107. *The Illinois Plan for Special Education of Exceptional Children: The Speech Defective*, Circular Series "E", #12, Revised (Illinois Department of Public Instruction: Springfield, Ill., 1952).
108. *Speech and Hearing Problems in the Secondary School*, Bulletin #173, v. 34 (National Association of Secondary School Principals: Washington, D.C., Nov., 1950).

109. Podolsky, E., *Music Therapy* (Philosophical Library: N.Y.C., 1954).
110. Gilliland, E. G., Editor, *Music Therapy*, 1952, 2nd Book of Proceedings of the National Assoc. for Music Therapy. Papers from the Third Annual Convention, 1953, Lawrence, Kansas. See also: "Proceedings of Mid-Atlantic Regional Conference, Mar. 2, 1954", *Bulletin of National Assn. for Music Therapy*, May 1953. 2:2.
111. Stafford, *op cit.*
112. *Exercise During Convalescence, A manual of Adapted Exercises* (A. S. Barnes: N.Y.C., 1947).
113. Buell, Charles, *Recreation for the Blind*, Educational Series 1 (American Foundation for the Blind: N.Y.C., 1951).
114. Dobbins, Eleanor C., *Physical Education Activities for Handicapped Children* (University of the State of N. Y.: Albany, N. Y., 1937).
115. Rathbone, J. L., *Corrective Physical Education*, 4th ed. (W. B. Saunders Co.: Philadelphia, 1949).
116. Stone, Eleanor, B., and Dyton, J. W., *Corrective Therapy for the Handicapped Child* (Prentice-Hall: N.Y.C., 1951).
117. Harrison, C. H., and Elkins, E. C., "Evaluation of Training of Physical Educationists for Reconditioning and Rehabilitation", *Archives Physical Medicine*, Feb., 1948. 29:2:99-107.
118. *A Bibliography on Camping With Handicapped Children* (National Society for Crippled Children and Adults: Chicago, Ill., 1951).
119. *Their Trail of Happiness With The Boy Scouts of America, A Review of Scouting With Physically Handicapped Boys* (Boy Scouts of America: N.Y.C., 1943).
120. Schlotter, B., and Svendsen, M., *An Experiment in Recreation With the Mentally Retarded*, Rev. Ed. (Illinois State Department of Public Welfare: Springfield, 1951).
121. Weiner, Bluma B., "Play and Recreational Activities of Young Mentally Retarded Boys", *American Journal of Mental Deficiency*, April, 1953, 57:4:594-600.
122. Pollock, M. P., and Pollock, M., *New Hope for the Retarded* (Porter Sargent: Boston, Mass., 1953).
123. Daniels, *op. cit.*
124. Durlacher, Ed., "Square Dancing for the Handicapped", *Crippled Children*, Feb., 1950. 27:3:16-17 29.
125. Terry, P. S., "Square Wheeling", *American Journal of Occupational Therapy*, July-Aug., 1950. 4:4:164-168.
126. Frampton, and Rowell, *Education of the Handicapped*.
127. *The Education of Exceptional Children*, 49th Yearbook, Part II, p. 24:
    "It is important that the philosophy of Special education in regard to segregation be explained to both teachers and parents. Segregation is not always a matter of separate rooms. It may be a matter of psychological or social repression. A child cannot be more cruelly segregated than to be placed in a room where his failures separate him from other children who are experiencing success. The nonreader, the deaf, or the mentally retarded may be segregated by placement in a regular classroom where his needs are not understood or met."
128. Frampton, M. E., and Kerney, E., *The Residential School* (Edwin Gould Printery: N.Y.C., 1953).
129. Heck, Arch O., *The Education of Exceptional Children* Rev. Ed. (McGraw-Hill: N.Y.C., 1953), Chapters 3-7.
130. Frampton, and Kerney, *The Residential School.*
131. *Special Education in the Chicago Public Schools, A Manual of Procedures and Policies*, pp. 103-116.
132. Hayes, E. Nelson, ed., *Directory for Exceptional Children*, 2d ed. (Porter Sargent: Boston Mass., 1955).
133. Carter, V. R., "Where Shall Blind Children Be Educated", *International Journal for the Education of the Blind*, Dec., 1954. 4:11:21-23.
134. See *Special Education for the Exceptional*, Vol. II, edited by Frampton, M. E., and Gall, E. D., and published by Porter Sargent, 11 Beacon St., Boston, Mass., Chapters on Blind and Sight-Saving, for further discussion on this topic.
135. Kirk, and Johnson, *Educating the Retarded Child*, Part I, Chapter I.

136. Worchester, D. A., "Clinical Services: Making the Best of Resources in the Rural Community", *Exceptional Children*, Jan., 1954. 20:4:176-179.
137. Several states, notably California, have established several types of mobile units for clinical services in speech, hard-of-hearing and control of communicable diseases. This type of service lends itself to the special needs of rural areas and should be more widely adopted as a method of servicing exceptional children in rural areas.—Editors.
138. Amoss, Harold E., and DeLaporte, L. Helen, *Training Handicapped Children* (The Ryerson Press: Toronto, 1933).
139. *Pupil Transportation* (National Education Association: Washington, D.C., 1953).
140. *National Conference on School Transportation*, 1954, Rev. Ed. (National Committee on Safety Education, National Education Association: Washington, D.C.).
141. Featherston, E. G., *Pupil Transportation in Cities*, Pamphlet #111 (U. S. Office of Education, Federal Security Agency: Washington, D.C., 1951).
142. *Ibid.*
143. *Ibid.*
144. Welfare and Health Council of New York City, Section on Services to Handicapped, *Report on Study of Transportation of the Handicapped, December, 1954*. Daily rates vary from $1.10 to $2.50 per child per day, various categories. This report also presents an excellent summary of basic problems of servicing, equipment, coordination, and financing.
145. Wheatley, G. M., and Hallock, G. R., *Health Observation of School Children* (McGraw-Hill: N.Y.C., 1951).
146. *Pupil Transportation in Cities.*
147. School Bus Body Manufacturing Association, 74 Trinity Place, N. Y. C., 6. Write the Secretary for full information as to types of busses for the handicapped now available.
148. New York State Department of Education, State Education Law, Transportation of Physically Handicapped Children.
149. *Pupil Transportation.*

A STATE PROGRAM OF SPECIAL EDUCATION

HAZEL G. MC INTIRE

In presenting a picture of services in special education, the program in operation in the state of Ohio is used as a framework in which the various phases of educating exceptional children are discussed. It is not intended that this state's special education services be taken as a pattern, but rather as a sample of an actual program in operation. It is presented as a movement rather than as a static picture of the educational services.

Beginnings of Special Education in Ohio

As in many other states, Ohio's first step in recognizing the needs of handicapped children was taken by building state residential schools for the deaf and blind. The school for the deaf was founded in 1829 and the State School for the blind in 1837. These state schools originally operated under the State Welfare Department,[1] but in 1927 they were brought under the Department of Education. The state residential schools for the deaf and the blind have recently moved into newly constructed plants; even though they are the oldest part of the special education program, they are still an essential part of it. Attendance in the state school for the deaf ranges around three hundred pupils, while the attendance at the state school for the blind is approximately two hundred pupils. The cost of education for deaf and blind children in the state residential schools is paid out of state funds. These state residential schools are each administered by a superintendent who is directly responsible to the state superintendent of public instruction.

In the period beginning about 1910, there began to appear in the larger cities of the state special classes and schools for physically handicapped children. In this movement it is noted that the local school districts not only set up special classes for deaf and blind children, but went a step further by setting up special classes for crippled children. Financial records for that period show that the State Department of Education granted "state aid" to these special classes from the funds available to the department.

It would be interesting to trace the development of some of these early public school classes for deaf, blind and crippled children. It is known that groups of mothers organized in the interest of handicapped children played a strong role. Service clubs and societies interested in blind and crippled children played their part. Out of these groups came the Ohio Society for Crippled Children, which for a generation has given strong support to state legislation and appropriation of funds for the education of handicapped children.[2]

Ohio's Special Education Law

By 1919 public interest in the education of physically handicapped children in the public school had crystallized to the point that there was strong demand for legislation that would recognize existing classes and provide a basis for the organization and financing of such classes throughout the state. The law enacted that year gave the state superintendent of public instruction authority to "grant permission to local boards of education" to set up special classes for deaf, blind or crippled children. These classes were to be operated under standards set by the state department of education; and excess costs in approved classes were to be paid by the state in an amount not to exceed $300 per child per year[3] (plus the cost of board or transportation for non-resident children) from funds appropriated for that purpose. This basic legislation recognized the provision of schooling for educable handicapped children as a function of the state and the local school district, not the responsibility of related agencies, such as health and welfare.

No major change was made in this original special education law until 1945, when it was broadened to include provisions for special classes for slow-learning children,[4] child study, and instructional services for any child whose learning is "retarded, interrupted or impaired by physical or mental handicap".[5] Financial aid from the state on this newer part of the program is paid on a teacher unit basis.[6]

Since 1945 there have been three additions to the law, each indicating the will of the people to extend special education. One of these provisions opened public school services to blind children at the age of 3 years instead of 5 as previously provided. A second opened public school education to persons over twenty-one years of age[7] who have not graduated from high school and are patients in public hospitals for the tuberculous. The other addition grew out of the need for expanding facilities for preparing more teachers for exceptional children. It permits the state department of education to contract with the education department of a university for in-classroom or in-service training of special education teachers and to pay as much as half the salary of college personnel doing the special training.[8]

Law in Operation

In the application of any legislation many problems arise which were not anticipated by the lawmakers and which are not fully and specifically covered in the law. Generally these problems are settled by legal opinions or by decision of the courts; and these opinions and decisions come to have the effect of broadening or narrowing the law. In this way law tends to take on meaning as questions arise, decisions are made, and opinions and rulings become the basis of practice.

When Ohio's original special education law was enacted, it was for the "deaf, blind and crippled", who because of the seriousness of their handicap presented an obvious problem. When the law was put into operation, it was soon found that there were many children who would not technically classify under any one of these three major handicap headings, but who were so handicapped that their normal school progress was seriously hampered.

In practice it was found that for every deaf child there were many partially hearing who needed special education, varying in amount and kind with the degree of hearing loss; for every blind child there were many partially seeing who needed different kinds of school facilities; while the original term crippled, applied to the orthopedically handicapped, closed the doors of special services to the heart damaged and even in some instances to the cerebral palsied. Through many experiences, while working to fulfill the special education needs of thousands of exceptional children, ways have been found to broaden the original concept of law until these children can take their rightful place in special education. Others, such as the tuberculous child, may attend a class in a hospital, or the child with epilepsy may have instruction at home while medical control is established. Thus we see that the law itself and meanings that come to be attached to it change slowly as the problems of children emerge. As solutions to these problems are worked out, they become precedent which serves as a basis for decision in future similar situations.

PHILOSOPHY OF SPECIAL EDUCATION

Before a statement of philosophy can be made, it is necessary to define special education. The definition that has come to be accepted in Ohio might be expressed as follows: "Special education is regular education custom-fitted to the individual limitations and potentialities of the exceptional child."

Custom-fitting means alterations or modifications in the regular pattern. The modification might mean the provision of transportation or physical therapy for the crippled child, or even bedside instruction. For the blind child it may mean Braille or reader service. For the deaf child it may mean that speech and language need to be developed. For the mentally retarded child it may mean that the timing of beginning reading and terminal expectancies for reading (or academic work) need to be different. For the speech handicapped child it may mean only some help from the speech correction teacher while he does his regular school work in regular class.

Any discussion of the philosophy of special education eventually leads to the question of segregation. On the one hand are those who believe that all of the needs of all children, including the handicapped, can be met in the regular classroom. Others feel just as strongly that the problems of the handicapped are so special that total segregation with special building, special teachers and special program is necessary. It appears that a better plan would consider only as much segregation as necessary for only as long as is necessary. One of the objectives of special education ought to be to bring the child to maximal realization of his potential for normal living. He may need a lot of special treatment in the beginning, but little or none in the end.

Another question that arises in connection with the education of exceptional children is that of responsibility. Are they the responsibility of the local community or of the state? Ohio's answer to this question is that both the state and the local school district have responsibility. Thus special education becomes a partnership in which the local district is responsible for normal costs of education while the state pays excess cost to a specified legal limit. The local school initiates special education while the state helps to plan and to pay.

ADMINISTRATION AND SUPERVISION

In the beginning, one high school supervisor was assigned the responsibility of inspecting special classes and distributing special funds to local school districts. The volume of work became too heavy to be handled in this manner, so in 1923 a director of special classes was appointed to devote full time to the problems incident to the education of physically handicapped children in public schools.

The function of the Director of Special Classes as viewed at that time, was primarily to organize and establish classes, to set minimum standards, to inspect existing classes and to distribute money. However, the concept of these duties soon was modified to include such matters as disseminating information about special classes, developing methods of finding exceptional children, coordinating the efforts of education with those of related state and local agencies in health and welfare, and all the other activities both official and volunteer that have come to be looked upon as essential in special education.

WHAT MAKES EDUCATION SPECIAL?

As the number and types of classes grew, the need for supervisory help became evident, so that one at a time, supervisors were added. The pattern followed in building a staff was that of employing a person with a background of regular teaching experience as well as training and experience in at least one special area. By 1936 the classes for the deaf, the blind and the crippled each had their own supervisors. Soon after this a psychologist was brought in to examine handicapped children and consult with school personnel and parents. In 1937 a supervising physical therapist was added to complete the list of special education personnel working with physically handicapped children.

When the special education law was broadened in 1945 to include the educable mentally retarded and other handicapped children, plus child study services for all handicapped children, three additional supervisory positions were added. These were in the areas of speech therapy, slow learning, and psychological services.

In the process of growth the functions of administration and supervision, which were at first carried by one person, have become more or less separated. The Director of Special Education carries the administrative responsibilities, while each supervisor works with teachers and children in a specific area of special education. The director establishes policy, prepares budgets and distributes funds, coordinates special education with the work of other state departments and in general directs the business and services of the division. The supervisors consult with local school personnel and parents, help teachers, participate in the training of special teachers, assist in surveys and the selection of children for special programs, and report to the director on problems and progress in his special area. Over the years the director and supervisors have given active help, on the spot, to local school districts in establishing new classes and services; and the supervisors spend almost full time in field service.

Special Classes and Programs

Ohio's program of special education began with special classes and special schools. It has moved in the direction of educating a handicapped child without breaking the contacts with brothers, sisters and normal classmates any more than is necessary. Thus the more recently established special classes are in regular school buildings, and as much as possible the participation of handicapped children with normal children in regular school activities is encouraged.

The Crippled. In four larger cities crippled children's classes are housed in a special school. In other cities and rural areas these classes are housed in regular school buildings. The special school offers the advantage of centralizing special equipment and services, while the special class or classes in a regular building offers the advantage of continued association with regular class children, and facilitates the return of the child to a regular class situation as soon as his physical condition makes this possible.

Crippled children's classes are for those children who need protection or therapy for a time. It is usually viewed as a temporary placement, often a stepping stone from the hospital back to the regular school.[9] It follows, then, that the curriculum for the crippled child is the regular school curriculum with the necessary modifications to meet the needs of the handicapped child. The special services, as required, are the therapies, the boarding home, transportation to school, and provision for rest during the school day.

Some crippled children are now receiving special education in hospitals where they are awaiting surgery or treatment, receiving treatment, or convalescing. This figure includes patients in hospitals both for the orthopedic and tuberculous. The number of children under this special instruction varies as children come and go, but the service is a regular part of special education. The local school district provides the instruction, with excess cost paid by the state.

Other children are provided with home instruction. This part of the special education services for crippled children is for those who are physically unable to attend class even if provided with transportation.

The Deaf in the Public School. In Ohio the education of deaf children is carried out in the public schools[10] by teachers trained not only in methods used for hearing children, but also in special techniques of teaching language and speech to the deaf. In the public school classes the oral method is used exclusively. The work is begun at as early an age as possible to at least partially overcome the child's speech and language retardation before he reaches regular school age. The deaf child is enrolled in a special class at the age of three, following advisory conferences with the parents, to prepare them to help in the child's school adjustment. The training of parents continues through all the early years of the child's education, for only as they carry on at home the work done at the school, can their child progress at a rate rapid enough to educate him in a reasonable number of years.

Even in the beginning the child is given as many contacts as possible with hearing children in the building in which his class is located. As he becomes more adept in the use of his special skills, he is placed in classes with hearing children for as much of his work as he can carry. Little by little, he makes the transition from special classes to regular classes. In the high school he carries his work—academic and vocational—with hearing students, being given counselling and tutoring services when needed. This helps him adjust more easily to community living.

The Hard of Hearing. Hard of hearing children are enrolled and do most of their work in the regular classes of a building where there is a resource room with a teacher prepared to teach the hard of hearing. Most of these children have or have had sufficient hearing to acquire some speech and language in the same way as hearing children. However, they are so seriously handicapped that they cannot compete with hearing children in a regular class.

The special teacher has each child (or a small group) a period or more a day to teach him lip reading, correct his speech if necessary, and advise on the use of his hearing aid. Occasionally she helps the regular teacher by tutoring the child if he is not succeeding.

With most of these children a year or two of this training is all that is necessary before the child can be returned to his own school district, with lip reading and his hearing aid (his tools of trade) and with confidence that he can now compete with hearing children. He is kept longer if doubly handicapped or if for some other reason he is not rehabilitated in the usual period. Differing from procedure in some states, Ohio children who become totally deafened after they have acquired speech and language are placed with hard of hearing children for education. Under this procedure they do not lose the language and speech acquired before they were deafened.

The Blind in the Public School. Early counseling services make it possible for blind children to come into nursery school at the age of three years. A feature of the nursery school program is the inclusion of a number of sighted children; this feature of association with normal children is continued through the kindergarten—where the blind child attends the public kindergarten in his home school district—and when the child is six years old he may go to a special Braille class located in a regular school. He has the services of this special class throughout elementary school, with emphasis on the development of the special techniques that he will need to carry out his academic program, and upon growing participation in activities with regular class children. In high school the blind student does not attend a special class but carries the regular program of courses with reader service and continued guidance from the special education supervisor or[11] the itinerant teacher trained to continue Braille and other necessary services.

The Partially Seeing. The program for visually handicapped children is one in which the possibility of meeting the needs of most partially seeing children in the regular class situation is being examined nation-wide. Most of the larger cities in Ohio operate "sight saving" classes with a special teacher in a special room. As with other special classes, the child remains here while he is acquiring those skills needed to help him adjust to his handicap in a school situation but participates in the regular classroom for much of his school work. In other districts the child is registered in his regular class, returning to a "sight saving" (or resource) room in the building for necessary help and materials. Few sight saving classes are found beyond the elementary and none beyond the junior high level; in the secondary school, reader service and guidance from the special education supervisor are maintained as needed, as with the blind pupils.

Two large and two smaller cities and a number of rural areas[12] are providing special service for partially seeing pupils through the itinerant teacher plan in which a specially trained teacher works with visually handicapped children and with their teachers in regular classrooms. This carries a vision conservation program into the regular class situation. Many children thus get the services they need while attending their neighborhood schools. The tendency at the present time seems to be in the direction of less separation from the regular school situation.

The Slow-Learning. Special classes for slow-learning pupils existed in some school districts in Ohio before the state began to assume financial or supervisory responsibility for them; 143 such classes were in operation in 1945, all of them housed in special class centers or in elementary schools. The provision of a small amount of financial aid to the program gave sufficient impetus that special classes have continued to develop at the rate of about 30 new classes each year, until at the present time there are 413 such groups, 98 of which are housed in junior and senior high schools.

Special education classes at the elementary level usually operate as self contained classroom units, as do other grades in the school. In secondary schools, the pupils are enrolled in regular home rooms and selected classes with regular students. The programs vary in the amount of time the pupils spend in the special class—not less than the equivalent of half the school day, since all of the academic work and what may be viewed as personal and occupational guidance takes place there—but, depending upon the abilities of the boys and girls and the facilities available in a given high school, the special class pupils participate in many activities with the regular high school students.

In general the trend in thinking about the education of slow learning children is in the direction of separation where necessary and for as long as necessary, participation when possible and as far as possible. Under this philosophy these pupils are proving to have relatively better potentialities than was recognized a generation ago. The program aims at general preparation for as normal and effective adult life as is possible for these young people.

Speech and Hearing Therapy. The speech correction program in the public schools of Ohio provides for instruction of children in small groups or individually. The child carries his full program of regular school work in his own grade, but reports to the speech teacher two or more times a week for half hour periods of instruction in his own school.

Hearing testing is generally considered the function of the health departments in Ohio. Since the speech correction teacher is trained in audiometric procedures, he sometimes assists the school nurse in the hearing testing program. He is also trained to teach speech reading, to give auditory training and to help adjust the child to the use of a hearing aid where indicated. Children whose hearing loss is less severe fall in the province of the speech correctionist. Provision for children with acute hearing loss is made under another program.

In addition to specialized training, the same basic background of courses in education is required as for the regular teacher in order that the speech correctionist may work effectively in the school situation. The speech correction teacher is usually employed by the local school district on the same basis and salary as any other teacher, based upon training and experience. An additional allowance for travel between schools is made, since most speech correctionists serve four to six buildings.

An important factor in the uniformity of policies and procedures throughout the state is the close working relationship between the staffs of the universities recognized by the Department of Education for the training of speech and hearing teachers and the Division of Special Education. By limiting the number of centers offering this specialized training, a high standard can be maintained. The locations of these speech training centers are so situated geographically that consultative and treatment services are available to most children in all parts of the state.

Psychological Services. The need for better understanding of the exceptional child's potentialities was recognized by Ohio's Education Department long before psychological services became generally available. The larger cities in the state were first to employ psychologists. The state division of special education sought service from state and local psychological clinics for some time and then began providing a limited amount of such service directly through a member of its own staff. For several years the idea of establishing in the state department of education a staff of psychologists to serve the public schools had considerable support. The viewpoint of the division has always been that to set up these services in the school districts is more effective.

When provision for subsidy of child study services in the public schools was made, the number of school psychologists began to grow rapidly. In 1954 there were ninety-eight state subsidized psychologists working in the public schools of the state. Each year finds this number growing even though the amount of financial aid is small.

The psychologist's role is that of measurement, diagnosis of mental abilities and prognosis for school progress. He is a member of the professional team that seeks to understand the child's disabilities and abilities and to map a program for his education.

The psychologist carries out the examinations of exceptional children for special services and serves as a consultant to parents and school personnel on matters of placement and adjustment in the special program. The general practice is for the psychologist to carry out his work in the schools rather than having the children brought to a central office. This procedure not only enables the school psychologist to see the child in his normal school situation but also allows ample opportunity for the principal or teacher to consult with the psychologist relative to the child and his problems.

Problems and Plans

The philosophy and practices in special education never become static. Certain basic principles remain constant but as progress is made in the fields of physiology, medicine and psychology, the forces of education need to reconsider and regroup in order to meet the needs of exceptional children effectively. What has happened in the development of control drugs and the treatment of children with epilepsy has made necessary a revision of thinking about the education of these children. Formerly the outlook for them was not very hopeful. Now that epilepsy can usually be treated effectively, most of these children can return to regular school after control is established through medication.

A few years ago, poliomyelitis was the great crippler of children. Improved methods of treatment of this disease seem to be greatly reducing its crippling effects and recent research findings offer promise that preventive measures may soon be effective in eliminating the problem.

While causes of crippling are being reduced by medical research on the one hand, a growing volume of knowledge and understanding of the problems of other children who have not been viewed very hopefully in the past brings new challenge to special education. Included in this category are the disturbed, the cerebral palsied, and those with neurological damage but no motor involvement.

In Ohio the cerebral palsied are provided for in the same general way as any other kind of crippled child. The educable cerebral palsied child attends regular school, class for crippled children, class for slow-learning children or has home instruction depending on the severity of his handicap. He is provided with therapies, transportation or boarding home as these services are required.

Special education is groping for ways of meeting the needs of other children with neurological damage and disturbed children. At present different programs are being tried on an experimental basis. Some children are on home instruction full time. Some have home instruction part time and attend regular school half time. Still others attend special class for a full school day. Whether the eventual answer will be one of these, or a combination, or something entirely different is not yet known.

Special education is also moving into the hospitals and home where numbers of disturbed children are housed and treated. Work with these children is also in the exploratory stage but it is felt this is an area needing much study.

Interest in the field of special education for the gifted has developed to the point that there is an organization of professional and lay people[13] exploring the needs of these children and current school practice in dealing with them. It is interesting to note that the same thing is happening here that has happened prior to the enactment of legislation for handicapped children. In each instance an organization concerned with children having a certain handicap —as crippled, blind, deaf—became interested in educational possibilities, gave the particular problem about which they were concerned sufficient publicity to develop public awareness and public support, then went to the General Assembly with a request for legislation to grant state subsidy and state direction through supervision for a program. If history repeats itself, we may therefore anticapte that in a very few years the Division of Special Education will have the responsibility of promoting a state philosophy, setting standards and otherwise encouraging the development of a program for this area.

At the present time gifted children are eligible for child study services in those districts having their own psychologist. In a few Ohio cities special programs for gifted already exist. Chief among these is the city of Cleveland, which did pioneer work in this area; its program of major work classes and enrichment classes is internationally known.

In addition to the need for special education to develop in new areas—as indicated in the foregoing paragraphs—there are certain continuing problems which are likely to be particularly pressing in the next few years, due to the general teacher shortage and the rapid increase in the elementary and secondary school population. These are: space to house special programs, teachers and other special personnel to carry on the instructional and correctional treatment programs needed by exceptional children, and funds to underwrite increased costs of special school services.

STATE PROVISION FOR EXCEPTIONAL CHILDREN IN THE PUBLIC SCHOOLS OF OHIO

Type of Handicap	Services	Subsidy
Crippled*	Special Class Therapies	Excess cost not exceeding $400.00 per child per year
Deaf	Special Class Tutors	Excess cost not exceeding $400.00 per child per year
Hard of hearing	Special Class or Resource Room Tutors	Excess cost not exceeding $400.00 per child per year
Blind	Special Class Tutoring	Excess cost not exceeding $400.00 per child per year
Partially Seeing	Special Class Resource Room Itinerant teacher Readers	Excess cost not exceeding $400.00 per child per year
Speech and hearing	Itinerant teacher	$1000.00 per year
Slow Learning	Special Class Psychological Services**	$750.00 per year $1000.00 per psychologist per year

*Home instruction available for homebound crippled children.
In addition to per pupil subsidy, funds are available to pay transportation or board when necessary for physically handicapped attending special classes.
**The school psychologist is available for work with all types of exceptional children.

During the current school year subsidized special education, including psychological and adjustment services, is reaching more than 50,000 children. Under instructional services one finds 4,106 crippled, 1,057 with serious hearing handicaps, 1,150 with visual handicaps, 7,700 mentally retarded and 13,921 speech handicapped.

FOOTNOTES

1. Ohio's schools "for the custody and training of the mentally deficient" are still under the jurisdiction of the State Department of Public Welfare, although these institutions do operate an educational program for patients who are classified as "educable mentally retarded". Similarly, the educational programs at the Boys' and Girls' Industrial Schools are under the supervision of the Department of Mental Hygiene and Corrections rather than under the Department of Education.
2. The National Society for Crippled Children and Adults was an outgrowth of the Ohio Society for Crippled Children; for many years the headquarters for the national organization was in Elyria, Ohio.
3. In 1953 the law was amended to allow $400 per child per year towards excess operating costs.
4. In Ohio the term "slow learning" applies to those children referred to as "educable mentally retarded" in much of the professional literature.
5. The Ohio School Code, revised edition, Section 3323.01.
6. There appears to be a trend under newer laws to pay on a per unit basis, although some states (as Illinois) pay on these newer services on a per child basis, and some (as California) pay a percentage of excess cost.
7. The public schools, in general, are open to youth from six to twenty-one years of age.
8. This service is further extended by the assignment of supervisors from the Division of Special Education to state universities for extension courses and summer courses dealing wih special education.
9. For certain children, such as the cerebral palsied, crippled children's class would probably provide a long term education program. It is interesting to note that since the early days of the program cerebral palsied children have been included in Ohio's classes for orthopedically handicapped boys and girls. In the mid 1940's a five year experimental program for a cerebral palsied unit was carried out under the joint auspices of the Division of Special Education, The Ohio Society for Crippled Children and Division of Crippled Children's Services, State Department of Welfare,—with the cooperation of the Toledo and Youngstown Public Schools. At the end of that period one of the conclusions reached was that it is better for cerebral palsied children to attend class with other crippled children than to be a part of a cerebral palsied group, per se.
10. In the organization of the state program, centers have been established in a number of city school districts which are open to deaf children in the area who are able to commute daily or who may be boarded through the school week.
11. Guidance is also given to faculty members and high school counsellors dealing with the blind student.
12. Cities: Cincinnati, Columbus, Marietta, Hillsboro.
13. The Ohio Association for Gifted Children.

BIBLIOGRAPHY

Allen, Amy A., *Let Us Teach Slow Learning Children* (State of Ohio, Department of Education: Columbus, 1950).

Bureau for Handicapped Children, *Helping Handicapped Children Move Ahead* (Department of Public Instruction: Madison, Wis., 1950).

The Educable Mentally Handicapped Child in Illinois (Commission for Handicapped Children, State of Illinois: Springfield, 1949).

Firestone, Sidney, H., and Orleans, Jacob S., *The Shortage of Special Class Teachers in Large Cities,* Research Publication #11 (Office of Research and Evaluation, Division of Teacher Education, College of the City of New York: N.Y.C., 1952).

Fiscal Survey of the State Department of Education (Ohio Public Expenditure Council: Columbus, 1946).

Helping the Physically Limited Child, Curriculum Bulletin 1952-53 Series #7 (Board of Education of the City of New York: N.Y.C.).

Hutchinson, Esther, Lanctot, Elizabeth M., and Phelps, Winthrop M., *Handbook on Physical Therapy for Cerebral Palsy* (The Ohio Society for Crippled Children, Inc.: Columbus, 1947).

Kilbane, Edward F., *New York State Law Pertaining to the Handicapped* (United Cerebral Palsy Associations of New York State, Inc.: N.Y.C., 1953).

Loviner, Della G., and Nichols, Edith C., *The Cerebral Palsied Child Goes to School* (The Ohio Society for Crippled Children, Inc.: Columbus, 1947).

MacLearie, Elizabeth C., *The Ohio Plan for Children with Speech and Hearing Problems* (State of Ohio, Deparment of Education: Columbus, 1953).

Ohio Commission on Children and Youth, Committee on Special Education, *The Status of the Gifted in Ohio* (Division of Special Education, Ohio Department of Education: Columbus, 1951).

Ohio Laws Governing Special Education under the State Subsidy for Handicapped Children (Division of Special Education, Ohio Department of Education: Columbus, 1954).

Report of the College Symposium on the Education of the Exceptional, February 25-28, 1952 (Hunter College of the City of New York: N.Y.C.).

State Legislation for Education of Exceptional Children, Bulletin #2 (Federal Security Agency, U. S. Office of Education: Washington, D.C., 1949).

Statistics of Special Education for Exceptional Children, Biennial Survey of Education in the United States, 1952-54, Chapter 5 (U.S. Department of Health, Education, and Welfare: Washington D.C., 1954).

A METROPOLITAN AREA PLANS FOR SPECIAL EDUCATION

FRANCES A. MULLEN

When Chicago plans current and future programs for exceptional children in the public schools, it does so from the perspective afforded by a long tradition of service. That tradition blossomed spectacularly as a result of the clear thinking of civic-minded Chicagoans at the turn of the century; it has flourished in a soil of community interest, fertilized with intelligence and vision The city of Jane Addams and Clarence Darrow has never lacked champions of the underprivileged.

Among American public school systems, Chicago claims the first class for crippled children (1899), the first child study clinic (1899), the first class for the blind (1900), and the first Parental School for court-committed truants (1902). Public school classes for the deaf were started in 1875; Chicago was an early exponent of the oral method of instruction of the deaf. Classes for the mentally retarded appeared in 1900. Public school teachers were sent into the hospitals to do bedside teaching in 1900, speech therapy began in 1910.

During the past half century, these programs have served increasing numbers of children with increasing effectiveness. Such programs have expanded upward into the secondary school for all types of handicapped children, and downward into the nursery for the cerebral palsied, the blind, and

The history of special education in Chicago is not solely a story of expansion. Rather it is one of continuous reappraisal as medical and psychological knowledge advances, urban culture develops, and the democratic philosophy of education is clarified. For example, as our understanding of the medical and social problems of tuberculosis changed over the years, Chicago first developed a program of open-air rooms in 1910, and in school building boom of the late twenties many specially designed rooms of this type were constructed in new buildings, just at the time that the concept of open-air rooms was being seriously questioned. Later the open-air aspects of these rooms were modified, and finally all special classrooms for delicate children were discontinued in 1942, but a program of "physical improvement centers" was substituted through which underweight children in under-privileged neighborhoods were given special services while remaining in their regular class groups. In 1951, The Physical Improvement Centers were closed with the advice of the medical profession. Similar changes in medical attitudes toward the handling of children with heart defects resulted in study of the policies for school placement of cardiac children. The Chicago Heart Association provided consultant medical service beginning in 1951, which resulted in the return of all but the most severe cardiac cases to the regular grades by 1952. Before 1950 heart disease accounted for 25% of the membership in the special schools; it now accounts for only 10% of the membership. Classes for pregnant girls have been discontinued. In these and many other instances there have been contractions of services, and changes of program and policy, paralleling expanding services in other areas.

Today Special Education Is Big Business

The Chicago public schools in January, 1955, make special provision for a large number of handicapped children. The detailed figures in Table I show that over 17,000 exceptional children are being served by approximately a thousand adults in seven special schools, in classes located in 173 of our 419 elementary and high schools, and in speech services to practically all schools, at a cost of seven million dollars in excess of what it would cost if these pupils could be educated in regular grades with no special services. The personnel figures do not include the services brought to exceptional children by 13 central office supervisors and administrators in special education, by 62 psychologists, by an increasing number of teacher-nurses; by adjustment teachers in all high schools and elementary schools, by placement counselors in the high schools, and by a host of other services in guidance, curriculum, subject supervision, and administration, which are shared with the non-handicapped. In costs some of this service is reflected in the auditor's calculation of overhead.

Services for gifted children are not included in Table I. The Department of Special Education has never had responsibility for them, except as gifted children have appeared among the physically handicapped, the deaf, or other special groups. The Chicago public schools however do give a great deal of attention to this group, through the administrative and instructional channels of the entire school system.

Special Education Is Intensely Personal

Every morning a fleet of 46 buses bring to four Chicago schools their cargoes of the physically handicapped, babies and high school seniors alike. Attendants help them to wheel chairs or crutches or walkers, see that they are toileted and helped to their classrooms if necessary. In the nursery Mary's interest in a game may lead her, in spite of her cerebral palsy, to take her first unaided step; in the physical therapy center a polio victim at age 10 and a recent amputee age 14 who has been struggling with the difficult art of using his new prothesis, may each achieve the same goal. At the afternoon assembly, others not so far along in rehabilitation will thrill to see crutches flying and amputees bouncing to the square dance tunes of the hill billy band led by an armless lad who plays the steel guitar with his toes. Fortunately most of the audience do not know that Theresa, who flinches just a little as her partner whirls her, must go back to the hospital next week to have a further amputation in a possibly fruitless effort to arrest a progressive disease process. Special rooms within the special schools provide for children with multiple handicaps, such as defects in mental capacity, vision or hearing associated with a crippling condition.

Visiting the deaf classes, we might find a group of three and four year olds learning to play together, while Billy on teacher's lap is exploring her lips and throat muscles and attempting joyously to imitate her actions though he cannot hear her voice; we see an older group moving from their session around the piano to vocabulary and language development exercises using group multiple hearing aid equipment; in Chicago's largest vocational school we find a deaf lad starring on the basketball team and another winning a prize in architecture, both in competition that makes no allowance for handicaps. Both have had continuous help in perfecting their speech reading abilities, and in improving the rhythm, tone, and pitch of their speech, as well as subject tutoring from a special home room teacher who has guided them through their four years, while their credits have been obtained in regular classes.

Blind babies gain much independence as they explore and enjoy their own nursery classroom, entertain and are entertained by their sighted kindergarten pals from across the hall at regular daily periods, and learn to care for their personal possessions, manage their outer clothing, and eat neatly. Before they begin first grade, they are familiar with the raised Braille dots on their blocks, some children have learned to name the letters and the numbers. Dottie in 3rd grade has learned to read Braille as rapidly as her sighted friends have progressed with ink-print. She is ready to join a regular third grade part of the day, returning to continue her special Braille training, to use the talking book and the Braille reference books, maps, and globes in her special room. By the time she reaches the upper grades she will be an expert typist both on the Braille writer and on a standard typewriter, and may have both machines at home as well as at school so that she may carry on her studies. She will go about the corridors of her elementary school unescorted; later she will take in stride the adjustment to a large city high school and a full program of integrated classes. The suite of rooms for the blind at Marshall High will provide her with an extensive library of Braille text books and reference materials; it is a popular center for social life, as the sighted students come in to read to blind students during study periods, or to dance with them; quiet cubicles for study via the talking book machine are available.

Henry's stuttering may have brought him agonies of frustration and humiliation whenever speech was required. With the help of the speech therapist he gains confidence and better control of his speech. Some youngsters formerly as handicapped as Henry have learned to participate fully in all oral activities to the extent of becoming class president or graduation speaker.

The schools for the physically handicapped have increased speech therapy service since cerebral palsied children, in particular, need intensive speech therapy. Other schools at present have speech therapy only one day per week.

Classes for the educable mentally handicapped face special problems of parental acceptance. When an ungraded division was first suggested to Harry's mother, she was horrified. Frequent counseling with her over a period of a year as Harry's lack of adjustment became more evident helped her to see that he needed more specialized educational assistance than the teacher of a large regular class could provide. Now mother is pleased with the change in Harry's personality, as he has blossomed under the warmth of Miss Sullivan's primary ungraded room, where 15 youngsters lose their fear of reading and find opportunity for success at their own levels. When he is twelve he will transfer to an advanced ungraded center where a departmental program including appropriate shop experience will give him wider opportunities and where his teachers will begin to focus on preparing him for problems of community and job adjustment. If he does well there, he may have opportunity to attend a modified high school program for perhaps a year. Many of his classmates will remain in the ungraded division housed in an elementary school until they drop out of school.

Truancy and other symptoms of maladjustment in the regular grades are problems every school must face. Frequency in certain schools, occasionally in any school, children will be found whose problems seem insoluble with the resources available to the regular school. Such pupils are given another chance in our day schools for the socially maladjusted. Here we reduce class memberships, add a variety of shops and other curricular opportunities, select teachers of proven ability in dealing with the most disturbed youngsters, and increase the staff of psychological, medical, and social workers available to focus their skills on a child's problems. About 15 per cent of the pupils enrolled will return successfully to regular grades, 20 per cent will "progress" to custodial institutions, and 65 per cent will complete their education in the special school. Records show that pupils in the social adjustment schools make significant gains in the skill subjects; improvement in social adjustment is harder to measure, but observers from the courts, the agencies, and the community agree that significant achievements are made.

Pupils who fail to respond to the program of the day school for social adjustment, and pupils who find their way into the courts for other reasons, may be committed to the Parental School. There they experience a period of clean, orderly living in cottage groups under the supervision of friendly cottage parents, with club and recreational programs, supplemented by psychiatric, psychological, medical, and religious resources. Effective religious programs are provided by Protestant and Catholic agencies according to the choice of the child's parents. All these, added to a school program emphasizing academic subjects, shop and agriculture for the boys, and personal grooming, household arts, and typing for the girls, start many potential delinquents on the road to wholesome home and community adjustment. Again evaluation is difficult; we know these youngsters gain weight and gain in reading and arithmetic skill; we know they become less tense and more responsive to human beings.

FRANCES A. MULLEN

Recent Metropolitan Trends

One step in planning for the future is careful reappraisal of the directions of recent changes.

One trend is the extension of services to new groups. Classes for the severely mentally handicapped were initiated as part of a state-wide experimental program two years ago, and are under careful evaluation. Homebound children were first served by one teacher in 1948; in 1955, 12 teachers are so employed. The schools for the physically handicapped have been accepting for trial placements children with more severe physical handicaps, including very difficult cerebral palsy cases. A class for mentally handicapped blind was opened in February 1955; other increases in provisions for pupils with two handicaps are under consideration. Hospital teaching has been extended to emotionally disturbed children in a psychiatric ward of a general hospital and in a special institution.

The age and grade range of provisions for the exceptional child has been widened. The nursery classes for the cerebral palsied were taken over from a private project in 1943, a vocational high school opened its doors to the deaf in 1950, four high school classes for educable mentally handicapped were instituted in 1952.

Secondly, a complementary trend has been the return to regular grades of certain types of children formerly offered special classes. The cardiac and the tuberculosis susceptible groups have been mentioned. The number of hospital teachers needed has decreased, partly as a result of the antibiotic drugs which have greatly reduced the period of hospitalization for some types of child patients. Fewer hard-of-hearing children are now referred to special classes, decreasing the membership of these classes from above 700 to under 500 during the past 12 years. Regular schools transfer fewer pupils to the social adjustment schools. Pregnant girls are no longer required to attend a special, stigmatized class, but are released from school attendance to the care of various social agencies, and may be returned to regular schools later.

Every child who can profit from education in the regular grades should be there. The line of demarcation between a handicap that can be accommodated in the regular grade and the more severe handicap requiring special placement is a flexible one, determined by the physical, mental, and emotional needs of each child. The change in the location of that line of demarcation reflects the increased skill of modern teachers in meeting varied needs within one room, and increased availability of psychological, medical and social consultants to the regular staff.

However, this trend, toward regular class placement for a child with a degree of handicap formerly thought to demand special placement, can be carried too far. Physicians and others not close to the educational needs of a child sometimes become over enthusiastic advocates of regular grade placement. The hard-of-hearing child, for example, whose language and speech development has not been normal will not necessarily be ready for a regular grade as soon as a hearing aid is fitted. He may need very skilled auditory training and special language work for several years before he can profit from a regular grade.

198

Thirdly, a trend toward closer integration of special programs with the rest of the school is clearly related to the trend to retain more pupils in the regular grades. Our two oldest schools for physically handicapped children are in separate buildings. Two others are remodeled sections within regular buildings. Now on the drawing boards is a new school for physically handicapped children to replace one existing school, and to relieve overcrowding in another. It will have both handicapped and non-handicapped pupils; library, gymnasium, lunchroom, and auditorium facilities will be shared. This sharing will provide benefits in human relations to both the handicapped and the non-handicapped.

Supplementing the work of the special schools for social adjustment is an expanding program of social adjustment centers, which are small classes for maladjusted youngsters in scattered elementary schools.

Classes for the mentally handicapped are widely scattered in many regular schools. Recent years have seen increased participation of the special pupils in the assemblies, student councils, and other educational aspects of the school. Fewer schools dismiss special classes at a different hour or provide different recess periods to "prevent conflicts" or appease disturbed parents or parent groups.

The blind and partially seeing are in fully integrated programs. The deaf are integrated in high school classes; in elementary schools so far integration has not been successful, although schools are endeavoring to provide increased contacts between deaf and hearing children in the upper grades.

Lastly, a continuing, but marked aspect, of the Chicago program is the interest of community and professional groups in the special education program. As has been indicated, this is not new. Special education in Chicago owed its origins around 1900 to the determined pressures, the careful study, the generous financial support, and the intelligent proposals of devoted citizens. The trend continues as we enter the second half of the century, The Chicago Hearing Society and the Illinois Society for Prevention of Blindness in 1950 spearheaded the drive and provided early financing for what is now an on-going vision and hearing survey, an integral part of the public school program. The Chicago Heart Association is now initiating an extensive vocational guidance service to cardiac pupils. The Council on the Educable Mentally Handicapped has focused the attention of medical and social experts on our ungraded program with fruitful results, particularly with regard to the vocational and medical problem of this group. The Illinois Society for the Crippled last year established a committee to plan a course for teachers of the physically handicapped; the chairman of their medical advisory board will offer that course under the auspices of Northwestern University. The parent-teacher movement, in the state and in the city has stepped up its interest in the exceptional child. An "Exceptional child chairman" has been appointed in most local school units of the Parent-Teacher Association; a continuing educational program is provided for those chairmen by district and region chairmen; great interest has resulted. Committee of the Welfare of Metropolitan Chicago are scrutinizing the school program for the physically handicapped. Contributions of the social and professional groups and of influential individuals are too many to enumerate.

Recent State Trends

A relatively recent trend is the rapid growth of special education in the state outside of Chicago, bringing increased state reimbursement and increased state activity in standard setting and in educational planning. Chicago's program antedates the state program and has not increased in size as a result of financial reimbursement for excess costs under progressively extended state legislation, except in speech correction, and small beginnings in provisions for the trainable mentally handicapped.

There have, however, been other impacts on the Chicago program from the developing state program. Teacher training standards have been raised, formalized, and adhered to more rigidly, most conspicuously in the speech therapy field. Other standards as to housing, equipment, curriculum, admission of pupils receive emphasis when incorporated in regulations of the state Department of Public Instruction, even though in large part the standards when established reflected existing practices in Chicago. Participation of Chicago staff members in the development of state standards has been stimulating, the visits of state supervisors have been helpful.

Specific results of state programs were anticipated in the city's relations with its suburbs. Chicago has always recognized a responsibility to accept suburban handicapped children provided the home community paid a share of the cost and no Chicago child was displaced. With state aid there have been steady increases in suburban provisions for the mentally and physically handicapped. Chicago therefore anticipated some decrease in requests for placement of suburban pupils. No decrease in actual numbers of applications has come about, perhaps because the growing state programs have made more school boards aware of their responsibilities to handicapped pupils and more willing to pay tuition to send them to Chicago classes.

In the next few years our public school program may be more affected by the growth of facilities for exceptional children in parochial and other private schools. The Catholic and Lutheran schools of Chicago are developing facilities for the mentally handicapped, the deaf, and other groups. The public schools have not yet felt much relief from these programs perhaps because of long waiting lists, especially in the area of the mentally handicapped. Pressure for school placement for the deaf has eased somewhat.

Recent National Trends

No local program develops in a vacuum. The trends noted in Chicago reflect national movements. The changes in thinking about segregation and integration, the interest in the severely handicapped and the multiply handicapped are instances. Chicagoans keep alert to national movements and national thinking through many channels of professional interchange. There are changes in method and philosophy primarily originating in the educational profession; special education finds particularly important also many advances in medicine, psychology, and social work, even changing concepts of the meaning of democracy in American political life. No attempt is made in this brief resume to trace the national trends reflected in the Chicago picture:

the reader will easily recognize them. As a local area plans to meet the particular needs of its own population, it must learn from the experience and knowledge accumulated in other geographical areas and other professional areas.

Crucial Problems

It is clear that there are many unsolved problems, many issues that need rethinking, in every aspect of special education.

The adolescent mentally handicapped group urgently needs attention. We have at present a good program for these pupils until they reach the age of 16, but few facilities that can offer helpful training to these youngsters beyond that age. Our own experience shows, and our friends in the welfare agencies, the rehabilitation agencies, and the state employment service constantly remind us that it is the unusual handicapped child who can find or hold employment below the age of 18. We need a combined program of work and school that develops good work habits and teaches the skills of job and community adjustment, that allows a pupil to try out a job and return to school when that job does not work out. It should be a program housed in a school with the pupil's social age mates; it should bear little if any resemblance to most current high school programs. We have been experimenting in may different patterns; a concentrated attack and a bold new program are indicated.

Juvenile delinquency is not on the decrease. The community rightly or wrongly looks to the school system for answers. How can our special schools and classes do a more effective job? What special services or adaptations of curriculum, method, and administration might be helpful to the regular school?

Housing of special education: Chicago like most of the nation has thus far been unable to keep up with the tremendous growth of the elementary school population. We are just completing a four-year fifty-million-dollar building program but still have ten thousand pupils on double shift, and a large number of outmoded school buildings. From the building program now being completed special education has benefited to the extent of one greatly needed building for physically handicapped children, some rehabilitation of the living quarters of the Parental School, and new Parental School quarters for girls.

If the City of Chicago is sufficiently alert to the school building crisis, another bond issue may be authorized this spring. In anticipation of such an event, the needs of exceptional children are being studied on a city-wide basis. Plans are being made for relocation and for additional facilities. Special education should serve the city more realistically than it has been able to do during the past decades, when special education had to be relegated to the space not desperately needed by the regular school, and areas of the city where special needs were most intense were left without facilities.

Teacher recruitment is another crucial problem, except in the field of speech correction. Although the number of blind babies has been increasing, it has been impossible to find an adequate supply of teachers competent in Braille and in teaching the blind. Four additional classes for the blind were opened in 1953 and one is being added in February 1955. The Parents of the Blind and other organizations are offering teacher scholarships. Our supervisor of the blind has a small group of teachers in training under the auspices of the Chicago Teachers College.

Staffing the 286 classes for the mentally handicapped is a constant problem, though several Chicago colleges and universities offer continuous training in this field and the number of vacancies has been decreased.

A new salary scale, ranging from $3500 to $6750 depending on training and experience will, it is hoped, help Chicago recruit teachers in all phases of the school program.

Pre-service and in-service teacher training need much attention. The Chicago Teachers College, a part of the public school system, and our neighboring universities offer intermittently some of the most essential courses. We certify teachers who have good general backgrounds plus a minimum of scattered special courses. In most areas of special education the need for coherent organized sequences of training, offered as integral parts of continuing graduate programs staffed by competent, permanent faculty members engaged in research as well as training is very great. Such programs exist in Urbana and Bloomington. Adequate programs in a number of special fields should be developed in Chicago where half the special teachers of the state are employed.

Curriculum planning has not been neglected in spite of the press of housing and staffing problems in recent years. Our teachers of the deaf organized a comprehensive course of language development in 1952; teacher committees in the mentally handicapped program with the cooperation of the Division of Curriculum Development, the Red Cross, and community representatives issued a course in home nursing for the mentally handicapped in 1953; newsletters carry exchange of ideas and suggestions between teachers in various fields; departmental meetings and ICEC meetings provide other stimuli to creative thinking and planning by teachers and administrators. Further work in curriculum development is desperately needed in many of the special fields.

How Is Planning Effected?

Faced with these crucial problems and many others, needing both immediate palliatives and long range planning, how does a large unwieldy metropolitan area achieve constructive planning, and insure acceptance and implementation of developing programs?

1. Teachers in their classrooms are the first and most important source of planning. As they are stimulated to creative experimentation under the guidance of local administrators with first-hand knowledge of the problems to be faced, channels of communication that bring their ideas to the central office, and that facilitate rapid exchange of suggestions between teachers and between schools must be developed. Newsletters, meetings, discussions, and visits can become effective if they are carried out in an atmosphere of mutual respect, understanding, and freedom, where honest criticism can be accepted and no suggestion is discarded without consideration. With the pressures under which both central office and local schools work, with time and dis-

taĥce barriers, this atmosphere is not easy to create and is easily disturbed. Here lies a crucial responsibility for all who hope to influence effective planning.

2. Special Education must keep close to regular education. Thinking and planning and discussion going on with respect to a special program must involve and draw upon the help of many persons not directly responsible for the special group, including principals, district and assistant superintendents, specialists in art or home mechanics, and many others. This too is not easy to achieve. Every school worker is busy in his own area; it is not always easy to find the time to think about a problem for which one is not immediately responsible. Yet all activities in a great school system are closely interlocked; the success of any program depends on the understanding, cooperation, and support of many individuals. When slow development of an idea carries many persons along in the planning process and incorporates the fruits of their experience, sounder growth will result.

3. Chicago is blessed with a bewildering array of community resources. Men and women of international reputation in medicine, psychology, speech pathology, audiology, and social work, in industry, commerce, labor and government, have time and again demonstrated that they are available at a telephone call to sit down with school people for detailed exploration of perplexing problems. Organizations interested in every conceivable type of handicapping condition, with emphases from the emotional to the scientific, abound. Welfare agencies, rehabilitation agencies, hospitals, and clinics need our advice as much as we need theirs on our overlapping responsibilities for individual clients and for creative planning. Yet the very plethora of helpers presents its problems. A woman's club gets excited about one aspect of one problem and becomes a pressure group for a plan which does not fit into the overall picture. A men's luncheon club wants to do so much for one particular group of handicapped children as to perhaps have unfortunate psychological effects on the youngsters. A respected professional agency makes requests that amount almost to exploitation of a group of pupils for the fund raising needs of the organization. Physicians seeing a child only in an individual setting, and unaware of the reaction of that child in a group, or the pressures on the teacher in a regular grade, make recommendations that are unrealistic. Parents grasp at any rationalization which will stave off the necessity of full acceptance of the child's handicap. How can the energies, the good will, and the skills and knowledge of these different groups be harnessed into effective working relationships from which will emerge better services to exceptional children?

Again the answer is not simple, but it is certainly not to be found in the closed door. Patient consultation and discussion will disabuse some of these people of their misconceptions. The educator must continue to be willing to study all criticisms, and to consider all suggestions no matter how contrary to current policy of the schools. Advisory committees and councils on a variety of levels, some acting as standing committees interested in a specific program, some as temporary groups to study an immediate problem, help to develop the atmosphere of confidence and mutual respect in which progress is made.

4. Planning that is to result in action must be channeled and must be based on facts, not opinions. Each school and each class must study its own local situation, and state in written or in graphic form, the changes which

TABLE I
SPECIAL EDUCATION IN CHICAGO — AS OF NOVEMBER, 1954

	No. of Pupils Enrolled	No. of Teachers, Therapists, House Parents	No. of Special Civil Service Attendants	No. of Special Schools	No. of Regular Schools Housing Special Classes Elem.	High School	Excess Cost Per Pupil 1953-1954
EDUCABLE MENTALLY RETARDED	4,554	282			133	4	$ 322.98
TRAINABLE MENTALLY RETARDED	48	4			2		322.98
PHYSICALLY HANDICAPPED	1,343	183	96	4			866.24
HOSPITAL INSTRUCTION	400	36					866.24
HOMEBOUND INSTRUCTION	125	12					866.24
SOCIALLY MALADJUSTED							
DAY SCHOOLS	1,671	108		2	5		628.15
PARENTAL SCHOOL	245	41		1			1,210.61
BLIND	113	14			12	2	Elem. 965.87 / H.S. 869.51
PARTIALLY SEEING	414	45			38	7	Elem. 965.87 / H.S. 869.51
DEAF AND HARD OF HEARING	602	76			69	7	Elem. 1,071.01 / H.S. 551.87
SPEECH DEFECTIVE	8,000	70					38.65
TOTALS	17,467	871	96		160*	13*	$ 6,128,835.00**
TOTAL FOR CHICAGO PUBLIC SCHOOLS	411,731	14,611			353	46	155,966,825.00***
PER CENT — SPECIAL EDUCATION	4.2%	5.8%			45.3%	28.2%	3.9%
TOTAL SCHOOL PROGRAM							

*Total number of schools housing special education classes, duplications excluded, and not counting speech therapy services.
***Chicago School Budget, 1954
**Total excess costs, 1953-1954.

have taken place in its population, in the problems of its students. Detailed maps may show just where the needs are; graphs can show whether a program is gaining or losing in pupil enrollment, in pupil achievement, in teacher recruitment, in equipment, or whatever constitutes a problem. In a small system, it may be adequate to have such information in the teacher's, the principal's or the supervisor's mind. In a big system, such information must be systematized, and passed both up and down the line and should result in recommendations embodying the boldest and most creative thinking of all concerned.

The schools of Chicago and the schools of the nation stand today at a crossroad. Never before has there been so much interest in the schools, so much bitter criticism, so much intelligent concern and support. To the extent that the schools of the nation fail to solve the problems of bringing effective educational services to all children, we endanger the America we believe in, the democracy we cherish, and the happiness of the children we love!

May we have the intelligence to analyze the criticisms, the courage to admit the failures of some of our pet ideas, the skill to help others understand the values of the ideas that have succeeded, and the imagination to plan boldly.

SPECIAL EDUCATION IN NEW YORK CITY

FRANK J. O'BRIEN

Children who have no handicapping disability, or who have one that does not interfere with or prevent them from participating in their regular life pursuits, are able to obtain maximum benefits from the general education that is provided by regular school programs.

The more seriously handicapped child, however, is not so fortunate. He must be given special educational opportunities and helps, the features of which are determined in each instance by the kind, severity, and number of his defects, deficiencies, and abilities.

The large number and variety of technical programs in special education that are provided, especially in public schools in the larger cities throughout the United States, bear eloquent testimony to the profound respect with which the individual is held and treated in our free society. These and other similar educational programs are made available to all children who can benefit from them, regardless of race, color, or creed, or the kind, severity or multiplicity of handicaps, abilities, and special talents.

The underlying and basic philosophy of an effective program of special education recognizes and emphasizes that the handicapped child is first and foremost a child. Consequently, the general features of his education must be fundamentally the same as those required by and provided for all children. In addition to these general educational provisions, however, the handicapped child must be provided additional helps such as modified teaching techniques, selected materials and equipment, transportation, and specially trained teachers. If his handicap is of a kind or severity that prevents him from attending school, even when transportation is available, and if he can benefit from an education, the "school should be brought to him" in his hospital, convalescent home, or other institution, or his own home. Education is provided this type of handicapped child by a well planned systematic program for 'the homebound'.

In our American way of life every individual is sacred, and those who can benefit have a right to an education adapted to their particular needs and abilities. For this reason society in general and the administrators of educational systems in particular, have a comparable responsibility to provide it. Such considerations as higher per capita costs and administrative difficulties and complications are of secondary importance.

As the fundamental aim of special education is identical with that of education in general, it must be predicated first and foremost upon the basic objectives that pertain to all children. These basic objectives that general and special education have in common include: helping each child develop his physical, mental, and moral potentialities to a maximum in order that he may acquire, improve, and preserve his total health, for the purpose of becoming an emotionally mature, morally motivated, integrated individual and at the same time, a worthy and contributing citizen.

Modern Education may be defined as that which accepts as its responsibility the healthy development of the total personality of each child. However, children of any given chronological age differ greatly in their intellectual endowment, functioning capacities, emotional and social maturity, and physical health, and in the degree to which spiritual and moral values motivate and direct their behaviour. It follows, then, that before an educational program can be organized and effectively adapted to the particular needs and potentialities of each individual, the total child must be thoroughly known and understood. Although this simple but fundamental principle applies, or should apply, to the planning for the education of all children, its necessity is more apparent and consequently more easily recognized as an important first step in any plan to provide an educational program for children who have outstanding physical or mental defects or deficiencies.

It is a truism, therefore, that to be successful, any educational program for handicapped children be predicated upon an accurate and complete knowledge of each child; this is obtained, as far as possible, from technical studies and scientific examinations. The acquisition of this necessary information, which is very extensive in scope, requires the services and contributions of individuals who are trained and experienced in various disciplines. As a result the 'teacher' in any modern educational program, and therefore in all special programs, is no longer the individual, but a 'team' which consists of all those, who can or should contribute to the understanding and education of the child. This team of educators consists primarily of the child's parents, religious counselors and classroom teacher; in addition, it may include a pediatrician, psychiatrist, cardiologist, or other medical specialist; nurse, psychologist, school social worker; family, child, or health case worker; educational and vocational guidance counselor; recreational worker, etc. The number of individuals who will constitute the team will vary according to the specific needs of the child and the extent to which all the necessary helps are available and can be organized into this particular cooperative effort. However, the mere existence or availability of a relatively large number of professional personnel and services does not, of itself, necessarily make for team action or guarantee maximum benefits to the child. The optimum educational benefits are achieved only when all members of the team work together harmoniously and effectively for the realization of its common goal, — the total needs, best interests, and highest good of each child.

To be effective, this team work, requires that each member, must be willing and able to make the required adjustments in his previously held professional philosophy and practices, in order that they may be adapted to and integrated with the other and equally valuable contributions of his colleagues.

Whether all of these various services are provided by the educational system, or whether some are provided by other community agencies, is of relatively minor significance. It is, however, very important that, in every instance, the proper means be provided for administering and coordinating them into a unified program.

In New York City, for example, the administration and coordination of the special educational and service programs is, from the viewpoint of education, accomplished primarily by two administrative devices. First, the Division of Child Welfare of the Board of Education, administered by an Associate Superintendent, was organized for the single purpose of coordinating, administering, and supervising the large number of special educational and service programs available in the Board of Education and which for the most part constitute the Division. Second, as the medical and nursing services to school children in New York City are provided by the Department of Health, a Coordinating Council on School Health has been organized. The regular membership of this council consists of the appropriate administrators who have been designated by the two agencies. However, when a problem arises in any aspect of a health or special education program, those concerned are asked to attend the meetings. For example, when the matter involves the education of the deaf, the appropriate specialist in the Department of Health and the Principal of the School for the Deaf of the Board of Education, neither of whom is a regular member of the council, are invited. If it seems desirable, a representative of some other community agency may also be invited to attend the Council's meeting and participate in the deliberations. By this simple administrative device, many inter-agency conflicts are prevented, and those that do arise are readily solved to the satisfaction of all and to the maximum benefits of the children.

If a request to conduct a survey or to provide some special service is made by an individual or agency representative, either to the Department of Health or the Board of Education, it is referred to the Coordinating Council on School Health for consideration, and a representative from the agency making the request is invited to attend the meeting and present his proposal.

Both these agencies have joint responsibility for other programs presented to the Coordinating Council for consideration and approval or implementation.

Examples of these projects are the experimental testing of children with the Salk Vaccine; the X-Raying of all school personnel; the detection and care of youths who are users of narcotics; podiatric examinations of high school children.

An instance of a practical administrative principle that can come out of this kind of joint partnership and planning is the policy in New York City that children are admitted to and discharged from special classes for the physically handicapped and the program for the education of the homebound only on the recommendation and approval of the Department of Health. If a child is recommended by a private or clinic physician for placement in a special class or for homebound instruction, the recommendation must be approved by the appropriate physician in the Bureau for Physically Handicapped of the Department of Health and sent to the appropriate Bureau in the Board of Education before the child is admitted. The educational personnel have exclusive responsibility during the period the child is in a special class or on homebound instruction for planning, providing and conducting the academic program that takes into consideration both the child's fundamental and special educational needs as well as the medical recommendations made by his physician.

Another example of the value of such joint planning is evidenced in the procedure established for keeping personnel in both agencies informed in regard to policy changes. If a new policy is established, or a change is made in an existing one, usually on the recommendation of the Coordinating Council on School Health, notices are sent out simultaneously by the Commissioner of Health to the school doctors and nurses and by the Superintendent of Schools to the assistant superintendents, directors, principals and teachers. This simple administrative procedure has proved most beneficial in maintaining team play, mutual confidence, and good morale between the staffs of both agencies. It also contributes to the prevention or solution of misunderstandings and, by so doing, to the continuous improvement of the quality of health and educational services for handicapped children.

The over-all administration and supervision of the various special educational and service programs require also that active liaison relationships be maintained by the Division of Child Welfare not only with the Department of Health and all other activities in the educational system, but also with teacher training institutions and professional and lay organizations such as the New York Heart Association, the several Tuberculosis and Health Associations, Cancer Committees, Cerebral Palsy Associations, and Parent Groups such as the Parents' Association of Homebound Children and the Association of Parents of Children in CRMD Classes (classes for children with retarded mental development), to mention only a few. This policy of maintaining and fostering favorable cooperative relationships with so many and varied community agencies contributes a great deal to the administrative efficiency and functioning effectiveness of all these programs and constitutes one of the unique features of this type of education. By participating actively in deliberations with members of other community organizations interested also in the education of handicapped children, school representatives are able to bring to these discussions a practical understanding of the special characteristics, needs, limitations, available facilities, and administrative requirements of the schools. At the same time, they help these agencies to increase the effectiveness of their own programs and to make greatly needed and valuable contributions to the schools. This broad and continuous program of participation in community organizational planning for special educational programs demands a great deal of the administrator's time. However, our experience in New York City convinced us that the time given to these deliberations is more than justified in terms of the resulting goodwill toward and constructive assistance to the schools.

All handicapped children have more characteristics in common with other children than they have differences. One important evidence of this is that the vast majority of them will ultimately take their places as members of society and associate with people who are not handicapped, at least not in the same way that they are. Consequently, every effort should be made during the school career of the handicapped to have them receive their education, as far as is practicable, in regular school buildings with other children. In other words, children with special educational or health problems should not be segregated for any greater length of time than is absolutely necessary. It should be evident that if a child is eventually to take his place with others in the community, he must have experience and help in learning how to associate happily and constructively with them. This can be accomplished best by seeing to it that he is an integral part of his general community during the formative school years.

In harmony with this principle, in New York City all classes for handicapped children, with two exceptions, are organized in regular schools. The two exceptions are the programs for the deaf and the emotionally disturbed. The reason for these exceptions is that the very special and intensive problems these children present, particularly during the early part of their education, require that the programs be conducted in highly specialized settings. However, as soon as these children have been benefited sufficiently from these programs so that they can maintain themselves with no or very little special help, they are returned to regular classes or to special classes in a regular school. Any special help that they still need in the regular school setting should, of course, be provided them.

For maximum educational results and supervisory efficiency, two or more classes should make up a special educational unit-organization in a regular school. The more special classes that can be organized in a school, which is determined in the final analyses by the amount of space that is available in each school, the more efficient is the special educational program from the viewpoint of benefits to children. For example, the larger the number of handicapped children in a given school, the greater is the opportunity to organize classes with the smallest possible grade range in each class and at the same time afford more opportunities for flexibility and for the organization of inter-departmental programs. In addition, children in these special classes can and do participate in selected aspects of the regular school program to the extent that their physical and mental conditions and the general school plant and program permit.

There is an unnecessarily wasteful expenditure of time out of the school day, and loss in his education that the handicapped child can ill afford to sustain, when he is required to go to a clinic or hospital for a special therapy. In this regular school setting, arrangements are made for the child to receive the therapies he needs to the extent that is possible with our existing staff. However, up to the present, it has unfortunately not always been possible to provide in the regular schools all of the therapies these children require. It is our plan and hope that in the not too distant future it will be possible to provide itinerant occupational and physio-therapists to the children who require these services as we now make available the services of speech therapists and itinerant teachers of the deaf, who give lip reading instruction to the hard of hearing children and to deaf children who have benefited sufficiently from the training they received in our School for the Deaf to be able to return to a regular class. Our Speech Improvement Program, through which help is provided by itinerant speech teachers to children in both regular and special classes, provides this type of special assistance to a large proportion of children who require it, although unfortunately, due to staff limitation, it does not reach all of them.

Without doubt one of the richest rewards that this broader kind of social experience with 'all children' brings to handicapped children who receive their education in a regular school environment, is the practical help they receive to minimize, if not completely eradicate, their feelings of 'being different' and, by so doing assist them in identifying themselves more readily and completely with other children.

From the experiences gained by attending a regular school and associating with so-called 'normal children', they gain positive and convincing evidence that their handicapped condition does not and therefore should not set them apart from other children any more than do differences in height, weight or color of eyes. Consequently, when they leave school to take up their responsibilities in society, they should have fewer handicapping psychological impediments that would stand in the way of their making successful and satisfying personal, social and employment adjustments than if they had received their entire education in a completely segregated school setting. This goal of helping handicapped children to accept themselves as they really are, and not resentfully and unfairly to compare themselves with their fantasy ideal of what they should like to be, or with others who do not seem to have such patent and limiting handicaps as they do, is, without any question, one of the most valuable contributions that special education can make to these children.

However, there are factors, or perhaps better, a constellation of conditions, that dictate that some handicapped children can best obtain the educational and medical therapies they need only in an institutional environment such as a resident school or hospital. Such considerations as the kind, severity and number of handicaps, the role of the family and especially its ability and willingness to help and make the necessary adjustments in its understanding of the child and how it can cooperate with the medical and educational people who are participating in the child's program, and the number and kind of therapeutic and educational facilities that the community offers, may point to the resident school or the hospital as the setting where certain children can receive most help rather than living at home and attending a special clinic-school program.

Thus, children who are extremely handicapped physically and require such costly facilities as therapeutic pools, cannot be admitted to special class programs that are organized in the average regular school building. They should receive their clinic-educational help either in special school buildings or hospitals that are equipped for this purpose.

The ultimate value of educational programs is enhanced greatly when children are admitted to special school at the youngest possible age. The chronological and mental age of three is not too young for many physically handicapped children of at least average intellectual endowment, to start their education. Among other very desirable results that can be achieved by making educational provisions for very young children is that academic retardation can be reduced significantly and in some conditions completely eliminated.

There are several factors that make this possible, not the least valuable of which is socialization, which includes learning how to associate and live happily and constructively with other children and adults. These social experiences also help in great measure to accelerate emotional maturation and thereby reduce or prevent the development of infantile fixation which can become a more far-reaching handicapping force than the original physical or intellectual deficiency or defect.

There is also the problem of providing the proper educational opportunities for children who have two or more major handicapping conditions. For example, if a child is both deaf and feebleminded, should he be placed in a program for the deaf and given, in addition, an educational program in harmony with his permanent intellectual deficiency, or should he be placed in a program for the education of the feebleminded and through the help of an itinerant teacher be given lip-reading and other special helps that deaf children need? There is, perhaps, no one answer and therefore no absolute criterion or rule based exclusively upon the co-existence of two or more handicaps in a child, that can be applied for the most advantageous educational placement of all multiple handicapped children. To the hypothetical question asked above, unless there are some unusual reasons that indicate otherwise, we should place the child in the School for the Deaf. The reason is that we consider his deafness the major handicap from the viewpoint of education, and in New York City we have classes for mentally retarded children in our School for the Deaf.

Each kind of special handicap presents its own particular problem and needs. It is not our purpose at this time to present a detailed analysis of the many physical and mental conditions that indicate the need for special programs. It will suffice to state that a complete program of special education would include provision for children with retarded mental deficiency (the feebleminded); those having cardiac, orthopedic and speech defects; children having cerebral palsy; children with visual and auditory deficiencies; and children presenting emotional disturbances. These special educational programs should be provided, whenever possible, in special classes in regular schools. When this is not possible or is specifically excluded, the appropriate educational program should be provided in hospitals, convalescent homes, treatment and remand centers and in the child's home when he is capable of benefiting from, but due to health status, is not able to attend school. In many instances when education is given under these conditions, it becomes a very helpful therapeutic as well as educational force.

Although each special educational program has many elements in common with all other special programs, each one, nevertheless, has its own particular characteristics that set it apart from the others. The reason why all special educational programs have common elements, even though the nature, number and severity of the handicap represents wide differences, is that the common denominator is the child and not a handicap or lack of one. This is the same reason why general education for the 'average' child and special education for the child with special needs also have more in common than they have that is different.

It must be accepted that the education of the total child is a much more costly operation than is the teaching of subject matter to children. For comparable reasons also, special education costs more per child than general education. However, the saving of individuals for themselves and for society as self-supporting, contented, loyal and contributing members of their community rather than their becoming personally disgruntled, unhappy, despondent, hostile and incompetent people and social liabilities, more than justifies the educational cost. Whether or not the cost of special education is excessive can be determined by comparing it, not with the per capita costs of general education but with what it costs the community if the child with handicaps is denied the special helps he needs to make him personally competent and socially desirable.

It is our belief that there is no one type of organization that should be provided or is best suited for all handicapped children or for all communities. What is most practical or what is all that can be provided in a given community at a given time may not always be in harmony with one's basic philosophy as to what constitutes the best setting for the best kind of education for specific types of handicapped children. What can be provided at a given time in any one community will be determined, in most instances perhaps, more by the facilities that are available or those that can be made available than by what is theoretically the most desirable for handicapped children. One has to be realistic, especially in initiating these programs, and not try to obtain the impossible. Naturally, anyone interested in handicapped children wants nothing less than the 'ideal'. However, it is administratively necessary, at times, to start at the level that one can and then continue to improve the program until the ideal, or as near the ideal as possible, is realized

It will be to the glorious credit of our American way of life when all children who can benefit, regardless of their needs, color, race, creed or extreme handicaps, receive an education that is best suited to each as an individual and as a contributing member of our free society.

SPECIAL CLASSES FOR HANDICAPPED CHILDREN*

HELEN M. WALLACE, J. WAYNE WRIGHTSTONE, AND ELENA GALL

The provision of adequate and equal educational opportunity for handicapped children is but one aspect of a program which should include prevention, early case finding, accurate diagnosis, prompt and maximum treatment and rehabilitation, and vocational guidance. The magnitude of the problem of education of handicapped children is illustrated by the fact that, as of 1948, 41 states had laws authorizing or requiring local school systems to provide special educational services for one or more types of children deviating seriously from what are supposed to be normal physical, mental, or emotional characteristics.[1]

It has been conservatively estimated that in the United States there are between 4,000,000 and 5,000,000 children of school age who are so exceptional as to need some adjustment in their school programs, if they are to attain optimum development.[2] In 1948 there were 378,059 exceptional children of various types reported as enrolled for special educational services in city school systems.[1] The problem then is large. It is of vital importance to the children concerned and their families, to the health, medical, and educational professions, and to the community because of the large expenditures of funds involved.

The types of handicapped children who are usually provided for through these special services may include those with cardiac, orthopedic, visual, or hearing problems; those considered to be "under par" physically; those who are mentally retarded; those who are gifted; and those who are socially and emotionally maladjusted. Special types of educational programs for these various types of exceptional children have existed in this country for over 50 years. The types of educational placement provided for handicapped children may consist of the following: regular classes in public and private schools; special classes in regular public and private schools, such as health improvement, cardiac, orthopedic, braille, sight conservation, and cerebral

*Reprinted from *American Journal of Public Health,* Vol. 44, No. 8, August, 1954 and used by special permission of the authors and the American Public Health Association, Inc., 1790 Broadway, New York City.

palsy; special separate day schools; special separate residential schools; educational service provided for children in hospitals and convalescent institutions; and home instruction for the homebound group.

Many of the educational programs now include similar services for preschool children. In addition , it has been the usual custom to provide special

TABLE 1 DATA ON SPECIAL CLASSES IN NEW YORK CITY PUBLIC SCHOOLS—1951-1952

	Type of Special Class			
	Cardiac	Orthopedic	Braille	Sight Conservation
Estimated number of handicapped children in school	7,000-10,000	4,200	?	?
Number of special classes	45*	39* **	12†	105†
Number of children registered	727	622**	105	1,334
Average register per class	16.2	15.9	8.8	12.7
Ratio of children in special class to:				
1. Total school population	10.5‡	8.9‡	1.2‡	14.6‡
2. Estimated number of handicapped children in school	Per cent 10.3–7.3	Per cent 14.8	?	?

School population in 1951–1952 was as follows:

Elementary schools	585,298	} 693,660
Junior high schools	108,362	
Academic high schools	166,234	} 209,847
Vocational high schools	43,613	
Special	4,134	
Total	907,641	

* In elementary and junior high schools only
† In all types of schools
‡ Per 10,000 school population
**In addition there are eight special cerebral palsy classes with a total registration of 100 children

transportation to school for those physically handicapped who otherwise might not find it possible to attend school.

Because of the size of the problem, the expense involved, the length of time special education services have existed, and the fact that there has been some lack of unanimous agreement on the relative values of special versus regular classes for handicapped children, this report is presented, using New York City data. We will attempt to discuss and answer certain basic questions: What is the extent of the problem in a local area? What are the costs involved in educating children in special classes? How appropriately from the medical viewpoint are children being placed in special classes? What are the principles from a public health viewpoint in the placement of children in special classes? What are thought to be the advantages and disadvantages of the placement of children in regular versus special classes?

Extent of the Problem

Table 1 demonstrates the size of the special class populations in New York City public schools for the cardiac, orthopedic, braille, and sight conservation groups. The ratios of the children in the special classes to the total school

TABLE 2—Comparison of Special Classes and Children in Them in New York City—1938-1939 and 1951-1952

| Type of Special Class | 1938-1939 | | 1951-1952 | |
	Number of Classes	Number of Children	Number of Classes	Number of Children
Cardiac	88	2,025	45	727
Orthopedic	123	2,423	39	622
Sight conservation	91	1,633	105	1,334
Braille	12	96	12	105

population are 10.5, 8.9, 1.2, and 14.6 per 10,000 school children for the cardiac, orthopedic, braille, and sight conservation groups, respectively. The percentage in special classes of the total numbers of handicapped children are 7-10 per cent for the cardiac group and 15 per cent for the orthopedic group. In addition, there were 318 cardiac children (3-5 per cent) and 781 orthopedically handicapped children (19 per cent) on home instruction. The numbers of such children in hospitals and convalescent institutions during this same period are unknown. Thus, the great majority of children in school handicapped with cardiac, orthopedic, or visual problems are in the regular classes. The average number of children per special class ranges from 8.8 in the braille group to 16.2 in the cardiac group, compared with a citywide average of 31.5 children per class, indicating that special classes are one-half to one-third the size of the regular classes in the public schools.

A comparison of these data for 1951-1952 with similar data in the city for 1938-1939 (Table 2) reveals significant decreases in all groups except the braille group, which increased in this 13-year period. The number of students per special class has also decreased in this period, except in the braille group. Whether these decreases are related to a decrease in the specific handicapping conditions in the general school population or to the placement of physically limited children in regular classes who previously were on the register of special classes, or both, is unknown.

What Are the Costs Involved?

Table 3 shows the annual cost per pupil in the regular and special classes in New York City. The most costly classes are those provided for children who are blind or deaf, as would be expected. These cost data are based upon pedagogical salaries only and do not include the cost of supplies and special equipment. The cost of the classes per child increased over a 13-year period approximately 50 per cent in all classes except at the School for the Deaf. Transportation is a separate costly item and increased in cost 231 per cent in this 13-year period.

APPROPRIATENESS OF PLACEMENT OF CHILDREN IN SPECIAL CLASSES

To date there have been very few reports on studies of the appropriateness of placement in special classes in schools. In 1940 and 1941 a series of studies of children in orthopedic and cardiac classes, and of children at the

TABLE 3—COST PER PUPIL IN SPECIAL CLASSES—NEW YORK CITY

Type of Class	1938	1951-1952	Per cent Increase	Ratio of Cost in Special Class to Regular Class in 1951-1952
Regular	$150.00	$228.83	52	
Cardiac	262.82	389.96	49	1.7
Orthopedic	267.86	440.48	64	1.9
Sight conservation	294.70	466.05	58	2.0
Braille	515.26	778.60	51	3.4
School for the Deaf	570.67	729.84	28	3.2
Cost of transportation	$ 45.00	$149.50	231	

special public school for the deaf, indicated that many of the children did not require placement in the special classes or in the special school.[3-6] In Chicago a study was conducted in 1951 which showed that "many children had remained in a special school for many years after a mild attack of rheumatic fever which left little or no heart damage. Many were able to assume full and normal activity even though a heart murmur persisted."[7]

Within the past two years in New York City special studies have been conducted jointly by the City Health Department and Board of Education on children currently placed in special cardiac, orthopedic, sight conservation, and braille classes. Because of the fact that New York City has 17 per cent of the children in the country's sight conservation classes, 15 per cent of the children in the country's braille classes, and 4 per cent of the children in the country's orthopedic classes,[1] any findings in the New York City group may be of significance to classes and programs elsewhere in the country. In each of the special studies at least one medical specialist in the respective medical specialty personally examined the children and reviewed the medical records of the children in the special classes.* The samples covered in the

---

*The medical aspects of these studies were conducted by the following personnel of the Bureau for Handicapped Children: Cardiologists: Adolph Berger, Stanley Greenfield, and Conrad Rosenberg; Orthopedic Surgeons: William Cooper and Victor Mayer; Ophthalmologists: Samuel Lossef and Walter Schachat; Pediatricians: Myra Palmer and Helen Palmer and Helen Wallace; Public Health Nursing Consultant: Leah Hoenig. In addition, in the cardiac study, four of the five Cardiac Consultation Service Clinics of the Bureau for Handicapped Children, Department of Health, participated.

studies are shown in Table 4. The percentages of special classes included in the studies ranged from 10.5 per cent to 64.4 per cent, and the percentages of children from 7.9 per cent to 31.4 per cent.

CHILDREN IN SIGHT CONSERVATION AND BRAILLE CLASSES

This study[8] was conducted by the Bureau for Handicapped Children of the City Health Department with the cooperation of the Bureau of School Health from November, 1952 to January, 1953. The ophthalmological diagnoses of the children in the classes are shown in Table 5. The greatest probable causes for placement were refractive errors (45 per cent), most of which were myopia with or without astigmatism; diseases of the choroid and retina

TABLE 4—CHILDREN STUDIED IN SPECIAL CLASSES IN PUBLIC SCHOOLS IN NEW YORK CITY—1951-1953

Type of Special Class	Classes			Children		
	Total Number	Number in Study	Per cent in Study	Total Number	Number in Study	Per cent in Study
Cardiac	45	29	64.4	727	74	10.2
Orthopedic	39	9	23.1	622	49	7.9
Sight conservation	105	11	10.5	1,334	149	11.1
Braille	12	4	33.3	105	33	31.4

(9 per cent), most of which were central choroiditis; congenital nystagmus (8 per cent); congenital cataracts (7 per cent); and amblyopia for occlusion (6 per cent). Together, these five diagnoses account for 75 per cent of all the probable causes. In the sight conservation group, these same five diagnoses are the important ones, accounting for 83 per cent of all the probable causes. In the braille group the greatest probable causes for placement were diseases of choroid and retina (20 per cent); congenital cataracts (13 per cent); optic atrophy (13 per cent); and retrolental fibroplasia (10 per cent). This distribution of probable causes in the sight conservation and braille groups in New York City in 1952 is similar to that reported by Kerby for the United States.[9,10]

For the entire group of 182 children included in the study, a minimum of 58 (31.9 per cent) did not require this type of placement on the basis of medical criteria (Table 6). Furthermore, of the entire group of 58 children inappropriately placed, 20 children never required this type of placement at all on the basis of the medical examination data. The percentages of children inappropriately placed, on the basis of medical criteria alone, were approximately 37 per cent in the sight conservation classes in elementary and junior high schools, and high schools. On the other hand, none of braille group in elementary and junior high was inappropriately placed, but 19 per cent of the braille high school group was inappropriately placed. In addition to the 58 children definitely known to be inappropriately placed, there were 19 children about whom it was impossible to make a decision concerning placement because of inadequate medical information.

TABLE 5—PROBABLE DIAGNOSIS ACCOUNTING FOR PLACEMENT

Diagnosis	Total Number	Sight Conservation	Braille
1. Refractive errors	89		
A. Myopia		73	70	3
B. Myopic astigmatism		14	14	
C. Hyperopia		2	2	
2. Diseases of choroid and retina	17		
A. Disseminated choroiditis		1		1
B. Central choroiditis		9	5	4
C. Hereditary macular degeneration		3	2	
D. Macular degeneration		2	2	1
E. Coloboma of macula		1		1
F. Retinitis pigmentosa		1		1
3. Congenital nystagmus		16	15	1
4. Congenital cataracts		14	9	5
5. Amblyopia for occlusion		12	12	
6. Optic atrophy	7		
A. Primary		4	2	2
B. Secondary to brain tumor		2		2
C. Secondary to craniostenosis		1		1
7. Albinism	7		
A. Complete		5	5	
B. Partial		2		2
8. Glaucoma	4		
A. Congenital		3	2	1
B. Secondary		1		1
9. Retrolental fibroplasia		4		4
10. Congenital amblyopia		4	4	
11. Esotropia		3	3	
12. Microphthalmus		3	1	2
13. Retinoblastoma		3	1	2
14. Corneal disease	3		
A. Leucoma		1		1
B. Nodular dystrophy		1	1	
C. Interstitial keratitis		1	1	
15. Detachment of retina		2	1	1
16. Uveitis		1		1
17. Atrophic globes		1		1
18. Hurler's disease		1		1
19. Ophthalmia neonatorum		1	1	
20. Exotropia		1	1	
21. No diagnosis		3	2	1
Total		196 *	156	40

*Fourteen children had 2 diagnoses (7 in sight conservation and 7 braille classes) of such major importance that it was impossible to determine which was the primary cause of special class placement.

Of the 58 children inappropriately placed at the time of the study, 54 in sight conservation classes belonged in regular classes, three in braille class belonged in sight conservation class, and one in sight conservation class belonged in braille class in the school system. Thus, 57 of the 58 children were overplaced and one underplaced.

The period of inappropriate placement is shown in Table 7. For the entire group of 58 children inappropriately placed whose period of inappropriate placement was known, the period of inappropriate placement was 1,283 calendar months, or an average of 23.3 calendar months per child inappropriately placed. The longest period of inappropriate placement was 74 calendar months for a child in braille class in high school.

For the entire group of 182 children studied, the medical agency is shown in Table 8. In the groups where the numbers are large enough to have statistical significance, the medical agent with the lowest percentage of inappropriate placement is the qualified ophthalmologist (17.0 per cent), with the accredited hospital second (28.6 per cent), and the Bureau for Handicapped Children's Eye Clinics third (43.8 per cent).

TABLE 6—APPROPRIATENESS OF PLACEMENT OF CHILDREN IN
SIGHT CONSERVATION AND BRAILLE CLASSES

Type of Grade and Class	Totals	Appropriate	Not Appropriate	Unknown	Minimum Per cent Inappropriately Placed
Sight Conservation					
Elementary and junior high school	115	58	43	14	37.4
High school	34	18	12	4	35.3
Braille					
Elementary and junior high school	17	17	..	..	0.0
High school	16	12	3	1	18.8
Total	182	105	58	19	31.9

CHILDREN IN CARDIAC CLASSES

This study[11] was conducted in 1951 by the Bureau of Educational Research of the New York City Board of Education with the cooperation and assistance of the City Health Department and the New York Heart Association. The significant medical findings of the 74 study children in the eighth grade in special cardiac classes are demonstrated in Table 9. Of the 74 children, three (4.1 per cent) were found to have no heart disease; 21 (28.4 per cent) were found to have possible and potential heart disease (patients in whom the symptoms or signs, though suggestive of heart disease, do not justify a definite diagnosis and from whom a history of an etiological factor which might cause heart disease is obtained); and 50 children (67.5 per cent) were found to have organic heart disease. Of the 50 children with organic heart disease, 37 had rheumatic heart disease, and 13 had congenital heart disease. Of the 50 children with organic heart disease, two were given A status (no limitation of physical activity) and 39 were placed in Class B (permitted to engage in all physical activities save violent competitive sports). Thus, 41 of the organic group, three noncardiacs, and 21 with possible potential heart disease (total of 87.9 per cent) probably did not require placement in the special classes on the basis of medical criteria. It is recognized, however, that for some of these children a limited period in special classes may assist in educational rehabilitation for instructional losses and in psychological rehabilitation for mental health losses caused by illness. Of the remaining nine children with organic heart disease, significant restriction was indicated for them; they included two children with tetralogy of Fallot, one child with interventricular septal defect, three children with rheumatic heart disease with marked cardiac enlargement, and three with organic disease who had had active rheumatic fever less than one year prior to the examination (Table 9).

In a subsequent smaller study in 1952 conducted[8] on all 19 children in two cardiac classes in an elementary school in Queens, six were over-restricted (32

TABLE 7—PERIOD OF INAPPROPRIATE PLACEMENT IN
SIGHT CONSERVATION AND BRAILLE CLASSES

Period Months	Sight Conservation		Braille	
	Elementary and Junior High School	High School	Elementary and Junior High School	High School
Under 6	6			
6-11	10	3		
12-17	6	1		
18-23	7	1		
24-29	1			
30-35	5	1		
36-41	4	2		
42-47				1
48-53		1		1
54-59	1	1		
60-65				
66-71		1		
72-77		1		1
Number of children inappropriately placed	40 *	12	..	3
Number of months of inappropriate placement	701	412	..	170
Average	17.5	34.3	..	56.7

* In addition there were three children of unknown duration

per cent) and one (5 per cent) was insufficiently restricted; 12 children (63 per cent) were appropriately placed. Of the 19 children, 13 had rheumatic heart disease, five had congenital heart disease, and one had no heart disease.

CHILDREN IN ORTHOPEDIC CLASSES

This study[8] was conducted by the Bureau of Educational Research of the New York City Board of Education with the cooperation and assistance of the City Health Department in 1952. The significant medical findings of the 49 study children in the eighth grade in special orthopedic classes are summarized in Tables 10 and 11. Thirty-one per cent of the children were found to be inappropriately placed, all in the direction of overplacement, i.e., they should have been in regular classes. The different types of medical treatment agencies made no difference in the appropriateness of class placement. While the numbers are small, the diagnostic condition seemed to be a factor in appropriateness of placement (Table 11). Of the 49 children, 18 had unlimited ability to climb stairs, three could climb three flights of stairs, 12 could climb two flights of stairs, 12 could climb one flight of stairs, and four could climb no stairs; thus 93 per cent could climb at least one flight of stairs.

In another study[8] in 1952 conducted on all 25 children in two orthopedic classes in one elementary school in Queens, nine (36 per cent) were appropriately placed; six (24 per cent) belonged in a class for mentally retarded children; five (20 per cent) belonged in regular class; for the five remaining children, no decision could be made because of the need for psychometric testing in four, and a hearing evaluation in one.

SOME PRINCIPLES IN THE PLACEMENT OF CHILDREN IN SPECIAL CLASSES

If special classes for handicapped children are to be maintained within the regular schools, it would seem desirable to establish certain principles under which they might operate for the maximum benefit of the children, their families, and the community as a whole. Most physically handicapped children will, upon reaching maturity, participate in the life of a community. Child life lived apart from normal children is not considered to be conductive to the development of the personality traits necessary for a shared social life. In so far as is possible, handicapped children should participate in the normal school activities. It is not enough to know that a child has a visual, cardiac, hearing, or orthopedic handicap; one also must know the degree, plus his social and psychological adjustment. The special classes should recognize the differences in children's needs, abilities, and interests, and the necessity for directing them toward ultimate adult adjustments compatible with their capacities. Modifications of the school program should not necessarily follow any standard pattern, but should be individualized in terms of the changing needs of individual children. Placement in a special class may be desirable at one time and unnecessary at another. The primary objective should be to return as many children as possible to regular classes in as short a time as possible. Vocational guidance, recreational activities, and a stimulating general educational program, with participation in many of the activities of normal children, can do much to safeguard the child against acquiring undesirable habits and attitudes.

The specific principles may be briefly summarized as follows: Special classes should be provided for those children who need them and who otherwise would not be able to attend school; special classes should provide the necessary services essential to meet the individual needs of the children in them; medical criteria should be established by medical experts for the admission

TABLE 8—ANALYSIS OF MEDICAL AGENCY AND APPROPRIATENESS OF PLACEMENT OF
CHILDREN IN SIGHT CONSERVATION AND BRAILLE CLASSES

		Inappropriately Placed	
Medical Agency	Total Number	Number	Per cent
DHEC	64	28	43.8
Qualified ophthalmologist	47	8	17.0
Accredited hospital	28	8	28.6
Optometrist	12	4	33.3
DHEC and optometrist	5	1	20.0
Nonaccredited hospital	5	2	40.0
DHEC and qualified ophthalmologist	4	2	50.0
Partly qualified ophthalmologist	4	2	50.0
DHEC and nonaccredited hospital	3	2	66.7
Accredited hospital and optometrist	2	1	50.0
" " " qualified ophthalmologist	1	0	0.0
Qualified ophthalmologist and optometrist	1	0	0.0
Neurologist	1	0	0.0
Unknown	5	0	0.0
Totals	182	58	31.9

Definitions
1. DHEC—Department of Health Eye Clinic
2. Qualified Ophthalmologist—A physician who is a diplomat of the American Board
   of Ophthalmology or who is an associate attending or better on the staff of a hospital
   approved by the American Medical Association for residency training in ophthalmology
3. Accredited Hospital—A hospital approved by the Council on Medical Education and
   Hospitals of the American Medical Association for residency training in ophthalmology
4. Partly Qualified Ophthalmologist—A physician who does not meet the qualifications
   of (2) above, but who has a rating of specialist in ophthalmology by the Workmen's
   Compensation Board and who has a rank lower than that of associate attending on
   the staff of a hospital approved by the American Medical Association for residency in
   ophthalmology.

TABLE 9—FUNCTIONAL AND THERAPEUTIC CLASSIFICATION* OF STUDY CHILDREN
BY AGE

| Age | Non-cardiac | Possible and Potential Heart Disease | IA | Organic Heart Disease | | | | | |
				IB	IC	IIB	IIC	IIE	Total
11	0	0	0	1	0	0	0	0	1
12	1	0	0	0	1	2	1	0	5
13	1	11	1	6	0	10	1	1	31
14	1	8	1	11	3	2	2	0	28
15	0	0	0	3	0	3	0	0	6
16	0	2	0	0	0	1	0	..	3
Total	3	21†	2	21	4	18	4	1	74
Per cent of Total	4.1	28.4	2.7	28.4	5.4	24.3	5.4	1.3	100.0

* Based on the Classification adopted by the New York Heart Association[12]
† Include 13 children with potential heart disease and eight children with possible
and potential heart disease

to, renewal of, and discharge from placement in special classes in order to serve as a general guide for physicians responsible for the care of handicapped children; children should be placed in special classes and their placement renewed only upon the recommendation of qualified medical specialists, and should remain under the guidance of well trained personnel in the various categories concerned, and with little or no segregation of children placed in the special classes. This principle is of major importance if children are to be given their opportunity of normal psychological growth and development. There should be a good record system to provide adequate data on each child's physical progress and emotional adjustment, and there should be easily accessible physical facilities for easy mobility of the children.

ADVANTAGES, DISADVANTAGES, AND VALUES OF SPECIAL CLASSES

Very few studies of a factual, objective nature have been performed to analyze the value of the special classes to the children in them. This lack of studies is surprising in view of the large numbers of children involved, the large amounts of funds expended, and the length of time special classes have been in operation. In 1916 in New York City the Association for the Prevention and Relief of Heart Disease studied the problem for a three-year period and in 1923 recommended that the segregated classes for children with rheumatic fever or heart disease be abolished, as they were considered unneces-

TABLE 10—APPROPRIATENESS OF PLACEMENT AND MEDICAL TREATMENT AGENCY—
CHILDREN IN ORTHOPEDIC CLASSES

Type of Medical Treatment Agency	Appropriate Placement		Inappropriate Placement		Total	
	Number	Per cent	Number	Per cent	Number	Per cent
Private physicians	9	69.2	4	30.8	13	100.0
Orthopedic surgeons	4	80.0	1	20.0	5	100.0
Other than orthopedic surgeons	5	62.5	3	37.5	8	100.0
Hospital clinics	25	69.4	11	30.6	36	100.0
With approved orthopedic residency	24	70.6	10	29.4	34	100.0
Without approved orthopedic residency	1	50.0	1	50.0	2	100.0
Total	34	69.4	15	30.6	49	100.0

sary for 92 per cent of the children.[13] In 1926 this same group reiterated that the cardiac segregated classes should be abolished and children classified as potential cardiacs, or Class I or II A should be transferred to the regular classes.[13] In 1941 a committee appointed by the New York City Board of Education concluded after another special study that the information and data available are inadequate for it to judge whether segregation of cardiac children in the public school system could be beneficial to them, whether such segregation is necessary, or whether they can be adequately cared for in regular classes.[13] In 1953 a report by Nebelung[14,15] in the San Francisco public schools describes the results of a study to attempt to answer the same question for the rheumatic fever and cardiac group. This report states that "despite the failure of either the health class or regular class to demonstrate a superior rate of growth in the majority of the years studied, the tendency favored the health class," although the differences are not statistically significant. Placement in a health class was more conducive for the child to work at or above his mental ability than in a regular class environment, even though the regular class group had more gifted and less mentally retarded children in terms of native ability.

The potential advantages of special classes for handicapped children in the public day schools are these: There is opportunity for more concentrated observation and supervision of the children by physicians, nurses, and teachers. There is opportunity for easier administration of special services, such as the use of physical therapists for children with orthopedic handicaps, or the control of upper respiratory infections in classes with children who have had rheumatic fever. There is opportunity to concentrate services more easily in the fields of rehabilitation, and the emotional and vocational aspects. The special classes have a smaller census, providing opportunity for more indi-

TABLE 11—APPROPRIATENESS OF PLACEMENT AND DIAGNOSIS
CHILDREN IN ORTHOPEDIC CLASSES

Diagnostic Group	Appropriately Placed		Inappropriately Placed		Total	
	Number	Per cent	Number	Per cent	Number	Per cent
Cerebral palsy	17	94.4	1	8.6	18	100.0
Poliomyelitis	14	77.7	4	23.3	18	100.0
Congenital dislocation of hip	3	60.0	2	40.0	5	100.0
Slipped epiphysis	2	66.7	1	33.3	3	100.0
Muscular dystrophy	2	100.0	0	0.0	2	100.0
Infection	1	33.3	2	66.7	3	100.0
Tuberculosis of bone	1	50.0	1	50.0	2	100.0
Osteomyelitis	0	0.0	1	100.0	1	100.0
Trauma	1	33.3	2	66.7	3	100.0
Atrophic limb	0	0.0	1	100.0	1	100.0
Amputation	1	100.0	..	0.0	1	100.0
Fracture ankle	0	0.0	1	100.0	1	100.0
Miscellaneous*	3	50.0	3	50.0	6	100.0
Total	34	69.4	15	30.6	49	100.0

* Composed one each of arthritis of spine, arthritis of hip, scoliosis, Perthes' disease, coxa vara, cavus foot.

vidual attention and making it potentially easier to modify the regime to meet the needs of the individual child. If special classes were not provided, some children might not be able to attend school who are now able to do so. There is opportunity to collect data on morbidity, or the prevalence of handicapping conditions of moderate to severe degree among children in school.

The potential disadvantages of special classes and the problems related to them can be summarized. Segregation is a serious problem because of two factors. First, there is the potential adverse psychological effect on the handicapped child and the limited opportunity for normal children to observe and realize the capabilities of the handicapped group and to develop some better understanding of them. Second, because of the pattern of concentrating special classes in a small number of schools, children in them must attend school at some distance from their home. This means longer time spent by the handicapped child in travel to and from school, possible increase in the cost of transportation for the handicapped child, and less opportunity for the handicapped child to attend the same schools as normal children with whom he might play in his own neighborhood.

There is also the problem of the wide age span and the wide range of educational ability in the special classes with the possibility that this might not be conducive to the best education of the handicapped child. In addition, there is the problem of inappropriate placement in special classes and sometimes difficulties in transferring children in and out of them, with the possibility that in a large school system some children may be "lost forever."

The cost of education of children in special classes is higher than in regular classes without much scientific objective evidence of some of the special classes' value to the children in them. Special health classes have a tendency at present to become a wastebasket for some children in a school who are thought to be socially unacceptable or mentally retarded. This, however, reflects the general need for additional adequate community services for both of these latter groups of children. Finally, there is a possibility that by placing handicapped children in a special classroom two undesirable results may occur: the segregated handicapped group may be relatively neglected by the general educational and school health services, and the handicapped group in the special classes may receive all or most of the services, to the detriment of the normal or mildly handicapped groups in the regular classes.

Suggested Pattern and Next Steps

It is likely that, with our current knowledge, special classes in the public schools for the blind, deaf, and mentally retarded groups of children should be continued, but on a modified basis with more opportunity for mixing in many of the school activities with normal children.

It is probable that there should be special classes in public schools for the severely physically disabled group of children. Possibly these services should not be limited to cerebral palsied children alone, but should include other severely disabled ones such as those with widespread congenital malformations, poliomyelitis, muscular dystrophy, etc.

For the sight conservation group, a few communities such as Oakland, Calif., Columbus, Ohio, and certain areas in Illinois have eliminated special sight conservation classes and have used the principle of the traveling special teacher to raise the visual standards of all schools in a district.[15,16] Apparently this plan is working well and has the added advantage of serving more children. Furthermore, a technical advisory ophthalmology committee in New York City stated recently that there was no scientific evidence that the use of special sight conservation classes contributed anything to the conservation of sight.

For other types of physically handicapped children, it is suggested that any school have one room where children with any type of health problem requiring modification of the school program may be placed temporarily. This should be looked upon as a highly flexible and fluid plan with easy and quick movement in and out.

Ideally, the regular classes should be smaller in registration and public schools should be one-story buildings or at least have elevators and ramps and easily accessible necessary physical facilities. It is possible that some of the problems in the education of handicapped children in schools are man-made, due to lack of foresight in planning adequate physical plants and facilities.

It is finally recommended that a series of carefully planned studies be made of the education of handicapped children in special versus regular classes in order to attempt to secure some final answers to this somewhat controversial and highly important subject.

FOOTNOTES

1. *Statistics for Special Schools and Classes for Exceptional Children—1947-1948.* (Office of Education, Department of Health, Education and Welfare: Washington, D. C., Gov. Ptg. Office, 1950).
2. *School Housing for Physically Handicapped Children,* Bull. 1951, No. 17 (Gov. Ptg. Office: Washington, D.C., 1950).
3. *Orthopedically Handicapped Children* (Board of Education, City of New York: N.Y.C., 1941), p. 43.
4. *Physically Handicapped Children in New York City* (Board of Education, City of New York: N.Y.C., 1941), pp. 64, 71, 89.
5. *The Crippled Child in New York City* (The Commission for the Study of Crippled Children: N.Y.C., 1940), p. 127.
6. *Acoustically Handicapped Children* (Board of Education, City of New York: N.Y.C., 1941), p. 41.
7. Marienfeld, Carl J., "Cardiac Aspects of School Health", *Am. J. Dis. Child.* 86:63-64 (July), 1953.
8. Bureau for Handicapped Children, New York City Department of Health. Unpublished data.
9. Kerby, C. Edith, "Causes and Prevention of Blindness in Children of School Age", *Sight-Saving Review* 22:1-12 (Jan.), 1952.
10. "A Report on Visual Handicaps of Partially Seeing Children", *Exceptional Children,* 18:137-142 (Feb.), 1952.
11. *Children with Cardiac Limitations: Studies of Pupils Enrolled in Special Classes* (Bureau of Educational Research, Board of Education of the City of New York: N.Y.C., 1952).
12. *New York Heart Association Nomenclature and Criteria for Diagnosis of Diseases of the Heart,* 4th ed. (Little & Ives, N.Y.C., 1943), pp. 9-10, 71-75.
13. *Cardiac Classes and the Care of Cardiac Children* (Board of Education, City of New York: N.Y.C., 1941).
14. Nebelung, Raymond G., "The Value of Segregated Classes Versus Regular Classroom Instruction for Post-Rheumatic Fever Children", *J. School Health,* 23:139-146 (May), 1953; and 23, 6:193-200 (June), 1953.
15. *Report of Workshop on Organization and Administration of Facilities for Partially Seeing Children. Educating Partially Seeing Children in the Public Schools, Exceptional Children,* 19, 7:269-288 (Apr.), 1953.
16. Tydyman, Al. and Bertram, Fredericka M., "Oakland's Sight Conservation Program", *Sight-Saving Rev.,* 22, 2:1-12, 1952.

THE DEVELOPMENT OF INSTRUCTIONAL MATERIALS FOR SPECIAL EDUCATION IN A CITY SYSTEM

HERMAN R. GOLDBERG

Because of the expansion of educational programs for exceptional children during the past decade, the total responsibility facing administrators of special education programs in city school systems is larger and more complex than that of any previous period. It has been generally determined that the administrator's responsibility includes effort in four major directions—community service, improvement of instruction in various areas of special education, recruitment, and in-service training of personnel, and general administration of the department, including finances, supplies, equipment and special education modifications in school housing.

Because of the urgency of the first and the last two of the above four areas, many administrators find that they have less time available to concentrate on the second, viz: the improvement of instruction. In the development of the concept which is to follow, a careful analysis of the administrator's total responsibility will be made, and some concrete suggestions offered for ways in which the special education administrator can contribute to leadership in the building of instructional materials.

RESPONSIBILITIES AND PROBLEMS

But special education administrators do not stand alone in all these problems. They take their place along with the administrators and supervisors of other areas of education and contribute to the solution of many common school problems. Peculiar to special education, however, are many problems not related solely to increased school enrollment or changing emphasis in curriculum. Many of those which can only be described briefly here become the daily agenda for the director of special education. But along with these lies the responsibility for development of instructional materials for more effective teaching programs. Among the responsibilities and problems which have to precede allocation of time for giving leadership to programs of development of instructional materials are the following:

1. Administration and Supervision of the department, including intake, maintenance of registers, transfers and individual pupil, parent and teacher problems, relationships with psychological services, school social work and medical services of the Health Bureau, the Courts, and probation departments.
2. Service on Local Superintendent's Committees, American Education Week, Cumulative Records Revision, General Curriculum and Instructional Materials, etc.
3. Community Service, including Community Chest, Red Cross, Civilian Defense, and other official, voluntary, fraternal, and philanthropic organizations, and agencies.
4. Research in Special Education.

A director of special education is in a strategic situation to assist in the programs of activities of many local agencies and organizations, including those with official, voluntary, fraternal, or philanthropic status. Because the special education administrator approaches many of the problems facing these agencies with a manner not charged with emotion, he is often able to help parents of exceptional children strike the balance between parent ambition and the pupil's limitations. To many of these organizations, the director will represent the public school system and will be called upon to interpret the total school program. Often these cooperative efforts of the director are carried to the point of serving as active contributing member on boards of directors or committees of these related agencies and organizations. Directors of special education are also frequently called upon to participate in public relations programs of the schools and are asked to prepare and participate in radio and TV programs and to prepare news releases and brochures and special reports.

A director of special education is also frequently called upon to participate in the preparation of professional articles, monographs, and texts for use by educators as well as the lay public. It is also expected that directors should be able to discover among their staff members those who can write meaningfully and succinctly, and must take the responsibility for encouraging staff members to participate in such projects. In addition to cooperation with local agencies, as described above, the director of special education of a local school system may be called upon to participate in conferences, forums, and institutes sponsored by local, state, and national agencies for similar or contemporary goals. Recent years have seen rapid growth in the number of private agencies interested in the exceptional child. The early goal of many of these groups was public information, thus creating a general awareness of the problem. The emphasis in the second phase of their operations was on raising of necessary funds. More recently, there has been the rapid growth of pilot or demonstration programs supported wholly or in part by these private agencies. It seems strongly indicated then that special education administrators should allocate some time to helping such groups through the influence they can exert through Board membership or active participation on key committees.

Since many directors of special education in local school systems have more than full time jobs carrying on the daily service functions of their departments, they have had little time for research activities. They are often called upon to cooperate with colleges and universities and to provide some assistance for graduate students engaged in research. In addition to this type of assistance, some administrators of special education in local school systems are initiating and completing their own studies and are providing encouragement and guidance for their staff members to do the same.

In addition, special education administrators are often required to prepare over-all budgets, cost sheets, and annual reports requiring understanding of financial matters. This includes an awareness of subsidies available through state budgets and reimbursement plans, as well as a general knowledge of transportation and city routing problems.

Perhaps the most crucial of all responsibilities for a director of special education lies in recruitment of candidates for teaching special education classes and in the contribution that can be made in the selection process of effective teachers. In many cities, directors of special education share in the teaching of extension courses to teacher candidates. The practical experience and wide knowledge attained by these specialists in the various fields of the exceptional can contribute significantly to effective teacher preparation and performance. From time to time, too, depending upon local conditions and variations in our national and local economy, directors of special education are drawn into service related to juvenile delinquency, the employment of the handicapped, and other over-all rehabilitation problems.

STAFF DEVELOPMENT OF INSTRUCTIONAL MATERIALS FOR SPECIAL EDUCATION

In recent years members of central office staffs of local school systems have taken a broader look at their responsibility and true function. And perhaps this broader look can be characterized by the frequent change of the title 'Supervisor' to 'Consultant'. More and more this gradual change has required that central office staff be chosen with the view toward assigning those people who have had a broad background of training and experience in education and who can see their roles as consultants in curriculum and instructional materials of the special area rather than as specialists in the subject matter area. In addition, the present day function of central office staff includes both that of initiating curriculum and of assisting programs already underway.

Before jumping in headlong and starting an extensive program of production of materials for instruction, staff members of a special education department should realize that sometimes it is more practical to obtain the materials or devices from other sources rather than to produce them themselves. The question of whether to produce your own materials, to adapt materials already at hand, or to buy new materials revolves on three factors: (1) the learning value of the materials required, (2) the availability of suitable materials, (3) the cost of new materials.

A local school system should not undertake the production of new materials of instruction before asking the following questions:

1. Will the material make a direct contribution to the instructional program?
2. Will the material really make the understanding of new or basic concepts earlier or quicker?
3. Will the materials be an in-service training activity for the teacher?

4. Will the material be better for the pupils' use than any other materials available?

5. Will the cost in both time and energy be less than the cost of comparable purchased material?

If, on the basis of the above criteria, the answers are in the affirmative, local production of instructional materials had better get underway. If the staff feels that the materials on hand are satisfactory or that materials could better be obtained from commerical sources, then no attempt to produce learning aids should be made. In screening available materials, departments of special education in local school systems should work closely with the department of instructional materials in its own school system.

More and more, departments formerly devoted to audio-visual materials, per se, are growing to include the broader function of evaluating all instructional materials. The skills and resources of such a department should not be by-passed in working toward the decision whether or not it is feasible for a local department to begin a project. It has been said by many audio-visual specialists that

too frequently they are recognized by their skill in threading a projector or teaching others how to thread the same, rather than for their ability to communicate ideas. They are called upon to solve a room darkening problem more often than a problem of bringing enlightenment to those who need it.[1]

The separateness of audio-visual materials is tending to disappear. They are no longer isolated.

There should be integrated selection, distribution, and use of all materials of instruction, including the printed word. Definitions of instructional materials occasionally have caused confusion. The broadest definition seems to be that instructional materials include anything which contributes to the learning process. In its broadest sense, this would include all environmental materials, too. It is generally recognized that the classroom and the school, together with their environs, including all the inanimate and animate resources of the community, offer a fertile field for enterprising teachers to find and put into use more worthwhile aids to instruction. The selection and use of environmental materials should include as broad a range of things, places, processes, and people as situations permit. One guiding principal in selection is that the experience should be as real and as much in its natural setting as is feasible under existing circumstances. The hit-or-miss approach to the study of instructional materials in the environment must be avoided, and can be when specific goals are set up in advance. The sources and variety of equipment and materials are limited only by the creative imagination of consultants, teachers and pupils.

How to Develop Teacher Competence in Providing Materials

The pre-service education of teachers actually begins early in life; it has its setting in the classroom of the public schools. If present or future teachers have had a more limited pattern of pupil services themselves, the cycle of uninspired teaching goes on like an endless chain. Teacher education institutions and leaders in public school systems will mutually profit by cooperative planning in which specific procedures in creation of instructional materials will meet part of the total educational planning. In addition, there should be in-service education in this area for more experienced teachers and those needing help. In discussing the role of courses in instructional materials' production on the teacher training levels, it is often suggested that at least three basic courses in production should be offered as electives to supplement the introductory course in audio-visual methods and materials. These would include:

1. A course in the preparation of graphic materials such as mimeograph and liquid stencils, construction of models, use of wood, metal, plaster, plastics, bulletin boards, posters, exhibits, dioramas, etc.
2. A course in elementary photography specifically set up for classroom teachers emphasizing use of photography in producing material for the classroom. This course should teach two basic skills, the ability to take good pictures and the ability to make photographic copies of materials useful in teaching. Many teachers find this skill particularly helpful in the construction of personalized readers and other charts which bring learning experiences very close to the child's family and community.
3. A basic course in production of instructional materials involving the printed word. This would include workshops or other types of courses where teachers get actual practice in creating and developing reading materials at three ability levels for use by the mentally retarded, and a variety of adapted reading materials for other types of exceptional children.

The first step, of course, is establishing a basic plan for concretely deciding upon those experiences which lead to maximum pupil growth and development, and upon materials that can help reach that goal.

How the Administrator Contributes to Leadership in the Building of Instructional Materials

There have always been two theories of administrative leadership; one based on command and observation, the other on example and participation. The success of many ventures is characterized by the latter, by the kind of leadership that takes off its coat and gets things done by doing them along with others.

While a scholarly study of the 'perspiration' required for success has never been made, it is a safe bet administrators of special education have expended at least as much effort in the fight to achieve recognition of their field as have pioneers in other fields of education. Performance above and beyond the call of duty has been the rule rather than the exception.

Somehow the progress toward maturity in professional performance seems to have led many to an increasing concern with philosophic abstractions at the expense of the concrete demands of reality. More time is likely to be spent conjuring over the philosophic implications of an often repeated and already belabored platitude rather than increasing the scope and effectiveness of the operating program. It may easily be argued that any worthwhile operating program cannot be built on a foundation of quicksand but rather must have a strong and proper philosophic structure if it is to survive. But when programs remain in the philosophical structure stage for too long, the development of effective programs are unduly delayed. Administrators should provide leadership by *Showing The Way*. Administrators who enter into programs of development and materials with their hats off and sleeves rolled up will not bring suffering to theory and philosophy. It is possible for those who are deeply occupied in the daily problems of an on-going program to make philosophic contributions to the field. Plain hard work is somehow necessary for the nourishment of the philosopher in man. Frequently, in discussing characteristics and abilities of administrators in special education, the question is asked, "Is he an *idea* man or a *technique* man?" And this is frequently followed by the question, "Can you count on him for a rich philosophical discussion or will he help to bring forth specific suggestions and materials for teachers' use now?"

It is interesting to note that in many branches of our Armed Services officers do more than lecture about tactical problems. In training maneuvers they lead their men and show leadership by example not merely encouragement;[2] while it may have been acceptable in the Gilbert and Sullivan operetta "Gondoliers" for the Duke to have "led his regiments from behind," special education administrators demonstrate the hallmark of the real contributing leader by working side by side with teachers and moving to the forefront when required.

As he works along with the staff, the administrator has three basic functions in the development of instructional materials: (1) motivation, (2) guidance, (3) coordination.

The administrator, especially one newly assigned, or one who is investigating new areas of learning, must move slowly. Changes to be brought about by the introduction of new ideas in curriculum must be carried on in relation to all the forces being exerted on the individual teacher or the departmental group. Some teachers feel change contrary to tradition is bad; others fear that change will cause them to lose control; others find it impossible to change; others look with contempt on those who are willing and anxious to try new things. All these teachers conspire against change and bring both actual and implied pressures of various sorts on individual teachers. The administrator must do all in his power to gain acceptance of his leadership and this is best done by first developing introductory ideas in those areas in which there is little controversy. If these preliminary relationships prove successful, confidence is more easily established for the more controversial areas to follow. Because new materials of instruction sometimes connote the questioning of formerly used techniques and materials, the wise administrator confines himself to small segments of the curriculum at first in order to avoid overwhelming opposition.

Anyone who has participated as a leader in workshops of various kinds will recognize that the mental hygiene of the participants is a matter of primary concern. In launching workshops designed for the cooperative building of instructional materials the administrator is faced with certain qualities of human nature in the group and must also be aware of certain weaknesses in the committee process as it is used in many school systems. It is important that committees not drag out their work, continuing from year to year in a half-hearted manner, with only an occasional meeting. This produces little of value and sets a bad morale example. In addition, the administrator must learn how to integrate those members of the staff identified as those who contribute too little, those who offer too much, those who are very slow to learn, those who seem to antagonize, and those who wander.

The above factors point out that while the committee process for the development of instructional materials is of recent vintage, committees per se are not substitutes for leadership talent. A committee operating without planning, executing, appraising, and rebuilding grows into a state of confusion in its ultimate decisions which is often difficult to modify. For the most part, in-service teacher workshop groups or working committees should be real workshops and real working committees and, in effect, be just what the name implies—a situation in which teachers get together to prepare the materials needed for classroom activities. This means that teachers must be given plenty of opportunity to work on their own, free from interference or influence from their consultants and administrators. On the other hand, a working committee would be to no purpose if there was no advantage taken of the stimulation that the administrator could give to the group or if his resource potential were ignored. Administrators, therefore, have the responsibility of adjusting the activities of committees so that all members may call upon them for assistance. The beginning of most effort of these committees is usually marked by a period of a certain amount of frustration. The competent administrator shuns being overdirective lest he destroy the group's spontaneity. It should be pointed out that these frustrations are a healthy sign and the administrator must not be tempted to do all the work in order to get things 'on the beam'. But because teachers are not all alike in either their ability or desire to contribute significantly, administrators often show more initiative in the early part of the project to ensure effective launching.

As indicated above, working committees contain many types of participants. There are those who are politely referred to as teachers with minimal energy threshold or with deficient volition. Administrators often find it necessary to work out special motivating approaches for them. These individuals need consideration and sympathetic guidance so that eventually their opposition can be overcome.

Teachers are frequently found in working committees who are afraid to speak up even in informal working groups. This may stem from previous squelching of their ideas. Such persons can be helped to contribute again if their suggestions are not forcefully negated as they are being given. For those teachers who seem to contribute too much a different approach is needed. The administrator must display great tact in helping the talkative member of the group to share the time with others. And the administrator, too, can set a good example by not monopolizing the discussion himself.

For those teachers who seem slow to learn about the value of new instructional materials, little can be done. Many of these teachers always see themselves in the role of followers. No amount of skillful motivation will change them. And in every working committee too, individuals are found who seek personal prestige rather than opportunity to contribute for the total benefit of the group. These people seem to work toward personal antagonisms. The responsibility of the administrator in these situations is to try to give these teachers more definite responsibilities and to team up with certain teachers who seem to be able to work along with them.

In planning for working committees, administrators need to make a decision as to whether an attempt will be made to work with all teachers concerned with the problem or just with those with whom a successful project can be predicted. Although all teachers are not equally gifted in the construction of new learning materials, it is important that all the teachers involved should be invited to make a study of their problem with real unity and then to go on to build instructional materials together. A teacher who is mentally or emotionally unable to make a significant contribution to the group can only be considered as 'also participating', but should not be condemned.

There are values in working out a combination of dominant and deferent teachers, as committee groupings are made. This balanced mixture of each type, under competent leadership, often produces good results.

Second only to personal characteristics of participating committee members in the list of problems connected with successful workshops is the lack of time allotted for the building of instructional materials. Although many authorities believe that work of this nature is important enough to be considered part of a teacher's regular day, committee assignments most frequently are added on at the close of the school day. Such meetings often run late in the afternoon or are held in the evening. Under these circumstances teachers find it difficult to bring a freshness of professional interest they might at other times. However, the extent of participation, the professional interest with which the staff often undertakes the work and the quality of the results are all the more remarkable when considered in the light of the fact that most of the contributions were made on the teacher's own time.

In some school systems attempts to alleviate this difficulty are made by the provision of substitute teachers who relieve teachers of classroom responsibility for study and planning. Some cities provide for summer employment at regular teacher salary for committees working on instructional materials; others dismiss classes forty-five minutes early on meeting days. Approval for many of the above plans has been gained in only a few school systems, since many recognize the value of the suggestions but few put them into actual practice. It seems inconsistent to expect instructors to teach effectively every hour of the school day and then to plan and produce effectively after a six to seven hour working schedule.

But one must not conclude that these difficulties should be a permanent barrier to further experimentation with teacher committees. Special education leaders must work with their local school superintendents and other administrative personnel toward receiving encouragement and approval for more efficient ways of obtaining teacher participation in building instructional materials.

How Teacher Workshops in Special Education Are Launched and Developed

As indicated above, groups of teachers meeting in committees to build instructional materials need to have a real purpose identified for them. Once this has been done, the workshop is ready to be launched. While it is probably wise for teachers actually to develop the scope of the workshop and the specific criteria for evaluating the materials, administrators have definite responsibilities for assisting with the work. To avoid weak or confused beginnings, administrators should come to the opening meeting with a working plan. It is up to the administrator, too, to provide some motivating force to bridge the opening remarks with the actual working effort. For example: in a workshop set up to prepare for the mentally retarded reading materials on bakeries, a freshly baked loaf of bread from a local trade school was placed at each working desk before the teachers arrived. Similarly, in preparing for the retarded reading materials in the general job area of gas stations, Kodachrome slides and films depicting some of the operational procedures which would form part of the background for the construction of the materials were used for motivation.

Too frequently workshops are launched with a statement attesting to the fact that the materials to be prepared are not available commercially. It is only in unusual situations commercial development companies or publishers will accept projects designed primarily for special education. They point out, time and time again, that because of the limited scope for eventual use of these materials they cannot justify the large expenditures for getting these materials into production. But this fact, per se, is not sufficient motivation for teachers to want to do something about the situation. At this point the motivation and continuing participation in the project by the administrator becomes a most essential ingredient for success.

Following the launching, administrators must be prepared to distribute, at the first session of the workshop, such information which will guide the development of the materials. In a workshop set up for the development of reading materials for the mentally retarded, for example, it is important to list the criteria for a good story, the length of the story, techniques of vocabulary control, including suggestions for repetition and recurrence of words and ideas, illustrations, etc. While many of these items are subject to change after discussion, their availability, at least in preliminary form, gives structure to the opening session. Following this, the large workshop group should be divided into smaller committees with the understanding that they may have a comfortable length of time to complete their project without the pressures of an absolute due date. Administrators should then be ready to accept invitations from individual committees to sit in on their preliminary sessions, not merely to approve what they have done to date, but to share in the building of scenarios and for overall guidance. Upon occasion, too, situations arise where the administrator plays the part of a referee in attempting to adjudicate both petty differences and major clashes. Finally, when the materials have been completed by the individual committees, administrators should exercise their obligation to do the final editing so that the group may have the benefit of this expert review.

The development of instructional materials for special education, in spite of all that has been said, is still only the first step in coordinating the total instructional program of special education in a city school system. The administrators and supervisors must work with the staff in seeing that the materials produced are used appropriately and effectively. It is important that units of work or suggestions for activities be used within the framework of a whole gamut of integrated learning activities. Administrators and supervisors need to be alert to those situations where teachers tend to use the materials produced in minimal fashion. It is only the proper use of such materials that can justify the effort expended in their construction. Then, and then only, can they be made challenging, interesting, realistic and stimulating, not only to the pupil but to the teacher as well.

FOOTNOTES

1. Reed, P. C. "Editorial," *Educational Screen,* XXXII (December, 1953), p. 432.
2. Witness the roles played by officers including chaplains in the U. S. Navy, especially those assigned to submarine service, who actually go through escape hatch training with each new group of recruits.

BIBLIOGRAPHY

Adams, Harold P., and Dickey, Frank G. *Basic Principles of Supervision* (American Book: N.Y.C., 1953).

Bartky, John A. *Supervision As Human Relations* (D. C. Heath: Boston).

Cain, Leo F. "General Problems and Administration of Programs for Exceptional Children", *Review of Educational Research,* XXIII, No. 5 (December, 1953).

Caswell, Hollis L., et al. *Curriculum Improvement in Public School Systems* (New York: Bureau of Publications, Teachers College, Columbia University, 1950).

"Group Processes in Supervision", *Journal of the Association for Supervision and Curriculum Development,* (1948).

Guide to Study and Experimentation in Cooperative Planning in Education (Bureau of Publications, Teachers College, Columbia University: N.Y.C., 1947).

"Improving Education in the Southern States," *Teaching Materials in the Modern School,* (Gainesville, Florida: State Department of Education, 1950).

Journal of the Association for Supervision and Curriculum Development, "Better Aids for Learning," *Educational Leadership,* IX, No. 7 (April, 1952).

Journal of the Association for Supervision and Curriculum Development, "Schools Foster Experimentation", *Educational Leadership,* IX, (May, 1952).

"Research in Action", *Journal of the Association for Supervision and Curriculum Development,* XI, No. 8 (May, 1954).

Miel, Alice, *et al., Cooperative Procedures in Learning,* (Bureau of Publications, Teachers College, Columbia University: N.Y.C., 1952).

COMMUNITY PLANNING FOR SPECIAL EDUCATION

MAMIE J. JONES

Often a State Director of Special Education or the State Superintendent of Schools gets a letter or a telephone call from a public school superintendent or a parent in a local community saying, "We are interested in starting a class for exceptional children. What is the first thing we do?" The individual may explain that he is particularly interested in a class for children who are crippled, or mentally retarded, or that his interest is in a speech correction program. On the other hand, he may not be at all sure of the type of unit he wants. But the first step toward the development of a special education program can be made from such a simple question as this, regardless of the originator of the idea. This one question may provide the yeast for changing community apathy and 'tolerance' toward inadequate services to community action for an adequate special education program.

Although the major responsibility for the development of a special education program rests with the members of the local board of education and with the local superintendent, community planning can bring about a sensitive awareness of the needs of such a service, its place in the total school program, its costs, and the importance of including this program in the regular school. It is difficult for one organization or one person to do the total planning. Our democratic way of life has shown us that group thinking, if inspired and adequately guided, can result in group action that will benefit both individuals and the community.

There is no one plan of community organization for the development of special education services. Since each community varies one from another, regardless of whether it is rural or urban, no one plan or pattern will fit every community. The ways of attacking and solving problems will vary from community to community, depending upon the people in each community, their professions, education, interests, needs, knowledge of problems, and leadership qualities. These things will also partially determine the quality of the program that will eventually be set up. If a special education program is going to be a part of and not apart from community life, then it is important that such a program be conceived through the efforts and interests of local citizens.

The following suggestions and ideas for community planning are given only as a guide, remembering that the pattern must be cut and fitted to each particular community or locality.

Form A Community Committee

A Community Committee should be formed to meet with the local school superintendent or his representative and the state director of special education. This committee should include professional people from both official and voluntary agencies as well as lay personnel. The size of the community will to some extent determine the number and types of available professional people. A community may not have either all of the professions, or all of the personnel in each profession as recommended in the following list. This should not be a deterent to the organization of a local committee of available professional and lay people. Regardless of the size and the number of professional services represented on a committee, much can be accomplished toward the development of special education services through the selection of a wisely chosen committee, with strong leadership, interested citizens, an alert and progressive local board of education, and a superintendent who tries to center his educational program around the interests and needs of individual children.

Members of Committee. A community committee should include members from the following groups:

Education: Board of Education, the local school superintendent, instructional supervisor, visiting teacher, principal, classroom teachers, psychologists, guidance and counselling personnel.

Medicine: Pediatrician, orthopedist, opthalmologist, otologist, laryngologist.

Dentistry: Orthodonist, general practitioner.

Health: Public health physician, public health nurse, school nurse, psychologist, psychiatric social worker, psychiatrist.

Welfare: Social worker, counsellor.

Juvenile Court: Judge, probation officer, psychologist, counsellors.

Private Agencies: Any representative of a private agency whose chief concern is the development of services for children.

Service Clubs: A representative of each club, having a major program of services to children.

Parent Organizations: A representative of parent groups developed in the mutual interest of children with special problems.

Individual Parents: There may be parents of exceptional children and of the "average" child who will not belong to a parent organization who should participate in the planning.

Youth: Teen-age children with special problems will have valuable ideas regarding their own program of education.

Vocational Rehabilitation: Since one of the aims of special education is to develop an individual who can be partially or totally economically independent, a member of the vocational rehabilitation staff should be concerned with the planning of a special education program.

Churches: A church leader can be a valuable contributor to the committee.

Recreation: The director of recreational activities or someone particularly interested in them since the activities and exceptional child engages in or doesn't engage in have a direct bearing on his personality adjustment.

The Local Parent-Teacher Association: A representative from this group because the State and National P.T.A. are committeed to plans of work for exceptional children.

Size of Committee. In urban communities this could mean the development of a large committee, as the number and variety of human resources exceed those of rural towns and communities. Regardless of the size, the committee should be organized for efficient work and so as to maintain good working relations. In rural communities this could mean the development of a small committee because of the lack of local resource personnel. It will then become particularly important for professional people from the region, state, or nation, to be invited to meet with the committee for particular sessions.

One of the main points to be stressed is that the committee should be made up of local citizens representing professional and non-professional organizations and agencies whose interests are in exceptional children, remembering always to include those with personal concern in this program. It is when knowledge and skills are effectively coordinated with interests, heartaches, and enthusiasms toward the development of a child-centered educational program that the best services will evolve. In this way the total child will be considered with due recognition of his physical, mental, emotional, as well as educational needs.

Regardless of the size of the committee, or the size of the community, it is necessary to have careful planning, wise selection of sub-committees, clarification of problems, the development of channels of communication to members of local organizations, and the subordination of individual interests to a common goal.

Committee Understanding. It is essential that the members of each profession recognize common interests and objectives as well as the specific part each plays in the development of a special education program. Each will have varying degrees of responsibility, but each will be equally important to the total planning of special education. Our world today has demanded the services of highly trained specialists and frequently it is necessary to stress the fact that a special education program is child centered; though each particular specialist has his part to play, this part must be interwoven with those of the other professions. From the first the discussions should be child-centered. Adequate time should be provided for each individual to explain the policies and the goals of the profession or agency which he represents. This kind of understanding can be an important first step in removal of barriers to thinking, planning, and working together.

Goals of Committee. One of the first jobs of the committee will be to define its goals, both immediate and long range. Immediate goals may be to stimulate interest in the development of special education services and to identify the need for such a program in the community. Long range goals may include planning and developing a special education unit and additional units which may be added later. In order to accomplish these goals, it is important for the committee to make specific plans to achieve basic aims.

Inform the Public Concerning Exceptional Children

Before a problem can be solved, there has to be an admission that it exists. Many people, perhaps including some on the planning committee, will not be familiar with these exceptional children as children, but will know them only as cases or as children to be pitied. They may not know what a child with severe cerebral palsy looks like, or the difficulty he has in performing simple tasks. Others may not have heard a child who has a severe speech problem, such as one who stutters. Some may not know that a deaf child can be taught to speak or that a child who is blind soon learns to listen for sounds in order to know from which direction the noise is coming. There are still people who think that you can tell whether or not a child is mentally retarded or mentally deficient by just looking at him.

Even some professional workers use the expression, "Oh, he'll grow out of it," concerning the child who stutters or the child who is mentally defective or some of the other exceptional children. Can attitudes like this be changed quickly? Is it strange that parents frequently seek help too late? Is it odd that they rationalize by saying, "Well, I had an aunt who stuttered when she was little but she talks perfectly alright now," or, "I knew he was slow, but I thought he would out-grow it."

Many people cut a rigid and stereotyped pattern to fit all children. When the pattern doesn't fit and someone deviates, they think he is 'strange and odd' and doesn't belong. It will require concentrated effort to remove the stigma that many people commonly attach to the epileptic, the mentally retarded, the mentally deficient, and others. It is not easy to break down prejudices. The old woman who said, "No'm, my child can't play with Joe cause he has fits and I know that's ketching," will not be easily convinced that Joe should be in the same class as her son. The school board member who said, "Why don't we put them all in institutions? Wouldn't that be cheaper?" or the school superintendent who said, "They can have a room in the public school if they will agree not to go on the playground when the other children are playing and if they will take the corner table in the lunchroom." Both should have factual data to stimulate interest and should know individual children of each different type of exceptionality in order to understand and accept them first of all as children and not just as categories.

Education is a slow process, but much can be accomplished through a planned procedure to inform the public. Study groups should be formed in the parent-teacher association and in other organizations. The various civic, professional, and religious organizations should hear informed speakers, have panel discussions, see films and film-strips, and have demonstrations presented to them if care is taken that no child is exploited. Both faculty data and human interest stories should be run in the local newspaper, presented over radio and television. Posters and materials on exceptional children should be attractively displayed in the local library and other public places.

The information to the public should include the numbers and types of exceptional children to be served, causes of these differences from the 'normal' growth and development, the importance of early detection, the need for adequate physical, mental, and educational diagnosis, treatment and educational services.

Inform the Public Concerning the Program for Special Education

Neither educators nor lay people are always informed concerning the advancement that has been made in the educational techniques for working with exceptional children. Frequently, they do not recognize the lack of facilities for these children in their home, school, and community, nor the advisability of starting special education units. Some do not care about the educational needs of exceptional children. Many have no understanding of the damage done these children when they are denied their rights of receiving an education. Others are chiefly concerned because they have heard that special education is a costly program. Many are not informed about available services in the state.

If there is a state director of special education, he should explain the state program, its policies and regulations. This can be done through talks, discussions, the showing of films, and the distribution of materials. In this way the planning committee as well as the general public will have a better idea of the needs, costs, and ways of developing each type of special education unit, as well as some understanding of the educational practices in each type of unit. State leadership is needed to help each community provide appropriate programs for all types of exceptional children. The following are some of the questions frequently asked of a State Supervisor or Consultant for Special Education:

- What is meant by the term "exceptional children?" What are the different types of exceptional children? How do you define each type? What percentage of each type would one find in a local community?
- What is the State Department of Education's (State Department of Public Instruction) plan for exceptional children? Do they have policies regarding the setting up of units for each type of child who is different?
- Who pays the salary of the special education teacher? Does he get a supplement? Is he paid more than the regular class-room teacher? Is this teacher a part of the regular teacher allotment?
- Is there money for transportation of the children? Is there money for transportation of an itinerant teacher? Is there money for equipment, materials?
- Who determines which children belong in a special class? Is it advisable to have a screening board?
- Will every candidate for a class need a psychological examination? Who gives these examinations? If there is no school psychologist where can a community find a psychologist to give the examinations? How much will they cost? Who pays for the examinations?
- What type of programs will need a special class-room? Does this class-room vary from the regular class-room? In what way? What type of toilet facilities should there be?
- Which types of programs can be started that will allow the children to remain in regular classes and receive special service?
- Should all classes for exceptional children be a part of the regular public school? Is it dangerous for children who are crippled to be in a school with "normal" children? Won't some of the exceptional children be teased and called names?
- Do teachers need special training to work with any or all types of exceptional children? If so, what kind? How long does it take for a certified class-room teacher to become qualified to teach each type of unit? Is teacher education given only at the graduate

level? Where does one find teachers who are qualified? Is there a special education program in the state that prepares teachers for these fields? Are special education teachers difficult to find?

- What do we mean by the term "motor involvement"? What type of equipment is needed for a class of children who are crippled? Does the school need to have the services of a physical therapist and an occupational therapist as well as a speech correctionist to adequately serve these children?
- If a child has speech that is different, does that necessarily mean that it is defective? Does the speech correctionist work in one school only? Does he work in a regular classroom? If he is an itinerant teacher, who pays for his transportation? What type of equipment does he need? What is meant by a hospital and home instruction program?
- Where should the child who is severely hard of hearing or deaf be placed? When should he be taught lip-reading?
- What is meant by the term "brain injured"?
- How can a school best serve the needs of a child who is emotionally disturbed?
- What is the best placement for a child with visual impairment? Does the state supply large-type edition books? When should a child be taught braille?
- What is the difference between a child who is educationally retarded and one who is mentally retarded? Is the "slow learner" a candidate for classes for children who are mentally retarded? Will the child who is mentally retarded be able to finish high school? Why should the child who is mentally retarded be taught in a special class? What is meant by the term "trainable"? Whose responsibility is the "education" or "training" of this child?
- How does one recognize a child who is gifted? Should the child who is gifted remain in the regular class-room or be taught in a special class?
- How many students can each teacher of exceptional children work with?
- How can a rural community plan to serve these children when there may not be sufficient numbers of a particular type to start a special unit?
- What help can be given children who are multiply handicapped?
- If a supplement is given to the teacher by a private agency or organization, or if special equipment is brought by them, will they be able to determine some of the policies for the development and running of the class?

Gather Statistical Information Concerning Resources Available

It is necessary not only to inform people in the community about exceptional children, but also to make them concerned over existing conditions. In order to plan a sound educational program, it is important to know what local resources are available and to be familiar with those at the regional, state, and national level. Although in some instances the local resources may seem meager, it is frequently found that the community has more resources available than are utilized. A detailed study should be made of the physical, mental, emotional, and educational resources both within the public school and in the community. This information may be obtained through:

1. *The School.* Finding answers to the following questions about the local public schools should emphasize the strengths and stress the weaknesses in the educational program. Does the superintendent feel that the school has a definite responsibility for the development of a program for exceptional children? Who constitutes the administrative staff? Is there a pre-school program? If so, does this include kindergarten and/or nursery school? Does the school have a visiting teacher to work with emotionally disturbed and other exceptional children and their families? Is there an instructional supervisor or some one on the school staff who can help teachers to meet the educational needs of individual children? Is there a psychologist to assess children's mental ability? Is there a guidance counselor in the school, and

if so, what are his duties? Does the physical education director take into consideration the needs of all children as well as the members of his football team? Is there a public school nurse? If so, does she give treatment, and what exactly is her job? Which classroom teachers pay particular attention to the physical, mental, educational and emotional needs of individual children and attempt to make some provision for meeting these needs? Is each principal sincerely concerned that each child have an opportunity to develop to the maximum of his ability?

2. *The Community*. Information should be obtained concerning:

Health and Welfare Department: Each of these departments is charged by law to be concerned about the needs of all children. If in any instance these service are lacking in a community, any citizen has the right to ask why they are lacking. The number and positions of the staff personnel and a description of their duties should be obtained. Information should be secured regarding the types of preventive, diagnostic, and treatment services as well as the kinds of consultative services made available through these departments. It is important to know the ages of the people served, the channel for receiving these services, the cost if any, and the possibility of receiving prosthetic devices without cost.

Child Guidance Clinics. Is there a child guidance clinic in the community or region? If so, information should be obtained regarding the number of psychologists and psychiatric social workers, and clinic hours, types of children served, costs, and the region served.

Private Agencies and Service Clubs. Find out the major as well as minor projects of each agency and club that sponsors services for exceptional children. Note if they are interested in children with particular problems; if so, which ones and the types of services they offer.

Juvenile Court. Get information on how often it meets, and know the individual staff members and their duties. Is there special provision for detention of juveniles other than in the county jail? If there is no Juvenile Court in the community, why isn't there one?

Dentistry. Information should be obtained on the number and frequency of dental clinics held in the community and on the types of services offered by dentists in private practice.

Medicine. Information should be obtained on the number of physicians in the community and their specialities.

Parent Organizations. The number and type of exceptionality which each represents. Does any organization sponsor or direct a special service?

Youth Organizations. Find the number of youth organizations in the community such as Boy Scouts, Girls Scouts, Camp Fire Girls, Future Farmers of America, Future Homemakers of America, and the like. It is important to know whether or not exceptional children are made welcome in these groups or if they are excluded from any of the organizations.

Recreational Facilities. List the number of tennis and badminton courts, swimming pools and other recreational facilities. If these facilities are available in the community, is there supervision by people with training in working with exceptional children?

Vocational Rehabilitation. The location of the regional office, the age and type of youth who can be served by them, and the kind of diagnosis, treatment, educational, and vocational services offered.

Churches. What are the types of youth organizations sponsored by each?

When this survey has been completed, the results should be an informative list of available resources with specific data concerning services for exceptional children. This should indicate gaps as well as duplication of services.

GATHER STATISTICAL INFORMATION CONCERNING THE NUMBER AND TYPES OF EXCEPTIONAL CHILDREN

Statistics concerning the number of exceptional children in the United States may be obtained from the United States Office of Health, Education, and Welfare, and applied to the number of children in a local community. The result for a particular community will not be accurate, but it will indicate the extent of the problem. Unless a survey will be followed by action, or is used as a type of pilot study, it is wise to plan and work from an estimated figure. Frequently, the estimated figure, the interest in the community, and the available physical, mental, and psychological diagnostic and treatment services will determine which type or types of units a school will give priority in starting. When this is true, then it will be necessary to survey only for a particular type or types of exceptionality. In gathering information concerning individual children, it is important that the person be trained in the procedure of interviewing. Otherwise, specific information may not be received, and there is a possibility that the reliability of some of it will be questionable. If there isn't a trained interviewer available, the data can still be collected, but it should be weighed with some care.

IDENTIFYING THE EXCEPTIONAL CHILDREN

So that all exceptional children within a community may be identified, it is necessary to complete inquiry forms calling for name, age, type of problem on each child. This information may be obtained through:

1. *The School.* Inquiry forms itemizing the type of exceptionality may be filled in by classroom teachers, visiting teachers, school psychologists, other members of the school staff, and others.

2. *The Community.* Inquiry forms may be filled in by individual members of each of the professions and organizations listed earlier, as well as any individual who may know of such a child.

When this survey has been completed the committee will have a list of names whom people think exceptional. With this basic information a Superintendent can start specific educational planning.

SUPERINTENDENT AND LOCAL BOARD OF EDUCATION FOLLOW THROUGH

1. *Professional Committee.* The Superintendent and local board of Education will need to recognize their responsibility in the development of special education services. This may mean the organization of a smaller professional committee composed predominantly of people from the field of education.

This group may serve in an advisory capacity and also do the actual screening of individual children who become applicants for a special class or a special service. They should be thoroughly informed concerning state policies and regulations and report to the Superintendent.

2. *Promoting In-service Training of Regular Classroom Teachers.* It may be advisable to promote an in-service program concerning exceptional children. The regular classroom teachers should be informed concerning the types of exceptional children and the means of identifying them in order to fill in inquiry forms. They should also know the services for the children in the school, the community, the region and the state. Teachers should know some of the ways that they may meet the individual needs of children, for whether they realize it or not, they are working with children who are exceptional.

3. *Finding Diagnostic Services.* Many communities have some type of medical and health service. Physical needs of children are often met without recognizing their other needs. When adequate medical diagnosis cannot be given locally, it may be possible to receive this help from a region or state service. Usually this can be channeled through the local counterpart. But many schools do not have a psychologist to examine the children and no budget to pay for such services. Since a psychological examination is often one of the requirements for admission to a unit, as well as one of the means of determining the educational needs of these children, the superintendent and local school board need to locate a psychologist to give this service and to find some means of paying him. Often a private club or organization will denote the money needed for such services if there is no way for the local school, through either local or state money, to provide them.

4. *Finding Adequate Physical Facilities.* Every effort should be made to house the unit in a classroom in a regular school. One administrator thought that the special education class should take the small dimly lighted and poorly ventilated basement room since there were only fifteen in the class. It is true that the finding of adequate space in the public school often poses a problem for the superintendent whose classrooms are overcrowded and whose schools are already bulging at the seams. Sometimes units may be started in rooms in a church, in a Boy Scout hut, or in some unused building or house when there is no place available. When this has to be done, the superintendent, the board of education, and the community need to understand and remember that it is only a temporary solution. Every effort should be made to make provision for these children to have a room in the public school.

5. *Finding A Qualified Teacher.* This will be one of the toughest jobs that will face the superintendent. There are not enough qualified special education teachers to meet the needs and demands. Recruitment of certified teachers who are willing to study in the field of special education may be a necessity. Scholarships should be obtained for interested people.

6. *Finding Adequate Transportation.* If a class for exceptional children is housed in a building near the center of a community or district, the regular school bus may not be able to transport all of the children. When the state makes no provision for a bus and driver for these children and the local budget will not permit this expenditure, it may be necessary to ask parents to bring their own children, or to form a car pool. In some communities local clubs

have bought station wagons for this purpose. In one city a business club not only bought the station wagon, but one of its members takes time from his business to bring the children to school in the morning and to take them home in the afternoon. Any form of transportation used should be under the direct sponsorship of the superintendent. If there is no public means of conveyance every effort should be made to make state funds available to provide the same service for exceptional children as exists for others.

7. *Getting Parents to Accept Exceptional Children Objectively.* Parents need to accept their children objectively. Frequently the Superintendent can help by seeing that his staff gives frank and objective information to parents. It is frequently difficult for parents to accept the mental limitations of a child. One parent put undue stress on a child by insisting that he could work arithmetic problems too advanced for his ability. On the other hand, parents need to objectively accept the child who is gifted without exploiting him. Everything possible must be done to get parents to know their child first of all as a child and not as a type of exceptionality.

Community planning for special education can be an exciting procedure when professional and lay people join in their efforts to serve children who are exceptional. The development of a sound program is aided through:

1. An informed and concerned public.
2. A knowledge of human and material resources in a community, region, and state.
3. Family and community acceptance of children who are different.
4. The Board of Education and local school Superintendent assuming responsibility of a program.
5. Individual teacher's emotional as well as intellectual acceptance of these children.
6. Adequate physical, mental, emotional and diagnostic and treatment services.
7. Adequate educational diagnostic services.
8. Qualified teachers.

RESEARCH IN SPECIAL EDUCATION

In the historical development of the field of special education one sees a pattern of growth quite similar to the course followed by older disciplines, such as medicine, biology, economics, psychology, sociology, general education, and other related sciences. This pattern has been one of an infant discipline growing out of a service need. In the initial stages of these services the motivations were humanitarianism and the stress of impelling necessities of the moment. Service programs and area content were almost wholly conditioned by immediate ameliorating solutions for pressing problems. For generations, medical research was but a short step from superstition and primitive alchemy. Economics, sociology and education, only in our century, have taken on aspects of research methodology worthy of the name research.[1-5] Special Education is still in swaddling clothes and has borrowed its research methodology largely from companion disciplines, copied good and poor methodology, and has as yet failed to present an acceptable or even standard research pattern.

Kirk gives a series of reasons why this condition has existed in the field of special education, and points out some basic problems amenable to research analysis.[6] Other recent studies[7-12] list sources for research materials, state problems and point up the need for an effective research program. The field itself does little to produce more than occasional articles worthy to be called research. What is needed is a definitive long range research program based on sound methodology applied widely and consistently to the manifold problems of our field. Our professional leadership in the medical, social, educational and rehabilitation areas must learn to distinguish clearly between monographic, qualitative and quantitative research projects, and properly evaluate the results of such studies. Research technicians in our field must utilize all reliable research techniques applicable from other fields, where needed, and develop new ones for a new profession.[13] University research centers, foundations, agency centers and field stations with trained research personnel and funds must give the research program for special education the painstaking objectivity of the abstract sciences before we can become enthusiastic about current or future research programs. Valid results in terms of improved service programs will not result from the continued practical, popular subjective materials which have in the past been presented to the field of special education as examples of valid research. Some of the areas within our discipline have made notable advances in recent years in the development of high quality research studies in the field of clinical psychology, protheses, control of communicable diseases, the deaf and hard of hearing, the cerebral palsied, poliomyelitis, the gifted, and the mentally retarded have produced acceptable research materials. The progress has been slow and it is hoped the next decade will see a marked advance in improved research methods and techniques. Kirk[14] has listed a vast number of pressing problems amenable to valid research study — the number and distribution of exceptional children, problems of administration and organization of programs for exceptional children and adults, financing, proper coordination, types of classes, mental hygiene and personality adjustment, curricular problems, accurate diagnosis for classification, technical aids for instruction and rehabilitation, intelligence, vocational and social aptitude tests and measurements, multiple handicaps and a wide variety of research studies for the field of the emotionally disturbed. The professional research personnel in special education have a virgin field for cultivation in the development of high quality research.[15-30]

FOOTNOTES

1. Jahodah, Deutsch and Cook, *Research Methods in Social Relations,* 2 vols. (Dryden Press: N.Y.C., 1951).
2. Freedman, Paul, *Principles of Scientific Research* (Public Affairs Press: Washington, D.C., 1950).
3. Huxley, Julian, *Scientific Research and Social Needs* (Watts: London, England, 1934).
4. Barr, Arvil; Dabis, Robert; Johnson, Palmer, *Educational Research and Appraisal* J. B. Lippincott: N.Y.C., 1953).
5. *Research Relating to Children; an Inventory of Studies in Progress,* Bul. II, Supp. I, reported Jan. 1, 1952, Mar. 31, 1954; Also Supp. II, reported Nov. 1, 1952, May 31, 1954 (Children's Bureau, Social Security Admin., U. S. Dept. Health, Educ. & Welfare: Washington, D. C. 1954).
6. *The Education of Exceptional Children,* 49th Yearbook, Part II, National Society for the Study of Education (University of Chicago Press: Chicago, 1950), pp. 320-21.
7. Barker, Harry J., "Administration of Special Education", *Review of Educational Research,* XIV, June, 1944, pp. 209-16.
8. Ziemer, Arthur C., "Suggested Research in Rehabilitation", *Jour. of Rehabilitation,* Sept.-Oct., 1952. 18:5:3-5, 24-25.
9. Bailey, Pearce, "Relationship of Research and Education in a National Program for Handicapped Children", *Exceptional Children,* Apr., 1954. 20:7:289-293.
10. Lord, F. E., Sources of Research Literature in Special Education", *Exceptional Children,* Vol. 19, #8, May 1953.
11. Cruickshank, William M. and Sprague, E., *A Survey of Exceptional Children in Three School Districts of Onondaga County, N. Y.* (Syracuse University Press: Syracuse, N. Y., 1948).
12. Kirk, Samuel, A. and Spalding, Willard B., "The Institute for Research on Exceptional Children at the University of Illinois", *Educational Forum,* May 1953, pp. 413-22. Reprint.

13. Barker, Roger G.; Wright, Beatrice; Meyerson, Lee; and Gonick, Mollie R., *Adjustment to Physical Handicaps and Illness; A survey of the Social Psychology of Physique and Disability*, Bul. #55, Rev. (Social Science Research Council: 230 Park Ave., N.Y.C., 1953).
14. *Education of Exceptional Children*, pp. 322-334.
15. Ivy, Andrew C., "The Importance of Research on the Prevention of Crippling Diseases", *Crippled Child*. Dec., 1951. 29:4:4-5.
16. Myklebust, Helmer R. and Brutten, Milton, "A Survey of Research Needs in the Education of the Deaf", *American Annals of the Deaf*, Nov. 1951. 96:5:512-523.
17. Garmezy, Norman, "Some Problems for Psychological Research in Cerebral Palsy", *American Journal Physical Medicine*, Dec., 1953. 32:6:348-355.
18. Lawrence, Ernest S., "Social Adjustment; an Area for Psychological Research in Mental Deficiency", *American Journal of Mental Deficiency*, Jan., 1954. 58:3:500-505.
19. *Symposium on Research into the Causes of Feeblemindedness*, 43rd Annual Report of the Board of Visitors of Letchworth Village (Dept. of Mental Hygiene, State of New York: Albany, N. Y.).
20. Raskin, Nathaniel J. and Weller, Marian F., *Current Research in Work for the Blind, Survey* (Am. Foundation for the Blind: N.Y.C., Oct., 1953).
21. *Research Suggestions on Psychological Problems Associated with Blindness* (Office of Vocational Rehabilitation, Federal Security Agency: Washington, D.C., 1955).
22. Haitema, John S., "Administrative Research Necessary to Special Education", *Jour. of Educ. Research*, LX, April 1947, pp. 628-37.
23. Baker, Harry J., "Administration of Special Education", *Review of Educational Research*, XIV, June, 1944, 209-16.
24. Kornitzer, Henrietta, "Problems for Research in Education of Partially Seeing Children", *Jour. of Educ. Research*, LX, April, 1947, pp. 592-97.
25. *Artificial Limb Program*, Five Years of Progress (National Research Council Advisory Committee on Artificial Limbs: Washington, D.C., Nov. 1951).
26. Weaver, H. E. and Young, J. L., *Annual Summary Report on Orthopedic Appliances* (Sarah Mellon Scaife Foundation, Pittsburgh, Pa., 1951).
27. Motes, G. M., *Final Report on Artificial Arm and Leg Research*, Jan. 1944, Dec. 1950, National Research Council Committee on Artificial Limbs, Advisory to Veterans Administration (Northrop Aircraft, Inc., 1951).
28. Buchwald, E.; Rusk, Howard A.; Draver, George; Covalt, Donald A., *Physical Rehabilitation for Daily Living*, (McGraw-Hill: N.Y.C., 1952).
29. *Self-help Devices for Rehabilitation*, Institute of Physical Medicine and Rehabilitation. New York University, Bellevue Medical Center, Pts. 1, 2, 3. (The Institute: N.Y.C.).
30. "Research Needs Related to Partially Seeing Children", National Society for the Prevention of Blindness, *Sight-Saving Review*, Summer, 1954. 24:2:94-99.

SECTION II

CHAPTER IV

TEACHER TRAINING

TEACHER TRAINING PROBLEMS

One of the greatest difficulties in a discussion of teacher training for work with the exceptional[1-8] is that the needs of the field are not clear to the general educator. A second difficulty is that many of those who are engaged in programs of training have in many instances built their own curriculum, and having done so, consider it ample and far-seeing. Another problem is created by a considerable divergence of opinion between persons engaged in teacher training and the actual employer of the teachers who are so trained.

A fourth difficulty arises from the feeling that it is necessary to put out special attractions, in terms of salary and of actual subsidy for training, if recruits are to be brought into this work. This difficulty is further complicated by the unwillingness of employers to insist on thorough training for the work. Likewise, there is a tendency toward hurrying teachers into the work before they have had experience instructing non-handicapped children.[9-12]

In preparing the program or curriculum for teacher training in a department of education of the exceptional, the following steps are necessary:

1. Analyses of both the apparent needs of each type of exceptional child and the existing teaching methods of meeting these needs.
2. An analysis of the special training the teacher needs for work with each type of the exceptional if she is to provide effective service.
3. A series of area curricula and admission standards based on 1 and 2 above.
4. A study of the situations and problems common to all areas and also of those distinctive of each area. To those horizontal and vertical courses an orientation course should be added.
5. The entire program must be in detail and must be submitted for criticism to a large number of experts in general education and also in special education, both teachers and administrators.

It is preferred that the student have a previous degree and also experience with non-handicapped students. The subsequent program consists of about

25 per cent in the foundations of education and 75 per cent in the major. The major includes: orientation courses covering all types of the exceptional; courses in organization, administration, and methods for the particular type of exceptional selected; field experience under close supervision in the chosen area; psychology of the exceptional; guidance, mental hygiene, and adjustments of the exceptional; and further electives in subject teaching, remedial instruction, music and the other arts, and such additional courses as are likely most to benefit the individual student.[13,14]

At present many excellent teachers of the exceptional have taken work for professional improvement in situations where academic credit and degrees were not available. However, this need not be a problem in the future, since there are now definitely organized programs in this field for full term, summer, and conference types offered by degree-conferring institutions.[15] "For the academic year 1953-54, 122 of the Nation's colleges and universities reported sequences of teacher preparation in one or more areas of exceptionality."[16]

Since in some instances there is a special increment of salary connected with work with the exceptional, it is reasonable to require that teachers of the exceptional conform to the usual practices in school systems, of spending some portion of their time in professional improvement through organized courses. These courses, while of necessity operated in the past by certain voluntary agencies, rightly belong in teacher-training institutions, and the student should look forward to obtaining a degree in one institution rather than following the plan, formerly in operation, of failing to secure a degree through taking work in various different setups. Granting a proper criticism of the undue worship of academic degrees, it must be borne in mind that they at least represent organized programs followed through for the most part under careful and competent advisors, as compared with sporadic, scattered personal efforts at meeting professional-improvement needs.[17,18]

In some teacher training centers it is the present practice to give work with the exceptional in the latter part of the graduate training years. It is debated at present whether it might not be better for the student to complete training for work with normals and serve a year or two as a regular classroom teacher before taking up work with the exceptional, which is possibly a graduate specialty, though the present emergency shortage of teachers may warrant senior college concentration in this area.[19]

Consideration should be given to starting some training on an undergraduate level in order to recruit interested and capable students into fields of specialization; and to inform students in general of the problems of the exceptional. The policy of many school systems of selecting for work in the field of the exceptional teachers with experience with normals supports this thought.

In recent years a good deal of attention has been centered on the training of teachers for the exceptional, due in no small measure to the acute shortage and the limited training facilities. Recent publications place in bold relief the most pressing problems.

The Need for Professional Standards for Teachers

The citizens of this country are almost universally interested in having the Nation's children taught by well-qualified teachers. Since the days of the Colonies, people have been searching for ways to select those teachers to whom they are willing to entrust the instruction of their children. This endeavor now takes on new meaning as local school systems attempt increasingly to provide opportunity for the four or five million exceptional children of school age. They are the boys and girls who, because of marked physical, mental, or emotional deviation, need something different from, or something in addition to, the usual school program if their development is to be as normal for them as possible.

Even with all that has been done, current statistics, both for local school systems and residential schools, indicate that less than one-fourth of the children in need of special services are receiving them. Many factors are responsible for this lag on the part of the schools. Among these are lack of personnel, inadequate housing, transportation problems, and difficulties encountered in screening, diagnosis, and placement. Most serious of all is the lack of *qualified* teachers who are able to bring to the schools the specialized and technical services which these children need.

The inadequate supply of teachers is only part of the problem. More basic is the need to select teachers who possess qualities, skills, and understandings which will make them successful in working with exceptional children. Many State departments of education now have special certification requirements aimed at achieving this goal; others are in the midst of developing and revising standards.[20]

In 1952, Hunter College of the City of New York held a College Symposium on the training of teachers and other professional personnel for the education of the exceptional. We quote at length the recommendations of this symposium covering twelve work conference areas:

HUNTER COLLEGE SYMPOSIUM

ON THE

EDUCATION OF THE EXCEPTIONAL

February 25-28, 1952

RECOMMENDATIONS OF THE TWELVE WORK CONFERENCE AREA GROUPS

Index to the Recommendations

(The arrangement of the Recommendations is by the stated Objectives for the Symposium)

These recommendations have been gathered together from the twelve groups, and will be detailed below according to the ten "Conference Objectives" proposed in the call which summoned the Symposium.

RECOMMENDATIONS REGARDING THE FIRST CONFERENCE
OBJECTIVE: "RECRUITMENT"

Under this objective, the recommendations of the twelve groups may be grouped as follows:

I. The Teacher
II. The Classroom
III. The Team
IV. Added Recommendations

I. *THE TEACHER*

A. *Recruiting in the High Schools*:

Vocational guidance
Films and Literature
Talks by visiting specialists
Field visits by the students to local community agencies and organizations, and guided participation therein
Educational guidance to Seniors; assemblies; information
Talks by successful and satisfied teachers
Voluntary services by students, in summer camps and extracurricular activities
Career-Day programs

B. *Recruiting from Undergraduates in College*:

Orientation —
........early in the education program
........course concerning exceptional children (their nature and need; modifying education programs accordingly; resources, medical, vocational, and community; and knowledge of pertinent legislation
........Freshman year
........Junior year
........obligatory—
........in all teacher education institutions in the United States
........for all majors in education, speech, and psychology
........including a unit on the partially seeing
........survey course covering all special areas
Present the need for teachers to teachers as well as other professionals
Paid advertising by colleges and normal schools
Field trips, obligatory on all majors in education, speech, and psychology; or simply, early field trips
Emphasize special values for teachers in the special education fields (small groups; individual and group instruction and counseling)
Recruitment committee in teacher education college
Talks — to assemblies, and by successful and satisfied teachers
Films, radio, and TV.
Local school boards, stressing the practical certainly to be appointed, due to shortage; superintendents and examiners also to stress this item
One session in each regular education course, on the mentally retarded
Guidance — to Freshmen
Organizations of future teachers

Rich curriculum in the field of the exceptional

All teachers to learn how to deal with those epileptic children who need to be kept in regular classes

Publicize — the need for, value of, and research opportunities in special education

Eliminate the requirement of 2-3 years of regular teaching before teaching in special education

Do not interrupt the five-year education program

Spend part of student teaching in the area of the handicapped

Gives laboratory experiences

No further recruitment of teachers of the partially blind, until the newer insights have been incorporated in their education courses

Courses in the psychology and education of exceptional children

Early in the program:

........visits to speech clinics

........assisting in speech clinics, with pay

........hospital work

........community centers

C. *Recruiting from Among Post-graduate Students* —

Paid advertising by graduate schools

Information for all professionals as to need of special teachers

Emphasize special values of special education, for a teacher

Cooperative license requirements to be made by college and board of examiners

Scholarships

At least one session in each regular education course, to consider the mentally retarded child

No further recruitment for teachers of the partially seeing until the newer insights are incorporated into courses

D. *Recruiting from Among In-Service Teachers* —

Salary differential —

........because of special license and certification

........because of extra training and added responsibility

........none for teachers of the gifted in special classes

........because of extra preparation, extra-curricular activities, difficulties, and complexities of the job, the added training and added experience

Teacher exchanges

Sabbaticals

Inform all professionals of need

Improved salaries for the teaching profession

Canvass the mature teachers and teachers who left teaching to raise families

Basic course on the exceptional required

........for all promotional licenses

........for in-service training of all regular teachers

........obligatory on all teachers

Visits to speech clinics

Short courses: in local areas and at educational conventions

Scholarships for advanced training

Visiting days, for all teachers, to observe special education activities

Reduction of the case-loads in speech therapy

Provide speech therapy rooms

Recruit such teachers through all professionals

E. *General Recommendations for Teachers*

(1) *Research and Recruiting* —

Further study of present methods of recruiting

(2) *Teachers* —

Educate the public and the teaching profession alike, as to the equal right of the gifted with other exceptional children

A liking for children of all degrees of brightness and learning potentialities, and patience and objectivity

Stress special compensations of teaching the mentally retarded: these pupils progress, not in spite of, but because of the teacher's efforts; teacher sees results before his (her) own eyes

Require of all teachers: orientation in the education of the exceptional

More consideration of mentally retarded children by educational organizations

Supervisors and school administrators: inform their groups

Realistic personality requirements

Specialized training

Unique qualifications

Enlarge regional training opportunities

More emphasis on summer school for trainees, for teachers of the blind, and for other teachers

(3) *Informing the Public* —

Educate the public and the teaching profession alike, as to the equal right of the gifted with other exceptional children

Local committees, support the development of school provisions for the gifted

Orientation —

........make the public more rehabilitation-minded

........data should be in the hands of various classes of educators and other professionals and laymen

........a nation-wide program of recruitment, led by the International Council for Exceptional Children and other agencies

........legislation to make internship possible, on local and State levels

........by organizations concerned with the mentally retarded, for all outside the field

........Statewide, by radio, etc.

........inform all professionals of the need

........more writings, giving information about all areas of the training program, and especially the blind

........a clearing-house for the dissemination of such writings; a central information and recruiting agency

Paid advertising by interested agencies, associations, and others

More public relations and public enlightenment

(4) *Scholarships* —

Try untapped sources: foundations? labor unions?

II. *THE CLASSROOM —*

[None of the "Recruitment" recommendations made by any of the twelve work-area groups mentioned the actual classroom teaching of the special child. Some of the groups, however, will mention classroom teaching under recommendations concerning Objective 3: Curriculum.]

III. *THE TEAM —*

Cooperative relationship in the school of education
Cooperation as to license requirements for teaching, between colleges and boards of examiners

IV. *ADDED RECOMMENDATION —*

Recruitment, guidance and counseling should constitute one continuous process

RECOMMENDATIONS REGARDING THE SECOND CONFERENCE OBJECTIVE: "SELECTION"

The candidate should have:
Integrated and stable personality, devoted and dedicated
All the qualities needed by a regular teacher
Emotional and intellectual maturity and stability
Ability to act as a member of the team
Sound mental hygiene for self and for children
Flexibility in adapting the curriculum and procedures to the individual needs of children
Acquaintance with special services and community resources
Ability to detect medical problem-cases
Warmth, humility, understanding of and liking for the individual child, and acceptance of him
Willingness to experiment
Prerequisite of 5 or at least 3 years of teaching in normal classes
Working knowledge of child development, needs, and growth
Understanding of family relations and the need for guidance of parents
Ability to provide fulfillment of the needs of the experientially deprived child at any level
Good judgment
Physical health
Selection on the basis of his (her) training and development, without regard to the physical handicap of the candidate
Foreign students — at home in the English language and in American customs
Supervised field work
Regional organizations to establish admission criteria for teacher education institutions
Research program, financed by Federal or State or foundation agencies
Personal interest in doing research
Good speech and no mouth deformities
Above-average intelligence and academic achievement
Quickness of response; intellectual curiosity; and sophistication

Prerequisite: successful experience with children

Ability to analyse and synthesize

Acquaintance with pertinent legislation

Ability to establish and maintain effective relationships; objectivity; organiz-
ability; and desire to work in the field

Good general education for teaching

Experience

Awareness of the individual child's home and social environments

Alertness for child fatigue or signs of malnutrition

Ability to help educate the community

Capability to detect cases fit for transfer to regular classes

Skill in all needed techniques

No serious eye difficulties; vision normal or correctable to 20/40

Willingness to invent instructional materials

Every State to certificate, qualify, and approve candidates

An accredited A. B. degree

Teaching certificate for the particular level

At least 6 semester hours of graduate work in the particular field

Training in urban centers only

Develop 6 to 8 regional centers for training

Ability to teach a handicapped child in normal classes

Continuous evaluation of the candidate's progress in training, and prompt
elimination of the unfit

Initiative and leadership

Optimism

Realistic thinking

Knowledge of job possibilities and vocational guidance

RECOMMENDATIONS REGARDING THE THIRD
CONFERENCE OBJECTIVE: "CURRICULUM"

These recommendations will be here classified as follows:

      I) Courses for teachers

     II) Methods for teachers

    III) Personal Qualities for Teachers

    IV) Courses Peculiar to the Area

     V) Curricula for Children of the Area

I) COURSES FOR TEACHERS

Same as required for all teachers

Psychology, Learning, Child Development

Orientation

........in special education

........survey: anatomy, physiology, kinesiology, and neurology

........in vocational rehabilitation

........concerning the handicapped

Observation

........in regular classes

........in special classes

........in hospitals
........of home instruction
........health needs as well as educational needs
........as integral part of teacher education programs
........to be begun not later than the third year
........to be begun as early as possible
Mental Hygiene
Guidance
........a sequence in
........at every level
........personal, educational, and vocational
Field experience
.... school activities
.... in varied schools
........begun in Sophomore year
Practica
Arts and Crafts (junior year)
Practical arts and leisure-time activities
Play techniques (junior year)
Group relations
Visual aids
Observation and practice teaching
Audiology (elective)
Remedial arts (elective)
Language arts (elective)
Psychology of special subjects (for teachers of the emotionally handicapped)
Psychology of exceptional children
Have a psychologist available
Education of children of multiple handicaps
Training centers should consider giving courses on the undergraduate level
Medical information by an M.D. on the teacher education faculty
Community projects and community resources and activities
Major in elementary education (preferred)
Health education
Physiology and anatomy
Social worker to be available
Student teaching
Variety of research techniques for different age-levels
Sociometry
Broad liberal education
Thorough, advanced preparation in one or more special fields
      (especially at the secondary level)
Mental and educational measurements
Family life
Study epilepsy in *all* undergraduate courses in college
Emphasize optimism regarding prevention and control of epilepsy
Biology and/ or physiology
Speech fundamentals (one year)
Speech (elective)

Psychology of personal adjustment
Mental Hygiene
Child development (required of all teachers of exceptional)
Psychology of the exceptional (ditto)
Principles and methods of education (ditto)
Psychology of speech (elective)
Tests and Measurements (elective)
Introduction to psychotherapy (elective)
Audio-visual aid (elective)
Language arts (elective)
(For graduate study)

> —Neuro-anatomy, with hospital affiliation
> —Advanced anatomy and physiology of the speech and auditory mechanisms
> —Seminar in brain-injuries: cerebral palsy; aphasia
> —Seminar in psychogenic disturbances in speech and language disorders: autism, stuttering
> —Seminar in voice disorders
> —Intellectual and perceptive problems (seminar)
> —Seminars should include individual research to develop critical analysis
> —Supervised clinical practice, including opportunities for diagnosis
> —Psychometric and projective testing
> —Advanced course in psychotherapeutic techniques

II) METHODS

Specialization in junior year
Group dynamics
Demonstration schools
Experimental classes for the gifted
Observation and practice teaching, with a variety of children
Special (such as "600" in N. Y. C.) schools required for some disturbed or maladjusted children
Interdisciplinary approach
Early childhood methods
Elementary school methods
Junior High School methods (optional)

III) PERSONAL QUALITIES

Continuous emotional development of teacher himself
Knowledge of his own limitations
Refer unsolved problems to other agencies, without a feeling of guilt in so doing
Learn to create a non-authoritarian school
Readiness to accept different kinds of people and children in abnormal environments
Self-direction and evaluation
Use of community and other resources
Ability to recognize a disturbed child

IV) *COURSES PECULIAR TO THE AREA, FOR TEACHERS*

Braille
Teaching methods for the blind
Physiology for special areas
History for a special area
Anatomy
Techniques
Public Attitudes
Speech
Language for an area
Elementary school subjects
Speech-reading
Phonetics
Speech
Measurement of hearing
Psychology of the physically handicapped
Practica, with first hand laboratory and practice teaching
Physiology of the human eye
History and psychology of blindness
Clinic
Orientation course in special education: should be compulsory for all
       teaching education institutions in the United States
Problems — physical, educational, and social
Mental hygiene
Vocational adjustment
Arts and crafts
More attention to case-finding activities in the schools of the United States
Know the number and location of all children needing service
Pool all community resources
Planned visits to clinics and hospitals of the orthopedic
Flexibility in adapting curriculum
Participation — teachers' workshop and conferences
                     leadership activities, special education
More courses in general guidance for physical handicapped
Materials of instruction
Observation experience
Internships
Sequence of electives, especially special education
Medical lectures and clinical observation
Phonetics
Anatomy of physiology of speech and auditory mechanisms
Physics
Voice and diction
Survey one year: speech disorders, including observations and field trips
Clinic supervisory practice
Participation in and organization of special education programs
Clinical courses in etiology, etc., of neurologically impaired
Student teaching of the neurologically impaired
Seminar in education of the neurologically impaired

Practice teaching in a group situation

Seminar for integration

Hearing problems and basic audiometry

Special consultations, with training in the field of the epileptic in schools, to advise on teaching those epileptic children who are in *regular* classes.
—PLUS:—Clinical abnormal psychology, 4 to 6 hours
  —Child guidance, 3-4 hours
  —Education of the brain-injured, 2-3 hours
  —Education of the mentally retarded, 2-3 hours
  —Education and vocational guidance of the handicapped, 3 hours

During the fifth year, part-time internship in a clinic for convulsive disorders

V) CURRICULA FOR CHILDREN OF A PARTICULAR AREA

A) *Curriculum for the Partially Seeing Child*

Do not educate him in schools for the blind, but in programs arranged by their own locality

B) *Curriculum for Children with Epilepsy*

To be shaped according to the type of epilepsy

Majority of epileptic children can and should be taught in *regular* classrooms *not* at home or in special classes

Teamwork by teacher, physician, psychiatrist, social worker, administrator, and all others who have worked with the child

Stimulate interest in epilepsy in high school

C) *Curriculum for Gifted Children*

For the present, for administrative reasons, keep them in heterogenous classes, for administrative reasons

Flexible program

Research techniques; also creative and recreational hobbies

Adequate, advanced learning resources to be provided

Promote individual creative abilities, develop social dedication and skills, and foster personal growth and development

Wide variety of experimental and pilot classes and schools

Individual instruction

Field experiences for these children, at all age levels

Advanced projects, supported by guidance by resource-persons such as research workers, professional men and women, and parents

Specialized learning and training at earlier age than for usual children

Based on continuing research on currently unsolved problems — e.g., acceleration vs. enrichment

Core experiences and individualized project work: *surely* for elementary educational level; *possibly* also for secondary level

Socializing experiences

RECOMMENDATIONS REGARDING THE FOURTH CONFERENCE OBJECTIVE: "FIELD AND LABORATORY EXPERIENCE"

Assign teaching and proctorial duties according to the abilities of the individuals

Field and laboratory experiences are more pertinent to teaching than to proctorial work

A continuing Symposium to study the whole program of selection of training for teachers of the deaf

Required field experience in school and community activities

Use field work experiences at Sophomore year for prospective trainee to learn to deal with normal and abnormal children and whether he (she) likes and has an aptitude for teaching

Required in methods courses for all teacher candidates: field trips, to learn how to recognize an emotionally disturbed and a normal child, and to adapt curriculum to practical situations in a given school

Laboratory experiences, together with observation and practice teaching

University or college should organize, where needed, a continuous program of education through use of community resources for the hard of hearing child, as a laboratory for the trainees

Early orientation, so that trainees may select this (retardate) area in time: field trips, visits to classes and schools for the mentally retarded, films, radio, and TV

Experimental laboratory units in teacher-education institutions, to deal with education of neurologically impaired children

Practice teaching in special classes, convalescent homes, hospitals, home instruction, etc.

Opportunities to participate in workshops for teachers and in conferences

Leadership activities in special education

Activities with exceptional children

.... summer camps

.... baby sitting

.... scouting

........the "Y"

........visits with the handicapped child and with the family

........visits to hospital clinics

........work in clinics and hospitals

.......recreational programs, especially with mentally retarded and cerebral palsied children

........observation in psychiatric clinics

.... films

.... guest lectures

.... observation of children in institutions

Undergraduate/graduate observation and supervised experience in schools, hospitals, or clinics, in a variety of speech situations

RECOMMENDATIONS REGARDING THE FIFTH CONFERENCE OBJECTIVE: "GUIDANCE AND COUNSELING"

Required college course in guidance and psychology

In regional training centers: courses in the guidance and the psychology of blind children

In training centers, suitable literature and guidance kits

Programs constructed for training psychologists and guidance workers, both for the field of the deaf

Required: field experience in school and community activities

Information in the curriculum concerning community resources and experience in community projects

All student teachers should have available counseling — personal, educational, and vocational

A social worker and a psychologist available when needed to all student teachers

Guidance and counseling needed at every level of training for teachers of emotionally disturbed and socially handicapped children

For guidance counselors, *et al.*, an orientation course in the problems of the hard of hearing (including lectures and observation)

A cooperative State Advisory Committee to be formed by guidance and counseling representatives and other professionals

Field experiences for gifted children at all ages, especially in socially useful fields

After the general preparation needed for all teachers of exceptional children, there should be, for candidates for teaching the mentally retarded, a sequence in guidance (guiding procedures, occupations, problems of placement and follow-up, etc.); totaling 2 credits. Require this for provisional appointment of teachers of mentally retarded children

Help the teacher in her role on "the team"

More courses in general guidance of the physically handicapped (for teachers of the orthopedically handicapped)

Educational and vocational guidance, as part of a 30 clock hour course on teaching methods for partially seeing children

Course in vocational adjustment, guidance, and counseling (for teacher of partially seeing child)

School-connected guidance clinics for epileptic children

Psychiatric or child guidance for *all* children with epilepsy

A course in "Introduction to psychotherapeutic techniques" for teachers of the speech handicapped)

Consultants in speech guidance and speech counseling should be provided by the educational departments of municipalities, counties, and States

Supervision to be continued after placement

Pilot-centers

Workshops

Conferences

RECOMMENDATIONS REGARDING THE SIXTH CONFERENCE OBJECTIVE: "IN-SERVICE EDUCATION"

Regional training centers and refresher courses

Guidance and supervision by school principal

Visitation and observation, oriented to the entire program of the school or agency

More married persons as teachers

Personnel not to lose seniority because of needed leaves of absence

Teaching and proctorial work should be apportioned according to individual ability

A program of In-Service training for housemothers, proctors, *et al.*

University or college should operate, where needed, a program of experiences, open to in-service teachers as well as trainees

Development of recreational skills in in-training courses for teachers of emotionally disturbed and socially handicapped children

Democratic participation by teachers in school policies and practices

Supervisors and other educational experts should be resource persons for teachers

Work-study groups, teacher-initiated and teacher-directed, by suitable levels and areas

Encouragement of teacher-visitation of other teachers and schools

Provision of newer materials on research, teacher practices, etc.; perhaps by regular news bulletins

College and university workshops, especially during summer, on teachers' own problems

Time during school day for study-work group and interschool visitations

Released time and funds for teacher attendance at frequent institutions, workshops, symposia, and conventions

Clearing-houses for dissemination of professional information

Supervisors should encourage teacher to explore ways and means of increasing the value of his (her) teaching services

Teacher should see to own professional growth

Periodic refresher courses and workshops dealing with problems of partially seeing children

Contacts with other professionals

Constructive supervision

Wide professional reading

Visitations, inter-school and inter-agency

Practical research

Participation in community activities

Films from field

Lists of suggested readings to be available to all school administrators

Continuing in-service education

Short courses, perhaps of one week's duration before or after conventions

RECOMMENDATIONS REGARDING THE SEVENTH CONFERENCE OBJECTIVE: "LEADERSHIP EDUCATION"

Encouragement of research and graduate study, by outstanding teachers, in leadership, supervision, and administration

Universities should encourage outstanding graduate students to develop adequate programs for children hard of hearing, where such programs do not exist

Course in organization and activation of these programs should be provided

The *Journal of Speech Correction and Hearing* ought to be less technical for speech correction teachers

Teachers of orthopedically handicapped should be able to help educate the community about the orthopedically handicapped child

Ability to pass on complete and up-to-date knowledge regarding epilepsy to others

Courses in leadership, parent education, and community organizations

RECOMMENDATIONS REGARDING THE EIGHTH OBJECTIVE: "LICENSING AND CERTIFICATION"

Certification of teachers of emotionally disturbed and socially maladjusted children only after special added courses, and with several years of experience with normal children and with emotionally disturbed and socially handicapped children

Professional associations to be advisory in setting up standards for teachers, although Licensing and Certification must remain a State and regional function

Colleges and boards of examiners should jointly confer, so that colleges could include courses required for license examination eligibility

Single license or certification for the teaching of the mentally retarded, regardless of chronological and mental age levels of the children in special classes

Permanent appointment as a teacher of mentally retarded should require 30 college credits, by taking 2 courses in each of 5 specified areas (foundations, clinic, guidance, methods, and electives in special education)

Provisional appointment as teacher of mentally retarded children should require 15 college credits, distributed among the first 4 of the above-mentioned areas (with over half the emphasis being on method)

Certification should be by both professional organizations and by State authorities

Required for a teacher of partially seeing children:

    (a) Same preparation as for a regular teacher (for example, diagnostic and remedial reading; mental hygiene; child psychology; mental testing; principles of elementary or secondary education, tests and measurements; guidance and counseling; child growth and development

    (b) At least three years of successful experience teaching normal children

(c) At least 6 semester hours of graduate work in the field of the partially seeing, preferably as an inclusive Practicum

(d) 20/40 vision, actual or corrected and

(e) Quick and efficient as typist

Certification for speech correctionists

Licensing of speech therapists

Training of speech clinicians not yet uniform enough to form a basis for licensing

Provisionally certified teachers of mentally retarded to be allowed three years to complete the 30 hours above specified

Such licensing and certification of teachers of the mentally retarded should follow either a B.S. program in a Department of the Education of the Exceptional Child or a program in the 5 specified areas on either the M.A. or the Doctorate level

Include in proposed study by the U. S. Office of Education, a study of desirable minimal standards for teaching in various areas of the education of the exceptional child

All States employing teachers for partially seeing should set up minimum essentials for certification of them

Restrictive laws should be changed to permit modern, acceptable programs for teachers of partly seeing children

RECOMMENDATIONS REGARDING THE NINTH OBJECTIVE: "PLACEMENT"

A clearing-house needed for placement services; to be established by recognized professional associations

Lists of available positions kept by university and college placement bureaus; also by national organizations and their local affiliates

A central placement bureau for all personnel of the hard of hearing should be established; possibly in the I. C. E. C.

Placement staffs in colleges and universities to list teachers trained in teaching of the mentally retarded

Placement should go beyond appointment in local school systems, and be concerned that the teachers are appropriately assigned

Supervision after placement is needed, and on a State basis

RECOMMENDATIONS REGARDING THE TENTH OBJECTIVE: "SUGGESTED CURRICULUM FOR PROFESSIONALS OTHER THAN TEACHERS"

Braille
Teaching methods for the area
Physiology for the area
History for the area
Psychology
Public Attitudes
Public Enlightenment
Internship (for psychologists and guidance workers)

Practica

Guidance (for counselors)

Occupational therapy (for counselors)

More travel opportunities for observation and study: by heads of departments; principals; and supervisors

In-service training for housemothers, proctors, and other workers

Psychologists and guidance workers should have special training for work with deaf

A standard curriculum should be created for psychologists and guidance workers

Study of epilepsy in all undergraduate courses preparing for the allied fields of social work, psychology, and medicine

The basic training for both the public school speech correctionist and the clinical therapist should be the same

Additional experience for clinical therapist in medicine and psychology

Required orientation course about the hard of hearing; for guidance counselors, psychologists, rehabilitation workers, administrators, supervisors, and auxiliary personnel; including tests and observation

Parent education by organizations of parents who know the needs of hard of hearing children, to lead to public recognition and acceptance of the problem of these children

Education of the public to special educational needs of gifted children

Study desirability of provisions for education of intellectually gifted children to be written into laws for exceptional children

Administrators and supervisors should take:

    (a) short area-conferences with professional leaders in the field

    (b) short summer workshops, dealing in orientation in the whole field of the exceptional and in the psychopathology of the neurologically impaired; and

    (c) periodic conference to receive advice from the teaching personnel

Superintendents, principals, and supervisors should take courses on the characteristics and education of atypical children

Supervisors in field of partially seeing children should have requirements of a certified, professionally trained teacher of those children

Orientation course in special education to be required of all principals, superintendents, and supervisors

This orientation course should include a unit on partially seeing children and be kept up-to-date

Administrators and supervisors should be offered a course in the psychology and education of exceptional children

Conference meetings between representatives of speech training centers and State officials

ADDED RECOMMENDATIONS OUTSIDE OF THE TEN CONFERENCE OBJECTIVES:

All the suggestions made by Work-Area Group I: The Blind are proposed only for future recruits and not for present personnel

Suggested topics for future research:

    (a) Qualities of successful teachers or workers in the field of the physically below par child

    (b) How can community programs for the coordination of services be strengthened and improved?

    (c) The relationship of health to behavior and learning

    (d) Differences in rate and in process of learning by children of different levels of intellectual ability

    (e) Follow-up studies of gifted children educated in various ways

    (f) Amount of social deviation shown by gifted children

    (g) Non-acceptance of gifted children as leaders by other children

A national campaign of public education

Train personnel for the special teaching of pre-school children, in classes where the hard of hearing children share the classroom with normally hearing children

Educational studies recommended:

    (a) Experimental programs for gifted children at all levels and in a variety of organizations

    (b) Survey of teacher education facilities for the teaching of the gifted

    (c) Problems of articulation of education of the gifted from nursery school through college

    (d) The survey conducted by Work-Area Group VII as to reasons why teachers of the mentally retarded chose their profession

Attendance at local and regional conferences, and make reports thereon

Support existing professional organizations

Encourage other professionals to give more attention to special education[21]

*   *   *

During the past three years the U.S. Office of Education, in cooperation with the Association for the Aid of Crippled Children, New York City, has made an extensive survey of state certification requirements for teachers of exceptional children and college and university programs for the preparation of teachers of exceptional children. From the bulletin, *State Certification Requirements for Teachers of Exceptional Children,* we quote the following important findings on existing State certification requirements:

1. Thirty-two States and the District of Columbia have special certification requirements for teachers in one or more areas of exceptionality.
2. More States have special standards for speech correctionists than for teachers in any of the other areas of exceptionality.
3. Next to speech correction, the areas in which the largest number of States have special teacher standards are, in order, the hard-of-hearing, the crippled, the mentally retarded, and the partially seeing.
4. The areas in which the least number of States have special requirements are for teachers of the blind, deaf, socially maladjusted, and the gifted.
5. Only one State has a special certificate for teachers of the gifted.
6. Sixteen States require teachers of exceptional children to hold only a regular teaching credential.
7. The majority of special education personnel believe that teachers of exceptional children should first possess the competencies needed by teachers of normal children.
8. Special education personnel favor the requirement of a regular teaching certificate plus a special credential (or special preparation) valid for teaching one type of exceptional child.
9. More than two-thirds of the speech correctionists believe that they too should hold a regular teaching credential.

10. Opinions indicate that State certification requirements should be set through the participation of representatives from a number of groups concerned with education and care of exceptional children.

11. State special educational personnel believe that the most effective method of developing State standards is through a systematic analysis of competencies needed by teachers of exceptional children.[22]

In the bulletin *College and University Programs for the Preparation of Teachers of Exceptional Children,* we note the important findings regarding teacher training shortages.

In the service of the Nation's schools there are perhaps 25,000 special teachers. The most recent Office of Education statistics [23] show 14,316 special education teachers in city school systems, an increase of 48 percent since 1947-48. In addition to these, there are approximately 3,000 teachers working in residential schools for the deaf, blind, and mentally retarded, and at least 2,500 giving hospital or home instruction. Still others not reported are employed by nursery schools and kindergartens, and in private schools. Another group works in small local school systems in rural areas. If allowance is made for the teachers not reported, the total number 25,000 is easily justifiable. Some of these teachers are well equipped professionally for service in their area of specialization; some are partially prepared; still others completely lack specialized preparation.

The literature in special education frequently suggests that at least 100,000 specialists (or four times the available number) would be required to staff the special day classes, hospitals, convalescent homes, and residential schools, and to provide the itinerant and consultative services needed.

When considering the establishment of special education programs in colleges and universities, administrators are interested in having some indication of the number of special teachers needed in each of the areas of the exceptionality. It would be excellent if it were possible to provide this information accurately. Because of variability of teaching load, varying degrees of handicapped conditions, individual community problems, and the many types of specialists needed, no firm estimates can be made. However, on the basis of the incidence figures and these factors, it is evident that many more teachers would be required for the mentally retarded, speech-handicapped, or crippled, for example, than for the blind or deaf.

It is particularly difficult to estimate the number of specialists who should be available to work with the gifted and the emotionally disturbed. The educational needs of these two types of children are met in various ways, and there are differing points of view concerning the kinds of programs which serve them most effectively.

It is probable that the teacher-need figure of 100,000 should be re-examined. One example will serve to illustrate this. On a basis of an average special class enrollment of 18, it seems reasonable to estimate that approximately 40,000 teachers are needed in the area of the mentally retarded alone. This leaves only 60,000 for all of the other types of exceptionality and personnel who would occupy administrative and college teaching positions. Many exceptional children are—and should be— enrolled for all or part of their schooling in regular classes with so-called normal children. Because of this, many educational leaders believe that the regular classroom teacher should have more understanding of the special needs of handicapped and gifted children. If this view is generally accepted, the colleges and universities of the Nation have still another responsibility in teacher-education."

For the academic year 1953-54, 122 of the Nation's colleges and universities reported sequences of teacher preparation in one or more areas of exceptionality.

The 122 centers with integrated programs today represent an increase of 45 institutions (58 percent) over the 77 reported in 1949. The 1949 study, however, included sequences offered during summer school sessions. Thus, it is seen that gains have been even greater in the last 5 years than the figures would suggest.

Little is known about the actual quality of the program. Furthermore, it is not within the scope of this study to make an evaluation of the quality of programs of teacher preparation. Techniques other than those employed in this project would be needed for such evaluation.

The rapid increase in number of centers with programs is viewed by many with both satisfaction and concern. Satisfaction comes from the recognition of the need for qualified persons to teach the Nation's handicapped and gifted children. Concern stems from the recognition of the need for evaluation of the facilities which should be available at colleges planning to develop programs. Later publications coming from the broader study will provide some information which will form a basis for planning.

There are more opportunities for the preparation of teachers of the physically and mentally handicapped than there are for those who wish to work with the emotionally disturbed and the gifted. More colleges (or 115) offer preparation for speech-correctionists than for teachers in any other area of exceptionality. In the closely allied field of the hard-of-hearing there are 68 sequences. A large number of centers have combined programs which equip a teacher to work both as a speech-correctionist and as a hearing specialist. Twenty-two colleges and universities prepare teachers in the somewhat related area of the deaf. As is to be expected, because of the size of the problem, many colleges have integrated curricula in mental retardation. In all, there are 40 programs of this type. In contrast only 2 centers meet the criterion for a sequence of preparation in the field of the gifted, only 3 in the blind, and not more than 13 in any other area.[24]

It is hoped, as projected in these reports, that future studies will "attempt to go beyond a status report" and that studies on teacher competencies, basic curricula requirements, recruitment procedures for teachers and other personnel needed in this rapidly growing field of special education will be forthcoming from our professional leadership.

FOOTNOTES

1. *College Symposium on the Education of the Exceptional—Teachers and Other Professionals, Their Selection and Education* (Hunter College Department of Special Education: N.Y.C., 1953).
2. Mackie, R. P., and Dunn, L. M., *College and University Programs for the Preparation of Teachers of Exceptional Children*, Bulletin #13 (U. S. Department of Health, Education, and Welfare: Washington, D. C., 1954), pp. 4-6
3. *The Education of Exceptional Children*, 49th Year Book, Part II, National Society for the Study of Education (University of Chicago Press: Chicago, 1950). Chapter 5 is an excellent treatment by Lord and Kirk of the basic principles of teacher training.
4. Tenny, John W., "Recruiting Teachers for Exceptional Children", *Crippled Child*, April, 1951. 28:6:6-7, 28. Reprint.
5. Lerner, Arthur, "Information and Responsibility—A Philosophy for Teachers of Exceptional Children", *Exceptional Children*, Oct., 1954. 21:1:8-9
6. Lord, F. E., and Wallace, M. M., "Recruitment of Special Education Teachers", *Exceptional Children*, March, 1949. 15:6:171-173.
7. *Opportunities for the Preparation of Teachers of Exceptional Children* (Chicago, 1949). Joint publication of National Society for Crippled Children and Adults, Inc., and U. S. Office of Education.
8. "Teacher Recruitment and Training, A panel—1952", *Volta Review*, Dec., 1952. 54:10:491-500, 512, 514.
9. Young, Marjorie, "Certification of Teachers of Partially Seeing Children", *Exceptional Children*, April, 1952. 18:7:207-15.
10. *Training Facilities for the Preparation of Teachers of Blind Children in the U. S.* (The American Foundation for the Blind: N.Y.C., 1953).
11. *Careers in Service to the Handicapped* (National Society for Crippled Children and Adults: Chicago, 1952).
12. Hawkins, Ruth, *Principles of Teaching Exceptional Children in the Elementary Schools*, Vol. III, No. 1 (Child Research Clinic, The Woods Schools: Langhorne, Pa.
13. *Certification for Teaching Services, Valid for Teaching Common Branch Subjects. Validation of Certificate for Teaching Special Classes and Other Subjects* (University of the State of New York, The State Education Department: Albany).
14. *Eligibility Requirements for License as Teachers of Health Conservation Classes in Day Elementary Schools; as Teachers of Classes for the Blind in Day Elementary Schools; as Teachers of Deaf and Hard-of-Hearing in Day Elementary Schools; as*

Teachers of Sight-Conservation Classes in Day Elementary Schools; as Teachers of Classes for Children with Retarded Mental Development; in the City of New York (New York Board of Education, Office of Examiners: 116 Livingston St., Brooklyn 1, N.Y.).

15. See list of colleges and universities offering courses during the academic year 1953-54 in the area of special education, in Section III of this volume.
16. Mackie and Dunn, *College and University Programs.*
17. Mackie, R.P., and Dunn, L.M., *State Certification Requirements for Teachers of Exceptional Children,* Bulletin #1 (U.S. Office of Education, U.S. Department of Health, Education, and Welfare: Washington, D.C., 1954).
18. *Opportunities for Preparation of Teachers of Exceptional Children.*
19. Firestone, S.H., and Orleans, J.S., *The Shortage of Special Class Teachers in Large Cities* (Division of Teacher Education, Office of Research and Evaluation, College of the City of New York: N.Y.C., 1952).
20. Rice, Mabel C., and Hill, Arthur S., "Statistics of Special Education for Exceptional Children, 1952-53", Chapter V, *Biennial Survey of Education in the United States, 1952-54* (U.S. Office of Health, Education, and Welfare: Washington, D.C., 1954).
21. *College Symposium,* pp. 60-80.
22. Mackie and Dunn, *State Certification Requirements.*
23. Rice and Hill, *op. cit.,* p. 15.
24. Mackie and Dunn, *College and University Programs.*

SOME BASIC NEEDS FOR THE EDUCATION
OF TEACHERS AND PERSONNEL FOR
SPECIAL EDUCATION

H. E. ROBINSON

In order to have clear objectives in teacher education for exceptional children, it appears obvious that a definite statement of the role of our public schools in modern society and an understanding of what constitutes adequate education are both a necessary foundation.

THE ROLE OF OUR PUBLIC SCHOOLS IN MODERN SOCIETY

Rather than espouse the interest of any organized social, economic, or political group, the major functions of our public schools should be to:

1. Provide an environment where all our children can acquire adequate mental, emotional, and physical health.
2. Make provision for acquiring adequate skills in expressing one's self effectively, both orally and in writing.
3. Help the child to know himself and his environment as a basis for a vocation; then help him acquire the necessary skills to do well some desirable job that will enable him to be self-sufficient in earning a living.
4. Teach the child to study, to use learning materials effectively, and to think, which includes distinguishing between propaganda and fact.
5. Show how to develop the habit of using leisure time properly, for so many people who long for immortality get bored when they have an idle afternoon.
6. Lead in cultivating desirable attitudes toward others of every sect, race, and land.
7. Emphasize appreciation for our homes, our churches, our schools, and the ideals of the American way of life.
8. Make democracy live by providing for and observing democratic techniques in the classroom and community.

In order to possess the above characteristics, most individuals must have all available assistance from the home, the church, and the school so that they will be able to make a living as they live with themselves and others peacefully. Some few individuals are so fortunate that in the absence of these organized efforts they can become self-educated citizens.

Present world conditions make it imperative that all of our local school officials and teachers carefully check their local situation and promptly eliminate any influence harmful to the welfare of any of our children or to our traditional American way of life as provided by the constitution.

What Makes Education Special?

This total environment for general education becomes special education when instruction and other assistance either in school, in the home, or in a hospital have been adjusted to fit the needs and capacities of the child who has a problem that interferes with learning to the extent that normal classroom facilities are either inadequate or unsafe. Such individualized instruction is enriched and supplemented by:

1. The use of music therapy, recreational therapy, physical therapy, occupational therapy, and speech correction as the child may need, and
2. The use of a variety of educational games that assist in teaching the basic subjects, or in providing needed therapies.

Special education is knowing the entire child, then teaching him. It is teaching the child subject matter rather than teaching subject matter to the child. It is tailoring good general education to fit the needs and capacities of each child. It is talking *to* the child rather than *about* him with every curious or interested individual or agency. It is not merely a knowledge of mental hygiene, abnormal or clinical psychology, tests and measurements, screenings, counseling and guidance. It is good stimulative teaching based on individual differences and a knowledge and appreciation of all these things.

Good teaching of any type of children is:

1. Having a personality that causes others to 'become',
2. Causing others to understand and know,
3. Showing how effectively,
4. Being an expert guide, and
5. Telling the truth attractively.

The regular teacher should attempt to provide these facilities as the child remains in the classroom with normal children. When the regular classroom facilities are inadequate or unsafe and the removal of the exceptional child from the regular classroom becomes necessary, a schoolroom with adequate teaching facilities should be provided and the instruction provided by a superior teacher with a cultured personality and specific knowledge and abilities. Thus, it becomes necessary to consider some of these basic needs for the education of such special teachers.

Opinion of Special Education Personnel in Texas Relative to Basic Education of Such Teachers and Personnel

In arriving at these needs, rather than use one man's opinion, the writer sent the following request on January 10, 1955 to 547 teachers of exceptional children in Texas, the 173 superintendents where the programs operate, and to the 28 colleges that have provided courses in the education of teachers for exceptional children in Texas.

I have been requested to prepare an article on Some Basic Needs for the Training of Teachers and Personnel for Special Education and this material will become available for consideration on a national basis. Rather than express my own opinion, I think it would be much more accurate and helpful if I had the composite thinking of people who are interested in this problem, therefore:

Please list briefly below some of the things you feel that a teacher should be and know in order to do a good job teaching exceptional children.

It will be noted that no suggestions nor outlines were provided to guide their reactions. Now, look at the following accompanying responses made simultaneously and individually from the 267 teachers, 78 superintendents, and 17 college professors. All of the college personnel contacted have a doctor's degree and practically all of the public school personnel contacted have at least a master's degree.

Suggestions Concerning Basic Educational Needs of Teachers of Exceptional Children

It will be noted that the ten most desirable personality traits and competencies mentioned by the respondents are:

1. Three hundred twelve of the respondents thought that the teachers of exceptional children should have a sincere regard and appreciation for the welfare of children especially those with handicaps. This does not include being "sorry for the poor little things".
2. Two hundred fourteen of the respondents stated that the ability to understand the nature and needs of children and wishes of parents is vital.
3. One hundred fifty three of the respondents mentioned that being able to wait faithfully, to be tolerant to the ungrateful, and to hope graciously for glimpses of even slight improvement of those children with serious limitations is very important.
4. One hundred fifty seven of the respondents rated as fourth the mastery of subject matter material of the core areas including proficiency in remedial reading.
5. One hundred thirty nine of the respondents felt that to be rated as an outstanding teacher, prior experience with normal children is imperative. Only three preferred young inexperienced college graduates with a major in special education.
6. One hundred twenty nine rated being mature, stable, and wholesomely sound mentally, emotionally, and physically as being very important.
7. One hundred twenty eight named the ability to master the use of all available resources and materials, and a variety of stimulating teaching methods as essential.
8. Ninety three thought that doing the proper thing on time and being courteous, mannerly and tactful in dealing with children and parents is a must.
9. One hundred eleven mentioned being kind, considerate and cooperative with initiative in working with everyone interested in exceptional children is imperative.
10. Sixty three said that having faith in self and recognizing and inspiring into action all the potentialities of children with limitations is very important.

Further study of items 1, 2, 5, 6, 7, 10, and 12 of Section A of the table reveals that of the seventeen personality competencies needed for efficient teaching, these seven are similar to the ones listed by Paul as "Fruits of the Spirit" in one of his letters to friends in Galatia (Gal. 5:22-23). These seven traits are generally regarded as the basic factors of a cultured personality. These seven personality traits may be acquired without residence on, or contact with college, campuses. Thus, what the teacher is must rate more important than her knowledge and skills. Since these important personality competencies are caught rather than taught, by being around others having such traits, it is important that all college personnel be outstanding in these respects.

RESPONSES OF 362 PROFESSIONAL PERSONNEL REGARDING BASIC EDUCATION
OF TEACHERS OF EXCEPTIONAL CHILDREN

A. The Teacher Should Be and/or Have (Habits-Attitudes-Appreciations)	Response of 267 Teachers	Response of 78 Supts.	Response of 17 Profs.	Opinion of U.S. Office of Education Competency Committee
1. Sincere regard and appreciation for children	223	72	17	1
2. Patient	115	28	9	
3. Rated as an outstanding teacher with prior experience with normal children	94	43	2	1
4. Mature and stable with M.P.E. health	87	39	3	1
5. Mannerly and tactful	69	20	4	1
6. Kind, considerate and cooperative	68	35	8	1
7. Faith in self and potential of children	48	11	4	
8. Original and resourceful with initiative	42	10	2	1
9. Poise with a calm pleasant voice	39	41	7	
10. Sympathetic yet realistic and objective	36	5	4	1
11. A sense of humor and common sense	27	11		
12. A happy-cheerful-optimistic attitude	25	32	14	1
13. Ability to inspire children to improve	21	10		
14. Intelligent observation with curiosity	15	5	4	
15. Scholarships to keep up-to-date	11	9	3	1
16. Be a parent	4			
17. Hobbies	1			

B. The Teacher Should Know and/or Be Able to (Her knowledge and skills)				
1. Understand the nature, and how to nurture the needs of exceptional children, and the wishes of parents	144	53	17	1
2. Master subject matter in the core areas, including remedial reading	111	39	7	1
3. Master the use of all available materials, and a variety of teaching methods	84	33	11	1
4. Use music, arts and crafts, and educational games	64	5	4	1
5. Know State law and plan for special education	23	24	5	
6. Have experience in practice teaching under supervision	15	3		
7. Use mental hygiene in classroom	5			

CONCLUSION

Summarizing the basic education needed by such a cultured personality as pointed out by the 362 professional people and covered in Section B of the table above, it will be noted that such a teacher of exceptional children should have the following knowledges and skills:

1. The ability to understand the nature and how to nurture the needs of exceptional children.
2. A mastery of the subject matter material in the core areas including remedial reading. A major in Elementary Education and a major in one of the subject matter areas including methods of teaching in the core areas would meet these needs.
3. Ability to master the use of all available resources and materials, and a variety of stimulating teaching methods.
4. The use of music, arts and crafts and educational games.
5. A thorough knowledge of the state law and the willingness and ability to follow the state plan for special education.

Mastery of the content of such titles as the following should adequately cover the six professional competencies deemed essential in the education of such teachers for exceptional children:

1. The survey of special education for exceptional children,
2. Child study, including the nature and needs of children at the various age levels,
3. Methods of teaching the various types of exceptional children,
4. The use of music, arts and crafts and educational games,
5. Remedial reading,
6. Tests and measurements,
7. Speech correction for the classroom teacher, including an improvement of her own voice,
8. Organization and administration of special education.

These eight items could very well be grouped into fewer than eight college courses, but all should be mastered thoroughly as additional education for experienced elementary teachers entering the field for exceptional children.

The local chapter of the Future Teachers of America now located in the high schools and colleges constitutes a golden opportunity for recruitment of outstanding young personalities who would enter the field and take their undergraduate work in special education.

SYRACUSE UNIVERSITY MEETS THE CHALLENGE OF THE EXCEPTIONAL CHILD*

WILLIAM M. CRUICKSHANK

The education of exceptional children is not a new public responsibility in the United States. It is an area of education, however, towards which the interests of higher education have turned only recently. The focus of two world wars upon the physically disabled individual, the advances of medical and psychological sciences, and the growing awareness that the education of exceptional children is a public school responsibility has stimulated teacher preparation centers to concern themselves with this important aspect of their over-all responsibility.

In 1946 Syracuse University, Syracuse, New York, through its All-University School of Education undertook a broad program of undergraduate and graduate experiences for individuals preparing for teaching careers with exceptional children. Curricula in several teacher preparation areas were established. The fields of education for the mentally retarded, the intellectually superior child and the crippled child, including those with cerebral palsy, were inaugurated. Likewise strong curricula were organized for the education of deaf children, those with lesser impairments of hearing, and children with speech disorders. Summer programs have been established for the education of the child with impaired vision and for teachers interested in the educational problems of the preschool blind child.

It was immediately obvious to the administrators of Syracuse University that this division of the teacher preparation program required facilities for clinical experience, for research, and for university instruction which differed markedly from many other phases of the general teacher education development. It was also immediately apparent that a teacher preparation program of this type involved expenditures in terms of personnel and equipment which were not normally assumed by a typical university budget. By 1950 developments at Syracuse University in the preparation of teachers, nurses, psycholo-

*Reprinted from 1954-55 *American School and University*. Photographs omitted. Used by special permission of American School and University and Dr. William M. Cruickshank, Professor of Education, Syracuse University, Syracuse, New York.

gists and general classroom teachers to answer the needs of exceptional children had progressed to the point where it was necessary to think of a central location for activity and of an expansion in facilities, equipment and research opportunities.

The Syracuse University Special Education Building was dedicated on February 27, 1953, and, in many of its features, is unique in institutions of higher education. At the outset certain facilities were excluded from plans for the building. The Syracuse Public Schools, through the Board of Education, provide facilities for numerous physically and mentally retarded children. Seventeen units for mentally retarded children include many classes which are outstanding in their effectiveness and which provide excellent pre-service observation and cadet teaching experiences. The Percy Hughes School for physically handicapped children, the Syracuse Cerebral Palsy Clinic, the Weiting-Johnson Hospital for children with rheumatic fever, the Onondaga Children's Court and its related agencies, the Syracuse State School, and other residential schools in neighboring communities provide rich resources for young teachers. The Syracuse Public Schools and other public and parochial school systems provide facilities for practice teaching and demonstration work.

A PLAN IS DECIDED UPON

It was thus not necessary to include these facilities in the plans for a projected building. It was agreed that there would be included in the Special Education Building only those facilities which were not currently available or which could not in the future be obtained by cooperating agencies, but which would strengthen both the university's and the general community program for exceptional children and adults. Thus a plan was envisioned to provide university classroom facilities, facilities for several types of direct clinical services to handicapped persons and their families, and facilities for research in the psychological, social and educational development of exceptional children. The Special Education Building was erected through the generosity of the James Foundation of New York, Incorporated, and the Association for the Aid of Crippled Children, Incorporated, of New York City. Additional funds from alumni and friends of the Syracuse University program for exceptional children ultimately made possible a $400,000 building. The professional staff, together with the university architects, Harry A. and F. Curtis King of Syracuse, visited numerous installations throughout the eastern and midwestern portions of the United States to determine the most effective ways in which to meet the requirements of the university program.

TYPES OF AREAS HOUSED

The Special Education Building houses services of a diverse nature. The facilities of the building make possible important research, teaching, and direct clinical services. The building contains more than two dozen rooms, including offices, classrooms and laboratories; rooms in which therapy, diagnosis, testing and evaluations are carried on; seminar rooms, lounges and other facilities. Many of the rooms are so constructed that dual or triple functions can be carried on simultaneously.

The building, contemporary in design and constructed of reinforced concrete faced with Glen-Gary brick, is conveniently located near the University Medical Center and a projected School of Education building. The present structure contains approximately 2,500 square feet of floor space on each of two floors. An excavated basement under approximately a third of the north end of the building houses air conditioning, heating and electrical equipment. It also contains janitorial office and supply space, adequate space for files, an area for a large tool bench, tool cupboards, power saws, drills and other equipment needed in the construction and repair of psychological and audiological equipment used in the clinics and in research.

Convenient Location of Offices

All faculty offices, seminar rooms and classrooms are located conveniently for incoming clients and students. Students need not walk through the entire building when interviews with their professors are desired. A pleasant lobby provides an enjoyable waiting room for both clients and students. The receptionist's window is placed at an angle to permit control of almost all traffic entering the building. This is important in view of the fact that an annual case load, exclusive of college students, of more than 6,000 exceptional children, adults and their families are and will be using the facilities of the building during individual appointments and regularly scheduled clinics.

Fifteen rich colors were used in painting the rooms. With the exception of rooms painted in greys and used on occasion by highly distracted children, two or three colors are employed in each room to give warmth and interest to the building. This has proven highly satisfactory to all who have used the facilities. Natural finished birch is used throughout for extensive prefabricated closets, bookshelves, doors and woodwork.

The north entrance of the building is reached by a sidewalk or driveway, ramp-type in nature and covered by a reinforced concrete canopy. This permits physically handicapped individuals who utilize wheelchairs or crutches to make use of the facilities of the building without experiencing the difficulties of many stairs. An elevator, placed just inside the north entrance, makes the second floor equally available and convenient.

The modern, well-lighted classrooms are equipped with light-proof curtains at the windows which, when lowered, make possible the use of two seven-foot, one-way vision windows. These windows permit the students to observe activities in the adjoining group auditory training room.

Group Auditory Room

The group auditory training room is equipped with air conditioning and has a sound treated ceiling. A heavy rug and rug pad cover the entire floor. Groups of from two to ten children or adults and an instructor can use this room in speech, lip reading and group auditory instruction. Microphones hidden in the ceiling with amplification in the adjacent classroom permit observing students not only to see instructional techniques, but also to hear what is taking place. The room can, of course, be used for many purposes other than auditory training with individuals who have impaired speech or hearing. It is frequently used for demonstrations of intelligence test administration and for similar purposes.

The second floor of the Special Education Building houses a variety of facilities. The Gordon D. Hoople Hearing and Speech Center is located here. A bank of thirteen rooms at the south end of the building is used for individual speech therapy, lip reading instruction, counseling, psychological evaluation, or other individual student-teacher or student-therapist work. Four of these rooms, partially sound-treated and covered with wall-to-wall carpets, are used as modifiable audiometric testing rooms. Each of the rooms contains a different type of audiometer so that students may receive a variety of experiences.

A medical diagnostic suite, including a clinic room, adjoining conference room and adjoining audiology laboratory, is located on the east side of the main corridor. All rooms in the building which are sound treated or which for various reasons have no windows are air-conditioned.

Testing and Evaluation Rooms

Two rooms, an audiometric testing room and a hearing-aid evaluation room, needed both in research and in clinic work, were carefully designed and planned by William A. Stanmyre, consultant to the Hearing and Speech Center. The goals which both architects and contractors kept in mind with respect to these two rooms were to provide a facility which was sound free from external noise and fully sound absorbent with respect to internal noise. The larger of these two rooms, 16 feet by 18 feet, is used for recording, for psychogalvanic skin reflex testing and ultimately will house electroencephalographic equipment. The smaller of the two, 11 feet 6 inches by 9 feet 9 inches, is used for hearing aid evaluations.

These two rooms rest upon steel springs with walls, ceiling and floor completely free from the remainder of the building. Air conditioning and hearing ducts leading to these two rooms are hung by springs from concrete supporting beams of the main structure. An observation window connects the control room with the sound-free room. This is composed of three panes of thermal glass set in rubber. Each pane is placed at a slightly different angle from the remaining two in order to avoid sound reflection as much as possible. Thus, the two rooms are almost completely free of contact with the building proper. Complete efficiency has been obtained. During daytime utilization of the rooms the sound level is less than 24 decibels. This is considered excellent in view of the fact that the building faces on an important street which itself has a long up-hill grade and which is utilized as a bus line and for heavy truck transportation.

Group-Play Therapy Facilities

In order to provide a suitable space for conducting individual and group-play therapy with young emotionally disturbed children, a special room was constructed. Frequently during play therapy sessions excessive amounts of water may be spilled on the floor, or highly disturbed children may smear paints and other substances on the walls purposively or accidentally. Such hard usage required serious thought in the construction of this room. To prevent water seepage through the floor only half of the reinforced concrete floor was poured originally. When this dried thoroughly a waterproof substance was spread over the entire area. The remainder of the concrete floor was was poured. Flexachrome tile (plastic asbestos) was placed on the floor for a finished surface.

A ceramic tile wainscoting was installed, permitting easy cleaning of wall areas. Counters, benches and tables are of hard maple to resist pounding and other unusual usage. The room is equipped with sandbox, sinks with running water, extensive toys and equipment. It also is utilized for a portion of the day as a nursery center for pre-school blind children. At the north end of the play-therapy area is an observation room seating twelve persons and equipped with one-way windows, amplification and apertures for motion picture cameras.

A second play room is also included on the second floor. This room is for diagnostic and educational purposes involving pre-school children. For example, a group of four pre-school mongoloid children utilize the facility two mornings a week during a speech improvement experiment. Pre-school deaf and hard-of-hearing children make use of this same room several half-days a week. The second floor also houses a well-equipped laboratory for research, a staff lounge, a small public waiting room and ample office space for eight doctoral candidates and clinical assistants.

A COSTLY UNDERTAKING

The education of exceptional children and teacher preparation in this important area is a costly undertaking. The total facilities of a major university are required to do the task competently. Full-time resident faculty are essential. The resources of many schools and colleges of the university are brought to bear directly upon the program. The assistance of private foundations and agencies is essential to the full development of the program and to the best type of teacher preparation program.

The Syracuse University program has been supported generously from time to time by such organizations as the New York State Association for Crippled Children, Inc., the Association for the Aid of Crippled Children, Inc., the National Society for the Prevention of Blindness, the American Foundation for the Blind, the National Society for Crippled Children and Adults, Inc., and from private funds of numerous individuals. The combined efforts of these many groups, together with the interest of the university itself, contribute to a program dedicated to the best in education for thousands of exceptional children throughout the United States and other countries of the world.

THE USE OF PANEL FORUMS IN SPECIAL EDUCATION SUBECTS AMONG COLLEGE STUDENTS

FRANCES KOENIG

When people gather together for any purpose and talk, a discussion group has been formed. When some in the group listen while others speak in turn, a panel has developed. When the audience then participates freely and discusses and questions openly what has been offered by the panel, a panel forum has come into being.

Utilization of panels as a form of disseminating knowledge resulted from the efforts of the American Association for Adult Education. Panels came to be an effective method of teaching through the leadership of Harry A. Overstreet, who felt that the panel is really a discussion held in the presence of a group and much could be learned through this form of educating young people.

It was in 1947 that the Hunter College Chapter of the International Council for Exceptional Children came into being. One of the major purposes of the Council is to offer information and stimulate growth among educators and others who work with all types of exceptional children and adults. This Chapter has utilized the method of panel forums in a yearly series since its inception. The aims stem from the position the Chapter holds in the College and in the community. It is one way to communicate and cooperate with other agencies for professional growth and development; it brings experts and authorities in the various fields; it stimulates the student body to some concern in the field of special education. Another purpose is to orient undergraduates to some understanding of exceptional children and to prepare them for graduate student status. Still another of its purposes is for teacher-recruitment in the field and for training in the several areas of study as preparation for teaching a specific type of exceptional child. The underlying emphasis has been in the growth and interplay of the dynamics that enter into all areas of endeavor with exceptional children and adults.

The series have been, in the main, panel forums which are held in a large lounge of Hunter College and are planned about a year in advance of the date of meeting. We rotate programs so that no area has been repeated for approximately four years. All types of exceptionality have been included: namely, the visually and acoustically handicapped, the orthopedic and cardiac, the gifted and mentally retarded, the cerebral palsied, the brain-injured, those with convulsive seizures and with special health problems, the emotionally disturbed and others. We have held panel forums concerning all of these, not only from the point of view of educators but also from the aspects of social workers, medical personnel and therapists of all types; not only in childhood but also into adulthood. Some of the programs have been titled: The Child in the Hospital; The Handicapped Speak for Themselves; Meeting the Needs of the Cerebral Palsied — Medically, Educationally and Socially; Parents Look at the Education of their Gifted Children; The Muscular Dystrophies; The Physically Handicapped Child from Two to Five; and The Prevention of Juvenile Delinquency.

It has been the practice to have a small program committee of from four to six people, since it is the membership of the Chapter which decides upon each year's plan in advance. Usually during the May business meeting the succeeding year's program is set up. On the whole, we have held panel forums in October, November and December of the fall semester, and in March, April and May during the spring term of the school year. On occasion we have found a need for and extreme interest in certain areas to be pursued further. For those we have found it expedient to hold two meetings on the same subject. This occurred at the time of the panel forums on The Brain-Injured Child and on The Child with Endocrine Disturbances.

The duties of the program committee are set by the executive committee and the chairman of programming. This committee is appointed by the executive and is directly responsible to her. The chairman invites speakers and moderators of note in their special fields several months in advance of the panel date.

Publicity for each panel is then set in motion through the efforts of one member of the committee whose task it is to send notices to other colleges, to schools, to boards of education in and around the metropolitan area, to newspapers that carry items of this type, and to the New York City radio and television stations. These announcements are usually placed so they are publicized both in advance of the panel date and on the day of the meeting. Another member sends notices to the evening session student newspaper and to the faculty newsletter of the college. A fourth member mails mimeographed copies of the panel program to chapter members, to other chapters, to a list of individuals, and to organizations and agencies interested in the field. A fifth member places all notices in the letter boxes of the instructional staff and on all bulletin boards of the college.

The sixth member of the program committee is the reporter, who summarizes the important elements of each panel forum for our annual publication, *Education Special* and who sends pertinent information concerning them to the national executive body of the International Council for Exceptional Children and to the New York State Chapters. They, in turn, print these items either in *Exceptional Children,* the journal of the Council, or in its monthly *Bulletin* for possible use in similar programs by other chapters throughout the country and Canada. At times, a reporter has been sent by the School of Journalism of Hunter College or Columbia University or by the Instructional Materials Center of the Board of Higher Education serving the four municipal colleges of New York City. Occasionally students are asked to report to class by their instructors or incorporate the information into term papers or studies. We have utilized these, too, as a part of our program of education, and have given these individuals a by-line in our own publication. This, we feel, is a fine method of training students professionally and of broadening the base of special education.

Arrangements for the use of the lounge are made several months in advance of the year's calendar and all physical needs are taken into account.

Seating arrangements are in the form of an L, with the speakers' table, chairs, microphone and podium at the meeting point of the L and the couches, chairs and folding chairs reaching out from that point in both directions of the lounge, so that all can see and hear equally well. The panel members are seated in a semi-circle at the table so that they can both see and hear the audience. When there is a motion picture or slides to be shown, a projector is brought in.

A table is placed near the rear entrance for literature, either Chapter or Council, or materials contributed by the agencies or organizations cooperating in the panel forum for that evening. All reading matter is free to the audience and no solicitation of any funds is permitted. The programs for the evening are distributed by chapter members as individuals enter the lounge.

The personnel involved in the actual panel includes the presiding chairman, who is ordinarily the president of the Chapter. It is his duty to introduce the speakers to one another before the meeting takes place and to explain the physical set-up, the time limits for each, and other data required for that particular evening. The chairman opens the meeting with greetings and announcements centering around the topic for discussion, and closes it with words of appreciation for the contributions made by the panelists and members of the audience. She mentions the topic and date for the following panel forum and invites all to partake in the social hour and refreshments which follow each meeting. Since this chapter functions under the aegis of the college, we have a faculty adviser. She comments upon the topic for discussion and coordinates some of the thinking in the area so that students either in graduate study in special education or those who plan to enter such study will find further clarification of the subject.

It is the moderator's task to act as middleman or mediator between the members of the panel and the audience. This is a person well-skilled in techniques of handling an audience and in stimulating participation in the forum phase of the evening; and is usually an expert in the area under consideration. The moderator plans with the panel members prior to the meeting, encourages and directs questions asked by members of the audience to the proper panelist, and summarizes the problem and possible solutions at the close of the meeting.

The panel members take their turns according to the program plan in expressing their views concerning the topics they had chosen in reference to the subject and then respond to questions from the audience as the moderator calls upon them.

The purposes have been carried out by the application of audience participation for the more complete realization of the learning process and for the expansion and clarification of the points of view expressed by the panelists. Audiences ask their questions from the floor and often direct them toward a particular speaker. It has been our experience that these questions are prefaced by a statement of belief or fact and are in themselves stimuli for further discussion not only by the speakers but also by other individuals in the audience. They add to the information which the speakers have proposed and sometimes present a refreshing and invigorating point of view concerning some phase of the topic.

Most meetings run for about an hour and a half; the social gathering lasts about three quarters of an hour. We generally request the use of the lounges for from seven to ten o'clock. The informal contact and manner lend a warm tone to the meetings and the resultant relationship continues into the refreshment hour. Panel members are approached for personal conversation and sometimes have difficulty in getting to their coffee or tea! This is also the time for light talk, fun and plans of various sorts.

We have employed audio-visual aids from time to time through the seven years of existence. The films or slides have been an excellent adjunct to the theme. We have not yet used the tape recorder sufficiently to warrant a good library of such material. It is our hope that the future will bring with it a permanent collection of panel forums in the form of tape recordings so that students and instructors may borrow them for classroom use in the four municipal colleges.

It has been our experience that the psychodrama or sociodrama is a fine springboard to bring to the audience and speakers thoughts for the panel to follow. On occasion we have called upon people who themselves deviate from the average physically to tell their own stories or to demonstrate some techniques or abilities which they have evolved, not only for themselves, but also for others similarly exceptional. Some of their techniques have been carried into the classroom with great success. Others have been modified by teachers for use with their own classes in grade schools and still others have been incorporated into several curricula for the education of physically exceptional children. At times we have had exhibits of materials for the exceptional along with the panel of the evening, and at others we have been fortunate to have children who exemplify the problem presented and the medical, educational and psychological methodology demonstrated to the audience introductory to the panel forum.

This form of adult education seems to have advantages that may outweigh other types. Panel forums influence and stimulate the audience to the point of actual participation in the meeting and discussion after the entire evening has passed. Frequently we receive mail from an observer or a request from another chapter for a complete panel forum-setup so that they, too, can hold a similar meeting in their own local chapter and city. Since members of the audience are inclined to declare their own ideas, they feel free to express themselves to the group. This informality lends itself to a solidification between the speakers and the audience and forms a bond of understanding at this meeting of the minds in the thinking through of a problem. Not only is this helpful for ease of discussion, but also it is an educational and social experience which grows with succeeding meetings. Interest in special education expands and requests are honored both for membership in the Hunter College Chapter of the International Council for Exceptional Children and for courses in special areas. This information is a spur to further investigation for some individuals and broadens their scope of knowledge in these fields. It also serves as a basis for research projects which our own chapter conducts.

However, there are limitations to this type of meeting. The limits imposed upon the question and answer period deter all audience members who wish to share in the discussion from having sufficient time for being heard. Sometimes a poorly trained moderator is inept in handling the forum element of the meeting or, without malice, attempts to answer the question rather than turning it over to the expert on the panel. Then, too, the timid in the audience may shy away from a question or from making a good point, and the aggressive may attempt a long-winded statement to show his erudition or to express some negative quality in his own personality. Such persons may antagonize the speakers or the audience. The need for an excellent moderator becomes quite apparent in these instances.

As in all endeavors there have been both successes and failures. It is a source of amazement to us that there has not been as much interest in the visually handicapped or in the muscular dystrophies as in convulsive seizures or in the orthopedically handicapped. It is ever a wonder and a challenge as the time for meeting approaches to see how many individuals are concerned with an area and yet not in another closely allied to it. Then, again, there are people who attend one or more meetings each year and there are others who have been present at many throughout the years. There are a few who have come once and have never returned. There are instructors at the college who attend these panel forums with their classes that would ordinarily be in session during those hours and whose subject would be aligned with the topic. Some of these classes have been in special education, while others have been in psychology, physical education, nursing education, early childhood education and music education.

This method of adult education has indeed been a remarkable experience for us of the Hunter College Chapter. Our sights are set and our ears are ever at the listening post for new and challenging areas to enter. We are constantly aware of and alert to the needs of the deviate. Our hopes are raised for the dynamic acceptance of that challenge by those whose life's work centers about those who are exceptional.

Sample Panel Progran

I

THE HUNTER COLLEGE CHAPTER

International Council for Exceptional Children
sponsors
"Opportunities in the Field of Special Education"
Third in a series of meetings in Special Education
during the school year of 1953-1954

MODERATOR

DR. FRANCIS P. CONNER - Instructor, Hunter College

PROGRAM

MR. SAMUEL STREICHER - Chairman of Committee on Licenses
for the Education of the Physically
Handicapped, Board of Education.
"Opportunities in Special Education Offered by the Board
of Education in the City of New York"

DR. JOSEPH FENTON - Department of the Physically Handicapped,
State Education Department.
"Opportunities in Special Education Offered by the State of New York"

DR. ELENA GALL - Coordinator of Special Education, Hunter College
"Some Competencies Which Are Being Sought in Teachers of
Exceptional Children"

DATE	TIME	PLACE
Dec. 14, 1953	7-10 p.m.	North Lounge - 3rd floor
Mon.		

REFRESHMENTS

Approved:
    Prof. Philip R. V. Curoe
    Chairman, Dept. of Education
Faculty Adviser:
    Dr. Elena D. Gall

Officers:
    Pres. - Frances G. Koenig
    Prog. - Sara Lopinto, Hilda Kash
    Secy. - Mary Fuccella
    Treas. - Hana Hartman

Sample Panel Program

II

THE HUNTER COLLEGE CHAPTER

International Council for Exceptional Children
in cooperation with the
National Society for Mental Health
presents
"Our Troubled Children"

FIRST in a series of meetings in Special Education, Hunter
College, during the school year of 1954-1955

MODERATOR:

Margaret T. Ross, M.D., - Director of the New York State Society for Mental Health

PROGRAM:

PSYCHODRAMA - WITH YOUR HELP - produced by the Denes Psychodramatic
    Theatre

CAST INCLUDES:
Psychiatrist - Reid Hanson
Father - Richard W. Schuman
Mother - Norma Leary
George - Robert Boucher
                John - Orlynn Bosse
                Betty - DeAnn Mears
                Rose - Lee Sanders
                Narrator - Frances Whiting

DIRECTOR - Gyula Denes   PRODUCTION ASSISTANT - Georgia Phillips

Discussion will be conducted by Lauretta Bender, M. D., Senior
Psychiatrist, Bellevue Hospital, New York City

DATE	TIME	PLACE
Mon., October 25, 1954	7:30-10:00 p.m.	3rd floor - North Lounge

REFRESHMENTS

Approved:
    Prof. Philip R. V. Curoe
    Chairman, Dept. of Education
Faculty Adviser:
    Dr. Elena D. Gall

Officers:
Pres. - Frances G. Koenig
Prog. - Hilda Kagan
        Sara Lopinto
        Miriam Ehrlich
Secy. - Mary Fuccella
Treas. - Hana Harman

SECTION II

CHAPTER V

PARENT EDUCATION

THE IMPORTANCE OF EDUCATION FOR
THE PARENTS OF EXCEPTIONAL CHILDREN
BY DOROTHY DAVIS SEBALD

SELF-UNDERSTANDING FOR THE PARENTS
OF HANDICAPPED CHILDREN BY JULIUS B.
RICHMOND

THE PARENTS OF EXCEPTIONAL CHILDREN
BY HENRY M. LIGHT

THE GROWTH AND DEVELOPMENT OF
EXCEPTIONAL CHILDREN BY ISAAC JOLLES

THE PRE-SCHOOL EXCEPTIONAL CHILD
BY VERNA S. CARLISLE

THE IMPORTANCE OF EDUCATION FOR THE PARENTS OF EXCEPTIONAL CHILDREN

DOROTHY DAVIS SEBALD

As the study of exceptional children progresses, the importance of the parent's role in the child's development and adjustment becomes more evident, and the need for increasing the parent's understanding of his exceptional child more apparent. The physical and emotional dependency of the exceptional child upon his parent and the parent's reaction to this dependency and to the fact of the child's deviation from normal are being recognized as important factors in the child's total life pattern. As a result of the increased knowledge of this interaction between the exceptional child and his parent, new and improved methods and techniques of parent education are being evolved and tested.

Definite programs of specialized parent education have been instituted by many of the foundations, associations, agencies and societies established to study and serve the deviate. Notable among these are the parent education programs of state and federal governments, and of such service organizations as the United Cerebral Palsy Association, Inc., the National Society for Crippled Children and Adults, Inc., the New York Association for the Blind, the National Tuberculosis Association, the American Heart Association, the Child Study Association of America. The parent education programs of the John Tracy Clinic and the Woods Schools exemplify work being done by schools for exceptional children.

These programs of parent education have been developed in the belief that the successful life adjustment of the exceptional child depends in large measure upon the successful life adjustment of his parents and the parent's ability to care for his child in ways proved fitting for the child's needs. Their purpose is to aid the parent in his understanding and acceptance of his exceptional child and to provide the parent with the specialized knowledge necessary for the child's training, care and education. It is hoped that through this approach the child's adjustment to society may be made easier and as free from conflict as possible.

It is generally agreed by psychologists that children reflect the social and emotional adjustment of their parents. This is true particularly of severely handicapped children who are of necessity bound closely to their parents emotionally and are dependent upon them for the simplest and most primal satisfactions. It is true, as well, of the gifted child whose deviation is so marked that it sets him apart from his peers, and who must seek stability and security from his parents to a greater extent than the normal child. The mental health of the parent thus becomes of paramount importance in the emotional and physical well-being of the child and hence should be the first and most important goal in parent education.

Most parents anticipate the birth of a child with high hopes for its future. They hope that their child will be well endowed with intelligence, physical attractiveness, health, and charm. They anticipate that their child will have good and satisfying social relationships, academic success, vocational satisfaction, spiritual well-being, and a wholesome development into adulthood with its associated self-sufficiency and independence.

When a child is born with a handicap or is handicapped by injury or disease, these anticipations of the parent are rudely disturbed. The parent must learn to live with the knowledge that many of the life satisfactions enjoyed by the average person will not be possible for his child. He anguishes both for his child and for his own frustrated hopes and dreams. Often he feels that he is in some way responsible for the handicap of his child and develops anxiety and guilt. It is necessary for him to resolve his own conflicting emotions regarding this unexpected and unwanted situation before he can begin to help educate his child toward the attainment of a reasonable adjustment to society within the framework of his handicap.

Parents of handicapped children, like the parents of all children, are striving to attain social and emotional security in their own lives. They are still in the process of learning to assume adult responsibility for the care and support of their new families. These adjustments to marriage and parenthood are a normal phase of living through which all parents pass. For many persons these adjustments are made easily and without undue strain, and the advent of a handicapped child in the family may not seriously or permanently affect them. Other parents make these adjustments precariously and the entrance of a handicapped child into the family under these conditions may be so traumatizing that those adjustments which have been made disintegrate.

The degree to which a child's handicap affects the parent's emotional and mental health depends not alone upon the nature or intensity of the handicap sustained by the child but also upon the personality structure of the parent. His past experiences, his emotional and social maturity, his present and potential economic condition, and his present life situation all contribute to his reaction to his child. One parent may feel that even a minor handicap suffered by his child is an overwhelming catastrophe; another is able to accept a child with marked deviation without appreciable loss to his security and serenity.

Whatever the parent's previous adjustments have been, a new adjustment consciously or unconsciously begins at the moment he is aware of his child's deviation from normal and continues in some measure throughout his life. Without guidance (and in many cases with it) the parent finds difficulty in achieving even a partially adequate adaptation to this new condition. It is important, therefore, that the planning for the initial education of the parent should be in terms of the parent himself and of the impact the handicapped child is making on his life.

Probably the greatest skill in parent education is needed at this point. In our culture most parents of handicapped children will accept, and assume responsibility for, the physical care and treatment of the child according to the socially approved practices in his community, but there are other problems, quite apart from the social, legal and physical aspects of responsibility which he may find difficulty in resolving. It is the intangible emotional acceptance or rejection of the child as a loved and respected member of the family that is so important to the life adjustment of both parent and child. The difference between a well-adjusted person with a handicap, sharing in a wholesome family relationship, and a person with a handicap perceived as a burden, a family liability and an object of perpetual sacrifice often lies in the initial rejection or acceptance on the part of the parent. This early rejection or acceptance, once determined, works toward the benefit or detriment of the child.
• When a parent can be helped, through psychiatric, psychological or spiritual processes, to examine and clarify his feelings about his child, he often finds that his child can be accepted wholeheartedly and welcomed into the family group. When the parent, by reason of his own insecurities and anxieties, is unable to accept his child he can be aided in the understanding of his emotional reactions and taught to deal with them in such a manner that the child will not be adversely and irreparably affected by them.

Relatively few persons are trained before parenthood in the care, education and discipline of children. Parent and child usually learn together as the child develops and grows. Mistakes that are made in child training are usually overcome by the successes achieved. With the exceptional child, however, the care, education and training are more difficult and more complex. The dynamic force of the handicap and its resultant effect upon the personality of the child may make each step in his training of utmost concern. Mistakes made with the normal child may be relatively harmless because of his strong drive toward normality and because of his flexibility in learning, unlearning, and relearning. The same mistakes made in the training of the handicapped child may be costly to the child's adjustment to life. Because parents realize the significance of mistakes in the care or training of the handicapped child they often become uncertain, confused, unduly apprehensive and overwhelmed with a sense of inadequacy and responsibility. Realistic teaching of the fundamentals of child development and training both for normal children and those with handicaps should be a part of all parent education programs. Knowledge of what can be expected of all children will help the parent to a better understanding of what he should expect of his own child.

Educating the parent in the physical care of his handicapped child is of extreme importance since his development, his well being and often his very life depend upon it. Many times the parent of a handicapped child must assume the physical care of his child within a very short period after his birth, and without adequate knowledge of the nature or extent of the handicap, the basic principles involved in its treatment, or the implications for harm inherent in deficient or insufficient care. The parent needs to be helped to gain the specific skills and techniques required to carry out the physical treatment prescribed and recommended by the physician. The education of the parent in the physical care of his child is usually begun by the physician, and his supervision and guidance are of inestimable value to the parent. His services are not always readily available, however, and often the physical therapist assumes the role of educator. In many instances the therapist is the only professional contact the parent has between infrequent visits to the physician, and must support, reassure, and counsel the parent as well as teach the techniques and skills of physical care. The therapist's attitude toward the child and his handicap may decisively determine the parent's actions and behavior. The objectivity, optimism, cheerfulness, naturalness, sympathetic care and realistic acceptance of the child shown by the therapist provide a pattern of behavior for the parent who, having no previous experience in this role, is striving for a mode of behavior which is good for his child and satisfying to his own needs.

There is great need in the life of the handicapped child to be able to enjoy satisfying social relationships with both his peer group and with adults. He reaches out with pathetic eagerness for the friendship and understanding he needs, yet may find great difficulty in forming the relationships he so ardently desires. The simplest relationships, taken for granted by the normal child and his parents, are often laboriously and painfully acquired by the handicapped child, and the parent needs to be educated in ways of teaching his child to behave which will be socially and emotionally acceptable to other children and adults. The parent needs help in the difficult task of making his child feel wanted, acceptable and lovable while coping with his bewilderment and unhappiness when his overtures of friendship are rejected and ignored. The parent may find that his own social adjustment is inadequate and his own ability to form satisfying and worthwhile relationships faulty. Often parent and child must learn simultaneously the arts of social amenity and friendship.

Despite continuous efforts to educate the general public toward an understanding of physical, intellectual or emotional deviation there still remains much to be accomplished before the handicapped child is accepted for himself alone. The parent of the handicapped child must be educated in ways of preparing the child for the varying reactions he will receive when he ventures into the community and attempts to engage in its activities. Communities differ in their acceptance of handicapped persons, and the parent may become bewildered, resentful, and embittered at the treatment accorded his child. Skilled education of the parent can prepare him for community reaction and can help him prevent situations from arising which could be harmful to the child's ego structure and to his future ability to take part in community life. Parent education can help the parent to understand and tolerate ignorance, superstition, and prejudice toward his child's handicaps and teach him ways of transmitting to his child the necessary recognition and acceptance of the vagaries of human attitudes toward handicaps.

New problems arise when the handicapped child reaches the age when he would normally be expected to attend school. Many handicapped children are able to take their places in a classroom and compete reasonably well in most of the classroom activities. For these children the problems of adjustment of academic life are relatively minor. For others the nature or severity of the handicap presents a much more serious problem in academic training. In many of our smaller communities, facilities for educating the handicapped are limited or non-existent. More serious, however, than the absence or presence of existing educational facilities is the attitude of the community toward the education of handicapped children. The parent, desiring educational opportunities for his child equal to those provided for the non-handicapped child, may encounter resistance, resentment, hostility and opposition to the inclusion of his child in classes of non-handicapped children, or to the education of his child in ways commensurate with the child's abilities and needs. Seeking educational opportunities for his handicapped child the parent may move his family to a less desirable community and sacrifice his family's comfort, pleasure and wellbeing for the desired education.

Educating the parent in ways of securing educational advantages for his child within his own community will often forestall loss of the desired goal through ineptness and inexperience. The specialized techniques of overcoming misunderstanding, prejudice or apathy toward the education of the handicapped child have been developed by trained workers laboring over the years, and timely and appropriate parent education in this area is especially important.

It is at this time in the child's life, also, that a reassessment of his potential educability is required, and the parent must be given help to understand the implications inherent in this. The parent of a handicapped child needs to be aware of the particular educational problems of his child. He needs to know how and what his child will be taught. He needs to know the special aims and goals of his child's education and something of the methodology that will be used to achieve them. Realistic appraisals made by the physician, the psychologist, and the educator demand an objective approach and understanding on the part of the parent. The parent must be educated to understand what the various measures of the child's abilities and aptitudes mean in terms of the child's educability, his social relationships and his vocational possibilities. Frequent conferences with all those engaged in the education of his child are desirable so that the parent is continuously aware of his child's achievements, his limitations and his abilities.

This phase of parent education, lasting over a period of many years, should be undertaken from both a long range view and from frequent evaluations of short term gains. An important point to be noted here is that parent education which has been consistently rejected by some parents may be acceptable to them at this time, since problems of education are encountered by almost all parents, and the parent may feel free to accept help in this area which he could accept in no other. Skillful help offered at this time may open the way for other important services to the child.

The adolescence of the handicapped child presents problems which are common to all children but may be exaggerated and intensified in children who have been denied the opportunity of leading normal lives. Often, however, it is the parent and not the child who finds the adolescent period difficult. Many parents who have been able to accept the limitations imposed upon their child during his early years resist the continued existence of the limitations as the child approaches adulthood. There is often a resurgence of the initial emotional reactions present at the time of the child's birth or injury, and the parent needs help in re-examining his emotions toward his child, himself and society. By this time in the child's life frustrations, irritations, disappointments, and sheer tiredness may have accumulated in the parent to a degree where he temporarily loses his objectivity, his equilibrium, his optimism and his perspective. On the other hand if the child's handicap has not been severe and the parent's overindulgence or overprotectiveness have been marked, the parent may find himself confronted by an adolescent who is retaining the prerogatives of childhood without accepting the concommitant responsibility of growing up. Relationships between parent and child that have been mutually satisfying may suddenly be recognized as emotionally harmful to both, and a new type of relationship developed which will be beneficial to both the older and younger adult. The physical and emotional approach to adulthood by the exceptional child demands from the parent new modes of behavior. Whatever the child's adjustment has been, this new period in his life is a critical one, and the parent needs help to understand it and to support his child through it.

The education of parents of handicapped children takes many forms. The first, and probably the most difficult, method is self-education. This may be the result of hard-won self-control and self-discipline, of independent study and research and of techniques learned through trial and error. Not all parents are capable of this type of education with its implications of high intelligence, diligence, perserverance, and strong motivation, although there are many that attempt it. Often such an attempt results in inadequate training and care of the child and discouragement and despair for the parent. Usually parents welcome help and guidance in acquiring the knowledge, skill, and understanding necessary for the training of their child if it is offered in a manner that implies no threat to their self-esteem and independence. In many isolated areas, however, there is little professional help available and many parents must depend upon self-education both for themselves and their child. In a few cases the parent may feel that the problem of the care and training of his child is a personal responsibility and prerogative and resent any implication that he is not fully capable of coping with the problem alone.

A second method of parent education is that of professional assistance by those persons especially trained for this task. Each handicapped child needs treatment that is unique to his particular handicap and unique to him as a person. No one person, however competent, is equipped to render so comprehensive a service as the child requires if his full potentials are to be realized. Team work of physician, therapist, psychologist, social worker and educator is necessary for the care of the child and for the education of the parent in implementing the recommendations and services of the team. The parent needs help in motivating his child to acquire and improve skills, to acquire knowledge, to form rich and lasting relationships and to develop the attributes of patience, perservance, diligence, optimism, cooperation and independence. He needs help to inculcate ethical values and standards of conduct appropriate to his abilities. Parents of handicapped children need help particularly in learning methods of effective discipline. The discipline of the handicapped child must be training in its finest sense, — consistent, firm guidance that will result in an emotionally secure child with realistic self-esteem, feelings of worth and adequacy and independence commensurate with his ability. These are teachings which the professional worker is trained to give in ways which will meet the needs of the parent as well as the child.

A third method of parent education is that which the parents of exceptional children give to each other. Increasingly this method is gaining in impetus and success. Parents meeting together discuss common problems, common needs, common aims and goals. They derive strength, understanding, knowledge and comfort from those who have actually lived through these same experiences or who are currently working their way through these experiences.

Groups of parents working together for the common good of their children are proving a powerful force in obtaining from the state and federal governments legislation designed to improve the treatment, care and education of all handicapped persons. Parents have formed study groups to improve their own understandings and skills, action groups to promote beneficial legislation, public relations groups to improve community understanding, and social groups to provide recreational opportunities for themselves and their children.

The education of the parent of the exceptional child who is gifted intellectually or in special aptitude is no less important than education for the parent of the handicapped child. Such a parent has a deep sense of responsibility to develop his child's talents to their optimal usefulness to society and at the same time to assure his child of a rich, satisfying personal life. The parent needs direction and guidance to achieve these ends.

The education of the parent depends increasingly upon the teaching done by professional personnel. Effective parent education is based on the sound knowledge of the principles of mental hygiene for both parent and child, of comprehensive knowledge of the nature and extent of the child's deviation, on knowledge of the appropriate treatment and care of the child and upon realistic knowledge of the child's strengths and weaknesses.

Education for parents of exceptional children is still in its beginning stages despite the rapid gains it has made in the past several years. It is still far from adequate both in scope and quality. Much needs to be learned of the parent's role in parent education and of the significance of parent reaction to the education available to him. More specialized knowledge as well as improved methodology is necessary on the part of those who would venture to help educate parents.

It is hoped that the time is not far off when every parent of an exceptional child will be able to obtain professional help that will enable him to assist his child in becoming an integral part of his family and his community, contributing to family and community life according to his abilities and receiving status and recognition from his family and community according to his needs.

SELF-UNDERSTANDING FOR THE PARENTS
OF HANDICAPPED CHILDREN*

JULIUS B. RICHMOND

The parents of all children—handicapped or normal—are interested in helping children grow into mature, self-reliant persons who have the capacity to contribute to, as well as to take from, the community in which they live. The success with which this objective is attained is to a considerable extent a reflection of the understanding which parents have not only of their children, but also themselves. For if parents do not understand themselves, they may, by superimposing emotional complications, increase the difficulties of children already subjected to a handicapping condition. This may minimize the child's effectiveness in dealing with his problems. Therefore, by increasing self-understanding of parents as individuals we in turn increase self-understanding among children with the result that better adaptation to the handicapping condition and to the community may be facilitated.

As parents grow in self-understanding, there are developed new and deeper insights into helping children to achieve their greatest potentialities. A parent may develop new skills with which to help the child, and also learn to provide realistically for many of the specific needs of the child. But perhaps most significantly a parent can begin to understand that he may be limiting the child too much and thereby thwarting growth, or he may make the child insecure by asking too much from him at another time. Parents may increase their understanding to the advantage of the child in various ways. These group themselves about the significance of physical care; the development of independence; and self-understanding by sharing.

SIGNIFICANCE OF PHYSICAL CARE

Parents of a handicapped child have basic concern about the full significance and extent of the child's handicap. This concern may be obvious; often it is subtle. Parents of a child with a deformity uneasily ask their physicians

---

*Used by special permission of the author, Julius B. Richmond, M.D., Prof. of Pediatrics, State University of N.Y., Syracuse, N.Y., and of the U.S. Department of Public Health.

rather diffuse and evasive questions about the condition when they really want to have some reassurance about not having any responsibility for the causation of the handicap. Particularly in the early days of adjustment to the full impact of the handicap, self-understanding stems from the sharing of one's doubts and anxieties.

The importance of an adequate program of medical care and ancillary services in all communities in order that all parents may be assured realistically that they are receiving the best possible help with their problems cannot be emphasized strongly enough. Certainly the impetus given by organizations such as the National Society for Crippled Children and Adults toward the nationwide attainment of high standards for the care of handicapped children has been a source of comfort to many parents. The program of providing scholarships of various kinds has made it possible for many communities to provide increasingly better services to the handicapped. Out of the continuity of care provided by professionally qualified personnel and from the reduction of doubts and anxieties, there develops a more effective relationship with children.

Out of an adequate medical program in which parents have invested energy —and often money—come feelings of security in relation to the management of the child and also the courage to face the future. These can come in no other way. To illustrate, when parents of a child with progressive muscular dystrophy come to a physician he may be often embarrassed by the gratitude extended to him as a physician who admittedly is powerless—as are all others —to interrupt the progress of the disease. Physicians can begin to understand that these expressions of gratitude have real meaning when they stop to realize that in these visits the parents have had an opportunity to share their anxieties with physicians who have the most information, that they have been able to ask questions which all parents want to ask, and perhaps most significantly— that they have received reassurance that everything possible has been done to help their child.

Parents have the further reassuring factor that medical science is constantly discovering and seeking new information through research. Although research isn't often translated into personal terms, the support of research by parents or groups of parents provides them with hope, without which it would be difficult to face the future. Resources and energy often are expended heavily in the direction of service to patients while research suffers. As a physician and investigator, I must call to your attention that research is a very personal investment of all. For when research dries up, hope for the future vanishes.

DEVELOPMENT OF INDEPENDENCE

To help children grow to maturity they need to be permitted to exercise increasing responsibility as age increases. Perhaps one of the greatest problems for parents in the rearing of handicapped children is the achievement of a delicate balance of understanding needed to determine how much responsibility is appropriate for the age and condition of the child. Over-protection ceases to be protection and may retard progress. Unfortunately, no rule of thumb can be employed with success; each child has his unique problems and rate of development.

Growth does not occur unless it is provided with building blocks. We have defined certain building blocks for physical growth which have become well known in the form of proteins, carbohydrates, fats, vitamins, and minerals. The psychological development of the child also has building blocks. These are evidenced in the form of a sense of trust in him, respect for his individual differences, and stimulation to develop his greatest potentialities. This latter point could be defined as "accentuating the positive."

A sense of trust in the child develops from the security he feels in those about him. The understanding which parents manifest; the capacity for patience which parents need to await progress, slow though it may be; the pleasure which they share as progress develops—all contribute to the development of the child's sense of trust in his parents first, and subsequently in the world about him. For if parents cannot be understanding, accepting, and patient, their anxieties are communicated to the child and have added to his burden.

Parents of handicapped children encounter problems similar to those parents of normal children face in dealing with individual differences. That no two so-called "normal" children are alike is now appreciated. An understanding of the unique problem of each child, his developmental rate, the fact that he may undergo a spurt at one time just as physical growth occurs in spurts, are all helpful. There is no normal level to which children and parents need aspire. "Mass-production psychology" which would tend to lower our sights to a "lowest common denominator" represents an unwholesome trend which we hope has been reversed. In order to understand the child's individual patterns, parents must learn to temper preconceived notions of what they expect children to do. This sometimes requires help from professional personnel outside the home who may provide us with a much more objective view of our relationships.

Out of a deeper understanding of the individual differences among children, parents can help children to develop the unique capacities they possess. Rather than being predominantly concerned with what the child can't do, parents can emphasize what he *can* do. With this emphasis we return to the importance of hope. Hope for the future must be placed in terms of positive achievement; it cannot be built on a psychology of defeat and despair. Emotions are contagious; a parent's feelings of defeat and despair are all too readily communicated to the child. The child cannot have high expectations when these are not shared by parents.

Self-Understanding by Sharing

Perhaps the greatest opportunities for parents to improve self-understanding arises from the sharing of experiences. Discussions of experiences and problems with other parents of handicapped children provide an opportunity for increasing the depth of understanding of problems. Physician parents of handicapped children with much knowledge of the handicapping condition of the child have often related how much help and support they have received from other parents. As a matter of fact, all physicians can learn from parents if they will afford themselves the inexpensive luxury of being good listeners. There is much the professional can learn from ordinary, everyday incidents.

In this connection the story related by a mother of a preschool deaf child at an institute for mothers is worth retelling. She had a large farm family. A considerable amount of washing and ironing had to be done each week. One day as she was about to start ironing one of the children proposed that they have a garden tea party. To this she acquiesced. Just as they were in the midst of having a delightful time, Mrs. Smith's mother dropped in. The mother noted the large ironing to be done and told the daughter that she could be using her time to better advantage. Mrs. Smith thought about it for a moment but replied that "the children would probably never remember whether the washing had been done that week, but they would never forget the tea party." The overtones and undertones of this story had great meaning for parents and professional staff alike.

A few words of caution are in order however. Occasionally, parents in their devotion to group activities may find an outlet for their problems at the expense of the child. The central focus of energies and activities of parents must be the the child, lest the child feel that his care has been relegated to a secondary position. Unfortunately, no one can provide the energy and understanding of which natural parents are capable. Children should, therefore, not need to settle for care which is second best.

The healthy sharing of experiences, supplemented by the sharing with professionally qualified people as indicated earlier results in ever increasing depth of understanding by parents. Out of such understanding emerges a more comfortable relationship which helps the child to attain his fullest potentialities. Parents who provide such understanding achieve gratifications which cannot be duplicated.

THE PARENTS OF EXCEPTIONAL CHILDREN*

HENRY M. LIGHT

As they are to all children, parents are of very great importance to the exceptional child. The child with a handicap is dependent on his parents for food, clothing, shelter; necessities of living—but children do not grow and flourish on necessities alone. The exceptional child is dependent on more—affection, love, understanding, attitudes and environment. These are the "extras." These are the things that children have a right to expect from parents, just as parents have the responsibility of giving them.

No teacher, doctor, professor, or nurse knows this as well as the parents of the exceptional child. A parent can better describe the importance, responsibility, joy, and work of guiding the exceptional child than can anyone else. For it is the parent who guides the deviate child in becoming a successful member of society. Successful in earning a dignified livelihood. Successful in the comradeship of a circle of friends. These are the aims of a parent who has an exceptional child.

PERSONALITY IS IMPORTANT

"Your child is spoiled—he is a little stinker!" Has a child psychologist ever given you that diagnosis? A little degree of spoiling in a child, as in good, wholesome fruit, is necessary. Over-pampering the handicapped child is frequently the rule. This is done to make-up to him some of the things he may be unable to do for himself. It is the degree of "spoiling" that may be permitted in any child, but this is where parents find their greatest difficulty. If a small degree of spoiling, prompted by love and affection, is permitted; it develops a child's maturity and personality just as fully ripened fruit becomes more luscious, more desirable.

---

*Used by special permission of the Dept. of Public Instruction, State of Illinois, and the author, who is President of Illinois Children's Hospital-School Parent-Teacher-Staff Association, Streator, Ill.

Let not the degree of spoiling imply that firm discipline and respect for authority do not apply to the exceptional child. These children must never be allowed to exploit their handicaps. They should be given certain responsibilities, certain jobs about the home; things, of course, which they are capable of doing. Parents must endeavor to create an interest in these jobs, in order to simulate the child's enthusiasm. As good work habits are important in our maturity, it is extremely desirable that the handicapped child learn them early.

We hear and read a great deal about the "I. Q."—Intelligence Quotient—particularly with regard to the exceptional child. There is another quotient that is very important and should be stressed more often. We refer to "P. Q." —Personality Quotient. If a likeable and charming personality can be developed in the handicapped child, it will go far in aiding his acceptance by the general public. There can be no denying that people are reticent about their contact with a handicapped person, both socially and in business. If a parent can develop in the child a warm, likeable personality, he has done as much for his future as all the aids; such as braces, glasses and forms of therapy can do for his physical rehabilitation.

When considering the future of the exceptional child, the question of paramount importance is how he will get along in society. How will he get along with people who we must expect to be in contact with each day of our lives? The fact that the child is exceptional or handicapped is not important; what is important is how his handicap affects his relationship with other people. Many parents avail themselves of every resource to rehabilitate the child physically, and neglect to develop his personality. The child's personality is an intangible thing, and we feel it is of such tremendous importance that parents should frequently seek the advice and council of an experienced and qualified child psychologist.

Attitudes Are Important

Parents frequently lack a constructive attitude toward their exceptional child; usually they are over-anxious or over-protective. Parents do not have any first hand experience with a handicapping condition until the catastrophe occurs in their own family. Then it is only natural that they become over-anxious and probably expend a good part of their physical and financial resources rushing from one charlatan to another, waiting for a miracle to happen. It certainly behooves the parents of normal children to learn about and participate in the programs as they are being developed for helping the exceptional or handicapped child.

It is a general observation that children experience their greatest success and accomplish most in the things they like, and that interest them most. Parents can do much to create an interest in the commonplace jobs about a child's home life that will stimulate his desire to do them well. The child who has learned to enjoy the responsibilities of which he is capable has added materially to his future growth.

Emotional Stability Is Important

In a recent issue of the *Psychiatric Review* appeared a paragraph which may well be repeated here: "It is not fantastic, when one examines the physiological and psychological situation of infancy, to trace the terrible insecurity in the soul of man today to the fact that his mother, having something else to do, didn't stay at home and love him."

Someone else has said that our first observation in visiting a backward country is that the children still obey their parents. The truth of this statement can be fully realized when considering the Eskimo. The Eskimo mother has no social life outside of her family. The mother's time and energies are devoted entirely to preparing the food, the clothing, and to the raising of her children who are emotionally stable. They grow into adult life respecting and obeying their parents.

Eskimo children are neither tense, sensitive, nor excitable. They withstand hardship and pain simply because they are emotionally stable. Any child, particularly the exceptional child, can profit immensely in social acceptability, from his childhood on into maturity, if his mother has successfully instilled into him the emotional stability that develops his growth of character.

Think for a moment how some children storm and fuss when they are taken to the dentist or even the barber. It hurts the emotionally stable child to have his teeth drilled; but he is relaxed, at ease, because of the security his mother's training his instilled within him. The development of the child's personality and character should begin with his birth. He should be fed whenever awakened. These are the two greatest needs of the infant. Can we expect the baby to smile and coo if he is hungry? Of course not; and how much character building can he get from a nursing bottle?

The exceptional child, because of his inability to perform certain functions, often becomes emotionally upset. He becomes sullen or develops temper tantrums. For the parents to guide the child through these periods properly is a serious problem and responsibility. Special techniques are necessary, and few parents are aware of how to go about this special training. It is plainly evident that if a parent wishes to be successful he must acquire some special training and instruction himself. There is much excellent material and help available. And the parent who fails to undertake a broadening of his own knowledge is definitely shirking his responsibility.

A few weeks hence, our small son will enter the hospital for an appendectomy. We are preparing him now, telling him what it will be like—not just the pleasant things, but that he will also experience a new kind of discomfort and hurt for a few days. He shall have the confidence that Mother will be nearby; that she will be able to spend some time with him reading his favorite stories. We look forward to this experience as being another step in the growth of his character building.

Responsibility

Child psychologists have said that the exceptional child should be brought up the same as any normal child. This may be true in a sense, but surely the exceptional child, due to his physical limitations, presents many problems with which his parents have had no previous experience. Parents could well profit by observing the example of professional workers in the field of special education, who must spend years of study at the college level before being allowed to work with the exceptional child. Parents too must become better informed if they are to discharge their responsibilities and mature in the satisfaction that they have successfully reared a handicapped child. There is much excellent material available for parent study. The division of special education of our state is recognized as one of the finest in the country. They have materials about exceptional children that could be used by interested parents. Another unending source of information for parents is the National Society for Crippled Children and Adults. You know it as the Easter Seal Agency. Through its 2,000 state and local units, it provides local groups with films, speakers, and other services. These services are designed to help all parents acquire the knowledge needed for successfully raising their handicapped child to a mature, acceptable adulthood.

THE GROWTH AND DEVELOPMENT OF EXCEPTIONAL CHILDREN*

ISAAC JOLLES

The most logical place to discuss the problem of the exceptional child is with the parents themselves, for they play such an important part in the shaping of their children's personalities. Just as the kindergarten child molds shapeless clay into a meaningful object, so do parents develop individual and distinct personalities out of their children by manipulating their environment.

ENVIRONMENT

Since parents are a definite part of their child's environment, their own feelings and attitudes tend to determine in one way or another the feelings and attitudes to be assumed by their child. Thus, a mother who has a fear of bugs will, by her behavior in the presence of bugs, teach the child to be afraid of them. A father who enjoys playing cards may very easily teach his child to have such an interest.

In the same way the general attitudes of parents towards the child, their aspirations for him, tend to determine in many ways the reactions and general behavior of the child. In order to understand the real importance of this, we must go back to the very moment when the child is conceived, for he actually begins to have experiences from that very moment. With these experiences he is getting some idea of what we call "contact with environment," even though he is growing inside the mother. Furthermore, these are comforting experiences because they meet all of the child's bodily or biological needs.

After nine months of this comforting contact with environment, something happens; the child is born. Birth is a shock to a child. He has been accustomed to the protection of his mother's womb. He has been fed constantly. He has been warm and happy. Then all of a sudden, this comfort is taken

*Used by special permission of the author, who is Staff Psychologist, Office of Superintendent of Public Instruction, Division of Special Education, State of Illinois, and of the Superintendent of Public Instruction and Division of Education for Exceptional Children, State of Illinois.

away; he is beset with countless new pressures and pains. The birth experience is just as hard on the baby as it is on the mother.

This shock is called the "birth trauma." "Trauma" is a Greek word meaning "wound." The period of the birth trauma is a critical one because the baby suddenly realizes that the temperature is not the same; it is not constant, and food does not come constantly. All of a sudden he begins to wonder what is going to happen. He begins to develop all kinds of fears.

Fortunately, the baby's mother is around. Her caresses and the feeding gives the infant the sense of security and love which he needs to overcome the traumatic experience he had at birth. In this way the child learns to seek security and help from first the mother and later the father. Parents thus become very important people to the child. The infant is very sensitive to all of their reactions because he is constantly looking to them for guidance.

Emotional Growth, Its Beginnings

Parental guidance becomes very important to the child in his efforts to mature emotionally and mentally. At birth, and for several years following birth, the infant has no control over his primitive impulses. If he is hungry, he cries or tries to eat anything within reach. If he feels like throwing something, he will throw it without any regard for the location of mother's vanity mirror. If he feels like pulling the cat's tail, he will do so without giving any thought to how the cat feels about it. This type of behavior is normal for the infant even though it is purely emotional without any intellectual control.

"No, no!" and spankings from mother as well as scratches from the cat begin to impress the child with the fact that others do not approve of what he is doing. Since he has a strong desire to win the approval of others so that he may continue to feel secure, he will try to conform. He tries to control his impulses; thus, his intellect begins to play a part in his emotional life. This is the beginning of emotional maturity. Nevertheless, for quite some time the child will forget and throw a block, thereby breaking mother's mirror. Immediately, he will regret it rather than delight in the noise of the breaking glass. His emotions dominated his behavior even though he knew the difference between right and wrong.

After starting to school restraints and rebuffs from the teacher and other pupils result in the final stage of emotional development. The child learns to think first and then to act. Destructiveness becomes very rare. In the meantime it is important to recognize that this emotional growth takes place because of the child's desire to win approval of his parents and his friends in order to make himself feel secure and wanted in his world.

This process of emotional growth implies that all children have a desire to conform, to be like others. As one grows up, one learns by being like others, by imitating. One only has to be a parent to know that children are great imitators. The child gets the feeling that he will be secure and welcomed by other people just as long as he is able to be like them. He especially wants to please and to be like his parents, for they are the people he sees most of the time. And, they are the ones who, more than anyone else, helped to cushion the shock he received at birth. Later he imitates his playmates as well as his parents. When something happens that he feels unaccepted by parents or friends, he will become emotionally upset. He will feel uneasy, insecure, and will hunt for some other methods of adjustment in order to protect himself.

All children try to avoid pain and seek pleasure in their attempts to adjust to the world around them. That is why the most important thing parents can do is to make their children feel loved and wanted. From the child's point of of view security does not necessarily mean money but rather a feeling of being loved and wanted. There are many secure and well adjusted children who come from homes of the lowest order of poverty just as there are badly adjusted and insecure children coming from homes of the highest order of wealth.

MENTAL GROWTH

We must recognize that as the child grows emotionally he also grows mentally, that is, in intelligence. Before a baby is born, he undergoes a certain amount of mental growth—not the kind of intellectual growth we usually think about, but the kind that enables him to move his hands and legs, to receive impressions from the outside world, and to make certain reactions in answer to these impressions. Nature prepares the child's mind before birth so that after birth he is able to adapt himself to his new and terrifying life outside the mother's womb.

But the parents have to prepare the child for his experiences in school, in social groups other than his family circle. In the very first stages of infancy the child learns by feeling and tasting. You have seen babies insist upon putting things in their mouth. That is how they learn about these objects. Later they learn from seeing and hearing. In this stage the deaf child has to depend entirely upon feeling and seeing, the blind child by feeling and hearing. These handicapped children make use of their normal senses to learn about their environment.

With the assistance of the parents the child then begins to develop language. Language becomes the symbol for the objects around him—objects which he has learned about through feeling, tasting, seeing, hearing, and eventually smelling. Language becomes a very important mental tool. Parents can help the child's mental growth through helping him develop his language. This is ordinarily done by talking with the child, showing him pictures and comparing them to actual things the child has seen. Finally, reading stories to the child from picture books helps him to realize that there is some relationship between the pictures and the printed words on the page. In this way parents are actually preparing the child for learning to read when he enters the first grade.

ACCEPTING THE CHILD

So far, it would seem that our discussion has been confined to the normal rather than to the exceptional child. Actually, it has applied to the exceptional child, for the things that apply to the normal individual also apply to the handicapped. The child who is born deaf, blind, crippled, or mentally deficient has the same problems of mental and emotional growth. He as the same need for security as does the normal child. The chief difference is in the way parents help the child to obtain this growth. The father and mother must learn how to capitalize on a child's assets rather than trying to work with his handicap.

Most important of all, parents must be able to accept the child for what he is, whether he be deaf, blind, crippled, or mentally deficient. Saying "I love my child in spite of his handicap" is not enough. The feeling of acceptance must be inside, not merely spoken. It should be remembered that very young children are sensitive to shame as far as love is concerned. Actions speak louder than words.

It is important that parents not be too optimistic about how their handicapped child will turn out. If they really accept him, they will accept him for better or for worse. Many parents of exceptional children think in idealistic terms—in terms of the exceptional things that some other handicapped persons have accomplished. These parents have read about outstanding handicapped people in novels. They have heard stories about the accomplishments of handicapped people. They have seen handicapped people portrayed in movies. They may have read the story of a deaf child who developed lip-reading to the point where he could read lips in seven different languages. Now it is possible that such a story is true, but most of the time they are nothing but fairy tales. Lip-reading is a great help to the deaf person; but so is the hearing aid. There is no getting away from the fact that deaf child is a handicapped child and will always be handicapped.

Pleasant or not, that is the attitude all parents must take if they expect to be at all helpful to their children. If a miracle does happen, and if it does turn out that the child gets along just the same as any non-handicapped person, it would be all to the good. It is really more likely to happen if the parents accept the fact that it probably will not happen.

This may sound strange to the parents of exceptional children. When one starts setting impossible goals for a child, he or she will tend to drive, drive, drive him. The more the child is driven beyond his abilities, the more he will resist. There is too much pressure being put on him. He begins to feel uncomfortable, and he develops what we call a *state of anxiety*. He worries. He begins to feel insecure, and one would be amazed at what such feelings can do to a child's ability to think. Pushing an exceptional child too much will reduce his chances of being outstanding rather than increase them.

This is part of the problem of accepting the child as he is, making him feel secure. It is rare that a parent drives a child to achieve beyond his ability for the benefit of the child. It is usually done because the parent is not satisfied with the child as he is. Of course, it is also rare that the parent is aware of this.

SIGNS OF INSECURITY

There are many symptoms of insecurity in a child's behavior. Temper tantrums, bed-wetting, shyness, stubbornness, and many others too numerous to mention are all signs of insecurity. The child who throws a temper tantrum when the parent denies him something is really saying, "You don't like me, I'll make you sorry." Punishment rarely puts a stop to a tantrum. The child's reasoning is, "You are spanking me. You don't like me. You don't like tantrums; therefore, I will continue to throw tantrums." This also explains why ignoring tantrums eventually proves to be very effective in stopping them. Here the child's reasoning is, "You don't seem to mind my tantrums. There is no point in my keeping it up." Then if the real cause of the tantrum, namely, the insecurity, is not dealt with, the child will quickly add, "I must think of some other way to make mama sorry."

The insecure child wets the bed. His reasoning is, "When I was a baby, mother had to pay more attention to me. I'll still be a baby. I'll wet the bed." Or, he will reason as does the child who throws tantrums—"My mother does not like me. She gets so upset when I wet the bed. Goodie! I can get even with her for not liking me by wetting the bed."

We must always be aware of the fact that the child may not know why he is wetting the bed or throwing tantrums. We must also be aware that a mother can love her child very much and still not give the child that impression. A mother who is very nervous, tense, and irritable because of some personal problems of her own may not be consistent in her dealings with her child. One moment she might not object to the child's jumping on the studio couch, but a short time later she may scold the child for jumping because she suddenly becomes confused. Enough of such instances will make the child very insecure.

Similar feelings arise in a child when the mother or father scolds him by saying, "You are a bad boy." This essentially means to the child, "I am bad; therefore, my father doesn't like me." How much better it would have been for father to have said, "Don't do that. It is bad," or "Don't do that; only bad boys do things like that."

It is so important for parents of exceptional children to avoid such instances as cited above. Exceptional children, because of their handicap, are more sensitive and more vulnerable to situations which produce feelings of insecurity. The infant usually is not aware of his handicap until he goes to school. Then he certainly becomes aware of it. It is so important to contribute much to his feelings of security during the pre-school years. It makes it easier for him to accept his handicap later.

Parents who make mistakes with their children are not unusual. They are human and entitled to mistakes, but they certainly should not be reluctant to seek help from experts—help on ways and means of aiding their children in their struggle for emotional and intellectual growth. Many of our schools in Illinois are sponsoring special programs for the exceptional child. These programs will assist exceptional children as much as possible towards a happy future.

THE PRE-SCHOOL EXCEPTIONAL CHILD*

VERNA S. CARLISLE

It is important to remember that children termed "exceptional" actually have more similarities too, than differences from other children. They are not "unusual" in all ways — mothers; working, playing, and caring for their children, have the opportunity to watch for and recognize symptoms that tell them their children are developing differently from the normal pattern.

WHO IS HE?

The pre-school age child is the before-school age child up to and including five years. During these first five years, children learn many things to help them make a happy adjustment when starting to school. It is at this time that their education begins at home—these years before he goes to school. He is "exceptional" in that he is "unusual." The term refers to children who are unusual physically, mentally, emotionally or socially from the average children.

These children require special treatment and knowledge, special services and programs. Exceptional children do not consist of a single group. Their "unusualness" may be one or a combination of several handicaps. Children with a physical handicap such as poliomyelitis, cerebral palsy, congenital deformities and other orthopedic handicaps; or children with impaired hearing, sight, speech, tuberculosis, epilepsy and endocrine disorders; or because of retardation in intellectual development; or because of exceptional gifts in talent and ability, fall into the class of "exceptional children." They may also be "unusual" because they are so emotionally disturbed they are unable to adjust harmoniously with family, school and community. The doctor, the psychologist and the educator are trained to note these differences; but many of them are not discovered until the child is in school. This is too late. It is

---

*Used by special permission of the author, Consultant, Child Development, National Society for Crippled Children and Adults, and of the Division of Public Instruction, Department of Special Education, State of Illinois.

vitally important that parents recognize, in the home and early in the child's life, some of the differences in children. If discovered in time, many physical handicaps can be remedied and other serious aspects prevented.

Whatever the type and degree of disability there is often some disturbing effect upon the emotional life of both the youngster and his family causing anxieties, stresses and strains which are bound up with his predicament. This is a continuing and perplexing problem day in and day out for anxious parents. Most bewildered parents have a keen desire to *do* the job, but this is sometimes limited by the uncertainty of *how* to do the job. To know how and what to do for the exceptional child, it is important to know the growth and needs of the normal child. For the exceptional child has the fundamental needs of all children in addition to his special needs.

SOME THINGS WE SHOULD KNOW ABOUT PRE-SCHOOL EXCEPTIONAL CHILDREN

The little child who squints, is clumsy, falls often may have *poor vision*. Prompt medical care frequently can mean the difference between a permanent disability and none when disease, infections, or injury affects the youngster's sight. It is important to take the child to an ophthalmologist (eye doctor) immediately to determine the extent and nature of the damage. Children can now wear glasses much earlier than they could a generation ago, and present medical science plus the new drugs can do more for defective vision. Some children are blind from birth. During infancy and early childhood, a blind child is better off at home where love and security can be given to him, than in any institution. It is especially important that he have daily routines, times of eating and going to bed, which will lessen his confusion and uncertainty. His clothes and the things he uses each day should be placed where they belong and where he can reach them without groping. It is important for his feelings of achievement to teach and encourage him to do some of the things babies who are not blind do by themselves. From the beginning, it is important never to do anything for him that he can do for himself; and though he may stumble and grope, it is wise for him to have the thrill of being successful in finding his blocks, rattle, or other simple toys. No matter how bright he is, he will be limited in his achievements—slow in walking and talking— because the pre-school child learns by seeing, hearing and through imitation. You may have to teach your baby to pull himself up and to lower himself, and almost surely he will need to be taught to creep and to walk. He has no experience of space and little urge to move from one place to another. As he begins to learn to walk, give him gentle support by holding his hands. This will give him confidence. He may also need to learn to hold his head up; and as soon as he learns to walk by himself, encourage him to explore and to get from one place to another. His sense of touch will help him greatly. Keep the furniture always in the same place to prevent unnecessary bumps and eliminate unnecessary articles and breakable objects. He will need to be taught to skip and to run and sufficient space must be provided so that he can do so without fear. Talking with him helps to increase his vocabulary and widen his horizons. Read to him from realistic books that inform him about things as they are. He must be able to connect words and associate in order to grasp what the rest of us get through seeing. He will need training in eating and dressing. Teach him to use a cup or glass and spoon and fork by placing his hands on it and helping him to take it to his mouth. Help him in the feeding motions over and over until they become simple to him. He can be taught to dress through his sense of touch and by guiding his hands, accompanying this with simple description of the article of clothing and the order in which it can be put on. Help him to help himself, always letting him feel the joy of accomplishment. Take him with you to places that would be suitable for young children, explaining beforehand what he is going to see and when he sees it. In planning for formal schooling, consult your local board of education or your state school for the blind to help you in preparing him for going away from home when the times comes.

The problem of *impaired hearing* in the young child is often difficult to recognize. A parent may wonder but go on hoping that the infant's failure to respond is due to some reason other than impaired hearing. Children who lack hearing very early in life do not talk because they have not had the opportunity to learn sounds and words; and where some speech has been developed, it may be far from perfect. Where a hearing loss is suspected, consult a reputable otologist (ear doctor) who can diagnose and measure the hearing capacity of your child. Skills have been developed in teaching a deaf child to speak, using the senses of touch and sight and sound. Using the voice pitch that the child hears best, speak clearly and distinctly assuming always that he will understand. The more you talk to your child, the more he will want to respond in speech. Avoid correcting him too often. Face him directly when you are speaking to him. Have your expression animated and pleasant, getting his attention before you speak to him. If a hearing aid will improve his hearing and your otologist has advised it, by all means see that your child gets it and that he is guided in the use and needs of it. This will require a long period of gradual and delicate adjustment.

When a pre-school child's *lack of speech* seems out of line with normal development—in the young child the average age of beginning speech is fifteen months—the pediatrician should give a thorough physical examination. Often a common cause of delayed speech is poor general health. An indirect cause of delayed speech is a hearing defect. Emotional problems may delay a child's speech. Illness may be responsible, or there may be a birth injury. An organic condition may be the cause. In many cases, speech therapy can be highly effective. The commonest speech defect is faulty pronunciation. A young child does not articulate (speak) well simply because he has not yet learned to do so. In stuttering, one of the common speech problems, no two cases are exactly alike. There are a number of theories as to its cause. We know that strain and tension aggravate stuttering. A pre-school child can be helped by harmony in the home, time for quiet play; activities and materials which he can manipulate successfully. At no time should emphasis be called to his speech defect. If the child has cerebral palsy, his speech may be delayed greatly and is often poorly articulated, slow, jerky and labored.

Rheumatic fever is a children's disease which usually occurs at about seven or eight years of age, later than the pre-school age. It varies in severity, appears in different ways and is often difficult for doctors to diagnose. The acute illness lasts for weeks or months, but convalescence is often a matter of months and perhaps years. It is important for the parent to cooperate in a program of physical hygiene made out by the doctor and hospital staff. A medical social worker can give counsel and help with important decisions as to whether the child should go to a convalescent home or convalesce at home. If at home, give the child the praise he deserves for cooperating with you in his daily health habits.

To the parent of the pre-school child who has *epilepsy*, it is comforting to know that the nature of seizures is now better understood; new medications, in most cases, can either completely eliminate or reduce them. Seizures arise from various causes and are evidence that something is out of order physiologically. They are not an indication of a mental or personality disorder. Although the child's handicap is not constant and though seizures may occur only rarely, it is important to get medical diagnosis and attention immediately as each seizure lowers the threshold for the next one. It is a mistake to treat the little child as an invalid or even as a semi-invalid, as the fuller, more active life an epileptic child can lead, the fewer seizures he is likely to have. He should be allowed to play freely, to be given a good nutritious diet and the usual amount of sleep for a normal child of his age. In some children, seizures appear early in life; others go through the normal infancy before the first one occurs. When the convulsion occurs, there is little a parent can do about it except to make the child comfortable. Seizures are not in themselves fatal. Although he has facial and bodily movements, there is no pain attached as the patient is unconscious. Sleep usually follows and is beneficial. The importance of proper diagnosis and medical care cannot be overemphasized.

The child who is *cerebral palsied* may be a much more complex problem than those with other handicaps. In the past, little encouragement was given to the parents of cerebral palsied children, but today the picture is different. The nature of cerebral palsy is understood, and it is known that cerebral palsy is caused by damage to the area of the brain that controls motor development. Methods have been devised to assist the needs of cerebral palsied children in the improvement of speech, use of hands and lower limbs. This multiple handicap, sometimes involving speech, hearing, vision and use of hands and legs, demands diagnosis by a team of medical specialists. State societies for crippled children, state crippled children's services and other state and local resources are cooperating to make available to parents; training and treatment services for cerebral palsied children. Here parents may receive the help and guidance of specialists in the field to begin the long, consistent program of therapy and training that is essential to progress. It is not the child's chronological age but his muscular condition that will determine what can be expected of him. With cerebral palsied children, as with all crippled children, the commonest mistake is in doing too much for him rather than encouraging the child to do everything for himself that he possibly can.

The *bright child* will need a carefully planned program of adequate physical care, playmates and play materials that will give him opportunity to explore and to experiment constructively. He will need the same consistent program that is desirable for all children. A good nursery school will recognize and provide for his individual abilities. The parent and the nursery school teacher working together should be able to plan a balanced program for the child's best development and talents.

The *slow learning child* needs what every child needs to become an agreeable, pleasant, well-adjusted person. Training must be geared to his capacity and given more slowly than it would be to a normal child. All parents are eager to find a reason for a child's slowness. It may be well to caution parents here not to be too concerned about the young pre-school child's lag in accomplishing one or two of the things that other children his age are doing. A child who has been babied or over-protected and not given the opportunity to develop his growing body and mind may be slow because of his limited environment and activities. Where a parent has serious doubts of his ability to estimate the child's true capabilities, it is essential to get the objective help of a competent psychologist or psychiatrist to estimate the child's capacity to learn and to help in planning future care and education for him. What he can or cannot do depends chiefly upon his degree of mental handicap. You will want to instill good habits in your child; and before habit is formed, you will have to repeat directions over and over again, giving only one direction at a time. Do not depend on your child to work out the best way of doing something but show it to him yourself in much detail. Even though he may be slow, once he has mastered the process of dressing, you should expect him to keep it up, if clothes are of a simple self-help type. Help him to establish routines where one act becomes associated with the other, giving him praise and recognition where he deserves it. Discipline will be as important for him as for any child and should never mean corporal punishment. Ordinarily a retarded child does not present many serious discipline problems as he does not have the initiative or imagination to be guilty of deliberate wrong doings. However, he cannot help being slow and forgetful and may have a number of irritating ways equally characteristic of retarded children. Contacts should be made with local schools and agencies regarding special classes or home training for your child. For children who are so retarded as to probably always need care and protection, the parent can work out with community sources a plan that will be most beneficial to the child when he reaches school age. At a very early age, the large majority of slow learning children can live comfortably and securely in the household, where there are many opportunities for friendly, interesting activities that can be enjoyed and participated in at the child's own rate of development.

Some Things You Can Do

Sometimes parents, in their anxiety over their child and their concern to "do something" for him, do not realize they can give him something as essential as medical care. A little child's mind and body are inseparable, and it is in the home in his very first months and years that he builds the attitudes and the personality that will be with him all his life.

How can one help him to live with his handicap and yet be able to live happily with the world in which he will grow up? There are a number of general but important things to do. Let him live in a home where there is a mother and father, harmony, respect and love. If he is in a happy family, he will he happy. He should feel a part of the family; and no matter what his handicap, share and have opportunities for responsibilities according to his age and ability. To have a job, even a small one, will give him a sense of security, of belonging, of helping. He needs attractive, nourishing food served in small portions in a pleasant leisurely atmosphere. All pre-school children need ten to twelve hours of sleep with an afternoon nap in a bed and room where he can relax and feel secure. You can help him by providing simple, self-help garments with front openings, large buttons or zippers and elastic waist bands that he can pull down himself. Low hooks for his clothes, his towel and a large shelf within reach for his books and playthings will help in developing orderliness and constructive play habits. He needs friends of his own age who will include him in their play and social learning situations, although he cannot actively participate. A "play hour" where he has some special toy will bring little friends who, though curious at first, will accept him as one of them, limited though his participation may be. He needs a mother and father who somehow, sometimes manage to find time to refresh themselves, to gain courage, to make friends, to have some outside interest, to gain perspective and to bring him wholesome and interesting parents to face each day.

BIBLIOGRAPHY

Almy, Milly, "Principles and Practices of Nursery Education", *Exceptional Children*, Oct., 1954. 21:1:18-20.

Armstrong, Keith S., "Parents and the Crippled Child", *Crippled Child*, Apr., 1955, pp. 11-13.

Burgess, Caroline B., "Counseling Parents of Handicapped Children", *The New Outlook for the Blind*, Jan., 1955, pp. 1-5.

Forest, Ilse, *The School for the Child from Two to Eight* (Ginn: Boston, 1935).

Gans, Roma; Stendler, Celia; and Almy, Millie, *Teaching Young Children* (World Book: Yonkers, N.Y., 1952).

Gesell, Arnold L., et al., *The First Five Years of Life,* A Guide to the Study of the Preschool Child (Harper: N.Y.C., 1940).

——, *Infant and Child in the Culture of Today.*

Gruenberg, Sidonie, *Our Children Today* (Viking: N.Y.C., 1952).

Jenkins, Gladys, et al., *These Are Your Children* (Scott, Foresman: Chicago, 1949).

Menninger, William C., M.D., "Angels Unaware", *Crippled Child*, Apr., 1955, pp. 4-7; 27.

Norton, Edith N., *Parent Education in the Nursery School* (Association for Childhood Education: Washington, D.C., 1949).

Reed, Katherine, *The Nursery School* (W.B. Saunders: Philadelphia, Pa., 1950).

Spock, Benjamin, *Common Sense Book of Baby and Child Care* (Duell, Sloan and Pearce: N.Y.C., 1946).

Wolff, Werner, *The Personality of the Pre-School Child* (Grune & Stratton; N.Y.C., 1946).

MAGAZINES AND PAMPHLETS

Child Study, a quarterly journal. The Child Study Association of American, 132 East 74th Street, New York 21, N.Y.

The National Association for Nursery Education, Roosevelt College, 430 S. Michigan Ave., Chicago Ill. Various publications.

Parents' Magazine, a monthly publication, Bergenfield, N.J.

Public Affairs Committee, Inc., 22 East 38th Street, New York 16, N.Y. publishes several pamphlets concerning young children.

The Child, monthly publication. U.S. Children's Bureau, Superintendent of Documents, U.S. Government Printing Office. Also publishes a series of free pamphlets available to parents.

Exceptional Children, a monthly magazine. International Council for Exceptional Children, National Education Association, 1201 16th Street, N.W., Washington, D.C.

SECTION II

CHAPTER VI

THE PREVENTION OF HANDICAPS

BY CHRISTINE P. INGRAM

THE PREVENTION OF HANDICAPS*

CHRISTINE P. INGRAM

Prevention! The need for focus on *prevention* of handicapping conditions in infants, children, youth, and adults is *now*. There is knowledge of causes and of measures which if applied would greatly reduce the number of handicapping conditions. Yet there has been too little attention to the matter in the development of programs, particularly for exceptional children and youth.[1]

Authentic figures and statements reveal the extent and increase of handicapping conditions when known preventive measures are not applied. Each year, for example, 22,000 Americans of all ages loose their sight. Experts are certain that 26% or 5,750 of this number could be saved if present sight-saving techniques were applied.[2]

It is estimated that one out of every twelve children born each year will sometime during his life suffer a mental illness severe enough to require hospitilization. Of the 15,000,000 men examined for service in World War II, 846,000 were rejected for neuro-psychiatric reasons. The present increase in delinquency rate for ages ten to seventeen years, exceeds the increase in child population.[3] A decade ago, however, the Children's Bureau stated that recognition and treatment of incipient symptomatic behavior could prevent serious social maladjustments of the majority of children brought to the attention of guidance clinics, juvenile court, police, and school authorities.[4]

SIGNIFICANT CURRENT TRENDS

There are four current developments which make prevention imperative.

1. The number of children with handicaps is increasing, due to the increased birthrate and lowered infant mortality resulting in increased population of pre-school and school-age children. For example, the estimated num-

---

*The author is indebted to Dr. Henry C. Schumacher, Medical Director, United States Public Health Service, Region IX, San Francisco, California who read the first draft of this chapter and made helpful suggestions.

ber of blind under twenty years of age was 10,800 in 1940 and 15,400 in 1955, or an increase of 4,600! On the basis of population increase alone the estimated increase is 3,500; the remaining 1100 is accounted for by recent increased rate of blindness in premature children under seven years of age.[5]

Benda calls attention to increase of handicaps due to lowered mortality rates.[6] Records of infant mortality for 1920 in New York City show that of every 1000 births, 85 died. Among the causes of death, congenital debility and malformation ranked first with a rate of 35.3 per 1000 live births. Twenty-nine years later, in 1949, the infant mortality rate had fallen to 25 and the mortality rate for malformations fell to 16.8 per 1000 live births indicating that 19 newborn per 100 live births who would have died in 1920 were saved in 1949. As a parallel to Benda's inference, the Children's Bureau reports that in the wide range of impairments cared for under the Crippled Children's Program, congenital impairments ranked highest in the numbers served.[7]

Although complete statistics on population increase and changing percentages in handicaps are not available, the literature generally reflects increased numbers.

2. The second development that augurs for prevention is the parent organization movement. The nationwide action for the care of children with cerebral palsy initiated more than a decade ago by parent groups and culminating in the United Cerebral Palsy Associations, Inc., brought to the attention of the medical, social work and educational professions the number and needs of children with these particular handicaps. This gave impetus to parents of children with mental retardation and to the organization of the National Association for Retarded Children. Parents of children with other deviations have organized locally in a number of places. They not only want study, diagnosis and treatment for their children, but ask: "Why?"—"What is the cause?"—"Does this condition have to be?"—"What can the medical profession do?"—"What can education do?"

3. The third development that creates a pressing need for prevention is the extension and the mounting cost of services to the handicapped which grow out of the first two trends. As the numbers increase, as more and more parents press for help, and as professional workers and the public recognize community responsibility in the matter, services are extended or initiated through public or private means. The financing of these services is costly. The following table illustrates the excess cost in one city of education for children with physical handicaps in comparison with the costs for non-handicapped children.[8]

TABLE 1

COST PER PUPIL IN SPECIAL CLASSES IN NEW YORK CITY FOR 1951-1952

Class	Cost	Ratio of Cost of Special Classes to Regular Classes
Regular	$228.83	
Cardiac	389.96	1.7
Orthopedic	440.48	1.9
Sight Conservation	466.05	2.0
Braille	778.60	3.4
School for Deaf	729.84	3.2

The expenditure to meet the many needs of children severely limited by cerebral palsy is much in excess of the above. A class unit for such children was established in a New York City school through the joint efforts of the Health and Education departments, voluntary agencies, and parents. Medical specialists, therapists, and special teachers served the unit. The cost of the combined medical and educational effort was approximately $2,300 annually per child.[9]

In a report on a state pilot-project for classes for trainable mentally retarded children carried out under public school auspices, the cost per capita ranged from $415 to $1,382.71, with an average of $765.71.[10]

4. The fourth development is the growing demand for specialists and the comparatively small number available or in training. With increase of the child population and with lengthened life-span, physicians, health and social workers, and teachers in general are greatly in demand. The shortage is critical, and despite the shortage in the regular ranks, the appeal must go out for specialists to serve the handicapped.

Nationwide drives for students in physical therapy, occupational therapy and medical social work were conducted in 1953 by the American Association of Occupational Therapists, American Physical Therapy Association, and the American Association of Medical Social Workers. It was estimated that an additional 5,200 physical therapists, 1,000 medical social workers and 2,900 occupational therapists were urgently needed to round out the treatment for polio and other handicapping conditions.[11]

It is estimated that 25,000 special teachers are employed in the instruction of exceptional children and that 100,000, or four times that number are needed to meet the national needs in full. Only 4,601 students are reported to be majoring in the various areas of special education in the 122 colleges and universities offering specialized curricula.[12]

Scholarships, fellowships, and internships for physicians, therapists, social workers and special teachers are offered through private agencies and government subsidy to stimulate recruitment. And yet the supply is far from adequate!

These four developments demand increased attention to prevention and to community responsibility for promoting prevention. Study and analysis of these four trends suggest that only through knowledge of developments and vigorous programs embodying prevention can the mounting problems and subsequent demands be abated.

The need for and the acceptance of responsibility for prevention of disabilities, moreover, is not solely national in scope but is recognized as international in importance. A recent United Nations publication on the subject of rehabilitation of the handicapped states:

> The prevention of disability and the rehabilitation of handicapped persons are problems in which the United Nations and several specialized agencies are taking great interest . . . it is just as important to prevent or limit disability as it is to rehabilitate and train those who are already disabled. From the viewpoint of a nation's total economy and the well-being of a maximum number of its citizens, preventive efforts deserve the very highest priority. Campaigns to improve public hygiene and sanitation, to spread knowledge on the prevention of disease and injury, deserve all possible encouragement and support.[13]

PREVENTION: THE FIRST LINE OF DEFENSE

There are four lines of defense for warding off the problems and hazards of handicapping conditions for the individual and for society: (1) prevention, (2) early case finding, (3) adequate medical, social, and educational treatment, and (4) rehabilitation or restoration for participation and competition with the non-handicapped in daily life activities.

The first line of defense is prevention, which in its broadest sense may be defined as the science and art of safeguarding the physical growth and development of the organism from conception through early infancy and of fostering the healthy development of physique and personality from infancy to adulthood. Prevention embraces the removal of causes which produce the initial onset of a handicapping condition or the occurrence of disease and of accidents at any age; the early arrest of a disease before it progresses, or the treatment of an accident before it disables. Particularly significant is early case finding of any deviation in infancy or the pre-school age that may be treated to give full restoration for normal development.

Prevention, furthermore, may be interpreted as functioning at any time in the individual's history if a persistent disease or disability is being alleviated or arrested through treatment. The interpretation in this chapter, however, relates mainly to knowledge of and measures for prevention which will safeguard health and eliminate the causes of the onset or development of handicapping conditions in infants, children, and youth.

PREVENTION OF HANDICAPS FROM INFECTIOUS DISEASES

The history of the search for microörganisms causing infectious diseases and the development of specific immunizing agents to prevent communicable diseases makes thrilling reading. Because of the victories of medical and related sciences, the dreaded inroads of small pox, typhoid, diphtheria, scarlet fever, and pertussis have disappeared.[14]

A prescribed routine of immunization and vaccinations offers every child, youth and adult protection from these once common infectious diseases and their untoward effects. Immunization is administered on a selective basis for persons exposed to typhus, typhoid, yellow fever, cholera, and tuberculosis.

The introduction of sulfa and penicillin for treatment of streptococcal infections has greatly reduced the incidence and the effects of influenza, pneumonia, rheumatic fever, meningitis and encephalitis. The American Heart Association states that the administration of a recommended procedure now available for giving prophylactic doses of penicillin to patients who are subject to repeated streptococcal infections would greatly reduce the number of children who suffer from heart conditions following rheumatic heart disease.[15]

Tuberculosis, through popular education, case findings, hospitalization, the administration of antibiotics and isoniazid, and through the protection of the uninfected from close contacts with those having the disease, has shown a marked decline. From 1945, when streptomycin first appeared, through 1952, deaths from tuberculosis dropped 58 per cent. Then the discovery of isoniazid proved additionally effective. It is said that, given time, the medical profession will remove the memories of the White Plague to the historical realm of the once dreaded Black Death.[16] Tuberculosis of the bones and joints is no longer one of the prevalent cripplers except in the outlying territory of Alaska.

A recent victory came in the announcement that the Salk polio vaccine has been proved effectual for prevention and was licensed by the Federal Government. There is promise that the crippling conditions of infantile paralysis will be greatly reduced.[17]

The percentage of blindness and partial vision from infectious diseases has noticeably decreased. In a sixteen year period the percentage occurring in new admissions to Schools for the Blind has been reduced from 29 to 14. In sight-saving classes the same category accounted for 3.4 per cent of the enrollment. Opthalmia neatorium, or blindness from eye infection at birth had been reduced to 1.2 per cent through legislation requiring the use of silver nitrate or penicillin in the eyes of all children at birth.[18]

In a ten-year period, deafness from infectious diseases in the enrollment of of the Clarke School for the Deaf was reduced from 28 to 14 per cent.[19] Although we have no comparable data for brain damage and neuro-muscular dysfunction resulting from infectious diseases contracted early in the life of the child, there is likely a similar decrease.

The defense lines for prevention are set for a high level in the ultimate elimination of infectious diseases and their deleterious effects, although the search must continue to discover better weapons against certain of the viral diseases such as measles, mumps, and influenza.[20]

PREVENTION OF CHRONIC DISABLING CONDITIONS

With infectious diseases so nearly under control, a campaign against the disabling and crippling ailments of chronic disease is underway. Heart disease, arthritis and rheumatism, muscular dystrophy, mental illness, cancer and neurological disorders such as cerebral palsy, epilepsy, and multiple sclerosis now demand the attention of science and medicine. These diseases affect children as well as youth and adults, although they take the greatest toll of life in adulthood. That the fight against these diseases is a present challenge is evidenced by the wide spread publicity accorded to sponsors of movements and to funds that are procured by both public and private agencies for research in causes and treatment, for training of personnel, and for treatment facilities.[21]

Heart Disease. Progress in prevention of rheumatic heart disease resulting from streptococcal infections has already been mentioned. The constellation of causes, however, which may be associated with malnutrition, unhygienic surroundings, or a possible hereditary factor is still undetermined. Penicillin has proven effective in treating subacute bacterial endocarditis, an infection of the heart valve, a disease which is much less common than rheumatic heart disease. Research in the mechanics of the heart and the painstaking work of cardiac surgeons have resulted in operative procedures for correcting the cardiac defect in the 'blue baby'. Other similar procedures correct a variety of defects in the heart's valves and arteries.[22]

Arthritis and rheumatism (excluding rheumatic fever). These diseases continue to defy the efforts of the scientists in search of cause and cure. Certain drugs, ACTH, cortisone, and hydrocortisone, arrest and give relief from further disabling in rheumatoid arthritis but do not cure. The older age groups are those generally affected. The Children's Bureau for the year 1950 reported that 2430 or 1.1 per cent of children served in the Crippled Children's Program were diagnosed under the classification of arthritis and rheumatism.[23]

Muscular dystrophy. This disease affecting as many children as adults has more recently attracted public attention due to the efforts of the Muscular Dystrophy Associations of America organized in 1950. Heredity has been proven a factor in the syndrome known as the pseudo hyperthropic type. Research in vitamin deficiency and the organisms's utilization of certain electrolytes such as sodium and potassium may afford other clues to causes.[24]

Cancer. This dread disease threatens childhood and youth. It is the fourth cause of death in children under fourteen years of age and ranks higher than the total deaths from several infectious diseases. While notable gains have been made in the arrest of cancer by means of surgery followed by radiation and drugs, the causes for cancer are as yet undefined. Extensive biochemical research is underway. The alarming increase in cancer incidence has led also to extensive studies of environmental factors such as smoking and air pollution.[52] A current survey of 25,000 households in 230 areas of the nation has been undertaken by the U. S. Census Bureau in cooperation with the National Cancer Institute of the U. S. Public Health Service.

Epilepsy. Scientists are still in search of the nature and causes of epilepsy or convulsive disorders. A predisposition or susceptibility to epilepsy may appear in more than one member of a family. Some of the precipitating causes may be brain injury due to infections, a severe head injury, or a tumor on the brain. One significant cause of a convulsive disorder came in the discovery of pyridoxine (Vitamin B_6) deficiency in the artificial feeding of young infants 8 to 16 months of age. Apparently normal in birth history and development to the time of onset, they responded normally following the inclusion of Vitamin B_6 in their feeding.[26] Continued biochemical research will likely reveal other causes.

PREMATURITY AND CONGENITAL MALFORMATIONS

Studies of prematurity, congenital malformations and birth injury have come to have particular significance due to the current wide-spread interest in children affected by cerebral palsy, brain-injury, and mental deficiency. There is a larger incidence of both cerebral palsy and mental deficiency in premature infants. There is accumulating evidence that these syndromes are associated with the same factors that produce prematurity, still births, and neonatal deaths.[27]

Congenital malformations such as club foot, dislocated hip, cleft palate, cerebral palsy, cataract, syanosis, cretinism, Mongolism and deafness and less well-known forms appear in 1 to 2 per cent of live born infants. Due to medical skill some of these defects, such as club foot, dislocated hip, cleft palate, cretinism and cataract, can be corrected early; but elimination of causes is the goal sought.

Prematurity and the extent and nature of anomalies, including neurological disorders appearing at or shortly after birth, have stimulated research in heredity and in ontogeny in utero, or the role of endogenous and exogenous factors in causing deviations. There is recognition of a constellation of factors that surround the developing organism from conception to birth. Research focused on the trimester periods of pregnancy show that not only specific agents such as infections, endocrine imbalance or irradiation, but the time of their action during embryonic development determine the defect. The first trimester is a particularly vulnerable period. This research is revealing also that exogenous factors may cause anomalies formerly believed to be hereditary in nature. Diagnoses are now being made based on deviations that are hereditary or eugenic, those that are congenital or secondary, and those that are undetermined.

Some of the more recent discoveries are already bearing fruit. Rh blood factor incompatibilities in the mother, and antibodies due to the Rh-negative factor in the mother's blood and Rh-positive in the unborn child's are causes of cerebral palsy. Through a process of exchange transfusion at birth the infant can be saved from negative effects.

Anoxia and hemorrhage are other causes of cerebral palsy or of brain damage without neuromuscular dysfunction and the syndrome of the brain-injured child described by Strauss.[28] Education of the mother in the natural course of pregnancy and child birth and improved obstetrical techniques are reducing the use of analgesic drugs in labor, and the incidence of head injuries which cause anoxia and brain hemorrhage.

Maternal protection from infections such as German measles during the first tri-semester may save the infant from defects of vision or hearing, mental defects, or other impairments. A controlled study in 18 hospitals has shown that retrolental fibroplasia, a condition of blindness developing in premature infants is caused by the administration of excessive exposures of oxygen in the first week of life. Safe standards of concentration and duration of oxygen intake established experimentally will protect the premature infant from loss of sight.[29]

Mongolism is a congenital growth deficiency having its onset in the early weeks of fetal development and producing characteristic physical anomalies observable at birth. The associated mental deficiency is due to the disturbance in the brain growth and development. Continued research, it is hoped, will lead to prevention.

Studies of effects of nutritional status during pregancy show that still-born and premature infants and those dying within a few days after birth are born to mothers whose diets were inadequate. Animal experiments with certain nutritional deficiencies in the pregnant female have produced certain anomalies such as cleft palate and brain abnormalities

The contemplation of future preventive research in the areas of prematurity and congenital malformations is stimulating.

HEREDITY

The role of heredity is proved in some diseases and conditions but in others is as yet undetermined. There are some persons who have a predisposition or a susceptibility to a particular disorder, such as epilepsy mentioned earlier.

The problem of hereditary deafness is far from solved. Hereditary nerve deafness or otosclerosis, in which there is a predisposition for the sense organ of hearing and the auditory nerve to degenerate at an early age has been established. The tentative conclusion drawn from an extensive study underway at the Clarke School for the Deaf is that a larger percentage of deafness at birth is due to heredity than had been judged so in the past; and that some cases are due to a hereditary factor coupled with a secondary cause.[30]

Eye diseases that have been proved to have certain patterns of inheritance are cataract, glaucoma, dislocated lens, corneal degeneration and macular degeneration. More research in congenital eye abnormalities is needed.[31] In any condition where heredity is a factor, individuals considering marriage should seek advice from a medical specialist.

ACCIDENT PREVENTION

There is a wealth of research in the field of accident prevention on extent, kind, and locale of accidents at various age levels from infancy to adulthood. There are excellent materials promoting safety and accident prevention.[32] Yet there continues to be an apathetic response on the part of parents and the public to education and safety means for reducing accident fatality and crippling. Forty thousand to 50,000 is a conservative estimate for the number of children permanently injured every year. Forty-three per cent of all deaths, ages 5 to 19, in 1951 were the result of accidents. While reduction in childhood accident rate has taken place in the last ten years, it is not comparable with what has been achieved for other causes. Despite many variables in the control of accidents, a concerted, united effort on this problem could greatly reduce crippling conditions and eye, ear and cosmetic impairments.

Dietrich, a Californian pediatrician, believes in the feasibility of accident prevention in childhood years, if it is attacked like any other public health or preventive medicine problem.[33] He recommends that public health departments and pediatricians cooperate in educating parents and public to the facts, in prescribing a plan for parent-teaching to condition the child early in concepts and safety habits in the home. Such teaching would 'immunize' the child as a safeguard for wider exploration and experiences outside the shelter of the home. Parents must take the initial responsibility for minimizing hazards, establishing necessary safety routines, and giving the child growing security in self-help and protection.

The school, then, in partnership with public health and the physician could undoubtedly contribute its share of protection and safety education more successfully. There are state laws requiring safety education in most of the states with teaching outlines and a wealth of appropriate materials supplied. Courses in driver-education are offered in many high schools.

As the child grows older, repeated accidents may call for psychological or psychiatric study.[34] The 'accident habit' may be a symptom of deep-seated emotional conflicts and a means of escaping responsibilities or of gaining attention.

Community programs, in which safety-engineering and law enforcement in the control of traffic, fireworks, and fire arms operate and in which public safety is adequate in fire and flood control, will contribute greatly to the reduction of accidents. While safety drives may have value, it is the over-all long-range program with consistent team work that is more likely to net results.

PREVENTION OF MENTAL ILLNESS AND DELINQUENCY

Mental illness and delinquency, two extremes of social maladjustment, loom larger in our society and are receiving wide publicity. The growing incidence in these two fields was mentioned earlier. The National Mental Health Act, which became effective in 1946, marked a new era, namely, the recognition of mental illness as a major public health problem in our nation. The recent Senate Inquiry into the extent and nature of delinquency may also lead to some national action for stemming the tidal waves of delinquent behavior. Findings indicate that betterment and increase of children's courts, and of appointment of judges and of probation officers would yield one source of prevention.[35]

Research Needed. The Mental Health Act authorized three major programs to be implemented through grants-in-aid to the states. These are training, research, and community mental health programs.

The provision for research[36] is timely because of the fact that some states allot no funds for research while others taken together spend less than one per cent of the vast amount expended for hospitalization. The identification of pellagra as a B vitamin deficiency disease which reduced mental illness caused by the scourge in the southern states is one illustration of the value of biochemical study in the field. Research is underway in the structure of the nervous system, in brain metabolism and electrical activity, and in the relationship of the endocrine system to certain syndromes. Studies of social and economic factors that may affect the development of schizophrenia and of drug addiction may prove a fruitful field for prevention. The refinement of psychological tools and techniques are needed to bring new and more efficient diagnosis of mental disorders. The recognition that a form of mental deficiency in childhood may be a symptom of a deep-seated emotional disorder calls for more intensive psychological research.

Progress in Understanding Personality. One encouraging trend is the progress that has been made and continues in the understanding of human nature's complexities. While eugenists, biologists, and biochemists have advanced knowledge of the developing physical organism, psychiatrists, anthropologists, psychologists, and sociologists have contributed greatly to our knowledge and understanding of personality and the dynamics of behavior.

The Mid-Century White House Conference for children and youth took as its theme the development of a healthy personality. Every area that affects the child's life in our nation was represented: home, school, church, recreation, correction, and vocation. Particular attention was given to the part that emotions play in the development of a worthy self ever growing in the ability to meet the developmental tasks that our society imposes. Much attention was given to the home as laying the foundation in the early years for the sense of trust and security and to the school's opportunity for guiding the child in the development of worthy tasks whereby he senses the feeling of achievement and finds group acceptance. The Conference stated that the development of a healthy personality is dependent on understanding the child and his motive, — how he grows, how he learns, how he develops values, and how he comes to regard himself as a social being and a 'self'. As such knowledge and understanding become the common core for all who guide children and youth in any way, we can look not only for improved attitudes and practices in building healthy personalities but for a sensitivity to behavior that may be symptomatic of maladjustment.

Public Health Services. The growth in public health programs over the past three decades has made possible substantial progress in the physical aspects of health and prevention. The concept of community public health service has gradually widened the scope and influence of health department staffs, both state and local. It is fitting, therefore, that stimulated by the provisions of the National Mental Health Act, public health services should grow to include the promotion of mental health and the prevention of social maladjustment.[37] Mental health principles can and should permeate every public health service. The public health worker who becomes sensitive to the mental and emotional well-being of the individual seeking help is better ready to administer whatever service he has to give. In every contact of the public health worker the positive traits of kindliness, understanding, and acceptance can be expressed toward the client. The public health department can become an agent, through example and through education, in promoting mental health principles in "the social structure of the community," in aiding the various social groups, parents, school, recreation, law enforcement, and job employment in understanding and in fostering conditions for "the constructive use of human relationships." Every community, furthermore, has need for the services of a mental health or guidance clinic for treatment of deviant behavior. The public health department may fittingly supply such a service or exercise leadership in cooperating with a treatment service offered through other community auspices.

The National Mental Health Act envisioned this broadening of public health programs. States generally have designated a state agency as the Mental Health authority, responsible for following through on the Federal grants available for training personnel, for conducting research, and for implementing carefully planned community programs. Since the National Mental Health Act recognizes private as well as public agencies and institutions as important contributors to the implementation of the Act's services, there is unparalleled opportunity for state and local planning to utilize whatever channels may be made available, public or private, for prevention and treatment. Progress thus far has been gratifying.[38]

PRESCHOOL AND SCHOOL-AGE PREVENTION

Infancy and the Preschool Child. Introduction and extension of the best known health practices in maternal and child welfare will greatly aid in prevention. Attention should be given on the part of public health departments, private physicians and parents to early prenatal care, obstetrical safeguards, the care of the premature, the early detection of deviations, periodic medical examinations and treatment, immunization, and the emotional aspects of child rearing. There is need for extension of maternal and child care centers, particularly well-baby and pre-school clinics. The introduction of parent education and nursery schools and the increase in provision of kindergartens are necessary steps toward recognition of understanding and of guidance in early years.

The School-age Child. The school-age period covers a span in which school health service in coordination with public and private health services can reach every child and his family through effective, efficient and up-to-date programs. Could the knowledge, forces and influences for shaping healthy physiques and healthy personalities be made available and utilized during the school-age periods, how much smaller would be the load for special education and rehabilitation services! A national committee appointed to build better health for all school-age children states:

> Some communities already are striding ahead in providing services and opportunities for at least some of their school-age children. Others are still carrying out the routine and less effective procedures of 50 years ago . . . . most communities can do something to step up the quality of the job now being done by building greater health opportunities for children.[39]

It was suggested that each community examine the health needs of its children. Of the fourteen priorities stated, those having the most direct bearing on prevention of handicaps are (1) better screening techniques, (2) follow-up diagnosis and treatment, (3) mental health, and (4) safety.

Studies have already proved the effectiveness of a thorough medical examination at school entrance and at three-year intervals, supplemented by examination at such time as the individual may need one. Screening techniques using height and weight measurements, vision and hearing tests, chest x-rays and other tests afford a means for discovering deviations early. Although present methods give fair returns, research continues to look for better means and methods of screening large groups in both hearing and vision at the several age periods. The need for detecting signs of social maladjustments during the child's school life is giving rise to studies designed to develop methods for mental health screening.[40]

Screening methods, however, are only a beginning. Recent studies stress the urgent need for follow-up with diagnosis and treatment. In an intensive study undertaken in 30 Pennsylvania communities, the findings showed the "present rate of correcting school children's medical and dental defects is far too low in all segments for society and all types of homes."[41] Experiments on methods of follow-up indicated that the "corrective action rate" can be significantly raised. "Long-range persuasive programs of public education" with support of private physicians as well as school physicians are needed. Individual cumulative health records are another 'must' for adequate follow-up. Awareness of health needs and follow-up treatment cannot be secured without education, planning, and teamwork of doctors, nurses, administrators, teachers, and parents.[42]

MENTAL HEALTH IN EDUCATION

The permeation of mental health in educational programs is essential in the prevention of the increasing incidence of social maladjustment.[43] Many school administrators have made provision for teacher study groups in the dynamics of child behavior. Others have promoted mental health institutes and courses in cooperation with university centers or psychiatric consultants. Home visitation, group work with parents, and parent conferences are growing in number.

Children and youth, too, need to be educated to understand and practice all-round health. It is encouraging to note that texts in health for the elementary and secondary school of today reflect the recognition that physical health and mental and social well-being go hand in hand. In one series, for example, a chart for the teacher outlines the text content from first to eight grade as follows: (1) physical health, learning about our bodies and how to care for them; (2) mental health, learning about how we think, feel, and act; (3) social health, learning to live in harmony with others; and (4) safety and first aid, learning to live safely.[44] At secondary level courses in personal and community health problems, family relationships, and child care lay the basis for college and parenthood. In day-to-day life in home and school, growth in knowledge, understanding and wholesome practices can be effectively guided.

Child guidance facilities to aid the school in prevention and treatment of behavior problems are woefully lacking. Facts gleaned from a questionnaire study of public school systems over the nation reveal that school administrators estimate ten per cent of the school population is emotionally disturbed and in need of treatment. But no school administrator stated that the number of psychiatrists, social workers, and psychologists available to him was adequate. Furthermore, his estimate of specialists needed was much below the number recommended by authorities.[45]

One of the greatest opportunities for promoting mental hygiene in education lies almost untapped in many teacher-training programs. Changes are overdue in the qualitative selection of candidates and personnel work, and in dynamic courses in the appropriate humanities, supplemented by laboratory methods and broadening experiences with children.

In summary, mental health movements should stimulate education at all levels to examine philosophy and practice. Education is only at the threshold of its opportunities in the field of mental health.

SUMMARY

The concept of prevention in medicine, in public health, in delinquency and in crime is not a new development, but its signficance and import to the nation and to the individual has taken on new meaning. The acceptance of the principle of prevention to which scientific research, medicine, public health, social work, and education can contribute is a product of the twentieth century. This chapter is focused on areas that have particular import for those who work with children and youth. The implications for all age groups are evident.

In summary, attention has been called to imperative needs in the following areas of prevention, the first line of defense in overcoming handicaps. (1) Progress in control of infectious diseases, which has markedly reduced illness and handicaps, has given increasing momentum to research which, in like manner, may discover causes and means of control for chronic and disabling diseases. (2) Research in prematurity, congenital malformations, and brain injury is defining better the role of hereditary and of secondary factors and is leading the way to improved control of abnormalities, if immunization, medical diagnosis and medical treatment are given at the proper periods in the life of the mother and child. (3) Education and concerted action for safety by school, home, and community can greatly reduce crippling, sensory, and cosmetic defects. (4) Mental health, geared at national and state levels to integration with public and private agencies for research, public education, and community service, gives hope for reducing social maladjustment and mental disorders. (5) The preschool and school periods in child life can afford far greater opportunity for developing healthy physiques and healthy personalities and for correcting defects than at present. (6) Mental health in education is a particular area which calls for greater knowledge, understanding, and implementation on the part of school personnel.

Special education calls for team work! Special education has joined forces with medical, health, child guidance, and social welfare agencies, public and private, in pursuit of better special education services for increased numbers of exceptional children and youth. To a greater or less degree these services have embodied elements of prevention. In a list of special education priorities where does prevention rank? If recognized as the first line of defense and attacked with concerted team action, how much greater the gains, not only for childhood and youth, but for adulthood, too!

FOOTNOTES

1. Some of the facts stated earlier in this text are restated here to give emphasis to the subject of prevention.
2. Cant, Gilbert, *Medical Research May Save Your Life!* Public Affairs Pamphlet #201 (Public Affairs Committee: N.Y.C., 1953), p. 22.
3. Puner, Helen W., *Children in Court*, Public Affairs Pamphlet #207 (Public Affairs Committee: N.Y.C., 1954).
4. "An Experiment in Child Welfare", The Child, Vol. II, Oct., 1946, pp. 70, 71, 79.
5. *Changing Problems in Prevention of Blindness*: U.S.A. 1940 vs. 1955 (National Society for the Prevention of Blindness: N.Y.C., 1955). Typed.
6. Benda, Clemens E. *Developmental Disorders of Mentation and Cerebral Palsies* (Grune and Stratton: N.Y.C., 1952), p. xx.
7. *Diagnosis of Children Served in the Crippled Children's Program* 1950, Children's Bureau Statistical Series, #21 (U. S. Department of Health, Education, and Welfare: Washington, D.C., 1954).
8. Wallace, Helen M., *et al.*, "Special Classes for Handicapped Children", *American Journal of Public Health*, Vol. 44, August, 1954, pp. 1045-1058.
9. Wilson, Charles, ed., *School Health Services* (National Education Association: Washington, D.C., 1953), p. 195.
10. *Report on Study Projects for Trainable Mentally Handicapped Children* (Office of Public Instruction: Springfield, Ill., 1954), pp. 14, 43.
11. *Sixteenth Annual Report—Polio* 1953 (National Foundation for Infantile Paralysis: N.Y.C., 1954).
12. Mackie, Romaine P., and Dunn, Lloyd M., *College and University Programs for the Preparation of Teachers of Exceptional Children*, Bulletin 1954 #13 (U. S. Office of Health, Education, and Welfare: Washington, D.C., 1954).
13. *Rehabilitation of the Handicapped*, United Nations Social Welfare Series, Special Issue (International Document Service, Columbia University Press: N.Y.C., September, 1953), pp. 3, 13.
14. Leavell, Hugh Rodman, and Clark, E. Gurney, *Textbook of Preventive Medicine* (McGraw-Hill: N.Y.C., 1953).
15. Cant, *op. cit.*, p. 16.
16. *Ibid.*, pp. 4-6.
17. *Ibid.*, p. 1.
18. Kerby, C. Edith, "Causes and Prevention of Blindness in Children of School Age", *The Sight-Saving Review*, Vol. XXII, April, 1952, pp. 1-10.
19. Hopkins, Louise A., "Heredity and Deafness", *Eugenics Quarterly*, Sept., 1954, pp. 193-199.
20. Cant, *op.cit.*, p. 10.
21. *Ibid.*, pp. 10-15.

22. *Ibid.*, pp. 15-17.
23. *Diagnosis of Children Served in the Crippled Children's Program* 1950.
24. *Muscular Dystrophy—The Facts* (Muscular Dystrophy Association of America: N.Y.C., 1954).
25. Cant, *op. cit.*, pp. 17, 18.
26. Molony, Clement J., and Parmelee, A. H., "Convulsions in Young Infants as a Result of Pyridoxine (Vitamin B6 Deficiency)", *Journal of the American Medical Association,* Vol. 154, Jan., 1954, pp. 405, 406.
27. *Prematurity Congenital Malformation and Birth Injury,* Proceedings of a Conference Sponsored by Association for the Aid of Crippled Children (Association for the Aid of Crippled Children: N.Y.C., 1953).
28. Strauss, Alfred A., and Lehtinen, Laura E., *Psychopathology and Education of the Brain-Injured Child* (Grune and Stratton: N.Y.C., 1947).
29. "Report on Retrolental Fibroplasia at AAOO" *The Sight Saving Review,* Vol. XXIV, Winter, 1954. pp. 212, 213.
30. Hopkins, *op. cit.*
31. Falls, Harold F., "Congenital and Heredity Eye Diseases", *The Sight-Saving Review,* Vol. XIX, Summer, 1949, pp. 67-78.
32. *Accident Facts: 1954 Edition* (National Safety Council: Chicago). The National Safety Council is a noncommercial, nonprofit cooperative organization furnishing leadership in the safety movement and providing services to meet the needs of groups and individuals in every area.
33. Dietrich, Harry F., "Prevention of Childhood Accidents", *The Journal of the American Medical Association,* Vol. 156, Nov., 1954, pp. 929-931.
34. Dunbar, Helen Flanders, "Mind and Body: Psychosomatic Medicine", *The Accident Habit* (Random House: N.Y.C., 1947), Chapter VIII.
35. Puner, *op. cit.*
36. *Health Inquiry: The Toll of Our Major Diseases, Their Causes, Prevention, and Control, House Report* No. 1338 (Government Printing Office: Washington, D.C., 1954), pp. 121-143.
37. Felix, R. H., "Mental Hygiene as Public Health Practice", *The American Journal of Orthopsychiatry,* Vol. XXI, Oct., 1951, pp. 707-716.
38. Dysinger, Robert H., ed., "Mental Health in the United States", *The Annals of the American Academy of Political and Social Science,* Vol. 286, March, 1953, pp. 167, 173, 174.
39. *Better Health for School-Age Children,* Children's Bureau Pamphlet (U. S. Department of Health, Education, and Welfare: Washington, D.C., 1951).
40. Ullmann, Charles A., "Mental Health Screening of School Children", *Public Health Reports,* Vo. 67, Dec., 1952, pp. 1219-1224.
41. *Rx for Healthier Children* (Health Information Foundation: N.Y.C., 1955).
42. Wilson, *op. cit.*, Chapter XV.
43. *Mental Health in Modern Education,* Part II, 54th Year Book of the National Society for the Study of Education (University of Chicago Press: Chicago, 1955).
44. *Health and Personal Development Series* (Scott, Foresman: Chicago).
45. Abrahamson, David, *et al.*, "Status of Mental Hygiene and Child Guidance Facilities in Public Schools in the United States", *Journal of Pediatrics,* Vol. 46, No. 1 (January, 1955), pp. 107-118.

ADDITIONAL REFERENCES

Foote, Franklin M., and Crane, Mariam M., "An Evaluation of Vision Screening", *Exceptional Children*, Vol. 20, Jan., 1954, pp. 153-161.

Grad, Marjorie A., "Congenital Anomalies", *Journal of the American Medical Women's Association*, Vol. 9, Dec., 1954, pp. 387-390.

Rankin, Paul T., and Dorsey, John M., "The Detroit School Mental Health Project: A Five Year Report, *Mental Hygiene*, Vol. 37, April, 1953, pp. 228-248.

Witmer, Helen L., and Katinsky, Ruth, *Personality in the Making*. The Fact-Finding Report of the Midcentury White House Conference on Children and Youth (Harper: N.Y.C., 1952).

Tufts, Edith, *et al.*, *The Effectiveness of Delinquency Prevention Programs*, Children's Bureau Publication #350 (U. S. Department of Health, Education, and Welfare: Washington, D.C., 1954).

Yahres, Herbert, *Epilepsy - The Ghost is out of the Closet*, Public Affairs Pamphlet #98 Public Affairs Committee: N.Y.C., 1954).

Gains for Handicapped Children, Public Affairs Pamphlet #212 (Public Affairs Committee: N.Y.C., 1954).

SECTION II

CHAPTER VII

VOCATIONAL REHABILITATION

VOCATIONAL REHABILITATION BY SALVATORE
G. DI MICHAEL

SPECIAL EDUCATION AND VOCATIONAL
REHABILITATION BY MARY E. SWITZER

VOCATIONAL REHABILITATION

SALVATORE G. DI MICHAEL

The essential purpose of rehabilitation programs is basically expressed in the following definition: Rehabilitation is the restoration of disabled persons to the fullest physical, mental, personal, social, vocational, and economic usefulness of which they are capable. Vocational rehabilitation emphasizes the ultimate goal of effective employment, with due consideration to the importance of other areas of life adjustment. In work with the very severely disabled of all ages, and with the aged, the term 'general rehabilitation' is used to signify a program primarily aimed to increase self-care and personal-social adjustment, with less need for family or professional resources. Recently, the educational literature makes increasing use of the term 'habilitation', to mean that disabled children are being prepared for proper adult living, a status not attained. Otherwise, the distinction has no force, since a child may become disabled and need 'rehabilitation'; likewise, an adult may actually be better adjusted and more effectively employed after 'rehabilitation'.

Many private and public agencies are involved in vocational rehabilitation. The current emphasis on the ideal of total community participation is a necessary result of the clearer perception that all areas of living contribute to a person's adjustment in any one or more phases of life. Although the author desires explicitly to recognize this fact, the treatment of vocational rehabilitation in this chapter must be limited. Accordingly, major consideration will be given to the public civilian program under state-federal auspices because of its greater potential and actual scope of clients and its close contact with many other public and private agencies in related work, and because of the difficulties of collecting comparable statistics and general data on the services of private agencies. The program of the Veterans Administration also is given only brief attention because its lesser role of influence in special education of the handicapped child, and because of limitations of space.

EXTENT OF DISABILITY

Although the disabled represent a minority in the total population, their numbers are considerable and represent a crucial social problem. In a certain sense, just as special education is an essential phase of a total school program, so is vocational rehabilitation a major factor in modern society. According to estimates based on the Public Health Survey of 1936, there are approximately 28,000,000 people in the United States with a disability of some degree. Included among these are about 2,000,000 with more severe physical and mental handicaps so as to be in need of special rehabilitation services in order to be prepared for and placed in suitable employment. Recent studies to support this estimate were made in 1949 and 1950 by the U.S. Department of Health, Education and Welfare in cooperation with the Bureau of the Census. Each year, an estimated 250,000 persons of working age become physically and vocationally handicapped because of congenital conditions, disease, or injury. These figures represent persons 14 years of age and over, not in the armed forces, with long-term rather than temporary disabilities, and not including people with very serious disabilities with no reasonable chance to rehabilitate them into employment, under our present knowledge.

SCHOOL PARTICIPATION IN VOCATIONAL REHABILITATION

Special efforts constantly have been made by rehabilitation counselors to work in close cooperation with the schools. This is the result of efforts to contact the disabled as early as possible, and of the recognized importance of training as a means of preparation for suitable employment. For example, in the fiscal year 1953, a total of $34,583,138 of state and federal funds was spent in the rehabilitation of 61,308 persons. Of the total expenditures, $17,096,369 was for purchased services (that is, exclusive of administration, counseling and placement costs). Of purchased services, 34 per cent was spent on training and supplies for 23,674 of the clients rehabilitated into gainful employment. This was the most money spent on a single category of services of the ten mentioned specifically in the report, *Facts and Figures on Vocational Rehabilitation*, 1953, a publication of the Office of Vocational Rehabilitation. It is also worthy of note that ten per cent of the clients rehabilitated, or 6,102 persons were initially referred by educational institutions. The latter figure is fourth in order of magnitude of the seven specifically designated categories of sources of referral.

Since the disabled persons eligible for services should be near or at working age, arrangements often have been made for the vocational counselor to contact the client in school at the age of 14 or 15. The policies and practices of establishing primary responsibility for the counseling of the client have depended upon the particular school, and the available personnel in the school and the rehabilitation agency. Many schools for the blind, for example, have few vocational counselors and have encouraged rehabilitation counselors to take primary responsibility for the student's terminal training and after-school adjustment. In many public schools, the rehabilitation personnel have an agreement with the school staff to speak to the high school classes and invite the physically disabled to talk with them and to undergo an evaluation for the purpose of determining their eligibility for vocational rehabilitation services. Because the rehabilitation of the mentally retarded and the emotionally disturbed have not been established on as firm a basis as with the physically handicapped, satisfactory arrangements for contacting them in the schools have not been widely made. An example of close cooperation in the Minneapolis schools has been described in "Vocational Rehabilitation of the Mentally Retarded" by Haasarud and Moore. Obviously, the retarded should be contacted initially in the schools by the rehabilitation counselor if the principle of early referral is to be effectively practiced.

The general policy to be followed is to have the schools maintain primary responsibility for counseling until the individual is almost ready to leave school or be graduated. The rehabilitation counselor acts as a consultant to the school counselor or as coordinate member of the team, ready to take over more actively from the school counselor at the appropriate time. As the student is preparing to leave the educational institution, the rehabilitation counselor becomes the client's main point of contact and coordination. In this way, the client's last years at school are planned in the light of maximum potential usefulness to later life adjustment, and a smoother transition is effected between school and community living. The more flexible is the curriculum, the greater opportunities for adaptations in the total plan for rehabilitation. In some cases, the plan may call for part-time work and additional educational courses in subjects specifically related to the future needs for employment. State and Federal laws on the employment of minors is one of the factors to be considered in the referral of handicapped students to the rehabilitation counselor.

Follow-up studies made by the rehabilitation agencies, or in cooperation with them, have materially influenced the curriculum in some situations. In the writer's observations, the schools for the blind have been more sensitive to the results of these studies than most other institutions of learning, although the total influence on curriculum changes is not as great as some authorities have hoped for.

Increasing attempts have been made to encourage vocational instructors in the regular schools to modify their teaching methods to the needs of the handicapped. This approach claims the desirable feature of integrating the handicapped with the non-handicapped, and of making available the better resources of regular schools without duplication of facilities, — a costly and usually less efficient arrangement from the overall social viewpoint. McAuley's recent publication, *Vocational Schools as Training Facilities for Blind Workers,* is a fairly complete exposition on the information and attitudes required by vocational teachers. Where occupational training is required on a semi-skilled level, as for the mentally retarded, the regular vocational schools have shown resistance to curricular or teaching adaptations in the belief that they are only set up to prepare journeymen for the skilled trades.

ELIGIBILITY AND BASIC SERVICES OF VOCATIONAL REHABILITATION

To be eligible for the state-federal program, the client should: (1) be at or near working age; (2) have a substantial job handicap because of physical or mental impairment; and (3) have a reasonable chance of becoming employable. After the applicant is contacted, it is necessary to evaluate him from the medical, personal, social, and vocational viewpoints. A general medical examination, and specialized examinations as needed, are obtained, while usually the counselor gathers together other data from various sources. When the person is deemed eligible, and with his consent, a rehabilitation plan is developed in terms of a judicious use of services arranged through the agency, with cooperation from community resources.

The state vocational rehabilitation agency provides medical and specialized examinations, counseling, assistance in placement, and follow-up at no expense to the client. Depending upon the need for other services, as well as a determination of financial ability of the client to pay some or all of the expenses for other services, the agency will arrange and provide for medical, surgical, and psychiatric treatment, hospital care, artificial appliances, living expenses and transportation during rehabilitation, occupational tools, equipment, and licenses.

During the 1953 fiscal year, the services of counseling and placement without other service was provided to 17.4 per cent of the rehabilitated clients, counseling and placement with training was given to 29.2 per cent of the group, physical restoration to 42.7 per cent, training and physical restoration to 9.3 per cent, and occupational equipment, tools, etc., to 1.4 per cent of the clients. Of the services purchased ($17,096,369), the amounts spent for various categories were: medical and psychiatric examinations, 4.1 per cent; psychological examinations, 0.4 per cent; transportation for diagnostic services, 0.2 per cent; surgery and treatment, 12.8 per cent; artificial appliances, 11.1 per cent; hospital and convalescent care, 12.8 per cent; training with training materials, 34.3 per cent; maintenance and transportation, 20.4 per cent; occupational tools, equipment and licenses, 3.1 per cent; equipment for business enterprises, 0.7 per cent; and other services, 0.1 per cent. Except for administration, counseling and placement services, almost all other services are purchased by the state rehabilitation agency through community facilities, by agreement in each individual area.

Training may be arranged in many ways. In most cases, regular training facilities are engaged, such as universities, colleges, commercial and business schools, high schools, and special educational institutions. In some cases, the training may be furnished by special tutors, correspondence or extension courses, or on-the-job.

LEGISLATIVE DEVELOPMENTS

The initial Vocational Rehabilitation Act was passed in 1920 "to provide for the promotion of vocational rehabilitation of persons disabled in industry or otherwise and their return to civil employment." For several reasons, the emphasis was on vocational training of persons disabled in industry. The program depended upon extensions of the Act until 1935, when Title V of the Social Security Act provided for permanent and continuing authorization by Congress of annual appropriations for grants to the states. The Social Security Act also provided for close liaison with the State Employment Services to place the handicapped. In 1936, the Randolph-Sheppard Act enabled the states to license qualified blind persons to operate vending stands in federal buildings. Although the Randolph-Sheppard Act contained no direct provision for financial participation, the activity gave impetus and example for the establishment of additional stands operated by the blind in state, municipal, and private buildings.

The enactment in 1943 of Public Law 113 resulted in a major expansion of the state-federal vocational rehabilitation program. The war had highlighted the needs of civilian disabled and their potential and real contributions to the total war effort. The Act considerably increased the scope of services, made the mentally retarded and emotionally disturbed eligible for all services on the basis of the same criteria as for the physically disabled, increased the annual authorized grants to the states, and permitted grants-in-aid to state commissions or agencies for the blind. Of the greatest importance was the provision which enabled the agencies to provide medical services of many kinds, a phase of the program frequently referred to as physical restoration. In July, 1945, authority contained in the yearly federal appropriation acts was responsible for the establishment of the controlled business enterprises program. It assisted state agencies to set up and maintain a system of suitable small businesses for eligible blind rehabilitation clients.

On August 3, 1954, President Eisenhower signed into law S.2759, the Vocational Rehabilitation Amendments of 1954. The specific intent was to expand the program over a period of years so that the goal of rehabilitating 200,000 persons a year might be reached by 1959, when federal and state governments might share equally in the total cost of the program. A three-part grant structure has been introduced with increasing authorization for federal funds up to $65 million in 1958, and subsequent amounts to be determined by Congress. The law outlines the three types of grants as follows: (1) basic support of the state-federal projects; (2) extension and improvement projects; (3) special projects. Under "extension and improvement" projects, the federal government desires to stimulate the state agencies to set up wider and better facilities by sharing in any one project for three years to the extent of paying 75 percent of the cost while the remainder is borne by the state. Under "special projects", the federal government makes grants to states and to public and other nonprofit organizations and agencies

to assist in meeting the costs of projects for research, demonstrations, training, traineeships and special projects which hold promise of making a substantial contribution to the solution of vocational rehabilitation problems common to a number of States, including temporary assistance in initiating a substantial nationwide expansion of vocational rehabilitation programs in the States.

The authority to make grants for special projects already has resulted in financial assistance to universities for graduate training in rehabilitation counseling, counseling psychology, vocational counseling, social work, and undergraduate training in physical and occupational therapy, as well as for short-term training. Educational benefits ranging from $1400 to $3700, with additional allowances of $350 a year for a dependent spouse and for each child under 18 years of age, have been made through arrangements with approved institutions of learning.

The Vocational Rehabilitation Amendments of 1954 included a number of other provisions which may be expected to influence the future course of the program. The Secretaries of Labor and of Health, Education, Welfare, together with the Chairman of the President's Committee on Employment of the Physically Handicapped were enjoined to cooperate in facilitating the employment of the handicapped. It also was stipulated that the Federal and State Employment Offices would have to furnish employment counseling and to provide at least one person in each state or Federal employment office with the specific duties of promoting and developing job opportunities. Another provision called for a thorough study of existing programs for teaching and training homebound handicapped persons, the report to be submitted to Congress, with the aim of expanding and improving such services. The Act authorized the licensing of persons to operate vending stands on any Federal property, with preference to blind persons licensed by a State Agency. Moreover, the Law encouraged the establishment of public and other non-profit rehabilitation facilities, with special mention of rehabilitation centers and workshops for the severely handicapped.

The Medical Facilities Survey and Construction Act of 1954, an amendment to the Hill-Burton Hospital Survey and Construction Act, includes authorization of $10 million in grants for rehabilitation facilities. The latter is defined as

a facility which is operated for the primary purpose of assisting in the rehabilitation of disabled persons through an integrated program of medical, psychological, social and vocational evaluation and services under competent professional supervision.

Rehabilitation Services by Private Agencies

Private agencies, as a whole, have made notable contributions in the development, improvement, and fuller scope of rehabilitation services. The public rehabilitation programs, both civilian and veteran, were influenced by the pioneering efforts of private organizations. It would take a careful and painstaking study to record the history of work by private agencies. Early in the century, the facility now known as the Cleveland Rehabilitation Center began a program considered ambitious by the standards of the time. The Institute of Crippled and Disabled of New York City, as well as the American Red Cross, participated actively in institutes during World War I, dealing with the problem of establishing a rehabilitation program for veterans and later for civilians.

The private agencies were unhampered by legislative restrictions and experimented with methods and techniques which later were incorporated in public programs. In more recent years, for example, the Institute of Physical Medicine and Rehabilitation, in New York City, did notable work with paraplegics, a group formerly considered non-feasible. The Altro Workshops helped to highlight the benefits of a work conditioning program for tubercular patients discharged from the sanatorium on a restricted-activity basis; more recently it has developed similar techniques for helping the emotionally disturbed in adjusting to community life after parole or discharge from mental hospitals. The Goodwill Industries of America have established a national network of sheltered workshop and training facilities. The National Society for Crippled Children and Adults, and later the United Cerebral Palsy Associations have fostered a program, including speech training and physical and occupational therapies, to demonstrate the possibilities of rehabilitating cerebral palsied persons. Similar examples could be mentioned at considerable length and would take in a very large number of private agencies.

The private organizations usually deal with one disability group. In so doing, they have conducted pilot studies which demonstrated improved methods of rehabilitating the people served, and then have eagerly sought to train personnel in public and private agencies in the newer principles and techniques. One great value, sometimes overlooked, is the fact that private agencies have solicited the interest of the lay and professional community and thus have been instrumental in proving to the public the values of rehabilitation. Legislative developments were the results of studies by Congressional committees, and their proceedings vividly testify to the factual data of demonstration projects, the encouragement and widespread backing of private organizations.

VOCATIONAL REHABILITATION OF VETERANS

With the passage, in 1917, of an amendment to the War Risk Insurance Act, the new concept of rehabilitation of the disabled veteran was adopted. Prior to this time, benefits were largely land grants, retirement pay, service pensions, and domiciliary care with some medical treatment. The concept of rehabilitation was expended in its current broad sense with the enactment of Public Law 16, in 1943. The purpose of the program was to restore employ-ability to those disabled in military service during the period of war or declared national emergency, and to integrate the veteran into regular com-munity living. Public Law 894, approved in 1950, provides essentially the same benefits as under Public Law 16 for veterans with active service during the period of national emergency commencing June 27, 1950. The date of January 31, 1955 has been established by proclamation of President Eisen-hower as the end of the Korean conflict period governing eligibility.

To be eligible for benefits under Public Law 16 and 894, the veteran must be in need of training to overcome the handicap of his service-incurred dis-ability. The Veterans Administration has not set up any special training facilities but has made use of established educational institutions and on-the-job, as well as home training for the homebound. The services include sub-sistence allowance payments, money for tuition, books and supplies, and other types of services necessary for the successful pursuit of the training program, such as speech correction, special restorative training, reader service, or special equipment.

The program is administered directly by 70 Veterans Administration re-gional offices. The disabled veteran must take training toward a goal con-sistent with his abilities, aptitudes, interests, previous training and disability. A vocational counselor is provided by the Veterans Administration either on its own staff or by contractual arrangements with educational institutions which operate guidance centers. On the basis of the chosen occupational goal, a Veterans Administration Training Officer assists in preparing a training program designed to bring the veteran to the goal of rehabilitation. As the individual becomes ready to seek employment, he is assisted by placement specialists in the Veterans Administration or the United States and States Employment Services, or by arrangement with the State-Federal program of vocational rehabilitation, or other suitable agencies.

Over 600,00 disabled veterans of World War II, or over one-fourth of the eligible group, have participated in the program under Public Law 16 since its inception. The peak was reached in December, 1947, when a total of

265,000 veterans were enrolled. Only 12,000 veterans remained in training in December, 1954. Approximately 25,000 veterans have been served under Public Law 894 since its inception in June, 1951, until December, 1954. The cost of benefits through Fiscal Year 1954 has approximated one billion, six hundred thousand dollars. About four-fifths of this cost represented subsistence allowance payments, and the remaining one-fifth was paid for tuition, books, supplies and equipment.

EMPLOYMENT OF THE HANDICAPPED

The cardinal aim of vocational rehabilitation has been to establish the handicapped into regular employment, side by side with the non-handicapped, and where this is not possible, into remunerative sheltered employment. Great strides have been made in developing techniques of placement that take into account the abilities as well as the limitations of the mentally and physically impaired. The present view is that every person has strengths and limitations so that the differences in employability between handicapped and non-handicapped are quantitative rather than qualitative. For example, it is as much of a handicap for a college-trained engineer to try to do bookkeeping, or for an automobile mechanic to try to construct a bridge, as it is for an amputee to undertake a job requiring considerable climbing or stooping.

The handicapped are to be found in all fields of employment. The yearly statistics of the Office of Vocational Rehabilitation have shown repeatedly that the disabled who were rehabilitated were employed in occupational groupings almost similar to those of the United States Labor Force. Moreover, studies of comparable groups of disabled and selectively placed non-disabled workers have shown almost similar records in such factors as production, job stability, absences, number of accidents, duration of illness due to accidents, earnings, and efficiency ratings. The small differences that appeared were sometimes in favor of one group, sometimes the other, with the possible exception that a small percentage of the handicapped needed to have some slight modification in job conditions. Although the point has not been proved, it is the opinion of some authorities that a slightly greater amount of supervisory time is required to assist the handicapped in initial adjustments to the total work situation.

Each handicapped group has a wide scope of jobs in which individuals have been, or may be placed. The studies of the United States Civil Service, the War and Navy Departments, United States Department of Labor, Veterans Administration, and Office of Vocational Rehabilitation, as well as others under private auspices, have attested to the wide range of jobs for any handicapped group. For the physically handicapped and the emotionally disturbed, one will find individuals in job categories ranging from the professional to the unskilled. For the mentally retarded, there are thousands of jobs in the semi-skilled and unskilled categories as has been shown in many studies. It is obvious, then, that the problem of suitable placement is dependent upon a skillful exploration of the field of work, and the strengths and limitations of the individual, with a matching between the two that also recognizes human adaptability to several kinds of jobs.

In spite of the evidence produced by many studies attesting to the economic usefulness of the handicapped, and their creditable performance as compared to the non-handicapped, resistance to the employment of the mentally and physically handicapped still exists, as was found by Barker and his associates in a critical summary of pertinent studies. This problem is not alone a condition which requires education of employers, but society as a whole, because the latter creates the social environment that is reflected in the attitudes of special social groups.

SPECIAL EDUCATION AND VOCATIONAL REHABILITATION

MARY E. SWITZER

In a very real sense, special education and vocational rehabilitation have a common purpose and a similarity of origin. Both deal with deviants for whom some special provision must be made if later life adjustment is to be healthy and successful. Both are products of our developing system of education, in which experience has taught us that variations in approach and in services must be made for certain of the population who, usually for reasons beyond their control, cannot participate in the benefits of standard instruction methods.

Just as the evolution of special education has taken it far beyond the rudimentary efforts of a few decades ago, so has vocational rehabilitation developed into a much broadened concept of what can and should be done for the disabled.

Scope of Vocational Rehabilitation Services

Vocational rehabilitation services to handicapped individuals are provided through eighty-eight State vocational rehabilitation agencies located in each State and Territory. Some States have two agencies, one specializing in the blind and another for the remainder of the disabled. They provide the 'core' services of counseling and placement and, as needed, physical restoration, vocational training, prosthetic appliances, transportation, occupational tools and equipment, and maintenance. Since the goal of all of these services is a suitable remunerative occupation, obviously the program is directed toward those of employable age. To be eligible for such services, there must be: (1) a physical or mental disability; (2) a limitation, imposed by the disability, which constitutes a handicap to employment; and (3) a reasonable expectation that the provision of rehabilitation services will make the individual fit to engage in remunerative work.

Vocational rehabilitation today has an exciting new charter. At the urging of the President, the 83rd Congress enacted Public Law 565, the Vocational

Rehabilitation Amendments of 1954. The framework for a much more complete vocational rehabilitation service now has the necessary legal foundation, with financial authorizations which point to a program three-fold and more larger. A tri-pronged attack on barriers to a more comprehensive program, — funds, facilities. and personnel, — is to be carried out through this legislation. Not only is provision made for supporting the present program operation, but the path to extending and improving rehabilitation services has been opened. Opportunity is presented for developing new methods and techniques of rehabilitation, for instituting new services to disabled people, for studying scientifically problems associated with disability, and for creating needed facilities for rehabilitation. To meet critical rehabilitation personnel shortages,. a training and traineeship program has been authorized.

Some Relationships

This newer dynamic framework of vocational rehabilitation has important implications for special education. For the estimated 700,000 children, many homebound, who are in special classes and schools or receive help from educational specialists, home or hospital teachers, vocational rehabilitation may well be the next step in the process of future gainful employment. For the estimated 4,000,000 children and youth, half of whom are physically handicapped, who have need for a special type of school program, an enlarged vocational rehabilitation program represents new hope for their future. While vocational rehabilitation services are available to a greater population than those who have been provided with special education, the relationship between them may be expressed as follows: Special education provides physically and mentally disabled children and youth with the broad foundation for maximum mental, physical, and emotional adjustment to disabling conditions that is consistent with the individual's abilities and capacities; upon this solid base vocational rehabilitation erects the superstructure of preparation for, entry into, and adjustment to an appropriate occupation, and assumes terminal responsibility with the disabled individual for such refinement and strengthening of his mental, physical, and emotional attributes as may be necessary. Obviously, the more closely planning and action are integrated, the more certain is it that needless duplication will be avoided, practical goals established, and clients time and energy used most advantageously and effectively for realization of these goals.

A fundamental technique in vocational rehabilitation frequently is used to study and solve problems among handicapped children and youth. An excellent illustration of this has been provided by the Children's Division of the Institute of Physical Medicine and Rehabilitation of the New York University — Bellevue Medical Center (a joint program of the Institute and the Association for the Aid of Crippled Children), in cooperation with the New York City Health Department. In 1952, the Institute initiated a team evaluation of a group of homebound handicapped school-age children in New York city. Permission for evaluation, as well as abstracts of medical records, were obtained from each child's physical or the hospital clinic where the child received care. In certain instances, some social data were provided by the hospital, the home teacher, or other agency interested in the family. Medical social workers discussed proposed evaluations with children and parents, analyzed home and family situations, and secured the permission of the family to have the child evaluated. The findings and recommendations of the evaluation team, which consisted of an orthopedic surgeon, a psychiatrist, a pediatrician, and a medical social worker, were sent to the child's private physician or hospital. Seventy-four orthopedically handicapped school-age children were evaluated by the team.

The outstanding result of the evaluation project[1] was the team's finding that one-half of these children were considered physically capable of returning to school immediately. Since some 1,100 similarly disabled children were receiving home instruction from teachers provided by the New York City Board of Education, the lessons to be learned from this approach have not only individual but also broad financial value.

This is not an isolated instance, as further demonstrated by a study of home instruction students made by the New York Division of Vocational Rehabilitation. In this study, a group of 246 students on home instruction in New York City were located by that Division and offered services. These students were under the care of private physicians, and it did not appear from the study that any special physical restorative services were provided after the beginning of the study. Through the provision of counseling and vocational training, 174 of the group successfully adjusted or were in the process of making an adjustment to the community. Thirty-one individuals were provided with vocational training and placed in employment, 16 were placed without further training, 16 were attending universities, 11 were attending either State Institutes or receiving special art instruction, and 15 were enrolled in a variety of private schools in the community. Sixteen of those in the study returned to high school or regular classes for the first time; 29 remained on home instruction. It is apparent from this study that factors other than physical account for a large part of the confinement of these individuals to the home for educational purposes, factors which have not been identified. On the other hand, it is reasonable to assume that a comprehensive and dynamic evaluation of the youngster's strengths and weaknesses would have led to the development of a more effective educational plan.

These studies impress one with the fact that individuals are homebound not only because of the nature or severity of their disabilities but often because of circumstances. This impression is fortified by the observations made in a study of disabled homebound persons conducted recently by the Office of Vocational Rehabilitation, pursuant to Section 7 of Public Law 565. This study suggests that "the same disability may cause a person to be homebound in one situation but not in another".[2] Some elements bringing this about are suggested.

1. Geographical factors often are instrumental in making a person 'shut-in', especially in rural areas where lack of transportation or distance to treatment centers and schools may keep one at home.

2. Lack of rehabilitation centers, workshops, special classes or personnel may force one into a homebound status.

3. Psychological components of disablement are often causative factors in confining an individual to his home.

While this study was limited to the homebound, the conclusions are sound for many types of services to the disabled and point to the comprehensiveness of the evaluation, planning, and programming needed to assist the disabled to make an adequate adjustment. It emphasizes the necessity of seeing the service, whether of special education or of vocational rehabilitation, in the perspective of the total individual with whom one deals. Thus, it is not enough to study the physical and mental abilities and disabilities of the handicapped child, or his educational growth and development. He must be studied as a total person with special emphasis on seeing him in his social setting. This is a perspective which is vital in both vocational rehabilitation and special education.

IMPORTANCE OF SELF-CARE

Rehabilitation has also learned that many disabled persons are seriously limited not because they are beyond help because help is beyond them. There is still a widespread lack of understanding of what modern methods of physical rehabilitation can contribute to making life for handicapped individuals more active and enjoyable. Dr. Howard A. Rusk, in the foreword to Edith Buchwald's *Physical Rehabilitation for Daily Living*, considers retraining in the physical activities of daily living the foundation of rehabilitation:

> The physician in the past has thought too much about the physiological and clinical aspects of the patient's disability and too little about the physical retraining in skills necessary for carrying out the basic activities of daily living. Except in a few isolated instances, the physically handicapped person must be retrained to walk and to travel, to care for his daily needs, to use normal methods of transportation, to use ordinary toilet facilities, to apply and remove his own prosthetic appliances and to communicate either orally or in writing. Too frequently, these basic skills are overlooked. The patient is given numerous medical, psychological and vocational services in preparation for employment or self-care, but retraining in the activities of daily living is overlooked with the result that the patient, being unable to walk or travel and care for himself, is also unable to utilize effectively the other medical, psychological, social and vocational services he has received for richer and fuller living. Retraining in the basic activities of daily living is primary; it is simple a matter of 'first things first', for daily activity skills are the basis for subsequent activities.[3]

That such emphases are decidedly lacking is made manifest in the 1950 survey of the Commission on Chronic Illness. Of 2,600 hospitals surveyed, only 65 reported having an organized rehabilitation service. Similarly, a survey by the Office of Vocational Rehabilitation in 1954 showed only 23 comprehensive rehabilitation facilities of varying sizes and major emphases. The unfortunate result of this situation is an increasing number of severely disabled individuals.

Fortunately special education can do much to prevent this from taking place since special classes for the handicapped may often prevent these individuals from becoming homebound. This can occur when special class teachers place maximum emphasis on the disabled child doing things for himself. In many instances, it is small favor to the disabled person, in the long run, to do things *for* him rather than *with* him. This often results in a one-sided educational process in which growth in information and intellectual knowledge proceeds without due attention to the other elements of a well-rounded life. Physical tasks involving activities of daily living should become a regular part of the classroom practice of special teachers. Such simple items as propelling one's wheelchair about the classroom or along school corridors rather than having it pushed by the teacher may be quite important for an individual, since it affects not only his present functioning but his future prospects for vocational rehabilitation as well. In like fashion, using crutches rather than being lifted, taking one's own class notes rather than using the services of a recorder, learning speech reading rather than depending upon an auditor, — all of these have significance to one's vocational future as well as to the educational present.

So important are these skills considered by some that they prefer to use the term 'habilitation' for them rather than 'rehabilitation'. In a real measure this is sound preference, since these skills enable a person to live rather than relive, to learn rather than relearn, to adjust rather than readjust. In this context, these skills take on a developmental meaning and educational significance, since they become part of a growth process.

The need to coordinate efforts and emphases in special education with those in physical rehabilitation is great. Thus the special teacher should make every effort to tie classroom activities into the physical goals set by the physician. In this way classroom and clinic become a total process in much the same way that vocation and physical therapy become integrated. Even in the absence of such a total process, however, an awareness of these goals and the methods of accomplishing them will contribute greatly to the child's achievement of capacity to meet the physical demands of daily life.

This effort will also be rewarding in the prevention of additional handicaps. The provision of appropriate medical and para-medical services in the functional activities of daily living may prevent many disabled individuals from becoming more severely handicapped. This is axiomatic in rehabilitaton and has important bearing for special education. The more special education can do to develop and maintain self-care ability, the greater will be the disabled individual's opportunity for self-support. The extent to which the disabled person is able to take care of his personal needs, ambulate, travel, and be independent conditions vocational potential greatly. The individual who is completely independent of assistance from others has greater potentiality for competitive employment, all other factors being equal, than those who are more limited in self-care. For those unable to care for themselves, some form of home employment would appear to be the highest attainable goal. Similarly, for those able to ambulate but who need assistance for travel, sheltered employment might be expected.

With these factors in mind, the special teacher has an unexcelled opportunity to be a constructive force in the lives of many handicapped children in ways which extend far beyond the usual sphere of the teacher's direct responsibility. Emphasis on academic learning may be joined with emphasis on the handicapped student's need to fully develop and maintain his skills in self-care and the general physical activities of daily living. The handicapped student needs to understand that one relates closely to the other, that educational progress may have little real meaning unless the person develops himself to the place where he will be able to use the knowledge acquired.

Paralleling this is the important responsibility of the teacher to help the disabled child or youth to accept educational fields and goals which correspond to the maximum physical potential of the person. For some persons, academic learning may suffice as a goal in itself. For the majority, however, completion of academic work implies a job, an income and self-sufficiency. There is cruel disappointment ahead for many severely handicapped young people when they are encouraged to pursue studies which they are mentally capable of completing, but which they may not, because of the severity of their disability, be able to put to use in the practical world of work.

EMOTIONAL ADJUSTMENT

Important as are these self-care activities, their achievement is conditioned by the extent of personality integration of the disabled individual. It is axiomatic that the disabled rehabilitate themselves, not the counselor, the physician, or the teacher. Dr. Rusk, in his *Evaluation of Rehabilitation,*[4] has pointed out that the degree of success of physical rehabilitation measures is usually influenced by the degree of individual motivation and social opportunity. Dr. Karl Menninger has also emphasized the role of adjustment in the extent to which the disabled person cooperates in the treatment process. In his chapter on "Psychiatric Aspects of Physical Disability"[5] in *Psychological Aspects of Physical Disability* he indicates that the disabled person must not only adjust to the physical limitations and changes imposed by his disability but also make a profound psychological adjustment involving his image of himself, his worth, and his place in society. The fact of physical dependency, he points out, must be accepted, not denied or yielded to, by the disabled person before he can make a realistic adjustment to his disability. Dr. Menninger also suggests that this acceptance is the basis for the personal motivation for improvement which is essential to successful rehabilitation.

The role of the special teacher in this area is of great importance. She may well serve as the catalyst for adjustment or maladjustment. As a positive force, she can readily lead the child to self-acceptance. Since the road to accepting oneself is through being accepted by others, the teacher must utilize all the techniques in her power to demonstrate her acceptance of the disabled youngster. She must keep in mind that disability does not change one's fundamental psychological needs, — security, sociability, approval, and the rest. Thus, while there is need for a supportive relationship between the special teacher and the child, emphasis must be placed on utmost participation by the child. The child, in other words, is to be looked upon as an active partner; he then begins to accept himself as a responsible individual with a resulting status position which will allow for action and acceptance of disability. It is well known that self-respect is built only when the individual feels that he has an important role in planning his life and when what he says and how he feels is respected. This is the technique of the rehabilitation counselor and is equally applicable to the special teacher.

The theory of this position is too often in contradiction with reality and nowhere is the dichotomy more clear-cut than in the case of the cerebral palsied. Thus, in a study of the *Vocational, Education, and Recreational Needs of the Cerebral Palsied Adult*[6] which investigated the adjustment of 200 ambulatory cerebral palsied adults in New York City, Selma J. Glick found that three-quarters of the cases interviewed presented a picture of emotional maladjustment. One out of five were judged severe enough to preclude the possibility of job placement. This judgment was based upon the presence of such factors as:

1. Unrealistic attitudes
2. Intense feelings of insecurity
3. Extreme immaturity
4. Excessive fears
5. Strong feelings or inferiority
6. Low frustration tolerance
7. Problems in interpersonal relationships, and
8. Lack of motivation.

Many of these conditions can be prevented or minimized when special teachers have both the opportunity and the vision to serve as positive forces. When individuals such as these come to vocational rehabilitation agencies, little can be accomplished without intensive social casework and even psychiatric help. On the other hand, a skilled and understanding special teacher can prevent many of these personality maladjustive patterns from forming and thus make simpler the later vocational adjustment of the youngsters.

COMMUNITY ACTION

Rehabilitation and special education have one other characteristic in common — they are both investments which the community can ill afford *not* to make. Experience has shown clearly that it is in the enlightened self-interest of the community to make funds available for vocational rehabilitation purposes. It has become increasingly apparent that disability and dependency run hand in hand and that many social problems arise in their wake. As a result, there has been a growing recognition that disability and dependency are largely community problems, and that they require the marshalling of the community's full health, welfare, educational, and employment resources if a solution is to be found.

Dr. Rusk has pointed out that, if something is not done about using the disabled, the chronically ill, and the older age group, by 1980 for every able-bodied worker in America, there will be one physically handicapped, one chronically ill, or beyond the age of 65 on that worker's back. Moreover, the States and the Federal Government are supporting almost one million men and women through the public assistance programs because of disability alone.

It has been demonstrated over and over again that in many instances, it costs substantially less to rehabilitate disabled persons on public assistance rolls than to maintain them on public aid. The taxes that such persons will pay during their lives will repay the Federal Treasury ten dollars for each one dollar invested.

A total approach to the problems of disablement is becoming available through cooperation between public and voluntary agencies. The goal is clearer than at any time in history. It has been well expressed in an address given at the November meeting of the National Society for Crippled Children and Adults by Nelson A. Rockefeller, then Under Secretary of the U. S. Department of Health, Education, and Welfare: "Today, *rehabilitation* . . . the process . . . is linked with *independence* . . . the goal. And in joining together these two symbolic terms, let us hope that some of the universal esteem in which all America holds *independence* will become associated in the public's thinking with *rehabilitation*."

FOOTNOTES

1. Wallace, Helen M.; Siffert, Robert S.; Deaver, George; and Pingitore, Eufelia, *The Homebound Child*, unpublished report of the Bureau for Handicapped Children, New York City Department of Health, and the Institute of Physical Medicine and Rehabilitation, New York University-Bellevue Medical Center.
2. *Report of Study of The Homebound - Programs for Physically Handicapped Homebound Individuals* (Office of Vocational Rehabilitation, Department of Health, Education, and Welfare: Washington, D.C., 1955), p. 113.
3. Buchwald, Edith, *Physical Rehabilitation for Daily Living*, with foreword by Howard A. Rusk (McGraw-Hill: N.Y.C., 1952).
4. Rusk, Howard A., and McCoy, Georgia F., *An Evaluation of Rehabilitation*, Rehabilitation Monograph I (Institute of Physical Medicine and Rehabilitation, New York University-Bellevue Medical Center, N.Y.C., 1953).
5. Garrett, J. R., ed., *Psychological Aspects of Physical Disability* (Office of Vocational Rehabilitation: Washington, D.C., 1952).
6. Glick, Selma J., *Vocational, Education, and Recreational Needs of the Cerebral Palsied Adult* (United Cerebral Palsy of New York City: N.Y.C., 1953).

SUGGESTED READINGS

Barker, Roger G., and others, *Adjustment to Physical Handicap and Illness: A Survey of the Social Psychology of Physique and Disability*, Rev. Bul. No.55. Social Science Research Council, N.Y.C. 1953).

Bauman, Mary K., *Adjustment to Blindness* (State Council for the Blind, Commonwealth of Pennsylvania: September 1954).

DiMichael, S. G., ed., *Vocational Rehabilitation of the Mentally Retarded* (Office of Vocational Rehabilitation, Federal Security Agency: Washington, D.C., 1951).

DiMichael, S. G., "Vocational Rehabilitation", *Social Work Year Book*, 1954, pp. 529-537.

Donahue, W. and D. Dabelstein, eds., *Psychological Diagnosis and Counseling of the Adult Blind* (American Foundation for the Blind: N.Y.C., 1950).

Garrett, James F., ed., *Psychological Aspects of Physical Disability* (Office of Vocational Rehabilitation, Department of Health, Education, and Welfare: Washington, D.C., 1952. Includes bibliography.

Hamilton, Kenneth W., *Counseling the Handicapped in the Rehabilitation Process* (Ronald Press: N.Y.C., 1950). Includes bibliography.

Handicapped Homemakers. Proceedings, Leader's Workshop on Principles of Work Simplification Applied to Problems of Physically Handicapped Homemakers. June 1953 (Univ. of Connecticut: Storrs).

Kessler, Henry H., *Rehabilitation of the Physically Handicapped*, Revised (Columbia University Press: N.Y.C., 1953).

Moore, Marjorie E., and Sanders, Barkev S., "Extent of Total Disability in the United States", *Social Security Bulletin*, November, 1950.

Naional Committee on Sheltered Workshops and Homebound Programs, *Sheltered Workshops and Homebound Programs.* (15 West 16th Street, New York 11, New York, 1952).

National Society for Crippled Children and Adults, *Bulletin on Current Literature.* Monthly bibliography for workers with the handicapped.

Redkey, Henry, *Rehabilitation Centers in the United States* (Office of Vocational Rehabilitation, Department of Health, Education and Welfare: Washington, D.C.).

Rennie, T.A.C., Burling, T. and Woodward, L. E., *Vocational Rehabilitation of Psychiatric Patients* (The Commonwealth Fund: N.Y.C., 1950).

Study of the Homebound: Programs for Physically Handicapped Homebound Individuals: A Report to the Congress (Office of Vocational Rehabilitation: Washington, D.C., February 2, 1955).

Switzer, Mary E., and Rusk, Howard A., *Doing Something for the Disabled*, Public Affairs Pamphlet No. 197 (Public Affairs Committee: N.Y.C., 1953).

United Nations, *Modern Methods of Rehabilitation of the Adult Disabled: Report of a Group Training Course Organized by the United Nations.* (Columbia University Press: New York, 1952).

SECTION II

CHAPTER VIII

ECONOMIC SECURITY BY GEORGE LAVOS

ECONOMIC SECURITY

GEORGE LAVOS

Keystone in the arch through which the exceptional youth passes when school days are finished is his vocational adjustment. The efforts of parents, teachers, and medical and guidance specialists as well as the exceptional youth himself focus with great intensity as the youth, leaving behind his adolescence, takes his first steps toward economic independence. His vocational adjustment is in part a measure of the success of the programs from which he has benefited and in part a return to his family and society for the habilitative steps they have taken on his behalf. Upon the freedom given him in his vocational adjustment he will be able to build his life and establish his own home.

The problems facing the counselor of a youth with some impairment of a sense organ or with a motor limitation are in numerous respects similar to those facing any counselor when he sits down to help a youth plan his future. Primarily the counselor must provide the youth with facts about his proposed goal, assist him in his planning without imposing his own thinking, and when a decision has been reached, aid in plans for attaining the goal. Concurrently with vocational adjustment the counselor must meet problems of emotional, social, leisure-time, and personal import to the youth. Vocational guidance cannot be wholly separated from other guidance needs in an integrated program of adjustment.

The counselor of the disabled will also find men and women coming to his desk who have suffered an impairment after taking on the responsibilities of adulthood. They, too, have their problems of security for their family, winning freedom from dependency, regaining confidence within, and other problems arising from the trauma of becoming impaired after life's patterns of behavior have become set and goals partially attained.

In guidance with the disabled, certain aspects are sharpened, certain decisions more crucial, and plans intensified in detail, for the world in which disabled men and women find themselves is more circumscribed than that of their former classmates, their fellow workers, friends, or brother; the alternative plans, less numerous. The limitations imposed by the impairment, the insecurities that develop through his relations with family, school, and neighborhood as well as in the world of work heighten the need for a firm footing beneath each step taken by such a person.

In his guidance program the counselor must channel several significant currents. Not only must he bring together an ordered array of facts about the individual and his goals, counsel for any needed attitudinal changes in the person himself, in his immmediate family, and secure needed services and appliances as well as training in their use, but he must be an advocate of programs for the disabled in his community, in industry, in research, and in government.

Today the breadth of the program for the adjustment of the disabled is so great that it cannot be carried on by one counselor alone. Doctors, appliance fitters, physical therapists, recreation specialists, social workers, psychologists, vocational counselors, job analysts, placement workers, and employers join talents in the program. The counselor, in many such programs, acts as the catalyst in the process. The approach, in the very core, is becoming a team attack. Although not all disabled need all services, and in some cases only a limited service is needed to set the individual on his way, in others an integrated program must be individually developed.

Evaluation and Counseling

In guidance with the disabled there are numerous functions which presuppose, on the part of the team member, definite professional preparation as well as a wide range of work experiences and personal attributes. In one respect he must come to terms with himself as in no other guidance work, and that adjustment lies in his philosophy about the status of disabled in the American Society of the 1950's. Actual attitudes of workers for the disabled and the general public from which such workers come are characterized more by their diversity than their coherence and by the contrast between verbalized statements and inner reactions.[1]

The member needs an insight into the emotional and social life of the disabled and tolerance for the many ways in which people in general behave and the disabled in particular insofar as their behavior may be out of the ordinary. Members of the team face one more demand. Disabled youth and adults are not a class unto themselves. In spite of the fact that they occupy a devalued status or, in some respects, a privileged one, each is an individual. Guidance with each individual, regardless how each is put into a class in a review such as this, is case work in its most intense techniques.

Evaluation. In the evaluation of the disabled, looking forward toward their habilitation into a working membership in the community, a wide range of services is called upon. There is a medical survey for treatment, surgery, appliances, and subsequent therapy ranging from physical exercises to strengthen muscles to auditory training to establish sound perception. There is a re-evaluation after all restoration is completed to determine capacities to sit, stand, walk, hear sounds of improperly operating machinery, sense depth visually, put forth sustained exertion, and so forth.[2–4] This evaluation sets the limits of physical versatility and highlights the remaining usable capacities.

A similar profile of abilities and disabilities is needed for psycho-social characteristics. Intelligence, educational level, talents, interests, attitude toward impairment, personal and family resources are among these. The goal is an appraisal of resources upon which a vocational plan may be built. The doctor, social worker, therapist, and psychologist must present their appraisals in language the job-placement import of which is clear to counselors, placement workers, and plant supervisors. For part of this appraisal, the physical capacity analysis as developed by the U.S. Employment Service and made specific in several industries is available.[5,6] The role of the psychologist and the social worker has been outlined, with specific suggestions for each area of impairment.[17]

Emotional Problems. Counseling, especially in the beginning stages of vocational adjustment, cannot escape the emotional problems a disabled person may have. He brings with him all the drives and barriers to their fulfillment that all people have. He comes with problems that arise from his particular disability. These problems, possibly, unverbalized, possibly easily expressed, come out of his reactions to himself as he learns that he cannot cope with all physical situations in which he would like to take part and as he sees himself as others do.

The normal childhood dependency was often heightened, possibly by numerous hospitalizations, or a special school with its unique habilitative steps, and by attitudes of chums, classmates, neighbors, and family friends. Although such forces may have given him a somewhat privileged position as a young child, as he grew he absorbed the physical and social goals of his immediate world. As he applied the yardsticks of physical versatility in ball games, hikes, and movie attendance, and of attractiveness in his social life, he found certain limitations in himself. At the same time he sought to measure up to the yardsticks of his world, he may have found himself the object of veering affection as parents shifted from oversolicitude to rejection, and brothers and sisters became resentful of him in a home in which he may have been given special status. In addition to these special liabilities, he had his share of soul-searching so common as adolescents become youths.

As he grew, these traits may have taken definite form. In terms of outward personality, he may be oversensitive, withdrawn, and self-conscious or their opposites. Inwardly he may be beset with feelings of dependency brought about by the many services he received and the restricted range of his activities; by feelings of doubt about his abilities because of the converse of the age-old association of a sound mind in a sound body; and by desires to appear like other people so often reiterated in inspirational talks.

In those who suffer a loss as an adult, the counselor will find no less problems, for such a person brings to his disablement all of the attitudes and beliefs of the physically normal without the years for reconciliation. In his own eyes, such a person has suffered a serious devaluation.

In spite of this generalized pattern, the counselor will find no fixed constellation of emotional problems. In the first place, and a point to remember, a substantial number, estimated at 35% to 40%, have no evidence of maladjustment. The maladjustments of the physically disabled are not different in kind from those who are not disabled. The type of disability has no relation to the type of adjustment attempted by the disabled except in a few extreme cases involving special ways of living. There is no personality type among the disabled, for their traits parallel those of the unimpaired.[8]

Experience Limitations. Disabled youths sometimes do not obtain the variety of experiences that their brothers and sisters do. Extended periods of hospitalization, residence at a school with its necessary rules of group conduct, limited travel capacities, and possible exclusion from youth groups tend to reduce the range of experiences, whether it be in sports, window shopping, social circles, or day-by-day travel. Not only is the physical environment possibly restricted, but contacts with other people on a casual basis are reduced. More particularly from a vocational viewpoint, the opportunities for part-time work are reduced. As a consequence, the youth has a limited range of experiences in which to try himself out and learn the give-and-take of every-day social intercourse.

Because of a serious motor or sensory limitation, he often may have been praised for even simple accomplishments. The untutored friend of the family or the teacher happy in seeing an accomplishment may praise an act or project beyond its merits. As an outgrowth of this, the youth may have unrealistic ideas about his capacities.

In tracing some of the pitfalls in the path of a disabled person, it can be seen that none is unique to him. His path is beset with more because of his physical limitations and the reactions of others as well as his own reactions to the two. To some extent the pitfalls are unavoidable. Although there are certain things he cannot do, he still must live in a world geared for those who can. On the other hand, some of the pitfalls become wider because of his own personality reactions to himself and deeper because of what others do to or for him.

Occupational Opportunities

The counselor cannot plunge from his evaluations and personal counseling into vocational training without facts about occupations. These facts control the directions the guidance takes because the vocational adjustment of the disabled is realized in the world of competitive jobs.

Job Analysis. Fortunately for the counselor, the growth of guidance in schools and colleges, the nation-wide expansion of a public employment service, defence manpower mobilization and demobilization as well as industrial expansion since 1945 have given impetus to occupational analysis. Not limited to a description of what the worker does and the tools he uses, it relates jobs into families, bringing together facts about industries and businesses in which jobs are. Trends in the future of the occupation and the supply of personnel for it are included.

One immediate source of such information is the state employment services which sometimes publish pamphlets on jobs outlining duties, working conditions, opportunities for promotion, and related topics.[9] Commercial material is also available.[10] This information must be evaluated, interpreted, and imparted to the counselee. Occupational information is a core extending through all vocational adjustment of the disabled to placement and follow-up.

A special feature in the growth of such analyses has been the increasing attention to physical demands in the performance of the duties of the job and the conditions under which the job is carried on. Job analysis, as developed by the public employment service, covers the need for walking, crouching, color vision, and other physical demands in jobs, as well as the physical conditions under which the job is carried on, — inside or outside, in damp surroundings, in cooperation with others, and so forth. Over 25 items are included in each aspect, and a specific review of special conditions is called for.[11] Other techniques are available, some more detailed in terms of safety to self and others or specialized for a particular class of work.[12,13] Such analyses are used in some government and private industry jobs. Training and placement plans can become more focalized, since this description of physical demands and conditions can be matched to the companion description of the physical capacities of the disabled job applicant.

Job analysis in the limited sense of physical demands and conditions as well as in a broader sense of difficulty analysis, time and motion studies is a possible approach to placement with such advantages as providing a tool to analyze any industry, a common specific terminology for doctor, job analyst, and placement worker. Analyses also provide a method by which jobs can be studied to determine whether the disability or some other factor caused a failure in a placement of a disabled worker.[15]

The first known attempt to analyze jobs from the view point of placement possibilities of the disabled was a pilot study in Minneapolis, in 1930.[16] Twenty-eight classifications of disabilities were used in analyzing over 20,000 jobs. A California study used the same classification with a few changes.[17] In both reports only summary tables of the number of feasible and conditionally feasible jobs for each type of disability were published. The job analysis technique used in these studies did not specifically define the disability or the working conditions; for example, 'partial vision' was used rather than specific levels of acuity, peripheral vision, depth perception, sustained acuity. The job itself was not described in terms of its physical demands; a generalized type of disability was applied to the performance of the job, and differentiation among various disabilities established.

The accompanying table presents some of the theoretical placement possibilities.[18]

TABLE I   PERCENTAGE OF THEORETICAL JOB POSSIBILITIES IN DIFFERENT AREAS OF WORK FOR SELECTED DISABILITIES.

Disability	Office Jobs	Commercial Jobs	Factory Jobs	Mechanical Jobs	Miscellaneous Jobs
Arm, right off above elbow	19	22	5	4	12
Cardiac	95	79	50	44	52
Partial deafness	61	47	90	71	55
Leg, right disabled	49	32	18	13	12
Pulmonary tuberculosis	93	75	34	42	53
Blind	0.5	1	0.6	0.4	0.2

Workers with a given disability are not handicapped equally in all areas of work, and all disabled are not equally handicapped. Those with right leg disabilities, for example, have twice as many office job possibilities as factory, nearly three times as many commerical as mechanical. The least limiting are cardiac and tuberculous disabilities; the most, blindness.

Theoretical possibilities can be enlarged in two technical ways. Jobs can be re-engineered. A right hand control, for example, can be shifted for use by a leg; a special jig can be made to hold a part for a missing hand. On the other hand, the worker can be trained to circumvent his disability in some specific way. For example, in training a blind worker to operate a stale baked-goods grinder, he can be taught to use the palm of his hand to force the material down the hopper with his fingers extending out over the edge.[19] In practice these two possibilities are used in times of tight labor markets or under other special circumstances.

Job Lists. In the pioneering efforts of vocational specialists, lists based on successful placements, not on job analyses, played a helpful role. While it was recognized in an early report that job lists, arranged by specific disability, were a static approach, the Federal Board of Control for Vocational Education, under which vocational rehabilitation once functioned, issued a lengthy listing.[20] Other reports followed, one in New York and one in California. For example, the California survey listed 207 office workers with such disabilities as hand, arm, leg, legs, partial vision, partial hearing, and so forth. Such lists were inadequate in their description of the disability, and they stereotyped vocational adjustment measures by limiting efforts only to areas of past placement, failing to recognize the range of abilities among those whose only common characteristic is a disability. Such a list was of limited usefulness in an industry in which no placements had already been made or under changing job conditions. The advantages included the fact that such lists were morale builders in showing the range of jobs a given disabled person could actually hold and in impressing laymen with the proved occupational versatility of a given disabled group. They may also be suggestive of related jobs in which disabled may be successful.

Occupational information whether in the form of lists, analyses, or possibilities for re-engineering or re-training cannot be concluded without placing it in its setting in guidance. On the one hand, the psychological assets of the counselee as well as local training opportunities must be meshed with such information; and on the other, the interest of employers in actual job analyses will govern the extent such techniques can be used. Psycho-social and economic factors probably play a more dominant role in actual placement than feasible job opportunities.

TRAINING

The individuality of each disabled person is recognized in the diversity of training opportunities given. No employment colonies have developed, and segregated training exists for only highly specific purposes. The range of physical capacities remaining after impairment, the profile of abilities, the depth of motivation and interest, the adaptability of personality, and the geographical distribution of the disabled require the use of training resources developed for all American youth. On the other hand, some special training centers exist, either dating from the time when such training was a distinct vocational asset because the able-bodied youth was untrained, or developed to meet a special need as in graduated work-exercise periods for convalescent cases.

Vocational Training. Vocational training is best demonstrated in the many opportunities offered under the Federal-state vocational rehabilitation programs, although such programs are much broader in scope including physical restoration, securing appliances, counseling, placement and follow up. Training has been offered in trade schools or colleges, on the job as an apprentice or more informally as a learner, through tutoring programs, and by correspondence. The program is selected in terms of the counselee's abilities, plans, work possibilities, and local resources. If the disabled are taken as a group, then training has been offered in every area of work represented by the thousands of entry jobs in the United States.

Specialized training has been developed for some groups of disabled. These are either residential schools or centers in large metropolitan areas. Virtually every residential school for the deaf or the blind has some form of training, although in practice this training is more often prevocational experiences rather than trade education. For the tuberculous, there are a few workshops or training centers which often combine increasing work tolerance with training and, in some instances, paid work. For the orthopedic and others there are workshops which provide training as well as employment, the most extensive of which are the Goodwill Industries.

Special Training Services. As the counselor moves toward the beginning of vocational training, he may have to develop several preliminary services of an instructional nature. His evaluation of the physical capacities of the individual may have revealed a need for training in meeting the numerous demands of daily living — dressing, holding the telephone, etc. A convalescent may need graduated work tolerance. If the individual had an appliance fitted, such as a hearing aid or an artificial limb, he most likely will need training in its use and care.[21,22]

Another group of preparatory training services includes those of exploratory experiences with power and hand tools as well as other types of work activity in a well-rounded program. In addition to the immediate value of uncovering some vocational interest, other values come out of such experiences. They can be used in conjunction with physical therapy measures, training in the use of appliances, and other aids to meeting the demands of daily living, and as a psychologically supportive technique for self-confidence.

Higher Education. A limited number of special aids are available for facilitating higher education for the disabled. For blind college students, some states provide readers, and there are also scholarship funds. Since the 1860's Gallaudet College, supported by the Federal government, has been operated for the deaf. Other disabled attend college as do the thousands of American young men and women, a few through the aid of vocational rehabilitation if their objective is primarily vocational in nature. Special problems in note taking, travel between buildings and within old buildings, sustained exertion, and so forth exist. Careful vocational planning is needed for college training as for any other kind of training.[23]

Training for job placement occupies a central place in the vocational adjustment of the disabled. It is a strong lever to pry open the occupational world.

Training not geared to abilities, capacities, and limitations is wasteful of talent; not in keeping with existing job opportunities, unrealistic; not thorough and comprehensive, misleading. The whole of general education, physical restoration, furnishing of appliances, and evaluation can bottleneck in ineffectual training.

PLACEMENT

Placement on a job is the conclusion to effective training. Training can be capitalized to its maximum values when placement is in line with such training. Placement, even in line with training, requires selective techniques for a variety of reasons. The applicant's disability may make employer acceptance of him difficult because of his appearance, imputed lack of ability commonly associated with a disability, or lack of experience in an entry job indicating he has not yet been tested in the world of work. The disability may be aggravated by improper working conditions or job demands. The disabled worker may be placed in a position in which he is a hazard to himself or others. If the applicant is an adult who was recently disabled, he may need a modified or changed job. The applicant may need adjustment services before he is ready for employment requiring referral elsewhere as a first step.

Behind these reasons for selective placement are the policies and beliefs of employers. One aspect of the policies was succinctly outlined by the Task Force on the Handicapped of the Office of Defense Mobilization in 1952:

When physical standards were drawn up during the first and second decades of this century, they were influenced by the anatomical concept of medicine which was then in sway. Competence was measured in terms of anatomical perfection. A man was either fit or unfit for work, depending on whether he was anatomically whole. It was all or none.

Undoubtedly the rise of workmen's compensation during the first decades of this century also influenced the policy of industrial medical examiners in establishing physical standards. As job subdivision reduced the need for physical versatility, as a functional concept gained prominence in medicine, and as modifications in compensation laws were made, the standard of a "whole man" for every job was changed especially during war stress.

The beliefs of employers are focused on their economic and social objectives. Employers are primarily producers of goods which must be sold profitably, in part by safeguarding investments and reducing manufacturing costs. In a secondary way they seek to enhance the community status of the company as well as to maintain harmonious relations among employees. To carry out these objectives employers must "attract a group of workers competent in production and capable of integration with their present team."[24]

In practice these policies and beliefs have been voiced in various objections to hiring disabled:

Increased accident risk to self and others; lessened productivity due to interference of the disability in the performance of the job and due to the absences and lower-than-normal physical stamina; limited versatility in carrying on different kinds of work because of the defect; increased insurance risks because of ill-health and because of the accident proneness of the disabled; increased compensation costs because of the demand that the combined effects of two or more injuries be compensated; past experience with the handicapped has proved them unsatisfactory workers and so all disabled applicants will prove unsatisfactory on the job; fear that the employer will show undue consideration and concern for the disabled worker and so reduce shop morale; and active dislike for the presence of a deformity or other visible defect on the part of fellow workers and employers.[25]

Beneath these voiced attitudes of employers are a variety of factors. Some of the objections may have their bases in ingrained emotions — the dislike of asymmetry; the inability to feel empathetic toward the deformed; the association of a deformity and an 'evil spirit.' Other objections are centered in maudlin pity, — fear of permitting the disabled worker to work on the employer's sympathies and so reduce morale; fear of permitting the disabled to carry out some function which may *appear* difficult or exploitive. A few have their source in facts, some true and some not, — increased accident proneness, extra compensation costs, costs of special job analyses and altered machines. Still others are the result of stereotyped thinking, — one inefficient disabled worker characterizes all disabled who have a smiliar disability. And yet others come out of common misconceptions, — an impaired body contains a peculiar personality, the intelligence of such a person is equally impaired.[26]

Employers who have hired disabled can usually match each objection with a contrary value. The studies of disabled workers on their jobs[27] contain answers to some of the objectives as do the facts about workmen's compensation and other laws and social welfare programs.[28]

To help the disabled secure employment, several programs have been developed. Two are nation-wide in their services. The first is the vocational rehabilitation service in each state. Placement in this program is part of the total case work given each counselee. Working with those who do not need the intense services of vocational rehabilitation as well as cooperatively with rehabilitation are the publicly supported state employment services.

In addition to these two nation-wide services, there are other public agencies which work with special groups. The various commissions for the blind provide specialized programs paralleling the work of vocational rehabilitation with other groups. Blind placement workers in these programs demonstrate the practicality of placing blind on the job by trying it out themselves. A few states, Michigan, Minnesota, and North Carolina, have special agencies for the deaf. Privately supported agencies for the disabled, such as the associations for the hard of hearing and the tuberculous, often include placement. Other community agencies and service clubs assist as well.

Placement for the disabled does not end with job location and referral to it. In-plant programs have been developed, especially during the war and as a part of the work for the returned disabled veteran. Several guides have been distributed as well as motion pictures for instruction of supervisors.[29-31] The in-plant program is premised on job analysis and pre-employment examinations designed to analyze the physical capacities of the applicant. After dovetailing job demands and the prospective worker's physical, psychological, and trained capacities, he is assigned a job. Transfers to other jobs or to other departments must be based on the dovetailed capacities and demands, usually only by approval of the personnel office.

Key-figure in the in-plant program is the foreman. He must not only instruct the disabled worker and properly introduce him to his fellow workers but as well create an atmosphere in which the disabled worker actually carries his share of the work. He must avoid excessive sympathy or overt rejection, the first of which would be detrimental to shop morale, and the second, to that of the disabled worker himself. Follow up by the personnel office is recommended.

In plants without special programs, close personal follow up by the placement agent is recommended for all disabled groups, especially those with severe disabilities and those with aggravatable defects. In follow up, misunderstandings can be straightened out, specific instructions given, especially in the case of the deaf whose communication problems may cause difficulties in the beginning days of work.

DISABLED AT WORK

Impelled by the need to present facts about the actual work efficiency of disabled to ascertain the bases for the objections to hiring disabled as well as to point the way to improved preparation and placement of disabled, public agencies, employers, colleges in research programs, and others have carried on studies to analyze the capacities of disabled workers. Such studies have provided a great deal of information to various specialists as well as the public.

Job Variety. Not too long ago, if not still today, an untutored layman's view of the work capacities of disabled might encompass only a few old-time standbys, such as chair caning for the blind, watch repair for the orthopedic, and printing for the deaf. In 1925, within five years of the start of the Federal program of aid to the states conducting vocational rehabilitation, the Federal agency carried on a study showing that over 6,000 disabled were engaged in 628 different jobs and that workers with specific disabilities were found in a variety of jobs; for example, over 200 jobs were listed for those with disabilities of both legs.[32] During the depression years of 1933-34 a study of deaf and hard of hearing revealed that such workers were in over 250 general occupational groups with many more specific jobs represented[33]. Disabled of all types were employed in nearly 300 different jobs in another survey of the depression years.[34] Much lengthier lists can be tabulated from data in the latest study, that of 11,000 seriously impaired workers in numerous industries.[35]

In spite of the very static approach inherent in defining a disability solely in terms of a part of the body, versatility among disabled workers as a group was demonstrated. The strength of individual characteristics as determinants for vocational versatility was indicated in the variety of jobs held.

Work Records. Going deeper into the occupational efficiency of the disabled, a number of studies have anlayzed the on-the-job efficiency of such workers. In 1929 the first study was made of the work records of disabled workers, and other studies followed in 1934, 1935, and 1938. The war gave impetus to this type of study; investigations came in rapid order, sometimes several in one year — 1943, 1944, 1945, 1946, and 1948. Most of these studies were summarized in two reports.[36-38]

The studies coming from a number of industries cover a wide range of disabilities ranging from hernias and varicose veins to epileptic conditions and including hearing, orthopedic, and other defects. The range in itself indicates that those considered disabled in the eyes of industrial medical examiners and employers are not always the same as those so considered by the lay public or specialists in the field of the disabled. The employment definition is more inclusive and the critical level at a higher point. Aspects of the on-the-job efficiency of the disabled analyzed in the studies include ratings of work quality, measures of production, injury rates, absenteeism, job versatility, turnover, advancement, insurance coverage, and personality-morale factors. The findings of the latest study, that of the U.S. Bureau of Labor Statistics,[39] which is based on the greatest number of workers in any report, will be cited, although only a limited number of items were used as measures of the work performance of disabled. Notes of special circumstances revealed in other studies will be added.

Eighteen thousand unimpaired workers were matched with 11,000 disabled workers who required special job placement considerations. All minor disabilities were excluded. The two groups were exposed to the same job incentives and the same industrial hazards.

Summary findings were: The disabled were absent .4 more days per 100 working days than the unimpaired. The two groups were identical in their accident rates. In terms of disabling injuries, the disabled had .6 less such injuries per 1,00,000 hours of work; .01 less days lost per 100 working days; and when out for the injury, .4 less days absent. The disabled exceeded the quantitatively determined output of the unimpaired by 1%. For each disabled worker there were 3.6 quits compared with 2.6 quits. All these facts were based on quantitative data taken directly from the records of cooperating firms. They contain no element of subjective valuation or selection on the part of foremen or supervisors or the investigators themselves. Similarity between the two groups of workers is emphasized.

Not all studies point to identical conclusions. Findings adverse to the disabled in one respect can be contrasted with favorable findings in another, often within the same study. In one study, 10% more disabled were absent for illness than unimpaired, but an identical percentage were less absent for unexcused reasons.[40] In another study, while the disabled and matched unimpaired had the same average number of injuries, the disabled had significantly a lesser number who sustained injuries.[41]

Because selective placement and in-plant procedures emphasize meshing remaining abilities and job demands, question may be raised about job versatility. Although no worker has unlimited versatility, the disabled, it is claimed, cannot shift jobs to meet production demands or promotional sequences. In a California study, three quarters of the group surveyed had equal promotional opportunities.[42] In a study of the deaf approximately three-eighths had difficulty in job shifts or starting unfamiliar jobs.[43] In a study of the orthopedic, restrictions in job performance did not arise from the location or degree of disability but from the age of the worker. Job changes after industrial accidents were required more frequently among those with hand-arm disabilities than leg disabilities.[43] The two latter studies were based on only a limited number of workers. Brighouse, with over 500 disabled workers, showed that, while fewer disabled were proportionately in supervisory or other responsible work, they took less time to move through the lower hourly-rated levels of promotion.[44] The disabled shifted jobs about as frequently as the unimpaired. but the facts are not clear as to the cause of the shift. While the disabled can be shifted, specific groups have unique problems with respect to job versatility.

Values apart from direct on the job efficiency come from the employment of disabled. Conscientiousness, loyalty, willingness to accept 'dead-end' positions, and less turnover for personal reasons characterize such workers. While data suggest that disabled workers have more internal emotional disturbances, they present such on-the-job efficiency that they were rated the same as matched unimpaired and significantly more in production quantity.[45] Compensatory efforts produce apparently satisfactory workmen.

As a general conclusion the fallacy of maintaining a single standard of physical perfection in workers is evident. While it is true that the disabled upon whom all these studies were based had qualities which impressed prospective employers with their future worth, thus constituting a selected group of disabled workers, and while it was also true that the unimpaired prospective worker was not scrutinized so carefully, the studies do reiterate the employability of such workers when properly placed. Inherent in the words "properly placed" are a great number of services which, if they have any values, should produce an acceptable worker. By the same token if the unimpaired worker received as much service, he may become a better worker than he is.

Civil Service. Although publicly supported programs sought to promote the employment of the disabled after the first World War, Federal civil service opened its doors during the second war and has held them open since. In 1950 the Federal Civil Service Commission stated "a program for selective placement of physically impaired persons . . . has been in effect eight years."[46] Dropping the all or none medical standard of prewar days resulted in the placement of 12,000 disabled between 1942 and 1944 and 37,700 veterans and 50,250 civilian disabled between 1944 and 1950. In 1948 a new law stabilized Federal policies by prohibiting discrimination if the disabled worker could perform the duties.[47] This policy change has resulted in continuing job analysis in classes of worker shortages, modifications in testing procedures (such as voice-transcribed examinations for the blind, large answer spaces for the arm disabled), modified medical examination forms although standards of job efficiency and retention have not been changed.

While no recent studies of the civil-service placement of disabled on a state or city level have been made, two studies, one in 1935 and the other in 1942, indicated that disabled had found a place for themselves, constituting for example nearly 6% of the state employees in California. While procedures at that time did not provide for dovetailing worker capacities and job demands, some adjustments were evident. For example, examining procedures were modified as they later were in Federal service. A few jobs, chiefly in special agencies, were reserved for disabled, and two jurisdictions allotted all feasible elevator operator jobs to orthopedic and dictaphone operation to the blind. Citations of on-the-job efficiency were made.[48]

Industrial Security Programs and the Disabled. It is almost a paradox that in industry, legislative and voluntary security programs, initiated and carried on to protect the workers, should injure the job security of disabled workers. Such has been the case in several programs, foremost of which is workmen's compensation. Minimum wage regulations, industrial homework limitations, and group insurance programs for health, accident, and death have also had repercussions in the vocational adjustment of the disabled. Because of feared or actual losses incurred by employers when one or another of these programs was carried out, the employer has applied keener standards of selection and retention resulting in curtailment of job openings for disabled.[49]

Workmen's compensation laws, introduced in the opening decades of this century, counterbalanced the unsure and costly ways of securing compensation by court action of earlier years. Because these compensation laws required automatic compensation for injuries on the job, employers sought to reduce injuries in every possible way. Safety programs were introduced. Medical standards were established to prevent hiring those with quiescent diseases or actual disabilities because court decisions had placed responsibility on the employer for payment of the cumulative effect of the pre-existing condition and the immediate industrial injury.

Several plans have been proposed to ameliorate this situation. The simplest plan was to grant the prospective worker the right to waive any compensation benefits. Another method limited the benefits to the effects of the last injury. Both negate the basic compensation philosophy.

Recognizing that the combined effect of two injuries may result in total disability, such as the loss of the remaining eye in a one-eyed worker, although the loss of each eye alone is considered partial, some laws have tried to apportion the costs. After determining the total incapacity and the incapacity resulting from the second injury, the latter was subtracted from the former, the difference being the employer's liability. In such a case he was responsible for more than he normally would be because a total disability is compensated for at a rate in excess of double that of a partial disability and the employee received less than his disablement warranted. Qualifying conditions were incorporated in some laws. However, in any situation in which there was likely to be an increased cost to a producer, he took advantage of his position and refused to hire disabled.

Later more equitable provisions were made. These are now known as second-injury funds. Under such funds, the employer is responsible for the second injury while payment for the difference between the compensation he paid and the total amount due is taken from the fund. Nearly every state with such a fund limits payment to total disability cases alone. Second-injury funds, raised with a minimum cost to industry and sometimes state subsidized, have grown in the past fifteen years. In 1939 there were 17 jurisdictions with such provision; in 1954, 47, including possessions and territories of the United States. Six states still lacked such funds.[50,51]

Mingled with the fear about responsibility for pre-existing disabilities is the fear that rates would be increased upon hiring disabled either by insurance company regulation or because of the imputed accident proneness of disabled workers. Immediate characteristics of employees do not determine rates inasmuch as rates are set by the industrial classification of the employment in question and the past accident experience. In some jurisdictions, the state superintendents of insurance, using standard forms, must approve the rates as "reasonable, adequate, and just" and in some cases "not excessive" or "not discriminatory." In two states specific prohibitions exist in the law against discrimination in rates because of the presence of disabled workers. Two associations of casualty insurance companies have made declarations clarifying the basis upon which rates are determined.[52]

As for the injury rates of the disabled, facts based on follow up studies have already been given. The Association of Casualty and Surety Companies, representing many insurance carriers, clearly indicated that the record of disabled "is as good as their able-bodied fellow workers . . . and is often superior" when they are properly placed.[53] In fact, the Association provided a guide for employing disabled.[54] In the Bureau of Labor Statistics study already cited, only one instance could be found in which the second injury was traceable to the pre-existing disability. And in that case the foreman had transferred the worker to a job from which he had been prohibited in his selective placement analysis.

As a general consequence of the trend toward second-injury funds and studies of the injury rates of disabled, compensation does not constitute an unanswerable objection to the employment of disabled as it once did. The present second-injury funds have certain limitations; i.e., total disability restrictions, restrictions on the origin of the pre-existing defect including only impairments arising from earlier employment, and neglecting those from disease and public accident. Cardiac conditions, occupational diseases, and other disorders may be excluded. As the population ages and the public-accident toll rises, these limitations will become more pressing.

Within industry there are several other security programs, some voluntary and some compulsory, which make more critical the scrutiny each employer gives his payroll. As it has become necessary to pay minimum wages, insurance, and pension premiums, he evaluates employees more carefully, for workers cost not only a daily wage but overhead as well.

Objection has been raised to hiring disabled because of the possibility that such workers may make untoward claims for health, accident and life coverage in group insurance. While the employer may not have to pay the claim directly, the insurance company does and its problem may be reflected in the employer's attitude. There is some evidence that the life expectancy of disabled granted life insurance is not as great as that of the unimpaired.[55] As for illness, the data are not conclusive. The Bureau of Labor Statistics study showed that disabled and unimpaired had equal absence rates for illness and quitting rates for health reasons. In another study it was found that 12% more disabled filed claims for illness, accident, and death than unimpaired, although the proportions of the two under the coverage was the same. The amount per claim was also greater. Further studies are needed.

Concession Employment. A very small number of disabled are provided for in jobs especially assigned them. Under the Randolph-Sheppard Act of Congress, vending stands in public buildings are given the blind. In some public and private agencies for the disabled, qualified impaired are sought for special needs such as the blind placement worker already mentioned and the deaf teacher of special classes.

There are a few industrial plans owned by disabled which seek to hire disabled.[56] War-time plans for action on a wide front in industries which have no special interest in the disabled have been reviewed in periodicals and the efforts of the Ford Motor Company to hire disabled in excess of their ratio in the general population are also known.[57] Other instances are the re-employment practices of many industries in rehiring workers disabled in their employ and in making special efforts to place disabled veterans.

Although the disabled have a certain degree of preference in being hired for these jobs, retention is based on efficiency. The number of such positions is extremely small.[58]

The Severely Disabled. While placement is crucial for all disabled, there are a certain number who are on the margin between competitive placement and sheltered employment. Although no census reports are at hand, various estimates have been made. Of the estimated 2,000,000 disabled needing habilitation into employment, 400,000 are severely disabled. Of these, half can be trained for placement in competitive industry, 40,000 would need custodial care, and the remainder, 160,000, cannot take the step from vocational training into competitive placement and need an opportunity for employment under sheltered conditions.[59]

While there are several programs for these severely disabled, only one is fairly extensive, that of sheltered workshops; yet it is limited to the metropolitan areas alone. Most of the shops are lay supported. Some have a public subsidy, especially those for the blind. Several states, such as New York, Massachusetts, and others, and the Federal government are required by law to purchase articles from such shops. Earnings from Federal purchasing during the war totaled over $5,000,000 for 2,500 blind workers.[60] In 1953 among the 104 Goodwill Industries 22,241 workers shared $13,421,048 in earnings. Some of these were self supporting.

Services for severely disabled in sheltered workshops may be expanded when recent changes in the basic vocational rehabilitation law are carried out. Although the founding law did not extend services to those who could not enter competitive employment, the 1954 amendments strengthened the provisions in the 1943 law to include those "homebound or otherwise whose rehabilitation is feasible through sheltered workshops or other rehabilitative treatment."

Among the problems facing such shops is that of meeting minimum wage laws. To aid in this problem a special workshop committee has advised the Federal administrator for over a decade. Minimum wage standards are met, and there is consequently no undercutting of industrial wages on subcontract work which would antagonize unions. Expanding the types of work performed and the sale of products are other problems.

Employment of disabled within their own homes is another type of sheltered employment. Home businesses have been established by resourceful disabled or developed by some workshops or private societies. In addition, industry has used homework as a means of reducing overhead costs, and regulations have been developed to control such work. Since control measures consisted largely of the elimination of home industries, exemptions were granted disabled.

In yet another way remunerative employment for the severely disabled can be maintained and, in this instance, the employment is performed within competitive industry. Wage payments given disabled are sometimes less than the standard wage for the job. In a California study, for example, 7% of the disabled did not receive a standard wage for the work they carried out.[61] Minimum wage laws make certain exemptions from such wages for the disabled. These exemptions are closely scrutinized. Minimum wage regulations affect the placement of disabled only if the minimum wage is the current wage. In an inflationary period current wages are often far above minimum wages, and wages below the standard wage may still be offered without violation of the law. A number of disabled may be employed at substandard wages.

Minimum wage regulations apply only to certain industries and under specified conditions. The mere presence of a severe disability is not grounds for an exemption from the minimum wage.[62,63]

At the core of the needs of the severely disabled is the extension of employment without the onus of charity and the need to live in one of the few areas with existing facilities. Among immediate possibilities in addition to the opening of more sheltered workshops, are increased self employment in businesses and the development of cooperatives for purchasing raw materials and sale of products in home industries. The exemption of such potential workers from measures designed to provide minimum needs is not in keeping with American principles.

NEW HORIZONS

Although there is virtually no history to be written of efforts toward vocational adjustment for disabled before 1900 except training in residential schools for deaf and blind, the pace of expansion has been accelerating rapidly since. Before the first World War there were a few private efforts. Civilian vocational rehabilitation, the strongest single force in vocational adjustment, followed that war. Growth continued in the generation between wars, and in the second world conflict the disabled demonstrated their work capacity. This growth has come about, not through compulsory employment laws as has been proposed in duplication of certain European efforts, but through voluntary and educative processes.

During and since World War II a nation-wide public and employer education program has grown from a week's observance in 1945 to a campaign carried on 52 weeks a year in 1954. This program, known as National Employ the Physically Handicapped Week and supported by community, state, and Federal committees, retells through many ways, even through a cancellation slogan on billions of envelopes, the message about the employment possibilities of the disabled.[64] Insurance companies such as the Association already cited, the Liberty Mutual Insurance Company with its two rehabilitation centers, and others, as well as the National Association of Manufacturers in several publications have joined hands with the American Federation of Labor in its support of selective placement and the United Mine Workers of America in its rehabilitation of disabled miners. Matching this is the Federal Office of Vocational Rehabilitation now empowered to expand facilities to rehabilitate 200,000 annually in the immediate future. Training of specialists and research is also on the rehabilitation agenda. Private societies, such as the National Society for Crippled Children, have expanded efforts. To give one instance, the Society has furthered the growth of rehabilitation centers. Such centers, applying the basic principles of guidance in psychological and physical evaluation, remedial steps, social service, vocational training, and placement adjustment, are dynamic in intent. Emphasizing the team approach, they will aid in resolving problems of the severely disabled. Although only a few are now in operation, notably in New York and Virginia, a minimum of 18 is recommended, located strategically through-out the country.[65]

Before the two wars and during them, as well as since the last war, the disabled themselves have taken many steps forward. They have many alumni, hospital, and local organizations, some knit together on a state and even national level. Recreation, promotion of their own social and economic interests, orientation to the problems of living with an impairment charac-terize their efforts. One of these, the American Federation of Physically Handicapped started the National Employ the Physically Handicapped Week. Another solved the life insurance problem over 50 years ago by creating its own company, the National Fraternal Society of the Deaf. Dis-abled have been called upon to take part in programs of specialists in their education and vocational adjustment thus becoming a force on a professional level.

The end result of these steps is the establishment of the disabled person as a productive member of his family and community. These workers are a reservoir for industrial production and national defense. They are a source of governmental support, for $10 million in income tax will be paid annually by those rehabilitated in one year alone. With the remaining $104 million earned, these workers will keep industry and business moving forward. And there are thousands more who achieve their own vocational adjustment each year and add to the wealth of the nation. As they win their economic secur-ity they blend into the mass of Americans managing their own personal welfare, raising their famililies, and supporting the churches of their choice.

FOOTNOTES

1. Barker, R., et al., *Adjustment to Physical Handicap and Illness*, Social Science Re-search Council Bulletin 55, 1953, pp. 67-86, 193-7, 273-8.
2. Bridges, C., *Job Placement of the Physically Handicapped* (McGraw Hill: N.Y.C., 1946).
3. Deaver, G., and Brown, M., *Physical Demands of Daily Life* (Institute for the Crippled and Disabled: N.Y.C.).
4. Harvey, V., and Luongo, E., "Physical Capacity for Work", *Occupational Medicine*, 1:1946:1-47.
5. Shartle, C., *Occupational Information* (Prentice-Hall: N.Y.C., 1946), Chapter 10.
6. *Selective Placement for the Handicapped* (U. S. Employment Security Bureau, Department of Labor: Washington, D. C., 1945).
7. Garrett, J., *Psychological Aspects of Physical Disability*, Series No. 210 (Office of Vocational Rehabilitation, U. S. Department of Health, Education, and Welfare: Washington, D.C., 1953).
8. *Ibid.*
9. *Occupational Guides for Various Occupations* (Michigan Employment Security Commission: Detroit). Published continuously.
10. Baer, M., and Roeber, E., *Occupational Information: Its Nature and Use* (Science Research Associates: N.Y.C., 1951).
11. *Selective Placement for the Handicapped.*
12. Shartle, *op. cit.*, p. 281.
13. *Operations Manual for the Placement of the Physically Handicapped* (U. S. Civil Service Commission: Washington, D.C., 1944).
14. *Approved Factory Jobs for the Physically Handicapped* (Industrial Relations Re-search, Vega Aircraft Corporation: undated).
15. Lavos, G., "Vocational Adjustment of the Handicapped", *Exceptional Children*, 7:1941:219-26.

16. *Report of the Study of Possibilities of Employment of Handicapped Persons in Minneapolis, Minnesota,* Bulletin #146 (Federal Board for Vocational Education: Washington, D.C., 1930).
17. *Census and Industrial Survey of the Physically Handicapped in California,* Bulletin #9 (California Department of Education: Sacramento, 1935).
18. *Ibid.*
19. *Handbook of Representative Industrial Jobs for Blind Workers,* Rehabilitation Service Series #58 (Office of Vocational Rehabilitation, U. S. Department of Health, Education, and Welfare: Washington, D.C.).
20. *A Study of Occupations at Which 6,097 Physically Disabled Persons are Employed afer Being Vocationally Rehabilitated,* Bulletin #96 (Federal Board for Vocational Rehabilitation: Washington, D.C., 1925).
21. Davis, H., ed., *Hearing and Deafness* (Rinehart: N.Y.C., 1947).
22. *Civilian Amputees in Action* (Office of Vocational Rehabilitation, U. S. Department of Health, Education, and Welfare: Washington, D.C., 1948).
23. Condon, M., "Helping the Handicapped Student", *Journal of Rehabilitation,* 17;1951:14-17.
24. Barker, *op.cit.,* p. 349.
25. Lavos, G., "Unfounded Objections to Hiring the Handicapped", *Journal of Consulting Psychology,* 7:1943:191-97.
26. *Ibid.*
27. See 'Work Records' discussed later in this chapter.
28. See 'Industrial Security Programs and the Disabled' discussed later in this chapter.
29. American Museum of Safety, "Industrial Rehabilitation", *Safety Training Digest,* New York University, 1945.
30. Bridges, *op.cit.*
31. *No Help Wanted* (National Association of Mutual Casualty Companies: undated).
32. *A Study of Occupations at Which 6,097 Physically Disabled Persons Are Employed after Being Vocationally Rehabilitated.*
33. Lavos, G., "The Work Efficiency of the Disabled", *Journal of Rehabilitation,* 13:1947:3-11.
34. *Census and Industrial Survey of the Physically Handicapped in California.*
35. *The Performance of Physically Impaired Workers in Manufacturing Industries,* Bulletin #923 (U. S. Bureau of Labor Statistics, Department of Labor: Washington, D. C., 1948).
36. Barker, *op. cit.*
37. Lavos, G., "The Work Efficiency of the Disabled".
38. Felton, J., "Job Performance of Physically Impaired Persons in Industry", *Occupational Medicine,* 5:1948:466-496.
39. *The Performance of Physically Impaired Persons in Industry.*
40. Brighouse, G., *The Physically Handicapped in Industry,* Bulletin #13 (California Institute of Technology: Sacramento, 1946).
41. Felton, *op. cit.*
42. *Census and Industrial Survey of the Physically Handicapped in California.*
43. Lavos, G., "The Work Efficiency of the Disabled".
44. Brighouse, *op. cit.*
45. Felton, *op. cit.*
46. *Hiring the Handicapped in the Federal Civil Service,* Pamphlet #16 (U. S. Civil Service Commission: Washington, D.C., 1950).
47. Harvey, V., "The 'How' of Hiring the Handicapped", *Public Personnel Review,* July, 1951, pp. 121-26.
48. Lavos, G., "The Employment of Physically Handicapped under Civil Service", *Outlook for the Blind,* 36:1942:4-15.
49. Lavos, G., *Social Welfare Programs and the Employment of the Physically Handicapped* (National Society for Crippled Children: Chicago, 1939).
50. *Ibid.*
51. *Workmen's Compensation Second Injury Fund* (U. S. Bureau of Labor Standards, Department of Labor: Washington, D.C., 1954).
52. *The Physically Impaired Can Be Insured Without Penalty* (Association of Casualty and Surety Companies: N.Y.C., undated).

53. *Ibid.*
54. *The Physically Impaired, A Guidebook to Their Employment* (National Conservation Bureau: 1952).
55. Lavos, G., *Social Welfare Programs and the Employment of the Physically Handicapped.*
56. President's Committee on National Employ the Physically Handicapped Week, "Leo Kuhn of Royal Oak", *Performance*, Oct., 1950.
57. "Industrial Rehabilitation".
58. Lavos, G., "Levels of the Aspiration for the Handicapped", *Exceptional Children*, 9:1943:169-75.
59. Committee on the Severely Disabled, *Rehabilitation Facilities for the Severely Handicapped* (National Society for Crippled Children and Adults: Chicago, 1947).
60. *Ibid.*
61. *Census and Industrial Survey of the Physically Handicapped in California.*
62. Lavos, *Social Welfare Programs and the Employment of the Physically Handicapped.*
63. *State Minimum Wage Laws and Orders as Supplemented* (Women's Bureau, U. S. Department of Labor: Washington, D.C., 1953). Bulletin #247.
64. McCahill, W., "Physically Handicapped Workers—10 Years of National Recognition", *Employment Security Review*, 21:1954:4-7.
65. *Rehabilitation Centers* (Office of Vocational Rehabilitation, U. S. Department of Health, Education, and Welfare: Washington, D.C., 1950).

SECTION III

CHAPTERS I - VIII

BIBLIOGRAPHIES FOR GENERAL USE IN
SPECIAL EDUCATION

DIRECTORIES. MANUALS. AND LISTS OF
AGENCIES FOR GENERAL REFERENCE

GENERAL READING BIBLIOGRAPHY

USEFUL REFERENCES IN THE FIELD OF
REHABILITATION FOR SPECIAL EDUCATION

LIST OF MAGAZINES AND PERIODICALS
SERVING THE FIELD OF SPECIAL EDUCATION

OFFICIAL AND VOLUNTARY AGENCIES

U. S. COLLEGES AND UNIVERSITIES
OFFERING COURSES IN SPECIAL EDUCATION.
PHYSICAL THERAPY, AND OCCUPATIONAL
THERAPY

GLOSSARY, PREPARED BY ELLEN KERNEY

BIBLIOGRAPHIES FOR GENERAL USE IN SPECIAL EDUCATION

BOOKS

Fishbein, Morris; Salmonsen, Ella M.; and Hektoen, Ludvig, editors, *A Bibliography of Infantile Paralysis, With Selected Abstracts and Annotations,* 1789-1949 (Lippincott: Philadelphia, 1951), 899 pp.

Forrester, Gertrude, *Occupational Literature, and an Annotated Bibliography* (H. W. Wilson Company: N.Y.C., 1954), 467 pp.

Lende, Helga, *Books About the Blind* (American Foundation for the Blind: N.Y.C., 1953), 357 p.

Literature and Materials on Occupational Therapy Available from the American Occupational Therapy Assn. (N.Y.C., 1954), 3 pp.

Riviere, Maya, *Rehabilitation of the Handicapped; a Bibliography,* 1940-1946 (National Council on Rehabilitation: N.Y.C., 1949), 2 volumes.

U. S. Public Health Service, *Catalog, Mental Health Pamphlets and Reprints, Available for Distribution,* 1951 (Washington, D.C., 1951).

PAMPHLETS

Basic List of Medical Books and Journals for VA Hospitals, Centers and Domiciliaries, revised October, 1952 (Library Service, U. S. Veteran's Administration: Washington, D.C., 1952), 22, 8 pp.

Bibliotherapy A bibliography 1900-1952 (Medical and General Reference Library Division, Veterans Administration: Washington, D.C., 1952), 18 pp.

Glossary; Definitions of Common Medical Terms in Orthopedics, Cardiology and Ophthalmology Frequently Encountered by Non-Medical Personnel Working with Exceptional Children (State Dept. of Education: Hartford, Conn., 1954), 25 pp.

Heinicke, Christoph and Whiting, Beatrice Blyth, compilers, *Bibliographies on Personality and Social Development of the Child* (Social Science Research Council: N.Y.C., 1953), 130 pp.

Hunter College, Dept. of Special Education, *General Bibliography; Education of the Exceptional Child* (N.Y.C., 1953).

Medical Care of Veterans in the United States, (1945-1950 (Medical and General Reference Library, Veterans Administration: Washington, D.C., 1951), 21 pp.

National Society for Crippled Children and Adults, *Bulletin on Current Literature; a Monthly Bibliography for Workers with the Handicapped* (Chicago, Ill.). The National Society for Crippled Children and Adults, 11 S. La Salle St., Chicago, Ill., also publishes, from time to time, reading lists in the various areas of Special Education. These special area bibliographies (i.e. Speech, Cerebral Palsy, etc.) are revised from time to time, and in ordinary compilation it is better to request the latest listing.

   A Bibliography on Camping with Handicapped Children, an Author-Subject Index to Literature in the Library of the National Society for Crippled Children & Adults (Chicago, 1951), 13 pp.

   Bibliography on the Deaf and Hard of Hearing (Chicago, 1951), 23 pp.

   A Bibliography on Recreation for Physically Handicapped Children and Adults (Chicago, Ill., 1954), 53 pp.

   Books and Pamphlets on Rehabilitation, A Selective Checklist of Publications in Print (Chicago, 1954), 12 pp.

A Brief List of Publications in Print on Cerebral Palsy (Chicago, Ill., 1954), 12 pp.

Employment of the Physically Handicapped, a Checklist of Publications in Print (Chicago, Ill., 1954), 8 pp.

Pamphlets in Print on Rehabilitation; a Checklist of Free and Inexpensive Materials (Chicago, 1951), 44 pp.

A Selected List of Periodicals that Publish Articles Concerning the Handicapped, Compiled & Distributed by the Library (Chicago, 1954), 8 pp.

A Selected List of Subject Headings on the Rehabilitation of the Handicapped (Chicago, 1954), 50 pp.

Selected References on Aphasia, Compiled by the Library, Oct., 1954, Thirty-first Convention, National Society for Crippled Children and Adults, Nov. 2-6, 1954, Hotel Statler, Boston; Occupational Therapy Seminar, *The Role of Occupational Therapy with the Aphasic Patient*, Wed. Nov. 3, 1954(Chicago, 1954), 7 pp.

Selected References on Hemiplegia, Compiled by the Library, Oct., 1954 Thirty-first Convention, National Society for Crippled Children and Adults, Nov. 2-6 1954, Hotel Statler, Boston; Occupational Therapy Seminar, *The Role of Occupational Therapy with the Aphasic Patients*. Wed. Nov., 3, 1954 Chicago, (Chicago, 1954), 7 pp.

A Special Education Bibliography; a Selection of Titles in the Library of the National Society for Crippled Children and Adults (Chicago, May, 1954), 57 pp.

A Speech Correction Bibliography; a Selection of Titles in the Library of the National Society for Crippled Children & Adults (Chicago, 1949).

A Speech Rehabilitation Bibliography, A Selection of Titles in the Library of the National Society for Crippled Children & Adults (Chicago, 1953).

Sources of Information about the Handicapped; a Guide to Non-technical Publications (Chicago, 1954), 21 pp.

Surveying Community Needs in Rehabilitation Services; a Checklist of Selected References in the Library; compiled March, 1954 (Chicago, 1954), 11 pp.

O'Conner, Thomas and Rothstein, Jerome H., *An Annotated Directory of Audio-Visual Aids Dealing with the Handicapped* (San Francisco State College: San Francisco, California, 1951), 53 pp.

Popular Books about the Physically Handicapped; First Supplement (Montclair Public Library: Montclair, N. J., 1954), 8 pp.

Poulos, Thomas H., *Selected Annotated Bibliography; Education of the Deaf* (Michigan School for the Deaf: Flint, 1953).

President's Committee on Employment of the Physically Handicapped, *Employing the Physically Handicapped: A Bibliography* (U. S. Bureau of Labor Standards: Washington, D.C.), 74 pp.

Publications of the U. S. Employment Service (U. S. Dept. of Labor, Bureau of Employment Security: Washington, D.C. 1953), 43 pp.

Ralya, Lynn L. and Lillian L., *Selected Sources of Free and Inexpensive Information Concerning Vocational Rehabilitation; a Bibliography Suitable for Use in Educational Institutions and by the Lay Public* (The Compilers: Santa Monica, California, 1953).

Rothstein, Jerome H., *Bibliography, Education of the Mentally Retarded* (State College: San Francisco, California, 1954), 65 pp.

Selected List of Acquisitions, May, 1954-Nov., 1954 (City College of New York Library, Russell Sage Collection: N.Y.C., 1954), 10 pp.

Speech Correction Techniques, Materials, References (Division of Speech Correction, Chicago Public Schools: Chicago, 1952), 71 pp.

Suggested Reading Bibliography, Area of the Physically Handicapped (Hunter College: N.Y.C., 1953), 17 pp.

U. S. Children's Bureau, *Selected References on Adoption* (Washington, D. C., 1953), 28 pp.

Weissberg, Albert O., *A Guide to Audio-Visual Materials on Speech and Hearing Disorders*, American Speech and Hearing Assn., *Journal of Speech and Hearing Disorders*, Supplement 2, Sept., 1952.

Wilson, Donald V., *The Crippled*. Reprinted by permission of American Association of Social Workers from *Social Work Year Book*, 1954.

ARTICLES

Busby, Dorothy Robinson and McMillan, Sherrill, "New Horizons; Readable Books about the Physically Handicapped, Adults and Young People", *Hospital Book Guide*, May, 1951. 12:5:27-31.

Dolphin, Jane E. and Kvaraceus, William C., "Selected References from the Literature on Exceptional Children", *Elementary School Journal*, April, 1954. 54:8:467-480.

Hollinshead, Merrill T., "The Orthopedically Handicapped", *Review, Educational Research*, Dec., 1953. 23:5:492-507.

Ingram, Christine P. and Kvaraceus, William C., "Selected References from the Literature on Exceptional Children", *Elementary School Journal*, April, 1952. Vol. 52, No. 8, pp. 471-483. Also: April, 1953. 53:8:462-476.

Strassler, Margaret G., "For the Handicapped", Junior Libraries, pp. 12-13, 15-16. (In: *Library Journal*, Nov. 15, 1954. 79:20).

Meyerson, Lee, "The Visually Handicapped", *Review, Educational Research*, Dec., 1953. 23:5:476-491.

ADDITIONAL REFERENCES

DIRECTORIES, MANUALS, AND LISTS OF AGENCIES FOR GENERAL REFERENCE

Address List of Field Stations (Excepting VA Offices) of the Veterans Administration, Names of Managers and Announcement of Changes (Veterans Administration: Washington, D.C., 1954), 19 pp.

American Annals of the Deaf, Annual January issue, (Gallaudet College: Washington, D.C.).

Annotated Directory of Films on the Handicapped (National Education Association of the U.S.A.: 1201 16th St., Washington, D.C., April, 1955).

Bluett, Charles G., *Handbook of Information for the Hard of Hearing* (California State Dept. of Education: Sacramento, 1947), 152 pp.

Directory of Services for Handicapped Children, State of Florida, 1954 (The Nemours Foundation and the Florida Children's Commission: 1954), 83 pp.

Directory of State and Local Employment Security Offices, March, 1954 (U. S. Department of Labor, Bureau of Employment Security: Washington, D.C., 1954), 50 pp.

Directory of State and Territorial Health Authorities (U. S. Public Health Service: Washington, D. C., 1954), 73 pp.

Directory of State Employment Security Agency Officials (U. S. Department of Labor, Bureau of Employment Security: Washington, D. C., 1954), 11 pp.

Directory, Private Foster Care Agencies for Children (Child Welfare League of America: N.Y.C., 1954), 84 pp.

Education Directory, Education, Associations (U. S. Dept. of Health, Education, and Welfare, Office of Education: Washington, D.C., 1954), 54 pp.

"Education Index." (H. W. Wilson: 950 University Ave., N. Y. C. 52).

Facts about the International Society for the Welfare of Cripples and its Affiliated National Organizations, Prepared for the Sixth World Congress, The Hague, Netherlands, Sept. 13-17, 1954 (The Society: N.Y.C., 1954).

Film Strip Guide (H. W. Wilson: 950 University Ave., N.Y.C. 52).

General Catalogue of Educational Films (U. S. Dept. H. E. W., Office of Education. Visual Education Service: Washington, D.C., Jan. 1955).

Graves, Eileen G., editor; Ulrich, Carolyn F., consulting editor, *Ulrich's Periodicals Directory* (R. R. Bowker: N.Y.C.).

Hayes, E. Nelson, editor, *Directory for Exceptional Children; Schools, Services and other Facilities*, with a preface by M. E. Frampton and E. D. Gall, 2nd Edition (Porter Sargent, Publisher, Boston, Mass., 1955).

Kurtz, Russell A., *Social Work Year Book*, 1954 (American Association of Social Workers: N.Y.C., 1954), 703 pp.

Lende, Helga, *Directory of Activities for the Blind in the United States and Canada* (American Foundation for the Blind: N.Y.C., 1954), 133 pp.

List of Special Schools, Boarding Homes for Handicapped Pupils, and Institutions for Further Education and Training of Disabled Persons in England and Wales (Published for the British Ministry of Education by Her Majesty's Stationary Office: London, England, 1953), 51 pp.

Medical Social Services for Children in the Maternal and Child Health and Crippled Children's Programs (U. S. Children's Bureau: Washington, D. C., 1953), 49 pp.

National Health Council Directory of Member Organizations (National Health Council: N.Y.C., 1954), 95 pp.

O'Connor, Thomas, and Rothstein, Jerome H., *An Annotated Directory of Audio-Visual Aids Dealing with the Handicapped* (San Francisco State College, Special Education Department: San Francisco, 1951).

O'Connor, Thomas and Rothstein, Jerome H., *Directory: Films on the Handicapped* (International Council for Exceptional Children: Washington, D.C., 1953), 56 pp.

Official Directory of State and Licensed Mental Institutions New York State Dept. of Mental Hygiene: N.Y.C., 1954), 115 pp.

Official Registry of Prosthetic and Orthopedic Appliance Facilities, 1954 (American Board for Certification of the Prosthetic and Orthopedic Appliance Industry, Inc.: Washington, D.C., 1954).

Orthopaedic Appliances Atlas, Vol. 1, "Braces, Splints, Shoe Alterations", (J. W. Edwards: Ann Arbor, Michigan, 1952), 588 pp.

Quarterly Cumulative Index Medicus (American Medical Association: Chicago, Ill).

Psychological Abstracts (American Psychological Associations, Washington, D.C.).

Rehabilitation Centers in the United States National Society for Crippled Children and Adults and Office of Vocational Rehabilitation, U. S. Dept of Health, Education and Welfare. (U. S. Government Printing Office: Washington, D.C. 1954), 128 pp.

Residential Treatment Centers for Emotionally Disturbed Children; a Listing (U.S. Children's Bureau: Washington, D.C., 1952), 78 pp.

Rusk, Howard A., and Taylor, Eugene J., *Directory of Agencies and Organizations Concerned with Rehabilitation and Services to the Handicapped* (New York Times: N.Y.C., 1947), 133 pp.

Swart, Dorothy M., editor; Lino, Edward N., assistant editor, *Directory of Social and Health Agencies of New York City, 1954-1955*. Prepared under the direction of the Committee on Information Services of the Welfare and Health Council of New York City. (Columbia University Press: N.Y.C., 1954), 594 pp.

Whitney, Helen Hay, *Directory of Care of Patients With Rheumatic Fever and Rheumatic Heart Disease* (The Helen Hay Whitney Foundation: 525 East 68th St., N. Y. 21, N. Y., 1954), 40 pp.

ternational Organizations (International Society for the Welfare of Cripples: N.Y.C., *1951 World Directory; Affiliated Organizations, Active Members, Correspondents, In-* 1951), 31 pp.

ADDITIONAL REFERENCES

GENERAL READING BIBLIOGRAPHY

GENERAL REFERENCES

BOOKS

American Academy of Political and Social Sciences, *Medical Care for Americans* (Philadelphia, Pa., 1951), 200 pp.

Bindt, J., *Handbook for the Blind* (Macmillan: N.Y.C., 1952).

Clarke, Joan Simeon, *Disabled Citizens* (Macmillan: N.Y.C., 1951), 237 pp.

Disabilities and How to Live with Them (Lancet Ltd.: London, England, 1952), 243 pp.

Dominick, Barbara, *Stuttering: A Psychodynamic Approach to its Understanding and Treatment* (Julian Press: N.Y.C., 1954), 304 pp.

Gilliland, Esther Goetz, editor, *Music Therapy*, 1951, Proceedings, National Association for Music Therapy, v. 1 (The Assn.: Chicago, Ill., 1952), 41 pp.

——, *Music Therapy*, 1952, Proceedings, National Assn. for Music Therapy, Papers from the Third Annual Convention, 1953, Lawrence, Kansas, 276 pp.

Gruenberg, Sidonie Matsner, editor, *The Encyclopedia of Child Care and Guidance* (Doubleday: Garden City, N.Y., 1954), 1016 pp.

International Children's Centre, *Readaptation des Enfants Atteints d' Infirmite Motrice, Cours du . . . Paris-London, 15 Octobre-15 Decembre, 1951* (The Centre: Paris, France, 1952).

International Society for the Welfare of Cripples, *The Disabled in the Modern World* (N.Y.C., 1951), 279 pp.

Klein, Alexander, editor, *Courage is the Key* (Twayne Publishers: N.Y.C.), 287 pp.

Lotz, Philip Henry, editor, *Unused Alibis* (Association Press: N.Y.C., 1951), 120 pp.

McMullin, M.D., *How to Help the Shut-in Child* (E.P. Dutton: N.Y.C., 1954), 192 pp.

National Association of Music Therapy, *Bulletin*. Proceedings of Mid-Atlantic Regional Conference, March 2, 1953. May, 1953. 2:2.

National Society for Crippled Children and Adults, *Nation-wide Report on: Building Happy, Useful Lives for the Handicapped*, A Record of the 1950 Convention, Hotel Stevens, Chicago, Ill., Oct. 26-28, 1950 (The Society: Chicago, Ill., 1951), 120 pp.

New York State Citizen's Committee of One Hundred for Children and Youth, *The Four Million* (N.Y.).

New York University-Bellevue Medical Center, *Self-help Devices for Rehabilitation* (Institute of Physical Medicine and Rehabilitation: N.Y.C., 1952).

Parker, C.S., *Your Child Can Be Happy in Bed* (Thomas Crowell: N.Y.C., 1952), 275 pp.

Podolsky, E., *Music Therapy* (Philosophical Library: N.Y.C., 1954), 335 pp.

Pollock, M.P. and Pollock M., *New Hope for the Retarded* (Porter Sargent: Boston, Mass., 1953), 176 pp.

---

*Area bibliographies for the various specializations, (i.e., Blind, Deaf, Gifted, etc.) will be found at the close of each chapter on the specific subject in *Special Education for the Exceptional*, vols. II & III, edited by M.E. Frampton and E.D. Gall and published by Porter Sargent, 11 Beacon Street, Boston, Mass.

Rusk, Howard A. and Taylor, Eugene J., *Living with a Disability* (Blakiston: N.Y.C., 1953), 207 pp.

Stafford, G., *Sports for the Handicapped*, 2nd ed. (Prentice-Hall: N.Y.C., 1947), 334 pp.

Stauco, Clarice, *The Atypical Child* (Catholic University of America Press: Washington, D.C., 1954), pp. 231 ff.

Stern, Edith M. and Castendyck, Elsa, *The Handicapped Child* (Wyn, Inc.: N.Y.C., 1950).

Stone, Eleanor B., and Deyton, John W., *Corrective Therapy for the Handicapped Child* (Prentice-Hall: N.Y.C., 1951), 315 pp.

Streng, Alice; Fitch, W.J.; Hedgecock, L.D.; Phillips, J.W. and Carrell, James A., *Hearing Therapy for Children* (Grune & Stratton: N.Y.C., 1955).

Stump, Al, *Champions Against Odds* (Macrae Smith: Philadelphia, Pa., 1952), 255 pp.

U.S. Children's Bureau, *Research Relating to Children, An Inventory of Studies in Progress*, Reported Nov. 1, 1952- May 31, 1954. (Washington, D.C., 1954), 195 pp.

U.S. Government Printing Office, *Assistance and Rehabilitation of the Physically Handicapped* (Washington, D.C., 1953).

U.S. National Institute of Mental Health, *Criteria for the Selection of Psychotic Patients for Psychosurgery*, Proceedings, First Research Conference of Psychosurgery, N.Y., Nov. 17 & 18, 1949 (Washington, D.C., 1951), 173 pp.

Viscardi, Henry, Jr., *A Man's Stature*, Intro. by Barnard M. Baruch (John Day Company: N.Y.C., 1952).

Wadia, A.R., editor, *The Handicapped Child* (Tata Institute of Social Sciences: Bombay, India, 1954), 171 pp.

Willard, Helen S. and Spackman, Clare S., editors, *Principles of Occupational Therapy*, 2 ed. (Lippincott: Philadelphia, Pa., 1954), 376 pp.

PAMPHLETS

American Medical Association, *Entertaining the Convalescent Child* (Chicago, Ill., 1944), 12 pp.

American Occupational Therapy Association, *Manual on the Organization and Administration of Occupational Therapy Departments* (McBrown: Iowa, 1951), 99 pp. Planographed.

American Public Health Association, *Committee on the Study of Education of Hospitalized and Crippled Children in Rural Areas; Preliminary Report* (N.Y.C., 1951), 4 pp.

Association for the Aid of Crippled Children, *Synthesis*, Annual Report of the Association for the Year Ending March 31, 1954 (The Assn.: N.Y.C., 1954), 32 pp.

Buell, Charles, *Recreation for the Blind*. Ed. Ser. #1 (American Foundation for the Blind: N.Y.C., 1951), 39 pp.

Boy Scouts of America, *Their Trail of Happiness with the Boy Scouts of America, A Review of Scouting With Physically Handicapped Boys* (N.Y.C., 1943), 61 pp.

Carrington, Evelyn M., *The Exceptional Child; His Nature and His Needs* (Texas State College for Women: Denton, 1951), 14 pp.

Child Research Clinic, Woods Schools, *The Exceptional Child in Infancy and Early Childhood* (Langhorne, Pa., 1950), 48 pp.

Commission for Handicapped Children, *Include All of the Children*, Biennial Report, 1951-1953 (Springfield, Ill., 1953).

——, *The Handicapped Child in His Home and His Community* (Chicago, 1952), 66 pp.

——, *The Handicapped Child in the Mainstream*, Proceedings, of the Tenth Governor's Conference on Exceptional Children, Palmer House, Chicago, Ill., Sept. 25, 1953 (Chicago, 1954), 111 pp.

Co-ordinating Council for the Study of Handicapped Children, *Kentucky Conference on Handicapped Children*. Sponsored by the Council and the Nemours Foundation, Oct. 22, 23, 1953, Seelbach Hotel, Louisville, Kentucky (The Council: Louisville, 1953), 119 pp.

De Whitt, Dorothy, *Survey of Handicapped Children in Nevada* (Legislative Counsel Bureau: Carson City, Nevada, 1952), Bul. No. 18.

Falkner, F., *The Convalescent Child* (University of Liverpool: England, 1952), 55 pp.

Gordon, E.E., *A Home Program for Independently Ambulatory Patients* (Nat. Multiple Sclerosis Society in Cooperation with the Institute of Physical Medicine & Rehabilitation — University-Bellevue Medical Center: N.Y.C., 1952), 16 pp.

Illinois Congress of Parents and Teachers, *Is Your Child Exceptional . . . Different from Other Children?* For parents and groups interested in the exceptional child (Springfield, Ill., 1950), 85 pp.

Indiana State Department of Public Instruction, *Is Your Child Exceptional . . . Different from Other Children?"* (Indianapolis, Ind., 1951), 76 pp.

International Council for Exceptional Children, *Report of the Inter. Council for Exceptional Children*, Western Regional Meeting, Nov. 1-4, 1953, Portland, Oregon; Conference Theme: "We Confront All Children." (Tacoma Public Schools: Tacoma, Washington, 1954), 48 pp.

——, *Third Annual Eastern II Regional Conference*, held at the Hotel Syracuse, Syracuse, N.Y., Nov. 5-6, 1954.

International Society for the Welfare of Cripples, *Facts About the . . . and its Affiliated National Organizations*. Prepared for the Sixth World Congress, the Hague, Netherlands, Sept. 13-17, 1954 (The Society: N.Y.C., 1954).

John Hancock Life Insurance Company, *Diversion for the Sick* (Boston, Mass., 1950), 28 pp.

Kentucky State Department of Education, *Exceptional Children; Administration, Supervision, Examination, Reporting, Identification, Housing, Curriculum, Aids to Instruction, Home Instruction, Consultation* (Frankfort, Kentucky, 1952), 19 pp.

Kirk, Samuel A. and Spalding, Willard B., *The Institute for Research on Exceptional Children at the University of Illinois*, reprinted from the *Educational Forum*, May, 1953, pp. 413-422.

Lutheran Education Association, *A Great Commission* (River Forest, Ill., 1953), 23 pp.

Martens, Elise H., *Needs of Exceptional Children* (U.S. Office of Education: Washington, D.C., 1952).

Mayo, Leonard, *The Art of Synthesis*, Assn. for the Aid of Crippled Children, Annual Report, Oct., 1954 (N.Y.C.).

National Conference of Catholic Charities, *Planning for the Exceptional Child* (Washingon, D.C., 1952).

National Society for Crippled Children & Adults, *A Bibliography on Camping with Handicapped Children* (Chicago, Ill., 1951), 13 pp.

Nickell, Vernon L., Supt. of Public Instruction, *Reimbursing for Excess Cost of Educating Exceptional Children, School Year Ending June 30, 1954. County Totals Special Education, State of Illinois*, 54 pp.

President's Committee on Employment of the Physically Handicapped, *Minutes of the Meeting of the President's Committee on Employment of the Physically Handicapped*, Fall Meeting, Aug. 26-27, 1954 (The Committee: Washington, D.C., 1954).

——, *Performance, the Story of the Handicapped* (Washington, D.C., 1954), 14 pp.

Schlotter, B. and Svendsen, M., *An Experiment in Recreation with the Mentally Retarded*, Rev. ed. (Dept. of Public Welfare, State of Ill.: Springfield, 1951), 142 pp.

Social Reference Center, United Nations, *Rehabilitation of the Handicapped* (N.Y.C., 1953), 85 pp.

South Africa, Inter-Departmental Committee on Deviate Children, *Report of the Inter-Departmental Committee on Deviate Children*, v. II, "Non-European Children" (Govt. Printer: Pretoria, S. Africa, 1950), 162 pp.

Special Services for Handicapped Children, Report of the Commission to Study Educational Needs of Handicapped Persons to the Governor and the General Assembly of Virginia (The Commonwealth of Virginia: Richmond, 1953), 18 pp.

Tenth Anniversary Celebration of the Alfred I. du Pont Institute of the Nemours Foundation, Wilmington, Del., Sat., June 17, 1950 (The Institute: Wilmington, 1951).

Texas Research League, *For Those Committed to Our Care*, Report No. 1 in a Survey of the Board for Texas State Hospitals and Special Schools (Austin, Texas, 1954), 124 pp.

United Cerebral Palsy Association, Inc., *Realistic Planning for Children with Cerebral Palsy* (N.Y.C., 1952-53), Pamphlets #1, 2, 3.

United Nations, *Services for the Physically Handicapped* (N.Y.C., 1954), 31 pp.

United Nations Economic and Social Council, *United Nations Economic and Social Council Aid to Programmes for the Care and Rehabilitation of Handicapped Children* (N.Y.C., 1954), 33 pp.

U.S. Department of Health, Education and Welfare, *Annual Report,* 1953 (Govt. Printing Office: Washington, D.C., 1953), 293 pp.

——, *Statistics of Special Education for Exceptional Children,* 1952-1953 (Office of Education: Washington, D.C., 1954), 78 pp.

U.S. Office of Defense Mobilization, *Report of the Task Force on the Handicapped* (Washington, D.C., 1952), Part VI, pp. 17 & 18, 45 pp.

U.S. Office of Vocational Rehabilitation, *Handicapped Homemakers,* Proceedings, Leader's Workshop on Principles of Work Simplification Applied to Problems of Physically Handicapped Homemakers, June 14-20, 1953. University of Connecticut, Schools of Home Economics, Business Administration and Physical Therapy (Washington, D.C., 1954), 97 pp.

——, *A Study of Home Bound Physically Handicapped Individuals* (U.S. Dept. of Health, Education and Welfare: Washington, D.C., 1954), 5 pp.

——, *Rehabilitation Programs for the Homebound Child* (Federal Security Agency: Washington, D.C., 1952), 76 pp.

Washington State Health Council, Committee on the Handicapped Child, *Help for Handicapped Children* (Seattle, 1952), 14 pp.

World Health Organization, *Joint Expert Committee on the Physically Handicapped Child, First Report* (Geneva, Switzerland, 1952).

Yahraes, Herbert, *Gains and Goals; Where We Stand in the Fight Against Some of the Crippling Conditions of Childhood and What We Still Must Do* (Assn. for the Aid of Crippled Children: N.Y.C., 1954), 34 pp.

ARTICLES

"A Better Chance for the Handicapped Child", *J., American Medical Association,* May 1, 1954. 155:1:39-39.

Abbott, Marguerite, "Professional C. P. Training for Occupational Therapists", *Cerebral Palsy Rev.* Jan. - Feb., 1953. 14:142:6-8.

"Administrative Practices and Personnel Policies", *American J. Occupational Therapy,* May-June, 1954. 8:3:128-129. Reprint.

Baker, L., "Personal Experience Books", *Hospital Book Guide,* 1952. 13:32-6.

Barton, Betsy, "If Your Child is Handicapped", *Child Study,* Spring, 1951. 28:2:12-14, 30-32.

Birch, Jack W., "Patterns of Clinical Services for Exceptional Children", *Exceptional Children,* March, 1953.

Brownell, Samuel Miller, "Needs for Services to Exceptional Children", *Exceptional Children,* Jan., 1955. 21:4:138-152.

Byran, Dorothy, "The Itinerant Teacher Plan for the Education of Partially-Seeing Children in Illinois", *Sight Saving Review,* Winter, 1953. 23:4:218-222.

Crawley, W. H., "Friends of the Homebound Disabled", Occupational Therapy, Oct., 1953. 16:4:211-214.

Curry, E. Thayer, "Analysis of Hearing Loss Patterns in a Rural Illinois School System: I. General Considerations", *Eye Ear, Nose and Throat Monthly,* July, 1950. 29:357-359. Reprint.

Dietrich, Harry F., "Prevention of Childhood Accidents; What Are We Waiting For?" *J. American Medical Assn.,* Nov. 6, 1954. 156:10:929-931.

——, "Accident Prevention in Childhood", *The Crippled Child Magazine,* Feb., 1955. Vol. 32, No. 5, p. 10.

Durlacher, editor, "Square Dancing for the Handicapped", *Crippled Children,* Feb., 1950. 27:3:16-17, 29.

Goldin, George J. (Kenosha County Schools, Kenosha, Wisconsin) "Rural, But Not Forgotten; Rural Areas, too, Can Provide for Handicapped Children", *NEA Journal,* Jan., 1955. 44:1:22-24.

Halstorm, Frances J., "Helping the Handicapped", *Junior Libraries,* pp. 11-12. Also: *Library Journal,* Feb. 15, 1955. 80:4.

Herdic, James F., Jr., "Swimming for Handicapped Children", *Recreation,* Feb., 1955. 48:2:84-85.

International Council for Exceptional Children, "By-laws . . . Adopted at the Delegate Assembly in Cincinnati, April 28, 1954", Committee on Constitution and By-laws, Ray Graham, chairman, *Exceptional Children*, Oct., 1954. 21:1:22-25.

Johnson, O., and Kirk, S., "Are Mentally Handicapped Children Segregated in Regular Grades?" *Journal of Exceptional Children*, 1950. 17:65-69.

Kerr, M., "A Program of Community Relationship Activities at the New Jersey School for the Deaf", *American Annals of the Deaf*, 1945. 90:193-305.

Laycock, S.R., "There Must Be No Forgotten Child", *Crippled Child*, Dec., 1953. 31:4:8-9.

Lesser, Arthur J., "The Nation's Handicapped Children", *American J. Public Health*, Feb., 1954. 44:2:166-170.

Lord, Francis E., "Sources of Research Literature in Special Education", *Exceptional Children*, May, 1953. 19:8:317-320, 322 pp.

Lowenfeld, B., "Effects of Blindness on the Cognitive Functions of Children", *The Nervous Child*, 1948. 47: 45-54.

Mayo, Leonard W., "Creed for Exceptional Children." *Exceptional Children*, Jan., 1955. 21:4:139.

Miers, E., "The Right To Be Different", *Exceptional Children*, 1952, 18:225-8.

Norris, Martha J., 'Cerebral Palsy Mobile Units." *Phys. Therapy Rev.*, Jan., 1953. 33:1:16-20.

Osborn, Courtney D., "Michigan's Mobile Hearing Units." *J. Speech and Hearing Disorders*, June, 1951. 16:2:140-147.

Outwitting Handicaps, 44th Issue, 1949. Entire issue devoted to brief articles on specialized equipment, biographical sketches, and other informational articles of interest to the severely handicapped.

Porter, Rutherford, B., "Clinical Service Extensions for Rural Area Exceptional Children", *Exceptional Children*, Dec., 1953. Dec., 1953. 20:3:105-110.

Robinson, H.M., "World Concern for the Exceptional", *Elementary School J.*, April, 1952. 52:437.

Shieff, F.L., "Occupational Therapy for the Chronically Ill Children", *Cerebral Palsy Rev.*, Nov., 1953. 14:11:8-9, 10.

Smock, C., and Cruickshank, W., "Responses of Handicapped and Normal Children to the Rosenzweig P-F Study", *Quarterly Journal of Child Behavior*, 1952. 4:156-64.

Terry, P.S., "Square Wheeling", *American J. Occupational Therapy*, July-Aug., 1950. 4:4:164-168.

Wallace, Helen M., "New York City's Program for the Handicapped Child", *N.Y. State J. Medicine*, Feb. 15, 1954. 54:4:512-18.

Weiner, Bluma B., "Play and Recreational Activities of Young Mentally Retarded Boys", *American J. Mental Deficiency*, April, 1953. 57:4:594-600.

Wendland, L., "Some Religious Feelings of the Post-Poliomyelitis", *Journal of Social Psychology*, 1953. 38:99-108.

Wilson, Donald V., "World Cooperation for Exceptional Children", *Exceptional Children*, May, 1953. v. 19, no. 8.

Woellner, R.C., "Care of the Deviates", *School Review*, Sept., 1954. 62:319-23.

Worcester, D.A., "Clinical Services: Making the Best of Resources in the Rural Community", *Exceptional Children*, Jan., 1954. 20:4:176-179.

EDUCATIONAL REFERENCES

BOOKS

Abraham, Willard, *A Guide for the Study of Exceptional Children* (The Author: Arizona State College, Tempe, 1955), 263 pp. Multilithed.

Amoss, Harold E. and De Laporte, L. Helen, *Training Handicapped Children* (The Ryerson Press: Toronto, 1933).

Amsterdam, Systemen Keesing, *Proceedings of the Second International Congress on Orthopedagogics, Amsterdam, 18-22 VIII, 1949* (1950), 534 pp.

Arizona State College, *Workshop in Education of the Exceptional Child* (Tempe, Arizona, 1954), 223 pp.

Baker, Harry J., *Introduction to Exceptional Children* (Macmillan: N.Y., 1953), 500 pp.

Bullis, N. Edmund and O'Malley, Emily E., *Human Relations in the Classroom* (Delaware Society for Mental Hygiene: Wilmington, 1948).

Cass, Marion T., *Speech Habilitation in Cerebral Palsy* (Columbia University Press: N.Y.C., 1951), 212 pp. Planographed.

Cutsforth, T.D., *The Blind in School and Society* (American Foundation for the Blind, N.Y.C., 1951), pp. 103-120.

Daniels, Arthur S., *Adapted Physical Education; Principles and Practice of Physical Education for Exceptional Students* (Harper: N.Y.C., 1954), 538 pp.

Dolch, Edmund William, *Helping Handicapped Children in School* (Garrand Press: Champaign, Ill., 1948), 349 pp.

Frampton, M.E., editor, *Education of the Blind, A Study in Methods of Teaching the Blind* (World Book: Yonkers, N.Y., 1940), 436 pp.

——, and Athearn, Clarence, *The School Assembly as an Educational Force* (Institute for the Blind: N.Y.C., 1944), 250 pp.

——, and Kerney, E., *The Residential School* (Edwin Gould Printery: N.Y.C., 1953).

——, and Rowell, Hugh Grant, editors, *Education of the Handicapped* (World Book: Yonkers, N.Y., 1940), 2 volumes.

Gaus, R.; Stendler, C.; and Almy, M., *Teaching Young Children* (World Book: Yonkers-on-Hudson, N.Y., 1952), 454 pp.

Gottlober, A.B., *Understanding Stuttering* (Grune & Stratton: N.Y.C., 1953), 274 pp.

Heck, Arch O., *Introduction to Exceptional Children* (McGraw-Hill: N.Y.C., 1953).

——, *The Education of Exceptional Children; Its Challenge to Teachers, Parents, and Laymen* (McGraw-Hill: N.Y.C., 1953), 513 pp.

Henry Nelson B., editor, *The Education of Exceptional Children*, 49th Year Book, Part II, National Society for the Study of Education (University of Chicago Press: Chicago, 1950), 346 pp.

Horn, John Louis, *The Education of Exceptional Children* (Century: N.Y.C., 1924), 343 pp.

Illinois Department of Public Instruction, *The Illinois Plan for Special Education of Exceptional Children; the Physically Handicapped, Exclusive of Children Who Are Handicapped with Vision, Hearing and Speech* (Springfield, Ill., 1952).

Jenks, William F., editor, *Special Education of the Exceptional Child*, Proceedings of the Workshop on Special Education of the Exceptional Child, Conducted at the Catholic University of America from June 12 to June 24, 1952 (Catholic University of America Press: Washington, D.C., 1953), 156 pp.

——, *The Atypical Child*, Proceedings of the Second Annual Workshop on Special Education of the Exceptional Child, Conducted at the Catholic University of America, from June 12 to June 23, 1953 (Catholic University of America Press: Washington, D.C., 1954), 302 pp.

Johnson, W., editor, *Speech Problems of Children* (Grune & Stratton: N.Y.C., 1950), 265 pp. Chs. 4, 5, 6, 7, 8, and 11.

Kirk, S. A. and Johnson, G. O., *Educating the Retarded Child* (Houghton, Mifflin: Cambridge, Mass., 1951), 434 pp. Pt. I, Ch. 1.

Lassman, Grace H., *Language for the Pre-School* (Grune & Stratton: N.Y.C., 1950), 263 pp.

Lindberg, Lucile, *The Democratic Classroom* (Teachers College, Columbia University: N.Y.C., 1954), 115 pp.

Lloyd, Frances, *Educating the Sub-normal Child* (Philosophical Library: N.Y.C., 1954).

MacKenzie, Gordon N.; Corey, Stephen M.; and associates, *Insructional Leadership* (Teachers College, Columbia University: N.Y.C., 1954), 209 pp.

McGeoch, D.M., *Direct Experience in Teacher Education* (Bureau of Publications, Teachers College, Columbia University: N.Y.C., 1953), 212 pp.

McNerney, C.T., *The Curriculum* (McGraw-Hill: N.Y.C., 1953), 292 pp. Ch. 1, 2, 13 and 14.

National Association of Secondary School Principals, Bulletin, *The Education of Handicapped and Gifted Pupils in the Secondary School* (Washington, D.C., Jan., 1955), Vol. 39, No. 207.

National Education Association, *Health in the Elementary School* (Washington, D.C., 1950).

National Education Association, Association for Supervision and Curriculum Development, *Fostering Mental Health in our Schools*, Yearbook, 1950.

New York City, Board of Education, *Helping the Physically Limited Child* (N.Y.C., 1953), 211 pp.

Olson, Willard C. and Hughes, Byron O., "Growth Patterns of Exceptional Children," in *The Education of Exceptional Children*, National Society for the Study of Education (University of Chicago Press: Chicago, 1950), Ch. 4.

Rathbone, Josephine Langworthy, *Corrective Physical Education*, Fifth ed. (W.B. Saunders: Philadelphia, 1954), 318 pp.

South Carolina University, School of Education, *Teaching Exceptional Children, the Physically Handicapped, and the Mentally Handicapped*, A manual prepared by the students of the Workshop on Orientation to Special Education. Sponsored by Crippled Children Society of South Carolina (The School: Columbia, S.C., 1954), 92 pp. Mimeo.

Strang, Ruth, *Role of the Teacher in Personnel Work* (Teachers College, Columbia University: N.Y.C., 1953), 507 pp.

Union of South Africa, Dept. of Education, Arts & Sciences, *Report of the Interdepartmental Committee on Deviate Children*, Vol. II. (Non-European Children) Pretoria, S.Af., 1950), 162 pp.

University of Minnesota, Center for Continuation Study, *Institute of the Education of Physically Handicapped Children*, Nov. 20-22, 1952 (Minneapolis, Minn., 1953), 47 pp.

U.S. Committee on Special Education, *Special Education; the Handicapped and the Gifted. Section III, Education and Training*, White House Conference on Child Health and Protection (Appleton-Century: N.Y.C., 1931), 604 pp.

Van Riper, Charles, *Speech Therapy, A Book of Readings* (Prentice-Hall: N.Y.C., 1953), 319 pp.

Wallin, J. E. Wallace, *Children with Mental and Physical Handicaps* (Prentice-Hall, N.Y.C., 1949), 549 pp.

——, *Education of Mentally Handicapped Children* (Harper: N.Y.C., 1955), 485 pp.

Wiley, R.D., *Guidance in Elementary Education* (Harper: N.Y.C., 1952).

Young, Leontine R., *Out of Wedlock, a Study of the Problems of the Unmarried Mother and Her Child* (McGraw-Hill: N.Y.C., 1954), 261 pp.

PAMPHLETS

A Decade of Progress in Special Education, Title of May, 1944 issue of *Journal of Exceptional Children*, 10:8:197-216.

American Foundation for the Blind, *Report of the National Work Session on the Pre-School Blind* (N.Y.C., 1951), 67 pp. Reprint.

——, *Training Facilities for the Preparation of Teachers of Blind Children in the U.S.* (N.Y.C., 1953), 38 pp.

American School Health Association, *A Study of Education of Hospitalized Children in Urban Areas* (Buffalo, N.Y., 1950), 10 pp., mimeo.

Association for Childhood Education International, *Educating for Healthful Living* Washington, D.C., 1950), 40 pp.

Barker, Felix S., *Special Education and its General Implications* (Division of Special Education: Raleigh, N.C., 1950), 21 pp.

Boyles, Iva Field and Green, Ruth E., *The Illinois Plan for Special Education of Exceptional Children, the Physically Handicapped* (Springfield, 1952), 69 pp.

Boynton, M.S. and Drennan, *The Pre-School Exceptional Child in Illinois* (Dept. of Public Instruction: Springfield, 1949), 78 pp.

Brieland, D. M., *A Comparative Study of Speech of Blind and Sighted Children*, Speech Monographs 17, #1, 1950, pp. 99-103.

Camp Fire Girls, *Services with and for Handicapped Children* (N.Y.C., 1952), 24 pp.

Cincinnati, Ohio, Public Schools, *Opportunities for the Handicapped in the Special Schools and Classes*, Report of the Supt., 1947-1948, 40 pp.

Cruickshank, William M. and Sprague, Elfleda, *A Survey of Exceptional Children in Three School Districts of Onondaga County, N.Y. State, Including a Study of Exception Status of Children Reported Not in School* (Syracuse University: Syracuse, N.Y., 1948), 50 pp.

Cruickshank, William M., *Syracuse University Meets the Challenge of the Exceptional Child,* 1954-55 (Syracuse University: Syracuse, N.Y., 1954).

——, *The Exceptional Child in Contemporary Education* (Syracuse University: Syracuse, N.Y., 1952), 26 pp.

Culbertson, Polly, *Kindergarten in the Kitchen* (Bancroft School: Haddonfield, N.J., 1954), 64 pp.

Dobbins, Eleanor C., *Physical Education Activities for Handicapped Children* (University of the State of N.Y.: Albany, 1937), 55 pp.

Educational Policies Commission, *Policies for Education in American Democracy* (NEA Assn.: Washington, D.C., 1946).

Featherston, E.G., *Pupil Transportation in Cities* (Federal Security Agency, U.S. Office of Education: Washington, D.C., 1951), Pamphlet #111.

Featherstone, W.B., *Teaching the Slow Learner,* Rev. Ed. (Bureau of Publications, Teachers College, Columbia University: N.Y.C., 1951), 118 pp.

Firestone, S.H. and Orleans, J.S., *The Shortage of Special Class Teachers in Large Cities* (Division of Teacher Education, Office of Research and Evaluation, College of the City of N.Y.: N.Y.C., 1952), 39 pp.

Gall, Elena D., *The Adult Education Program at Goldwater Memorial Hospital,* Doctoral Thesis (Teachers College, Columbia University: N.Y.C., 1949), 147 pp.

Girl Scouts, *Girl Scouting for the Handicapped* (N.Y.C., 1951).

Great Britain, Ministry of Education, *List of Special Schools, Boarding Homes for Handicapped Pupils, and Institutions for Further Education and Training of Disabled Persons in England and Wales* (His Majesty's Stationery Office: London, England, 1953), 51 pp.

Heilman, G. C., *Needs and Resources for Group Learning of Cerebral Palsied Children of Pre-Elementary School Age in N.Y.C.* (Coordinating Council for Cerebral Palsy, in N.Y.C., 1954), 47 pp., mimeo.

Hopkins, Thomas W.; Bice, Harry V.; and Calton, Kathryn C., *Evaluation and Education of the Cerebral Palsied Child,* N.J. Study (International Council for Exceptional Children: Washington, D.C., 1954), 114 pp.

Hunter College, *College Symposium on the Education of the Exceptional,* Feb. 25-28, 1952; *Teachers and Other Professional Personnel, Their Selection and Education* (N.Y.C., 1953), 84 pp.

——, *Education of the Homebound,* Dept. of Spec. Ed., N.Y.C., E.D. Gall, Coordinator, 1953. 37 pp.

——, *Summer Vacation and Demonstration School for the Exceptional* (Office of Special Education: N.Y.C., 1953), 40 pp.

Illinois, Chicago Board of Education, *Special Education in the Chicago Public Schools,* A manual of procedures and policies, Revised (Chicago, 1953), 116 pp., pp. 103-116.

Illinois, Department of Public Instruction, *The Illinois Plan for Special Education of Exceptional Children; the Speech Defective,* Rev. (Springfield: 1952), Circular Series "E", #12, 1952.

International Council for Exceptional Children, *What Is Special about Special Education?* (Washington, D.C.: 1954), 46 pp.

Iowa, State University, *Iowa Hospital School for Severely Disabled Children* (Iowa City: 1950), 18 pp.

Irwin, R. B., *Special Education for Children with Speech and Hearing Disorders* (Division of Special Education: Columbus, Ohio, 1948), 65 pp.

Jenks, William, "Homebound Catholic Children Take on New Hope", *The Catholic Educator,* Oct., 1953. Reprint. 3 pp.

Kansas, Division of Special Education, *The Kansas Plan for Home and Hospital Instruction for Homebound and Hospitalized Children* (Topeka: 1951), #4.

Kilander, H.F., *Health Services in City Schools,* in Bul. #20 (Federal Security Agency, Office of Education: Washington, D.C., 1952), 68 pp.

Los Angeles, Calif., City School Districts, *We Serve the Exceptional Child,* Publication #555, 1953.

Lubeck, Alvin S., *Juvenile Delinquency Rates,* 1953 and Socio-Economic Characteristics for New York City (Youth Board: N.Y.C., 1954), 64 pp.

Mackie, Romaine P., *Crippled Children in School* (U.S. Office of Education: Washington, D.C., 1948), 37 pp.

——, *Education of Visually Handicapped Children* (U.S. Office of Education: Washington, D.C., 1951), 46 pp.

——, *School Housing for Physically Handicapped Children* (U.S. Office of Education: Washington, D.C., 1951).

——, *Some Problems in the Education of Handicapped Children* (U.S. Office of Education: Washington, D.C., 1952), 12 pp.

Mackie, Romaine P. and Dunn, Lloyd M., *College and University Programs for the Preparation of Teachers of Exceptional Children* (U.S. Office of Education: Washington, D.C., 1954), Bul. #13, 93 pp.

——, *State Certification Requirements for Teachers of Exceptional Children* (U.S. Office of Education, U.S. Dept. of Health, Education and Welfare: Washington, D.C., 1954), Bul. #1, 60 pp.

Mackie, Romaine P. and Fitzgerald, M., *School in the Hospital* (U.S. Office of Education: Washington, D.C., 1949), Bul. #3, 54 pp.

Martens, Elise H., *Coordination of Effort for the Education of Exceptional Children; Report of a Conference Called by the Office of Education* (U.S. Office of Education: Washington, D.C., 1935), 82 pp.

——, *Organization for Exceptional Children within State Departments of Education* (U.S. Office of Education: Washington, D.C., 1933), Pamphlet #42.

Mathesson, L., *Hospital Schools in the U.S.* (U.S. Office of Education: Washington, D.C., 1939), Bul. #17.

McIntire, Hazel C., *Highlights of Special Education* (Division of Special Education, Commission on Children & Youth: Columbus, Ohio, 1951), 16 pp.

Michigan Department of Public Instruction, *State Plan for Education of Physically Handicapped Children* (Lansing, 1952), 11 pp.

——, *The Exceptional Child; Summary of Public School Education Programs for Physically Handicapped Children and/or Speech Defective for the Year 1951-1952* (Lansing: 1952), 9 pp.

Michigan. Superintendent of Public Instruction, *Education of the Homebound Child* (Lansing, 1952).

National Education Association, *What the Classroom Teacher Should Know about the Child with Polio, with Epilepsy, with Cerebral Palsy, with Partial Sight, with Rheumatic Fever, with Impaired Hearing* (Washington, D.C., 1952).

——, National Committee on Safety Education, *National Conference on School Transportation* (Washington, D.C., 1954).

——, Rural Education Department, *Pupil Transportation, Yearbook* (Washington, D.C., 1953).

National Foundation for Infantile Paralysis, *Advancing the Education of the Hospitalized Child* (N.Y.C., 1948), Publication #72. 96 pp.

National Society for Crippled Children and Adults, *Speech Problems of School Children, a Symposium* (Chicago, 1953), 60 pp.

——, *Opportunities for the Preparation of Teachers of Exceptional Children* (Chicago, 1949), 99 pp.

National Tuberculosis Association, *Children with Special Health Problems; Educational Adaptations in School, Home and Hospital* (N.Y.C., 1948), 24 pp.

Nebraska, Department of Public Instruction, *Special Education; Children with Cerebral Palsy* (Division of Supervision and Curriculum: Lincoln, 1951), 185 pp.

New York City Board of Education, *Eligibility Requirements for License as Teacher of Health Conservation Classes in Elementary Schools* (N.Y.C., 1954), 4 pp.

New York City Board of Education, Bureau of Educational Research, *The Child with Orthopedic Limitations*, Pub. #33 (N.Y.C., June 1954), 132 pp.

——, Bureau of Educational Research, *The Child with Cardiac Limitations*, Pub #32 (N.Y.C., June, 1953), 154 pp.

New York City Board of Higher Education, Division of Teachers Education, *The Employment Outlook in Teaching for Those Students in the Municipal Colleges of New York City Who Will Complete Teacher Education Programs during the Period 1955-58* (Committee on Coordination of Teacher Education: N.Y.C., Dec., 1954), 8 pp.

——, Bureau of Health Education, *The Activities of the School Health Education Program in the Public Schools of the City of New York. Joint Policy on Procedures for Health Services in Secondary Schools*, Rev. ed. (N.Y.C., Oct., 1954).

New York State Department of Education, *State Education Law; Transportation of Physically Handicapped Children.*

North Carolina: Division of Special Education, *Proceedings of the First Annual Special Education Conference* (Raleigh, 1950), 102 pp.

Oklahoma Division of Special Education, *A Program of Education for Exceptional Children in Oklahoma* (Oklahoma City, 1951), 69 pp.

Oregon State Department of Education, *Special Education; Your Question Answered* (Salem, 1948), 24 pp.

Oregon: Superintendent of Public Instruction, *Home Instruction for Crippled Children — A Handbook for Parents* (Salem, 1951), 13 pp. mimeo.

Parker, Rose E., *Undergraduate Preparation for Teachers of Exceptional Children* (National Society for the Prevention of Blindness: N.Y.C., 1948), 8 pp.

Putnam, Rex, *Fifth Biennial Report of the Program for the Education of Handicapped Children,* as Provided for by Chapter 480, Oregon Laws, 1941 and Amended in 1943, 1945, 1949 and 1951, to the 47th Legislative Assembly, Submitted by Rex Putnam, Supt. of Public Instruction, Jan., 1953 (Dept. of Public Instruction: Salem, 1953).

Schleier, Louis, *Problems in the Training of Certain Special-Class Teachers* (Teachers College, Columbia University: N.Y.C., 1931), 138 pp.

Scottish Education Department, *Pupils with Physical Disabilities,* a Report of the Advisory Council on Education in Scotland (His Majesty's Stationery Office; Edinburgh, Scotland, 1951), 72 pp.

Texas Education Agency, *A Guide for Organizing and Providing Special Education for Exceptional Children* (Austin, 1951), 73 pp.

University of the State of New York, *Certificates for Teaching Services, Valid for Teaching Branch Subjects. Validation of Certificate for Teaching Special Classes and Other Subjects* (State Educ. Dept.: Albany, N.Y.).

U.S. Congress, *Hearings Before a Subcommittee of the U.S. Congress Senate, Committee on Labor and Public Welfare,* 81st Congress, 2nd Session, on S. 3102, a Bill to Enable the States to Make More Adequate Provision for Special Services Required for the Education of Physically Handicapped Children of School Age, and for other Purposes, May 16, 17, and 18, 1950 (Government Printing Office: Washington, D.C., 1950), 148 pp.

U.S. Federal Security Agency, Office of Education, *Health Services in City Schools* (Washington, D.C., 1952), 68 pp.

U.S. Office of Education, *Curriculum Adjustments for the Mentally Retarded* (U.S. Department of Health, Education and Welfare: Washington, D.C., 1953), Bul. #2, Reprint, 199 pp.

——, *Statistics of Special Education for Exceptional Children,* 1952-53. Biennial Survey of Education in the U.S., Chapter 5. (U.S. Department of Health, Education and Welfare: Washington, D.C., 1954), 78 pp.

——, *Teachers of Children Who Have Special Health Problems; Their Qualification and Professional Preparation* (Washington, D.C., 1954), 70 pp.

——, *The Forward Look, The Severely Retarded Child Goes to School* (U.S. Dept. of Health, Education and Welfare: Washington, D.C., 1953) Bul. #11, Reprint, 54 pp.

Westlake, H., *A System of Developing Speech with Cerebral Palsied Children* (National Society for Crippled Children & Adults: Chicago, 1952), 16 pp.

Whitehurst, M.V. and Morisees, E.K., *Auditory Training for the Deaf* (The Volta Bureau: Washington, D.C., 1952), 99 pp.

Woods Schools, *Adolescent Exceptional Child, Realistic Approach to Treatment and Training;* Proceedings of the 1954 Spring Conference of the Child Research Clinic of the Woods Schools, New Orleans, April 9-10 (Langhorne, Pa., 1954), 79 pp.

——, *An Educational Philosophy for Exceptional Children,* Proceedings of the Spring Conference on Education and the Exceptional Child of the Child Research Clinic of the Woods Schools, Langhorne, Pa., 1947 (Langhorne, Pa., 1947).

——, *Exceptional Child in Infancy and Early Childhood,* Proceedings, May, 1950, Conference on Education and the Exceptional Child (Child Research Clinic: Langhorne, Pa., 1950).

——, *The Emotional Climate of the Exceptional Child,* Proceedings of the Spring Conference on Education and the Exceptional Child of the Child Research Clinic (Langhorne, Pa., 1949).

——, *The Pre-Adolescent Exceptional Child*, Proceedings 35th Conference of the Child Research Clinic of the Woods Schools, Langhorne, Pa., held in Philadelphia, Pa., May 23, 1953 (Langhorne, Pa., 1953), 66 pp.

ARTICLES

Almy, M., "Principles and Practices of Nursery Education", *J. Int. Council for Exceptional Children*, Oct., 1954. v. 21, #1, pp. 18-21.

Barckley, V., "They Go to School in the Hospital", *Amer. J. Nursing*, March, 1954. 54:3:328-330.

Cain, Leo F., "General Problems and Administration of Programs for Exceptional Children", *Review, Educational Research*, Dec., 1953. 23:5:391-399.

Carter, V.R., "Where Shall Blind Children Be Educated?" *Int. J. for the Ed. of the Blind*, Dec., 1954. 4:11:21-23.

Cianci, V., "A Program for the Home Training of Mentally Retarded Children", *Training School Bul.*, June, 1948. 45:4:63-68.

——, "Objectives of Home Training", *Training School Bul.*, April, 1953. 50:2:23-29.

Cruickshank, William M., "Strengthening the Core of Special Education", *Exceptional Children*, Jan., 1954. 20:4:146-152, 183.

Dabney, R.S., "Responsibility of the School in the Education of the Exceptional Child", *Exceptional Children*, Nov., 1953. 20:87-88.

Davies, E. A., "Rehabilitation in the Schools", *Teach. Col. Rec.*, Nov., 1954. 56:92-7.

Denhoff, E., "The Physically Handicapped Child and the Nursery School", *J. Int. Council for Exceptional Children*, Feb., 1954. 20:5:202-208.

Dry, L.O., "A School to Hospital", *Telephone Service Hospitals*, June, 1952. 26:6 pt. 1:52-54.

Duggins, L. A., "Exceptional Children in the Classroom," *J. of Ed.*, Oct., 1950. 133:200-202.

Dunn, L. M. and McNeil, W.W., Special Education in Canada as Provided by Local School Systems", *Exceptional Children*, Feb., 1954. 20:5:209-215.

"Education of Exceptional Children; Reviews of the Literature in this Area for the 9-Year Period Since June, 1944", *Rev. of Educational Research*, Dec., 1953. 23:391-507.

Ellis, Vivian, "Some Changing Concepts in the Education of Physically Handicapped Children", *J. of School Health*, Nov., 1948. 18:9:241-247.

Featherstone, W.B., "Education of Exceptional Children", *Teach. Col. Rec.*, May, 1950. 51:512-19.

Fladeland, and Waterhouse, S.V., "Speech Therapy for Blind Pupils", *Outlook for the Blind*, 1951. 45. pp. 22-23.

Fouracre, Maurice, "Educational Opportunities for the Handicapped Child", *Cerebral Palsy Rev.*, Dec., 1953. 14:12:7-10.

Gwens, George W., "The Speech Pathologist Looks at the Mentally Deficient Child", *Training School Bul.*, April, 1951. 48:2:19-27.

Hill, Arthur S., "Extending Special Education Through State Legislation", *School Life*, June, 1953. 35:9:140-142. 144.

——, "Preparing Teachers for Exceptional Children", *Crippled Child*, July-August, 1949. 27:2:16-17, 30.

——, "Special Education Comes of Age", *Crippled Child*, April, 1952. 29:6:4-5.

"Implementing 'The Framework' Through Special Education for Exceptional Children and Youth", *California Schools*, May, 1952. 23:5:181-197.

Jenks, W.F., "Exceptional Child in Catholic Education", *Nat. Catholic Ed. Assn. Bul.*, May, 1954. 50; 7-21.

Jochem, Charles M., "State Survey on the Education of Handicapped Children", *Educ. Bul.*, N.J. Dept. of Ed., May, 1954. 25:3:151-52.

Karlin, Isaac W. and Strazulla, M., "Speech and Language Problems of Mentally Deficient Children", *J. Speech & Hearing Disorders*, Sept., 1952. 17:3:286-294.

Kelly, Elizabeth, "Curriculum Planning for Exceptional Children", *J. of Exceptional Children*, Feb., 1948. 14:5:130-133, 152.

Kille, E. C., "Therapy and Training Programs for Middle Grade Epileptic, Physically Handicapped, and Emotionally Disturbed Children", *Amer. J. Mental Deficiency*, July, 1953. Reprint. 58:1:88-92.

Kirk, S. A., "How Fare the Handicapped and the Gifted in Today's Crowded Schools?" *Educational Leadership*, Oct., 1954. 12:15-17.

Lerner, Arthur, "Information and Responsibility—A Philosophy for Teachers of Exceptional Children", *Exceptional Children*, Oct., 1954. 21:1:8-9.

Lesser, Arthur, "The School Health Program and the Handicapped Child", *Amer. J. of Public Health*, August, 1953. 43:8:1023-1029.

Leventhal, Eugenia G., "Positive Factors in a Multiple Grade Classroom for the Physically Handicapped", *Exceptional Children*, May, 1953. v. 19, n. 8.

Lord, F.E. and Wallace, M.M., "Recruitment of Special Education Teachers", *Exceptional Children*, March, 1949. 15:6:171-173.

Mackie, Romaine P. and Dunn, Lloyd M., "State Standards for Teaching Our Nation's 5,000,000 Exceptional Children", *School Life*, Oct., 1953. 36:1:8-10.

Mackie, Romaine P. and Fitzgerald, M., "Enriching the Curriculum of the Hospitalized Child", *J. Exceptional Children*, Nov., 1950. 17:2:33-34; 61-62.

McGrath, E. J., "Crucial National Problems in Education", *School Life*, April, 1953. 35: 99-101 plus.

Meyers, Allen, "Music Education and Music Therapy in Facilities Educating Physically Handicapped Children", *Bul., National Assn. for Music Therapy*, Jan., 1955. 4:1:7-8.

National Association of Secondary School Principals, "*Bulletin*, Speech and Hearing Problems in the Sceondary School", Nov., 1950. 34:173:4-139.

——, "*Bulletin*, Supervised Correspondence Instruction in the Secondary School", *National University Extension Assn*, Dec., 1952. 36:190:4-151.

"Nursery and Pre-School Panel—June, 1952", *Volta Review*, Nov., 1952. 54:9:421-434, 464.

Otto, Henry J., "Texas School Provides Normal Classroom Situations in Teaching Handicapped Children", *The Nation's Schools*, July, 1952. 50:1:38-43.

Porter, Rutherford B., "Clinical Service Extensions for Rural Area Exceptional Children", *Exceptional Children*, Dec., 1953. 20:3:105-110.

Reynolds, Maynard C., "Minnesota Has Done Well in Education for the Handicapped but We Must Do More", *Minnesota Journal of Education*, Feb., 1954. 34:7:24-25, **36.**

Richards, J. A., "Teaching Homebound Children by Telephone", *J. Exceptional Children*, Dec., 1953. v. 20, #3.

Salmon, F. Cuthbert, "Schools for the Handicapped", *School Executive*, Feb., 1952. 71:6:46-53.

Schlanger, Bernard B., "Speech Examination of a Group of Institutionalized Mentally Handicapped Children", *J. Speech and Hearing Disorders*, Dec., 1953. 18:4:339-49.

Severson, Ingeborg, "Philosophy of Special Education Cited", *Teaching Progress*, Nov., 1952. v. 8, no. 1.

Shane, P.J., "Slow Learning Pre-School Child", *American Childhood*, May, 1953. 38:14-15.

Simpson, R.E., "Some Children Require Special Help", *California Teacher's Assn. J.*, Sept., 1954. 50:26-27.

"Teacher Recruitment and Training—A Panel—1952", *Volta Rev.*, Dec., 1952. 54: 10:491-500, 512, 514.

Tenney, John W., "Recruiting Teachers for Exceptional Children", *Crippled Child*, April, 1951. 28:6:6-7, 28. Reprint.

Van Kleeck, E. R., "Special Education's Forgotten Child", *Nations Schools*, Oct. 1954. 54:52-4.

Wallace, Helen M.; Wrightstone, J. Wayne; and Gall, Elena D., "Special Classes for Handicapped Children", *American Journal of Public Health*, Aug., 1954. v. 44, no. 8.

Westlake, H., "What Is Special about Special Education? The Speech Defective Child", *Exceptional Children*, Nov., 1953. 20;2:56-60, 86.

Widdowsen, D.C., "30 Cardinal Requisites for an Adequate Educational Program for Hospitalized Children", *Exceptional Children*, March, 1954. 20:6:251-252, 258.

Willoughby, M. G., "Education of the Physically Homebound Child", *Occupational Therapy and Rehabilitation*, June, 1948. 27:3:186-190.

Young, Marjorie, "Certification of Teachers of Partially Seeing Children", *Exceptional Children*, April, 1952. 18:7:207-15.

LEGISLATIVE AND SOCIAL WORK REFERENCES

BOOKS

American Association of Social Workers, *Social Work Year Book*, 1953. A Description of Organized Activities in Social Work and in Related Fields. 12th ed. (N.Y.C., 1954), 703 pp.

American Parents Committee, *Handbook on Federal Grants-in-Aid* (N.Y.C., 1953), 216 pp.

Goldstine, Dora, ed., *Expanding Horizons in Medical Social Work* (Univ. of Chicago Press: Chicago, 1955), 288 pp.

Konopka, Gisela, *Group Work in the Institution; a Modern Challenge*, Intro. by Fritz Redl (Whiteside, Inc. & William Morrow: N.Y.C., 1954), 304 pp.

Somers, Herman Miles and Somers, Anne Ramsey, *Workmen's Compensation; Prevention, Insurance and Rehabilitation of Occupational Disability* (John Wiley & Sons, N.Y.C., 1954), 341 pp.

U.S. Bureau of Public Assistance, *Characteristics of Recipients of Aid to the Permanently and Totally Disabled, Mid-1951* (Washington, D.C., 1953).

PAMPHLETS

American Parents Committe, Inc., *The U.S. Program for Crippled Children, What It Does, and What Congress and the States Need to Do About It* (N.Y.C.), 24 pp.

California State Department of Education, *Laws and Regulations Relating to Education and Health Services for Exceptional Children in California* (Sacramento: 1954), 73 pp.

Committee on Education and Labor, on H.R. 3095, *Hearings, U.S. Congress, House of Representatives*. A Bill to Establish a Federal Commission on Services for the Physically Handicapped, to Define its Duties, and for Other Purposes, Hearings Held at Washington, D.C., July 12-15, 1949 (Govt. Printing Office, Washington, D.C., 1949), 202 pp.

Commonwealth of Virginia, *Special Services for Handicapped Children* (Richmond, 1953), 18 pp.

Frampton, M.E., *Assistance and Rehabilitation of the Physically Handicapped*, Hearing Before a Special Sub-Committee of the Committee on Education & Labor, House of Representatives, 83rd Congress, First Session, July and August, 1953, pp. 79 ff.

National Council of Churches of Christ, *The Church and the Handicapped* (The Council: 1954).

Montreal Council of Social Agencies, *Handbook on Services to the Physically Handicapped, Montreal and Region* (Montreal, Canada, 1952), 36 pp.

New York City Department of Health, *Service for the Handicapped Children*, Manual of Procedures for Participating Hospitals, Convalescent Institutions, and Rehabilitation Services (Bureau for Handicapped Children, N.Y.C.).

New York City Welfare and Health Council, Section on Services to the Handicapped, *Report on Study of Transportation of the Handicapped*, Dec., 1954.

New York City Welfare and Health Council, *Score Card for Welfare and Health Service* (May, 1954).

New York State Department of Social Welfare, *Amendments to N.Y. State Social Welfare Laws*, Article 10A, Chapter 418-419, and 420 of the Laws of 1954 (Albany, N.Y.).

New York State Joint Legislative Committee on Charitable and Philanthropic Agencies and Organizations, *Report of the . . . Legislative Document #26*, 1954 (William Piers: Albany, N.Y.).

The Woods Schools, *Some Contemporary Thinking About the Exceptional Child*, Proceedings of a Special Conference on Education and the Exceptional Child of the Child Research Clinic of the Woods Schools (Langhorne, Pa., 1949), 64 pp.

U.S. Children's Bureau, *Medical Social Services for Children in the Maternal and Child Health and Crippled Children's Programs* (Washington, D.C., 1953), 49 pp.

——, *Services for Children; How Title V. of the Social Security Act Benefits Children* (Washington, D.C., 1952), 9 pp.

U.S. Congress, *Public Law 565, 83rd Congress, Chapter 655, 2nd Session, Vocational Rehabilitation Amendments of 1954.*

U.S. Federal Security Agency, *Federal Grants-in-Aid in Health, Social Security, Education, Vocational Rehabilitation, Selected References,* 1938-1951 (Washington, D.C., 1952), 37 pp.

ARTICLES

Cruickshank, William M., "Team Action with Exceptional Children", *Exceptional Children,* May, 1952. 18:8:242-244.

Higgins, Lawrence E., "The Exceptional Child", *Louisiana Welfare,* April, 1954. 15:2:5-8.

Hill, Arthur S., "Legislation Affecting Special Education Since 1949", *Exceptional Children,* Dec., 1951. 18:3:65-67, 90.

Kershaw, J.D., "The Handicapped Child; a World Problem", *Special Schools Journal,* July, 1953. 42:3:4-8.

Laycock, Samuel R., "Community Understanding of the Exceptional Child", *Exceptional Children,* Nov., 1954. 21:2:47-49.

Lee, John J., "Landmark on the Highway of Social Advance", *Exceptional Children,* Oct., 1953.

Richard F., "What Would Happen if Community Agencies Worked Together?" *Illinois Education,* March, 1953. 41:264-8 plus.

Tenney, John W., "The Minority Status of the Handicapped", *Exceptional Children,* April, 1953. 19:7:260-264.

Worchester, D.A., "Clinical Services: Making the Best of Resources in the Rural Community", *Exceptional Children,* Jan., 1954. 20:4:176-179.

MEDICAL REFERENCES

BOOKS

American Medical Association, *Handbook of Physical Medicine and Rehabilitation* (Blakiston: N.Y.C., 1950), 573 pp.

Association for the Aid of Crippled Children, *Prematurity, Congenital Malformation, and Birth Injury,* Proceedings of a Conference sponsored by the Assn. at the N.Y. Academy of Medicine, June 5 & 6, 1952 (The Assn., N.Y.C., 1953), 255 pp.

Cruickshank, William M. and Raus, George M., editors, *Cerebral Palsy Its Individual & Community Problems* (Syracuse University Press: Syracuse, N.Y., 1955), 560 pp.

Dorland, W.A. Newman, *The American Illustrated Medical Dictionary* (WB. Saunders: Philadelphia, Pa., 1944), 1668 pp.

Exercise During Convalescence, A Manual of Adapted Exercises (A.S. Barnes: N.Y.C., 1947), 281 pp.

Health in Later Years, Report of the Third Annual Southern Conference on Gerontology, Held at the University of Florida, Jan. 26-27, 1953 (University of Florida Press: Gainesville, 1953), 123 pp.

Kiernander, Basil, editor, *Physical Medicine and Rehabilitation,* with an introduction by Lord Horder (Charles C. Thomas: Springfield, Ill., 1953), 610 pp.

Michal-Smith, H., editor, *Pediatric Problems in Clinical Practice; Special Medical and Psychological Aspects* (Grune & Stratton: N.Y.C., 1954), 310 pp.

National Health Council, *Health Careers Guide Book* (National Health Council and The Equitable Life Insurance Co.: N.Y.C., 1955), 154 pp.

——, *Partners for Health* (National Health Council and The Equitable Life Ins. Co.: N.Y.C., 1955), 406 pp.

Olson, Willard C., *Child Development* (Heath: Boston, Mass., 1949), 417 pp.

Presidents Commission on the Health Needs of the Nation, *Building America's Health.* Vol. 1, "Findings and Recommendations"; Vol. 5, "The People Speak; Excerpts from Regional Public Hearings on Health" (Washington, D.C., vol 1, 1952, 80 pp.; vol. 5, 1953, 521 pp.

Ridenour, Nina, *Health Supervision of Young Children* (Committee on Child Health, American Public Health Association: N.Y.C.), 180 pp.

West, Jessie Stevenson, *Congenital Malformations and Birth Injuries; a Handbook on Nursing* (N.Y. Assn. for the Aid of Crippled Children: N.Y.C.), 178 pp. illus.

Wheatley, G.M. and Hallock, G.R., *Health Observation of School Children* (McGraw-Hill: N.Y.C., 1951), 401 pp.

PAMPHLETS

American Medical Association, *Today's Health* (Chicago, Nov., 1954), 76 pp.

American Physical Therapy Association, *Physical Therapy—A Service and a Career* (N.Y.C., 1953).

——, *The Job of the Physical Therapist* (N.Y.C., 1954), 14 pp.

British Journal of Physical Medicine, Issue of Nov., 1954. 17:11. Entire issue devoted to subject of the blind.

Dublin, Louis I., *Health Progress, 1936 to 1945.* A supplement to 25 *Years of Health Progress* (Metropolitan Life Insurance Company: N.Y.C.).

Federal Security Agency, *The National Health Survey, 1935-1945, Scope, Method, and Bibliography* (Washington, D.C., 1951), 67 pp.

Great Britain, Ministry of Education, *The Health of the School Child,* Report of the Chief Medical Officer, Ministry of Education for Years 1950-1951 (London, 1952).

Hunter College, Department of Special Education, *Diseases and Disabilities of the Homebound Child* (N.Y.C., 1952), 61 pp.

New York University-Bellevue Medical Center, *Manual of Procedures of the Children's Division, Including Objectives, Philosophy, Policies, and Staff Functions of the Children's Division* (Institute of Physical Medicine and Rehabilitation, and Assn. for the Aid of Crippled Children, N.Y.C., 1952), 43 pp.

Smiley, Dean F., M.D. and Hein, Fred V., *Health Appraisal of School Children,* A report of the Joint Committee on Health Problems in Education of N.E.A. and the A.M.A.

U.S. Women's Bureau, Federal Security Agency, *The Outlook for Women as Occupational Therapists* (Washington, D.C.), Medical Services Series, #203-2, Rev., 51 pp.

U.S. Public Health Service, *Distribution of Health Services in the Structure of State Government—1950,* Public Health Service Publications no. 154, pt. 3 (Washington, D.C., 1953).

Walton, M.H., Chairman, *Report on a Survey of 559 Hospitals in the U.S.* (Committee on the Hospitalized Child, International Council for Exceptional Children, Washington, D.C., 1954), 9 pp. Mimeo.

ARTICLES

Brooks, G.L., Chairman, "The Care of Children in Hospitals", *Pediatrics,* Oct., 1954. 14:4:401-419.

Cholden, L., "Group Therapy with the Blind", *Group Psychotherapy* 1953. 6:21-29.

Culbert, R.W.; Jacobziner, H.; Ollstein, P., "Training Programs in School Health Service", *American J. of Public Health,* Feb., 1954. 44:2:228-234.

Harrison, C.H. and Elkins, E.C., "Evaluation of Training of Physical Educationists for Reconditioning and Rehabilitation", *Archives, Physical Medicine,* Feb., 1948. 29:2: 99-107.

Hessler, H.E., "The Relationship of Dentistry to Speech", *J. American Dental Assn.,* Jan., 1954. Reprint. 40:44-49.

Krusen, F. H., "Relationships Between Occupational Therapy and Physical Medicine and Rehabilitation", *Canadian J. Occupational Therapy,* March, 1954. 21:1:3-9.

Quibell, E.P., "The Child in the Long Stay Hospital, a Medical Social Problem", *Almoner,* July, 1954. 7:4:142-149.

Roberts, Grace, O.T.R., "Toys . . . tools for training", *The Crippled Child Magazine,* Feb., 1955, Vol. 32, No. 5, p. 4.

Schwartz, F.F., "Physical Therapy for Children with Cerebral Palsy" *J. Int. Coll. Surgeons,* Jan., 1954. Reprint. 21:1:84-87.

Wade, B., "Organizing an Occupational Therapy Department", *Hospitals,* Nov., 1954. 28:11:92-96, 98.

MENTAL HYGIENE AND PSYCHOLOGICAL REFERENCES

BOOKS

Bakwin, Harry, and Bakwin, Ruth Morris, *Clinical Management of Behavior Disorders in Children* (W.B. Saunders: Philadelphia, 1952), 495 pp.

Barker, Roger C., and others, *Adjustment to Physical Handicap and Illness; a Survey of the Social Psychology of Physique and Disability* (Social Science Research Council: N.Y.C., 1953), 440 pp.

Bett, W.R., *The Infirmities of Genius* (Philosophical Library: N.Y.C., 1952).

Blair, Glenn Myers, and others, *Educational Psychology* (Macmillan: N.Y.C., 1954), 601 pp.

Brower, D., and Abt, L., *Progress in Clinical Psychology* (Grune and Stratton: N.Y.C., 1952), Vol. I, Sec. 2.

Carmichael, Leonard, editor, *Manual of Child Psychology*, 2d ed (John Wiley: N.Y.C., 1954), 1295 pp.

Cavan, Ruth Shonle, and others, *Personal Adjustment in Old Age* (Science Research Associates: Chicago, 1949), 204 pp.

Cleugh, M.F., *Psychology in the Service of the School* (Philosophical Library: N.Y.C., 1954).

Garrison, Karl G., *The Psychology of Exceptional Children* (Ronald Press: N.Y.C., 1950).

Gesell, Arnold, and Amatruda, Catherine, *Developmental Diagnosis; Normal and Abnormal Child Development, Clinical Methods and Pediatric Applications* (Harper: N.Y.C., 1947), 426 pp.

Gesell, A., and Ilg, F.L., *The Child from Five to Ten* (Harper: N.Y.C., 1946).

Cruickshank, William M., editor, *Psychology of Exceptional Children and Youth* (Prentice-Hall: N.Y.C., 1955).

Guilford, J.P., *Psychometric Methods* (McGraw-Hill: N.Y.C., 1954), 597 pp.

Harms, Ernest, *Essentials of Abnormal Child Psychology; Survey Representing Twenty-five Years' Work in the Field of Child Psychology* (Julian Press: N.Y.C., 1953), 265 pp.

Harriman, Philip Lawrence, *The New Dictionary of Psychology* (Philosophical Library: N.Y.C., 1954).

Jersild, Arthur, *Child Psychology* (Prentice-Hall: N.Y.C., 1954).

Katz, B. and Lehner, George F., *Mental Hygiene in Modern Living* (The Ronald Press: N.Y.C., 1953), 544 pp.

Littledale, Harold A., *Mastering Your Disability* (Rinehart: N.Y.C., 1952), 224 pp.

Moloney, James Clark, M.D., *The Battle for Mental Health* (Philosophical Library: N.Y.C., 1954).

Pinter, R.; Eisenson, J.; and Stanton, M., *The Psychology of the Physically Handicapped* (Crofts: N.Y.C., 1941).

Sarason, Seymour B., *Psychology Problems in Mental Deficiency*, 2d edition (Harper: N.Y.C., 1953).

Seidenfeld, Morton A., *Psychological Aspects of Medical Care* (Chas. C. Thomas: Springfield, Ill., 1949), 61 pp.

Stinchfield, Sara M., and Hawk, S.M., *Psychology of Speech* (Boston Expression Company: Boston, 1928), 331 pp.

Strauss, Alfred A. and Lehtinen, Laura E., *Psychopathology and Education of the Brain-injured Child* (Grune & Stratton: N.Y.C., 1947), 206 pp.

Thom, Douglas A.; Von Salzen, Charles F.; Frommer, Allan, *Psychological Aspects of the Paraplegic Patient* (Saunders: Philadelphia, 1946).

PAMPHLETS

American Foundation for the Blind, *Attitudes toward Blindness* (N.Y.C., 1951), 32 pp.

Bauman, M., *A Comparative Study of Personality Factors in Blind, Other Handicapped, and Non-Handicapped Individuals* (U.S. Office of Vocational Rehabilitation, Dept. of Health, Education & Welfare: Washington, D.C., 1950), Rehab. Series #134.

Bauman, Mary K. and Hayes, Samuel P., *A Manual for the Psychological Examination of the Adult Blind* (Psychological Corp.: N.Y.C., 1951), 58 pp.

Council of State Governments, *The Mental Health Programs of the Forty-eight States; Summary and Recommendations* (Chicago, Ill., 1950), 10 pp.

Federal Securiy Agency, *Mental Health Pamphlets and Reprints, Public Health Service Series* #2 (Washington, D.C., 1951), 53 pp.

Garrett, James F., editor, *Psychological Aspects of Physical Disability* (U.S. Office of Vocational Rehabilitation, U.S. Dept. of Health, Education & Welfare: Washington, D.C., 1952), 195 pp. Also Service Bul. #210, 1954.

Grayson, Morris, in collab. with Powers, Ann, and Levi, Joseph, *Psychiatric Aspects of Rehabilitation* (N.Y. University-Bellevue Medical Center: N.Y.C., 1952), 86 pp.

Greenleigh, Lawrence F., M.D., *Psychological Problems of Our Aging Population* (National Institute of Mental Health: Washington, D.C., 1952).

Hayward, E., *Psychological Problems of the Physically Disabled* (U.S. Office of Vocational Rehabilitation, Dept. of Health, Education & Welfare: Washington, D.C., 1947).

Hobby, O.C., *Address Before Arizona's Third Annual Mental Health Institute, Nov. 8, 1954* (U.S. Dept. of Health, Education and Welfare: Washington, D.C., Nov., 1954). Mimeo.

Hynes, James L., Jr., *A Pound of Prevention* (N.Y. Comm. on Mental Hygiene of the State Charities Aid Assn.: N.Y.C.)

Kuder, G. Frederic and Paulson, Blanche B., *Exploring Children's Interests* (Science Research Associates: Chicago, 1951), 49 pp.

Myerson, Lee, issue editor, *The Social Psychology of Physical Disability*, Fall 1948. Vol. IV, No. 4 (Association Press: N.Y.C., 1948).

National Association for Mental Health, Inc., Proceedings, Third Annual Meeting of the National Association for Mental Health, Inc., Oct. 31, Nov. 2, 1953. *Mental Health — Everybody's Business* (N.Y.C., 1954), 126 pp.

National Society for Crippled Children and Adults, *The School Psychologist Aids the Parent of the Crippled Child*. A Symposium Co-Sponsored by the Division of School Psychologists and Division of Educational Psychology of the . . . , American Speech & Hearing Assn. and the. . . . (Chicago, 1954), 38 pp.

New York State Charities Aid Association, N.Y.C. Committee on Mental Hygiene, *Psychiatric Needs in Rehabilitation* (N.Y.C., 1948), 72 pp.

New York State Education Department, Mental Health Committee, *Removing Blocks to Mental Health in School; Suggestions for Faculty Study of School Situations that Prevent Optimum Mental Health* (1954).

Prat, Dallas, M.D. and Neher, Jack, *Mental Health is a Family Affair* (Public Affairs Committee: N.Y.C.).

Rennie, Thomas A.C. and Bozeman, Mary F., *Vocational Services for Psychiatric Clinic Patients* (The Commonwealth Fund: Cambridge, Mass., 1952), 100 pp.

The Social Psychology of Physical Disability, Title of fall 1948 issue of the *Journal of Social Issues*. 4:4:1-115.

Stern, Edith M. and Hamilton, Samuel W., *Mental Illness; a Guide for the Family* (The Commonwealth Fund: N.Y.C., 1942), 134 pp.

Thorman, George, *Toward Mental Health* (Public Affairs Committee: N.Y.C.).

Ullmann, Charles A., *Identification of Maladjusted School Children; a Comparison of Three Methods of Screening* (U.S. Public Health Service: Washington, D.C., 1952).

U.S. Children's Bureau, *The Adolescent in Your Family* (Washington, D.C., 1954), 110 pp.

U.S. Children's Bureau, *Emotional Problems Associated with Handicapping Conditions in Children* (Washington, D.C., 1952), 19 pp.

U.S. Federal Security Agency, Office of Vocational Rehabilitation, *Research Suggestions on Psychological Problems Associated with Blindness* (Washington, D.C.), 20 pp.

U.S. Federal Security Agency, Public Health Service, Catalog. *Mental Health Pamphlets and Reprints, Available for Distribution*, 1951 (Washington, D.C., 1951), 53 pp.

U.S. Office of Vocational Rehabilitation, "Counseling for Psychological Acceptance of Disability," Washington, D.C., 1953. 38 pp.

Ware, E. Louise, "Mental Hygiene of the Orthopedically Handicapped Child," Assn. for the Aid of Crippled Children, N.Y., 1947. 16 pp.

——, *The Mental Hygiene Consultant; Role, Basic Concepts and Functions* (Assn. for the Aid of Crippled Children: N.Y.C., Oct. 1950), 24 pp.

Young, Marjorie A.C., *The Partially Seeing—Psychological Aspects* (National Society for the Prevention of Blindness: N.Y.C., 1953).

ARTICLES

Abt, Lawrence Edwin, "The Psychology of Physical Handicap; a Statement of Some Principles", *Orthopedic & Prosthetic Appliance Journal*, June, 1954. 8:2:19-22.

American Cancer Society, "Psychological Aspects of Cancer", *Public Health Reports*, Oct., Nov., 1952, and Feb., 1953. 67:10 & 11; 68:2. 3 pts.

Barker, Roger G., "The Social Psychology of Physical Disability", *J. Social Issues*, 1948. 4:28-35.

Barnes, Robert H., "Psychological Problems in Physical Rehabilitation, a Review", *Am. J. Med. Sciences*, Jan., 1952. 223:106-112.

Bender, Lauretta, "Psychological Problems of Children with Organic Brain Disease", *Am. J. Orthopsychiatry*, July, 1949. 19:3:404-415.

Berko, Frances Giden, "Classroom Case Studies", *Cerebral Palsy Review*, Mar., 1954. 15:3:7-10, 13.

Berger, Stanley and Garrett, James F., "Psychological Problems of the Paraplegic Patient", *J. Rehabilitation*, Sept.-Oct., 1952. 18:5:15-17.

Berreman, J.V., "Some Implications of Research in the Social Psychology of Physical Disability", *Exceptional Children*, May, 1954. 20:347-50 plus.

Bird, H. Waldo; Teitelbaum, Harry; and Dunn, M.B., "Psychosomatic Aspects of Encephalomyelopathy with Muscle Atrophy", *Psychosomative Medicine*, May-June, 1952. 14:3:161-173.

Block, W., "Personality of the Brain Injured Child", *Exceptional Children*, 1954. 21:91-100.

Blodgett, Harriet E., "Psychology Points the Way", *Crippled Child*, June, 1953. 31:1:19-20.

Brown, William, and Pisetsky, Joseph E., "Sociopsychologic Factors in Hysterical Paraplegia", *J. Nervous & Mental Diseases*, April, 1954. 119:4:283-98.

Blom, Gaston E., and Nicholas, Grace, "Emotional Factors in Children with Rheumatoid Arthritis", *Am. J. Orthopsychiatry*, July, 1954. 24:3:588-601.

Cayley, Camille K., "Psychiatric Aspects of Rehabilitation of the Physically Handicapped", *Am. J. Psychotherapy*, July, 1954. 8:3:518-539.

Clotheir, F., "Education for Mental Health", *Mental Hygiene*, Oct., 1951. 35:560-70.

Cruickshank, W., "Relation of Physical Disability to Fear and Guilt Feelings", *Child Development*, 1951. 22:291-98.

——, "A Study of the Relation of Physical Disability to Social Adjustment", *Am. J. Occupational Therapy*, May-June, 1952. 6:3:100-109, 141.

——, and Dolphin, Jane E., "The Educational Implications of Psychological Studies of Cerebral-palsied Children", *Exceptional Children*, Oct., 1951. 18:1:1-8.

Di Carlo, Louis M. and Dolphin, Jane E., "Social Adjustment and Personality Development of Deaf Children; a Review of the Literature", *Exceptional Children*, Jan. 1952. 18:4:111-18, 28.

Doll, Edgar A., "Mental Evaluation of Children with Cerebral Palsy", *Crippled Child*, June, 1952. 30:1:6-7, 28.

Drewry, Henry M., "Emotional Needs of Children", *Exceptional Children*, Feb., 1955. Vol. 21, No. 5, p. 178.

Feast, Howard F., "Foster Homes — a Substitute for Dormitory Care", *Crippled Child*, April, 1952. 29:6:6-7, 30.

Felix, R.H., "For the Mental Health of Children in our Smaller Communities", *Children*, May, 1952. 16:132-6 plus.

Grossman, M., "Emotional Aspects of Rehabilitation", *American Journal of Psychiatry*, 1953. 109:849-52.

Heilman, Ann, "Intelligence in Cerebral Palsy . . . a New Interpretation of Research Studies", *Crippled Child*, Aug., 1952. 30:2:11-13.

Heiser, Karl F., "Applications of Clinical Psychology to Mental Deficiency", *Training School Bul.*, Feb., 1953. 49:10:235-244.

——, "Psychotherapy in a Residential School for Mentally Retarded Children", *Training School Bul.*, Feb., 1954. 50:10:211-218.

Hohman, Leslie B., "Intelligence Levels in Cerebral Palsied Children", *Am. J. Phys. Med.*, Oct., 1933. 32:5:282-290.

Ignotus, Pastor, "Some Psychological and Spiritual Aspects of Acute Anterior Poliomyelitis", *Mental Health*, Summer, 1953. 12:3:95-98.

International Council for the Mental Health of Children, "Mental Health of Children in the World of Today; International Reports", *Nervous Children*, Oct., 1950. 8:407-523.

Kanner, L., "Mental Health in Child Rearing", *Children*, March, 1953. 17:116-17.

Laycock, S.R., "Have Your Pupils Sick Feelings?" *Exceptional Children*, Feb., 1954. 20:5:223-225.

——, "Problems in the Adolescence of Exceptional Children", *Journal of Exceptional Children*, 1943. pp. 263-7.

Lennox, William G., and Markham, Charles H., "The Sociopsychological Treatment of Epilepsy", *J. Am. Med. Assn.*, Aug. 29, 1953. 152:18: 1690-1694.

Liber, B., "Behavior Problems of the Pre-school Child; a Radio Interview", *Understanding the Child*, Oct., 1952. 21:121-5.

Lindsay, Mary M., "The Physically Handicapped Child and his Family; the Influence of his Environment on the Behavior of the Physically Handicapped Child", *Courrier*, Nov.-Dec., 1953. 3:10:541-547.

Lorenze, Edward J., "The Role of the Psychiatrist in a Convalescent Hospital", *Arch. Phys. Med. & Rehabilitation*, Oct., 1954. 35:10:652-656.

MacGregor, F.C., "Some Psycho-social Problems Associated with Facial Deformities", *Amer. Sociol. Rev.*, 11:629-38, 1951.

McGrath, F., "The Psychology of the Hard of Hearing", *Handbook of Information for the Hard of Hearing*. California State Dept. of Education, 1947.

McClelland, E.S., "Minor Plastic Surgery and its Relation to Inferiority Complexes", *Med. Rec.*, 146:419-24, 1937.

Melnick, Arnold, "Psychological Aspects of the Cerebral Palsied Child", *J. Am. Osteopathic Assn.* June, 1954. 53:10:592-94.

Meyer, E., "Psychological and Emotional Problems of the Deaf Child", *American Annals of the Deaf*, 1953. 98:472-77.

Meyer, Edith and Crothers, Bronson, "Psychological and Physical Evaluation of Patients with Cerebral Palsy Studied for Periods of Ten Years or More. I. 'Psychological Evaluation' by Edith Meyer. II. 'Physical Evaluation, with Motion Pictures' by Bronson Crothers", *Am. J. Phys. Med.*, June, 1953. 32:3:153-158.

Misbach, Dorothy L., "Happy, Gracious Living for the Mentally Retarded Blind Child", *New Outlook for the Blind*, March, 1953. 47:3:61-66.

Mullen, Francis A., "Therapy and the School Psychologist", *Exceptional Children*, 21:7:257, 1955.

Peck, H.B., ed., "Planning for the Mental Health Needs of New York City Children", *J. Ed. Sociol.*, May, 1951. 24:497-557.

"Pills for Mental Illness? Help for Multiple Sclerosis?" *Time*, Nov. 8, 1954.

Podolsky, Edward, "How the Child Reacts to His Physical Defects", *Mental Hygiene*, Oct., 1953. 37:4:581-84.

Prugh, D.G., "A Study of the Emotional Reaction of Children and Families to Hospitalization and Illness", *American Journal of Orthopsychiatry*, Jan., 1953. 23:1:70-106.

"Psychiatric Problems of Interest for the Psychiatrist", *Arch. Phys. Med. & Rehabilitation*, June, 1953. 34:6:353-358.

Ravinovitch, Ralph D., "An Evaluation of Present Trends in Psychotherapy with Children", *J. Psychiatric Social Work*, Oct., 1954. 24:1:11-19.

Roach, Robert E., "The Meaning of Severe Deafness in the Life of the Young Child", *Cerebral Palsy Review*, Sept., 1953. 14:9:8, 12-14.

Rush, H. and Taylor, E., "Team Approach in Rehabilitation and the Psychologists' Role", in Garrett, J.F., ed., *Psychological Aspects of Physical Disability* (U.S. Office of Educational Rehabilitation, Dept. of Health, Education and Welfare: Washington, D.C., 1954), Bul. #210, Ch. 1.

Ryan, W.C., Jr., "School and Mental Health", *Understanding the Child*, Oct., 1954. 23:112-16.

Schlanger, Bernard B., "Environmental Influences on the Verbal Output of Mentally Retarded Children", *J. Speech and Hearing Disorders*, Sept., 1954. 19:3:339-343.

Seidenfeld, Morton A. and Abt, L.E., "Application of Clinic Psychology in Physical Handicaps", *Progress in Clinical Psychology*, 1953. pp. 430-42.

Sloan, William and Bensberg, Gerard J., "An Exploratory Study of the Full-Range Picture Vocabulary Test with Mental Defectives", *Am. J. Mental Deficiency*, Jan., 1954. 58:3:481-485.

Smith, Alan P., Jr., "The Psychiatric Approach to Rehabilitation", *J. National Medical Assn.*, Sept., 1953. 45:5:340-344.

Solomon, Mildred White, "Post-operative Social Adjustment of Blue Babies", *Smith College Studies in Social Work*, June, 1949. 19:3:180-192.

"Symposium on Psychologists and Psychiatrists in the Child Guidance Service", *Brit. J. Ed. Psych.*, Nov., 1951- Feb., 1953. 21:167-71; 22:1-29, 79-88, 155-9; 23:1-28.

Turrell, E.S., "Parental Influences in the Social Adjustment of the Handicapped Child", *Speech and Hearing Therapist*, Feb., 1954, pp. 4-12.

Whitley, H.E., "Mental Health Problems in the Classroom", *Understanding the Child*, Oct., 1954. 23:98-103.

Yost, Charles O., "Who Are the Children in Foster Care?" *Louisiana Welfare*, Jan., 1952. 12:1:14-16, 23.

PARENTAL EDUCATION AND PRESCHOOL REFERENCES

BOOKS

Hathaway, Winifred, *Education and Health of the Partially Seeing Child* (Columbia University Press: N.Y.C., 1954), 277 pp.

Kawin, Ethel, *A Guide for Child-Study Groups* (Science Research Associates: Chicago, 1952).

Kennedy, Millicent, V., and Somerset, H.C.D., *Bring Up Crippled Children, Suggestions for Parents, Teachers, and Nurses* (Council for Educational Research: Wellington, New Zealand, 1951), 94 pp.

Leonard, Edith M.; Vandeman, Dorothy D.; and Miles, Lillian E., *Counseling With Parents In Early Childhood Education* (The Macmillan: N.Y.C., 1954), 330 pp.

Stern, Edith M. and Castendyck, Elsa, *The Handicapped Child. A Guide for Parents* (A.A. Wyn: N.Y.C., 1950), 179 pp.

PAMPHLETS

Brown, Muriel W., *Partners in Education* (Assn. for Childhood Education International: Washington, D.C., 1950), 36 pp.

Drennan, Genevieve, editor, *Is Your Child Exceptional, Different?* For Parents and Groups Interested in the Exceptional Child (Illinois Congress of Parents and Teachers: Springfield, 1950), 85 pp. illus.

Eckert, Ralph G., *Handbook on Parent Education* (California Dept. of Education, Sacramento, California, 1950), Bul. of the Calif. State Dept. of Education. v. 19, no. 5, Nov., 1950, 74 pp. illus.

If You Have a Deaf Child, A Collection of Helpful Hints to Mothers of Deaf Children. Annual School for Mothers of Deaf Children (University of Illinois Press: Urbana, 1951), 134 pp. illus.

Keaster, Jacqueline and Holversten, Gloria, *Suggestions to the Parents of a Deaf Child*, Reprint from *American Academy of Opthalmology and Otolaryngology*, Sept.-Oct., 1953, 16 pp.

Metropolitan Life Insurance Company, *Preparing for Parenthood* (N.Y.C., 1953), 31 pp.

Miles, Madeline, *Do You Know Your Cleft Palate Child?* A Handbook for Parents (The Author: 23 Williams St., Bradford, Pa., 1953), 15 pp.

Minnesota Department of Public Welfare, *You Are Not Alone.* Information Helpful to Parents of Retarded Children (St. Paul, Minn., 1954).

Myklebust, Helmer R., *Your Deaf Child* (Chas. C. Thomas: Springfield, Ill., 1950), 133 pp.

National Congress of Parents and Teachers, *Study-Discussion Group Techniques for Parent Education Leaders*, Rev. ed. (The Congress: Chicago, Ill., 1951), 64 pp.

National Foundation for Infantile Paralysis, *When Your Child Has Infantile Paralysis, Suggestions for Parents*, Pub. no. 37, rev. (N.Y.C., July, 1952).

National Society for Crippled Children and Adults, Inc., *Parent's Study Guide; A Manual for Parents of Cerebral Palsied Children* (Chicago, 1951), 68 pp.

——, Division of Psychologists and Division of Educational Psychology, of the American Psychological Assn., American Speech & Hearing Assn., *The School Psychologist Aids the Parents of the Crippled Child* (Chicago, Ill., 1954).

Nelson, Boyd E., *Talks with Parents and Teachers of Deaf Children*, Part III, 47 pp.; Pt. IV, 27 pp.; Pt. V, 47 pp. (Utah Schools for the Deaf and Blind: 1954).

Norton, Edith N., *Parent Education in the Nursery Schools* (Assn. for Childhood Education International: Washington, D.C., 1949).

John Tracy Clinic, *Correspondence Course for Parents of Little Deaf Children*. Designed to be used with Preschool Children from Two to Five Years of Age (Los Angeles, California, 1951).

Ware, E. Louise, *Parents of the Orthopedically Handicapped Child*, Mental Hygiene Series No. 3 (N.Y. Assn. for the Aid of Crippled Children: N.Y.C., 1950), 21 pp.

Woods Schools, Child Research Clinic, *Helping Parents Understand the Exceptional Child*, Proceedings, May 1952. Conference on Education and the Exceptional Child (Langhorne, Pa., 1952).

ARTICLES

Axline, Virginia M., "Understanding and Accepting the Child Who Is Blind", *Childhood Education*, May, 1954. 30:9:427-430.

Bancroft, Frances L., "You Are Not Alone", *Crippled Child*, Aug., 1954.

Bidwell, Barbara, "Problems of Families with Epileptic Children", *Mental Health*, Summer, 1952. 11:3:104-110.

Burgess, Caroline B., "Counseling Parents of Handicapped Children", *New Outlook for the Blind*, Jan., 1955. 49:1:1-15.

Chapin, May Bishop, "Parent Education of Preschool Speech Defective Children", *Exceptional Children*, Jan., 1949. 15:4:75-80.

Child Study Association of America, "Conference on Parent Education", *Child Study*, 31, No. 3:34-6, 1954.

Cobb, Katharine, "Selected References on Preschool and Parental Education", *The Elementary School Journal*, Feb. 1955, pp. 351-358.

Denhoff, Eric and Holden, Raymond H., "Family Influence on Successful School Adjustment of Cerebral Palsied Children", *Journal International for Exceptional Children*, Oct., 1954. Vol. 21, No. 1, pp. 5-7.

Doll, Edgar A., "New Hope for Parents", *Am. J. Orthopsychiatry*, April, 1954. 24:2: 416-20.

Engel, Anna M., "How to Help Parents of Physically Handicapped Children", *N.E.A. Journal*, Oct., 1952. 41:7:432-433.

Gane, Grace M., editor, "Cleft Palate; a Guide for Parents and Teachers", *New Zealand Speech Therapist's Journal*, Supp., Nov., 1953. n.p. mimeo.

Gillette, Harriet E., "Preschool Training for Cerebral Palsy", *Arch. Physical Medicine Rehabilitation*, Jan., 1955. 36:1:34.

Greenberg, H., "Problems of Parents of Handicapped Children", *Journal of Exceptional Children*, 1950. 17:1-7.

Held, Marian, "New York Association Faces Challenge of the Preschool Child", *New Outlook for the Blind*, Dec., 1954. 48:10:363-368.

Ikeda, Hannah, "Adapting the Nursery School for the Mentally Retarded Child", *Exceptional Children*, Feb., 1955. 21:5:171-173, 196.

Jackson, Claire, "The Blind Child in the Nursery School", *New Outlook for the Blind*, Feb., 1955. 49:2:39-45.

Levy, Joseph H., "Study of Parent Groups for Handicapped Children", *Exceptional Children*, Oct. 1952. 19:1:19-26.

Mecham, Merlin J., "A Letter to the Parents of a Brain-injured Child", *Cerebral Palsy Review*, Jan.-Feb., 1955. 16:1:25-26.

"Parents of the Mentally Retarded Child", *J. Pediatrics*, April, 1954. 44:4:486-489.

Rankin, Carl E., "The Parent and the Deaf Child", *North Carolina Medical Journal*, Sept., 1954. 15:9:445-47.

Richmond, Julius B., "Self-understanding for the Parents of Handicapped Children", *Public Health Reports*, July, 1954. 69:7:702-4.

Roberts, Grace, "Toys — Tools for Training", *Crippled Child*, 1955. 32:5:4.

Shands, A.R., Jr., "Parents, Teachers; Partners in a Job Better Done", *Crippled Child*, 1955. 32:5:8-9.

Vorce, Eleanor C., "Your Child Is Deaf; Advice for Parents", *Volta Review*, May, 1954. 56:5:201-204.

Ward, Moira M., "Group Therapy for Eleven Preschool Cerebral Palsied Children", *Exceptional Children*, 1955. 21:6:207.

Weingold, Joseph T., "Parents' Groups and the Problem of Mental Retardation", *Am. J. Mental Deficience*, Jan., 1952. 56:3:484-492.

Zwerling, Israel, "Initial Counseling of Parents with Mentally Retarded Children", *J. Pediatrics*, April, 1954. 44:4:469-79.

VOCATIONAL GUIDANCE AND EMPLOYMENT REFERENCES*

BOOKS

Forrester, Gertrude, *Occupational Literature, an Annotated Bibliography* (H.W. Wilson: N.Y.C., 1954), 467 pp.

Hamilton, Kenneth W., *Counseling the Handicapped in the Rehabilitation Process* (Ronald Press: N.Y.C., 1950).

International Labor Office, *Vocational Training of Adults in the United States* (Geneva, Switzerland, 1948), 223 pp. Vocational Training Monograph no. 3.

Vocational Advisory Service, *Where to Find Vocational Training in New York City. A Directory*. Vocational Advisory Service (432 Fourth Avenue, New York City 16, 1954), 208 pp.

Warters, Jane, *Techniques of Counseling* (McGraw-Hill: N.Y.C., 1954).

PAMPHLETS

Association for New York City Teachers of Special Education, *Job Area Analysis for Occupational Education* (1948), 46 pp.

Blackburn, Alan R.; Athearn, Clarence R.; and Shoesmith, Marion, *Report on the Vocational Training and Guidance Program of the N.Y. Institute for the Education of the Blind* (The Institute: N.Y.C., 1943), 104 pp.

Brinn, Carolyn and Smith, Esther Elder, *Opportunities Limited; a Study of Employment Problems of the Cerebral Palsied and Epileptic* (California Society for Crippled Children: San Francisco, California, 1951), 116 pp.

California, Centinela Valley Committee for the Employment of the Physically Handicapped, *Two Doctors Report on the Employment of the Handicapped* (Inglewood, California, 1952), 12 pp.

Chappell, J. Hiram, *Counselor's Guide; How to Analyze the Rehabilitation Needs of Blind Persons on the Farm* (U.S. Office of Vocational Rehabilitation: Washington, D.C., 1954), 30 pp. Rehab. Ser. no. 160.

Curtis, Linn W., *Vocational Placement of the Cerebral Palsied: a Brief Experience in Dealing with the Vocational Problems of 200 Cerebral Palsied Adults* (United Cerebral Palsy of New York City: 1953), 13 pp.

Federal Security Agency, U.S. Office of Vocational Rehabilitation, *Instructional Guide for Use in Vocational Schools Providing Training for Blind Persons* (Washington, D.C., 1950), 45 pp.

---

*See Section III, Chapter IV, for further references on employment of the exceptional.

Fitting, Edward A., *Evaluation of Adjustment to Blindness* (American Foundation for the Blind: N.Y.C., 1954), 84 pp.

Fusfeld, Irving, *Counseling the Deafened; Developing Psychological Acceptance of the Disability in Counseling Adolescents and Young Adults* (Gallaudet College: Washington, D.C., 1954), 22 pp.

Gallaudet College, *Diversification of Employment for Deaf College Graduates; Symposium* (Washington, D.C., 1951), 37 pp. Bul. no. 4, vol. 1, Oct., 1951.

——, *Government Employment for the College-Trained Deaf Person* (Washington, D.C., 1952), 38 pp.

Gange, Harold, *Vocational Guidance of the Physically Handicapped* (The Author: Detroit, Michigan, 1942), 125 pp. Typed.

Hunter College Chapter, International Council for Exceptional Children; United Cerebral Palsy of New York City, Inc., *Vocational, Educational, and Recreational Needs of the Cerebral Palsied Adult; a Survey of a Sampling of 200 Ambulatory Cerebral Palsied Adults in New York City.*

Hyde, James F.C., Jr., *Law as a Profession for the Blind* (American Foundation for the Blind: N.Y.C., 1954), 67 pp.

Indiana State Board of Health, *Monthly Bulletin*, Jan., 1953. 56:1. Entire issue devoted to the subject of rehabilitation.

Mahoney, Harold J., *Occupational Information for Counselors; Essential Content for Training Courses* (World Book: N.Y.C., 1952), 70 pp.

McAulay, John H., *Vocational Schools as Training Facilities for Blind Workers* (American Foundation for the Blind: N.Y.C., 1954), 95 pp.

McIntire, Hazel C., *Vocations for Sight-Saving Class Children* (National Society for the Prevention of Blindness: N.Y.C., 1951), 4 pp.

McKay, Evelyn C., *Vocational Guidance of the Blind* (American Foundation for the Blind: N.Y.C.), 12 pp.

National Society for Crippled Children and Adults, *Careers in Service to the Handicapped.* Information for Vocational Guidance Specialists on the Professions of Physical Therapy, Occupational Therapy, Speech and Hearing Therapy, and Special Education (Chicago, 1952), 52 pp.

National Society for Crippled Children and Adults, *Conserving Human Resources; Proceedings*, 1952, Annual Convention, Oct. 26-29, 1952, Fairmont Hotel, San Francisco, California (Chicago, Ill., 1953), 107 pp.

Newman, Harry W.; Hoard, Seth W.; and Wodtke, Henry S., "Beekeeping for the Blind." New York Institute for the Education of the Blind, N.Y., 1947. 43 pp.

New York City Institute for the Crippled and the Disabled, *The Rehabilitation of Industrial Hand and Arm Disabilities;* a Series of Papers Presented at the Second Annual Conference and Demonstration for Compensation Insurers and Physicians, sponsored by the. . . . (N.Y.C., 1953), 47 pp.

New York Institute for the Education of the Blind, *A Study of Vocational Guidance Training and Placement Needs of the Blind and Deaf in New York State* (N.Y.C., 1942).

Ralya, Lynn L. and Ralya, Lillian L., *Selected Sources of Free and Inexpensive Information Concerning Vocational Rehabilitation—a Bibliography* (The Authors: Santa Monica, California, 1953), 8 pp.

Rennie, Thomas A.C., and Bozeman, Mary F., *Vocational Services for Psychiatric Clinic Patients* (The Commonwealth Fund: Cambridge, Mass., 1952), 100 pp.

United Cerebral Palsy Associations, Inc., United Cerebral Palsy Educational Advisory Board, *Realistic Educational Planning for Children with Cerebral Palsy; Guidance and Counseling*, Pamphlet no. 6.

U.S. Civil Service Commission, *A Guide for the Placement of the Physically Handicapped*, Pt. I, 'Aircraft Positions,' 1952; Pt. II, 'Ordnance and Ordnance Stores Positions,' 1953 (Superintendent of Documents: Washington, D.C., 1952-53).

U.S. Congress, *Public Law 565, 83rd Congress, Chapter 655, 2d Session, Vocational Rehabilitation Amendments of 1954.*

U.S. Department of Health, Education, and Welfare, *The Adolescent in Your Family* (Social Security Administration, Children's Bureau: 1954), pub. 347.

U.S. Employment Service, *Counseling and Employment Service for Special Work Groups* (Washington, D.C., 1954), 123 pp.

U.S. Office of Defense Mobilization, *Report to the Chairman,* Manpower Policy Committee by the Task Force on the Handicapped (Washington, D.C., 1951), 63 pp.

U.S. Office of Vocational Rehabilitation, *Counseling for Psychological Acceptance of Disability* (Washington, D.C., 1954), 38 pp. Rehabilitation Serv. Ser. no. 260.

———, *Proceedings:* Third Annual Workshop for Guidance, Training and Placement Supervisors, Washington, D.C., April 24-28, 1950. Rehabilitation Serv. Ser. no. 150.

———, *Proceedings:* Fourth Annual Workshop of Guidance, Training, and Placement Supervisors, Washington, D.C., April 23-27, 1951. 69 pp.

———, *Report on Proceedings:* Fifth Annual Workshop on Guidance, Training and Placement, Washington, D.C., 1952. 3 pts. Rehabilitation Serv. Ser. 188.

Usdane, William M., *Client Employability and the Therapeutic Community* (Institute for the Crippled and the Disabled: N.Y.C., 1954), 2 pp. Rehabilitation Ser. no. 7.

ARTICLES

Bloom, Mildred L., "Vocational Counseling with the Paraplegic", *Vocational Guidance Quarterly,* Winter, 1953, pp. 46-49.

Bongard, M.M., "Placing the Disabled", *Rehabilitation,* Nov., 1952. 6, 15-19.

Boyland, Laurence C., "Counseling the Physically Handicapped", *Progressive Physical Educator,* May, 1948. 30:2:53-55, Reprint.

Buchwald, L. C., "Counselor's Role in Identifying and Guiding the Superior Pupil", *Baltimore Bul. Ed.,* June, 1954. 31:16-17.

Delp, Harold and Hawk, Lewis, F. W., "Vocational Training of the Mentally Retarded", *Training School Bul.,* March 1953. 50:1:3-12.

Di Michael, Salvatore G., "Vocational Rehabilitation for the Mentally Retarded." *Personnel and Guidance J.,* April, 1953. 31:7:428-432.

Fantl, Kurt; Small, Leonard; Robinson, Richard, "Vocational Counseling in the Rehabilitation of Disturbed and Delinquent Boys", *Mental Hygiene,* Oct., 1949. 33:4:615-628.

Ferson, Regis F., "A School Vocational Guidance Program", *New Outlook for the Blind,* Jan., 1955. v. 49, no. 1, pp. 6-14.

Fleischer, Ernest, "Developing Occupational Information Programs for Adults with Cerebral Palsy", *Cerebral Palsy Rev.,* Sept., 1954. 15:9:4-6.

Fowlks, Everill W.; Cooper, Albert L.; Shumaker, L. Kenneth, "The Role of Vocational Adjustment in Rehabilitation", *Archives of Physical Medicine,* March, 1952. 33:3: 137-147.

Gellman, William, "A Workshop for Overcoming Barriers to Employment", *Vocational Guidance Quarterly,* Summer, 1953.

Geyer, Miriam A., "Counseling for Physically Impaired Students in High School", *Personnel and Guidance J.,* Dec., 1953. 32:4:214-216.

"Industrial Rehabilitation Units", *Rehabilitation,* Dec., 1953. 9:11-17.

Jansson, Kurt, "The Employment of Handicapped Workers in Industry", *Internat'l. Labour Rev.,* Aug., 1953. 68:2:16 pages.

Lamber, Gerald F., "The Counselor as Placement Specialist", *J. Rehabilitation,* July-Aug., 1952. 18:4:3-6, 29-30.

Lerner, Ruth S., "Rehabilitation at Hunter College", *Exceptional Children,* April, 1949. 15:7:199-202, 217.

Massee, Joseph C., "Vocational Rehabilitation of Cardiac Patients", *J. Med. Assn. Georgia,* Jan., 1952, 41:1:7-9. Reprint. 1952. 31:3:159-161.

McCahill, William P., "The So-Called Handicapped", *Personnel & Guidance J.,* Dec., 1952. 31:3:159-161.

Mowrer, G.E., "Guidance Services for Exceptional Children", *Am. Voc. J.,* March, 1952. 21:11-12.

Novis, Frederick W., "Job Readiness in Rehabilitation: What Are the Essential Objectives?" *Personnel and Guidance J.,* Nov., 1952. 31:2:83-86.

Olshansky, Simon S., "Three Views of Job Placement of the Handicapped", *Am. J. Occupational Therapy, Sept.-Oct.,* 1951. 55:5201-202,220-221.

Perry, Virginia, "Curriculum Planning for the Cerebral Palsied Child", *Crippled Child.* Oct., 1950. 28:3:20-21, 29. Reprint.

Pindell, Howard D., "Home Visitation in Counseling the Handicapped", *J. Rehabilitation*, Sept.-Oct., 1954. 20:5:15-16.

Poulos, Thomas, "Vocational Adjustments for Hearing Handicapped Children; a Public School Service", *Hearing News*, Dec., 1948. 16:12:10, 14.

Rusalem, Herbert, "Is There a Place for You in State Rehabilitation; Vocational Information for the Counselor", *Personnel and Guidance J.*, Nov., 1952. 31:2:113-115.

Rusalem, Herbert, "Vocational Adjustment of the Handicapped Child", *Cerebral Palsy Review*, Jan., 1954. 15:1:11-13.

Scherer, Isador W., "Vocational Planning for the Cerebral Palsied", *Cerebral Palsy Rev.*, August, 1952. 13:8:3-5, 16-17, 19.

Schowe, B. M., "Guide Lines for the Employment of Deaf Workers", *Employment Security Review*, Dec., 1951. 18:12:30-31.

Sylvester, C.W., "What Vocational Education Offers the Superior Pupil", *Baltimore Bul. Ed.*, June, 1954. 31:21-2.

Tenney, John W., "The Minority Status of the Handicapped," *Exceptional Children*, April, 1953. 19:7:260-264.

Thompson, Caroline Gross, "Prevocational Activities for the Physically Handicapped", *Am. J. Occupational Therapy*, June, 1947. 1:3:152-154.

Trachtman, Alvin, "An Exploratory Program for the Vocational Adjustment of Mentally Handicapped Adolescents", *Am. J. Mental Deficiency*, Jan., 1954. 58:3:424-430.

Usdane, William M., "Vocational Counseling with the Severely Handicapped", *Arch. Phys. Med. & Rehabilitation*, Oct., 1953. 34:10:607-16.

Wenkert, Walker, "Community Planning for Rehabilitation", *Amer. J. Public Health*, July, 1952. 42:7:779-783.

Whitehouse, Frederick A., "Teamwork: Clinical Practice in Rehabilitation", *Exceptional Children*, Jan., 1953. 19:4:143-148, 150-153.

Whitehouse, Frederick A., "When Does Vocational Preparation Start?" *Cerebral Palsy Rev.*, Jan., 1951. 12:1:7-8, 14. Reprint.

ADDITIONAL REFERENCES

USEFUL REFERENCES IN THE FIELD OF REHABILITATION FOR SPECIAL EDUCATION

GENERAL REFERENCES

BOOKS

Buchwald, Edith; Rusk, Howard A.; Deaver, George; and Covalt, Donald A., *Physical Rehabilitation for Daily Living* (McGraw-Hill: N.Y.C., 1952), 183 pp.

Davis, John Eisele, *Rehabilitation; Its Principles and Practice* (Barnes and Company: N.Y.C., 1946).

Kessler, Henry H., *Rehabilitation of the Physically Handicapped* (Columbia University Press: N.Y.C., 1953), 275 pp.

——, *The Principles and Practices of Rehabilitation* (Lea and Febiger: Philadelphia, 1950), 448 pp.

Krusen, Frank H., editor; Elkins, Earl C., and Deaver, George G., associate editors, *The 1950 Year Book of Physical Medicine and Rehabilitation* (*December, 1949-1951*) (Year Book Publishers: Chicago, 1951), 328 pp.

Littledale, Harold, *Mastering Your Disability* (Rinehart: N.Y.C., 1952), 224 pp.

Redkey, Henry, *Rehabilitation Centers in the United States*, a Compilation of Information Submitted by 40 Rehabilitation Centers for the 1st National Conference on Rehabilitation Centers, Dec. 1-3, 1952, Under the Sponsorship of the Nat. Soc. for Crippled Children & Adults and the Office of Vocational Rehabilitation, U.S. Dept. of Health, Education, & Welfare (National Society for Crippled Children & Adults: Chicago, Ill., 1953), 128 pp.

Rusk, Howard A., and Taylor, Eugene J. (and others), *Living with a Disability* (Blakiston Company: N.Y.C., 1953).

Soden, William H., ed., *Rehabilitation of the Handicapped* (Ronald Press: N.Y.C., 1949), 399 pp.

Technische Arbeitshilfen fur Schwerbeschadigte Ereste Zusammenstellung von Beispielen aus der Praktischen Vermittlungsarbeit in Norhein-Westfalen (Landesarbeitsamt: Dusseldorf, 1952).

PAMPHLETS

American Rehabilitation Committee, Inc., Bulletin No. 6, Vol. 2, May, 1954. *Rehabilitation Review.*

——, Bulletin No. 2, Vol. 3, Sept., 1954. *Rehabilitation Review.*

Florida Children's Commission, *Florida's Sunshine Story* (Nemour Foundation: Wilmington, Del., 1954), 73 pp. illus.

Garrett, James F., *Rehabilitation of the Paraplegic*, Danville, Ky., State Hospital Mental Health Bulletin, No. 1, Vol. 30.

Gingras, G.; Dallain, Leo; Mongeau, M.; and Rusk, Howard A., *The Rehabilitation Centre* (Rehabilitation Society for Cripples: Montreal, Canada, 1953).

Kabat, Herman; Huddleston, O. Leonard; and Vivino, Jean, *A Physical Medicine and Rehabilitation Center as a Private Enterprise and a Non-profit Organization* (Kabat-Kaiser Institute: Vallejo, California, 1951), 49 pp.

LeTourneau, Charles U., *Rehabilitating the Handicapped* (Rehabilitation Society for Cripples: 1951).

National Rehabilitation Association, *Conference Proceedings,* Hotel Statler, New York City, Oct. 23, 24, 25, and 26, 1950. (The Association: N.Y.C., 1951), 169 pp.

National Headquarters, Disabled American Veterans, Ohio, *Special Study Unit on the Disabled Veteran.*

Rehabilitation Center for the Physically Handicapped, Stamford, Conn., *Steps Toward Rehabilitation* (Stamford, Conn., 1949), 17 pp.

Svenska Vanforevardens Central-Kommittee, *Litteratur-Fortechning Rorande Vanfore- vard Och Annan Invalidvard* (Stockholm, Sweden, 1953), 59 pp.

ARTICLES

Bateman, Charles, "To See and Hear", *Exceptional Children,* Feb., 1955. 21:5:187-190, 192-194.

Cobalt, Donald A., "Rehabilitation of the Amputee Patient", *Archives, Physical Medi- cine and Rehabilitation,* April, 1953. 34:4:235-239.

Di Michael, S.G., ed., "Vocational Rehabilitation of the Mentally Retarded", *American Journal of Mental Deficiency,* Oct., 1952.

——, and Terwilliger, W.B., "Counselors' Activities in the Vocational Rehabilitation of the Mentally Retarded", *Journal of Clinical Psychology,* Monograph Supplement No. 9, April, 1953.

Feuer, Samuel G.; Chrystal, Murry; and Kaufman, Harriet, "A Realistic Approach to Rehabilitation", *Physical Therapy Review,* June, 1953. 33:6:304-305.

Fielding, B.B., "Two Approaches to the Rehabilitation of the Physically Handicapped", *Exceptional Children,* May, 1954. 20:336-41.

Kessler, Henry H., "Rehabilitation of the Severely Disabled", *Journal, International College of Surgeons,* Sept., 1953 20:3:370-373.

Mecham, Merlin J., "A Habilitation Program for the Adolescent and Adult with Cere- bral Palsy", *Cerebral Palsy Review,* Oct., 1954. 15:10:11-12, 14.

Rusk, Howard A. and Taylor, Eugene J., "Man's Fight Against Disability", *Crippled Child,* April, 1953. 30:6:10-12.

Rusk, Howard A., "Rehabilitation-Reconstruction", *Missouri Medicine,* May, 1954. 51:5:391-393.

——, "Total Rehabilitation", *Journal, National Medical Association,* Jan., 1953. 45:1: 1-16.

Swartz, Frederick C., "Some of the Problems Encountered in Setting Up a Rehabilita- tion Center", *Journal, Michigan State Medical Society,* May, 1953. 52:5:511-512, 515.

Zinovieff, A., "The Relationship of Physiotherapy to Occupational Therapy in Rehabili- tation", *Canadian Journal of Occupational Therapy,* June, 1953. 20:2:29-34.

EDUCATIONAL REFERENCES

PAMPHLETS

Strom, Ralph J., *The Disabled College Veteran of World War II* (American Council on Education: Washington, D.C., 1950).

ARTICLES

Rusk, Howard A., "Physical Medicine and Rehabilitation, the Problems of Education", *Archives, Physical Medicine and Rehabilitation,* Mar., 1951. 32:3:137-141.

Worden, Ralph E. and Hamilton, Kenneth W., "The Use of University Facilities in a Broad Rehabilitation Program for the Disabled", *Archives, Physical Medicine and Rehabilitation,* Oct., 1954. 35:10:621-626.

LEGISLATIVE AND SOCIAL WORK REFERENCES

BOOKS

American Association of Medical Social Workers, *Handbook on Services to the Physically Handicapped, Montreal and Region* (The Association, Eastern Canada District: Montreal, Canada, 1952).

United Nations, *Modern Methods of Rehabilitation of the Adult Disabled*. Report of a Group-Training Course Organized by the United Nations, with the cooperation of the World Health Organization and the International Labor Organization, held in Sweden, Finland, and Denmark, Sept. 8-Nov. 7, 1952 (United Nations: Geneva, Switzerland, 1952).

PAMPHLETS

Committee on Education and Labor, *Assistance and Rehabilitation of the Physically Handicapped*, Hearings before a special Subcommittee, House of Representatives, 83rd Congress, First Session, Pursuant to House Resolution 115, a resolution authorizing the Committee "to conduct studies and investigations relating to matters within its Jurisdiction", hearings held at Washington, D.C., July 14, 16, 17, 20, 21, 22, 23, 24, 27 and 28, 1953 (U.S. Government Printing Office: Washington, D.C., 1953), 361 pp.

The Community Chest and Council of Hennepin County, *Resources for the Handicapped; a Survey of Hennepin County, May,* 1952 (Hennepin County, Minnesota, 1952).

National Society for Crippled Children and Adults, *Rehabilitation Centers in the United States; a Compilation of Information* (Chicago, Ill., 1952).

Switzer, Mary E., and Rusk, Howard A., *Doing Something for the Disabled* (Public Affairs Committee: New York, 1953), 28 pp.

ARTICLES

Brodkin, Henry A., "New Jersey Service to the Physically Handicapped", *Journal, Medical Society of New Jersey*, April, 1953. 50:3:135-137.

International Society for the Welfare of Cripples, "International Circulation of Films on Services for the Disabled", *News Letter, International Society*, Nov. 10, 1952.

Kratz, John A., "How Federal Laws Made Vocational Rehabilitation History", *Journal of Rehabilitation*, Jan.-Feb., 1951. 17:1:16-19, 30.

Kratz, John A., "Vocational Rehabilitation, Past, Present, and Future in the United States", *Bulletin, American Rehabilitation Committee*, May, 1954. 2:6:1-6.

Krusen, Frank H., "Rehabilitation; Simplification and Public Assistance", *Minnesota Welfare*, May, 1953. 8:11:12-15.

Moore, Marjorie E., and Sanders, Barkev S., "Extent of Total Disability in the United States", *Social Security Bulletin*, Nov., 1950, 13:11:7-14.

Pellegrin, Margaret D., "Venture in Rehabilitation Planning", *Louisiana Welfare*, July, 1954. 14:3:17-20.

Pohlmann, Kenneth E., "Rehabilitation of the Severely Disabled: UMWA Welfare and Retirement Fund Experience", *American Journal of Public Health*, April, 1953. 43:4:445-451.

Redkey, Henry, "The Community Rehabilitation Center", *Journal of Rehabilitation*, May-June, 1954. 20:3:14-15, 18-20, 29-30.

Wenkert, Walter, "Community Planning for Rehabilitation", *American Journal of Public Health*, July, 1952. 42:7:779-783.

MEDICAL REFERENCES

BOOKS

Clark, Marguerite, *After the Doctor Leaves; a Practical Guide to Approved Post-Medical Care and Treatment of Chronic Diseases for the Patient and His Family*, Foreword by Howard A. Rusk (Crown Publishers: New York, 1954), 310 pp.

Dening, Kenneth A.; Deyoe, Frank S.; Ellison, Alfred B., *Ambulations; Physical Rehabilitation for Crutch Walkers* (Funk & Wagnalls: New York, 1951).

Krusen, Frank H., ed., *Physical Medicine and Rehabilitation for the Clinician* (W. B. Saunders: Philadelphia, 1951).

McBride, Earl D., *Disability Evaluation; Principles of Treatment of Compensable Injuries* (Lippincott: Philadelphia, 1953), 715 pp.

PAMPHLETS

British Medical Association, *The Rehabilitation and Resettlement of Disabled Persons; Memorandum of Evidence Submitted by the Council of the British Medical Association to the Interdepartmental Committee* (London, England, 1954), 80 pp.

Institute for Physical Medicine and Rehabilitation, New York University-Bellevue Medical Center, *Rx for the Disabled Housewife* (N.Y.C., 1952), 14 pp.

McCoy, Georgia F. and Rusk, Howard A., *An Evaluation of Rehabilitation; a Study of 476 Cases, with a Detailed Follow-up Study of 208 Cases Discharged from the Physical Medicine and Rehabilitation Services of the New York University-Bellevue Medical Center* (The Institute of Physical Medicine and Rehabilitation: N.Y.C., 1953).

Rusk, Howard A., "The Teaching of Rehabilitation and Physical Medicine" (an abstract), *Proceedings, Annual Congress on Medical Education and Licensure*, Feb. 9-10, 1948. 6 pp.

U.S. Bureau of Medicine and Surgery, *The Rehabilitation Program of the Medical Department, United States Navy* (Washington, D.C., 1945).

U.S. Federal Security Agency, Office of Vocational Rehabilitation, *Medical Information for Vocational Rehabilitation Officers* (Washington, D.C., 1947), 88 pp.

ARTICLES

Gifford, Yale W., "Notes on the New Provisions of the Vocational Rehabilitation Act of 1954", *Cerebral Palsy Review*, Mar., Apr., 1955. Vol. 16:2:21.

Institute of Physical Medicine and Rehabilitation, New York University-Bellevue Medical Center, "Self-help Devices for Rehabilitation", New York, 1953. Part 6.

Krusen, Frank H., "Physical Medicine and Rehabilitation as Related to Industrial Health", *Archives, Industrial Hygiene and Occupational Medicine*, July, 1953. 8:1:61-69.

——, "Relationships Between Occupational Therapy and Physical Medicine and Rehabilitation". Read at the meeting of the Canadian Association of Occupational Therapy, Toronto, Canada, Oct. 31, 1953.

Neu, Harld N., "Rehabilitation; the Third Phase of Medical Care", *Nebraska State Medical Journal*, Sept., 1953. 38:9:315-320.

Poole, F.E. and Bent, J.R., "The Employment of Cardiacs", *Industrial Medicine*, Dec., 1943.

Schiffer, Doris Marie, "Liberty Mutual's Rehabilitation Program", *American Journal of Nursing*, July, 1953. 53:7:834-837.

Shands, Alfred Rives, "Diagnostic Clinic for Rehabilitation", *Journal, American Medical Association*, July 16, 1949. 140:11:937-940.

Solomon, Walter M., "Progress in Physical Medicine and Rehabilitation", *Journal, American Medical Association*, Oct. 23, 1954. 156:8:753-755.

MENTAL HYGIENE AND PSYCHOLOGICAL REFERENCES

BOOKS

Bauman, Mary K., *Adjustment to Blindness* (State Council for the Blind, Department of Welfare: Harrisburg, Pa., 1954), 198 pp.

Donahue, W. and Dabelstein, D., eds., *Psychological Diagnosis and Counseling for the Adult Blind* (New York, 1950), 173 pp.

Garrett, James F., ed., *Psychological Aspects of Physical Disability* (Office of Vocational Rehabilitation, Federal Security Agency: Washington, D.C., 1952), 195 pp. Includes bibliography.

Rennie, T.A.C., and Bozeman, H.F., *Vocational Services for Psychiatric Patients* (Harvard University Press: Cambridge, Mass., 1952), 100 pp.

PAMPHLETS

New York State Charities Aid Assn., New York City, Committee on Mental Hygiene, *Psychiatric Needs in Rehabilitation* (N.Y.C., 1948), 72 pp.

ARTICLES

Barnes, Robert H., "Psychological Problems in Physical Rehabilitation: a Review", *American Journal of Medical Sciences*, Jan., 1952. 223:106-112.

Grossman, Maurice, "Emotional Aspects of Rehabilitation", *American Journal of Psychiatry*, May, 1953. Vol. 109, No. 2.

Smith, Alan P., Jr., "The Psychiatric Approach to Rehabilitation", *Journal, National Medical Assn.*, Sept., 1953. 45:5:340-344.

VOCATIONAL GUIDANCE AND EMPLOYMENT REFERENCES

BOOKS

Hamilton, Kenneth W., *Counseling of the Handicapped in the Rehabilitation Process* (Ronald Press: N.Y.C., 1950), 296 pp. Includes bibliography.

MacDonald, Mary E., *Federal Grants for Vocational Rehabilitation* (University of Chicago Press: Chicago, Ill., 1944), 404 pp. Includes bibliography.

Rennie, T.A.C.; Burling, T.; and Woodward, L. E., *Vocational Rehabilitation of Psychiatric Patients* (The Commonwealth Fund: N.Y.C., 1950), 133 pp. Includes bibliography.

Rusk, Howard A. and Taylor, Eugene J., *New Hope for the Handicapped; the Rehabilitation of the Disabled from Bed to Job*, Foreword by Bernard M. Baruch (Harper: N.Y.C., 1949), 231 pp.

U.S. Veterans Administration, *Manual of Advisement and Guidance* (Superintendent of Documents, U.S. Government Printing Office: Washington, D.C., 1945), 233 pp.

PAMPHLETS

American Federation of Labor, *Jobs for the Handicapped through Union-Management Cooperation* (Washington, D.C., 1954).

American Management Association, *Solving Office Staffing Problems; Some Current Approaches* (N.Y.C., 1952), 44 pp.

Brighouse, G., *The Physically Handicapped Workers in Industry*, Bulletin #13 (California Institute of Technology, Industrial Relations Section: Pasadena, California, 1946).

Canada: Department of Labour, *Survey of Disabled Persons Registered with the National Employment Service*, Montreal, P.Q. Prepared by the Rehabilitation Society for Cripples and the Occupational Therapy and Rehabilitation Centre, in collaboration with the Special Placement Units of the National Employment Service. (Montreal, Canada, 1953), 45 pp.

Finland, Ministry of Social Affairs, *Return to Work: Vocational Rehabilitation of the Physically Handicapped in Finland* (Helsinki, Finland, 1952), 43 pp.

Hochhauser, Edward, *The Sheltered Workshop in a Program for the Rehabilitation of the Chronically Ill* (N.Y.C., 1951), 16 pp.

Jewish Occupational Council, *A Survey of Sheltered Workshops Operated by Jewish Vocational Service Agencies* (N.Y.C., 1954), 31 pp.

McAulay, John H., *Vocational Schools as Training Facilities for Blind Workers* (American Foundation for the Blind: N.Y.C., 1954), 95 pp.

National Committee on Sheltered Workshops and Homebound Programs, *Sheltered Workshops and Homebound Programs; A Handbook on Their Establishment and Standards of Operation* (N.Y.C., 1952), xiii, 71 pp.

President's Committee on Employing the Physically Handicapped, *Performance, the Story of the Handicapped*, Nov., 1954. Vol. 4, no. 5.

United Mineworkers of America, Welfare and Retirement Fund, *Rehabilitation of the Disabled* (Cornelius Printing Company).

U.S. Bureau of Labor Statistics, *The Performance of Physically Impaired Workers in Manufacturing Industries*, Bul. No. 923, 1948. 132 pp.

U.S. Civil Service Commission, *A Guide for the Placement of the Physically Impaired*, Pamphlet No. 14, 4th ed., 1947. 337 pp.

U.S. Department of Health, Education, and Welfare, *National Conference of Rehabilitation Centers, Second Annual Meeting, October, 1953, Selected Papers*. Co-Sponsors: Office of Vocational Rehabilitation and National Society for Crippled Children and Adults (Washington, D.C.).

U.S. Department of Labor, *Employing the Physically Handicapped: A Bibliography*, Bul. No. 146, 72 pp.

——, Bureau of Employment Security, Employment Service Program Letter No. 596 to State Employment Security Agencies, "Expansion of Program of Services to the Handicapped", (Washington, D.C., Dec., 1954).

U.S. Office of Defense Mobilization, *Report of the Chairman, Manpower Policy Committee by the Task Force on the Handicapped* (Washington, D.C., Dec 28, 1951), 63 pp.

U.S. Office of Vocational Rehabilitation, *Directory, Rehabilitation Centers* (Washington, D.C., 1953), 12 pp.

——, *Psychiatric Information for the Rehabilitation Worker*, Rehabilitation Standard Memo. No. 118, 1948. 77 pp.

——, *Rehabilitation Centers; a Report to the States' Vocational Rehabilitation Council* (Washington, D.C., 1950), 65 pp.

——, *Rehabilitation Centers in the United States* (U.S. Department of Health, Education, and Welfare: Washington, D.C., 1954), 128 pp.

——, *Rehabilitation of the Mentally Retarded and Emotionally Disturbed* (Washington, D.C., 1952), 62 pp.

——, *Report of Proceedings, Fifth Annual Workshop on Guidance, Training, and Placement* (Washington, D.C., 1952).

——, *Selected Papers, National Conference of Rehabilitation Centers, Oct., 1953* (Washington, D.C., 1954).

U.S. Veterans Administration, *Review of Vocational Rehabilitation and Training Programs Administered by the Veterans Administration for Disabled Veterans* (Office of Vocational Rehabilitation and Education Service and Evaluation Service, Veterans Administration: Washington, D.C., Oct., 1954).

ARTICLES

Felton, Jean S., "Job Performance of Physically Impaired Persons in Industry", *Occupational Medicine*, May, 1948.

Hunt, Joseph, "President's Program for the Disabled", *America*, Nov 27, 1954.

Krusen, Frank H., "Physical Rehabilitation and Reemployment of the Handicapped", *Archives, Industrial Hygiene and Occupational Medicine*, July, 1954. 10:1:11-15.

Lee, John J., "Workshops, How They Help Train Workers for the Handicapped", *Crippled Child*, Feb., 1951. 30:5:16-17, 30.

Lesser, Marion S. and Darling, Robert C., "Factors Prognostic for Vocational Rehabilitation among the Physically Handicapped", *Archives, Physical Medicine and Rehabilitation*, Feb., 1953. 34:2:73-81.

Markham, Margaret E. H., "The Place of Occupational Therapy in the Rehabilitation Programme", *Canadian Journal of Occupational Therapy*, March, 1953. 20:1:11-17.

Novis, Frederick W., "Job Readiness in Rehabilitation; What Are the Essential Objectives?", *Personnel and Guidance Journal*, Nov., 1952. 31:2:83-86.

Switzer, Mary E., "New Trends in Vocational Rehabilitation", *American Journal of Public Health*, July, 1952. 42:7:784-786.

———, "Ten Years of Rehabilitation Under Public Law 113", *Journal of Rehabilitation*, July-August, 1954.

ADDITIONAL REFERENCES

LIST OF MAGAZINES AND PERIODICALS
SERVING THE FIELD OF SPECIAL EDUCATION

AGING

Aging, U.S. Department of Health, Education, and Welfare, Washington 25, D.C.
Geriatrics, 84 South Tenth St., Minneapolis 2, Minn.
Journal of Gerontology, Gerontological Society, 660 S. Kingshighway Blvd. St. Louis 10, Mo.

BUILDING AND EQUIPMENT, SCHOOLS

Guide for Planning School Plants, National Council on Schoolhouse Construction, State Department of Education, Los Angeles, Calif.

CAMPING

Camping Magazine, American Camping Association, 343 Dearborn St., Chicago 4, Ill.

CANCER

Cancer News, 521 W. 57th St., New York 19, N.Y.

CARDIAC

The American Heart Journal, C. V. Mosby Company, 3207 Washington Ave., St. Louis 3, Mo.

CEREBRAL PALSY

Cerebral Palsy Review, 2400 Jardine Drive, Wichita 14, Kans.

CHARITIES

The American Legion Magazine, American Legion, 700 N. Pennsylvania St., Indianapolis 6, Ind.
Catholic Charities Review, The National Conference of Catholic Charities, 1346 Connecticut Ave., N.W., Washington, D.C.
Red Cross Newsletter, American National Red Cross, 17th and D Streets, N.W., Washington 13, D.C.

---

*A listing of magazines and periodicals for each area of Special Education will be found at the close of each chapter in Vols. II and III *Special Education for the Exceptional*, edited by M.E. Frampton and E.D. Gall, published by Porter Sargent, 11 Beacon St., Boston, Mass.

CHILDHOOD EDUCATION AND WELFARE .

The American Child, National Child Labor Committee, 419 Fourth Ave., New York 16, N.Y.

The Child, Government Printing Office, Washington 25, D.C.

Child Development, Society for Research in Child Development, Fayerweather Hall, Northwestern Univ., Evanston, Ill.

Child Family Digest, 5320 Danneel St., New Orleans, La.

Child Study, Child Study Association of America, Inc., 132 E. 74th St., New York 21, N.Y.

Child Welfare, Child Welfare League of America, Inc., 345 E. 46th St., New York 17, N.Y.

Childhood Education, Association for Childhood Education International, 1200 M St. N.W., Washington 5, D.C.

Nane Bulletin, National Association for Nursery Education. Distribution Center, College of Home Economics, University of Rhode Island, Kingston, R.I.

Understanding the Child, 1790 Broadway, New York 19, N.Y.

CHRONICALLY ILL

Chronic Illness News Letter, Commission on Chronic Illness, 615 N. Wolfe St., Baltimore 5, Md.

Journal of Chronic Diseases, C. V. Mosby Company, 3707 Washington Blvd., St Louis 3, Mo.

DEAF

A. M. A. Archives of Otolaryngology, American Medical Association, 535 N. Dearborn St., Chicago 10, Ill.

American Annals of the Deaf, Gallaudet College, Kendall Green, Washington 2, D.C.

Hearing News, American Hearing Society, 817 14th St., N.W., Washington, D.C.

Volta Review, Alexander Graham Bell Association for the Deaf, 1537 35th St., N.W., Washington 7, D.C.

DENTAL EDUCATION

American Dental Association Proceedings, 222 E. Superior St., Chicago 11, Ill.

DIABETICS

Ada Forecast, American Diabetes Association, Inc., 1 E. 45th St., New York 17, N.Y.

EMPLOYMENT

Employment Security Review, U.S. Bureau of Employment Security, United States Department of Labor, Washington, D.C.

International Labor Review, International Labor Office, 1262 New Hampshire Ave., N.W., Washington 6, D.C.

Labor Market and Employment Security, U.S. Bureau of Employment Security, United States Department of Labor, Washington, D.C.

Nacca Law Journal, National Association of Claimants' Compensation Attorneys, 6 Beacon St., Boston 8, Mass.

EPILEPTICS

Epilepsia, International League Against Epilepsy, c/o Veterans Administration Hospital, 150 S. Huntington Ave., Boston 30, Mass.

GENERAL

American Journal of Diseases of Children, 535 N. Dearborn St., Chicago 10, Ill.

American Journal of Sociology, University of Chicago Press, 1126 E. 59th St., Chicago 37, Ill.

Child Development Abstracts and Bibliography, Child Development Publications, School of Medicine, Louisiana State University, New Orleans 12, La.

Disabled American Veterans Semi-Monthly, Disabled American Veterans, Washington, D.C.

Jewish Education, The National Council for Jewish Education, American Association for Jewish Education, 15th Floor, 1776 Broadway, New York, N.Y.

Journal of Educational Psychology, 10 E. Centre St., Baltimore 2, Md.

Public Welfare, American Public Welfare Association, 1313 E. 16th St., Chicago 37, Ill.

Social Statistics: Supplement to *The Child*, Superintendent of Documents, Washington 25, D.C.

UNESCO Courier, UNESCO, United Nations, Columbia University Press, 2960 Broadway, New York, N.Y.

U.S. Naval Medical Bulletin, U.S. Government Printing Office, Washington, D.C.

U.S. Public Health Reports, U.S. Department of Health, Education, and Welfare, Public Health Service, Washington 25, D.C.

Valor, American Federation for the Physically Handicapped, National Press Building, Washington, D.C.

Journal of the American Association for Health, Physical Education, and Recreation, American Association for Health, Physical Education and Recreation, 1201 16th St., N.W., Washington 6, D.C.

GENERAL EDUCATION

American Childhood, Milton Bradley Co., 44 Cross St., Springfield, Mass.

The American Teacher, American Federation of Teachers, 28 E. Jackson, Chicago, Ill.

The Bulletin, published by National Association of Secondary-School Principals, 1201 16th St., N.W., Washington 6, D.C.

Catholic School Journal, Bruce Publishing Co., 400 N. Broadway, Milwaukee 1, Wis.

Children, Superintendent of Documents, Washington 25, D.C.

Christian Education, National Protestant Council on Higher Education, 808 Witherspoon Bldg., Philadelphia 7, Pa.

The Clearing House, 207 Fourth Ave., New York, N.Y.

Education, The Palmer Co., 349 Lincoln St., Hingham, Mass.

Educational Forum, Kappa Delta Pi, Heidelberg College, Tiffin, Ohio

The Educational Record, The American Council on Education, Washington 6, D.C.

Educational Screen, 64 East Lake Street, Chicago 1, Ill.

The Education Digest, Ann Arbor, Mich.

Elementary School Journal, University of Chicago Press, Chicago 37, Ill.

Harvard Educational Review, Lawrence Hall, Kirkland St., Cambridge 38, Mass.

The Independent School Bulletin, Secondary Education Board, Milton, Mass.

International Journal of Religious Education, International Council of Religious Education, 79 E. Adams, Chicago 2, Ill.

Journal of Education, 334 Bay State Road, Boston 15, Mass.

Journal of Educational Research, Dembar Publications, Inc., 303 E. Wilson St., Madison 3, Wis.

Journal of Experimental Education, Dembar Publications, Inc., 303 E. Wilson St., Madison 3, Wis.

The Journal of General Education, University of Chicago Press, Chicago 37, Ill.

The NEA Journal, National Education Association of the United States, 1201 16th St., N.W., Washington 6, D.C.

National Parent-Teacher, 700 N. Rush St., Chicago 11, Ill.

The Nation's Schools, 919 North Michigan Ave., Chicago 11, Ill.

The Parents' Magazine, 52 Vanderbilt Ave., New York 17, N.Y.

Peabody Journal of Education, Published by the faculty of George Peabody College for Teachers, Nashville, Tenn.

The Progressive Teacher, Morristown, Tenn.

Religious Education, 545 West 111th St., New York 25, N.Y.

Research Bulletin, National Education Association of the United States, 1201 16th St., N.W., Washington 6, D.C.

School and Society, The Society for the Advancement of Education, Inc., 1834 Broadway, New York 23, N.Y.

The School Executive, 470 Fourth Ave., New York 16, N.Y.
School Life, Office of Education, U.S. Department of Health, Education, and Welfare, Superintendent of Documents, Government Printing Office, Washington 25, D.C.
The School Review, Univ. of Chicago Press, Chicago 37, Ill.
Student Life, Published by National Association of Secondary-School Principals, 1201 16th St., N.W., Washington 6, D.C.
Understanding the Child, National Assn. for Mental Health, 1790 Broadway, New York 19, N.Y.

GUIDANCE

Personnel and Guidance Journal, American Personnel and Guidance Association, 1534 O St., N.W., Washington 5, D.C.

HEALTH

American Journal of Public Health, American Public Health Association, Inc., 1790 Broadway, New York 19, N.Y.
Health Education Journal, Central Council of Health Education, Tavistock Square, London, England
Journal of School Health, American School Health Association, 33 Colonial Terrace, East Orange, N.J.
Journal of Social Hygiene, American Social Hygiene Association, 1790 Broadway, New York 19, N.Y.
Workshop Report, Society of State Directors of Health, Physical Education, and Recreation, Indiana State Board of Health, Indianapolis 7, Indiana

HEREDITY

Journal of Heredity, 1507 M St., N.W. ,Washington 5, D.C.
Pedagogical Seminary and Journal of Genetic Psychology, The Journal Press, 2 Commercial St., Provincetown, Mass.

JUVENILE DELINQUENTS

Focus, National Probation and Parole Association, 1790 Broadway, New York 19, N.Y.
The Prison World, American Prison Association, in cooperation with National Jail Association, 135 15th St., New York 3, N.Y.

MEDICINE

A. M. A. Archives of Industrial Hygiene and Occupational Medicine, American Medical Association, 535 N. Dearborn St., Chicago 10, Ill.
American Journal of Nursing, 2 Park Ave., New York 16, N.Y.
American Journal of Public Health and the Nation's Health, American Public Association, 1790 Broadway, New York 19, N.Y.
Canada's Health and Welfare, Information Services Division, Department of National Health and Welfare, Ottawa, Canada
Hospitals, American Hospital Association, 18 E. Division St., Chicago 10, Ill.
Journal of the American Medical Association, 535 N. Dearborn St., Chicago 10, Ill.
Journal of Medical Education, Association of American Medical Colleges, 185 N. Wabash Ave., Chicago 1, Ill.
Journal of Pediatrics, 3207 Washington Blvd., St. Louis 3, Mo.
Nervous Child, Child Care Publications, 30 W. 58 St., New York 19, N.Y.
Neurology, American Academy of Neurology, 84 S. 10th St., Minneapolis 3, Minn.
Nursing Outlook, National League for Nursing, 2 Park Ave., New York 16, N.Y.
Pediatrics, 301-327 E. Lawrence Ave., Springfield, Ill.
Spastics Quarterly, British Council for the Welfare of Spastics, 26 Cranleigh Parade, Limpsfield Rd., Sanderstead, Surrey, England
Today's Health, American Medical Association, 535 N. Dearborn St., Chicago 10, Ill.

MENTAL HEALTH

Mental Hygiene, National Association for Physical and Mental Rehabilitation, 1472 Broadway, New York 19, N.Y.

MENTALLY RETARDED

American Journal of Mental Deficiency, American Association on Mental Deficiency, Inc., Mansfield Depot, Conn.

Children Limited, National Association for Retarded Children, 129 E. 52nd St., New York 22, N.Y.

Journal of Nervous and Mental Disease, New Jersey Neuro-Psychiatric Institute, Box 1000, Princeton, N.J.

Training School Bulletin, Training School, Vineland, New Jersey

MULTIPLE SCLEROSIS

AARMS Forward, 270 Park Ave., Suite 7G, New York 17, N.Y.

OCCUPATIONAL THERAPY

American Journal of Occupational Therapy, 33 W. 42nd St., New York 36, N.Y.

ORTHOPEDICALLY HANDICAPPED

Artificial Limbs

Braces Today, Pope Foundation, 197 S. West Ave., Kankakee, Ill.

Bulletin International Society for the Welfare of Cripples, 127 E. 52nd St., New York 22, N.Y.

Bulletin National Society for Crippled Children and Adults, 11 S. La Salle St., Chicago 3, Ill.

The Crippled Child, National Society for Crippled Children, Inc., 11 S. La Salle St., Chicago 3, Ill.

Journal of Bone and Joint Surgery, 8 The Fenway, Boston, Mass.

Journal of Paraplegia, National Paraplegia Foundation, Broad Grace Arcade, Richmond, Va.

PARENT EDUCATION

National Parent-Teacher: The P.T.A. Magazine, National Congress of Parents and Teachers, 700 N. Rush St., Chicago 11, Ill.

Parents' Magazine, 52 Vanderbilt Ave., New York 17, N.Y.

PHYSICAL MEDICINE

American Journal of Physical Medicine, The Williams and Wilkins Co., Mt. Royal and Guilford Aves., Baltimore 2, Md.

Annals of Physical Medicine, British Association of Physical Medicine, Headley Brothers Ltd., 109 Kingsway, London, W. C. 2, England

Archives of Physical Medicine and Rehabilitation, American Congress of Physical Medicine and Rehabilitation; American Society of Physical Medicine and Rehabilitation, 30 N. Michigan Ave., Chicago 2, Ill.

British Journal of Physical Medicine, Butterworth & Co., Ltd., 88 Kingsway, London, W. C. 2, England

Physical Therapy Review, American Physical Therapy Association, 1790 Broadway, New York 19, N.Y.

PSYCHOLOGY AND PSYCHIATRY

American Journal of Orthopsychiatry, 1790 Broadway, New York 19, N.Y.

American Journal of Psychiatry, 1270 6th Ave., New York, N.Y.

American Journal of Psychotherapy, North Queen Street and McGovern Ave., Lancaster, Pa.

American Psychologist, The American Psychological Association, 1333 16th St., N.W., Washington, D.C.

Educational and Psychological Measurement, Box 6907, College Station, Durham, N.C.

International Journal of Group Psychotherapy, International Universities Press, Inc., 227 W. 13th St., New York, N.Y.

Journal of Clinical Psychology, 5 Pearl St., Brandon, Vt.

Journal of Consulting Psychology, American Psychological Association, 1515 Massachusetts Ave., N.W., Washington 5, D.C.

Journal of Educational Psychology, Warwick & York, Inc., 10 E. Centre St., Baltimore 2, Md.

Journal of Psychiatric Social Work, American Association of Psychiatric Social Workers, 1860 Broadway, New York, N.Y.

Pastoral Psychology, Great Neck, L.I., N.Y.

Psychiatry, The William Alanson White Psychiatric Foundation, 1711 Rhode Island Ave., N.W., Washington 6, D.C.

The Psychoanalytic Review, New Jersey Neuro-Psychiatric Institute, Box 1000, Princeton, N.J.

Psychological Abstracts, The American Psychological Association, Inc., Wayne University, Detroit 1, Mich.

RECREATION

Parks and Recreation, American Institute of Park Executives, 30 N. La Salle St., Chicago, Ill.

Recreation, 315 Fourth Ave., New York, N.Y.

REHABILITATION

Bulletin American Rehabilitation Committee, 28 E. 21st St., New York 10, N.Y.

Journal of the Association for Physical and Mental Rehabilitation, 1472 Broadway, New York 36, N.Y.

Journal of Rehabilitation, 1025 Vermont Ave., N.W., Washington 5, D.C.

Performance: The Story of the Handicapped, U.S. Printing Office, Washington 25, D.C.

Selected Rehabilitation Abstracts, U.S. Office of Vocational Rehabilitation, Washington, D.C.

The World Veteran, The World Veteran Federation, 27, rue de la Michodiére, Paris (2e) France.

RESEARCH

Review of Educational Research, American Educational Research Association, 1201 16th St., N.W., Washington 6, D.C.

SIGHT-SAVING

American Journal of Opthalmology, Ophthalmic Publishing Company, 664 N. Michigan Ave., Chicago 11, Ill.

Better Light Better Sight News, Better Light Better Sight Bureau, 420 Lexington Ave., New York 17, N.Y.

Elemenary School Journal, University of Chicago Press, 5750 Ellis Ave., Chicago 37, Ill.

Eye, Ear, Nose and Throat Monthly, Professional Press, Inc., 5 N. Wabash Ave., Chicago 2, Ill.

Illuminating Engineering, Illuminating Engineering Society, 1860 Broadway, New York 23, N.Y.

Magazine of Light, Lamp Department, General Electric Company, Nela Park, Cleveland 12, Ohio

Optical Journal and Review of Optometry, Chilton Company, Inc., Chestnut and 56th Sts., Philadelphia 39, Pa.

Sight-Saving Review, National Society for the Prevention of Blindness, 1790 Broadway, New York 19, N.Y.

SOCIAL WORK

Bulletin of the National Association of School Social Workers, 1 Park Ave., Room 810, New York 16, N.Y.

Conference Bulletin, National Conference of Social Work, 22 W. Gay St., Columbus, Ohio

Conference News, U.S. Com., International Conference of Social Work, 345 E. 46th St., New York, N.Y.

Journal of Social Issues, Society for the Psychological Study of Social Issues, Department of Psychology, Columbia University, New York, N.Y.

Journal of Social Work Process, 2410 Pine St., Philadelphia, Pa.

Quarterly Bulletin, New York State Welfare Conference, Capitol Station Annex, Box 26, Albany, N.Y.

Social Casework, 192 Lexington Ave., New York, N.Y.

Social Work Education, Council on Social Work Education, 345 E. 46th St., New York, N.Y.

Social Work Journal, American Association of Social Workers, 1 Park Ave., New York, N.Y.

SPECIAL EDUCATION

Exceptional Children, The International Council for Exceptional Children, 1201 16th St., N.W., Washington 6, D.C.

The Exceptional Children's Foundation Bulletin, 2225 W. Adams Blvd., Los Angeles 18, Calif.

The Gifted Child, American Association for Gifted Children, Inc., 15 Gramercy Park, New York 3, N.Y.

ICEC Bulletin, The International Council for Exceptional Children, 1201 16th St., N.W., Washington 6, D.C.

SPEECH

Journal of Speech and Hearing Disorders, Speech and Hearing Association, 321 Illini Hall, University of Illinois, Urbana, Ill.

TUBERCULOSIS

Bulletin National Tuberculosis Association, 1790 Broadway, New York 19, N.Y.

VISUAL EDUCATION

Audio-Visual Communication Review, Department of Audio-Visual Instruction, 1201 16th St., N.W., Washington 6, D.C.

Audio-Visual Guide, 1630 Springfield Ave., Maplewood, N.J.

EFLA Bulletin, Educational Film Library Association, Inc., 345 E. 46th St., New York 17, N.Y.

Educational Screen, Department of Audio-Visual Instruction, 1201 16th St., N.W., Washington 6, D.C.

Film Counselor, Film Council of America, 600 Davis St., Evanston, Ill.

New Bulletin, Film Council of America, 600 Davis St., Evanston, Ill.

VOCATIONAL GUIDANCE

American Vocational Journal, American Vocational Association, Inc., 1010 Vermont Ave., Washington 5, D.C.

The Personnel and Guidance Journal, American Personnel and Guidance, 1534 O St., N.W., Washington 5, D.C.

OFFICIAL AND VOLUNTARY AGENCIES

OFFICIAL AGENCIES

U.S. Department of Health, Education, and Welfare, Washington, D.C.
Public Health Service, Washington, D.C.
National Institute of Public Health, Washington, D.C.
Social Security Administration, Washington, D.C.
Children's Bureau and Bureau of Public Assistance, Washington, D.C.
U.S. Office of Education, Washington, D.C.
Food and Drug Administration, Washington, D.C.
U.S. Department of Labor, Washington, D.C.
Bureau of Employment Security, Washington, D.C.
Bureau of Apprenticeship, Washington, D.C.
Bureau of Labor Standards, Washington, D.C.
Bureau of Labor Statistics, Washington, D.C.
Womens' Bureau, Washington, D.C.
The President's Committee on National Employment of the Physically Handicapped
U.S. Veteran's Administration, Washington, D.C.
Department of Defense, Washington, D.C.
U.S. Civil Service Commission, Washington, D.C.
Federal Inter-Agency Group, Washington, D.C.

* * *

Office of Vocational Administration, Washington, D.C.

REGIONAL OFFICES
OF THE
OFFICE OF VOCATIONAL REHABILITATION

Region I	Boston, Mass.
Region II	New York, N.Y.
Region III	Washington, D.C.
Region IV	Atlanta, Ga.
Region V	Chicago, Ill.
Region VI	Kansas City, Mo.
Region VII	Dallas, Texas
Region VIII	Denver, Colorado
Region IX	San Francisco, Calif.

Each region employs a regional director.

VOLUNTARY AGENCIES

ACCIDENTS

National Safety Council, Inc., 425 N. Michigan Ave., Chicago 11, Ill.

ALCOHOLICS

Alcoholics Anonymous, c/o Alcoholic Foundation, Inc., P.O. Box 459, Grand Central Annex, New York 17, N.Y.

National Committee on Alcoholism, Suite 564, 2 E. 103 St., New York 29, N.Y.

National States' Conference on Alcoholism, Division on Alcoholism, State Department of Health, 66 South St., Concord, N.H.

U.N. World Health Organization, Palais des Nations, Geneva, Switzerland; Dr. M. G. Candau, Director-General; Dr. R. L. Coigny, Chief, Liaison Office with United Nations, New York 17, N.Y.

ARTHRITICS

American Rheumatism Association, Inc., 620 W. 168 St., New York 32, N.Y.

Arthritis and Rheumatism Foundation, 23 W. 45th St., New York 36, N.Y.

Canadian Arthritis and Rheumatism Society, Inc., 270 MacLaren St., Ottawa, Canada

BLIND

American Association of Instructors of the Blind, State School for the Blind and Deaf, Raleigh, N.C.

American Association of Workers for the Blind, 15 W. 16th St., New York 11, N.Y.

American Foundation for the Blind, Inc., 15 W. 16th St., New York 11, N.Y.

American Printing House for the Blind, Inc., 1839 Frankfort Ave., Louisville 6, Ky.

Braille Institute of America, Inc., 741 N. Vermont Ave., Los Angeles 29, Calif.

National Council of State Agencies for the Blind, 416 Monroe St., Montgomery, Ala.

National Council of State Executives for the Blind, c/o Bureau for the Blind, Providence, R.I.

National Society for the Prevention of Blindness, Inc., 1790 Broadway, New York 19, N.Y.

BUILDING AND EQUIPMENT, SCHOOLS

National Council on Schoolhouse Construction, State Department of Education, Los Angeles, Calif.

CAMPING

American Camping Association, Inc., Room 1706, 343 S. Dearborn St., Chicago 4, Ill.

Canadian Camping Association, 40 College St., Toronto, Canada.

Canadian Youth Hostels Association, 1-A Classic Ave., Toronto 5, Canada

National Catholic Camping Association, 1312 Massachusetts Ave., N.W., Washington 5, D.C.

CANCER

American Cancer Society, Inc., 47 Beaver St., New York 4, N.Y.

American Society for the Control of Cancer, 350 Madison Ave., New York 17, N.Y.

Canadian Cancer Society, Inc., 800 Bay St., Toronto, Canada

---

*Special Agency lists for areas in Special Education, (i.e., Blind, Deaf, Speech, etc.) will be found at the end of each chapter in Vols. II and III, *Special Education for the Exceptional*, edited by Frampton, M. E., and Gall, Elena D., and published by Porter Sargent, 11 Beacon Street, Boston, Mass.

CARDIAC

American Heart Association, Inc., 44 E. 23rd St., New York 10, N.Y.
Helen Hay Whitney Foundation, 525 E. 68th St., New York 21, N.Y.

CEREBRAL PALSIED

American Academy for Cerebral Palsy, Inc., 4743 N. Drake Ave., Chicago 25, Ill.
Association for the Aid of Crippled Children, 345 E. 46th St., New York, N.Y.
National Society for Crippled Children and Adults, Inc., 11 S. La Salle St., Chicago, Ill.
United Cerebral Palsy, Inc., 50 W. 57th St., New York 19, N.Y.

CHARITIES

American Legion, Inc., 700 N. Pennsylvania St., Indianapolis 6, Ind.
American National Red Cross, 17th and D Sts., N.W., Washington 13, D.C.
Community Chests and Councils of America, 345 E. 46th St., New York 17, N.Y.
Imperial Shriners Council, Box 2028, Richmond 16, Va.

CHILDHOOD EDUCATION AND WELFARE

American Academy of Pediatrics, 636 Church St., Evanston, Ill.
Association for Childhood Education International, 1200 M St., N.W., Washington 5, D.C.
Child Welfare League of America, Inc., 345 E. 46th St., New York 17, N.Y.
Department of Kindergarten-Primary Education, 1201 16th St., N.W., Washington 6, D.C.
International Council for Exceptional Children, 1201 16th St., N.W., Washington 6, D.C.
National Association for Nursery Education, Distribution Center, College of Home Economics, University of Rhode Island, Kingston, R.I.
National Kindergarten Association, 8 West Fortieth St., New York 18, N.Y.

CHRONICALLY ILL

Commission on Chronic Illness, 615 N. Wolfe St., Baltimore 5, Md.

DEAF AND HARD OF HEARING

Alexander Graham Bell Association for the Deaf (formerly Volta Speech Association for the Deaf), 1537 35th St., N.W., Washington 7, D.C.
American Hearing Society, Inc., 817 14th St., N.W., Washington 5, D.C.
American Speech and Hearing Association, Inc., Wayne University, Detroit 1, Mich.
Conference of Executive of American Schools for the Deaf, Inc., Faribault, Minn.
Convention of American Instructors of the Deaf, Inc., New Mexico School for the Deaf, 1060 Cerrillos Rd., Santa Fe, N.M.
National Association of the Deaf, Inc., 121 W. Wacker Dr., Suite 1020, Chicago 1, Ill.
National Society of the Deaf and the Hard of Hearing, Inc., 2 Bloor St., East Toronto 5, Canada
John Tracy Clinic, 806 W. Adams Blvd., Los Angeles, Calif.

DENTAL EDUCATION

American Dental Association, Council on Dental Education, 222 E. Superior St., Chicago 11, Ill.

DIABETICS

American Diabetes Association, Inc., 1 E. 45th St., New York 17, N.Y.

DIETETICS

The American Dietetic Association, 620 N. Michigan Ave, Chicago 11, Ill.

EMPLOYMENT

Bureau of Apprenticeship, United States Department of Labor, Washington 25, D.C.

Bureau of Employment Security, United States Department of Labor, Washington, D.C.

Bureau of Labor Standards, United States Department of Labor, Washington 25, D.C.

Bureau of Veterans' Reemployment Rights, United States Department of Labor, Washington 25, D.C.

Goodwill Industries of America, Inc., 1222 New Hampshire Ave., N.W., Washington, D.C.

International Association of Industrial Accident Boards and Commissions, Bureau of Labor, Washington 25, D.C.

National Association of Claimants' Compensation Attorneys, 6 Beacon St., Boston 8, Mass.

National Association of Manufacturers, 14 W. 49th St., New York 20, N.Y.

National Child Labor Committee, Inc., 419 4th Ave., New York 16, N.Y.

National Committee on Sheltered Workshops and Homebound Programs, 15 West 16th St., New York 11, N.Y.

President's Committee on Employment of the Physically Handicapped, Bureau of Labor Standards, U.S. Department of Labor, Washington 25, D.C.

Social Work Vocational Bureau, 192 Lexington Ave., New York 16, N.Y.

EPILEPTICS

American Branch, International League Against Epilepsy, National Veterans Epilepsy Center, Boston VA Hospital, Boston, Mass.

National Committee on Social Aspects of Epilepsy, c/o Muscatatuck School, Butlerville, Ind.

National Epilepsy League, Inc., 130 N. Wells St., Chicago 6, Ill.

GENERAL

American Academy of Political and Social Science, 3937 Chestnut St., Philadelphia, Pa.

American Association of Industrial Nurses, 645 Madison Ave., New York 21, N.Y.

American Association of School Administrators (NEA), 1201 16th St., N.W., Washington 6, D.C.

American Council on Education, Inc., 1785 Massachusetts Ave., N.W., Washington 6, D.C.

American-Korean Foundation, Inc., 345 E. 46th St., New York 17, N.Y.

American National Red Cross, 17th and O Sts., N.W., Washington 13, D.C.

American Neurological Association, 710 W. 168th St., New York 32, N.Y.

American Nurses' Association, Inc., 2 Park Ave., New York 16, N.Y.

American Optometric Association, Council on Education and Professional Guidance, 404 Wilmac Building, Minneapolis 2, Minn.

American Sociological Society, Inc., New York University, Washington Sq., New York 3, N.Y.

Association of the Junior Leagues of America, Inc., Waldorf Astoria, 305 Park Ave., New York 22, N.Y.

Association for the Study of Community Organization, Inc., 1 Park Ave., New York 16, N.Y.

Association of Volunteer Bureaus, 345 E. 46th St., New York 17, N.Y.

Canadian Red Cross Society, Inc., 95 Wellesley St., E., Toronto 5, Canada

Central Department of Church World Service, National Council of the Churches of Christ, in the United States of America, 120 E. 23rd St., New York 10, N.Y.

Chamber of Commerce of the United States, 1615 H St., Washington 6, D.C.

Children's Bureau, Social Security Administration, United States Department of Health, Education, and Welfare, Washington 25, D.C.

Conference for Health Council Work, c/o Council of Social Agencies of New Haven, 397 Temple St., New Haven 10, Conn.

Elizabeth McCormick Memorial Fund, Inc., 848 N. Dearborn St., Chicago 10, Ill.

Elks National Foundation, 16 Court St., Boston 8, Mass.

Institute of Child Welfare, University of Minnesota, Minneapolis, Minn.

International Union for Child Welfare, 16 rue du Mont Blanc, Geneva, Switzerland (New York Office, 129 E. 52nd St., New York 22, N.Y.)

Iowa Child Welfare Research Station, Iowa Univ., Iowa City, Iowa

Kaiser Foundation, 368 42nd St., Oakland, Calif.

The Kellogg Foundation, 250 Champion St., Battle Creek, Mich.

League of Red Cross Societies, 26 avenue Beau-Séjour, Geneva, Switzerland

Liberty Mutual Insurance Company, 10 Rockefeller Plaza, New York, N.Y.

Metropolitan Life Insurance Company, 1 Madison Ave., New York, N.Y.

National Catholic Welfare Conference, Inc., 1312 Massachusetts Ave., N.W., Washington 5, D.C.

National Child Welfare Division, American Legion, Inc., 700 N. Pennsylvania St., Indianapolis 6, Ind.

National Committee on Homemaker Service, 3715 Penn Ave., Pittsburgh 1, Pa.

National Council on Chief State School Officers, Office of the Commissioner of Education, Little Rock, Ark.

National Council on Physical Fitness, 700 Jackson Building, Ottawa, Canada; the Physical Fitness Division of the Department of National Health and Welfare.

National League for Nursing, Inc., 2 Park Ave., New York 16, N.Y.

National Social Welfare Assembly, Inc., 345 E. 46th St., New York 17, N.Y.

National Society for the Study of Education, Inc., 5835 Kimbark Ave., Chicago 37, Ill.

Office of Education, United States Department of Health, Education, and Welfare, Washington 25, D.C.

Russell Sage Foundation, Inc., 505 Park Ave., New York 22, N.Y.

The Salvation Army, 120 W. 14th St., New York 11, N.Y.

Save the Children Federation, Inc., 345 46th St., New York 17, N.Y.

Social Science Research Council, Inc., 230 Park Ave., New York 17, N.Y.

Society for the Psychological Study of Social Issues, Department of Psychology, Columbia University, New York 27, N.Y.

Spokesmen for Children, Inc., Suite 407, 654 Madison Ave., New York 21, N.Y.

United Mine Workers of America, Welfare and Retirement Fund, Terre Haute, Ind.

United Nations Children's Fund, United Nations Building, New York 17, N.Y.

United Nations Department of Social Affairs, Division of Social Welfare, United Nations Building, New York 17, N.Y.

United Nations Economic and Social Council, United Nations Building, New York 17, Secretariat of the Council

United Nations Educational, Scientific and Cultural Organization, 19 Avenue Kleber, Paris 16, France; United Nations Building, New York 17, N.Y.

United States Civil Service Commissioner, 80th and F Street, N.W., Washington 25, D.C.

The Woods Schools, Child Research Clinic, Langhorne, Pa.

GENERAL EDUCATION

National Education Association of the United States, 1201 16th St., N.W., Washington 6, D.C.

HEALTH

American Public Health Association, Inc., 1790 Broadway, New York 19, N.Y.

American School Health Association, 33 Colonial Terr., E. Orange, N.J.

American Social Hygiene Association, 1790 Broadway, New York 19, N.Y.

National Health Council, Inc., 1790 Broadway, New York 10, N.Y.

Society of State Directors of Health, Physical Education, and Recreation, Indiana State Board of Health, Indianapolis 7, Ind.

HOMEBOUND

Shut-In Society, Inc., 221 Lexington Ave., New York 16, N.Y.

HOSPITALS AND CONVALESCENT CARE

American Hospital Association, 18 E. Division St., Chicago 10, Ill.

American Protestant Hospital Association, Station A, Drawer 7, Evansville 11, Ind.
Catholic Hospital Association of the United States and Canada, 1438 Grand Blvd., St. Louis 4, Mo.
National Association of Methodist Hospitals and Homes, 740 Rush St., Chicago 11, Ill.

JUVENILE DELINQUENTS

American Prison Association, Inc., 135 E. 15th St., New York 3, N.Y.
Big Brothers of America, Inc., 1347 Suburban Station Building, Philadelphia 3, Pa.
Board of Parole, United States Department of Justice, Washington 25, D.C.
Bureau of Prisons, United States Department of Justice, Washington 25, D.C.
Canadian Penal Association, Inc., 340 Jarvis St., Toronto 5, Canada
Conference of Superintendents of Correctional Institutions for Girls and Women, 10 Greenwich Ave., New York 11, N.Y.
Correctional Service Associates, c/o National Training School for Boys, Bladensburgh, Washington 16, D.C.
Federal Bureau of Investigation, United States Department of Justice, 9th St. and Pennsylvania Ave., N.W., Washington 25, D.C.
John Howard Association, Inc., 608 Dearborn St., Chicago 5, Ill.
National Conference of Juvenile Agencies, Woodbine, N.J.
National Conference of Superintendents of Training Schools and Reformatories, The Children's Village, Dobbs Ferry, N.Y.
National Probation and Parole Association, Inc., 1790 Broadway, New York 19, N.Y.
Osborne Association, Inc., 114 E. 30th St., New York 16, N.Y.
Society for the Prevention of Crime, Inc., 114 E. 30th St., New York 16, N.Y.
United States Probation System, Administrative Office of the United States Courts, Supreme Court Building, Washington 13, D.C.

MEDICINE

American Industrial Hygiene Association, Mellon Institute, Pittsburgh, Pa.
American Medical Association, 535 N. Dearborn St., Chicago 10, Ill.
Canadian Public Health Association, 150 College St., Toronto 5, Canada
Industrial Medical Association, 28 E. Jackson St., Chicago, Ill.
National Conference for Cooperation in Health Education, 1790 Broadway, New York 19, N.Y.
National Medical Association, 1108 Church St., Norfolk, Va.
Planned Parenthood Federation of America, Inc., 501 Madison Ave., New York 22, N.Y.
Public Health Service, United States Department of Health, Education, and Welfare, Washington 25, D.C.
Society for Public Health Educators, Inc., c/o National Tuberculosis Association, 1790 Broadway, New York 19, N.Y.

MENTAL HEALTH

Alabama: Alabama Society for Mental Health, P.O. Box 2591, Birmingham
Arizona: Association for Mental Health, Professional Building, Phoenix
Arkansas: Mental Health Society, Veterans Administration Office, 211 Broadway, Little Rock
California: Mental Health Society of Northern California, 2015 Steiner St., San Francisco 2
California: Southern California Society for Mental Hygiene, 3067 W. 7th St., Los Angeles 5
Colorado: Association for Mental Health, 314 14th St., Denver
Connecticut: Connecticut Association for Mental Health, 956 Chapel St., New Haven 10
Delaware: Mental Health Association of Delaware, 1404 Franklin St., Wilmington
District of Columbia: Exceptional Children and Youth, Section, Division of State and Local School Systems, Office of Education, Federal Agency, Washington 25
District of Columbia: Mental Health Association, 227 M. Street, N.W., Washington
Florida: Association for Mental Health, 122 Wall St., Orlando
Florida: Florida Association for Mental Health, Box 3208, University Station, Gainesville

Georgia: Association for Mental Health, 502-3 Kemzer Insurance Building, 41 Exchange Pl., Atlanta

Georgia: Georgia Association for Mental Health, 89 E. Park Lane, N.E., Atlanta

Hawaii: Mental Hygiene Society of Hawaii, 1407 Kalakaua Ave., Honolulu, Hawaii

Idaho: Idaho Mental Hygiene Society, 615 S. 20th Ave., Caldwell

Illinois: Association: for Family Living, 28 E. Jackson St., Chicago 4

Illinois: Illinois Society for Mental Health, 123 W. Madison St., Chicago 2

Illinois: National Council on Family Relations, 1126 E. 59th St., Chicago 37

Indiana: Indiana Mental Health Association, 2331 N. Meridian St., Indianapolis 4

Indiana: Mental Healh Association, 331 English Foundation Building, 615 N. Alabama St., Indianapolis

Iowa: Association for Mental Health, 1027 High St., Des Moines

Iowa: Iowa Mental Health Authority, 1027 Des Moines Sts., Des Moines

Iowa: Iowa Society for Mental Hygiene, 314 19th St., S.E., Cedar Rapids

Kansas: Association for Mental Health, Masonic Temple, 10th and Van Buren, Topeka

Kansas: Kansas Association for Mental Health, 917 Cambridge Ave., Topeka

Kentucky: Association for Mental Health, Hopkinsville Milling Company, Hopkinsville

Kentucky: Kentucky Association for Mental Health, Barry Bingham, c/o The Courier Journal, Louisville

Louisiana: Louisiana Society for Mental Health, 816 Hibernia Bank Building, New Orleans 12

Maryland: National Institute of Mental Health, Public Health Service, Federal Security Agency, Bethesda 14

Maryland: Maryland Mental Hygiene Society, 317 E. 25th St., Baltimore 18

Massachusetts: Massachusetts Association for Mental Health, 41 Mt. Vernon St., Boston 8

Michigan: Michigan Society for Mental Health, 153 E. Elizabeth St., Detroit 1

Minnesota: Citizen Mental Health Association of Minnesota, 309 E. Franklin Ave., Minneapolis

Minnesota: Division of Public Instruction, Globe Building, 4th and Cedar, St. Paul 1

Minnesota: Minnesota Mental Hygiene Society, 309 E. Franklin Ave., Minneapolis 4

Mississippi: Mental Hygiene Association, 1404 Woolfolk State Office Building, Jackson

Missouri: Missouri Association for Mental Hygiene, 1210 E. University St., Springfield

Montana: Montana Society for Mental Hygiene, Montana State University, Missoula

Montana: Society for Mental Hygiene, 315 Spruce, Anaconda

New Jersey: Association for Mental Health, 12 Kimball Circle, Westfield

New Jersey: New Jersey Association for Mental Health, Park Hotel, W. 7th St., Plainfield

New York: American Association of Psychiatric Clinics for Children, 1790 Broadway, Rm. 916, New York 19

New York: American Foundation for Mental Hygiene, 1790 Broadway, Rm. 916, New York 19

New York: National Association for Mental Health, Inc., 1790 Broadway, New York 19

New York: New York State Society for Mental Health, 105 E. 22nd St., New York 10

North Carolina: North Carolina Mental Hygiene Society, P.O. Box 2599, Raleigh

North Dakota: Mental Health Association, 1006 9th St., Bismarck

Ohio: American Association on Mental Deficiency, Cambridge State Hospital, Cambridge

Ohio: Ohio Mental Health Association, 503 Chamber of Commerce Bldg., Columbus 15

Oklahoma: Oklahoma Association for Mental Health, P.O. Box 1672, Oklahoma City 3

Oregon: Mental Health Association of Oregon, 429 Park Bldg., Portland 5

Pennsylvania: Mental Health, Inc., 1 N. 13th St., Philadelphia 7

Pennsylvania: Pennsylvania Mental Health, Inc., 311 S. Juniper St., Philadelphia 7

Rhode Island: Rhode Island Society for Mental Hygiene, 19 Wingate Rd., Riverside

Rhode Island: Society for Mental Hygiene, 100 N. Main St., Providence

South Carolina: Mental & Social Hygiene Society, Drawer 189, Columbia

South Carolina: South Carolina Mental & Social Hygiene Society, Mental Hygiene Division, c/o State Hospital, Columbia

South Dakota: Mental Health Association, 827 S. Dakota Ave., Sioux Falls

South Dakota: South Dakota Mental Health Association, 1369 5th St., Brookings

Tennessee: Mental Hygiene Society, 303 Inter State Bldg., Chattanooga

Tennessee: Tennessee Mental Hygiene Society, 4175 Lyons View Pike, Knoxville
Texas: Texas Society for Mental Health, 2504 Jarratt Ave., Austin 3
Texas: Hogg Foundation for Mental Hygiene, University of Texas, Austin 12
Utah: Utah Society for Mental Health, c/o Family Service Society, 112 S. State St., Salt Lake City
Vermont: Association for Mental Health, c/o Department of Social Welfare, Montpelier
Vermont: Vermont Association for Mental Health, Vermont State Hospital, Waterbury
Virginia: Mental Hygiene Society of Virginia, 1105 W. Franklin St., Richmond 20
Washington: Association for Mental Health, 2245 Crescent Dr., Seattle
West Virginia: Davis & Elkins College, Elkins
Wisconsin: Association for Mental Health, 119 E. Washington Ave., Madison
Canada: Canadian Mental Health Association, 11 St. George St., Toronto 5

MENTALLY RETARDED

American Association of Mental Deficiency, Inc., Mansfield Depot, Conn.
National Association for Retarded Children, 129 E. 52nd St., New York 22, N.Y.

MULTIPLE SCLEROSIS

National Multiple Sclerosis Society, 270 Park Ave., New York 17, N.Y.

MUSCULAR DYSTROPHY

Muscular Dystrophy Association of America, 39 Broadway, New York 6, N.Y.

NUTRITION

The American Dietetic Association, 620 N. Michigan Ave., Chicago 11, Ill.
American Home Economics Association, 1600 20th St., N.W., Washington 9, D.C.
Bureau of Human Nutrition and Home Economics, Agricultural Research Administration, United States Department of Agriculture, Washington 25, D.C.

OCCUPATIONAL THERAPY

American Craftsmen's Educational Council, Inc., 32 E. 52nd St., New York 22, N.Y.
American Federation of Arts, 1083 5th Ave., New York 28, N.Y.
American Occupational Therapy Association, Inc., 33 W. 42nd St., New York 36, N.Y.

ORTHOPEDICALLY HANDICAPPED: INTERNATIONAL AGENCIES

ARGENTINA: Asociacion de Ayuda y Orientacion al Invalido (Association for the Aid and Orientation of the Disabled) Calle Humberto 1, 1284, Buenos Aires
AUSTRALIA: Australian Advisory Council for the Physically Handicapped, Box 3545, G. P. O., Sydney
AUSTRIA: Arbeitsgemeinschaft fuer die Fuersorge fuer Koerperund Sinnesbehinderte, (Society for the Welfare of Physically and Mentally Handicapped), 4, Hegelgasse, Vienna
BELGIUM: Association National d'Assistance aux Engants Estropies, (Association for the Care of Crippled Children), 9 Quai de Flandre, Charleroi
BRAZIL: Associacao de Assistencia a Crianaca Defeituosa (Association for the Aid of Crippled Children), Rua Xavier de Toledo, 98-8 Andar, Sao Paulo
CANADA: The Canadian Council for Crippled Children and Adults Incorp., 52 St. Clair Ave., E., Toronto
CHILE: Sociedad Pro-Ayuda al Nino Lisiado (Society for Aiding the Crippled Child), Genova 2037, Santiago
CUBA: Centro de Rehabilitacion de Lisados "Franklin D. Roosevelt", Calle 23, No. 508, Vedado, Havana
DENMARK: Samfundet og Hjemmet for Vanfore (The Society and Home for Cripples), Esplanaden 34, Copenhagen

FINLAND: Finnish Committee for the International Society for the Welfare of Cripples, Tenholantie 11, Helsinki-Toolo

FRANCE: Federation des Associations de Post-Cure et de Reeducation Fonctionnelle et
Professionnelle des Diminues (Federation of Associations of Post-Cure and Functional
and Professional Reeducation of the Physically Handicapped), 6 Rue de Seine, Paris

GERMANY: Deutsche Vereinigung fur Krueppelfursorge (German Association for
Crippled Care), Harlachingerstrasse 12, Munich

GREECE: Hellenic Society for Crippled Children, 41, Stavropoulou St., Athens

HAITI: L'Association Haitienne pour la Rehabilitation des Handicapes (The Haitian
Association for the Rehabilitation of the Handicapped), Box 1319, Rue de Interne-
ment, Port-au-Prince

INDIA: Society for the Rehabilitation of Crippled Children, Haji Ali Park, Clerk
Road, Mahaluxmi, Bombay

JAPAN: Japanese Society for Crippled Children, 15 Ichigaya-Hachiman-cho, Shinjiku-
ku, Tokyo

MEXICO: Associacion Mexicana de Rehabilitation, (National Rehabilitation Association of Mexico), Tonalla No. 16, Mexico

NETHERLANDS: Nederlandse Centrale Vereniging voor Gebrekkigenzorg, (Netherlands Central Society for the Welfare of Cripples), Pieter Lastmankade 37, Amsterdam Zuid

NEW ZEALAND: New Zealand Crippled Children Society, P.O. Box 6025, Te Aro,
Wellington, C. 2

NORWAY: Norwegian Committee for the International Society for the Welfare of
Cripples, Boks 65, Refstad pr. Oslo

SWEDEN: The Swedish Committee for the International Society for the Welfare of
Cripples, c/o SVCK, Jutas Backe 1, Stockholm

SWITZERLAND: Schweizerische Arbeitsgemeinschaft fur Invalidenhilfe (Swiss Federation or Organization for the Welfare of the Crippled), Hohenbuhlstrasse 15,
Zurich

UNION OF SOUTH AFRICA: National Council for the Care of Cripples in South
Africa, P.O. Box 10173, Johannesburg

UNITED KINGDOM: Central Council for the Care of Cripples, 34 Eccleston Square,
London, S. W. 1

URUGUAY: El Asociacion Nacional Para el Nino Lisiado, (National Association for
Crippled Children), Avenida Millan 4205, Montevideo

ORTHOPEDICALLY HANDICAPPED: NATIONAL AGENCIES

American Federation of Physically Handicapped, National Press Bldg., Washington 4,
D.C.

Association for the Aid of Crippled Children, 345 E. 46th St., New York 17, N.Y.

Bureau of Public Assistance, Social Security Administration, United States Department
of Health, Education, and Welfare, Washington 25, D.C.

Institute for the Crippled and Disabled, Inc., 400 1st Ave., New York 10, N.Y.

International Society for the Welfare of Cripples, 70 First Ave., New York 17, N.Y.

The National Paraplegia Foundation, Broad-Grace Arcade, Richmond 19, Va.

National Society for Crippled Children and Adults, Inc., 11 S. La Salle St., Chicago 3,
Ill.

PARENTS

American Parents Committee, Inc., 52 Vanderbilt Ave., New York 17, N.Y.; 132 3rd
St., S.E., Washington 3, D.C.

Child Study Association of America, Inc., 132 E. 74th St., New York 21, N.Y.

National Committee for Parent Education, Inc., 71 E. Ferry, Detroit 2, Mich.

National Congress of Colored Parents and Teachers, Inc., 123 S. Queen St., Dover, Del.

National Congress of Parents and Teachers, 700 N. Rush St., Chicago 11, Ill.

National Council on Family Relations, Inc., 5757 S. Drexel Ave., Chicago 37, Ill.

PEDIATRICS

The American Academy of Pediatrics, 636 Church St., Evanston, Ill.

PHYSICAL EDUCATION

American Academy of Physical Education, University of Utah, Salt Lake City 1, Utah

American Association for Health, Physical Education, and Recreation, 1201 16th St., N.W., Washington 6, D.C.

Central Association for Physical Education of College Women, College of St. Scholastica, Duluth, Minn.

College Physical Education Association, University of Pennsylvania, Philadelphia 4, Pa.

Eastern Association for Physical Education of College Women, Vassar College, Poughkeepsie, N.Y.

Midwest Association for Physical Education of College Women, Illinois Normal University, Normal, Ill.

National Association for Physical Education of College Women, University of Illinois, Urbana, Ill.

National Collegiate Athletic Association, 209 Fairfax Building, 11th and Baltimore, Kansas City 5, Mo.; University of Alabama, Tuscaloosa, Ala.

National Federation State High School Athletic Associations, Benton Harbor High School, Benton Harbor, Mich.

Southern Association for Physical Education of College Women, Alabama College, Montevallo, Ala.

Western Society Physical Education of College Women, Oregon State College, Corvallis, Ore.

PHYSICAL MEDICINE

American Congress of Physical Medicine, 30 N. Michigan Ave., Chicago 2, Ill.

Baruch Commission on Physical Medicine, 597 Madison Ave., New York 22, N.Y.

PHYSICAL THERAPY

American Physical Therapy Association, 1790 Broadway, New York 19, N.Y.

POLIOMYELITIS

National Foundation for Infantile Paralysis, Inc., 120 Broadway, New York 5, N.Y.

Sister Elizabeth Kenny Foundation, Inc., 507 Fifth Ave., New York, N.Y.

PSYCHOLOGY AND PSYCHIATRY

American Association of Psychiatric Clinics for Children, 1790 Broadway, New York 19, N.Y.

American Group Psychotherapy Association, Inc., 228 E. 19th St., New York 3, N.Y.

American Orthpsychiatric Association, Inc., 1790 Broadway, New York 19, N.Y.

American Psychiatric Association, Inc., 1270 Avenue of the Americas, New York 20, N.Y.

American Psychological Association, Inc., 1333 16th St., N.W., Washington 6, D.C.

Midwestern Psychological Association, 1007 S. Wright St., Champaign, Ill.

National Council of the Churches of Christ in the United States of America, 297 4th Ave., New York 10, N.Y.

Western Psychological Association, Institute of Child Welfare, University of California, Berkeley 4, Calif.

World Federation for Mental Health, 19 Manchester St., London, W. 1, England

RECREATION

Amateur Athletics Union of the United States, 233 Broadway, New York 7, N.Y.

American Institute of Park Executives, Inc., 30 N. La Salle St., Chicago 2, Ill.

American Planning and Civic Association, Inc., 901 Union Trust Bldg., Washington 5, D.C.

American Recreation Society, Inc., 1420 New York Avenue, N.W., Washington 5, D.C.

American Youth Hostels, Inc., 6 E. 39th St., New York 16, N.Y.

Boy Scouts of America, Inc., 2 Park Ave., New York 16, N.Y.

Boy Scouts Association, Canadian General Council, Inc., 306 Metcalfe St., Ottawa, Canada
Boys' Clubs of America, Inc., 381 4th Ave., New York 16, N.Y.
Camp Fire Girls, Inc., 16 E. 48th St., New York 17, N.Y.
Canadian Association for Health, Physical Education, and Recreation, 320 Sherbrook St., Winnipeg, Canada
Conference of National Agencies and Schools of Group and Recreation, 345 E. 46th St., New York 17, N.Y.
Cooperative Recreation Service, P.O. Box 333, Delaware, Ohio
Episcopal Service for Youth, Inc., 118 E. 22nd St., New York 10, N.Y.
Federal Inter-Agency Committee on Recreation, 2649 S. Interior Bldg., Washington 25, D.C.
Folk Arts Center, Inc., 271 Hicks St., Brooklyn 2, N.Y.
Girl Guides Association, Canadian Council, 891 Yonge St., Toronto 5, Canada
Girl Scouts of the United States of America, 155 E. 44th St., New York 17, N.Y.
Girls Clubs of America, Inc., 115 State St., Springfield 1, Mass.
Girls' Friendly Society of the United States of America, Inc., 345 46th St., New York 17, N.Y.
Junior Achievement, Inc., 345 Madison Ave., New York 17, N.Y.
Knights of Columbus, Inc., 71 Meadow St., New Haven 7, Conn.
National Committee on Boys and Girls Work, Inc., 59 E. Van Buren St., Chicago 5, Ill.
National Conference on State Parks, Inc., 901 Union Trust Bldg., Washington 5, D.C.
National Council of Catholic Youth, 1312 Massachusetts Ave., N.W., Washington 5, D.C.
National Federation of Settlements and Neighborhood Centers, Inc., 129 E. 52nd St., New York 22, N.Y.
National Industrial Recreation Association, Inc., 203 N. Wabash Ave., Chicago 1, Ill.
National and Inter-American Music Week Committee, 315 4th Ave., New York 10, N.Y.
National Park Service, United States Department of Interior, Washington 25, D.C.
National Parks Association, Inc., 1840 Mintwood Pl., N.W., Washington, 9, D.C.
National Parks and Historic Sites Division, National Parks Branch, Department of Resources and Development, Ottawa, Canada
National Recreation Association, Inc., 315 4th Ave., New York 10, N.Y.
National Recreation Policies Committee, c/o Recreation Department, School of Education, Indiana University, Bloomington, Ind.
Parks and Recreation Association of Canada, Inc., City Hall Annex, 465 Bay St., Toronto 2, Canada
Play Schools Association, Inc., 119 W. 57th St., New York 19, N.Y.
Society of State Directors of Health, Physical Education, and Recreation, c/o State Department of Education, Olympia, Wash.
United Service Organizations, Inc., 500 5th Ave., New York 36, N.Y.
Y.M.C.A.'s of Canada, National Council, 15 Spadina Rd., Toronto 4, Canada
Y.M.-Y.W.H.A.'s of Canada, National Council, 493 Sherbrooke St., Montreal 2, Canada

REHABILITATION

American ORT Federation, Inc., 212 5th Ave., New York 10, N.Y.
American Rehabilitation Committee, Inc., 28 E. 21st St., New York 10, N.Y.
American Veterans Committee, Inc., 1751 New Hampshire Ave., N.W., Washington 9, D.C.
Disabled American Veterans, Inc., 1423 E. McMillan St., Cincinnati 6, Ohio
Orthopedic Appliance and Limb Manufacturers Association, 336 Washington Bldg., Washington, D.C.
Federation for the Handicapped, 241 W. 23rd St., New York, N.Y.
Institute of Physical Medicine and Rehabilitation, New York University-Bellevue Medical Center, 400 E. 34th St., New York, N.Y.
National Rehabilitation Association, Inc., Rm. 614, 1025 Vermont Ave., N.W., Washington 5, D.C.
National Rehabilitation Commission, American Legion, Inc., 1608 K St., N.W., Washington 6, D.C.

Office of Vocational Rehabilitation, United States Department of Health, Education, and Welfare, Washington 25, D.C.

Veterans Administration, Vermont Ave., between H and Eye Sts., N.W., Washington 25, D.C.

Veterans of Foreign Wars of the United States, Inc., Broadway and 34th Sts., Kansas City 2, Mo.

World Veterans Federation, 27 rue de la Michodiere, Paris 2, France

RESEARCH

American Educational Research Association (NEA), 1201 16th St., N.W., Washington 6, D.C.

National Research Council, 2101 Constitution Ave., N.W., Washington 25, D.C.

National Society for Medical Research, 208 North Wells St., Chicago 6, Ill.

Science Research Associates, 57 W. Grand Ave., Chicago 10, Ill.

Society for Occupational Research, Ltd., 518 Solway St., Glendale 6, Calif.

RHEUMATIC FEVER

The American Council on Rheumatic Fever of the American Heart Association, 44 E. 23rd St., New York, N.Y.

RURAL

National Sharecroppers Fund, Inc., 40 E. 49th St., New York 17, N.Y.

Rural Youth of the United States of America, Inc., 224 5th St., Marietta, Ohio

SECONDARY EDUCATION

Council for Advancement of Secondary Education, Inc., 1201 16th St., N.W., Washington 6, D.C.

National Association of Secondary School Principals, 1201 16th St., N.W., Washington 6, D.C.

SHELTERED WORKSHOPS

National Committee on Sheltered Workshops and Homebound Programs, 15 W. 16th St., New York 8, N.Y.

SOCIAL WORK

American Association of Group Workers, 129 E. 52nd St., New York 22, N.Y.

American Association of Medical Social Workers, Inc., 1834 K St., N.W., Washington 6, D.C.

American Association of Psychiatric Social Workers, 1860 Broadway, New York 23, N.Y.

American Association of Social Workers, Inc., 1 Park Ave., New York 16, N.Y.

American Public Welfare Association, Inc., 1313 E. 16th St., Chicago 37, Ill.

Association of Jewish Community Relations Workers, Rm. 801, 9 E. 38th St., New York 16, N.Y.

Association of State Conferences, 22 W. Gay St., Columbus 15, Ohio

Canadian Association of Social Workers, 18 Rideau St., W., Ottawa, Canada

Canadian Conference on Social Work, 245 Cooper St., Ottawa, Canada

Christian Social Welfare Associates, 297 4th Ave., New York 10, N.Y.

Council on Social Work Education, Inc., 345 E. 46th St., New York 17, N.Y.

Family Service Association of America, Inc., 192 Lexington Ave., New York 16, N.Y.

International Conference of Social Work, 22 W. Gay St., Columbus 15, Ohio

International Federation of Social Workers, 3 rue de Stockholm, Paris 8, France; (c/o National Foundation for Infantile Paralysis, 120 Broadway, New York 5, N.Y.)

National Association of School Social Workers, Inc., 1 Park Ave., New York 16, N.Y.

National Conference of Catholic Charities, 1346 Connecticut Ave., N.W., Washington 6, D.C.

National Conference of Jewish Communal Service, 1841 Broadway, New York 23, N.Y.

National Conference of Social Work, Inc., 22 W. Gay St., Columbus 15, Ohio
Social Work Research Group, c/o School of Social Work, University of Pittsburgh, Pittsburgh 13, Pa.

SPECIAL EDUCATION

American Association for Gited Children, Inc., 15 Gramercy Park, New York 3, N.Y.
American Federation of the Physically Handicapped, 1379 National Press Bldg., Washington 4, D.C.
Department of Vocational Education (NEA), 1201 16th St., N.W., Washington 6, D.C.
Exceptional Children's Foundation, 225 W. Adams Blvd., Los Angeles 18, Calif.
The International Council for Exceptional Children, 1201 16th St., N.W., Washington 6, D.C.
National Association of State Directors of Special Education, State Department of Education, Oklahoma City, Okla.
National Association of State Directors of Vocational Education, State Department of Education, Raleigh, N.C.

SPEECH

Cleveland Hearing and Speech Center, Western Reserve University, Cleveland, Ohio

SPEECH EDUCATION

American Speech and Hearing Association, Wayne University, Detroit, Mich.
American Speech Correction Association, Box 3066, Ohio State University, Columbus, Ohio
Central States Speech Association, University of Wisconsin, Madison 5, Wis.; University of Illinois, Navy Pier, Chicago, Ill.
Speech Association of America, Department of Speech, University of Illinois, Urbana, Ill.
Western Speech Association, University of Southern California, Los Angeles 7, Calif.

TUBERCULOSIS

Canadian Tuberculosis Association, 265 Elgin St., Ottawa, Canada
National Conference of Tuberculosis Workers, 1790 Broadway, New York 19, N.Y.
National Tuberculosis Association, Inc., 1790 Broadway, New York 19, N.Y.

UNWED

Florence Crittenton Homes Association, 608 S. Dearborn St., Chicago 5, Ill.
Foster Parents' Plan for War Children, Inc., 55 W. 42nd St., New York 36, N.Y.
Maternity Center Association, Inc., 48 E. 92nd St., New York 28, N.Y.
National Association on Service to Unmarried Parents, 1881 Torbenson Dr., Cleveland 12, Ohio

VISUAL EDUCATION

Department of Audio-Visual Instruction (NEA), 1201 16th St., N.W., Washington 6, D.C.
Educational Film Library Association, Inc., 345 E. 46th St., New York 17, N.Y.
Film Council of America, 600 Davis St., Evanston, Ill.

VOCATIONAL GUIDANCE

Alliance for Guidance of Rural Youth, Inc., 1201 16th St., N.W., Washington 6, D.C.
American Association of Marriage Counselors, Inc., 270 Park Ave., New York 17, N.Y.
American Personnel and Guidance Association, Inc., 1534 O St., N.W., Washington 5, D.C.
American School Health Association, Kent State University, Kent, Ohio

American Vocational Association, Inc., 1010 Vermont Ave., Washington 5, D.C.
Eastern College Personnel Officers Association, Tufts College, Medford 55, Mass.
Jewish Occupational Council, Inc., 1841 Broadway, New York 23, N.Y.
National Association of Guidance Supervisors and Counselor Trainers, c/o Iowa State Board for Vocational Education, Des Moines, Iowa
National League to Promote School Attendance, 110 Livingston St., Brooklyn 1, N.Y.
National Vocational Guidance Association, 1434 O St., N.W., Washington 5, D.C.
Pathfinder of America, Inc., 335 Bulkley Bldg., Cleveland 15, Ohio

ADDITIONAL REFERENCES

U. S. COLLEGES AND UNIVERSITIES OFFERING COURSES IN SPECIAL EDUCATION, PHYSICAL THERAPY, AND OCCUPATIONAL THERAPY

COLLEGES AND UNIVERSITIES REPORTING SEQUENCES OF PREPARATION FOR TEACHERS OF EXCEPTIONAL CHILDREN DURING THE ACADEMIC YEAR 1953-54*

Number of institutions reporting sequences 1953-54 (exclusive of summer sessions) 122
Number of institutions reporting sequences 1949 (excluding summer school sequences) 77

STATE AND INSTITUTION

Alabama
University of Alabama (University)

Arizona
University of Arizona (Tucson)

Arkansas
University of Arkansas (Fayetteville)

California
Chico State College (Chico)
College of the Pacific (Stockton)
Fresno State College (Fresno)
Los Angeles State College (Los Angeles)
Occidental College (Los Angeles)
San Diego State College (San Diego)
San Francisco State College (San Francisco)
San Jose State College (San Jose)
Stanford University (Palo Alto)
University of California (Berkeley)
University of California (Los Angeles)
University of California (Santa Barbara)
University of Redlands (Redlands)
University of Southern California (Los Angeles)
Whittier College (Whittier)

Colorado
University of Denver (Denver)

Connecticut
New Haven State Teachers College (New Haven)

Florida
Florida State University (Tallahassee)
University of Florida (Gainesville)
University of Miami (Coral Gables)

Georgia
Emory University (Emory University)
University of Georgia (Athens)

Illinois
Bradley University (Peoria)
College of St. Francis (Joliet)
Eastern Illinois State College (Charleston)
Elmhurst College (Elmhurst)
Illinois State Normal University (Normal)
Northern Illinois State Teachers College (De Kalb)
Northwestern University (Evanston)
Rockford College (Rockford)

---

*From Mackie, R.P., and Dunn, L.M., *College and University Programs for the Preparation of Teachers of Exceptional Children* (U.S. Office of Education, U.S. Department of Health, Education, and Welfare, Washington, D.C., 1954), Bulletin # 13, pp. 12-19.

Southern Illinois University (Carbondale)
University of Chicago (Chicago)
University of Illinois (Urbana)

Indiana
Ball State Teachers College (Muncie)
Indiana State Teachers College (Terre Haute)
Indiana University (Bloomington)
Purdue University (Lafayette)

Iowa
Grinnell College (Grinnell)
Iowa State Teachers College (Cedar Falls)
State University of Iowa (Iowa City)

Kansas
Fort Hays Kansas State College (Hays)
Kansas State Teachers College (Emporia)
Municipal University of Wichita (Wichita)
University of Kansas (Lawrence and Kansas City)

Kentucky
University of Kentucky (Lexington)

Louisiana
Louisiana State University (Baton Rouge)

Maryland
University of Maryland (College Park)

Massachusetts
Boston University (Boston)
Emerson College (Boston)
Smith College (Northampton)

Michigan
Central Michigan College of Education (Mount Pleasant)
Michigan State College (East Lansing)
Michigan State Normal College (Ypsilanti)
University of Michigan (Ann Arbor)
Wayne University (Detroit)
Western Michigan College of Education (Kalamazoo)

Minnesota
State Teachers College (St. Cloud)
University of Minnesota (Minneapolis)

Mississippi
Mississippi Southern College (Hattiesburg)
University of Mississippi (University)

Missouri
Central Missouri College (Warrensburg)
St. Louis University (St. Louis)
Southwest Missouri State College (Springfield)

University of Missouri (Columbia)
Washington University (St. Louis)

Nebraska
University of Nebraska (Lincoln)

New Jersey
New Jersey State Teachers College (Newark)

New York
Brooklyn College (Brooklyn)
City College of the City of New York (New York)
Hunter College of the City of New York (New York)
New York University (New York)
Queens College of the City of New York (Flushing)
State University of New York College for Teachers (Buffalo)
State University of New York Teachers College (Geneseo)
Syracuse University (Syracuse)
Teachers College of Columbia University (New York)
University of Buffalo (Buffalo)

North Dakota
State Teachers College (Minot)
University of North Dakota (Grand Forks)

Ohio
Bowling Green State University (Bowling Green)
Kent State University (Kent)
Ohio State University (Columbus)
Ohio University (Athens)
Western Reserve University (Cleveland)

Oklahoma
Oklahoma College for Women (Chickasha)
University of Oklahoma (Norman)
University of Tulsa (Tulsa)

Oregon
University of Oregon (Eugene)

Pennsylvania
Duquesne University (Pittsburgh)
Franklin and Marshall College (Lancaster)
Marywood College (Scranton)
Mount Mercy College (Pittsburgh)
Pennsylvania State University (State College)
State Teachers College (Bloomsburg)
State Teachers College (California)
State Teachers College (Indiana)
Temple University (Philadelphia)
University of Pennsylvania (Philadelphia)
University of Pittsburgh (Pittsburgh)

South Dakota
University of South Dakota (Vermillion)

Tennessee
George Peabody College for Teachers (Nashville)
University of Tennessee (Knoxville)
Vanderbilt University (Nashville)

Texas
North Texas State College (Denton)
Southern Methodist University (Dallas)
Southwest Texas State Teachers College (San Marcos)
Texas State College for Women (Denton)
University of Houston (Houston)
University of Texas (Austin)

Utah
University of Utah (Salt Lake City)

Virginia
University of Virginia (Charlottesville)

Washington
University of Washington (Seattle)

Wisconsin
Marquette University (Madison)
Wisconsin State College (Milwaukee)

Wyoming
University of Wyoming (Laramie)

District of Columbia
Catholic University of America (Washington)
Gallaudet College (Washington)
George Washington University (Washington)

SCHOOLS OFFERING COURSES IN OCCUPATIONAL THERAPY

Boston School of Occupational Therapy
   7 Harcourt St., Boston 16, Mass.
      Affiliated with Tufts College
Colorado Agricultural and Mechanical
College
   School of Home Economics
      Ft. Collins, Colo.
Columbia University
   College of Physicians and Surgeons
      630 W. 168th St., New York 32, N.Y.
Illinois, University of
   College of Medicine
      1853 W. Polk St., Chicago 12, Ill.
Iowa, State University of
   College of Liberal Arts and College of
   Medicine
      Iowa City, Iowa
Kalamazoo, School of Occupational Ther-
apy of Western Michigan
   College of Education
      Kalamazoo 45, Mich.
New York University
   School of Education
      Washington Sq., New York 3, N.Y.
Ohio State University
   College of Education
      Columbus 10, Ohio
Pennsylvania, University of
   School of Auxiliary Medical Services
      419 S. 19th St., Philadelphia 46, Pa.

Physical and Occupational Therapy,
School of
   Affiliated with the University of Puerto
   Rico
      Bldg., 8th Fl., Santurce, Puerto Rico
Pudget Sound, College of
      Tacoma 6, Wash.
Richmond Professional, Institute of the
   College of William and Mary
      Richmond 20, Va.
Saint Catherine, College of
      St. Paul 1, Minn.
San Jose State College
      , San Jose 14, Calif.
Southern California, University of
   College of Letters, Arts and Sciences
      Box 274, Los Angeles 7, Calif.
Texas, University of
   Medical Branch
      Galveston, Tex.
Texas State College for Women
      Denton, Tex.
U.S. Medical Service
   School of Occupational Therapy
      Address Inquiries: The Surgeon Gen-
      eral, Department of the Army
      Washington 25, D.C.
      Attn.: Chief, Personnel Div.
Washington University
   School of Medicine
      4567 Scott Ave., St. Louis 10, Mo.

PHYSICAL THERAPY PROGRAMS—1955

APPROVED BY THE COUNCIL ON MEDICAL EDUCATION AND HOSPITALS
OF THE AMERICAN MEDICAL ASSOCIATION

DEGREE and CERTIFICATE PROGRAMS—Information on specific entrance requirements should be obtained from the schools listed below. Schools offering a degree will
accept high school graduates for the four year program leading to a baccalaureate degree,
as well as transfer students. A certificate program is a concentrated course of study offered
to those who have completed all or most of their undergraduate work before declaring
a major in physical therapy. Graduates of either the degree or certificate programs are
equally qualified.

California

School of Physical Therapy
Childrens Hospital Society
(Univ. of California at Los Angeles)
4614 Sunset Boulevard
Los Angeles 27

School of Physical Therapy
College of Medical Evangelists
White Memorial Hospital
Boyle and Michigan Avenues
Los Angeles 33

Department of Physical Therapy
University of Southern California
University Park
Los Angeles 7

Curriculum in Physical Therapy
School of Medicine
University of California
3rd and Parnassus
San Francisco 22

Division of Physical Therapy
Stanford University
Stanford

Colorado

School of Physical Therapy
School of Medicine
University of Colorado
4200 East 9th Avenue
Denver 7

Connecticut

School of Physical Therapy
University of Connecticut
Box U 101
Storrs

Illinois

Course in Physical Therapy
Northwestern University Medical School
303 East Chicago Avenue
Chicago 11

Iowa

Department of Physical Therapy
State University of Iowa
University Hospitals
Iowa City

Kansas

Section of Physical Therapy
University of Kansas Medical Center
39th and Rainbow Boulevard
Kansas City 3

Louisiana

School of Physical Therapy
Charity Hospital of Louisiana
1532 Tulane Avenue
New Orleans 12

Massachusetts

Department of Physical Therapy
Boston University
Sargent College of Physical Education
6 Everett Street
Cambridge 38

*Course in Physical Therapy
Bouve-Boston School
Tufts College
Medford 55

*Programs in Physical Therapy
Simmons College
The Fenway
Boston

Michigan

Curriculum in Physical Therapy
University of Michigan
1313 East Ann Street
Ann Arbor

Minnesota

School of Physical Therapy
Mayo Clinic
102-110 Second Avenue, S.W.
Rochester

Course in Physical Therapy
860 Mayo Memorial
University of Minnesota
Minneapolis 14

Missouri

Division of Health and Hospital Services
St. Louis University
1325 South Grand Boulevard
St. Louis 4
Department of Physical Therapy
School of Medicine
Washington University
660 South Kingshighway
St. Louis 10

New York

*School of Physical Therapy
Albany Hospital (Russell Sage College)
New Scotland Avenue
Albany 8

Courses for Physical Therapists
Columbia University
College of Physicians and Surgeons
630 West 168th Street
New York 32
Physical Therapy Division
School of Education, New York
   University
Washington Square East
New York 3

Program in Physical Therapy
University of Buffalo
2183 Main Street
Buffalo 14

North Carolina

Physical Therapy Course
School of Medicine
Duke University
Durham

Ohio

Course in Physical Therapy
Frank E. Bunts Ed. Inst.
Cleveland Clinic Hospital
2020 East 93rd Street
Cleveland 6

Pennsylvania

Division of Physical Therapy
School of Auxiliary Medical Services
University of Pennsylvania
1818 Lombard Street
Philadelphia 46

Division of Physical Therapy
The D. T. Watson School of Psychiatrics
(In affiliation with the University of
   Pittsburgh)
Sunny Hill
Leetsdale

Puerto Rico

School of Physical and Occupational
   Therapy
Commonwealth of Puerto Rico
State Insurance Fund
San Juan, P.R.

Texas

Grady Vaughn School of Physical
   Therapy
Baylor University
University Hospital
Dallas

Hermann School of Physical Therapy
Hermann Hospital
1203 Ross Sterling Avenue
Houston 5

Division of Physical Therapy
University of Texas
   School of Medicine
Galveston

Virginia

School of Physical Therapy
Baruch Center of Physical Medicine
   and Rehabilitation
Medical College of Virginia
1203 East Broad Street
Richmond 19

Wisconsin

Course in Physical Therapy
Medical School, University of
   Wisconsin
Madison 6

U. S. Army Medical Service

*Physical Therapy Course
Medical Field Service School
Brooke Army Medical Center,
Fort Sam Houston, Texas and
Brooke, Letterman and Walter Reed
Army Hospitals
   Write to: The Surgeon General
   Department of the Army
   Washington 25, D.C.
   Att: Personnel Division

---

*Accepts women students only.
Used by Permission of the American Physical Therapy Association, New York City, N.Y.

GLOSSARY, PREPARED BY ELLEN KERNEY

A

abduction: drawing away from median line

abductor: muscle or nerve that abducts

accommodation: increase of refractive power of crystalline lens for vision at various distances

Achilles tendon: tendon at back of heel connecting calf muscle with tuberosity of calcaneus (heel bone)

achondroplasia: fetal rickets, skeletal disease starting in fetal life and causing dwarfism

achromatic: characterized by lack of color

acquired deafness: hearing impairment acquired after birth

acromegaly: a chronic nervous disease characterized by enlargement of extremities

acuity: amount of sensory perception

acuity of hearing: ability to hear; sharpness of hearing

Addison's disease: a disease caused by disturbance of the suprarenal glands

adduction: drawing toward median line

adiposogenital syndrome: disease of anterior lobe of pituitary occurring during adolescence, resulting in obesity and arrested development of sex glands

adjudication: decision or settlement by law; in case of disabled veterans, establishment of claim under law

adjustment: process or result of accepting environment, facing up to life, taking things in stride

affect: feeling or emotions

aggression: action bordering on hostility, with the infliction of physical or psychological injury

agnosia: inability to attach meaning to sensory stimuli

agraphia: difficulty with writing symbols

air conduction: normal way in which most people hear (sounds being carried by air to ear)

akinesia: loss or impairment of motor function

albinism: lack of pigment, abnormal whiteness of skin, hair, and eyes

albino: person presenting abnormal whiteness of skin, hair, and eyes

alexia: word blindness; inability to read, due to brain injury

amaurosis: blindness due to disease of optic nerve

amblyopia: dimness of vision without any apparent disease of eye

amblyopia ex anopsia: dimness of vision due to disuse of eye

amentia: lack of mental development (to be distinguished from dementia)

ametropia: refractive defect which prevents eye, in state of rest, from focusing image of distant objects upon retina; includes hyperopia, myopia, and astigmatism

amnesia: lack or loss of memory

ampere: unit of measurement of electric current

amplified sound: any sound when made louder

amputee: person who has suffered amputation (surgical cutting-off of limb)

amyotonia congenita: Oppenheim's disease, congenital general hypotonia of muscles in children

anarthria: loss or impairment of ability to articulate words

aniridia: congenital absence of iris

ankylosis: frozen joint, abnormal immobility and consolidation of joint

anomaly: deviation from natural order

anophthalmos: absence of true eyeball

anoxia: oxygen deficiency; suffocation from lack of oxygen

anterior chamber: space in anterior portion of eye, bounded in front by cornea and behind by iris; filled with aqueous

anxiety neurosis: worry amounting to psychoneurosis, with irritablity, excitability, and depression

aphakia: absence of lens of eye

aphasia: defect or loss of power of expression by speech, writing, or signs, or of comprehending spoken or written language

aphasia, expressive: inability to express ideas in speech

aphasia, receptive: inability to understand meaning of words

apraxia: motor disturbance, or difficulty in performing skilled motor acts

aqueous: clear, watery fluid which fills interior and posterior chambers within front part of eye

arrhythmia: variation from normal rhythm of heart beat

arteriosclerosis: hardening of arteries

arthritis: inflammation of joint

arthrodesis: surgical fixation of joint by fusion of joint surfaces, artificial ankylosis

aseptic: free from septic (putrefying) material

assymetry: lack or absence of symmetry (right proportion)

asthenopia: eye fatigue caused by tiring of internal or external muscles

astigmatism: defective curvature of refractive surfaces of eye, as result of which a ray of light is not sharply focused on retina but is spread over a more or less diffuse area

ataxia: failure of mucular coordination characterized by lack of balance

athetoid: resembling or affected with athetosis

athetosis: involuntary movements of head, body, extremities, or tongue; subclassification of cerebral palsy

atonicity: lack of normal muscle tone

atrophy: wasting away or diminution in size of cell, tissue, organ, or part

atrophine: drug which dilates pupil, increases frequency of heart's action, and checks sweating and salivation

audiogram: chart or record indicating child's ability to hear as compared with ability of known normal listeners; chart or graph is generally used to indicate at what intensity child is just able to hear tones of pure-tone audiometer

audiology: science of hearing

audiometer: instrument for testing hearing

auditory training: educational method by which child is taught to use to best advantage any hearing that he has

automatic control: electric switch, utilizing light-sensitive tube as signal device, which turns artificial lights on and off, respectively, when daylight falls below or rises above limits for which it is set

B

Babinski reflex test: test for confirmation of lesions of pyramidal tract; stimulation of sole of foot produces extension of toes instead of flexion

basal: at the base

B. M. R.: basal metabolic rate

basal metabolism: basal metabolic rate

basal metabolic rate: minimal heat produced by individual 14-18 hours after eating with individual at rest but not asleep; it represents energy expended to maintain respiration, circulation, peristalsis, muscle tonus, body temperature, glandular activity, and other vegetative functions

benign: not malignant

benzedrine: drug used to stimulate cerebral activity by producing wakefulness, feeling of well being, and loss of appetite

bilateral: having two sides, pertaining to both sides

binocular: characterized by functioning of two eyes together

binocular vision: ability to use two eyes simultaneously to focus on same object and fuse two images into single image which gives correct interpretation of its solidity and position in space

blepharitis: inflammation of eyelid

blepharospasm: spasm of orbicular muscle of eyelids

blue baby: baby born with cyanosis due to congenital heart lesion or to congenital atelectasis (imperfect expansion of lungs)

bone conduction: transmission of sound waves to hearing mechanism through bones of head

brace: appliance for support of body part, to relieve weakness or to maintain alignment

brachial birth palsy: paralysis or partial paralysis of arm resulting from injury to nerves at birth, and affecting forearm, upper arm or whole arm

Bradford frame: rectangular frame of gas pipe, to which sheet of heavy canvas is attached: used as bed frame in spinal tuberculosis and fracture of thigh to maintain position

brightness: (1) brightness of primary light source is determined by intensity of light emitted from that source; (2) brightness of any other surface is product of illumination it receives and percentage it reflects

brightness ratio: relative brightness of any two objects, areas, or spaces

bulbar conjunctiva: part of conjunctiva covering anterior surface of eyeball

buphthalmos: large eyeball (infantile glaucoma)

C

C. A.: chronological age

C, CC (cum correction): with correction (wearing lenses prescribed)

calcaneo valgus deformity: deformity of the foot; turning it upward and outward.

calcaneus: heel bone

calcaneus deformity: heel-walking deformity

Calvè-Perthes disease: disease characterized by softening and crumbling of head of femur that fits into hip socket

canal of Schlemm: circular tube at junction of sclera and cornea through which aqueous passes out of eye

canthus: angle at either end of slit between eyelids, specified as outer (temporal) and inner (nasal)

cardiac: relating to the heart: person with organic heart disorder

cardiogram: tracing produced by means of cardiograph

cardiograph: instrument placed over heart to indicate force and form of heart's movements

cardiologist: heart specialist

cardiotomy: incision of heart

cardiovascular: relating to heart and blood vessels

carditis: inflammation of heart

cartilage: gristle or white elastic substance attached to joint surfaces and forming certain parts of skeleton

cast: rigid dressing made of bandage impregnated with plaster of paris or other hardening materials, used for immobilizing parts of body

catalepsy: waxiness and rigidity of muscles, which maintain limbs in any position in which they are placed

cataract: opacity (cloudiness) of crystalline lens or its capsule; two of its many types are senile (in older people) and congenital (in most partially sighted children)

catatonia: variety of schizophrenia (dementia praecox) involving negativistic reactions, phases of stupor or excitement, and impulsive or stereotyped behavior

catharsis: purification; getting rid of disturbing conflicts and complexes

central visual acuity: ability of eye to perceive shape or form of objects in direct line of vision

cerebellum: part of brain behind cerebrum, occupying back part of skull and concerned in balance or coordination of movements

cerebral: relating to brain or to cerebrum

cerebral palsy: term applied to group of diseases in children, marked by paralysis or disturbances of motion; weakness or paralysis due to brain lesion

cerebrospinal: relating to brain and spinal cord

cerebrum: main portion of brain, occupying upper part of cranium

chalazion: inflammatory enlargement of a meibomian gland in eyelid

choked disk: noninflammatory swelling of optic nerve head

chorea: St. Vitus's dance; conclusive nervous disease, with involuntary and irregular jerking movements, irritability, depression, and mental impairment; it occurs in children and is often associated with rheumatic fever

chorea minor: ordinary chorea

choroid: vascular, intermediate coat which furnishes nourishment to other parts of eyeball

choroidal: relating to choroid

choroiditis: inflammation of choroid

chronic chorea: hereditary disease of adults, marked by irregular movements, speech disturbances, and dementia

cila: eyelashes

ciliary body: portion of vascular coat between iris and choroid; it consists of ciliary processes and the ciliary muscles

claimant: veteran who claims right to certain compensation or benefits from government on basis of service record

claustrophobia: fear of being in confined or closed places

clavicle: collarbone

clear-type book (large-type book): book in 18-point or 24-point type of clear, simple design without many serifs, produced especially for education of partially seeing pupils

cleft lip: cleft in the upper lip

cleft palate: roof of mouth may be split part way or full length; nasal cavity opens into mouth; faulty union of two sides of lip or mouth

clerestory window: one cut in a set-back wall rising above roof of room below it, to provide additional light in inner portion of room below

clinician: practising physician, psychiatrist, or psychologist who examines, diagnoses, and treats individuals presenting emotional and mental disorders

clonic: pertaining to clonus (series of alternating contractions and partial relaxation of same muscle)

close work: such work as reading, sewing, drawing, normally done at short distance from eyes and hence requiring effort of accommodation

clubfoot: talipes; deformity of foot in which it is twisted out of shape or position

coccyx: small bone situated caudad to sacrum; in man, caudal end of spinal column

coefficient of utilization: proportion of light that reaches plane of work from any light source; it depends on type of diffusing and reflecting equipment, color and maintenance of walls and ceilings, and proportions of room

coloboma: congenital cleft due to failure of eye to complete growth in part affected

color blindness: diminished ability to percieve differences in color

coma: loss of consciousness

compensable: receiving compensation or remuneration to make up for loss or injury

compensation: whatever offsets any defect of structure or function; mechanism of putting forward approved trait of character to hide existence of undesirable trait

complex: Freudian term for series of emotionally accentuated ideas in repressed state

concave lens: lens having power to diverge rays of light; also known as diverging, reducing, negative, myopic, or minus lens, denoted by sign

conduction deafness: hearing impairment due to interference of sound waves in their progress to inner ear

cones: together with rods, they are receptors for optic nerve; they are light-perceiving layer of retina; cones concentrated at macula are concerned with sharp vision and perception of shape

congenital: existing at or before birth

congential deafness: hearing impairment present from birth

conjunctiva: mucous membrane which lines eyelids and covers front part of eyeball

conjunctivitis: inflammation of conjunctiva

contact lens: lens so constructed that it fits directly on eyeball; used chiefly in connection with cone-shaped cornea and high myopia

contraction: shortening of muscle

contracture: shortening or distortion (from shrinkage of muscles, scars, or from sudden stimulus)

control: experiment to test correctness of observations; person, animal, group subjected to conditions of original test with exception of one factor under study

convergence: ability to direct visual lines of two eyes to near point

convex lens: lens having power to converge rays of light and to bring them to a focus; also known as converging, magnifying, hyperopic, or plus lens, denoted by sign+

convulsion: violent involuntary contraction of muscle

cornea: clear, transparent ("watch crystal") portion of external coat of eyeball forming front of aqueous chamber

cortex: outer layer of organ

coxa: hip or hip joint

coxa plana: osteochondrosis of capitular epiphysis, flattening and broadening of head of femur in Legg-Calvé-Perthes disease

coxa valga: exaggerated angle of neck of femur

coxa vara: diminished angle of neck of femur

cretinism: arrested physical and mental development, due to lack of thyroid

crutch palsy: paralysis, chiefly of musculospiral nerve, from pressure of crutch in armpit

crystalline lens: transparent, colorless body suspended in anterior portion of eyeball between aqueous and vitreous chambers, whose function is to bring rays of light to a focus

cyanosis: blueness of skin, often due to cardiac malformation (causing insufficient oxygenation of blood)

cybernetics: Norbert Wiener's term for study of what, in a human context, is sometimes loosely described as thinking and, in engineering, is known as control and communication; study of striking similarities between human brain and calculating machines; "machine thinking"

cyclitis: inflammation of ciliary body

cycloplegic: drug which temporarily paralyzes accommodation and dilates pupil

cylindrical lens: segment of cylinder, whose refractive power varies in different meridians; used in correction of astigmatism; cylinders are convex or concave

D

dacryocystitis: inflammation of lacrimal sac

dark adaptation: power of eye to adjust itelf to dim light

daydreaming: indulging in dreams while awake, building castles in the air; brown study, abstraction, absent-mindedness; escape from reality to dream world of easy success

deaf and dumb: term often used to describe those with congenital deafness, or those whose deafness is acquired before speech is developed; this term has fallen into disrepute, since most deaf children can be taught to talk if given appropriate instruction; today, in colloquial use, the word **dumb** is usually associated with stupidity, whereas the hearing loss alone does not affect a child's intelligence; properly speaking, a child is said to be **deaf,** not **deaf and dumb**

deafness: hearing impairment so severe that person cannot understand speech, no matter how loud it is rendered.

decibel: term named after Alexander Graham Bell around 1935, used in measurement of sound; unit employed to express comparison between two amounts of power in any field in which power is measured, as in telephony, radio, and acoustics; basic unit "bel" is exponent to which 10 must be raised to equal ratio between two amounts of power

delirium: mental disturbance marked by illusions, hallucinations, delusions, cerebral excitement, physical restlessness, and incoherence, and of short duration

delusion: false belief that cannot be corrected by reason

dementia: insanity, being out of touch with reality

dementia praecox: term for large group of psychoses of psychogenic origin, often recognized during or shortly after adolescence and also occasionally in later maturity; characteristics are disorientation, loss of contact with reality, splitting of personality

depression: absence of cheerfulness or hope, emotional dejection

depth perception: ability to perceive solidity of objects and their position in space

Descenet's membrane: thin membrane between substantia propria and endothelial layer of cornea

diagnosis: distinguishing one disease from another; determining nature of case of diease

diaphragm: musculomembranous partition that separates abdomen from thorax (chest)

diathermy: generation of heat in body tissues due to resistance offered by tissues to high-frequency electric currents forced through them

diffusion (of light): scattering of light rays by reflecting surface or by transmission through translucent material

diopter: unit of measurement of strength or refractive power of lenses

diplegia: paralysis of corresponding parts of the body

diplopia: seeing of single objects as two

direct illumination: type of electric lighting in which major portion of light falls directly on surface to be illuminated

disabled veteran: person who (1) has been wounded, gassed, or injured in mind or body, or (2) was a victim of disease while serving in armed forces of U. S. during wartime

discission (or needling): operation in which lens capsule is broken up with knife-needle, so that its contents may be absorbed

distribution: term used to describe uniformity of or variations in quantity of illumination available in various parts of room

domiciliary: concerning home for incapacitated veterans, where they are cared for and receive treatment, but which is not a veteran hospital

dorsal: concerning the back or any dorsum

dorsiflexion: bending (as of toes) toward dorsum

dorsum: the back; also, any part corresponding to the back in position, as of the foot or hand

drop foot: paralysis of the muscles which dorsiflex the ankle and thereby raise the foot

duction: stem word used with prefix to describe turning or rotation of eyeball (abduction, adduction)

dumb: characterized by mutism (lack of speech)

dysarthria: stammering

dyschondroplasia: abnormal growth of cartilage at diaphyseal (shaft) end of long bones, with formation of cartilaginous and bony tumors on shafts of bones near epiphyses

dysfunction: partial disturbance, impairment, or abnormality of functioning of organ

dysgraphia: impaired ability to write

dysplasia: abnormality of development

dyspnea: difficult or labored breathing, shortness of breath

dysrhythmia: disturbance in rhythm

dystrophy: defectve nutrition

E

echolalia: meaningless repetition of words

ectropion: condition in which there is eversion (turning inside out) of eyelids

edema: localized fluid in tissue

educable mentally retarded: persons with IQ's in 50 to 75 range

electrocardiogram: graphic picture of electrical charges caused by contraction of heart muscle

electroencephalogram: record of brain waves

electrotherapy: treatment of disease by means of electricity

embolus: clot or plug that obstructs blood vessel

emmetropia: condition of normal refraction of eye; images of distant objects are focused exactly upon retina when eye is in state of rest

empyema: accumulation of pus in cavity of body, especially chest

encephalitis: inflammation of brain

endocarditis: inflammation of endocardium (endothelial lining membrane of heart), generally associated with acute rheumatism

endocrine gland: ductless gland

endogenous: originating within organism (said of retarded mental development due to cultural-familial causes)

endothelium: layer of simple squamous (scaly) cells that lines inner surface of circulatory organs and other closed cavities

entropion: condition in which there is inversion (turning inward) of eyelids

enucleation: complete surgical removal of eyeball

enuresis nocturna: bedwetting at night and during sleep

epilepsy: occasional lack of consciousness resulting from brain injury

epiphora: overflowing of tears due to malfunction of lacrimal gland or lacrimal duct

epiphyseal arrest: epiphyseal-diaphyseal fusion, operative establishment of bony union between epiphysis and diaphysis of bone, aimed at arresting growth of bone at epiphysis

epiphysis: piece of bone separated from long bone in early life by cartilage, but later becoming part of larger bone

episcleritis: inflammation of outermost layers of sclera

equitable: fair, just

Erb's palsy: birth palsy, due to cerebral hemorrhage occurring at birth; also partial paralysis of brachial plexus, affecting various muscles of arm and chest wall

erythroblast: one of nucleated cells of type from which red blood corpuscles are developed

esophoria: tendency of eye to turn inward

esotropia: manifest turning inward of eye (convergent strabismus or crossed eyes)

etiology: science or study of causes of disease, both direct and predisposing, and mode of their operation

exogenous: originating outside body (said of retarded mental development due to brain injury)

exophoria: tendency of the eye to turn outward

exophthalmos: abnormal protrusion of eyeball

exostosis: bone tumor; simple growth on bone; a sort of spur

exotropia: abnormal turning outward from nose of one or both eyes (divergent strabismus)

extrinsic muscles: external muscles of eye which move eyeball; each eye has four recti and two oblique muscles

eye dominance: tendency of one eye to assume major function of seeing, being assisted by less dominant eye

F

farsightedness: hyperopia

fascia: sheet or band of tissue that invests and connects muscles

febrile: relating to high fever

feeblemindedness: mental deficiency; social incompetence due to mental retardation

femur: thigh bone

festinating gait: incoordinated, hurried, uncertain walk in paralysis agitans

fibroplasia: formation of fibrous tissue, as in healing of wounds; in eye, retrolental fibroplasia occurs in premature babies of low birth weight and is cause of much infant blindness

fibula: outer and smaller of two bones of leg

field of vision: entire space within which eye is able to perceive objects at one time; it extends outward from line of direct vision to approximately 90°, but brows, cheeks, and nose restrict it to approximately 60° upward, downward, and nasally

fifth-year program: accelerated course in teacher training for liberal-arts graduates who seem to be good teacher material

fit: convulsive seizure

fixation: in psychiatry, cessation of development of personality at stage short of maturity

flaccid: characterized by lack of muscle tone

flatfeet: pronated feet; weak arches

flexion: act of bending or condition of being bent

flexor: any muscle that flexes a joint

flexure: bending of body

fluorescent lighting: illumination produced by Mazda F (fluorescent) lamps, popularly known as bulbs or tubes

focus: point to which rays are converged after passing through a lens; focal length is distance rays travel after refraction before focus is reached

foot candle: amount of light falling on surface one foot from standard candle (used as unit of measurement of quantity of light)

footlambert: unit of measurement of amount of illumination resulting from number of footcandles multiplied by reflection factor of surface illuminated

fornix: loose fold connecting palpebral and bulbar conjunctiva

fourth level of learning: adult education

fovea: depression or pit in retina at posterior part of eye (temporal of optic disk), most sensitive part of retina

fragilitas ossium: abnormal brittleness of bones (subject to fracture from slight violence)

Friedreich's disease: family or hereditary ataxia; inherited disease, usually beginning in childhood or youth, with sclerosis of dorsal and lateral columns of spinal cord, attended with ataxia, speech impairment, lateral curvature of spinal column, and peculiar swaying and irregular movements, with paralysis of muscles, especially of lower extremities

frustration: prevention of act which, if carried out, would produce gratification of desire; feeling of being thwarted

functional: pertaining to or affecting functions, but not structure; caused by inefficient use of organism

functional murmur: cardiac murmur due to anemia or excited action of heart

fundus: posterior part of eye within its coats

fuse: plug or bar of soft metal that melts or fuses when too great strength of current causes too much heat for safety

fusion: co-ordination by brain into one image of separate images formed on retinas of two eyes

G

gamma globulin: part of blood containing most antibodies (it protects against paralytic poliomyelitis)

ganglion: any collection or mass of nerve cells that serves as center of nervous influence

gastrocnemius: muscle whose action extends foot, flexes leg, et cetera

gene: carrier of hereditary factor in chromosome

genu-recurvatum: backward curvature of the knee joint

genu-valgum: inward curving of the knee; knock-knee

genu-varum: a curvature of the knee sometimes referred to as bowleg

geriatrics: geriatric medicine; department of medicine which treats of clinical problem of senescence and senility

gerontology: scientific study of aging process, its phenomena, diseases, et cetera

gibbous: humpbacked

gigantism: abnormally large development in size or stature of the whole body, or of parts of body, usually due to dysfunction of the pituitary gland

gland: organ which secretes

glare: discomfort and interference with vision caused by any excessive brightness within field of vision

glass area: total area of window panes of given room (measurement used particularly in relation to floor area)

glass blocks: constructed of prismatic glass to redirect daylight rays upward toward ceiling

glaucoma: eye disease caused by fluid pressure in eye and frequently resulting in hardening of eyeball

glioma: malignant tumor (as of retina)

gluteus maximus: muscle whose action extends, abducts, and rotates thigh outward

grand mal: major epileptic attack

granular conjunctivitis: trachoma

H

hallux valgus: displacement of the great toe

hamstring: either of tendons that laterally bound popliteal space (at back of knee and thigh)

hard of hearing: presenting impairment of hearing (term ordinarily employed in connection with persons whose hearing is impaired but not absent)

harelip: roof of mouth split part way or full length; nasal cavity opens into mouth; faulty union of two sides of lip or mouth

hearing aid: device which amplifies sounds and is consequently used to enable a person to hear better; receiver of aid may be worn in ear (air conduction aid) or on head (bone conduction aid), depending on type of hearing loss

hebephrenia: clinical form of dementia praecox, appearing soon after puberty and marked by rapid deterioration, hallucinations, absurd delusion, senseless laughter, and silly mannerisms

heliotherapy: treatment of disease by exposing body to sun's rays; therapeutic use of sun bath; use of ultraviolet lamp

hemianopsia: blindness of one half of field of vision of one or both eyes

hemiatrophy: marked discrepancy of size of lateral halves of body

hemiplegia: paralysis of one side of body

hemoglobin: oxygen-carrying red pigment of red blood corpuscles

hemophilia: hereditary condition characterized by delayed clotting of blood and consequent difficulty in checking hemorrhage; it is inherited by males through mother as sex-linked character

heredity: organic resemblance based on descent; inheritance of qualities or diseases from ancestry

heterophoria: constant tendency of eyes to deviate from normal axis, counterbalanced by simultaneous fixation forced by muscular effort (prompted by desire for single binocular vision); deviation is not usually apparent, hence is said to be "latent"

heterotropia (strabismus, squint): manifest deviation of axis of eyes, making single binocular vision impossible; fixation is maintained with either eye, but not simultaneously with both

hip disease: tuberculosis of the round head of the thigh bone at the hip; head of bone decays and socket is destroyed; stiffness of joints

hip dislocation: one or both hips with limp or waddling gait; more frequent in girls than in boys

Hodgkin's disease: pseudoleukemia (blood disease)

Holmgren wool test: test for color blindness based on ability to match correctly wool samples from a set especially dyed in various shades and colors

hordeolum (stye): acute inflammation of sebaceous gland in margin of eyelid, due to infection and usually resulting in formation of pus

humerus: bone that extends from shoulder to elbow

Huntington's chorea: chronic chorea

Hutchinson's teeth: notched or peg shaped teeth; due usually to congenital syphilis

hydrocephalus: increase in size of skull due to cerebrofluid pressures

hydrotherapy: use of water in treating disease

hyperemia: reddening and swelling of margin of eyelid

hyperopia (farsightedness): refractive error where, because eyeball is short or refractive power of lens is weak, point of focus for rays of light from distant objects (parallel light rays) is behind retina; thus accommodation to increase refractive power of lens is necessary for distant as well as near vision

hyperphoria: tendency of one eye to deviate upward

hyperpituitarism: overactivity of the pituitary gland

hyperplasia: increase in number of cells of a part

hyperthyroidism: condition due to excessive functional activity of thyroid gland

hypertonia: excess tension, activity, or tone of muscles

hypertrophy: morbid enlargement or overgrowth of organ or part due to increase in size of its constituent cells

hypertropia: elevation of one of visual axes

hypopituitarism: abnormally diminished activity of the pituitary gland

hypotonia: diminished tension or tonicity, reduction in muscle tone; arterial hypotension; low intraocular tension

I

idiopathic: self-originated; of unknown cause

idiot: low-grade mental defective

imbecile: defective mentally; one mentally defective; feebleminded person with mental age between two and seven years

incandescent lamp: glass bulb in which filament (usually of tungsten) is heated to whiteness and maintained at high temperature by electric current

indirect illumination: type of illumination in which 90 percent or more of light is directed toward ceiling for diffused reflection over room area

infantile paralysis: poliomyelitis (disease of spinal cord)

infrared: concerning rays of energy beyond limit of vision and below red rays, employed in heat therapy

injection: usually congestion of ciliary or conjunctival vessels

innate: present at birth

insanity: social and legal term, rather than medical one; condition which renders affected person unfit to enjoy liberty of action because of unreliability of his behavior, with concomitant danger to himself and others

IQ: intelligence quotient, calculated by formula of mental age divided by chronological age

internist: physician who treats diseases of internal organs

interstitial keratitis: affection of middle layer of cornea (substantia propria), disease found chiefly in children and young adults; usually caused by transmission of syphilis from mother to unborn child

intraocular tension: pressure or tension of contents of eyeball

introvert: person given to introspection, often concerning himself alone

invert: person whose sexual interests and impulses are homosexual (directed toward same sex)

iridocyclitis: inflammation of iris and ciliary body

iris: colored, circular membrane, suspended behind cornea and immediately in front of lens, which regulates amount of light entering eye by changing size of pupil

iritis: inflammation of iris

Ishihara color plates: test for color blindness, based on ability to trace patterns in series of multicolored charts

J

jacksonian epilepsy: partial epilepsy, marked by localized spasm, and mainly limited to one side and often to one group of muscles

Jaeger test: test for near vision; lines of reading matter printed in a series of various sizes of type

jaundice: accumulation of bile resulting in yellowness of skin and eyes

K

keratitis: inflammation of cornea

keratoconus: cone-shaped deformity of cornea

kyphosis: rounded deformity of back, humpback

L

lacrimal gland: gland which secretes tears; it lies in outer angle of orbit

lacrimal sac: dilated upper end of lacrimal duct

lacrimation: production of slightly alkaline liquid known as "tears"

lagophthalmos: condition in which lids cannot be completely closed

large-type book (clear-type book): book in 18-point or 24-point type of clear, simple design without many serifs, produced especially for education of partially seeing pupils

larynx: the cavity at the upper end of the human trachea or windpipe, containing the vocal cords and acting as the organ of voice

lens: refractive medium having one or both surfaces curved

lesion: an injury; a hurt; a wound

leukemia: cancer of blood cells

leukocyte: white blood corpuscle

ligament: tough, fibrous band connecting bones or supporting viscera

light adaptation: power of eye to adjust itself to variations in amount of light

light perception (L. P.): ability to distinguish light from dark

L. P.: light perception, ability to distinguish light from dark

limbus: boundary between cornea and sclera

lordosis: curvature of spine

lumbar: concerning the loins or lower back

lumbar puncture: spinal puncture; tapping of spinal membranes in lumbar region, usually between third and fourth lumbar vertebrae

lumen: unit of measurement of light output of light source; modern lamps are rated in lumens

luminaire: lighting fixture or complete unit (including lamp, shade, and other accessories)

M

M. A.: mental age

macrocephaly: abnormal largeness of the head

macrophthalmus: abnormally large eyeball, resulting chiefly from infantile glaucoma

macula (yellow spot): small area of retina which surrounds fovea; with fovea, it is area of distinct vision

maladjustment: in psychiatry, defective adaptation to environment, marked by anxiety, depression, and irritability

malignant: virulent and tending to go from bad to worse

malnutrition: imperfect assimilation and nutrition

malocculsion: faulty occlusion, closing, or meeting, as of opposing teeth in the upper or lower jaw

mandible: bone forming lower jaw; inferior maxilla

mat(te) surface: dull or non-glossy finish which diffuses light reflected from it, thereby preventing reflected glare from surface

maxilla: one of two bones forming upper jaw; superior maxilla

mechanism: method unconsciously used to keep self-respect or prestige in presence of obstacles and conflicts impossible for individual to overcome (as by rationalization)

megalophthalmus: abnormally large eyeball, resulting usually from infantile glaucoma

membrane: thin layer of tissue that covers surface or divides space or organ

meninges: membrane covering brain

meningitis: inflammation of membrane covering brain

mental age: level of intellectual development in terms of level of average person of same chronological age

mental deficiency: feeblemindedness; social incompetence due to mental retardation

mental hygiene: science which deals with development of healthy mental and emotional reactions and habits

metabolism: process of converting food into energy

metastasis: transfer of disease from one organ or part to another

microcephalous: presenting abnormal smallness of head

microphthalmus: eyeball congenitally abnormally small in all its meridians

miotic: agent that causes pupil to contract

Mongolism: condition of a child born with a wide, flattened skull, narrow, slanting eyes, and generally a mental deficiency

monoplegia: paralysis of single part (brachial, facial, central, peripheral, et cetera)

moron: feebleminded person whose IQ is between 50 and 75 and whose mental age is between 8 and 12 years

motivation: reason or group of reasons inducing a person to act in a certain way

multiple sclerosis: disease marked by sclerosis occurring in sporadic patches throughout brain or spinal cord or both

muscular distrophy: a primary wasting disease of muscles characterized by progressive muscular weakness

mutism: a conscious or unconscious refusal to respond verbally to intertogation

mydriatic: drug that dilates the pupil

myelitis: inflammation of bone marrow (osteomyelitis) or spinal cord (poliomyelitis)

myocarditis: inflammation of myocardium (heart muscle)

myopia (nearsightedness): refractive error where, because eyeball is too long, point of focus for rays of light from distant objects (parallel light rays) is in front of retina; thus, to obtain distinct vision, object must be brought nearer to take advantage of divergent light rays (those from objects less than twenty feet away)

myositis: inflammation of voluntary muscle

myotonia: inhibition of voluntary movements due to increase in muscle tonus; tonic spasm of muscle

N

near point of accommodation: nearest point at which eye can perceive an object distinctly; it varies according to power of accommodation

near point of convergence: nearest single point at which the two eyes can direct their visual lines, normally about three inches from eyes

nearsightedness: myopia

near vision: ability to perceive objects clearly at normal reading distance (usually considered to be approximately fourteen inches from eyes)

nephritis: inflammation of kidney

nerve deafness: hearing impairment caused by damage to perceptive mechanism of ear; perception deafness

neuritis: inflammation of nerve

neurologist: expert in neurology or in treatment of nervous diseases

neuropsychiatry: branch of medicine which deals with cases that are both neurologic and mental or bordering thereon

neurosis (psychoneurosis): relatively minor disorder of psychic constitution; in contrast with the psychosis, it is less incapacitating, and in it the personality remains more or less intact

neurosurgery: surgery of nervous system

neurosyphilis: syphilis affecting the central nervous system

night blindness: condition in which sight is good by day, but deficient at night and in any faint light

nystagmus: involuntary movement of muscles of eye

O

obstetrical paralysis: palsy due to injuries received at birth

obstetrics: art of managing childbirth cases

occipital: concerning occiput (back of head)

occupational therapy: use of any occupation for remedial purposes, especially of arts and crafts to promote relaxation, coördination, et cetera

oculist (ophthalmologist): physician who is specialist in diseases and defects of eye

O. D. (oculus dexter): right eye

ophthalmia: inflammation of eye or conjunctiva

ophthalmia neonatorum: acute, purulent conjunctivitis in newborn; for control purposes, it is sometimes legally defined as "an inflamed or discharging eye in a newborn baby under two weeks"

ophthalmologist (oculist): physician who is specialist in diseases and defects of eye

ophthalmoscope: instrument having perforated mirror, used in examining interior of eye

Oppenheim's disease: amyotonia congenita, congenital general hypotonia of muscles in children

optic atrophy: atrophy of optic nerve

optic chiasm: crossing of fibers of optic nerves on ventral surface of brain

optic disk: head of optic nerve

optic nerve: second cranial nerve, special nerve of sense of sight

optic neuritis: inflammation of optic nerve

optician: maker of eyeglasses

optometrist: technician in measurement of refraction and fitting of eyeglasses

organic: caused by maldevelopment or impairment of organism

orientation: determination of one's position with respect to time, place, and identity of persons

orthopedics: branch of medicine dealing with deformities and diseases of bones and joints

orthopsychiatry: study and treatment of disorders of behavior and personality, particularly in youth

orthoptic training: series of scientifically planned exercises for developing or restoring normal teamwork of eyes

O. S: (oculus sinister): left eye

Osgood-Schlatter disease: osteochondrosis of tuberosity of tibia (just below kneecap)

Osler's disease: chronic blueness with enlarged spleen and excess of red corpuscles in blood

osteitis: inflammation of bone

osteitis fibrosa cystica: bone cyst; sac or cavity filled with fluid material

osteochondritis: inflammation of both bone and cartilage

osteogenesis imperfecta: fragilitas ossium, abnormal brittleness of bones (subject to fracture from slight violence)

osteoma: bone tumor

osteomyelitis: inflammation of bone caused by pyogenic organism

osteopetrosis: thickening of the bone cortex throughout the bones of the body including the pelvis, vertebrae, and skull

otitis media: inflammation of middle ear

otological examination: medical examination of ear

otologist: physician who specializes in diseases of ear

O. U. (oculus uterque): both eyes

out-patient: patient receiving treatment at hospital but not staying there

output: light given off by lighting unit of any kind after deduction of losses due to reflection and transmission

P

palate: the roof of the mouth, consisting of bone (hard palate) in front and of a fleshy structure (soft palate at the back)

palpebral: pertaining to eyelid

palsy: synonym of paralysis, used only in connection with certain special forms

pannus: invasion of cornea by infiltration of lymph and formation of new blood vessels

panophthalmitis: inflammation of entire eyeball

papilledema: choked disk, noninflammatory swelling of optic nerve head

paralysis: loss or impairment of motor function in part, due to lesion of neural or muscular mechanism; also, by analogy, impairment of sensory function

paraplegia: paralysis of lower part of body

paresis: incomplete motor paralysis

Parkinson's disease: paralysis agitans, shaking palsy (disease of late life)

patella: kneecap

pathology: branch of medicine which treats of essential nature of disease, especially of structural and functional changes caused by disease

pavor nocturnus: nightmare; night terror

pediatrician: specialist in treatment of children's diseases

pellagra: noncontagious disease caused by deficient diet

pelvis: basin-shaped ring of bone at posterior extremity of trunk, supporting spinal column and resting upon lower extremities

perception deafness: hearing impairment caused by damage to perceptive mechanism of ear; nerve deafness

pericarditis: inflammation of pericardium (membranous sac containing heart)

perimeter: instrument for measuring field of vision

periosteum: tough fibrous membrane surrounding bone

peripheral: relating to the boundary; relating to nerves outside the central nervous system

peripheral vision: ability to perceive presence, motion, or color of objects outside of direct line of vision

pesplanus: flatfoot

perseveration: involuntary persistence of one reply or one idea in response to various questions; when neural stimulation toward goal lasts too long, individual cannot put aside one task when he needs to do another, is almost obsessed by unfinished tasks, and cannot give vigorous attention to any one task because of residual stimulation from previous tasks

personality: what constitutes, distinguishes, and characterizes a person; total reaction of a person to his environment

petit mal: a relatively mild form of epilepsy involving a temporary partial lapse of consciousness

phalanx (plural phalanges): any bone of finger or toe

phlyctenular keratitis: variety of keratitis characterized by formation of pustules or papules on cornea; usually occurs in young children and may be caused by poor nutrition; many physicians believe it to be a tubercular condition

phoria: root word denoting latent deviation in which eyes have constant tendency to deviate from normal axis; used with prefix to indicate direction of such deviation (hyperophoria, esophoria, exophoria)

photometer (light meter): device for measuring illumination

photophobia: abnormal sensitivity to light

physiotherapy: physical therapy; treatment of disease by physical (nonmedical) means, such as heat, massage, hydrotherapy, exercise, rest, occupational therapy, radiation, and electricity

pinkeye: acute contagious conjunctivitis

pneumoencephalogram: record of shaddows of brain following injection of air or other gas into brain through spinal column

pneumothorax: collapse of lung induced intentionally by artificial means (as by injection of nitrogen gas) in treatment of pulmonary tuberculosis; also accumulation of air or gas in pleural cavity

poliomyelitis: infantile paralysis (disease of spinal cord)

polydactylism: occurrence of more than usual number of fingers or toes

posterior chamber: space between posterior surface of iris and anterior surface of lens, filled with aqueous

Pott's disease: tuberculosis of the spine

prebyopia: loss of accommodation due to advanced age

prognosis: forecast as to probable result of attack of disease; prospect as to recovery from disease afforded by nature and symptoms of case

progressive muscular atrophy: chronic disease marked by progressive wasting of muscles with paralysis, due to degeneration of ventral gray horns of spinal cord, followed by degeneration of anterior nerve roots and muscles

pronation: act of turning palm of hand downward

properdin: protein believed important in immunity to disease

prosthesis: artificial part of body

pseudohypertrophic muscular dystrophy: dystrophy of muscles of shoulder girdle and sometimes of pelvic girdle, beginning with hypertrophy and followed later by atrophy; it begins in childhood

psychiatry: branch of medicine dealing with behavior disorders

psychoanalysis: method of eliciting from nervous patients an idea of their past emotional experiences and the facts of their mental life, in order to discover the mechanism by which a pathologic mental state has been produced, and to furnish hints for psychotherapy

psychologist: one trained in psychology (branch of science that treats of mind and mental operations, especially as reflected in behavior)

psychomotor epilepsy: state of disturbed consciousness in which individual may perform various activities for which he is later amnesic

psychoneurosis (neurosis): relatively minor disorder of psychic constitution; in contrast with the psychosis, it is less incapacitating, and in it the personality remains more or less intact

psychosis: one of deeper, more far-reaching and prolonged mental disorders

psychosomatic: concerning mind-body relationship; having bodily symptoms of psychic, emotional, or mental origin

psychotherapy: form of therapy employing psychologic methods in treatment of functional nervous disorders (including suggestion, persuasion, psychoanalysis, reëducation, et cetera)

pterygium: fold of mucous membrane consisting of subepithelial growth of vascular connective tissue of conjunctiva which may extend into cornea; it occurs most frequently on nasal side

ptosis: drooping of upper eyelid

pure-tone audiometer: audiometer for testing hearing by means of pure tones

pyemia: pus in blood stream

pyogenic: pus-forming

Q

quadriplegia (tetraplegia): paralysis of all four limbs

R

radiology: science of radiant energy and radiant substances; especially that branch of medical science which deals with use of radiant energy in diagnosis and treatment of disease

radius: bone on outer or thumb side of forearm

rationalization: mental process by which plausible explanation is concocted for ideas, beliefs, or activities that one wishes to hold or do, whereas real motivation is subconscious or at least obscure

recidivism: a repeated or habitual relapse into crime

reflection factor (reflectance) of any surface: percentage of incident light reflected

reflex: reflected action or movement; sum total of any particular involuntary activity; it is often elicited by tapping a muscle tendon

refraction: (1) deviation in course of light rays in passing from one transparent medium into another of different density; (2) determination of refractive errors of eye and their correction by glasses

refractive error: defect in eye which prevents light rays from being brought to single focus exactly on retina

refractive media: media of eye having refractive power (cornea, aqueous, lens, and vitreous)

rehabilitation: restoring disabled person to his best possible mental and physical condition, aiding him in preparing for and getting into employment, and making him a "plus" quantity in his community

residual: remaining; left behind

retardation of thought: delay in thinking, in which either process of thought is set in motion slowly (initial retardation), or thought or action once having started, is performed slowly (executive retardation)

retina: innermost coat and perceptive structure of eye formd by expansion of optic nerve

retinitis: inflammation of retina; it is marked by impairment of sight, perversion of vision, edema, and exudation into retina, and occasionally by hemorrhages into retina

retinitis pigmentosa: chronic degenerative disease of retina having hereditary tendency

retinopathy of infancy: retrolental fibroplasia

retinoscope: instrument for determining refractive state of eye by observing movements of lights and shadows across pupil by light thrown onto retina from moving mirror

retrolental fibroplasia (retinopathy of infancy): considered disease of retina; occurs in premature babies of low birth weight; may cause hemorrhages into retina and vitreous, detachment of retina, and hazing of vitreous; so called because of fibrous membrane that forms behind lens; is cause of much infant blindness

Rh factor: Rhesus factor, agglutinogen first found in Rhesus monkeys (Landsteiner and Wiener, 1940) and normally present in most persons; it may cause hemolytic transfusion reactions in adults, especially in pregnancy and after multiple transfusions and hemolytic anemias in infants; individuals who show this agglutination (86%) are Rh positive, while those who do not (14%) are Rh negative

rheumatic fever: disease of unknown cause resulting in heart injury

rheumatic heart disease: permanent damage of heart valves (usually mitral or aortic ones) as result of rheumatic fever in past

rheumatoid arthritis: disease of joints, usually polyarticular, marked by inflammatory changes in synovial membranes and articular structures, and by atrophy and rarefaction of bones

rickets: deficiency disease of infancy and childhood, in which normal process of ossification is disturbed, due to lack of vitamin D; it is marked by bending and distortion of bones under muscular action, by formation of nodular enlargements on ends and sides of bones, by delayed closure of fontanels, pain in muscles, sweating of head, and degeneration of liver and spleen

rigidity: tenseness on movement of part

rods: together with cones, they are receptors for optic nerve; they are light-perceiving layer of retina, concerned with seeing light and motion

roentgen ray: X ray

roentgenology: branch of radiology that deals with diagnostic and therapeutic use of roentgen rays

rubella: German measles

S

sacrum: triangular bone situated dorsad and caudad from two ilia, formed of five united vertebrae wedged in between two innominate bones

St. Vitus's dance: chorea

Salk vaccine: vaccine that stimulates production of antibodies in bloodstream against all three poliomyelitis viruses; this vaccine is made of viruses "killed" by addition of formaldehyde (named for Dr. Jonas E. Salk)

sarcoma: any of various malignant tumors originating in the connective tissue, attacking especially the bones

scapula: shoulder blade

schizophrenia: Bleuler's term for dementia praecox

scissor gait: gait in which one foot is passed in front of the other, producing cross-legged progression

sclera: membrane which, with cornea, forms external, protective coat of eye

scleritis: inflammation of sclera

sclerosis: hardening

scoliosis: abnormal curvature of vertebral column, especially lateral curvature

scotoma: blind or partially blind area in visual field

semantics: science of meaning of words, influence of language on thought, symbolism

semi-indirect illumination: type of illumination in which between 60 percent and 90 percent of light is reflected toward ceiling; it increases quantity of illumination received on work areas, without objectionable high brightness of unit

senile: concerning old age

septic: produced by putrefaction

sequela: lesion or affection following or caused by attack of disease

siblings: brothers and sisters

SC, S (sine correction): without correction; that is, not wearing eyeglasses

Snellen chart: chart to measure visual acuity

spasm: sudden, violent, involuntary contraction of muscle or group of muscles

spasticity: hyper-irritable condition of muscle resulting from brain injury

speech and hearing consultant: teacher trained in speech correction and services for hard of hearing; consultant not only works with children presenting speech and hearing problems, but also is available for consultation with classroom teachers, parents, physicians, or anyone responsible for welfare of such children

spherical lens: segment of sphere refracting rays of light equally in all meridians

spina bifida: congenital cleft of vertebral column with meningeal protrusion

spinal meningitis: inflammation of meninges of spinal cord

spinal puncture: lumbar puncture; tapping of spinal membranes in lumbar region, usually between third and fourth lumbar vetebrae

splint: rigid or flexible appliance for fixation of displaced or movable parts

Sprengel's deformity: one shoulder blade or scapula is abnormally small, elevated with respect to the level of the other shoulder blade, and displaced slightly forward in its upper part

statutory: concerning law enacted by legislative body

stenosis: narrowing or stricture of duct or canal

sternum: breast bone

Still's disease: inflammatory arthritis severely involving multiple joints: permanent damage and deformity occur

strabismus: squint; failure of two eyes to direct their gaze at same object because of muscle imbalance

stuttering: a hesitation in speech due to an inability to enunciate the syllables without repeated efforts

subluxation: incomplete or partial dislocation

supination: turning of palm of hand upward

sweep-check: screening method for detecting child with hearing loss, in contrast to child with normal hearing

Sydenham's chorea: chorea minor

GLOSSARY

sympathetic ophthalmia: inflammation of one eye due to infection in other eye (usually traumatic iridocyclitis from perforating injury)

syndactylism: webbed fingers or toes; common; union between sometimes extends to tip ends

syndrome: a pattern of symptoms in a disease or the like; a number of characteristic symptoms occurring together

synechia: adhesion (usually of iris to cornea or lens)

syphilis: congenital deformity of bones and joints: paralysis, stunted growth; often mentally deficient; some hereditary quality

T

talipes: clubfoot; deformity of foot in which it is twisted out of shape or position

Talking Book: phonograph record made from text read aloud; it can be played to a class or an individual and is usually for entertainment or instruction of blind or partially seeing persons

tarsus: framework of connective tissue which gives shape to eyelid

Taylor brace: steel back brace for support in cases of tuberculosis of the spine

telescopic glasses: spectacles founded on principles of telescope; occasionally prescribed for improving very poor vision which cannot be helped by ordinary glasses

tetraplegia (quadriplegia): paralysis of all four limbs

therapeutic: concerning treatment

therapist: person skilled in treatment of disease

therapy: attempt to cure or treat

thorax: chest

thrombosis: formation, development, or presence of thrombus (plug or clot) in blood vessel or in one of cavities of heart, formed by coagulation of blood and remaining at point of formation

thyroid: large ductless gland in front of and on either side of trachea, containing thyroxin (organic iodine compound)

tibia: inner and larger bone of leg below knee

tic: currenty, psychoneurosis marked by quick, sudden spasms that are identical with movements of volitional intent; formerly, any spasmodic movement or twitching (as of face)

tinnitus: ringing or buzzing in the ear; subjective noise generated somewhere wihin individual's own hearing mechanism, as after riding in airplane

tonic: characteristic of muscle tone or tension

tonometer: instrument for measuring tension

torticollis: wryneck; contracted state of cervical muscles, producing twisting of neck and unnatural position of head

trachoma: chronic form of infectious conjunctivitis, which may also seriously affect other parts of eye

traction: act of drawing or pulling

transistor: pea-sized bit of germanium, a semi-conductor, which can supplant the vacuum tube, as in a hearing aid; also a mixture of aluminum and antimony, or indium and antimony, et cetera

trauma: injury

tremor: involuntary trembling or quivering

triplegia: hemiplegia (paralysis of one side of body) with paralysis of one limb on opposite side

tuberculosis: infectious disease caused by Koch's bacillus and characterized by formation of tubercles in tissues

tuberculosis of the knee and other joints: increase in joint fluid; painful; prevention of motion is essential; germs lodge in growing portion of bone (epiphysis) and involve joints

tuberosity: broad eminence situated on a bone

Tuition Plan: monthly payment by parents for education of their children, while school receives its fees in full before beginning of each term (founded by Rudolf Neuburger in 1938)

tumor: a swollen part; a swelling or protuberance

tunnel vision: contraction of visual field to such an extent that only central visual acuity remains, thus giving affected individual impression of looking through tunnel

U

ulna: inner and larger bone of forearm, on side opposite that of thumb

uniaural: hearing in one ear

uvea: entire vascular coat of eyeball (iris, ciliary body, and choroid)

uveitis: inflammation of uvea

V

ventricle: small cavity

verbigeration: prolonged and monotonous repetition of meaningless words, phrases, sounds, or sentences

vertebra: small bone in spinal column

vertigo: dizziness

viable: capable of living

visual purple: pigment of outer segment of visual rods

vitreous: transparent, colorless mass of soft, gelatinous material filling eyeball behind lens

volt: unit of measurement of electromotive force

W

watt: unit of measurement of electric lamps

working plane: plane on which work requiring eye use is done (such as desk top, chalkboard, easel, et cetera)

wryneck: torticollis; contracted state of cervical muscles, producing twisting of neck and unnatural position of head

X

X ray: roentgen ray

Z

zygote: fertilized egg cell